TYPE SPECIMENS

120 POINT VERSATILE INITIALS

120 Point, per set (twenty-four characters) $12.10

Color, per set (twenty-four characters) $12.10

Single character: one color 85c; two colors $1.55

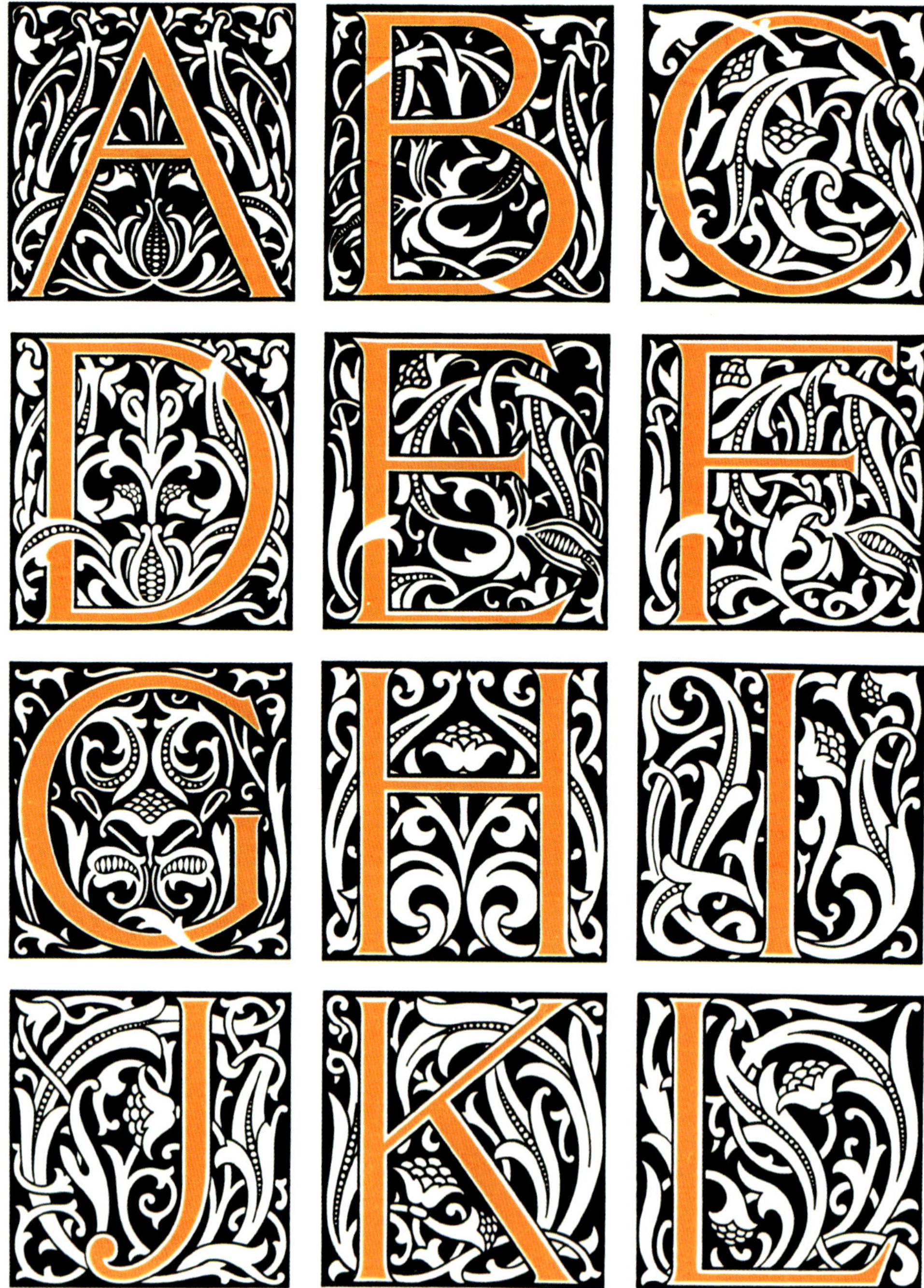

No. 12040 A	No. 12043 D	No. 12046 G	No. 12049 J	No. 12052 M	No. 12055 P	No. 12059 T	No. 12062 W
No. 12041 B	No. 12044 E	No. 12047 H	No. 12050 K	No. 12053 N	No. 12057 R	No. 12060 U	No. 12063 X
No. 12042 C	No. 12045 F	No. 12048 I	No. 12051 L	No. 12054 O	No. 12058 S	No. 12061 V	No. 12064 Y

TYPE SPECIMENS

A Visual History of Typesetting and Printing

Dori Griffin

BLOOMSBURY VISUAL ARTS
LONDON • NEW YORK • OXFORD • NEW DELHI • SYDNEY

Previous page
***American Specimen Book of Type Styles*, American Type Founders, 1912.**

BLOOMSBURY VISUAL ARTS
Bloomsbury Publishing Plc
50 Bedford Square, London, WC1B 3DP, UK
1385 Broadway, New York, NY 10018, USA
29 Earlsfort Terrace, Dublin 2, Ireland

BLOOMSBURY, BLOOMSBURY VISUAL ARTS and the Diana logo are trademarks of Bloomsbury Publishing Plc

First published in Great Britain 2022

Cover design: Louise Dugdale
Cover image: Antique wood type © kjohansen/iStock.

A catalogue record for this book is available from the British Library.

Library of Congress Cataloging-in-Publication Data
Names: Griffin, Dori, author.
Title: Type specimens : a visual history of typesetting and printing / Dori Griffin.
Description: New York : Bloomsbury Visual Arts, 2021. | Includes bibliographical references and index.
Identifiers: LCCN 2021023396 (print) | LCCN 2021023397 (ebook) | ISBN 9781350116603 (hardback) | ISBN 9781350116597 (paperback) | ISBN 9781350116610 (epub) | ISBN 9781350116627 (pdf)
Subjects: LCSH: Type and type-founding--Specimens. | Typesetting--History. | Typesetting--History--Pictorial works. | Printing--History. | Printing--History--Pictorial works.
Classification: LCC Z250 G85 2021 (print) | LCC Z250 (ebook) | DDC 686.2/24--dc23
LC record available at https://lccn.loc.gov/2021023396
LC ebook record available at https://lccn.loc.gov/2021023397

ISBN:
HB: 978-1-350116-60-3
PB: 978-1-350116-59-7
ePDF: 978-1-350116-62-7
eBook: 978-1-350116-61-0

Typeset by Struktur Design
Printed and bound in India

To find out more about our authors and books visit www.bloomsbury.com and sign up for our newsletters.

CONTENTS

INTRODUCTION

***Desktop Specimens*, US Government Printing Office, 1896-1981.**

The United States Government Printing Office's desktop reference specimens offer a snapshot view of changing typographic technologies. The 1896 edition offered type from individual foundries, with a few display faces from the newly-formed American Type Founders corporate trust. In 1912, mechanized typesetting warranted its own specialized *Specimen Book of Monotype Faces*. The 1916 specimen indicated whether a typeface originated from Monotype or Linotype, appending M or L to its catalog listing. In 1950, Linotype, Monotype, Intertype, and Ludlow faces were available, plus a section of foundry type for special purposes, but the new technology of phototype wasn't yet represented. By 1962, though, all of this material was supplemented by an extensive selection of Fotosetter phototype faces. 1962's Jobbing section still included "miscellaneous fonts of script, text, and wood type" which printers were advised to avoid "unless absolutely necessary" due to limited supply. By 1981, phototype required its own volume, *United States Government Photocomposition Type Faces*. Overt visualizations marked none of these swift changes in technology, however. Page composition reflected evolving design tastes, but the differences between foundry, hot metal, and photo type remained all but invisible on the printed page. Cover images occasionally provided more robust clues. Photocomposition simulated moving the negative during printing plate exposure, one of the physical contortions available with film type—unlike metal, a physically flexible medium.

36 Point, Gothic, No. 1. Caps, lower case,

37—10
A D F—6

ABCDEF
abcdefghij

48 Point, Gothic, No. 1. Caps, lower case,

39—10
A D F—6

ABCDal

MONOTONE GOTHIC (Fotosetter—Photocomposition) FOR SMITHSONIAN USE ONLY

ABCDEFGHIJKLMNOPQRSTU
VWXYZ 1234567890
abcdefghijklmnopqrstuvwxyz

ABCDEFGHIJKLMNOPQ
RSTUVWXYZ 1234567890
abcdefghijklmnopqrstuvwx
yz

MISCELLANEOUS SORTS (Fotosetter—Photocomposition)

PIECE FRACTIONS

300

GARAMOND ITALIC

157

CENTURY BOLD

ABCDEFGHIJKLMNOPQRSTUVWXYZ
abcdefghijklmnopqrstuvwxyz1234567890
ABCDEFGHIJKLMNOPQRSTUVWXYZ1234567890

51

48 Point, Doric. Caps, lower case, and figures.

ABCDEFGHI
abcdefghijkl

48 Point, Extended. Caps and figures.

ABCD
12345

15-Line Pica Clarendon. Caps.

ABCDE

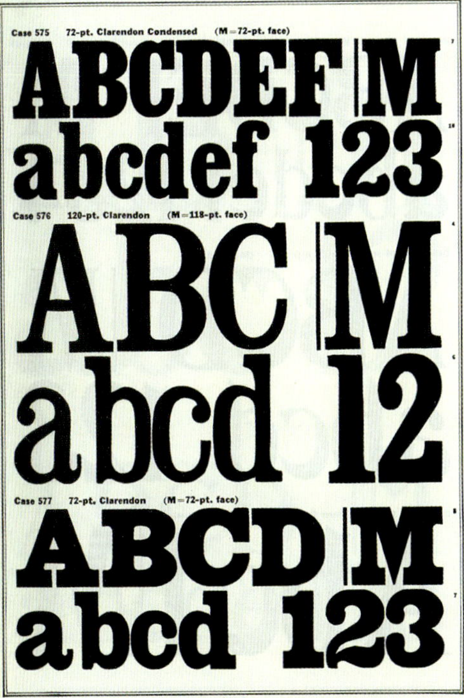

Case 575 72-pt. Clarendon Condensed (M=72-pt. face)

ABCDEF M
abcdef 123

Case 576 120-pt. Clarendon (M=118-pt. face)

ABC M
abcd 12

Case 577 72-pt. Clarendon (M=72-pt. face)

ABCD M
abcd 123

[95]

ABCDEFGHIJKLMNOPQRSTUV
abcdefghijklmnopqrstuvwxyz

ABCDEFGHIJKLMNOP
abcdefghijklmnopqrstuvwxy

ABCDEFGHIJKL 2
abcdefghijklmnopqrst

ABCDEFG
abcdefghijk

7890 1234

45678

67890 12

567890

SUPERIORS AND INF
Use superior figures for ref-
$12345 erences 67890

VOTES, BALLOTS, ETC.
To be expressed
$12345 in figs 67890

MONOTYPE SEC.
Many keyboards and
$123 casters 456

FOUNDRY TYPE IN JOB SECTION 203

60 pt. Cheltenham Condensed (Caps only)

ABCDEFG 12

72 pt. Cheltenham Condensed (Caps only)

ABCDEF 12

60 pt. Cheltenham

ABCDEF G
abcdefghijkl m
Qu 12345678
fi fl ff ffi ffl ct st ¶

Also on Ludlow from 6 pt. to 48 pt., see pages 162 and 163.

otocomposition Type

mposition / United States Government Printing Offi
ited States Government Printing Office / Photocom
vernment Printing Office / Photocomposition / Unit

Who is this book's audience?

If you're a student or teacher of design, I wrote this book for you. The first time I taught a type specimen project in the university design studio, my students and I needed access to useful historical images in color, accompanied by accurate contextual information, with bonus points for relevance to contemporary studio practice. Though a quick Google search for "type specimen" lent plenty of images, few included context. At conferences, colleagues suggested we should "just go see the real thing at a local archive," which would have worked if I were teaching in a major metro area. But I was teaching at a public university in southern Mississippi, and there weren't any such archives in the entire state. So I asked my students if they'd be interested in a book about type specimens, at least enough to pick it up and look at the pictures. They said yes, and I started researching and writing this book. In it, I've prioritized the following goals:

1: Wide access. I want as many people as possible to be able to find, afford, and enjoy this book. It won't replace the experience of viewing printed artifacts in person. But it can enable students, teachers, practicing designers, and design-curious readers to access resources otherwise unavailable because of constraints in time, money, or geographical location.

2: Historical context. Graphic design notoriously lacks a diverse, carefully researched body of disciplinary literature. Introductory survey textbooks and specialized academic monographs certainly address typographic history, but there aren't many resources in the space between these two extremes. As a teacher, I believe we can do a better job of solving today's design problems and anticipating tomorrow's if we understand yesterday's problems and solutions. This book provides context for understanding typographic design and communication practices.

3: Diverse global geographies. The type specimen—as both a visual form and a professional practice—has intrinsically Eurocentric beginnings. Its historical roots are neither value-neutral nor culturally diverse. In choosing images, though, this book seeks to be as global and inclusive as possible. At the same time, it's important to acknowledge the exclusion, discrimination, settler colonialism, and cultural imperialism that have accompanied the spread of western print capitalism, a problem this book takes seriously, but doesn't pretend to solve.

4: Visual reference. Designers tend to be visual thinkers. This book treats images as equally important to words, reading them with just as much care and affording them equal space. We see type, as well as reading it, so this book takes the act of seeing seriously. The images aren't illustrations; they're part of the text.

What's a type specimen?

Typographic specimens display the design of typefaces, what everyday users now call fonts.[1] Today's specimens are often digital, but historically specimens were printed. The most famous examples are attributed to white, western European men, often those who practiced their craft on behalf of religious and state authorities.[2] Originally, type foundries—producers of metal type—designed specimens for their customers, printers who needed to know how the types they purchased would look when printed. Printers in turn produced specimens for their customers, including civil and religious institutions, publishing houses, newspapers, and advertisers.[3] Specimens functioned as catalogs, and as such most were intended to be used, then discarded upon arrival of a new edition.[4] Today's type designers still need to answer the essential questions of the very first specimens: what does a specific typeface look like, what sizes and styles are available for purchase or use, and in what situations will the type be functional and context-appropriate?

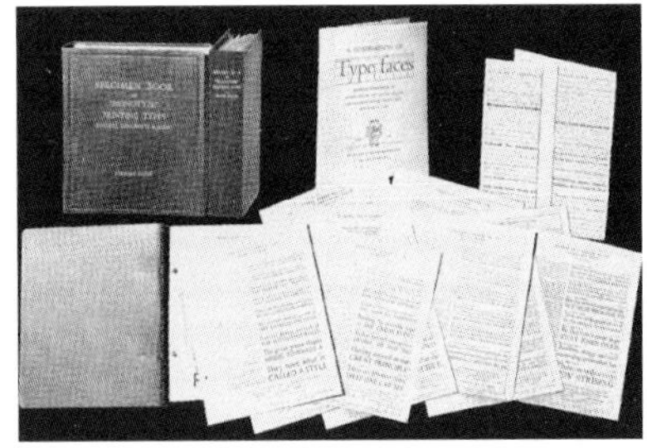

Type specimens were distributed by founders, printers, and publishers to show customers what types for purchase or use looked like and in what sizes, styles, and weights they were available. Historical printed forms include large and small broadsides (posters), books, booklets, magazines, pamphlets, brochures, and advertisements within larger publications. These Monotype specimens were photographed in 1937.

How are historical specimens relevant to design practice now?

During the early twentieth century, printer-historians Stanley Morison (English) and Daniel Updike (American)—along with many of their international contemporaries—introduced the idea that typographers, printers, librarians, and historians could learn a great deal from a systematic visual study of type specimens.[5] Yet because they were originally designed and distributed as ephemeral documents, surviving specimens weren't abundant. Considering limited access to original sources, early type historians advocated the production of annotated facsimile editions to widen availability and offer context for historical specimens. Their premise—that practitioners can design more effectively and communicate in more context-specific ways if they understand the history of their discipline—holds true for designers today.

Specimens provide contemporary designers with several useful tools. Because typography still uses a specialist vocabulary developed in the context of early printing with metal types, a basic understanding of printing technologies and processes can be helpful in navigating contemporary typographic tools, including digital tools. Typefaces connote meaning through their visual form and historical associations, and awareness of these meanings can inform designers' type choices. Specimens succinctly capture historical styles which contemporary revivalism re-visits regularly, and successful quotation—or parody—requires acquaintance with the original. These very pragmatic questions can be addressed through studying typographic specimens.

Specimens illuminate larger questions, too—questions of professional and cultural identity, human relationships to technology, and global networks of communication. How, and in what contexts, have typographic technologies, practices, and styles evolved? How do they circulate? How have changes in technology impacted typography? How have printing and type-founding shaped contemporary definitions of visual communication design? How has typography been used to communicate visual messages and cultural identities? How has typographic printing been used to disseminate and support religious and political ideologies? Type specimens offer insight into all of these questions, but to learn from images, it's vital to see them in chronological and cultural context. The specimens reproduced here offer brief introductions to the visual forms and professional practices that have undergirded what we now think of as "graphic design" from the inception of western European typographic printing. These abridged histories are the typographic equivalent of speed dating, and there's much more to know about every specimen and its context. The notes and bibliography represent a rich trove of typographic knowledge; whenever possible, they include URLs for open source online documents.

How is this book organized?

Type specimens take many forms, and those physical differences provide a structure for this book. Chapter 1 explores large-format broadsides, the earliest known type specimens produced. Chapter 2 considers multi-page specimens appended to printers' instruction manuals. Chapter 3 examines specimen books representing a single foundry's or printer's stock before the advent of mechanized typecasting. Chapter 4 surveys developments in technologies and materials that pre-dated Linotype and Monotype, including early experiments with mechanization, electrotyping, and mass-produced wood type. Chapter 5 continues by considering specimens from Linotype and Monotype, as well as their smaller competitors also producing "hot metal type." Chapter 6 looks at small-format ephemera—booklets, brochures, trade journal ads, and small broadsides designed to be folded and shipped through the mail. Chapter 7 provides an overview of phototype and explores how this "cold type" technology led to today's digital types. The postlude showcases examples by contemporary global typographers. Within this form-based framework, examples trace technological developments, following a generalized chronology: type-founding as a secretive individual craft and then as a product of organized manufacture—literally, making by hand; type as an industrialized, mechanized product in individual metal sorts, metal slugs (lines of type cast as single units), metal plates, and wood; and type dematerialized through photographic technologies and democratized through digital tools. Physical formats, visual styles, and professional typographic practices evolved in dialogue with each other, and approaching type specimens from this multivalent position allows us to see them not only as beautiful objects, but as visual evidence of physical processes, cultural contexts, and professional identities.

Acknowledgements

Throughout the writing process, I've benefited profoundly from the deep knowledge of scholars, practitioners, and archivists who have devoted their careers to questions I've been able to engage only briefly in this text. Thank you to all the brilliant, patient librarians and curators around the world who have shared their specialized knowledge—especially Steven Galbraith and Amelia Hugill-Fontanel at the Rochester Institute of Technology's Cary Graphic Arts Collection. There, as the first Cary Research Fellow in 2015, I jump-started this project with a month in the archives.

Thanks also to the Design Incubation Fellowship, where in 2017, veteran writers and editors (plus a delightful cohort of fellow educators) workshopped the book proposal; and to the Scholarship Enhancement Fund grant at the University of Florida College of the Arts, which partially funds reproduction of the book's many images.

Many thanks to the practicing typographers whose work appears in the postlude; its working title, "the afterword of pure awesome," describes how I feel about including each of you. A special shout-out to Megan McCormick, an MFA candidate in graphic design at Ohio University, where she worked with me as a research fellow in 2019. Her image management expertise, digital-archival research contributions, and collaborative energy made finishing this book on time possible.

Cheers to my former typography students at the University of Southern Mississippi—teaching you made me passionate about this book.

Finally, thanks to my teachers—you're the reason I chose to teach.

1 Specifically, "In hand composition, a font is a set of printing types that gives rise to character images of a particular size, with a particular set of appearance characteristics." Richard Southall, *Printer's Type in the Twentieth Century: Manufacturing And Design Methods* (New Castle, DE: Oak Knoll, 2005), 47.

2 Of course, women and people of color have long participated in type-founding and printing, and their histories are beginning to be acknowledged. An influential early effort to expand historical views of printing was Janet Higgins, "'And the Wife Helped Also,'" *Southeastern College Art Conference Review* 11, no. 3 (1988): 201-6.

3 Birrell & Garnett and Henry Graham Pollard, *Catalogue of I Typefounders' Specimens II Books Printed in Founts of Historic Importance III Works on Typefounding Printing & Bibliography* (Brighton: Tony Appleton, 1928), v.

4 James Mosley, *British Type Specimens Before 1831: A Hand-List*, Occasional Publication 14 (Oxford: Oxford Bibliographical Society, 1984), 7, https://catalog.hathitrust.org/Record/000569676.

5 Mosley, 7-8. Daniel Berkeley Updike, *Printing Types: Their History, Forms, and Use; a Study in Survivals*, vols. 1 & 2 (Cambridge: Harvard University Press, 1922), http://archive.org/details/printingtypesthe01updi. Stanley Morison's essay "On the Classification of Typographical Variations" is reprinted in John Dreyfus, Harry Carter, and Hendrik D.L. Vervliet, *Type Specimen Facsimiles: Reproductions of Fifteen Type Specimen Sheets Issued between the Sixteenth and Eighteenth Centuries*, vol. 2, 2 vols. (London: Bodley Head, 1972).

1: EARLY BROADSIDES

A Specimen of Printing Types,
Joseph Fry, 1785

Founded in 1764, Joseph Fry's type foundry was predated by the noted British foundries of Caxton (1477) and Caslon (1720), among others. Fry's 1785 broadside includes an extensive selection of sizes, styles, and scripts. It's printed recto and verso (front and back) to accommodate all of them. In the Latin script, sizes range from Four Lines Pica, ≈48 modern American points, to Diamond, ≈3 points. Notice that Fry calls this "the smallest type in the world." Fry's foundry stocks Latin romans and companion italics, as well as English blackletter. Like many early printers in England and Europe, Fry also stocked scripts useful to the study of biblical history: Arabic, Greek, Hebrew, Persian, and Samaritan. A small sample of borders, rules, and ornaments provides a preview of the more extensive selection shown in Fry's early specimen books.

New Long Primer, No. 3. on Burgeois Body.

Quousque tandem abutêre, Catilina, patientia nostra? quamdiu nos etiam furor iste tuus eludet? quem ad finem sese effrenata jactabit audacia? nihilne te nocturnum præsidium palatii, nihil urbis vigiliæ, nihil timor populi, nihil consensus bonorum omnium, nihil hic munitissimus habendi senatus locus, nihil horum ora vultusque moverunt? patere tua consilia non sentis? constrictam jam omnium horum conscientia teneri conjurationem
ABCDEFGHIJKLMNOPQRSTUVWXYZÆ

Burgeois, No. 1. on Long Primer Body.

Quousque tandem abutêre, Catilina, patientia nostra? quamdiu nos etiam furor iste tuus eludet? quem ad finem sese effrenata jactabit audacia? nihilne te nocturnum præsidium palatii, nihil urbis vigiliæ, nihil timor populi, nihil consensus bonorum omnium, nihil hic munitissimus habendi senatus locus, nihil horum ora vultusque moverunt? patere tua consilia non sentis? constrictam jam omnium horum conscientia teneri conjurationem tuam non vides?
ABCDEFGHIJKLMNOPQRSTUVWXYZÆŒ

Burgeois Roman, No. 1.

Quousque tandem abutêre, Catilina, patientia nostra? quamdiu nos etiam furor iste tuus eludet? quem ad finem sese effrenata jactabit audacia? nihilne te nocturnum præsidium palatii, nihil urbis vigiliæ, nihil timor populi, nihil consensus bonorum omnium, nihil hic munitissimus habendi senatus locus, nihil horum ora vultusque moverunt? patere tua consilia non sentis? constrictam jam omnium horum conscientia teneri conjurationem tuam non vides?
ABCDEFGHIJKLMNOPQRSTUVWXYZÆŒ

Burgeois Italic, No. 1.

Quousque tandem abutêre, Catilina, patientia nostra? quamdiu nos etiam furor iste tuus eludet? quem ad finem sese effrenata jactabit audacia? nihilne te nocturnum præsidium palatii, nihil urbis vigiliæ, nihil timor populi, nihil consensus bonorum omnium, nihil hic munitissimus habendi senatus locus, nihil horum ora vultusque moverunt? patere tua consilia non sentis? constrictam jam omnium horum conscientia teneri conjurationem tuam non vides? quid proxima, quid superiore, nocte egeris, ubi fueris, quos convocaveris,
ABCDEFGHIJKLMNOPQRSTUVWXYZÆŒ

Burgeois, No. 1. on Brevier Body.

Quousque tandem abutêre, Catilina, patientia nostra? quamdiu nos etiam furor iste tuus eludet? quem ad finem sese effrenata jactabit audacia? nihilne te nocturnum præsidium palatii, nihil urbis vigiliæ, nihil timor populi, nihil consensus bonorum omnium, nihil hic munitissimus habendi senatus locus, nihil horum ora vultusque moverunt? patere tua consilia non sentis? constrictam jam omnium horum conscientia teneri conjurationem tuam non vides? quid proxima, quid superiore nocte egeris, ubi fueris, quos convocaveris, quid consilii ceperis, quem nostrum ignorare arbitraris? O
ABCDEFGHIJKLMNOPQRSTUVWXYZÆŒ

New Burgeois Roman, on Long Primer Body.

Quousque tandem abutêre, Catilina, patientia nostra? quamdiu nos etiam furor iste tuus eludet? quem ad finem sese effrenata jactabit audacia? nihilne te nocturnum præsidium palatii, nihil urbis vigiliæ, nihil timor populi, nihil consensus bonorum omnium, nihil hic munitissimus habendi senatus locus, nihil horum ora vultusque moverunt? patere tua consilia non sentis? constrictam jam omnium horum conscientia teneri conjurationem tuam non vides? quid proxima,
ABCDEFGHIJKLMNOPQRSTUVWXYZÆ

Burgeois Roman. No. 2. (New)

Quousque tandem abutêre, Catilina, patientia nostra? quamdiu nos etiam furor iste tuus eludet? quem ad finem sese effrenata jactabit audacia? nihilne te nocturnum præsidium palatii, nihil urbis vigiliæ, nihil timor populi, nihil consensus bonorum omnium, nihil hic munitissimus habendi senatus locus, nihil horum ora vultusque moverunt? patere tua consilia non sentis? constrictam jam omnium horum conscientia teneri conjurationem tuam non vides? quid proxima,
ABCDEFGHIJKLMNOPQRSTUVWXYZÆ

New Brevier Roman, No. 2. on Burgeois Body.

Quousque tandem abutêre, Catilina, patientia nostra? quamdiu nos etiam furor iste tuus eludet? quem ad finem sese effrenata jactabit audacia? nihilne te nocturnum præsidium palatii, nihil urbis vigiliæ, nihil timor populi, nihil consensus bonorum omnium, nihil hic munitissimus habendi senatus locus, nihil horum ora vultusque moverunt? patere tua consilia non sentis? constrictam jam omnium horum conscientia teneri conjurationem tuam non vides? quid proxima, quid superiore, nocte egeris, ubi fueris, quos convocaveris, quid
ABCDEFGHIJKLMNOPQRSTUVWXYZÆ

Brevier Roman, No 2. (New)

Quousque tandem abutêre, Catilina, patientia nostra? quamdiu nos etiam furor iste tuus eludet? quem ad finem sese effrenata jactabit audacia? nihilne te nocturnum præsidium palatii, nihil urbis vigiliæ, nihil timor populi, nihil consensus bonorum omnium, nihil hic munitissimus habendi senatus locus, nihil horum ora vultusque moverunt? patere tua consilia non sentis? constrictam jam omnium horum conscientia teneri conjurationem tuam non vides? quid proxima, quid superiore, nocte egeris, ubi fueris, quos convocaveris, quid
ABCDEFGHIJKLMNOPQRSTUVWXYZÆŒ

Brevier Italic, No. 2. (New)

Quousque tandem abutere, Catilina, patientia nostra? quamdiu nos etiam furor iste tuus eludet? quem ad finem sese effrenata jactabit audacia? nihilne te nocturnum præsidium palatii, nihil urbis vigiliæ, nihil timor populi, nihil consensus bonorum omnium, nihil hic munitissimus habendi senatus locus, nihil horum ora vultusque moverunt? patere tua consilia non sentis? constrictam jam omnium horum conscientia teneri conjurationem tuam non vides? quid proxima, quid superiore, nocte egeris, ubi fueris, quos convocaveris, quid consilii ceperis, quem nostrum ignorare
ABCDEFGHIJKLMNOPQRSTUVWXYZÆŒ

New Brevier Roman, No. 2. on Minion Body.

Quousque tandem abutêre, Catilina, patientia nostra? quamdiu nos etiam furor iste tuus eludet? quem ad finem sese effrenata jactabit audacia? nihilne te nocturnum præsidium palatii, nihil urbis vigiliæ, nihil timor populi, nihil consensus bonorum omnium, nihil hic munitissimus habendi senatus locus, nihil horum ora vultusque moverunt? patere tua consilia non sentis? constrictam jam omnium horum conscientia teneri conjurationem tuam non vides? quid proxima, quid superiore, nocte egeris, ubi fueris, quos convocaveris, quid consilii ceperis,
ABCDEFGHIJKLMNOPQRSTUVWXYZÆŒ

New Brevier Roman, No. 2. (Close).

Quousque tandem abutêre, Catilina, patientia nostra? quamdiu nos etiam furor iste tuus eludet? quem ad finem sese effrenata jactabit audacia? nihilne te nocturnum præsidium palatii, nihil urbis vigiliæ, nihil timor populi, nihil consensus bonorum omnium, nihil hic munitissimus habendi senatus locus, nihil horum ora vultusque moverunt? patere tua consilia non sentis? constrictam jam omnium horum conscientia teneri conjurationem tuam non vides? quid proxima, quid superiore, nocte egeris, ubi fueris, quos convocaveris, quid consilii ceperis, quem
ABCDEFGHIJKLMNOPQRSTUVWXYZÆŒ

New Brevier Italic. No. 2. (Close)

Quousque tandem abutere, Catilina, patientia nostra? quamdiu nos etiam furor iste tuus eludet? quem ad finem sese effrenata jactabit audacia? nihilne te nocturnum præsidium palatii, nihil urbis vigiliæ, nihil timor populi, nihil consensus bonorum omnium, nihil hic munitissimus habendi senatus locus, nihil horum ora vultusque moverunt? patere tua consilia non sentis? constrictam jam omnium horum conscientia teneri conjurationem tuam non vides? quid proxima, quid superiore, nocte egeris, ubi fueris, quos convocaveris, quid consilii ceperis, quem nostrum ignorare
ABCDEFGHIJKLMNOPQRSTUVWXYZÆŒ

Nonpareil Roman, on Minion Body.

Nonpareil Roman.

Nonpareil Italic.

Pearl Roman, on Nonpareil Body.

Pearl Italic, on Nonpareil Body.

Pearl Roman.

Pearl Italic.

Diamond.

ABCDEFGHIJKLMNOPQRSTUVWXYZÆŒ

N. B. This is the Smallest Letter in the World.

Arabic, on English Body, with Points.

لا تلخذ لك صورة * ولا تمثيل كل ما في السماء من فوق *
وما في الارض من اسفل * ولا ما في الماء من تحت الارض *
لا تسجد لهن * ولا تعبدهن * فاني انا الرب الاهك الاه
غيور * اجتزي ذنوب الاباء من الابناء الي ثلثة و(الي)
اربعة اجيال للذين يبغضونني * وافعل الحسنة الي الف
(جيل) لاحبائي وحافظي وصاياي * آمين

Persian.

اين سخن بر دل دهقان كاركر آمده بلبلرا آزاد كرد بلبل زباني
بازادي كشاد و بگفت چون با من نكوي بحكم هل جزا الاحسان
الا الاحسان مكافات آن بايد كرد بدان كه در زير درخت كه ايستادهٔ
آفتابهٔ است پر از زر بردار و در حوايج خود صرف كن دهقان آن
محلرا بكاويد و سخن بلبل درست يافت گفت اي بلبل عجب
كه آفتابهٔ زررا در زير زمين مي بيني و دام در زير خاك.

Two Lines Great Primer Black.

And be it further hereby enacted, That

Double Pica Black.

And be it further hereby enacted, That the Mayors, Bailiffs, or other head Officers,

Great Primer Black.

And be it further hereby enacted, That the Mayors, Bailiffs, or other head Officers of every Town and place corporate, and City wit-

English Black, No. 1.

And be it further hereby enacted, That the Mayors, Bailiffs, or other head Officers of every Town and place corporate, and City within this Realm, being Justice or Justices of Peace, shall have the same au-

English Black No. 2.

And be it further hereby enacted, That the Mayors, Bailiffs, or other head Officers of every Town and place corporate, and City within this Realm, being Justice or Justices of Peace, shall have the same authority by virtue of this

Pica Black, No. 1.

And be it further hereby enacted, That the Mayors, Bailiffs, or other head Officers of every Town and place corporate, and City within this Realm, being Justice or Justices of Peace, shall have the same authority by virtue of this
ABCDEFGHIJKLMNOPQRS

Small Pica Black.

And be it further hereby enacted, That the Mayors, Bailiffs, or other head Officers of every Town and place corporate, and City within this Realm, being Justice or Justices of Peace, shall have the same authority by virtue of this Act, within the limits and precincts of their Jurisdictions, as well out of Sel-
ABCDEFGHIJKLMNOPQRSTUWXYZ

Long Primer Black.

And be it further hereby enacted, That the Mayors, Bailiffs, or other head Officers of every Town and place corporate, and City within this Realm, being Justice or Justices of Peace, shall have the same authority by virtue of this Act, within the limits and precincts of their Jurisdictions, as well out of Sessions, as at their Sessions, if they hold any, as is herein limited, prescribed and appointed to Justices of
ABCDEFGHIJKLMNOPQRSTUWXYZ

Brevier Black.

And be it further hereby enacted, That the Mayors, Bailiffs, or other head Officers of every Town and place corporate, and City within this Realm, being Justice or Justices of Peace, shall have the same authority by virtue of this Act, within the limits and precincts of their Jurisdictions, as well out of Sessions, as at their Sessions, if they hold any, as is herein limited, prescribed and appointed to Justices of Peace of the County, or any two or more of them, or to the Justices of Peace in their
ABCDEFGHIJKLMNOPQRSTUWXYZ

Two Lines Great Primer Hebrew.

בראשית ברא אלהים
את השמים ואת
הארץ: והארץ היתה

Double Pica Hebrew. No. 2.

בראשית ברא אלהים את השמים
ואת הארץ: והארץ היתה תהו ובהו
וחשך על־פני תהום ורוח אלהים
מרחפת על־פני המים: ויאמר אלהים

Double Pica Hebrew. No. 2. with Points.

בְּרֵאשִׁית בָּרָא אֱלֹהִים אֵת הַשָּׁמַיִם
וְאֵת הָאָרֶץ: וְהָאָרֶץ הָיְתָה תֹהוּ וָבֹהוּ
וְחֹשֶׁךְ עַל־פְּנֵי תְהוֹם וְרוּחַ אֱלֹהִים
מְרַחֶפֶת עַל־פְּנֵי הַמָּיִם: וַיֹּאמֶר אֱלֹהִים

English Hebrew. No. 2.

בראשית ברא אלהים את השמים ואת הארץ:
והארץ היתה תהו ובהו וחשך על־פני תהום ורוח
אלהים מרחפת על־פני המים: ויאמר אלהים יהי
אור ויהי־אור: וירא אלהים את־האור כי־טוב ויבדל
אלהים בין האור ובין החשך: ויקרא אלהים לאור
יום ולחשך קרא לילה ויהי־ערב ויהי־בקר יום

Pica Hebrew.

Small Pica Hebrew.

Long Primer Hebrew.

Burgois Hebrew.

Brevier Hebrew.

Small Pica Rabbinical Hebrew.

Brevier Rabbinical Hebrew.

Nonpareil Rabbinical Hebrew.

Great Primer Greek.

Πάτερ ἡμῶν ὁ ἐν τοῖς οὐρανοῖς· ἁγιασθήτω τὸ ὄνομά σου. Ἐλθέτω ἡ βασιλεία σου· γενηθήτω τὸ θέλημά σου, ὡς ἐν οὐρανῷ, καὶ ἐπὶ τῆς γῆς. Τὸν ἄρτον ἡμῶν τὸν ἐπιούσιον δὸς ἡμῖν σήμερον. Καὶ ἄφες ἡμῖν τὰ ὀφειλήματα ἡμῶν, ὡς καὶ ἡμεῖς ἀφίεμεν τοῖς ὀφειλέταις ἡμῶν. Καὶ μὴ εἰσενέγκῃς ἡμᾶς εἰς πειρασμόν, ἀλλὰ ῥῦσαι ἡμᾶς ἀπὸ τοῦ πονηροῦ· ὅτι σοῦ ἐστιν ἡ βασιλεία, καὶ ἡ δύναμις, καὶ ἡ δόξα εἰς τοὺς αἰῶνας. ἀμήν.

Pica Greek.

Πάτερ ἡμῶν ὁ ἐν τοῖς οὐρανοῖς· ἁγιασθήτω τὸ ὄνομά σου. Ἐλθέτω ἡ βασιλεία σου· γενηθήτω τὸ θέλημά σου, ὡς ἐν οὐρανῷ, καὶ ἐπὶ τῆς γῆς. Τὸν ἄρτον ἡμῶν τὸν ἐπιούσιον δὸς ἡμῖν σήμερον. Καὶ ἄφες ἡμῖν τὰ ὀφειλήματα ἡμῶν, ὡς καὶ ἡμεῖς ἀφίεμεν τοῖς ὀφειλέταις ἡμῶν. Καὶ μὴ εἰσενέγκῃς ἡμᾶς εἰς πειρασμόν, ἀλλὰ ῥῦσαι ἡμᾶς ἀπὸ τοῦ πονηροῦ· ὅτι σοῦ ἐστιν ἡ βασιλεία, καὶ ἡ δύναμις, καὶ ἡ δόξα εἰς τοὺς αἰῶνας. ἀμήν.

Pica Samaritan.

Long Primer Samaritan.

King's Arms, Five Lines Pica.

Ships, Five Lines Pica. No. 1.

Two Lines Double Pica.

Two Lines Great Primer.

Check, Four Lines Pica.

Two Lines Great Primer.

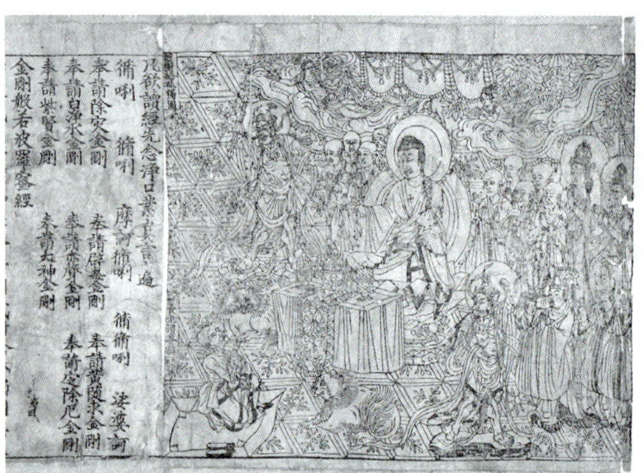

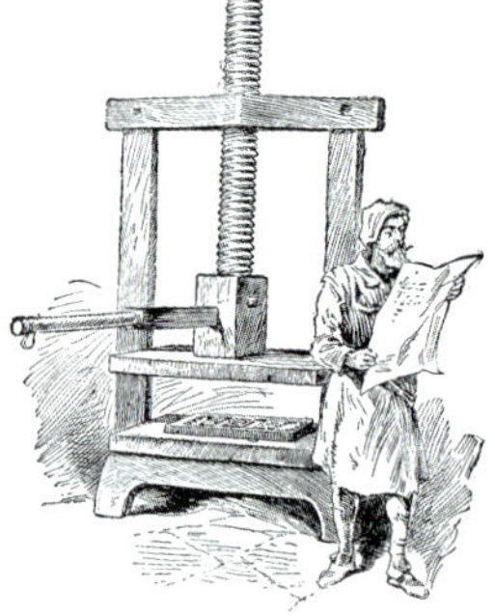

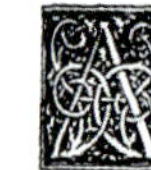

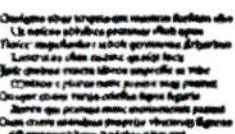

Aue maria gra plena dominus tecū benedicta tu in mulierib' et benedictus fruct' uentris tui: ihesus christus amen.

868 CE — China

The woodblock-printed Diamond Sutra, world's first extant printed book, produced.

1438-44 — Germany

Adjustable type mold and movable metal type introduced to Western Europe.

1486 — Italy

Printer Erhardt Ratdolt issues the first known type specimen broadside.

1377 — Korea

First known printing with movable metal type.

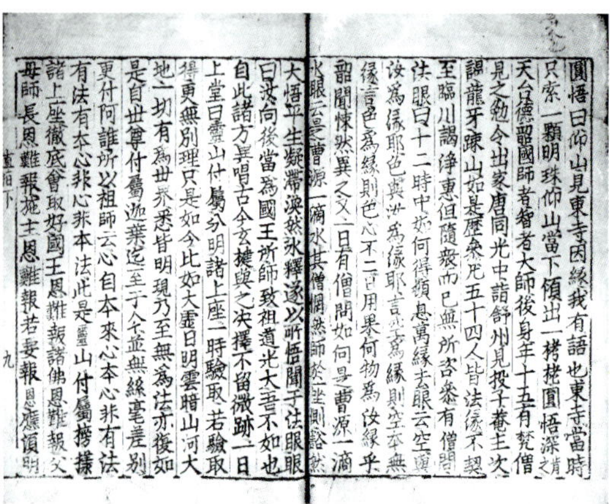

1567 — Belgium

First known type specimen book.

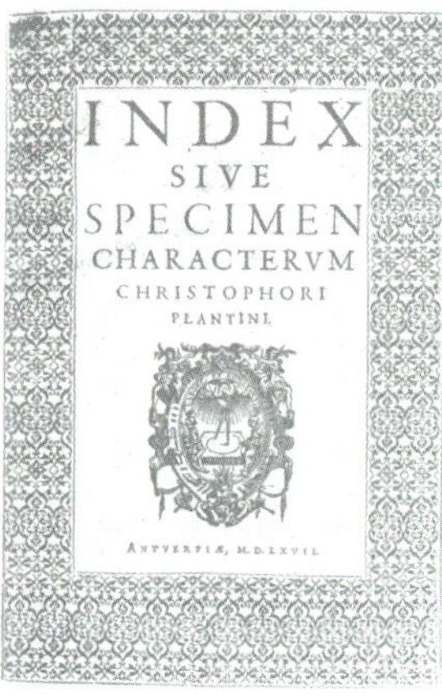

INDEX SIVE SPECIMEN CHARACTERVM CHRISTOPHORI PLANTINI.

ANTVERPIÆ, M.D.LXVII.

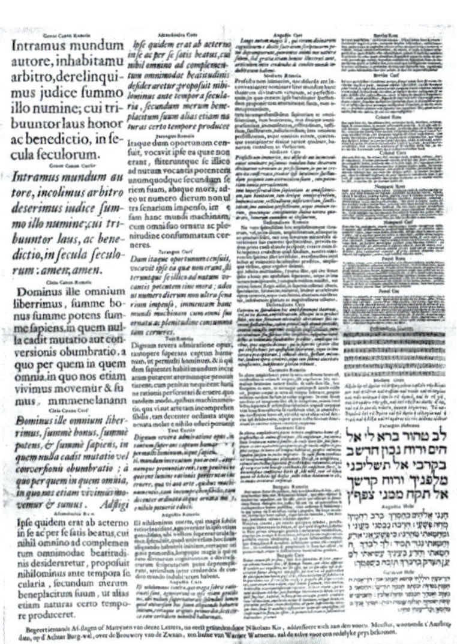

Intramus mundum autore, inhabitamu arbitro, derelinqui-mus judice summo illo numine; cui tri-buuntor laus honor ac benedictio, in se-cula seculorum.

Intramus mundum au tore, incolimus arbitro deserimus iudice sum-mo illo numine; cui tri-buuntor laus, ac bene-dictio, in secula seculo-rum: amen, amen.

Dominus ille omnium liberrimus, summe bo-nus summe potens fum-me sapiens, in quem nul-la cadit mutatio aut con-versionis obumbratio, a quo per quem in quem omnia, in quo nos etiam vivimus movemur & su mus, mmmenelanann

Bominus ille omnium liber-rimus, summe bonus, summe potens, & summe sapiens, in quem nulla cadit mutatio vel conversionis obumbratio; a quo per quem in quem omnia, in quo nos etiam vivimus mo-vemur & sumus. Adsig

Ipse quidem erat ab aeterno in se ac per se satis beatus, cui nihil omnino ad complemen-tum omnimodae beatitudi-nis desideraretur, propfuit nihilominus ante tempora fa culari, secundum merum beneplacitum suum, ut aliis etiam naturas certo tempo-re produceret.

Ipse quidem erat ab aeterno in se ac per se satis beatus, cui nihil omnino ad complemen-tum omnimodae beatitudi-nis desideraretur propositum nihi-lominus ante tempora secula-ria, secundum merum bene-placitum suum aliis etiam na turas certo tempore producere

לב טהור ברא לי אל
הים ורוח נכון חדש
בקרבי אל תשליכני
מלפניך ורוח קדשך
אל תקח ממני צפתי

1685-6 — Netherlands

Type founder Miklós Kis' broadside, printed 200 years after Ratdolt's, employs a similar design strategy.

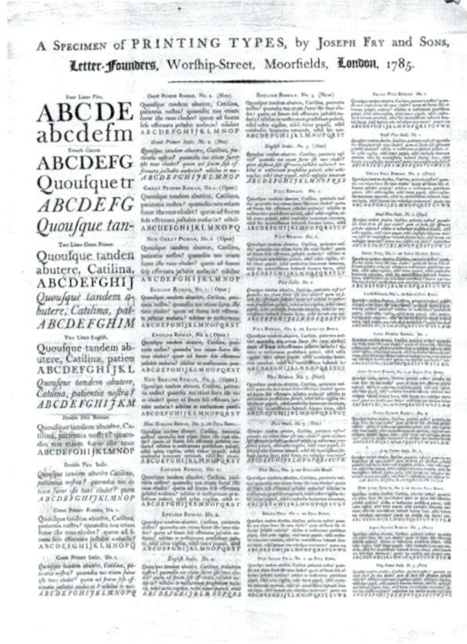

A SPECIMEN of PRINTING TYPES, by JOSEPH FRY and SONS, Letter-Founders, Worship-Street, Moorfields, London, 1785.

ABCDE abcdefm

ABCDEFG Quousque tr

ABCDEFG Quousque tan-

Quousque tandem abutere, Catilina, ABCDEFGHIJ

Quousque tandem a-butere, Catilina, pat-ABCDEFGHIM

Quousque tandem ab-utere, Catilina, patien ABCDEFGHIJKL

Quousque tandem abutere, Catilina, patientia nostra? ABCDEFGHIJKM

1785 — England

Type founder Joseph Fry continues a well-established tradition.

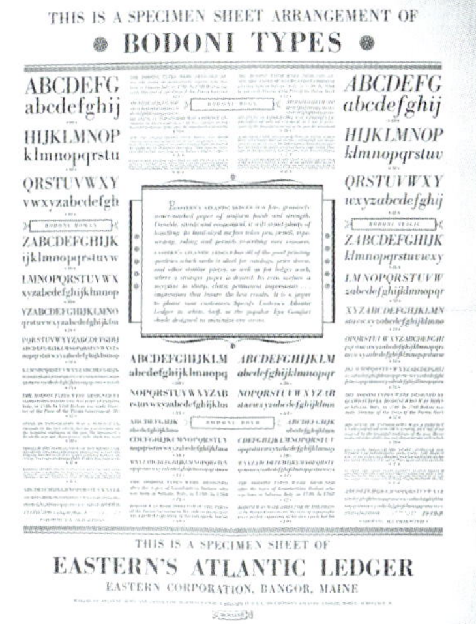

THIS IS A SPECIMEN SHEET ARRANGEMENT OF

BODONI TYPES

ABCDEFG abcdefghij HIJKLMNOP klmnopqrstu QRSTUVWXY vwxyzabcdefgh

ABCDEFG abcdefghij HIJKLMNOP klmnopqrstuv QRSTUVWXY uvxyzabcdefghij

THIS IS A SPECIMEN SHEET OF

EASTERN'S ATLANTIC LEDGER

EASTERN CORPORATION, BANGOR, MAINE

1947 — USA

Types by Giambattisa Bodoni (Italy, 1798) sell "fine paper" 2 years before phototype's introduction.

1605 — Germany

First recorded newspaper printed.

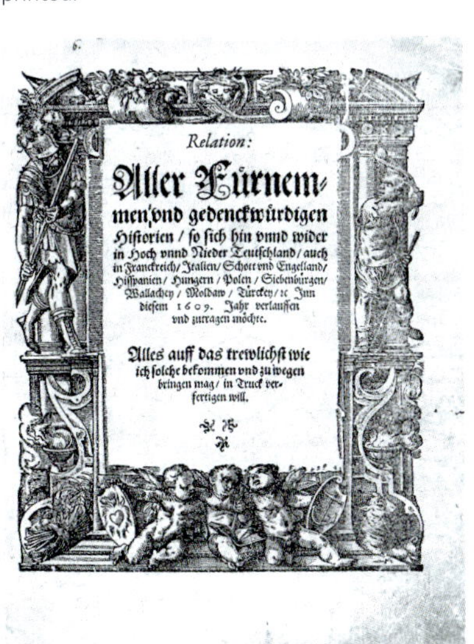

Relation:

Aller Fürnemmen, und gedenckwürdigen Historien / so sich hin unnd wider in Hoch unnd Nieder Teutschland / auch in Franckreich / Italien / Schott und Engelland / Hispanien / Hungern / Polen / Siebenbürgen / Wallachey / Moldaw / Türckey / etc. Inn diesem 1609. Jahr verlauffen und zutragen möchte.

Alles auff das trewlichst wie ich solche bekommen und zu wegen bringen mag / in Truck ver-fertigen will.

1683 — England

First known printer's manual.

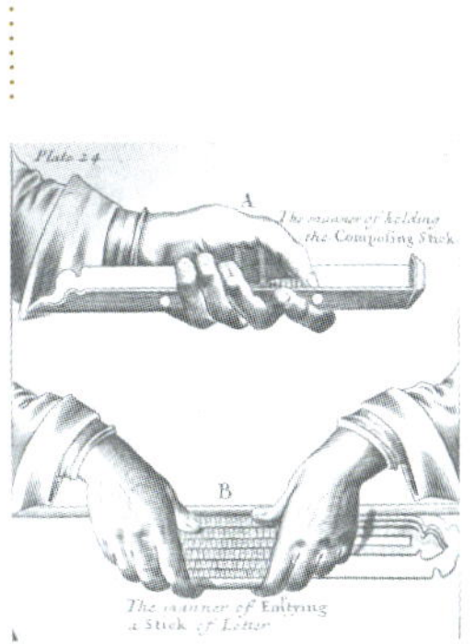

1886 — USA

Mechanical type-casting and typesetting introduced.

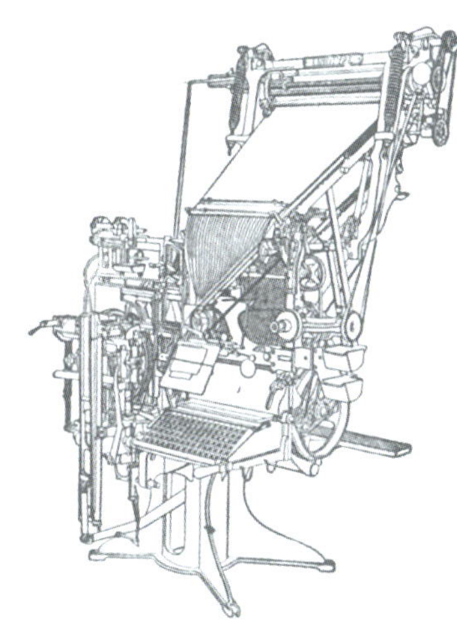

Typographic broadsides appeared in western Europe soon after the introduction of movable metal type and the **screw press**. Broadsides provided an important source of income for early printers, because they were quick and cheap to produce. Typically printed on a single side in black ink, these large-format documents ranged in size from foolscap (13×16 inches) up to almost five feet. Broadsides met time-sensitive needs like advertising, news, and public notices, most from religious and civil authorities. A significant market for news-sheets meant that many printers published them to increase their profit margin.[1] Localized uses emerged, too. Germany, Belgium, and Switzerland embraced academic broadsides, most familiarly Martin Luther's ninety-five theses, and wall charts for schoolroom use circulated, as well. Meanwhile, illustrated **broadside ballads** flourished in England, demonstrating how the format served multiple purposes within early print culture.[2] Typographic specimens in broadside format emerged concurrently with these other kinds of single-sheet printing, and they shared common compositional strategies. The physical framework of the printing press lent itself to rectilinearity and modularity, while paper-making molds and press beds determined maximum page size. Stylistic decisions regarding the use of **borders**, rules, ornaments, headlines, the combination of multiple typefaces, and proportional relationships among elements were influenced both by necessity—the need to fit all of the desired information onto a single sheet of a given size—and by local or regional visual traditions. Thus, type specimen broadsides weren't unusual in their physical characteristics or their basic function as advertisements.

The type specimen's specialized audiences differentiated it from other kinds of broadsides. **Type founders** produced specimens for printers (who were often publishers too), and printers produced them for their clients. With some famous exceptions, most printers didn't make their own type; rather, they purchased it from foundries specializing in type design and manufacture. Specimen broadsides displayed the type styles and sizes available for purchase or use. Writers comprised an important audience for both founders and printers, and some early specimens addressed authors directly. Hamburg type founder Bartholomeus Voskens published his sheet (c.1600) "for the convenience of all authors, printers and booksellers and other customers, so that they may see which best to select for their work."[3] Display occurred at booksellers' fairs, most famously in Frankfurt, and in printers' offices.[4] Indirectly, specimen sheets also addressed other typefounders, as a means for circulating typographic styles.

Despite the format's apparent widespread use among early typefounders, surviving examples are rare, even compared to early printed books like Gutenberg's Bible. Single, oversized sheets were easily damaged, and many examples survive in a single copy, often through accidental circumstances rather than archival efforts. Frequently, broadsides were unsigned and undated, further impeding the cataloging process for surviving copies.[5] Broadside specimens were designed for **ephemeral** use, and they became outdated with the introduction of new types or the removal of old ones. The *Catalogue of Typefounders' Specimens* (1928) first recognized what Stanley Morison called the "scientific value" of specimens for tracing the origins of individual typefaces or styles and the evolution of broader printing and typefounding practices.[6] Today, broadsides remain an important source of historical information and contemporary visual inspiration.

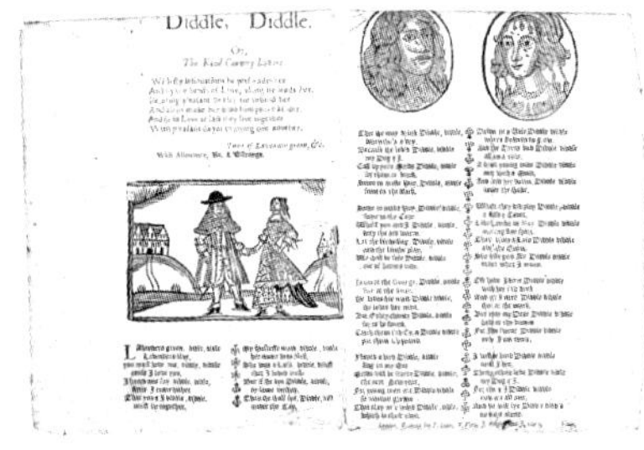
Diddle, Diddle.

Broadside ballads were popular 17 and 18 c. songs printed on one side of a cheap sheet of paper. Drinking ditties, love songs, and sensationalist news stories were set to familiar tunes. As affordable, populist entertainment, they were often lamented as immoral or vulgar. "Diddle, Diddle" (English, 1681–4) sung to the folk tune "Lavendar's Blue," opens with the line "With sly insinuations he perswades her."

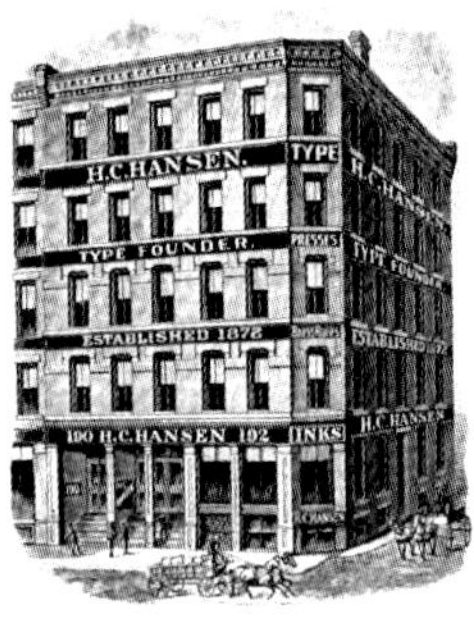

Type founders actually produced lead type, often overseeing the design of the typefaces being made, as well. Unlike print shops or publishing houses, which used type, a foundry manufactured type. These three operations might be combined within a single business, but didn't have to be.

Early broadsides: form and function

The compositional and content decisions made by early printers and typefounders established lasting visual conventions, and the format they initiated persists over 500 years later. These early specimens also framed dialogues during their own time, facilitating conversations among typefounders, type designers, printers, publishers, and the reading public. Along the way, the broadsides contributed to the formation of visible and distinct professional identities for the typographic trades. During the late nineteenth and early twentieth centuries, flourishing scholarly and trade-based interest in the history of typography led to numerous annotated facsimiles of early typographic specimens. In 1896, British librarian Gordon Duff wrote that "[t]he want of reliable **facsimiles** has been a great hindrance to the study of early printing."[7] Subsequent publications from leading voices in printing history—Theodore Low De Vinne and Daniel Updike (American printers), Beatrice Warde (an American archivist writing under the male pseudonym Paul Beaujon), Gustav Mori (a German type designer), Graham Pollard (an English bookseller and bibliographer), and Hendrik Vervliet (a Belgian professor and librarian)—played an important role in establishing the foundations of contemporary research in typographic history. The facsimiles in their books provided wider access to previously inaccessible historical documents.

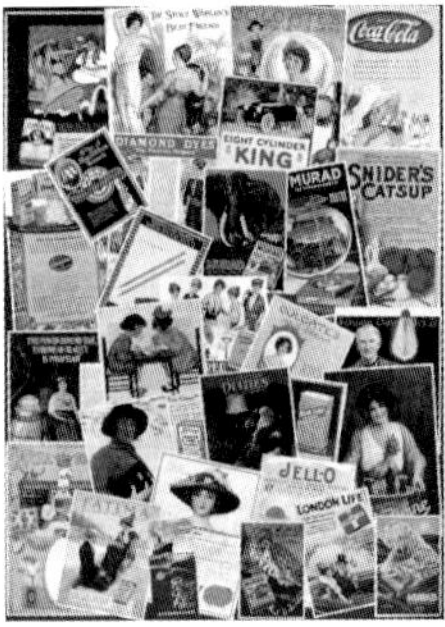

Ephemera is made to be used for a short time, perhaps only once, then discarded. Newspapers, magazines, ads, posters or broadsides, brochures, postcards, train tickets, postage stamps—cheap, widely available printing made these ephemeral documents possible.

Fig. 1.1 (right)

Reproduction of *Indicis Characterum* (Erhardt Ratdolt, Augsburg, 1486). Ratdolt's printer's specimen displayed the types he owned so customers could make visually informed decisions; his work as a printer, for instance the 1482 edition of Euclid's *Elements* shown here, made good use of his types. The *Inland Printer* reproduced *Indicis Characterum* in monochrome (January 1922), calling it "the earliest known specimen sheet." *Specimens of Type in General Use at the Condé Nast Press* (forwarded by Douglas C. McMurtrie, 1923) discussed it as the "first specimen showing more than one typeface."

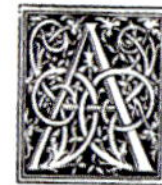

ue maria gr̄a plena dominus tecū benedicta tu in mulierib⁹ et benedictus fruct⁹ ventris tui : ihesus christus amen.

Gloria laudis resonet in ore omniū Patri genitoq3 proli spiritui sancto pariter Resultet laude perhenni Laboribus dei vendunt nobis omnia bona. laus: honor: virtus potētia: ꝛ gratiaꝝ actio tibi christe. Amen.

Vive deū sic ꝛ vives per secula cuncta. Providet ꝛ tribuit deus omnia nobis. Proficit absque deo null⁹ in orbe labor. Illa placet tell⁹ in qua res parva beatū. De facit ꝛ tenues luxuriantur opes.

Indicis characteꝝ diversaꝝ manerierū impressioni paratarū: Finis.

Erhardi Ratdolt Augustensis viri solertissimi: preclaro ingenio ꝛ mirifica arte: qua olim Venetijs excelluit celebratissimus. In imperiali nunc vrbe Auguste vindelicoꝝ laudatissime impressioni dedit. Annoq3 salutis. M.CCCC.LXXXVI. Calē. Aprilis Sidere felici compleuit.

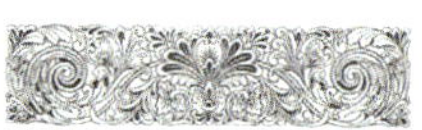

ON TYPES AND TYPE SPECIMENS

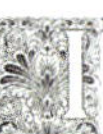

NTELLIGENT selection of types, either by printers or the users of printing, is largely contingent on the availability of type specimens so arranged as to show not only the design and size of the type but also the appearance it presents in actual composition. It therefore came about quite naturally, soon after the invention of movable types, that type specimens began to make their appearance. The earliest showing of a single type face apart from the volume which was printed with it, occurred at the bottom of a list of books printed and published by Peter Schœffer, one of Gutenberg's associates at Mainz. Here we find a line in larger type than the rest of the circular: *hec est littera psalterii*—"this is the type used in the psalter."

The first specimen showing more than one type face was issued by Erhard Ratdolt at Augsburg, Germany, in 1486, and was entitled: *Indicis characterum diversarum manerierum impressioni paratarum*. This was the Ratdolt who later printed at Venice and used in his books such distinguished borders and decorative initials. Another specimen sheet is said to have been issued

[5]

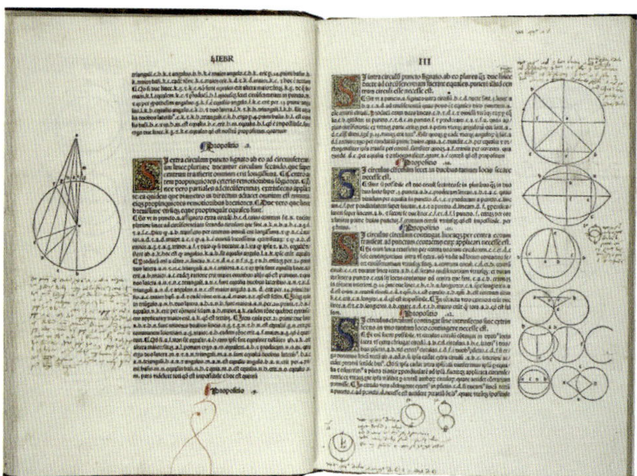

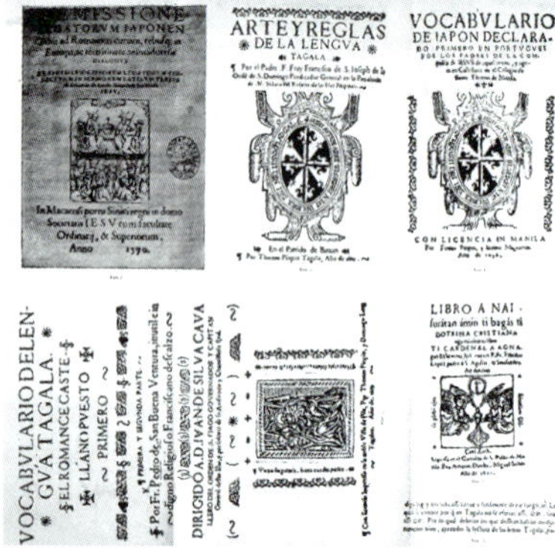

Facsimile editions faithfully reproduce original documents for the purpose of study—or, sometimes, decoration. The facsimiles in *La imprenta en Filipinas* (Madrid, 1897) reproduce important early printed documents from the Philippines.

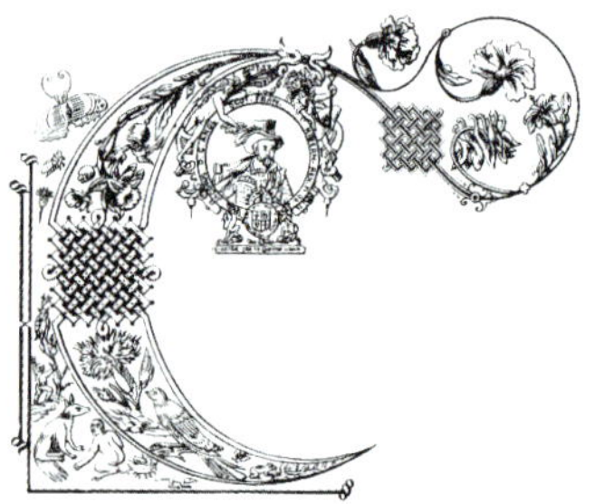

Versals, today known as drop caps, draw attention to the beginning of the text or passage. They might be a large but fairly standard letter; or they might be decorative, historiated (with narrative illustrations), or illuminated—hand colored, often decoratively or illustratively, like the manuscript letters the printed form originally echoed.

Pragmatic beginnings—the Ratdolt specimen of 1486

The first datable specimen sheet of printed types dates from the Incunabula: the Indicis characterum (Ratdolt, 1486). Its maker, printer Erhardt Ratdolt (1447-1527/8), was born in Augsburg, a city known for its printing even before movable metal typography. Ratdolt trained as a printer in Mainz, printed in Venice from 1477-86, then returned to Augsburg at the invitation of that city's Bishop. His type specimen of April 1486 survives today only because it was pasted into the cover of another book, where it was rediscovered in Munich in 1887.[8] Ratdolt's sheet displays fourteen fonts ranging in body size from about nine to thirty contemporary points. Importantly, Ratdolt described his purpose with the word "index," explicitly indicating a visual catalog of his wares.[9] The sheet's straightforward design directs the gaze to the fonts themselves: ten Gothics, three Romans, and one Greek, set in two generously spaced columns [Fig 1.1]. Ratdolt returned to Augsburg as the liturgical printer for the diocese, so unsurprisingly, the sample texts are short religious excerpts in Latin. The *Ave Maria*, the first and largest text, opens with a **versal**—like many features of early letterpress printing, rooted in the manuscript tradition.

In a dated statement at the bottom-right corner of the sheet, printed in **Gothic** type, Ratdolt sings his own praises; he's "an expert," known in Venice for his "illustrious genius and wonderful art" as a printer, and a businessman now ready for work in Augsburg. As a printer—not a type founder—Ratdolt didn't design the types he showed. Rather, his specimen displayed the stock of types available to his customers. Early twentieth century typographer Henry Lewis Bullen praised Ratdolt's wide selection; though Bullen found the types less readable than those of Ratdolt's famous peer, Nicholas Jenson, they were functional. Ratdolt also owned more fonts, and in smaller sizes, then any other printer working at the time—though the 1486 specimen didn't show all of these.[10] At its earliest, then, the specimen broadside filled a pragmatic function that remains relevant today: it displayed type **sizes and styles** for the benefit of users.

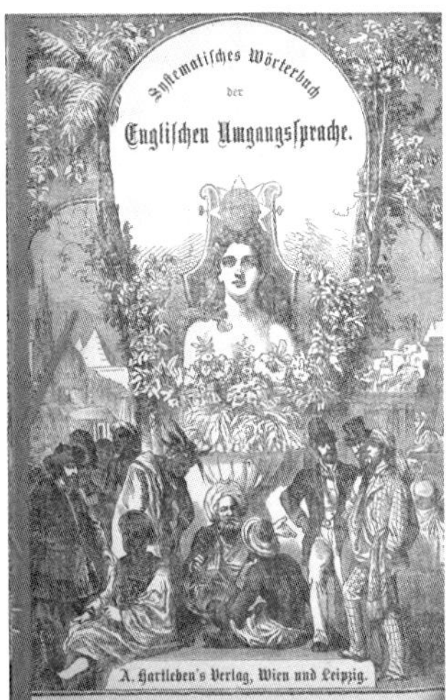

Gothic can refer to early sans serif faces like Century Gothic or to blackletter faces. Blackletters were common throughout western Europe during the Middle Ages and early Renaissance. They remained popular in Germany well into the twentieth century; this German-English dictionary title page dates to 1910. Blackletters can be further divided into many categories, the most common being Cursiva, Fraktur, Textura, and Schwabacher.

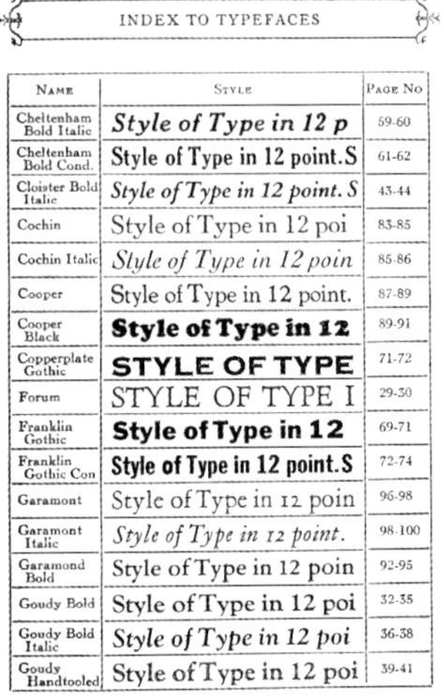

INDEX TO TYPEFACES

Name	Style	Page No
Cheltenham Bold Italic	*Style of Type in 12 p*	59-60
Cheltenham Bold Cond.	Style of Type in 12 point.S	61-62
Cloister Bold Italic	*Style of Type in 12 point. S*	43-44
Cochin	Style of Type in 12 poi	83-85
Cochin Italic	*Style of Type in 12 poin*	85-86
Cooper	Style of Type in 12 point.	87-89
Cooper Black	Style of Type in 12	89-91
Copperplate Gothic	STYLE OF TYPE	71-72
Forum	STYLE OF TYPE I	29-30
Franklin Gothic	Style of Type in 12	69-71
Franklin Gothic Con	Style of Type in 12 point.S	72-74
Garamont	Style of Type in 12 poin	96-98
Garamont Italic	*Style of Type in 12 point.*	98-100
Garamond Bold	Style of Type in 12 poin	92-95
Goudy Bold	Style of Type in 12 poi	32-35
Goudy Bold Italic	*Style of Type in 12 poi*	36-38
Goudy Handtooled	Style of Type in 12 poi	39-41

Size and style as illustrated by an index from a New York foundry's specimen (Gildea & Co, 1923). Garamont [Roman], Garamont Bold, and Garamont Italic at 12 points are three different styles of the same root typeface design, all at the same size.

This detail from the Guyot specimen shows handwritten **annotations** which give prices and other notes on the type.

Patterns of circulation

The Guyot specimen (c.1565), displaying for the English market types by French punch-cutter François Guyot, shows how type designs and designers circulated internationally. Unsigned and undated, it too survived because it was bound into another text in 1618. The sheet's history emerged thanks to John Dreyfus' research for *Type Specimen Facsimiles* (1963), which reproduced it and fourteen other 16–18c. sheets. The Guyot sheet's types saw use in France, Belgium, England, Holland, Portugal, and even Japan, where missionaries imported it in 1588. The Folger Shakespeare Library's copy contains **annotations** with English prices and notes on the type, and coupled with the fact that Guyot worked briefly as a printer in London, this indicates the sheet was probably used to market Guyot's types to London printers.[11]

Fig 1.2 (right)

Type specimen (François Guyot, c.1565). Guyot, a French punch-cutter, marketed his types to English customers with this sheet.

Cl. Garamond in Verwendung 1640				Grandjean u. Alexandre 1693/1714				Marcellin-Legrand 1825			
A	a	*A*	*a*	A	a	*A*	*a*	A	a	*A*	*a*
B	b	*B*	*b*	B	b	*B*	*b*	B	b	*B*	*b*
C	c	*C*	*c*	C	c	*C*	*c*	C	c	*C*	*c*
D	d	*D*	*d*	D	d	*D*	*d*	D	d	*D*	*d*
E	e	*E*	*e*	E	e	*E*	*e*	E	e	*E*	*e*
F	f	*F*	*f*	F	f	*F*	*f*	F	f	*F*	*f*
G	g	*G*	*g*	G	g	*G*	*g*	G	g	*G*	*g*
H	h	*H*	*h*	H	h	*H*	*h*	H	h	*H*	*h*
I	i	*I*	*i*	I	i	*I*	*i*	I	i	*I*	*i*
	j		*j*	J	j	*J*	*j*	J	j	*J*	*j*
K	k	K	*k*	K	k	*K*	*k*	K	k	*K*	*k*
L	l	*L*	*l*	L	l	*L*	*l*	L	l	*L*	*l*
M	m	*M*	*m*	M	m	*M*	*m*	M	m	*M*	*m*
N	n	*N*	*n*	N	n	*N*	*n*	N	n	*N*	*n*
O	o	*O*	*o*	O	o	*O*	*o*	O	o	*O*	*o*
P	p	*P*	*p*	P	p	*P*	*p*	P	p	*P*	*p*
Q	q	*Q*	*q*	Q	q	*Q*	*q*	Q	q	*Q*	*q*
R	r	*R*	*r*	R	r	*R*	*r*	R	r	*R*	*r*
S	s ſ	*S*	*s ſ*	S	s ſ	*S*	*s ſ*	S	s	*S*	*s*
T	t	*T*	*t*	T	t	*T*	*t*	T	t	*T*	*t*
	u		*u*	U	u	*U*	*u*	U	u	*U*	*u*
V	v	*V*	*v*	V	v	*V*	*v*	V	v	*V*	*v*
X	x	*X*	*x*	X	x	*X*	*x*	X	x	*X*	*x*
Y	y	*Y*	*y*	Y	y	*Y*	*y*	Y	y	*Y*	*y*
Z	z	*Z*	*z*	Z	z	*Z*	*z*	Z	z	*Z*	*z*

The mid-sixteenth century saw the decline of italicized body copy—originally an early 16 c. strategy to save space on the printed page—and the rise of pairing **companion italics** with romans for emphasis or visual variety, a well-established practice by the seventeenth century as shown in this chart of romans and italics by Garamond [Garamont], Grandjean, and Marcellin-LeGrand from *Illustrierte Geschichte der Buchdruckerkunst* (Faulmann, 1882).

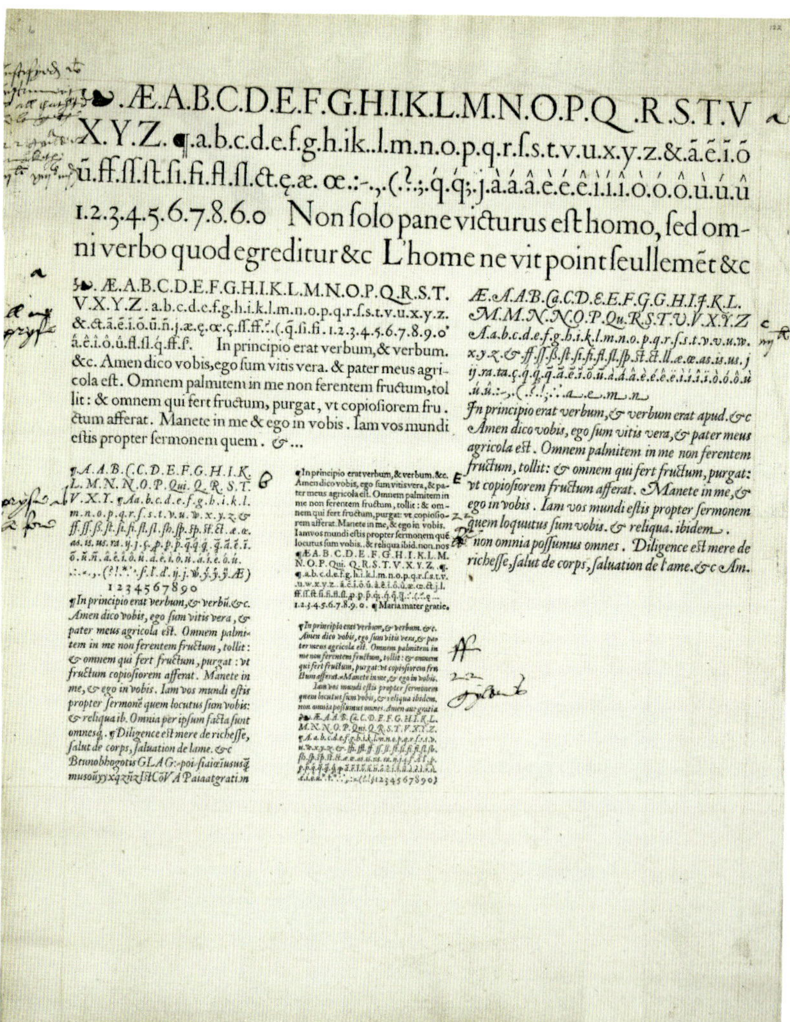
Æ.A.B.C.D.E.F.G.H.I.K.L.M.N.O.P.Q .R.S.T.V X.Y.Z. a.b.c.d.e.f.g.h.ik..l.m.n.o.p.q.r.ſ.s.t.v.u.x.y.z.&.ã.ẽ.ĩ.õ ũ.ff.ſſ.ſt.ſi.fi.fl.ſl.ct.ç.æ. œ.:-.,.(.?.;.q́.q̃;.j.à.á.â.è.é.ê.ì.í.î.ò.ó.ô.ù.ú.û

1.2.3.4.5.6.7.8.6.0 Non ſolo pane victurus eſt homo, ſed omni verbo quod egreditur &c L'home ne vit point ſeullemẽt &c

Æ.A.B.C.D.E.F.G.H.I.K.L.M.N.O.P.Q.R.S.T. V.X.Y.Z. a.b.c.d.e.f.g.h.i.k.l.m.n.o.p.q.r.ſ.s.t.v.u.x.y.z. &.ct.ã.ẽ.ĩ.õ.ũ.ñ.j.æ.ç.œ.ç.ſſ.ff.(.q̃.ſi.fi. 1.2.3.4.5.6.7.8.9.0 â.ê.î.ô.û.fl.ſl.q́.ff.ſ. In principio erat verbum, & verbum. &c. Amen dico vobis, ego ſum vitis vera. & pater meus agricola eſt. Omnem palmitem in me non ferentem fructum, tollit: & omnem qui fert fructum, purgat, vt copioſiorem fructum afferat. Manete in me & ego in vobis. Iam vos mundi eſtis propter ſermonem quem. &...

In principio erat verbum, & verbum erat apud. &c Amen dico vobis, ego ſum vitis vera, & pater meus agricola eſt. Omnem palmitem in me non ferentem fructum, tollit: & omnem qui fert fructum, purgat: vt copioſiorem fructum afferat. Manete in me, & ego in vobis. Iam vos mundi eſtis propter ſermonem quem loquutus ſum vobis. & reliqua. ibidem. non omnia poſſumus omnes. Diligence eſt mere de richeſſe, ſalut de corps, ſaluation de l'ame. &c Am.

In principio erat verbum, & verbum. &c. Amen dico vobis, ego ſum vitis vera, & pater meus agricola eſt. Omnem palmitem in me non ferentem fructum, tollit: & omnem qui fert fructum, purgat: vt copioſiorem afferat. Manete in me, & ego in vobis. Iam vos mundi eſtis propter ſermonem quẽ locutus ſum vobis.

The Guyot specimen featured three romans with **companion italics** [Fig 1.2].[12] Though the sheet itself doesn't specify the types' origins, two of the faces appeared around the same time in Antwerp printer Christophe Plantin's inventory as *Ascendonica Cursive and Texte Italique*, both attributed to Guyot.[13] The Guyot specimen used a four-column grid, with the largest roman almost spanning the sheet's width; the double pica roman and great primer italic run in two columns beneath it. The smallest types, subdivided again in two columns, nest beneath the double pica roman. Much of the text simply repeated the letters of the latin alphabet, A-Z, uppercase followed by lowercase, special characters, and numerals, with a period (full stop) after each letter. Brief biblical quotations made up the remainder of the text. There are no rules or decorative borders, only a single printer's flower and the paragraph symbol used to mark each paragraph's beginning; the bottom-right quadrant of the sheet is empty. Functional display, rather than impressive beauty, determined the page design strategy.

The Guyot specimen documented patterns of circulation, showing types designed by a French **punch-cutter** for a foundry in Belgium then sold to printers in England. But it's not unusual within the landscape of early western European printing. As specimens moved between places and times, so too did the types they showed. Sometimes the type itself was imported, like Guyot's to England, and sometimes local punch-cutters or foundries drew inspiration (or copied directly) from types seen on imported specimens. By typographic historian Harry Carter's count, Nicholas Jenson's 1476 **roman** face, for instance, directly inspired upwards of thirty faces used in various Italian printing houses before 1520.[14] It's easy to overlook these connections, especially those obscured over time. Some typefaces now known as **Garamond** weren't designed by Claude Garamont at all, for instance, but by Jean Jannon some sixty years after Garamont's death. Jannon's types were shaped in part by the Garamont types shown on another early specimen, the Egenolff-Berner specimen.

The first known type founder's specimen sheet, the Egenolff-Berner sheet (1592), drew the attention of English-language typographers in 1926. Beatrice Warde, writing under the male pseudonym Paul Beaujon, traced its complicated lineage for the typographic journal the *Fleuron*.[15] Later research proved some details of her account inaccurate, but she illuminated how marriage and inheritance played a role in the circulation of type designs, as well as opening up the question of "Garamond's" origins. After Frankfurt printer Christian Egenolff's death in 1555, his heirs expanded the family printing business into a typefounding operation, marketing their types at the city's famous book fairs. French type-cutter Jacques Sabon, after being employed by Egenolff's widow and later marrying Egenolff's granddaughter, acquired the foundry in 1572. Subsequently, Conrad Berner married Sabon's widow, acquiring the foundry and its types in 1591.[16] Later sources mis-attributed Jean Jannon's derivatives of the Egenolff-Berner Garamonds to Garamont, a fact initially brought to wide attention by Warde's inspection of the specimen.[17] While Berner's 1592 sheet displayed his collection of types, its typographic material was produced and/or commissioned primarily by his predecessors—about whose work subsequent generations weren't always clear.

Designed to attract visual attention in a crowded commercial environment like the Frankfurt Book Fair, the Egenolff-Berner broadside nonetheless utilized

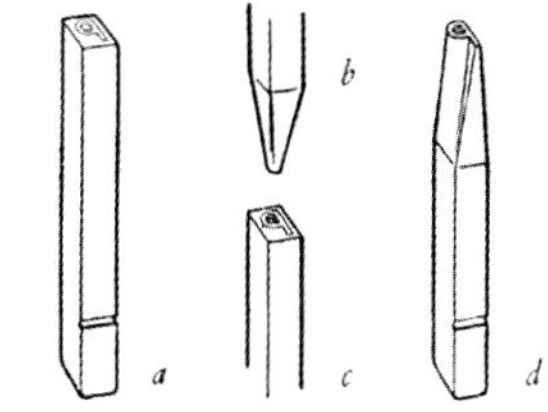

STEPS IN CUTTING THE TRADITIONAL PUNCH

Punch-cutters cut the steel punches used to strike the form of the character into softer metal to form the matrix, which was then used to cast individual sorts of type; essentially, this person was the designer of the typeface, as he controlled what the letters on the punch looked like.

altiſſimi dei ſacerdos iuſtiti
bræorũ appellatus eſt:apud
ulla mentio erat. Quare ne
gentiles:quoniam non utg
hebræos proprie noĩamus a
tranſitiuos ſignificat.Soli c
nõ ſcripta ad cognitioné ue
ad rectam uitam pueniſſe ſ

Nicholas Jenson's **roman** types, unlike the Gothic blackletters that preceeded them, were based on Roman inscriptions and seemed light and open.

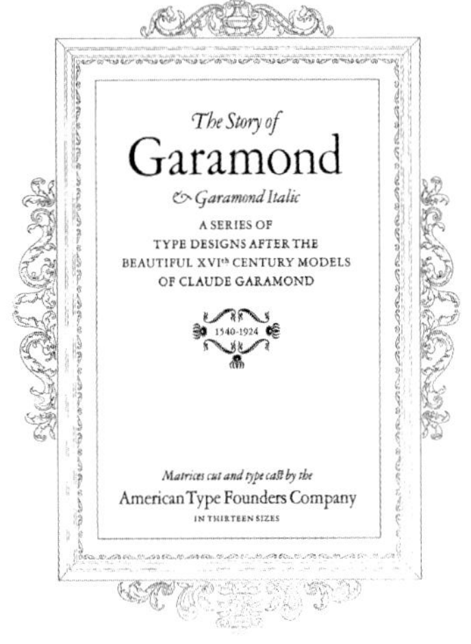

Garamond is the familiar name for types designed by or inspired—sometimes mistakenly, through mis-attribution—by French punch-cutter and type founder Claude Garamont (1499–1561). The *Monotype* journal's first 1923 issue documented what little was known of Garamond [sic] at the time.

compositional strategies familiar from its less elaborate forerunners [Fig 1.3]. A four-column grid organized the body copy, chiefly biblical quotations; the largest types occupied a single column, book faces two columns, and the smallest types four columns. The specimen displayed a work-horse collection of printing types, primarily romans and italics by French typographers Claude Garamont and Philippe Grandjean. Greek and Cyrillic alphabets, **manicules**, borders, and **fleurons** rounded out the selection. A decorative border composed of individual sorts framed the page; blackletter type differentiates a description of the foundry. Notably, this advertising copy highlighted the *writer's* role in selecting suitable typefaces. It offered:

Fig 1.3 (right)

***Specimen Characterum* (Conrad Berner, Frankfurt, 1592). Berner's is the first known type founder's specimen sheet, but it primarily displays types he acquired from Jacques Sabon, who had in turn acquired many from Christian Egenolff.**

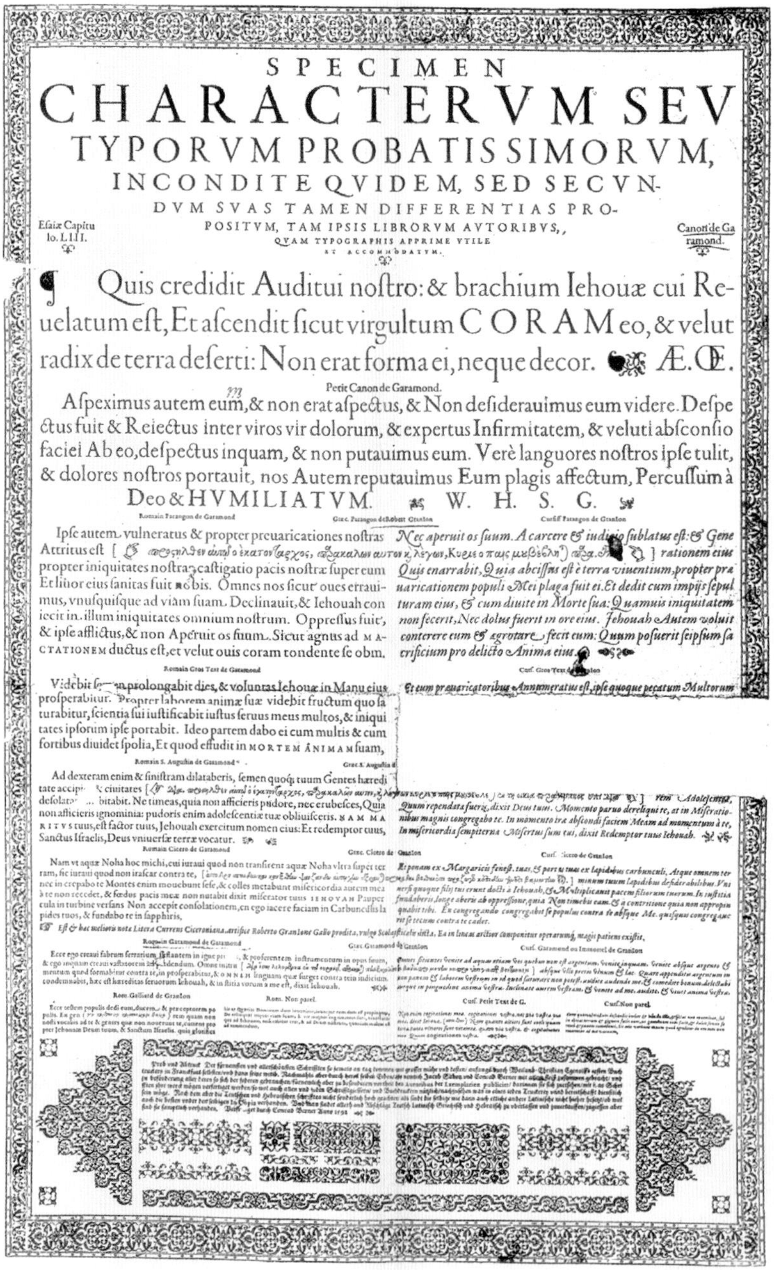

SPECIMEN CHARACTERVM SEV TYPORVM PROBATIS SIMORVM, INCONDITE QVIDEM, SED SECVNDVM SVAS TAMEN DIFFERENTIAS PROPOSITVM, TAM IPSIS LIBRORVM AVTORIBVS,, QVAM TYPOGRAPHIS APPRIME VTILE ET ACCOMMODATVM.

Esaiæ Capitu lo. LIII.

Canon de Garamond.

Quis credidit Auditui noſtro: & brachium Iehouæ cui Reuelatum eſt, Et aſcendit ſicut virgultum CORAM eo, & velut radix de terra deſerti: Non erat forma ei, neque decor. Æ. Œ.

Petit Canon de Garamond.

Aſpeximus autem eum, & non erat aſpectus, & Non deſiderauimus eum videre. Deſpectus fuit & Reiectus inter viros vir dolorum, & expertus Infirmitatem, & veluti abſconſio faciei Ab eo, deſpectus inquam, & non putauimus eum. Verè languores noſtros ipſe tulit, & dolores noſtros portauit, nos Autem reputauimus Eum plagis affectum, Percuſſum à Deo & HVMILIATVM. W. H. S. G.

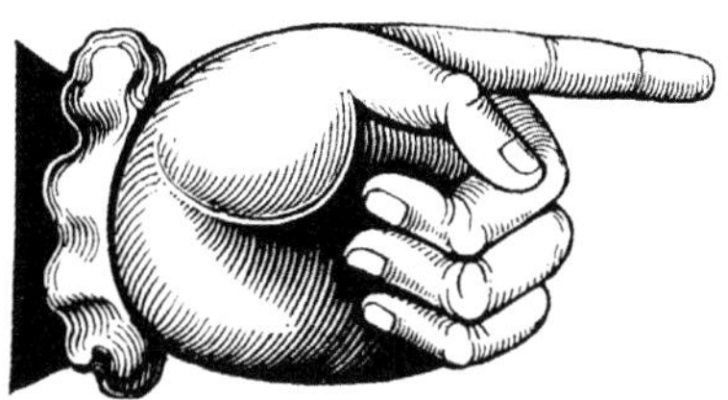

The **manicule** can also be called a fist, pointing fist or pointing finger, or index. Manicules can be in any style or size, suited to a footnote or a poster.

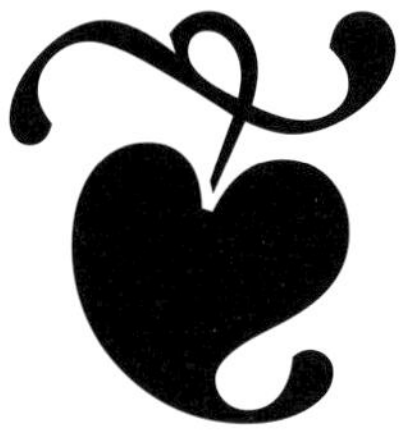

The **fleuron** above, designed by Hermann Zapf for the International Typeface Corporation (ITC) in 1978, draws on centuries-old typographic conventions.

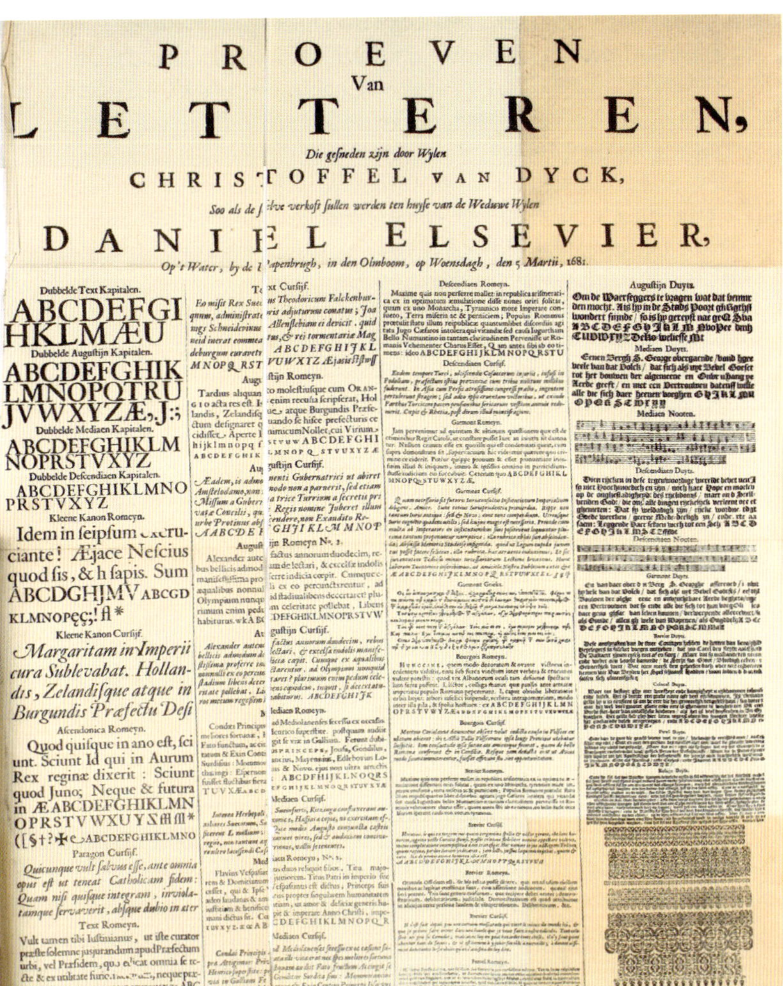

PROEVEN
Van
LETTEREN,
Die gesneden zijn door Wylen
CHRISTOFFEL VAN DYCK,
Soo als de selve verkoft sullen werden ten huyse van de Weduwe Wylen
DANIEL ELSEVIER,
Op't Water, by de Papenbrugh, in den Olmboom, op Woensdagh, den 5 Martii, 1681.

Fig 1.4 (left)

***Proeven van Letteren* (Elsevier & van Dyck, Amsterdam, 1681). Printer Daniel Elsevier's widow used this specimen to advertise and sell types her late husband had purchased from Christoffel Van Dyck, a well-known punch-cutter.**

> the finest and most beautiful types ever yet seen ... Published for the benefit of all who use a pen, but more especially for the advantage of authors of printers' copy, so that they may judge in what type their work may best be done, but equally useful to type-casters and printers as showing what may be of service in every printing-office and business. ... you may have all manner of strikes, German, Latin, Greek, or Hebrew, for hire or sale, notwithstanding that all are kept at hand for casting.[18]

As the Egenolff-Berner specimen demonstrates, the idea that different typefaces perform different jobs and connote different meanings dates from the earliest chapter of printing history.

Inheritance and marriage played a significant role across the typefounding trade, not just at the Egenolff-Berner foundry. The 1681 Van Dyck [or Van Dijck] specimen was issued by the widow of Amsterdam printer Daniel Elsevier, who had purchased well-known punch-cutter Christoffel Van Dyck's inventory in 1673 following the death of Van Dyck and his only son. Designed on a four-column grid, the sheet includes types by Van Dyck, Van den Keere, Garamont, and Granjon, representing both local Dutch and imported French

Fig 1.5 (opposite)

***A Specimen* (William Caslon, London, 1734). Caslon's first known specimen, this broadside established him as a central figure in English typography, a reputation still intact today.**

Great Primer Greek.

ΠΑτερ ἡμῶν ὁ ἐν τοῖς οὐρανοῖς· ἁγιασθήτω τὸ ὄνομά σου. Ἐλθέτω ἡ βασιλεία σου. γενηθήτω τὸ θέλημά σου, ὡς ἐν οὐρανῷ, καὶ ἐπὶ τῆς γῆς. Τὸν ἄρτον ἡμῶν τὸν ἐπιούσιον δὸς ἡμῖν σήμερον. Καὶ ἄφες ἡμῖν τὰ ὀφειλήματα ἡμῶν, ὡς καὶ ἡμεῖς ἀφίεμεν τοῖς ὀφειλέταις ἡμῶν. Καὶ μὴ εἰσενέγκῃς ἡμᾶς εἰς πειρασμὸν, ἀλλὰ ῥῦσαι ἡμᾶς ἀπὸ τοῦ πονηροῦ. ὅτι σοῦ ἐστιν ἡ βασιλεία, καὶ ἡ δύναμις, καὶ ἡ δόξα, εἰς τοὺς αἰῶνας. ἀμήν.

The **Greek** alphabet has 24 letters, each with an upper- and lower-case form. This Great Primer Greek, roughly equal to today's 18 points, is from Caslon's 1785 specimen book.

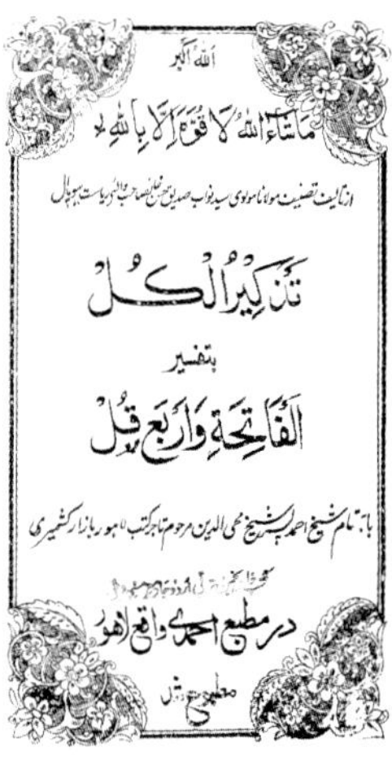

Arabic poses specific challenges for typesetting, and local text production often occured by hand or via lithography, as in the case of this Quranic commentary published in nineteenth century Pakistan.

ARMENIAN

Although there are two kinds of lower case to Armenian, the caps used for both are identical. A complete font includes the caps and both lower cases, the sloping lower case being known as No. 1 and the upright as No. 2..

10 Point Armenian—464

Figure size, .0761. Code word, SPAHEFT

ՀԱՑ ԿԻՐ ԵՒ ՎԱՐԴԱՆԱՆՑ Մեր պատմ ութեա , · :—«» ' '.
ՀԱՑ ԿԻՐ ԵՒ ՎԱՐԴԱՆԱՆՑ Մեր պատմ ութեա 1234567890

Exotics is one of many antiquated terms historically used for writing systems unfamiliar to readers, printers, and type designers who used the Latin alphabet. Above: 10pt. Linotype Armenian, 1913.

types [Fig 1.4].[19] The title at the top spans the sheet's width and takes up eight lines. Excerpts from Classical texts display primarily roman and italic types (*Romeyn* and *Cursijf*, in Dutch) but also eight blackletters, a **Greek** attributed to Garamont, two musical note faces, and floral ornaments—useful for constructing borders, though the sheet doesn't demonstrate this. Hairline rules divide the four columns, and the tightly-packed composition uses space efficiently, with compact leading and inter-column spacing. Though the sheet was designed to advertise the sale of Elzevier's business after his death, the auction never took place.[20] But this practical purpose made displaying the range of types more important than elaborate decoration or an airy composition. A late nineteenth century history of the Elzevier house contained a facsimile of this specimen, a seminal document in the history of what eventually became—after a series of purchases and inheritances—the venerable Enschedé foundry. Enschedé (est. 1743) retained the punches and matrices for only one italic type shown on the 1681 specimen, the rest having been discarded over time.[21] The decisions and preferences of successive founders shaped the survival of historical types, as the Van Dyck specimen testifies.

William Caslon's 1734 specimen sheet established him as a preeminent figure in English typography. The introductory note in Caslon's first specimen book (1785) credited his own foundry—accurately—with "transferr[ing] the letter-foundry business from Holland to England."[22] Prior to Caslon's success as the first major English type founder, printing relied primarily on imported Dutch matrices and types, explaining Caslon's reliance on Dutch models for his earliest typeface designs.[23] Apprenticed to a metal engraver, Caslon entered the printing trade via the bookbinders whose tools he made. His first reliably recorded type, a 1724 **Arabic** for the Society for Promoting Christian Knowledge (SPCK), was commissioned to print a psalter and New Testament for Arabic-reading Christians. In 1725, a pica roman modeled on a c.1695 Dutch face followed.[24] The 1734 broadside is Caslon's earliest known specimen, showing just under fifty typefaces: fourteen romans and italics, an array of **exotics**, and floral ornaments and borders [Fig. 1.5]. Like many early broadsides, most of its copy uses a four-column grid, with title and attribution spanning the entire width and text faces set in four narrow columns below. This decision emphasizes the point size of the smallest of these fonts. Size mattered; the SPCK commissioned the novice Caslon's 1724 Arabic because the extant local source of Arabic type could supply only a larger (Great Primer) face, which would have caused the project to exceed its budget.[25] Showing a wide selection of sizes emphasized to potential customers the comprehensive breadth of the Caslon foundry.

A SPECIMEN

By WILLIAM CASLON, Letter-Founder, in Chiſwell-Street, LONDON.

ABCD
ABCDE
ABCDEFG
ABCDEFGHI
ABCDEFGHIJK
ABCDEFGHIJKL
ABCDEFGHIKLMN

French Cannon.

Quouſque tandem abutere, Catilina, pati-
Quouſque tandem abutere, Catilina, patientia noſtra?

Two Lines Great Primer.

Quouſque tandem abutere, Catilina, patientia noſtra? quamdiu nos etiam
Quouſque tandem abutere, Catilina, patientia noſtra? quamdiu nos etiam furor

Two Lines Engliſh.

Quouſque tandem abutere, Catilina, patientia noſtra? quamdiu nos etiam furor iſte tuus elu-
Quouſque tandem abutere, Catilina, patientia noſtra? quamdiu nos etiam furor

DOUBLE PICA ROMAN.

Quouſque tandem abutere, Catilina, patientia noſtra? quamdiu nos etiam furor iſte tuus eludet? quem ad finem ſeſe effrenata jac-
ABCDEFGHJIKLMNOP

GREAT PRIMER ROMAN.

Quouſque tandem abutêre, Catilina, patientia noſtra? quamdiu nos etiam furor iſte tuus eludet? quem ad finem ſeſe effrenata jactabit audacia? nihilne te nocturnum præſidium palatii, nihil urbis vigiliæ, nihil timor populi, nihil con-
ABCDEFGHIJKLMNOPQRS

ENGLISH ROMAN.

Quouſque tandem abutêre, Catilina, patientia noſtra? quamdiu nos etiam furor iſte tuus eludet? quem ad finem ſeſe effrenata jactabit audacia? nihilne te nocturnum præſidium palatii, nihil urbis vigiliæ, nihil timor populi, nihil conſenſus bonorum omnium, nihil hic munitiſſimus
ABCDEFGHIJKLMNOPQRSTVUW

PICA ROMAN.

Melium, novis rebus ſtudentem, manu ſua occidit. Fuit, fuit iſta quondam in hac repub. virtus, ut viri fortes acrioribus ſuppliciis civem pernicioſum, quam acerbiſſimum hoſtem coërcerent. Habemus enim ſenatuſconſultum in te, Catilina, vehemens, & grave: non deeſt reip. conſilium, neque autoritas hujus ordinis: nos, nos, dico aperte, conſules deſumus. De-
ABCDEFGHIJKLMNOPQRSTVUWX

Double Pica Italick.

Quouſque tandem abutere, Catilina, patientia noſtra? quamdiu nos etiam furor iſte tuus eludet? quem ad finem ſeſe effrenata jac-
ABCDEFGHJIKLMNO

Great Primer Italick.

Quouſque tandem abutêre, Catilina, patientia noſtra? quamdiu nos etiam furor iſte tuus eludet? quem ad finem ſeſe effrenata jactabit audacia? nihilne te nocturnum præſidium palatii, nihil urbis vigiliæ, nihil timor populi, nihil con-
ABCDEFGHIJKLMNOPQR

Engliſh Italick.

Quouſque tandem abutere, Catilina, patientia noſtra? quamdiu nos etiam furor iſte tuus eludet? quem ad finem ſeſe effrenata jactabit audacia? nihilne te nocturnum præſidium palatii, nihil urbis vigiliæ, nihil timor populi, nihil conſenſus bonorum omnium, nihil hic munitiſſimus habendi ſe-
ABCDEFGHIJKLMNOPQRSTVU

Pica Italick.

Melium, novis rebus ſtudentem, manu ſua occidit. Fuit, fuit iſta quondam in hac repub. virtus, ut viri fortes acrioribus ſuppliciis civem pernicioſum, quam acerbiſſimum hoſtem coërcerent. Habemus enim ſenatuſconſultum in te, Catilina, vehemens, & grave: non deeſt reip. conſilium, neque autoritas hujus ordinis: nos, nos, dico aperte, conſules deſumus. Decrevit quondam ſenatus
ABCDEFGHIJKLMNOPQRSTVUWXYZ

Pica Black.

And be it further enacted by the Authority aforeſaid, That all and every of the ſaid Exchequer Bills to be made forth by virtue of this Act, or ſo many of them as ſhall from
ABCDEFGHIJKLMNOPQRST

Brevier Black.

Pica Gothick.

Pica Coptick.

Pica Armenian.

Engliſh Syriack.

Pica Samaritan.

SMALL PICA ROMAN. No 1.

At nos vigeſimum jam diem patimur hebeſcere aciem horum autoritatis. habemus enim hujuſmodi ſenatuſconſultum, verumtamen incluſum in tabulis, tanquam gladium in vagina reconditum: quo ex ſenatuſconſulto confeſtim interfectum te eſſe, Catilina, convenit. Vivis: & vivis non ad deponendam, ſed ad confirmandam audaciam. Cupio, P. C., me eſſe clementem: cupio in tantis reipub. periculis non diſ-
ABCDEFGHIJKLMNOPQRSTVUWXYZ

SMALL PICA ROMAN. No 2.

At nos vigeſimum jam diem patimur hebeſcere aciem horum autoritatis. habemus enim hujuſmodi ſenatuſconſultum, verumtamen incluſum in tabulis, tanquam gladium in vagina reconditum: quo ex ſenatuſconſulto confeſtim interfectum te eſſe, Catilina, convenit. Vivis: & vivis non ad deponendam, ſed ad confirmandam audaciam. Cupio, P. C., me eſſe clementem: cupio in tantis reipub. periculis non diſſolutum
ABCDEFGHIJKLMNOPQRSTVUWXYZ

LONG PRIMER ROMAN. No 1.

Verum ego hoc, quod jampridem factum eſſe oportuit, certa de cauſſa nondum adducor ut faciam. tum denique interficiam te, cum jam nemo tam improbus, tam perditus, tam tui ſimilis inveniri poterit, qui id non jure factum eſſe fateatur. Quamdiu quiſquam erit qui te defendere audeat, vives: & vives, ita ut nunc vivis, multis meis & firmis præſidiis obſeſſus, ne commovere te contra rempub. poſſis. multorum te etiam oculi & aures non ſentientem, ſicut adhuc fecerunt, ſpeculabuntur, atque cuſtodient. Etenim quid eſt, Cati-
ABCDEFGHIJKLMNOPQRSTUVWXYZÆ

LONG PRIMER ROMAN. No 2.

Verum ego hoc, quod jampridem factum eſſe oportuit, certa de cauſſa nondum adducor ut faciam. tum denique interficiam te, cum jam nemo tam improbus, tam perditus, tam tui ſimilis inveniri poterit, qui id non jure factum eſſe fateatur. Quamdiu quiſquam erit qui te defendere audeat, vives: & vives, ita ut nunc vivis, multis meis & firmis præſidiis obſeſſus, ne commovere te contra rempub. poſſis. multorum te etiam oculi & aures non ſentientem, ſicut adhuc fecerunt, ſpeculabuntur, atque cuſtodient. Etenim quid eſt, Cati-
ABCDEFGHIJKLMNOPQRSTVUWXYZÆ

BREVIER ROMAN.

Nonpareil Roman.

Pearl Roman.

Small Pica Italick. No 1.

At nos vigeſimum jam diem patimur hebeſcere aciem horum autoritatis. habemus enim hujuſmodi ſenatuſconſultum, verumtamen incluſum in tabulis, tanquam gladium in vagina reconditum: quo ex ſenatuſconſulto confeſtim interfectum te eſſe, Catilina, convenit. Vivis: & vivis non ad deponendam, ſed ad confirmandam audaciam. Cupio, P. C., me eſſe clementem: cupio in tantis reipub. periculis non diſſolutum videri: ſed jam
ABCDEFGHIJKLMNOPQRSTVWUXYZ

Small Pica Italick. No 2.

At nos vigeſimum jam diem patimur hebeſcere aciem horum autoritatis. habemus enim hujuſmodi ſenatuſconſultum, verumtamen incluſum in tabulis, tanquam gladium in vagina reconditum: quo ex ſenatuſconſulto confeſtim interfectum te eſſe, Catilina, convenit. Vivis: & vivis non ad deponendam, ſed ad confirmandam audaciam. Cupio, P. C., me eſſe clementem: cupio in tantis reipub. periculis non diſſolutum videri: ſed jam meipſum inertiæ
ABCDEFGHIJKLMNOPQRSTVUWXYZ

Long Primer Italick. No 1.

Verum ego hoc, quod jampridem factum eſſe oportuit, certa de cauſſa nondum adducor ut faciam. tum denique interficiam te, cum jam nemo tam improbus, tam perditus, tam tui ſimilis inveniri poterit, qui id non jure factum eſſe fateatur. Quamdiu quiſquam erit qui te defendere audeat, vives: & vives, ita ut nunc vivis, multis meis & firmis præſidiis obſeſſus, ne commovere te contra rempub. poſſis. multorum te etiam oculi & aures non ſentientem, ſicut adhuc fecerunt, ſpeculabuntur, atque cuſtodient. Etenim quid eſt, Catilina, quod jam
ABCDEFGHIJKLMNOPQRSTVUWXYZÆ

Long Primer Italick. No 2.

Verum ego hoc, quod jampridem factum eſſe oportuit, certa de cauſſa nondum adducor ut faciam. tum denique interficiam te, cum jam nemo tam improbus, tam perditus, tam tui ſimilis inveniri poterit, qui id non jure factum eſſe fateatur. Quamdiu quiſquam erit qui te defendere audeat, vives: & vives, ita ut nunc vivis, multis meis & firmis præſidiis obſeſſus, ne commovere te contra rempub. poſſis. multorum te
ABCDEFGHIJKLMNOPQRSTVUWXYZÆ

Brevier Italick.

Nonpareil Italick.

Pearl Italick.

Engliſh Arabick.

Hebrew with Points.

Hebrew without Points.

Brevier Hebrew.

Engliſh Greek.

Pica Greek.

Long Primer Greek.

Brevier Greek.

Long Primer Saxon.

Pica Saxon.

This SPECIMEN to be placed in the Middle of the Sheet 5 U u, VOL. II.

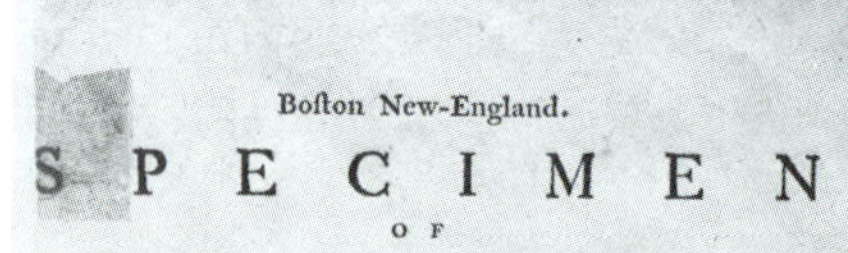

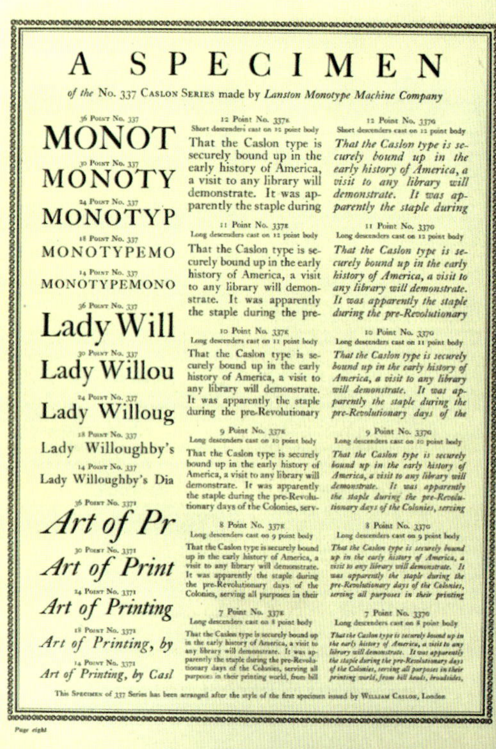

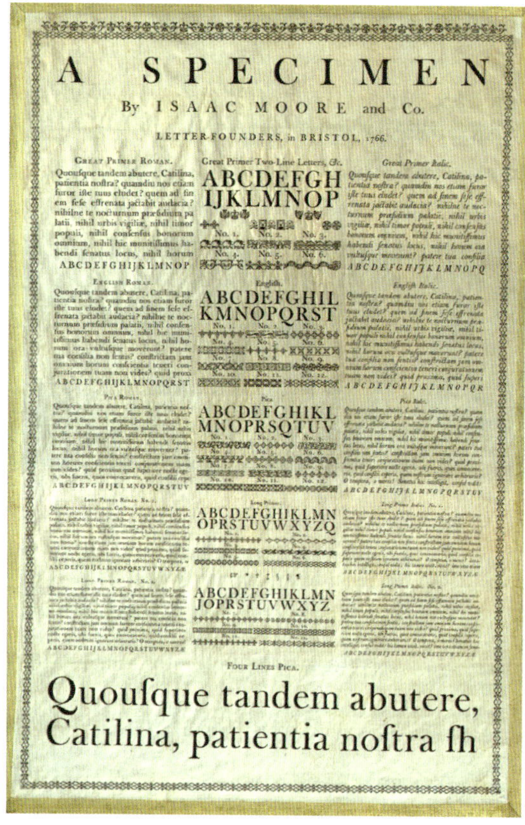

Fig 1.6 (above)

A Specimen **(Lanston Monotype Company, Philadelphia, 1922). Promotional material for Monotype's Caslon series was "arranged in the style of the first specimen issued by" Caslon.**

Fig 1.7 (top right)

Specimen of Mein & Fleeming's Printing Types **(John Mein & John Fleeming, Boston, 1765-9). All the types on this printers' specimen were imported from England; the first American type founders' sheets wouldn't follow until 1815.**

Fig 1.8 (right)

A Specimen **(Isaac Moore & Co., Bristol, 1766). Moore's specimen, though not ostentatious, offers a wide selection of type and ornament. The centered, symmetrical composition reflects the Neoclassical taste of the period.**

Along the bottom of the sheet, Caslon's ornaments align into a single rule, the only decorative element. The restrained page design underscores the types' functionality and clarity, characteristics admired during Caslon's time and long thereafter. Rival type founder Joseph Fry's first specimen book (1785) boasted that his typefaces weren't discernable from Caslon's—though if he admired Caslon or knew this claim would boost sales, he didn't say. The Caslon foundry, in turn, accused Fry of being an envious maker of cheap imitations.[26] Two centuries after their design, a 1924 **trade journal** article praised Caslon's types as useful, beautiful, proportional, and instinctually fit for their purpose, as well as singularly popular and widely employed.[27] As the display copy for his 1734 broadside, Caslon made another influential decision, choosing Cicero's first oration: *Quousque tandem abutere, Catilina.* Typographic historian Daniel Berkeley Updike credited Caslon as the first to do so, arguing that Caslon's choice exerted "considerable influence on the shape of the capital letter Q; for this sentence became so consecrated to type specimens that most eighteenth century type founders felt it necessary to employ it, and in order to outdo each other, they elongated the **tails** of the Q's more and more."[28] The design of the specimen sheet itself also influenced specimens to follow. Almost two centuries later, Lanston Monotype based the design of the specimen material for their "real Caslon"—not an imitation, however good, but the *original* letterforms—on Caslon's design strategy [Fig. 1.6].[29]

In the Colonial United States, printing was an infant industry in the eighteenth century. Even Americans eager to bestow praise admitted that the chief virtue of American printing (and American type) lay in the fact that it wasn't **imported** from England. The *Boston New-England Specimen of Mein and Fleeming's Printing Types* (1765-9) demonstrates the pragmatic design that dominated in New England long after more elaborate specimens, displaying a larger number of types and styles, became common elsewhere [Fig. 1.7]. A comparison to Bristol type founder Isaac Moore's concurrent *Specimen* (1766) underscores the Colonial American prioritization of function [Fig. 1.8]. Bookseller and publisher John Mein published the Loyalist newspaper the *Boston Chronicle* (1767-70) with his business partner John Fleeming. Their printer's specimen displayed the imported types their print shop owned. Successful typefounding in the American Colonies originated with Abel Buell in Connecticut in 1769, but the first dated founder's (as opposed to printer's) specimen sheets, from the Bruce foundry in New York, weren't printed until 1815.[30] Mein and Fleeming's compositional approach embraced function, avoiding any hint of embellishment. The centered title sat above six roman faces of different sizes; the title word *specimen* showed a seventh, larger type. At the bottom of the sheet, a small manicule quite literally pointed toward what was, for a printer's advertisement of the time, a rather modest statement: "Mein and Fleeming execute all sorts of printing work in the best and most reasonable manner, and with the utmost expedition." Like Caslon and Moore, Mein and Fleeming chose Cicero for their sample copy, but used the third oration instead of the first. Fortunately, it too contained an uppercase Q, the tails of which enlivened the six sample texts. Though Mein and Fleeming's aesthetic prioritized American pragmatism, they elected to participate in this typographic fashion of their day.

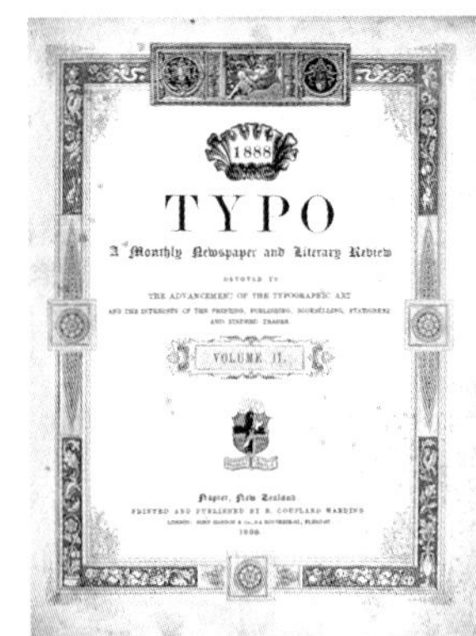

Trade journals are periodical publications for members of a specific trade, like printing. Typically they contain articles, advice columns, and advertisements pertinent to practitioners. *Typo* addressed the printers of New Zealand (and beyond) around the turn of the twentieth century.

Quoufque tan-
dem abutere,

Quoufque tandem
abutere, Catilina,

The **tail** of the uppercase Q appears at the beginning of one of the eighteenth century's most popular specimen texts, the opening line of first-century Roman statesman Cicero's first oration against Catiline, here from Caslon's 1785 specimen. Tail also refers, sometimes, to the leg of the uppercase R or K.

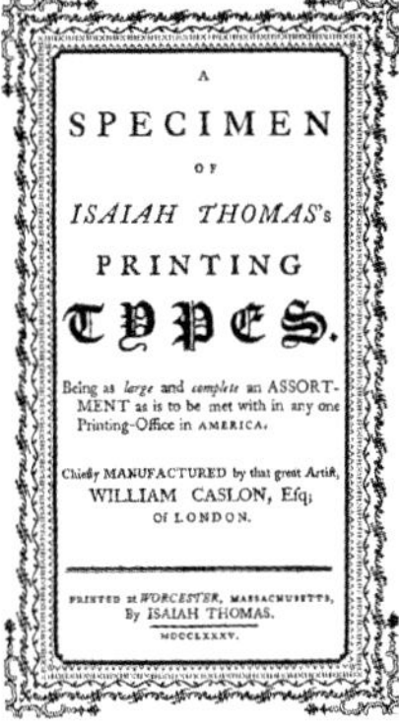

A
SPECIMEN
OF
ISAIAH THOMAS's
PRINTING
TYPES.

Being as large and complete an ASSORTMENT as is to be met with in any one Printing-Office in AMERICA.

Chiefly MANUFACTURED by that great Artist, WILLIAM CASLON, Esq; OF LONDON.

PRINTED at WORCESTER, MASSACHUSETTS, By ISAIAH THOMAS.
MDCCLXXXV.

Printing in the early United States relied on **imported** types, as the title page of Isaiah Thomas' printing office specimen (Massachusetts, 1785) attests by describing the types it shows as "chiefly manufactured" by Caslon.

HYMN 6 12,9

Psalm 5

Liturgical texts are produced for religious purposes, like this 1909 hymnal for Cherokee congregations published by the Presbyterian Dwight Mission Press. This text was produced to prostelytize Cherokee Nation citizens who had been forcably removed from their homelands in the Southeast United States to Oklahoma reservations by the United States government.

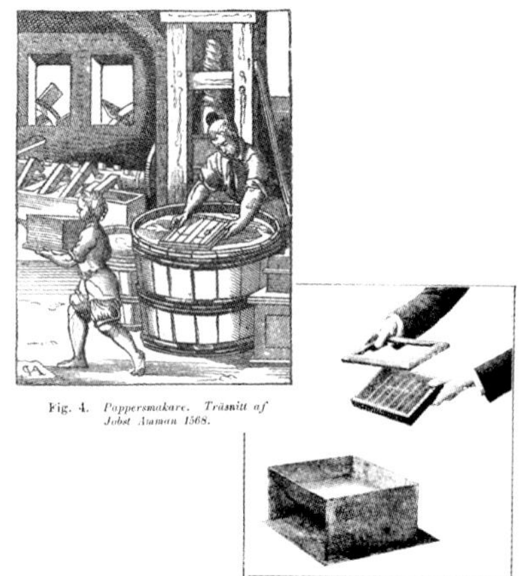

A **folio** is a full sheet of paper folded or cut in half; a foolscap sheet measured 13.5x17 inches and a foolscap folio 8.5x13 inches. As this 1568 illustration of a papermaker at work shows, paper sizes were originally determined by the maximum size of the paper mold, which needed to be held between the papermaker's two hands.

Multi-tasking—specimens serving multiple purposes

Excerpts from **liturgical** texts (Ratdolt, Guyot, Egenolff-Berner) and Classical literature (Van Dyck, Caslon, Mein & Fleeming) were common as specimen texts. But other kinds of copy could facilitate additional uses for the specimen. Specimen broadsides always served as advertisements for the types they displayed; founders deployed them to cultivate custom among printers and publishers, printers to cultivate authors, religious and civil entities, and commercial businesses. Yet some broadsides cleverly exploited their medium to sell additional products or claimed alternate, often scholarly, purposes for documents that functioned essentially as ads for type. Swiss scholar J.J. Bodmer's *Elementale quadrilingue* (Zürich, 1654) ostensibly provided an educational guide (a *ratio legendi*) to reading then-called exotic types, though functionally it advertised new faces commissioned by Bodmer and Swiss philologist J.H. Hottinger, and designed and cut by Balthasar Köblin.[31] The broadside exhibited the Zurich School's unusual (in Northern Europe) capacity to print texts in multiple scripts. The years-long, expensive production process of Köblin's types, intended to establish Zurich as a leading and financially lucrative center for "oriental" scholarship, failed when Hottinger relocated to the University of Heidelberg in 1655.[32] Few copies of the sheet survived; Harvard's Houghton Library houses one, where it was re-discovered after lying forgotten with a donated set of seventeenth-century pamphlets on Semitic languages.[33] *Elementale quadrilingue* visually recorded the role typography and type-founding have played in scholarship, leveraging the form of the specimen to highlight its makers' roles in scholarly dialogues.

Proves of Several Sorts of Letters Cut by Joseph Moxon (1699) likewise served a dual purpose. The sheet claimed to display Moxon's types, and showed eleven of these—which early typographic historians judged "poor in face and uneven in line."[34] But it also advertised his business as a dealer of scientific and mathematical instruments, including "Globes Celestial and Terrestrial, [and] Large Maps of the World."[35] Long thought England's first specimen broadside, Moxon's *Proves* was almost certainly preceded by two undated single-sheet specimens printed by Nicholas Nicholls, probably in 1656 and 1665, and by the Fell specimen of 1685 [Fig. 1.9]. Like Moxon's, it served a dual advertising purpose. Named after Dr. John Fell, supervisor of printing at Oxford University from 1671, it advertised books "lately printed at the Theatre in Oxford"; significant contextual evidence suggests a publication date of 1685.[36] Its headline explained that "a specimen of the letter on which every book is printed followeth underneath." The types weren't labeled with name, size, or designer; rather, each named the book in which it was used. For instance, the header "a Church-Bible in large **Folio**, on this Letter following" appeared above two verses from Titus, printed in the type used for the large folio Bible. This ingenious format addressed both book-buyers and potential printing clients. The heading spanned the page, with sample texts set in two

labeled, and some sample texts advertised the *Times*, but most of the copy repeated the alphabet A–Z. Masthead, typographic sorts, and **linear rules** were the only compositional elements. This reflected Morison's approach to typographic craft; he admired mid nineteenth-century English printing that displayed "the durable charm of all good craftsmanship, for their beauty [was] achieved entirely by their use of types and a few printers' flowers."[42] His specimen sheet reflected this philosophy and avoided decorative embellishment.

A later Times New Roman broadside from the San Francisco foundry McKenzie & Harris (1960) both echoed and contrasted with Morison's approach [Fig. 1.12]. Like Morison's, the composition used only the Times New Roman types and hairline rules. As a framing device around the perimeter of the composition, the letters of the alphabet were printed in black (upper case) and red (lower case) and their baseline followed the rectangular hairline frame around the specimen text—again, echoing Morison, the alphabet running A–Z. Inverting Morison's original approach, a smaller inset frame showed the larger sizes, 42–72 **points**. A footnote in small italic type read:

> The design of this broadside and the presswork, by letterpress, have been accomplished for us by Taylor & Taylor of San Francisco. With the exception of the title ... all the type used has been cut in our foundry from Monotype matrices cut from the original design and obtained by us from England. Naturally, the typography has been done in our composing room.

This text contained multiple signals of the broadside's role as a vehicle for communication among professionals. It referenced casting and printing technologies (**Monotype**, letterpress), articulated the typographic process (matrices, composing room), and underscored the type's legitimacy by specifying its origins (England). By situating itself within a particular lineage, the specimen imparted validity on the type it showed and the foundry it represented.

Fig 1.12 (opposite)
***The Times New Roman and Italic* (McKenzie & Harris, San Francisco, 1960). This later interpretation of Morison's typeface quotes both his 1948 broadside and the more generalized and very long-standing conventions of the specimen as a form.**

KEGLERNES STØRRELSEFORHOLD
indbyrdes, i typografiske enheder og i millimeter.

DIDOT·BERTHOLDS			LEIPZIGER SYSTEM		
Antal metriske punkter	Keglernes størrelser i millimeter	Keglernes almindelige typografiske betegnelser	Antal kvartpetit	Svarende til metriske punkter	Keglernes størrelser i millimeter
4	1,504	······ Diamant ······	2	3,85	1,44
5	1,879	········· Perle ·········	2,5	4,80	1,80
6	2,256	······ Nonpareil ······	3	5,75	2,17
7	2,632	Mignon ··· Kolonel ···	3,5	6,70	2,53
8	3,008	········· Petit ·········	4	7,65	2,89
9	3,383	······ Bourgeois ······	4,5	8,60	3,15
10	3,759	······· Korpus ·······	5	9,60	3,61
12	4,511	······· Cicero ·······	6	11,50	4,33
14	5,263	······· Mittel ·······	7	13,40	5,05
16	6,015	······· Tertia ·······	8	15,30	5,78
20	7,519	······· Tekst ·······	10	19,15	7,22
24	9,023	····· Dobbelcicero ·····	12	23,00	8,66
28	10,526	····· Dobbelmittel ·····	14	26,80	10,10
32	12,030	Dobbeltertia Lille kanon ·	16	30,60	11,56
36	13,534	Trecicero ··· Kanon ····	18	34,50	12,99
40	15,038	Dobbelttekst Grov kanon	20	38,30	14,44
48	18,046	Firecicero ·· Missal ····	24	46,00	17,32
60	22,555	Femcicero ·· Grov missal	30	57,50	21,66
72	27,066	Sekscicero ·· Sabon ····	36	69,00	25,98

Basis: meteren. 2660 Didot-Bertholdske punkter = 1 meter; 133 nonpareil = 798 metriske punkter = 300 millimeter. Papirhøjde: 62,67 metriske punkter.

Basis: ubekendt. 72 cicerolegemer = 828 metriske punkter = 311,28 millimeter. 231,30 cicerogevierter = 1 meter. Papirhøjde: 5¾ cicerolegemer = 66 metriske punkter.

The Didot and American **point systems** are–as this Danish chart shows–only two of many systems historically deployed to measure type size (*Typografi for Saettere*, Selmar, 1913).

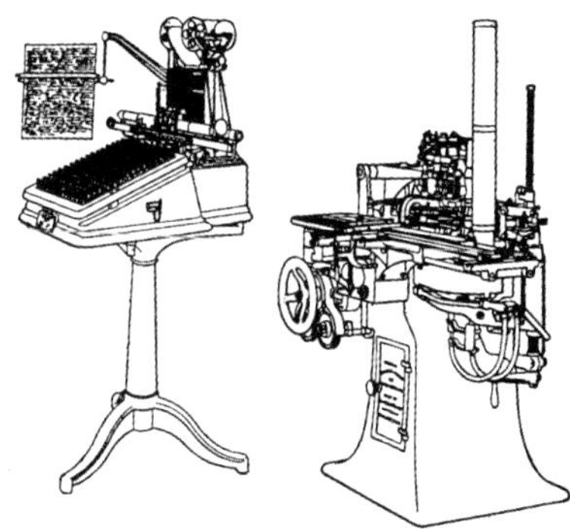

Monotype machines produced individual sorts of type in the order determined by the keyboard operator. The caster was a separate unit. This system meant individual letters could be added or removed to already-cast lines of type and allowed finer letterspacing control.

Fig 1.13 (opposite)
***Pasto specimen* (Julia Martínez Diana, Antipixel, Argentina, 2019). Even in today's digital environment, the printed specimen remains an important signifier of professional identity. Like many digital foundries, Antipixel markets not only Pasto, a digital typeface, but also the printed specimen designed to display it.**

The printed specimen broadside remains familiar even in the twenty-first century, when much of the typography in our everyday environment is selected, set, and consumed on screens. Because the format has a long and distinguished history within the profession, type designers continue to engage with it as a way to participate in an historically situated field of practice and address community members within that field. Broadsides continue to emerge from traditional centers of typography and printing in Western Europe and North America. But given globalized type design practices in the digital era, broadside specimens are also produced in locations and languages once represented almost exclusively by imported metal type. For contemporary digital foundries like Argentinian type designer Julia Martínez Diana's Antipixel [Fig. 1.13], the production of printed broadside specimens no longer serves as a primary means of display or circulation. Martínez describes the specimen for her typeface Pasto (2019) as a visual representation of "the overall look of the type family, its playfulness, and its graphic universe." She writes about the work the specimen does:

> With the desire to display every essential aspect of the typeface and the details that stand out, one of the main goals of Pasto's type specimen was to show its language support. The reason for this is that I find it necessary to include diacritics that make the font versatile and available for as many people as possible. It was also very important to highlight the available Open Type Contextual Alternates. These may not be noticeable at first sight thanks to their subtlety, but they provide a more natural handwritten feel because the letterforms differ slightly from each other. Pasto has three alphabet variants that automatically alternate to avoid repeating the same letterforms and textures in close proximity. The specimen is available online for purchase as a printed poster since it is not only a type specimen but a design object itself.[43]

As Pasto demonstrates, the specimen format remains a lovingly crafted signal of professional identity for both producers and consumers of specimen broadsides.

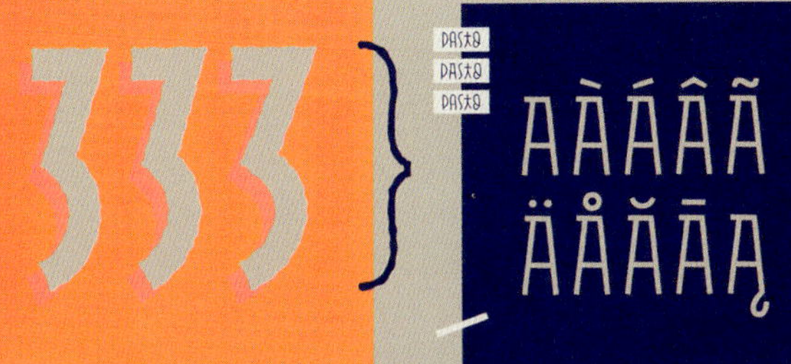

PASTO

¡AMSTERDAM!

A24, AN AMERICAN INDEPENDENT ENTERTAINMENT FILM COMPANY

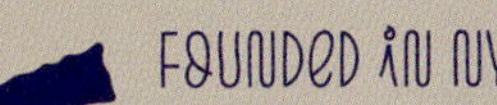

FOUNDED IN NY

PAMPAHÚM

M&M'S

(EGGGS)

THECUSTOMSKATEDECKS

ACTRESS GRETA GERWIG CO-WROTE AND STARRED IN THE 2013 ACCLAIMED FRANCES HA

1 Andrew Pettegree, ed., *Broadsheets: Single-Sheet Publishing in the First Age of Print* (Leiden: Brill, 2017), 17–26, 114.

2 Pettegree, *Broadsheets*. See particularly the editor's introduction and chapters 5 (Drew Thomas), 14 (Richard Kirwin), 15 (Malcolm Walsby), and 16 (Saskia Limbach). On broadside ballads, see Paula McDowell, "'The Manufacture and Lingua-Facture of Ballad-Making': Broadside Ballads in Long Eighteenth-Century Ballad Discourse," *The Eighteenth Century* 47, no. 2/3 (2006): 151–78, https://www.jstor.org/stable/41467998; Katie Sisneros, "Early Modern Memes: The Reuse and Recycling of Woodcuts in 17th-Century English Popular Print" (The Public Domain Review, June 6, 2018), https://publicdomainreview.org/2018/06/06/early-modern-memes-the-reuse-and-recycling-of-woodcuts-in-17th-century-english-popular-print/.

3 Hendrik D.L. Vervliet, Harry Carter, and John Dreyfus, eds., *Type Specimen Facsimiles* (London: Bowes & Bowes, 1963), 10.

4 Harry Carter, *A View of Early Typography: Up to about 1600* (London: Hyphen, 2002), 98. John A. Lane and Mathieu Lommen, *Dutch Typefounders' Specimens: From the Library of the KVB and Other Collections in the Amsterdam University Library, with Histories of the Firms Represented* (Amsterdam: De Buitenkant, 1998), 12.

5 Lane and Lommen, *Dutch Typefounders' Specimens*, 9–12; Pettegree, *Broadsheets*, 4–6.

6 Graham Pollard, *Catalogue of I Typefounders' Specimens; II Books Printed in Founts of Historic Importance; III Works on Typefounding Printing & Bibliography Offered for Sale* (London: Birrell & Garnett, 1928); Dreyfus, Carter, and Vervliet, *Type Specimen Facsimiles*, 2:xxv.

7 E. Gordon Duff, *Early English Printing: A Series of Facsimiles of All the Types Used in England during the XVth Century* (London: Kegan Paul, Trench Trubner and Company, Ltd, 1896), n.p.

8 Henry Lewis Bullen, "Erhard Ratdolt, of Venice and Augsburg, and His Improvements in Typography," *The Inland Printer* 68, no. 4 (January 1922): 489–91.

9 Dreyfus, Carter, and Vervliet, *Type Specimen Facsimiles*, 2:ix.

10 Bullen, "Erhard Ratdolt," 491.

11 Sarah Werner, "Guyot's Specimen Sheet" (Folger Shakespeare Library: The Collation, September 22, 2011), https://collation.folger.edu/2011/09/guyots-speciman-sheet/.

12 Vervliet cites Italian printer Aldus Manutius' 1500/01 Italic as the first in this new style; Hendrik D. L. Vervliet, *The Palaeotypography of the French Renaissance: Selected Papers on Sixteenth-Century Typefaces* (Leiden: Brill, 2008), 287. Morison credits French punchcutter Claud Garamont with being the first to design a companion italic; Stanley Morison, *A Brief Survey of Printing: History and Practice*, (New York: A.A. Knopf, 1923), 27, http://hdl.handle.net/2027/mdp.39015008145081.

13 Werner.

14 Carter, *A View of Early Typography*, 71.

15 Paul Beaujon [Beatrice Warde], "The Garamond Types: Sixteenth and Seventeenth Century Sources Considered," *The Fleuron*, no. 5 (1926): 131–79.

16 John A. Lane, "Egenolff-Sabon-Berner-Luther Typefoundry," in *The Oxford Companion to the Book* (Oxford: Oxford University Press, 2010), http://www.oxfordreference.com/view/10.1093/acref/9780198606536.001.0001/acref-9780198606536-e-1559.

17 Vervliet, *The Palaeotypography of the French Renaissance*, 157.

18 Carter, *A View of Early Typography*, 98–99.

19 Jan Middendorp, *Dutch Type* (Rotterdam: 010 Publishers, 2004), 23; Hendrik D.L. Vervliet, *Sixteenth Century Printing Types of the Low Countries* (Amsterdam: Menno Hertzberger, 1968), vi.

20 Middendorp, *Dutch Type*, 23.

21 Middendorp, 24; Alphonse Willems, *Les Elzevier: histoire et annales typographiques* (Bruxelles: G.A. van Trigt, 1880), http://archive.org/details/leselzevierhisto00will.

22 William Caslon, *A Specimen* (London: W. Caslon, 1734), http://archive.org/details/McGillLibrary-rbsc_caslon-william-speciman-colgate3-C377C377S51734-17593.

23 Enschedé en Zonen and Harry Carter, *The House of Enschedé, 1703–1953* (Haarlem, Netherlands: Joh. Enschedé en Zonen, 1953), 419–28; Stan Knight, *Historical Types: From Gutenberg to Ashendene* (New Castle, Delaware: Oak Knoll Press, 2012), 61–63..

24 James Mosley, "Caslon, William, the Elder (1692–1766), Typefounder," in *Oxford Dictionary of National Biography* (Oxford: Oxford University Press, 2008), https://www.oxforddnb.com/view/10.1093/ref:odnb/9780198614128.001.0001/odnb-9780198614128-e-4857.

25 James Mosley, "Caslon, William, the Elder (1692–1766), Typefounder," in *Oxford Dictionary of National Biography* (Oxford: Oxford University Press, 2008), https://www.oxforddnb.com/view/10.1093/ref:odnb/9780198614128.001.0001/odnb-9780198614128-e-4857.

26 Edmund Fry and David Chambers, *Specimen of Modern Printing Types by Edmund Fry 1821: A Facsimile with an Introduction and Notes by David Chambers* (London: Printing Historical Society, 1986), 5.

27 J.L. Frazier, "Popular Types—Their Origin and Use, No. VI. Caslon," *Inland Printer, American Lithographer* 72, no. 6 (March 1924): 945.

28 Updike, *Printing Types*, 1922, 1:20.

29 Lanston Monotype Machine Company, *The Monotype Specimen Book of Type Faces. A Complete Catalog of Matrices Made for Use with the Monotype Composing Machine and with Type & Rule Caster* (Philadelphia, 1922), 2–12, (Individually paginated insert.) http://archive.org/details/monotypespecimen00lansrich.

30 Rossiter Johnson and John Howard Brown, *The Twentieth Century Biographical Dictionary of Notable Americans* (Boston: Biographical Society, 1904); Binny & Ronaldson and Carl Purington Rollins, *The Specimen Books of Binny and Ronaldson, 1809–1812, in Facsimile; with an Introduction by Carl Purington Rollins, and Facsimiles of Some Early American Types* (Columbiad Club: New Haven, 1936), 5, 13–14; Rollo Silver, *Typefounding in America, 1787–1825* (Charlottesville: University Press of Virginia, 1965), 79.

31 Johann Heinrich Hottinger et al., *Elementale Quadrilingue: A Philological Type-Specimen (Zürich 1654)* (Oxford: Jericho Press, 2005).

32 Jan Loop, *Johann Heinrich Hottinger: Arabic and Islamic Studies in the Seventeenth Century* (Oxford: Oxford University Press, 2013), 52–53.

33 *Elementale quadrilingue* catalog record; http://id.lib.harvard.edu/alma/990094120200203941/catalog

34 William Blades, *Some Early Type Specimen Books of England, Holland, France, Italy, and Germany* (London: J.M. Powell, 1875), 4–5, http://archive.org/details/someearlytypespe00bladrich.

35 Joseph Moxon and Theodore Low De Vinne, *Moxon's Mechanick Exercises, or, the Doctrine of Handyworks Applied to the Art of Printing: A Literal Reprint in Two Volumes of the First Edition Published in the Year 1683*, vol. 1 (New York: Typothetæ, 1896), ix–x, https//catalog.hathitrust.org/Record/008411043.

36 Philip Hofer, *A Newly-Discovered Broadside Specimen of Fell Type Printed at Oxford about 1685* (Cambridge: Cambridge University Press, 1940), http://hdl.handle.net/2027/uiug.30112108344406; Stanley Morison and Harry Graham Carter, *John Fell: The University Press and the "Fell" Types; the Punches and Matrices Designed for Printing in the Greek, Latin, English, and Oriental Languages Bequeathed in 1686 to the University of Oxford by John Fell, D. D., Delegate of the Press, Dean of Christ Church, Vice-Chancellor of the University, and Bishop of Oxford* (Oxford: Clarendon Press, 1967).

37 J.L. Frazier, "Popular Types—Their Origin and Use, No. VI. Caslon," *Inland Printer, American Lithographer* 72, no. 6 (March 1924): 946-47.

38 Oxford UP's website offers a summary: https://global.oup.com/about/oup_history/?cc=us

39 A representative overview would be prohibitively massive. Reproductions exist, often in editions limited enough to warrant archiving in special collections, for instance: Dreyfus, Carter, and Vervliet, *Type Specimen Facsimiles.*

40 Robin Kinross, *Modern Typography, 2nd Edition,* (London: Hyphen, 2004), 68-69.

41 Stanley Morison, *The English Newspaper, 1622-1932: An Account of the Physical Development of Journals Printed in London between 1622 & the Present Day* (Cambridge: Cambridge University Press, 1932); Stanley Morison, *The History of the Times,* vol. 1, 7 vols. (London: Office of the *Times,* 1935). Morison wrote v.1-4 of the *Times'* series, 1935-52.

42 Morison, *A Brief Survey of Printing,* 16.Stanley Morison, *A Brief Survey of Printing: History and Practice,* (New York, 1923), 16, http://hdl.handle.net/2027/mdp.39015008145081.

43 Julia Martínez Diana, email to the author, August 19, 2020.

KLINGSPOR TYPEFOUNDERS

R.D.1. MORRISTOWN N.J.
TELEPHONE: MEndham 3-0298

presents

Salut

designed by H. Maehler

12 point — 22 A · 43 a · 8 Fig. 1
Be not a baker, if your head be of butter

14 point — 19 A · 37 a · 7 Fig. 1
Mainly in Malay many mammals

18 point — 12 A · 22 a · 5 Fig. 1
A word to the wise is enough

24 point No. 1 — 8 A · 15 a · 4 Fig. 1
Berlin Frankfurt Bern

24 point No. 2 — 8 A · 15 a · 4 Fig. 1
Haunt Mohammed

30 point — 6 A · 12 a · 3 Fig. 1
Parry Darkness

42 point — 5 A · 10 a · 3 Fig. 1
Saloon Roost

54 point — 4 A · 7 a · 3 Fig. 1
Maid Woe

This type needs little introduction; it speaks for itself in no uncertain voice. It can give you heavy weight plus a most original form – in fact, the advantages of an extra-bold and a casual script combined in one type. It has an important part to play in advertising, where a few words in Salut are bound to command attention. Can't you visualize how it would liven up your publicity printing? Salut insists on being read!

CHARACTERS IN COMPLETE FONT

Cap Fonts
ABCDEFGHIJKLMNO PQRSTUVWXYZ& .,-':;()!?

Lowercase Fonts
abcdefghijklmnopq rstuvwxyz.,-':;()!?

Figure Fonts
1234567890

Extra Characters
bfjpqs

RELATED TYPES

Kabel medium
Kabel bold
Steel
Steel italic
Steel bold

Klingspor Foundry types bring Distinction to Your printing

***Salut*, Klingspor Typefounders, 1931-c.1945**

Heinrich Maehler designed Salut for the German foundry Klingspor in 1931. During World War II, American imports of European—and particularly German—types halted. After the war, though, American typographers embraced the notion of "sophisticated" European typography with deep historical roots and American foundries and speciality importers once more stocked English, German, Dutch, French, and Italian types for the discerning American printer. Producing, advertising, and consuming commercial goods played a large role in the post-war American economy. This small-format broadside described Salut as "extra bold and casual," promising that "a few words" set in Salut are "bound to command attention" and "liven up your publicity printing." A small inset offers the "related types" Kabel and Steel as companion text faces.

2: PRINTERS' MANUALS

History of the Russian Book,
Fedor Bulgakov, 1880

One of the first comprehensive histories of Russian books and printing was written by a Russian journalist. Bulgakov's history isn't a printer's manual—it doesn't include practical trade-based instructions or typographic specimens from local printers' offices. But its concept of trade history is expansive. Some images, like the medieval scribe at work or Gutenberg's press, are familiar illustrations in the histories included in Western European printing manuals. But many of Bulgakov's choices frame Russian printing in a much wider context. Early Japanese, Chinese, and Egyptian texts place Russian books in a global context. With a focus on Slavic languages and the Cyrillic alphabet, Bulgakov offers a view of manuscripts, incunabula, and fine printing that departs from the formulaic narrative of many of his contemporaries elsewhere.

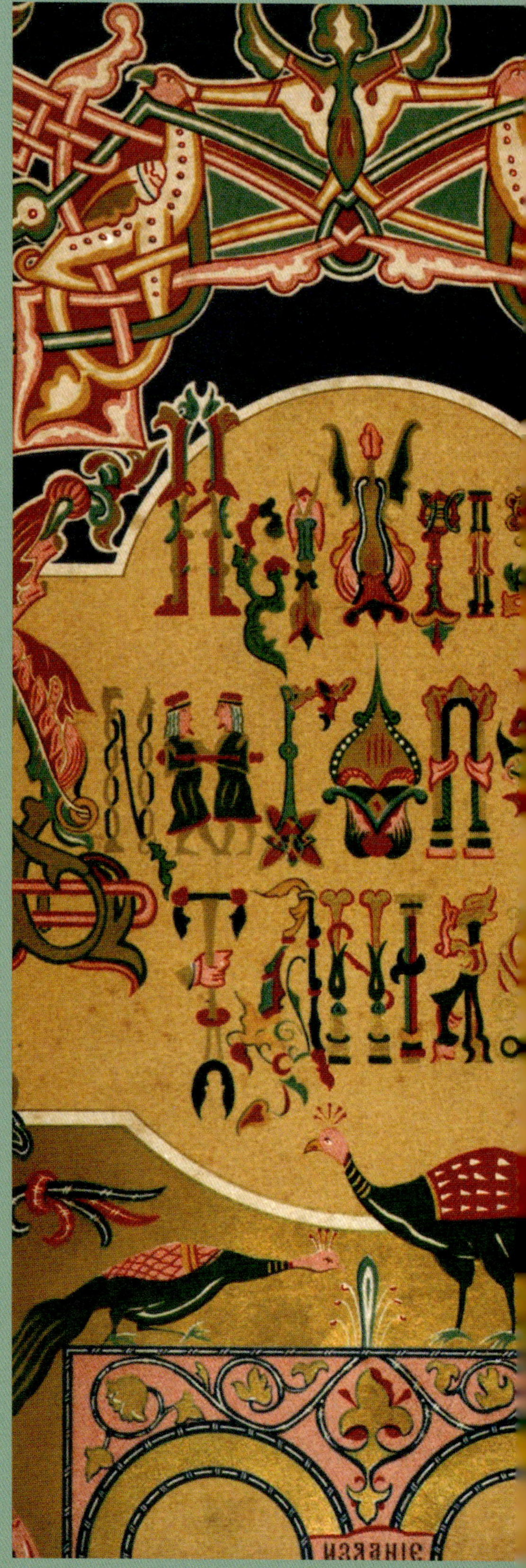

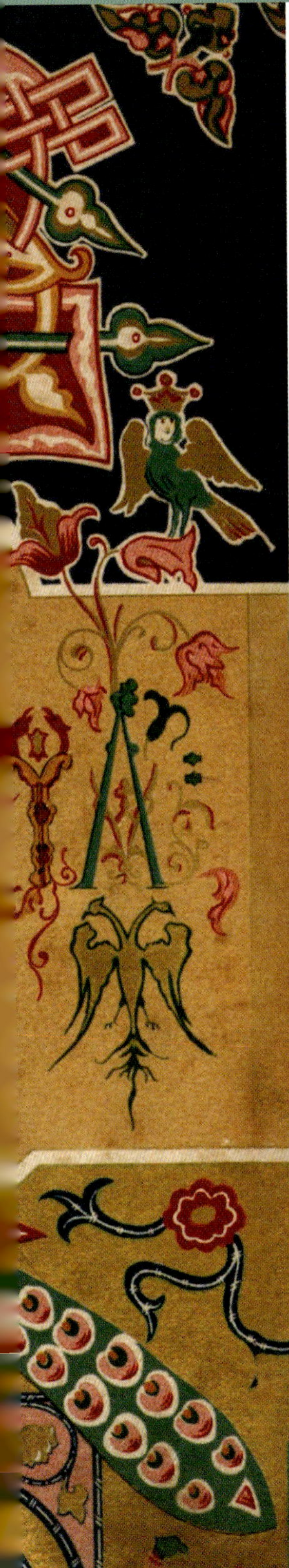

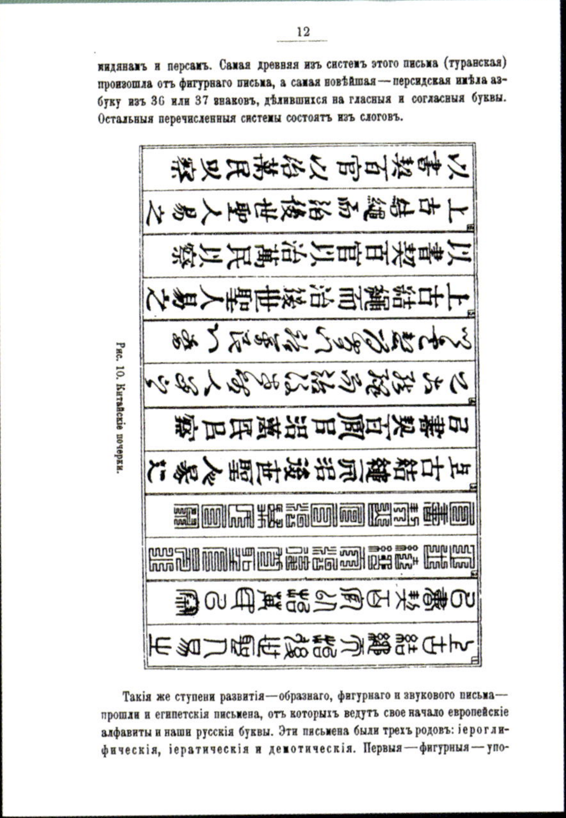

12

мидянамъ и персамъ. Самая древняя изъ системъ этого письма (туранская) произошла отъ фигурнаго письма, а самая новѣйшая — персидская имѣла азбуку изъ 36 или 37 знаковъ, дѣлившихся на гласныя и согласныя буквы. Остальныя перечисленныя системы состоятъ изъ слоговъ.

Рис. 10. Китайскіе почерки.

Такія же ступени развитія—образнаго, фигурнаго и звукового письма—прошли и египетскія письмена, отъ которыхъ ведутъ свое начало европейскіе алфавиты и наши русскія буквы. Эти письмена были трехъ родовъ: іероглифическія, іератическія и демотическія. Первыя—фигурныя—упо-

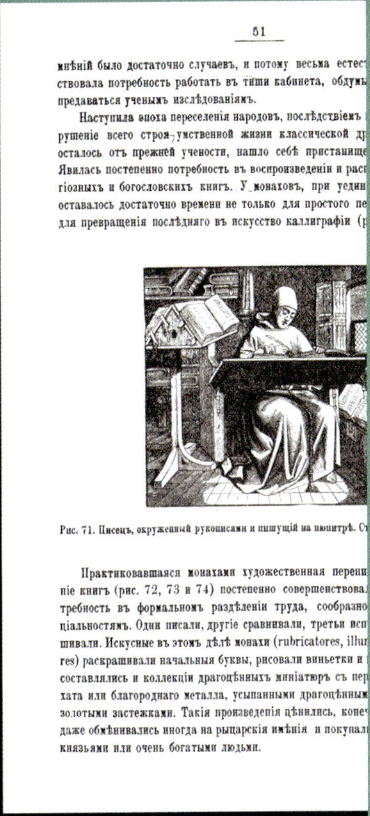

51

мнѣній было достаточно случаевъ, и потому весьма естес
ствовала потребность работать въ тиши кабинета, обдумы
предаваться ученымъ изслѣдованіямъ.

Наступила эпоха переселенія народовъ, послѣдствіемъ
рушеніе всего строя умственной жизни классической др
осталось отъ прежней учености, нашло себѣ пристанище
Явилась постепенно потребность въ воспроизведеніи и рас
гіозныхъ и богословскихъ книгъ. У монаховъ, при уедин
оставалось достаточно времени не только для простого пе
для превращенія послѣдняго въ искусство каллиграфіи (р

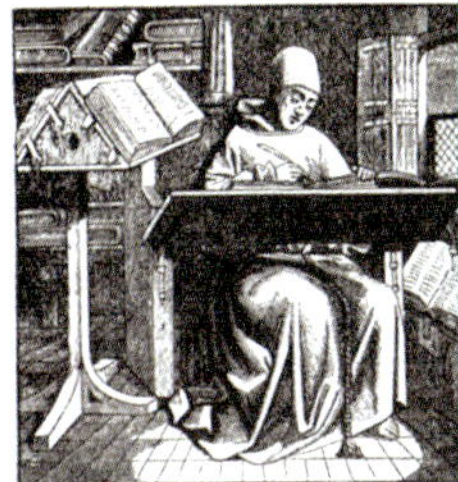

Рис. 71. Писецъ, окруженный рукописями и пишущій на пюпитрѣ. Ст

Практиковавшаяся монахами художественная перепи
ніе книгъ (рис. 72, 73 и 74) постепенно совершенствова
требность въ формальномъ раздѣленіи труда, сообразно
ціальностямъ. Одни писали, другіе сравнивали, третьи исп
шивали. Искусные въ этомъ дѣлѣ монахи (rubricatores, illu
res) раскрашивали начальныя буквы, рисовали виньетки и
составлялись и коллекціи драгоцѣнныхъ миніатюръ съ пер
хата или благороднаго металла, усыпанными драгоцѣнным
золотыми застежками. Такія произведенія цѣнились, конеч
даже обмѣнивались иногда на рыцарскія имѣнія и покупал
князьями или очень богатыми людьми.

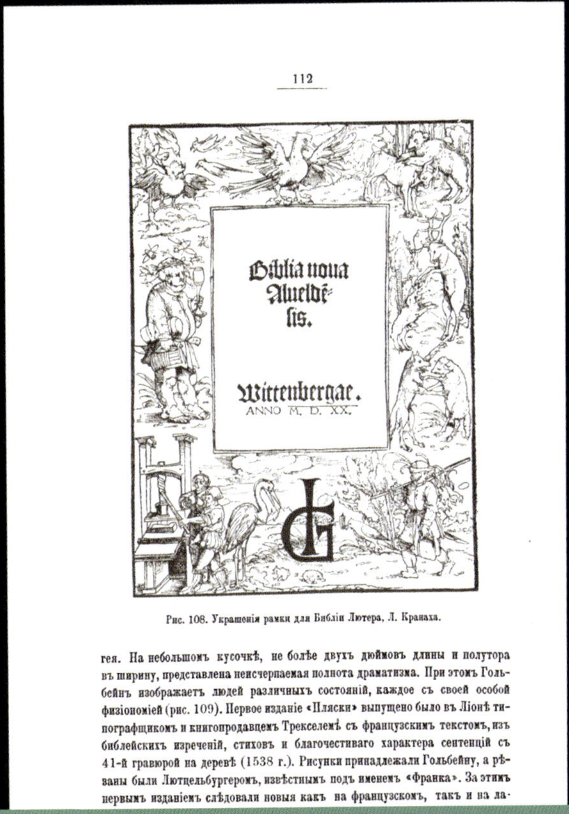

112

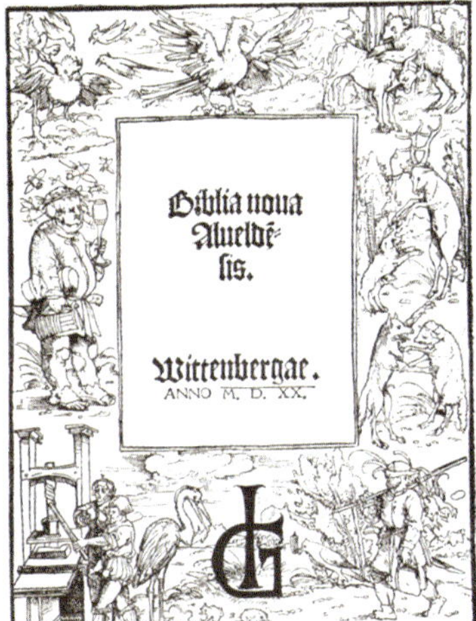

Рис. 108. Украшенія рамки для Библіи Лютера, Л. Кранаха.

гея. На небольшомъ кусочкѣ, не болѣе двухъ дюймовъ длины и полутора въ ширину, представлена неисчерпаемая полнота драматизма. При этомъ Гольбейнъ изображаетъ людей различныхъ состояній, каждое съ своей особой физіономіей (рис. 109). Первое изданіе «Пляски» выпущено было въ Ліонѣ типографщикомъ и книгопродавцемъ Трекселемъ съ французскимъ текстомъ, изъ библейскихъ изреченій, стиховъ и благочестиваго характера сентенцій съ 41-й гравюрой на деревѣ (1538 г.). Рисунки принадлежали Гольбейну, а рѣзаны были Лютцельбургеромъ, извѣстнымъ подъ именемъ «Франка». За этимъ первымъ изданіемъ слѣдовали новыя какъ на французскомъ, такъ и на ла-

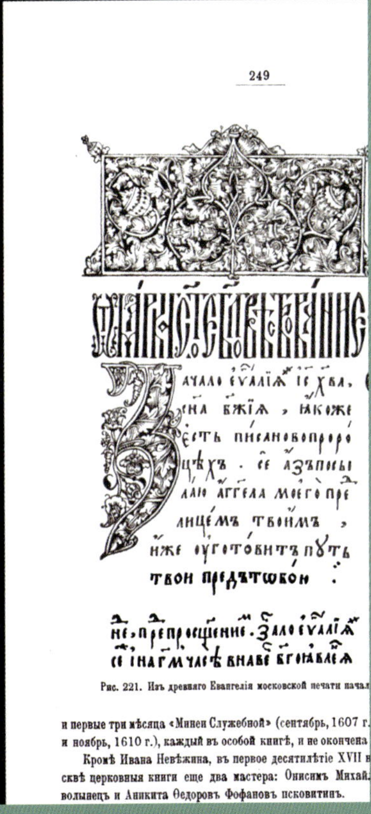

249

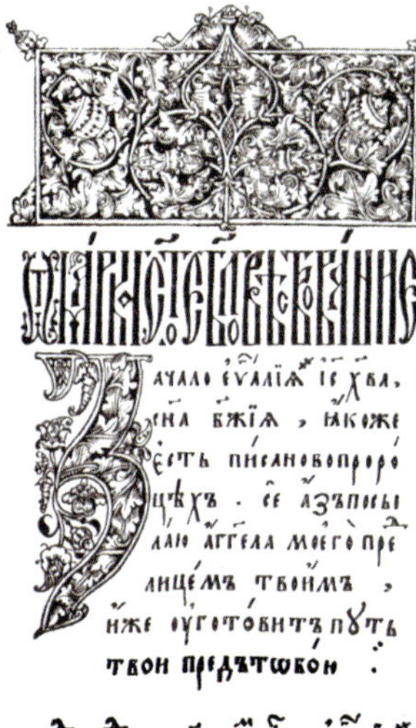

Рис. 221. Изъ древняго Евангелія московской печати начал

и первые три мѣсяца «Минеи Служебной» (сентябрь, 1607 г.
и ноябрь, 1610 г.), каждый въ особой книгѣ, и не окончена

Кромѣ Ивана Невѣжина, въ первое десятилѣтіе XVII в
сквѣ церковныя книги еще два мастера: Онисимъ Михай
волынецъ и Аникита Өедоровъ Фофановъ псковитинъ.

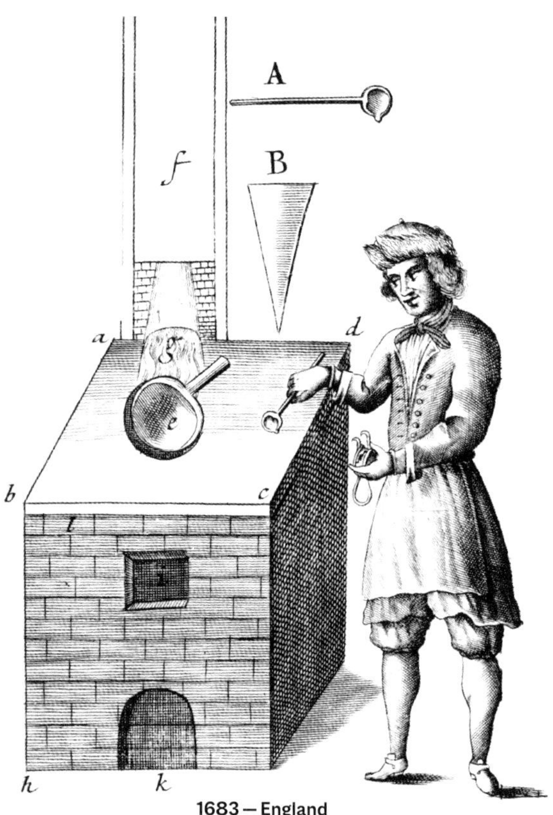

DE L'IMPRIMERIE. 109

PARTIE I. CHAP. II. ARTICLE V.

Démonstration d'un Titre de These.

ILLUSTRIS. ECCLESIÆ PRINCIPI

MARTINO DE RATABON

IPRENSIUM EPISCOPO.

PHILOSOPHIA RATIONALIS.

LOGICA. | MORALIS. | METAPHISICA.

1. *De Natura Logicæ.* 1. *De primis Qualitatibus.* 1. *De Natura Metaphisicæ.*

Quant aux Titres d'en bas, où sont le *nom* & *qualitez* du *Professeur*, *&c.* on les doit faire de caractere italique, plus gros que celui de la matiere de la *These*; & le petit sommaire, ou est le *nom* de celui qui soutient la *These*, doit être de roman, & de plus petit caractere, comme il se voit ici.

Præside Rev. D. ANTONIO MARESCHAL, Artium Doctore, Regio, Historiæ, atque Philosophiæ Professore Primario.

Propugnabit in Aula Collegii Regii D. JACOBUS ANTONIUS DEFFOSSE, Audomarensis, Primum Baccalaureus, Die 29. Junii ad medium nonæ matutinæ.

DUACI, Typis &c.

Lettres de deux points.

Titelschriften und Capitailgen.

Gaillarde.	AABCDEFGHIKLMNOPQRSTV
Petit Romain.	AABCDEFGHIKLMNOPQRSTV
Philosophie.	AABCDEFGHIKLMNOPQR
Cicero.	AABCDEFGHIKLMNOPQR
St. Augustin.	AABCDEFGHIKLMN
Gros Romain.	AABCDEFGHIKLMNOP
Petit Parangon.	AABCDEFGHIKLM
Gros Parangon.	AABCDEFGHIJKL
Palestine.	AABCDEFGHI
Petit Canon.	AABCDEFGH

Sur PETIT PARANGON.

A B C D E F G H I K

A B C D E F G H I

1683 — England

Apparently self-taught type founder and printer Joseph Moxon publishes *Mechanick Exercises in the Whole Art of Printing*.

1723 — France

First printer's manual to address jobbing work, Fertel's *La science pratique de l'imprimerie*.

1740 — Germany

Gessner's "useful & necessary" manual lists types by size, Gaillarde through Petit Canon.

1477 — England

William Caxon prints the first book printed with movable metal type in England, *Dictes and Sayings of Philosophers*.

1615 — Japan

The Edo period (ends 1868) witnesses a thriving commercial publishing scene, facilitated almost entirely by woodblock printing.

1751 — France

Denis Diderot's *Encyclopédie* codifies the biological and natural world, including printing.

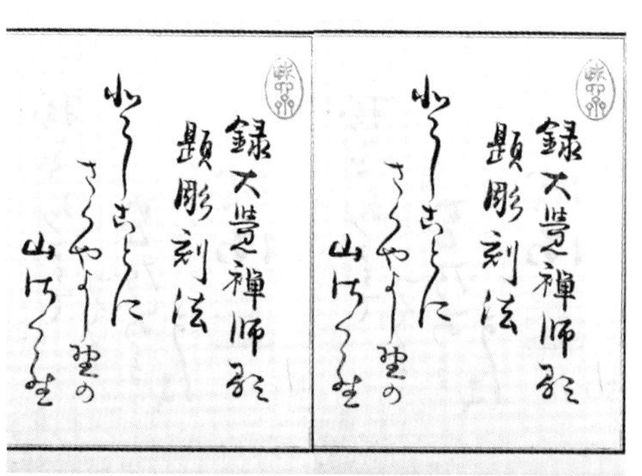

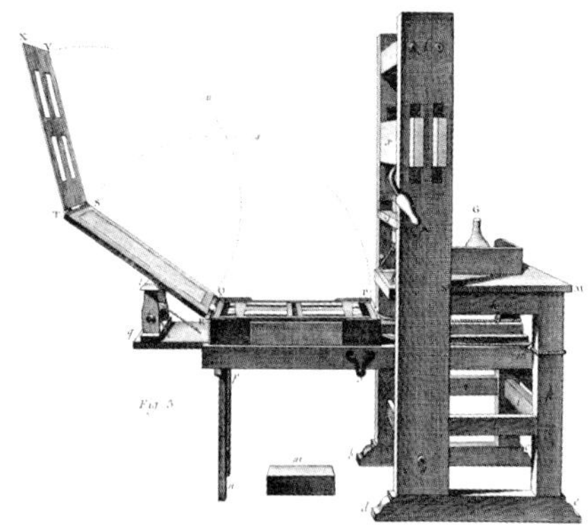

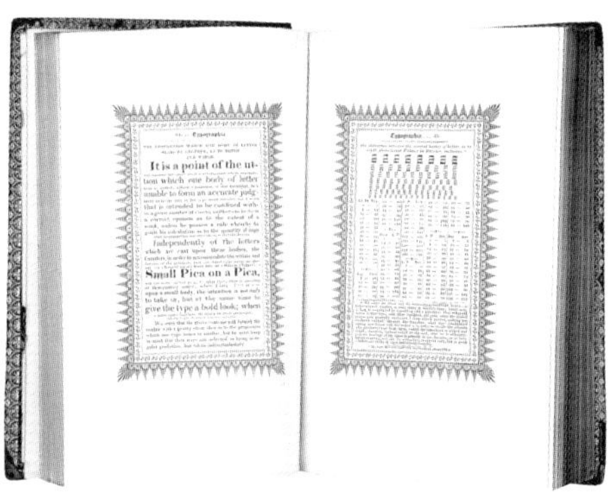

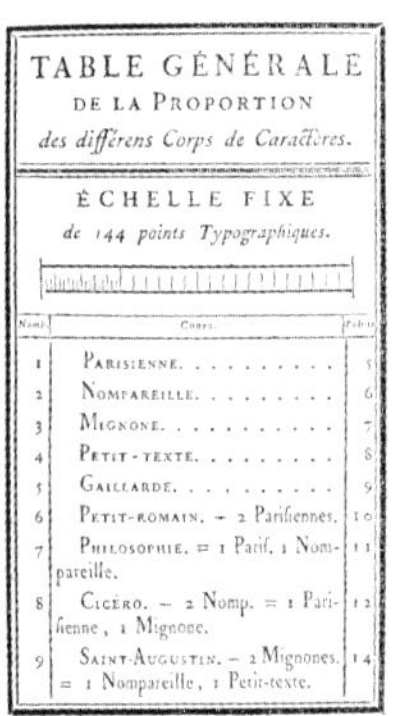

TABLE GÉNÉRALE
DE LA PROPORTION
des différens Corps de Caractères.

ÉCHELLE FIXE
de 144 points Typographiques.

Noms		Corps
1	Parisienne.	5
2	Nompareille.	6
3	Mignone.	7
4	Petit-texte.	8
5	Gaillarde.	9
6	Petit-romain. = 2 Parisiennes.	10
7	Philosophie. = 1 Paris. 1 Nompareille.	11
8	Cicéro. = 2 Nomp. = 1 Parisienne, 1 Mignone.	12
9	Saint-Augustin. = 2 Mignones. = 1 Nompareille, 1 Petit-texte.	14

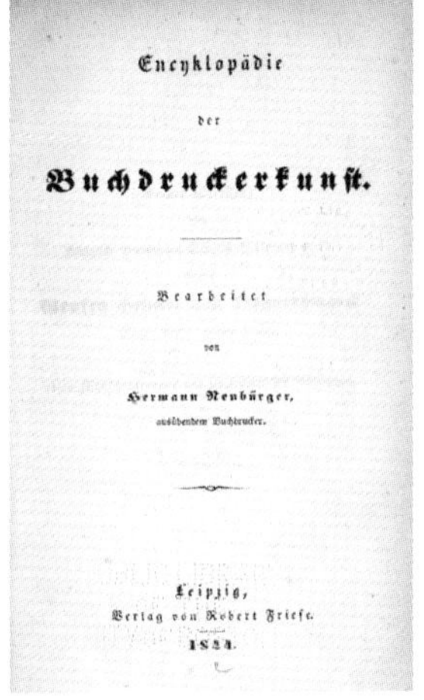

Encyklopädie
der
Buchdruckerkunst.
Bearbeitet
von
Hermann Neubürger,
ausübendem Buchdrucker.
Leipzig,
Verlag von Robert Friese.
1844.

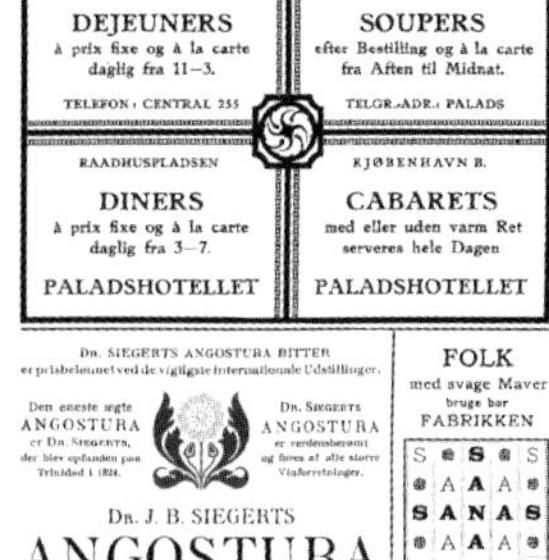

PALADSHOTELLET
DEJEUNERS
à prix fixe og à la carte
daglig fra 11–3.
TELEFON: CENTRAL 255

PALADSHOTELLET
SOUPERS
efter Bestilling og à la carte
fra Aften til Midnat.
TELGR.-ADR.: PALADS

RAADHUSPLADSEN
DINERS
à prix fixe og à la carte
daglig fra 3–7.
PALADSHOTELLET

KJØBENHAVN B.
CABARETS
med eller uden varm Ret
serveres hele Dagen
PALADSHOTELLET

DR. J. B. SIEGERTS
ANGOSTURA
URTE-BITTER

Leverandør til
Deres Majestæter Kejseren af Tyskland
og Kongen af Spanien.

FOLK
med svage Maver
bruge bør
FABRIKKEN
S A N A S
FØDEMIDLER
FABRIKKEN
SANA
KJØBENHAVN
2 FREDERIKSBERGGADE 2

1764 — France

Fournier's *Manuel* begins to popularize the idea of numerical point sizes.

1824 — England

Johnson's *Typographia* is full of what his critics called useless matter, glaring errors, and frivilous decoration.

1841 — Germany

Neubürger's *Encyklopädie der Buchdruckerkunst* is criticized for being too practical; second edition issued 1844.

1913 — Denmark

Typografi for saettere, like most printers' manuals of its day, gives many practical, commercial examples.

1790 — England

Cylindrical press patented.

1803 — England

Lighter, sturdier Stanhope press facilitates global spread of letterpress printing.

1809 — USA

Handlever press invented.

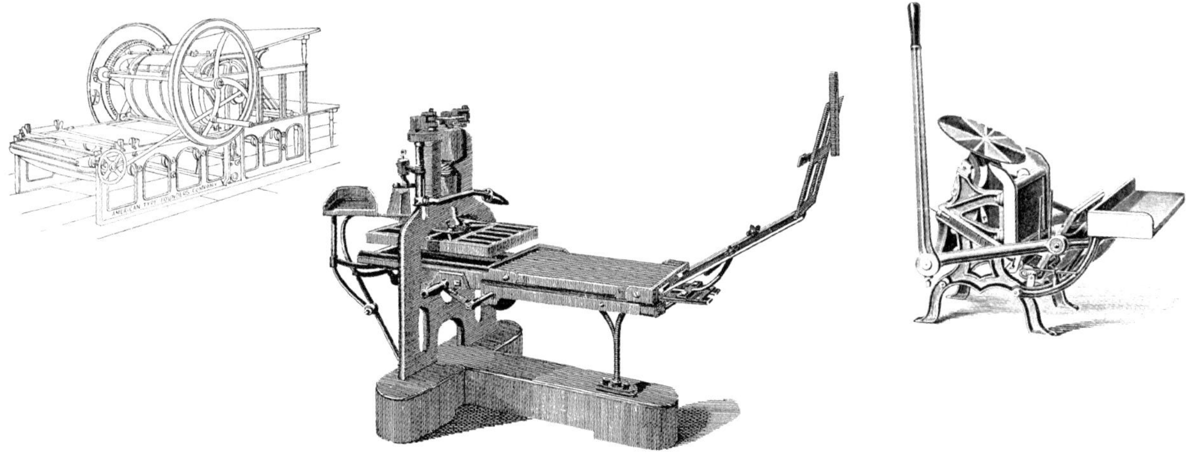

Printers' manuals, unlike ephemeral broadsides, were designed for continued use. These books offered instruction in the art and craft of printing and documented the tools of the trade. Early manuals revealed previously secretive practices to a general readership. From mixing **type metal**, making matrices, and casting type to organizing an upper and lower type **case** and pulling a printed proof, printers' manuals offered sometimes excruciating detail. The profound practical and economic value of the earliest manuals lay in their divulgence of new information never before shared in a public context. Many manuals included type specimens in their appendices, documenting the evolving form and function of specimens during the late seventeenth through nineteenth centuries.

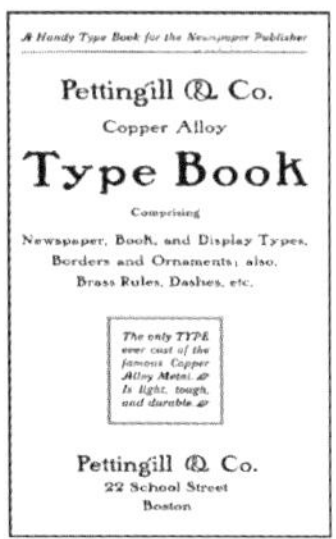
A Handy Type Book for the Newspaper Publisher

Pettingill & Co.

Copper Alloy

Type Book

Comprising

Newspaper, Book, and Display Types, Borders and Ornaments; also, Brass Rules, Dashes, etc.

The only TYPE ever cast of the famous Copper Alloy Metal. Is light, tough, and durable.

Pettingill & Co.

22 School Street

Boston

Type metal is an alloy, or mixture of metals — often proprietary and marketed as the strongest or best, as in the case of Pettingill's "famous copper alloy."

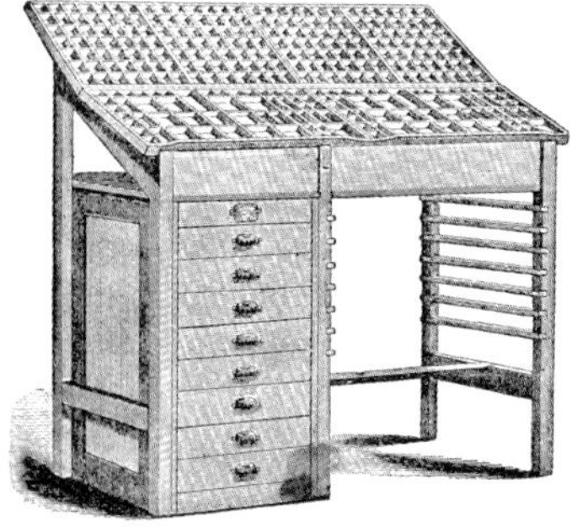

The **case** stores sorts—all the individual characters of a single face at a single size—with majuscules (or capitals) in the upper case and miniscules in the lower case.

Printers' manuals: form and function

Printers' manuals appeared toward the end of the seventeenth century, and they served multiple purposes, functioning as teaching tools, trade histories, and encyclopedic references.[1] English hydrographer, businessman, and apparently self-taught printer Joseph Moxon's revolutionary *Mechanick exercises on the whole art of printing* (1683) revealed closely-guarded trade secrets to a wide reading audience. Until that time, financially motivated printers' guilds carefully guarded their knowledge, which traveled with printers trained in Mainz and then with their apprentices, not through written texts. As the sixteenth century dawned, over 1,000 print shops had been established in roughly 200 European cities, primarily in Germany, France, Italy, and Spain.[2] Yet in 1683, more than two centuries after Gutenberg, Moxon's was the first printer's manual in any language. Ostensibly, it provided instruction for novice printers. Yet there's evidence that early manuals, like Moxon's, were written not for tradesmen but for well-educated, upper class readers, imparting them with a text-based power over the printing trade and the laboring class that supported it. Printers' manuals removed sole ownership of trade-based knowledge from guilds, which transferred knowledge orally and through the embodied experience of apprenticeships, and shared it with gentlemen-scholars.[3] Regardless of audience, manuals itemized each step in the printing process, gathering a vast body of knowledge into a single, accessible, transferable volume.

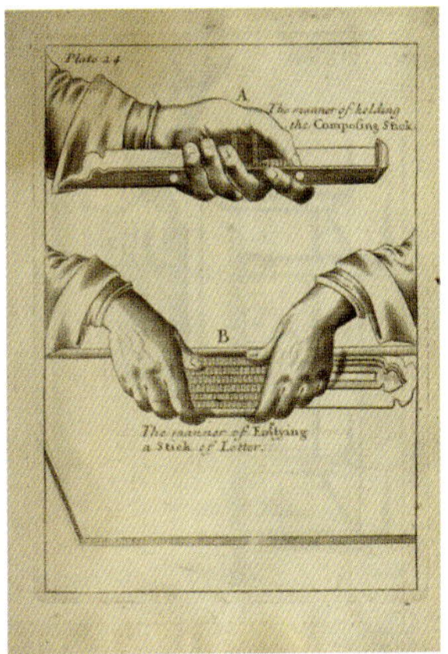

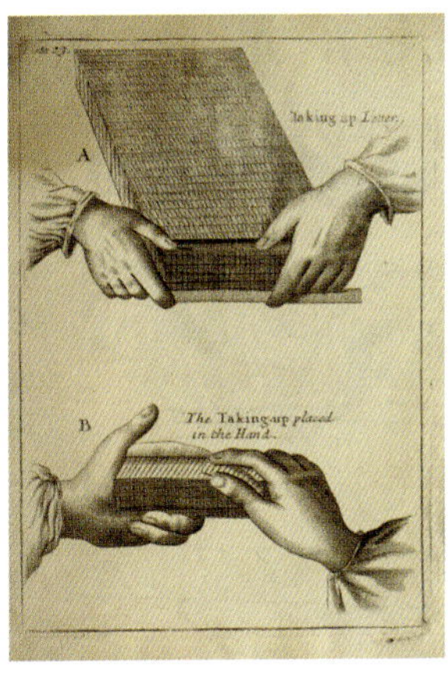

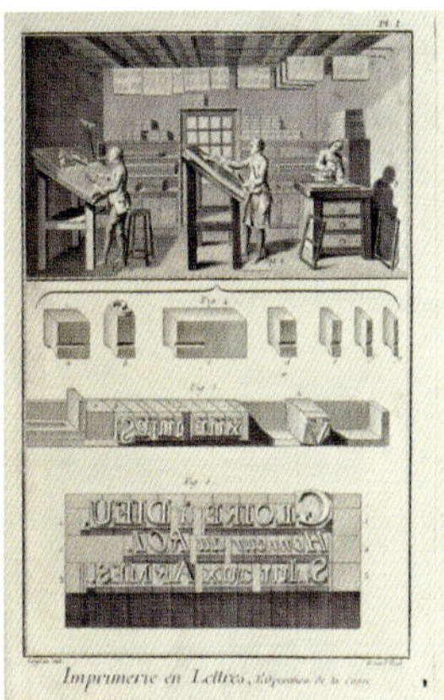

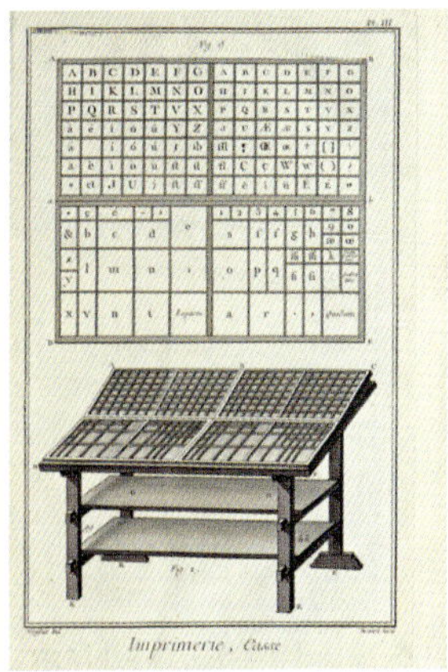

Fig 2.1 (above)

Plates from *Mechanick Exercises on the Whole Art of Printing* (Joseph Moxon, London, 1683; left) and v. 7 of Diderot's *Encyclopedie* (Denis Diderot, Paris, 1769). Printers' manuals, like other rationalist explorations of the physical world, sought to document and explain the mechanics of printing from beginning to end.

That Moxon didn't include a type specimen points to another important fact about manuals: their primary purpose was the documentation of the printing trade's history and equipment, with specimens as supplements. Histories typically started with the western "invention" of typographic printing, then cataloged famous printers up to the author's present day. Historical accuracy varied. Moxon dismissed Chinese **xylography** as irrelevant to western printing, then pondered (inconclusively, for four pages) if the first movable metal type should be credited to Johann Gutenberg in Meinz, Germany, or to Laurens Jansz Koster in Haarlem, the Netherlands.[4] Cornelius Van Winkle, writing in the United States in the early nineteenth century, glibly informed his readers that historians didn't know if "John Guttenberg" or "John Faust" [sic]—Fust was Gutenberg's financial backer—had first practiced "the art of printing by moveable types" and said no more about the matter. But he devoted three pages to listing early printers in America, a decision which included and excluded information based on how engaging anticipated readers might find it.[5]

Finally, manuals functioned as encyclopedias, documenting tools and processes and contributing to western European scholarship's Enlightenment project [Fig. 2.1]. Like Denis Diderot's quintessential 28-volume *Encyclopedie* (1751-72), manuals sought to provide rational explanations and accurate descriptions. They concentrated exclusively on the histories and tools of the printing trade, while Diderot extended his scope to the entire natural and constructed world. But the *Encyclopedie*'s treatment of typography and printing followed the format standardized by printers' manuals; it laid out a history starting with Gutenberg and provided a detailed explanation for each piece of equipment in the typefounding and printing processes.[6]

Generally speaking, specimens in printers' manuals differed from specimens designed as broadsides in several important ways, chief among these durability. As appendices to larger instructional works, specimens in manuals weren't freestanding objects. The books they were bound into protected them from damage and loss. As well as being sturdier than broadsides, books cost more upon initial issue; thus they were more likely to be cataloged and archived. Finally, while broadsides usually displayed types from a single foundry or printer, specimens appended to manuals could and often did include multiple foundries.

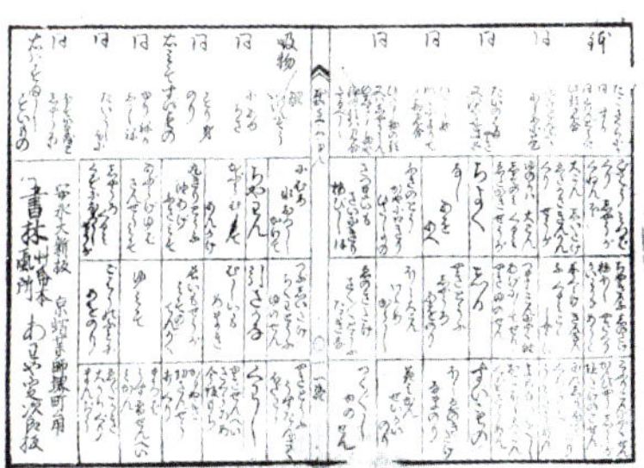

Xylography, or woodblock printing, originated in China before 220 BCE, saw common use in Japan, was used in Egypt by the 10 c. BCE, and didn't arrive in western Europe until about 1423. It remained a popular, efficient, economical printing method for many logographic languages until the middle of the nineteenth century. Above: *Kondate shinan* 献立指南, a book about diet habits, published in Kyoto, Japan (1772-80).

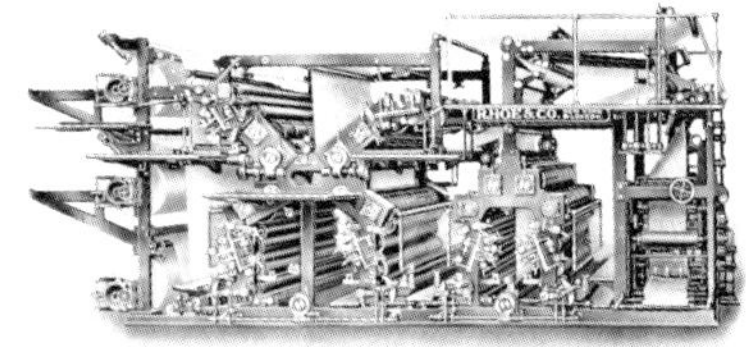

Steam-powered rotary presses sunbstantially increased the number of printed pages per hour: about 8,000 compared to the 1,100 for Koenig & Bauer rotary presses (1814), 480 for the Stanhope press (1803), and 25 for the first screw presses (1436-9), such as the one Gutenberg used.

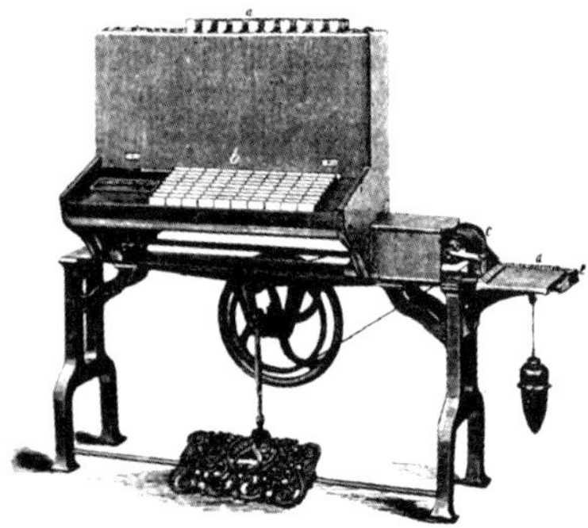

Mechanized typecasting and typesetting automated the process of casting and setting type. Many non-operational and/or commercially unsuccessful attempts predated the Linotype and Monotype machines, such as this Setzmachine (Germany, 1882).

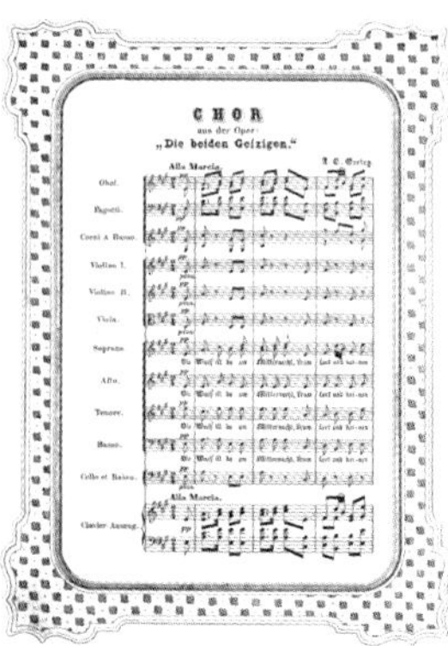

Frames like this one in a German music printer's specimen from the 1860s added visual interest to the printed page, or subdivided it to indicate different kinds of content.

Shaping print culture

Early examples of printers' manuals were revolutionary because they revealed trade secrets. But the mechanics of the type-casting and printing process changed very little between Gutenberg and the late nineteenth century introduction of **steam-powered presses** and **mechanized typecasting**. Once in wide circulation, the genre could reveal few secrets, though the scope of manuals increased over time. The first to include advice on job printing (ads and single sheets rather than books) was Martin Fertel's *La science pratique de l'imprimerie* (1723), for instance.[7] In the mid-eighteenth century, typographic nomenclature began standardizing, though slowly. Manuals established and reinforced industry norms. Meanwhile, typographic options expanded, and concepts of national taste informed the language of visual style. Manuals and their appended specimens proved valuable to both mechanical standardization and stylistic variety, introducing new practical functions—uniform names for type sizes, pairing romans with italics to create the forerunners of the type family—and reinforcing national styles through page layout and typeface design. Since publishers often relied on nearby foundries for specimen material, the types could reflect (or help to construct) local and regional typographic preferences. With space at a premium, function drove page design. Title pages embraced current aesthetic fashions, while the remainder of a specimen's pages demonstrated logical efficiently. Rows of type in ascending or descending size, often labeled with the name and/or size of the face, proved effective and therefore common. Rules and **frames**, from simple to ridiculously complex, sometimes added period style and visual interest. By the middle of the nineteenth century, an "entirely practical" printer's manual was the object of scorn rather than a notable technical advancement. Taste in type specimens had likewise moved on, favoring elaborate and often expensive specimen books. But for a century and a half, the brief specimens appended to printers' manuals offered a practical way to display new types—often from newly-established foundries—to their most important audience: printers.

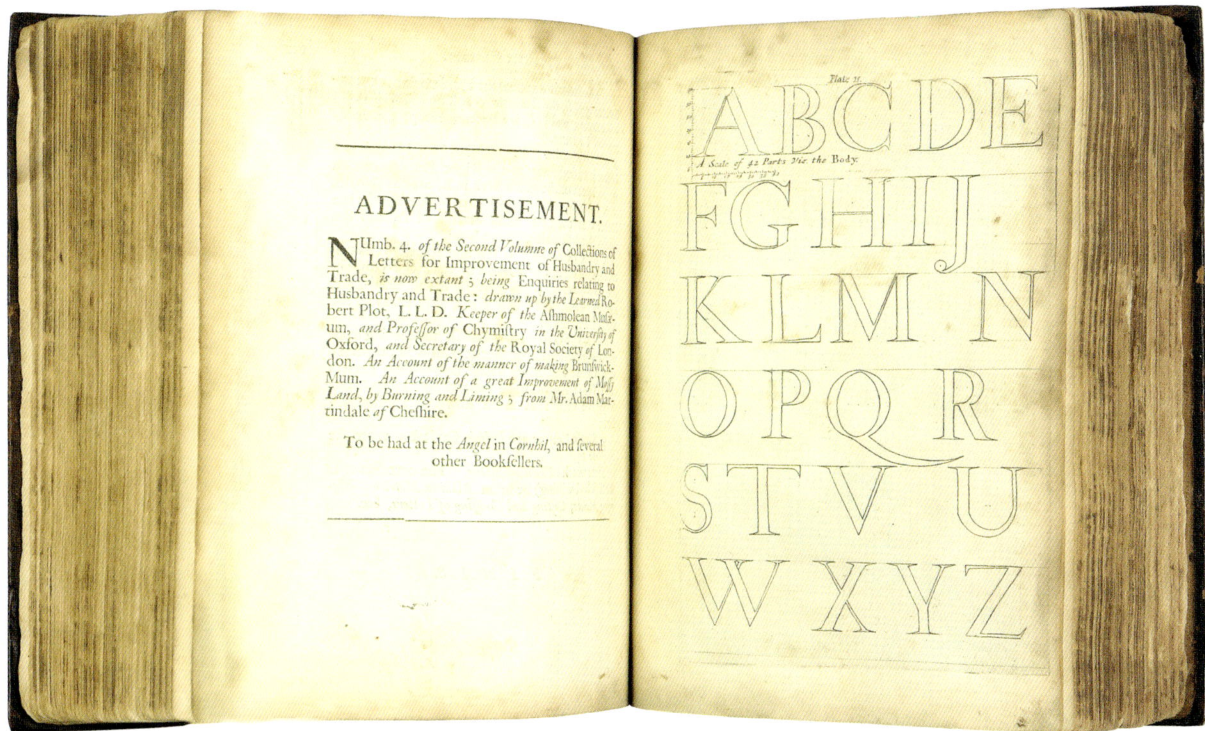

Establishing shared knowledge and expectations

Moxon's 1683 *Mechanick Exercises* didn't include a type specimen, but it did illustrate his ideas about the geometric construction of letterforms—a subject he'd explored at book length in 1676.[8] He believed the alphabet should be constructed geometrically, built on a foundation of circles, triangles, and squares within a square grid [Fig. 2.2]. Moxon's text indicated a master printer should have "a Fount of Letter of all **Bodies** ... Pearl, Nomparel, Brevier, Long-Primmer, Pica, English, Great-Primmer, Double-Pica, Two-Lin'd-English, Great-Cannon." Moxon's list ran from smallest to largest, providing a range of sizes roughly 5–48 modern American points. All required both a roman and italic, with some sizes in English (blackletter), Greek, Hebrew, and Syriack alphabets.[9] The last three would have been particularly useful for printing biblical and classical texts, a mainstay of early printing, and Moxon left it to individual printers to decide which were needed. A chart showed how many of each roman "body" fit into one foot to indicate the relative size of each typeface, a tactic that eventually informed the development of the Fournier, Didot, and American point systems. Moxon failed to mention that typographic measurement systems varied widely—between countries, cities, even foundries in the same city. Without a universal standard for measurement, descriptive names like *Pearl* or *Pica* might correspond to types of different absolute physical measurements. Type size turned into a guessing game without knowledge of a local printer's stock—a problem specimens could help to solve. Moxon's lengthy descriptions of typeface selection, type size, and the qualities of a well-designed fount were detailed and pragmatic, but not illustrated.

Fig 2.2 (above)

***Mechanick Exercises on the Whole Art of Printing* (Joseph Moxon, London, 1683). The first printers' manual in any language didn't include a type specimen, but it did illustrate Moxon's ideas about the geometric construction of letterforms.**

View of body inclined to show the face.

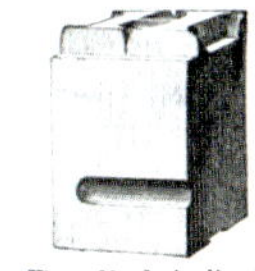

Letter H, from a type of canon body.

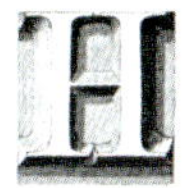

Face of the letter on the body.

The **body** of a letter is the block of type metal on which an individual character sits.

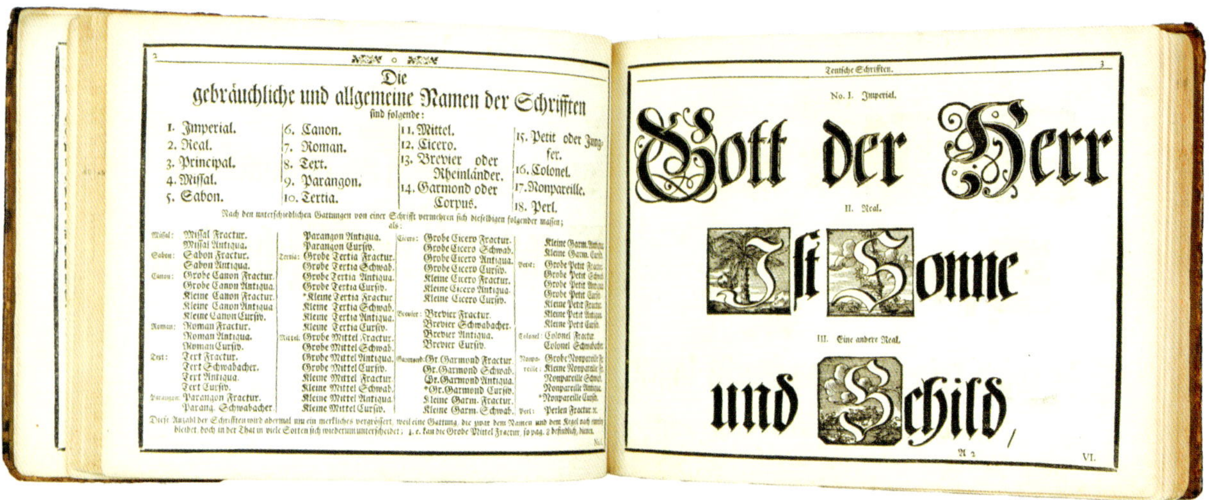

Die
gebräuchliche und allgemeine Namen der Schrifften
sind folgende:

1. Imperial. 2. Real. 3. Principal. 4. Missal. 5. Sabon. 6. Canon. 7. Roman. 8. Text. 9. Parangon. 10. Tertia. 11. Mittel. 12. Cicero. 13. Brevier oder Rheinländer. 14. Garmond oder Corpus. 15. Petit oder Jungfer. 16. Colonel. 17. Nonpareille. 18. Perl.

Teutsche Schrifften.

No. I. Imperial.

Gott der Herr

II. Real.

Ist Sonne

III. Eine andere Real.

und Schild

Fig 2.3 (above)

***Die wol-eingerichtete Buchdruckerey* (Johann Ernesti, Nürnberg, 1721). This early German manual includes a 44-page type specimen.**

10 Teutsche S

XLI. Grobe Petit Fractur, auf Cicero Kegel.

Ich will nun preisen des Herrn Werk/ und aus der heiligen Schrifft seine Werke verkündigen/ wie ichs gelesen habe. Die Sonne ist aller Welt Licht/ und ihr Licht ist das allerhelleste Licht. Es ist auch den Heiligen von dem Herrn noch nie gegeben/ daß sie alle seine Wunder aussprechen könnten; denn der allmächtige Herr hat sie so groß gemacht/ und alle Dinge sind zu groß/ nach Würden zu loben. Er allein erforschet den Abgrund/ und der Menschen Herzen/ und weiß/ was sie gedenken: denn der Herr weiß alle Dinge/ und siehet/ zu welcher Zeit ein jegliches geschehen werde. Er verkündiget/ was vergangen/ und was zukünfftig ist/ und offenbaret/ was verborgen ist/ er verstehet alle Heimlichkeit/ und ist ihm keine Sache verborgen. Er beweiset seine grosse Weisheit herrlich/ und er ist von Ewigkeit bis zu Ewigkeit. Man kan ihn weder grösser noch geringer machen/ und er bedarf keines Raths. Wie lieblich sind deine Werke/ wiewol man kaum ein Fünklein davon erkennen kan. Es lebet alles/ und bleibet für und für/ und worzu er ihrer bedarf/ sind sie alle gehorsam.

XLII. Grobe Petit Fractur.

Wer kan sich seiner Herrlichkeit satt sehen? Man siehet seine Herrlichkeit an der mächtigen grossen Höhe, an dem hellen Firmament, an dem schönen Himmel. Die Sonne, wenn sie aufgehet, verkündiget sie den Tag, sie ist ein Wunderwerk des Höchsten. Im Mittage trocknet sie die Erde, und wer kan für ihrer Hitze bleiben? Sie machts heisser denn viel Oefen, und brennet die Berge, und bläset eitel Hitze von sich, und gibt so hellen Glanz von sich, daß sie die Augen blendet. Das muß ein grosser HERR seyn, der sie gemacht hat, und hat sie heissen so schnell lauffen. Und der Mond in aller Welt muß scheinen zu seiner Zeit, und die Monat unterscheiden, und das Jahr austheilen. Nach dem Mond rechnet man die Feste es ist ein Licht das abnimmt und wieder zunimmt.

Gothic was the word used for sans serifs at the turn of the twentieth century, but more commonly refers to Germanic blackletters, including Cursiva, Fraktur, Textura, and Schwabacher.

Printer Johann Ernesti's *Die wol-eingerichtete Buchdruckerey* (1721), conversely, included forty-four pages of specimens [Fig. 2.3]. Ernesti's manual, the third published in German, echoed Moxon in giving a history of printing and offering practical advice for printers, explaining tasks like handling page imposition and arranging type cases.[10] Unlike Moxon, Ernesti was concerned not only with the history and practice of printing, but also with the varying aesthetic and functional qualities of specific typefaces, which he displayed very intentionally. The composition of the specimen pages, particularly those for text faces, helped viewers understand how a single typeface would look and work when used. A straight-forward page design strategy made use of bold lines to frame two columns of text, with a running header and page number above. These functional navigational aids guided viewers through a range of blackletters, romans, and italics (*cursiv*) at varying sizes, including **Gothic Frakturs** clearly intended to be functional as body copy. The specimen labeled each typeface by name and size, further evidence of its functional purpose. It also included decorative capitals and large romans for titles and display; Hebrew, Greek, and Arabic alphabets; **musical notation**; Zodiac signs; and liturgical **calendar symbols**. Some of these graphic elements were printed in red ink to add to their visual appeal. Yet these pages utilized the same functional approach as the rest of the specimen, organizing the graphic material into ordered rows and columns arranged by size. The specimen's generous length indicated that printers should expect type-casters to provide a range of typographic options—just as Moxon had written, but not shown.

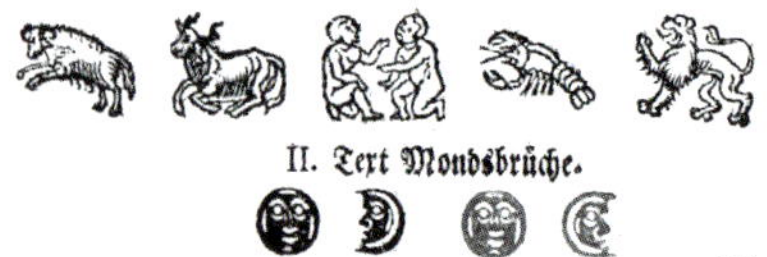

Calendar symbols might include Zodiac signs, the phases of the moon, days of the week, months of the year, and sacred or national holidays. This detail shows part of the calendar symbols segment from the specimen in Johann Ernesti's 1721 printer's manual.

Expanding typographic options

Moxon's advice that a printer should offer a variety of typographic options reflected evolving industry standards and a steady increase in the number of types being designed and produced. When Christian Friedrich Gessner wrote about "the necessary and useful art of printing" (*Die so nöthig als nützliche Buchdruckerkunst und Schriftgiesserey*) in 1740, he reprinted a 1739 specimen by noted German type founder Bernhard Christian Breitkopf.[11] The twenty pages of specimen signatures, as Gessner called them, showed roman, italic, blackletter, Hebrew, and Greek faces at multiple sizes. Four folded out for larger display, boosting their impact within the modestly-sized manual [Fig. 2.4]. Breitkopf's Frakturs demonstrated their utility as both display and text faces, a typographic choice that would remain common in Germany until the twentieth century. Throughout, a simple rule separated the running head and page number from the single-column text below; there was no other ornament. Gessner's choice to reprint a commercially produced type specimen in an instructional manual indicated that typefounding was no longer a closely-guarded practice of individual artisan-craftsmen. Rather, it had become a well-documented industry with a flourishing trade literature.[12]

Fig 2.4 (above)

***Die so Nöthig als Nützliche Buchdruckerkunst und Schriftgiesserey* (Christian Friedrich Gessner, Leipzig, 1740). This 1740 manual on "the necessary and useful art of printing" reprints a 1739 specimen by noted German type founder Bernhard Christian Breitkopf.**

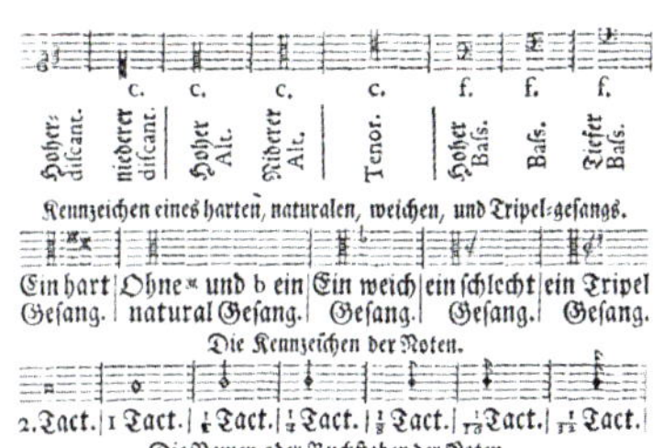

Printed **musical notation** presented its own particular typographic challenges and eventually became something of a niche market. Pictured above, Ernesti's 1721 German notation.

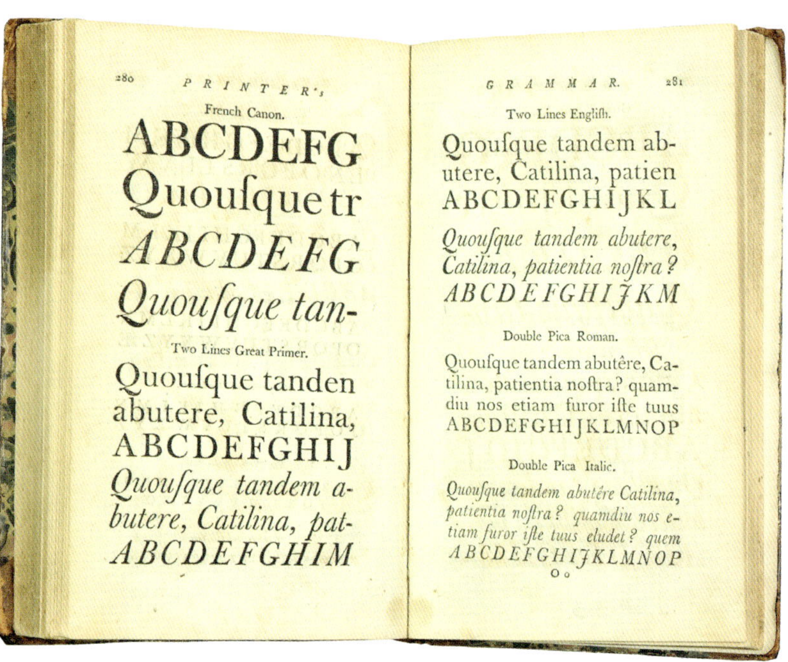

Fig 2.5 (right)

***The Printer's Grammar* (John Smith [pseud.?], London, 1787). This second edition of a 1755 manual was prepared quickly, primarily so the publisher could include an abridgement of the Fry foundry's 1785 specimen book.**

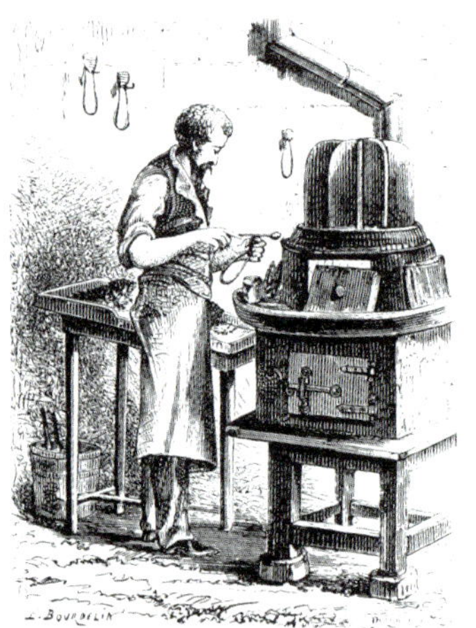

The **typecaster** poured molten metal into the adjustable type mold, where it filled the matrix and resulted in a single sort of type. Mechanized typecasting replaced human type-casters in short order.

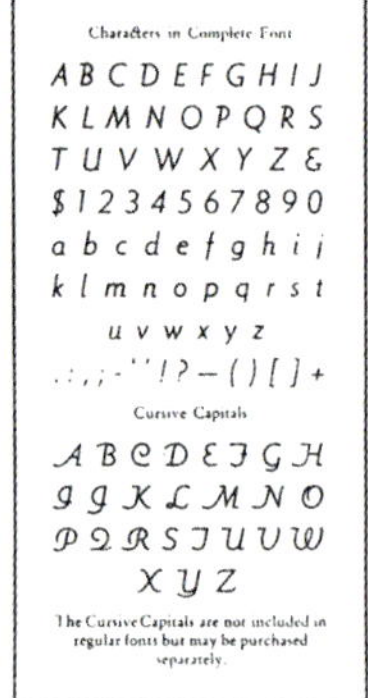

A **fount** of type is a full set of the characters in a given face at a given size, with the number of sorts per character designed to accommodate everyday printing needs. A fount of type needs more As than Zs, for instance. Originally interchangable with font as it's used today.

Several influential printing manuals post-dating Gessner's adopted and popularized the custom of reprinting commercial type specimens. By the second half of the eighteenth century, type founders regularly produced entire specimen books, often expensive showcase pieces. Specimens in manuals tended to be more humble, and thus more accessible. In 1755, John Smith (possibly a pseudonym) published *The Printer's Grammar*, an influential text reprinted multiple times under different "author's" names. Smith focused almost entirely on the practicalities of typesetting rather than history: how many of each character to cast for a complete **fount** of type, how to set up a letter-case, handle page imposition, abbreviate words, and so forth. Though he showed full alphabets in Saxon, English and German blackletter, and Roman faces, he didn't include a formal specimen. The 1787 edition, however, included a specimen from Edmund Fry & Company's London foundry (est. Joseph Fry, 1764) with typefaces inspired by Baskerville and Caslon [Fig. 2.5]. The Fry foundry published its first specimen book in 1785, and two years later the introduction to the forty-four-page abbreviation in the *Printer's Grammar* glowed with praise for the

> many very useful improvements [which] have been made in the Letter Foundery [sic] of Messrs. Fry and Son, which was begun in 1764. They have at present Twenty-seven complete Founts in Punches and Matrices of Roman and Italic … also an elegant assortment of Blacks, with Hebrews and Greeks, and many other **Orientals** [… and] a greater variety of Flowers than are to be met with in any other Foundery in this Kingdom. The following short Specimen may serve to convey some idea of the Perfection to which that Manufactory [Fry & Son] is arrived.[13]

Typographic historian David Pankow described the 1787 *Printer's Grammar* as "a hastily improvised vehicle for the type specimen."[14] Certainly the specimen was the most notable addition to the text, and the book's title page acknowledged that it was "chiefly collected from Smith's edition."

Fry & Company took pride in serving as the royal letter-founder to the Prince of Wales—and chocolatier to the Queen and Prince of Wales. (Like many members of the Society of Friends—Quakers, in America—Joseph Fry was also a chocolatier.) Yet despite this accolade, the straightforward design of the specimen presented Fry's types and ornaments pragmatically. It used a running header and page number as its only page-framing device. Romans and italics of the same size appeared together, though type sizes still bore descriptive names rather than numerical sizes. (The precise physical size of type varied slightly by foundry, though Fry did claim to match Caslon exactly.) A small, single-column block of body copy and a full alphabet represented each typeface, with four or five types to the average page. The ornaments received similarly functional treatment, with a stark page design that focused attention on the types themselves, unobstructed by any decorative flourishes or framing devices.

London printer Caleb Stower's 1808 edition of *The Printer's Grammar* included new specimens from two foundries: Fry & Steele and Caslon & Catherwood [Fig. 2.6]. Isaac Steele joined Fry in 1794; Nathaniel Catherwood joined Caslon in 1799. Stower chose foundries proximate to his own print shop, praising the extensive selections available to modern printers like himself. "Every one must observe, with increasing admiration, the numerous and elegant founts of every size, which have with rapid succession been lately presented to the public," he wrote. Stower didn't judge the competitors' relative merits, leaving that to his audience. "On the beauty, variety, or just arrangement of the following specimens, it is unnecessary for us to enlarge, or to make comparisons, wishing to leave that to the judgment or fancy of our brother printers." But he couldn't help sharing his opinion of detailed and decorative ornaments, called **printer's flowers**; in 1808, he already found their use outmoded. Yet he showed a modest selection of Fry & Steele's flowers, saying they were "still used in some of the country towns of England, but principally as borders to cards." Stower, a sophisticated Londoner, found this countrified practice undesirable. Elsewhere in his text, he wrote, "the present

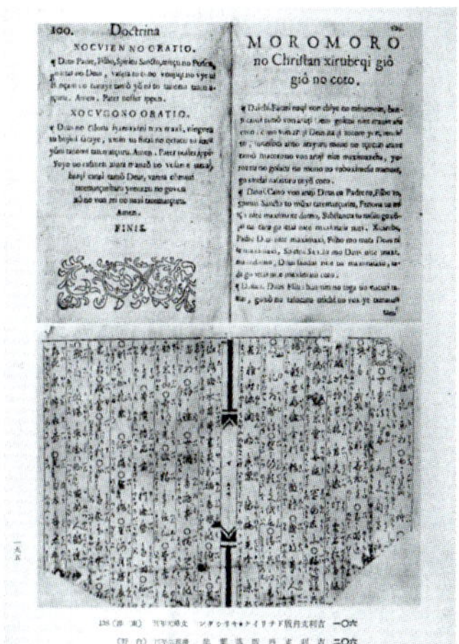

Orientals once referred to scripts from China, Japan, Korea, and other locations in Eastern Asia. East Asian types were also frequently grouped with "exotics" or "foreign language faces"—other antiquated and ultimately inaccurate terms, generally referring to any alphabet other than the Latin. Illustration from *A Brief History of Early Japanese Typography* (Kazuma Kawase, 1937).

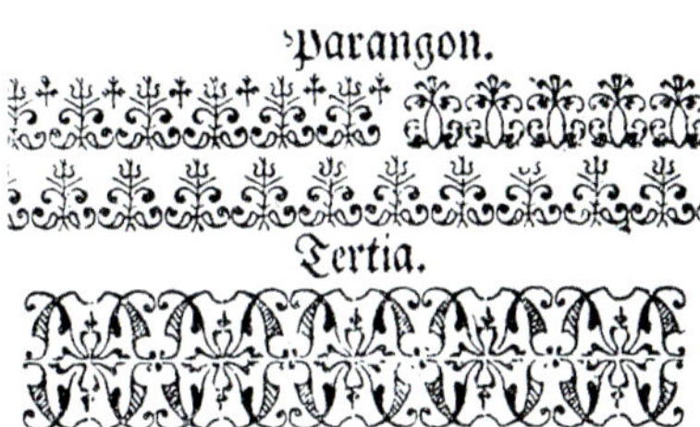

Printer's flowers—*auerhand roslein* in German and *fleurons* in French—are decorative ornaments, often floral or foliate.

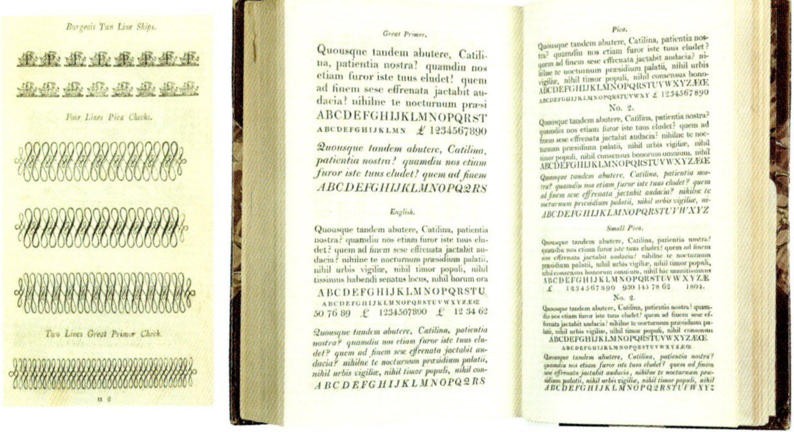

Fig 2.6 (left)

This new edition of an oft-reprinted classic included specimens from two foundries: Caslon & Catherwood and Fry & Steele. Like the manual's publisher, the foundries were located in London.

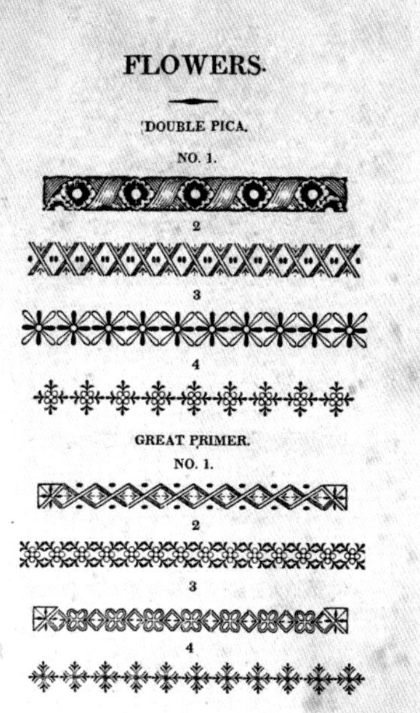

Fig 2.7 (above)

***The Printer's Guide* (C.S. Van Winkle, New York, 1818). This early American manual featured short specimens from the New York foundries of David & George Bruce and Elihu White.**

improved mode of printing has eased [master-printers] of the burthen [sic] of expensive founts of flowers and cases."[15] The type specimens Stower included focused on variety in sizes and styles, rather than extensive range of ornament, as its predecessor had. Nothing in the page design differentiated Caslon's pages from Fry's. The foundry name appeared only on each segment's title page. If randomly opening to a single page, viewers had no way of knowing which foundry had produced the type.

Pragmatically, Stower included neighboring London typefounders in his 1808 manual. Meanwhile, in America, New York printer C.S. Van Winkle chose specimens from New York's Bruce and White foundries for his popular and influential 1818 *Printer's Guide* [Fig.2.7].[16] Scottish-born brothers David and George Bruce opened their foundry in 1806 and released a specimen book in 1815; American-born Elihu White established his foundry in 1810, releasing a specimen book in 1817.[17] Van Winkle's abbreviated versions of these specimens prioritized function, presenting the types on unornamented pages, with landscape-oriented display sizes and text types shown in compact blocks of copy. Of White, Stower noted: "We regret that the size of this work will not admit specimens of all the variety of type cast at this foundry." Instead, it presented "the sizes most generally in use" and referred the reader to White's own 1817 book to see the remainder.[18] Van Winkle's choices reiterated the introductory role and geographic convenience of specimens in manuals.

Standardizing printing vocabularies

In addition to documentary and commercial purposes, specimens in printers' manuals contributed to the increasing standardization of the printing trade and its professional vocabulary. Type size offers a clear demonstration, with eighteenth century typefounders using different descriptive names for the physical sizes of type. What's now 12pts. to American and British typographers was *Pica* to English, *St. Augustin* to French, and *Cicero* to German typesetters. Further complicating matters, absolute physical measurements of a single size weren't standard across foundries, even within the same country. Only using founts of type from a single type founder ensured uniformity in the size of printed letters and the height of the metal sorts used to print them. Early correctional efforts gained traction in France when type founder Pierre-Simon Fournier published his first specimen book to wide acclaim in 1742. In it, Fournier paired descriptive names in French with specific physical measurements expressed numerically, a system he'd first published in 1737.[19]

Specimens appended to manuals tended to adopt local or regional convention, often without discussion. Jean-Raymond de Petity's *Encyclopedie Elementaire* (1767) did this, featuring Fournier's types [Fig. 2.8]. Petity described his nine pages of Fournier types as "a table to acquaint the reader with the names and sizes of twenty different typeface proportions."[20] Yet Petity identified the romans and matching italics by Fournier's descriptive *names* rather than his numerical point sizes. *Parisienne* (roughly 5pts.) was the smallest and *Grosse Nompareille* (roughly 96pts.) the largest size. Though retrospectively he left out one of Fournier's most lasting contributions, Petity used Fournier's types—and Fournier's vocabulary for describing their size—to teach readers how typographic proportional systems worked. As similar choices played out in other manuals, authors and publishers of these instructional texts played a role (if indirect) in standardizing the vocabulary of typography.

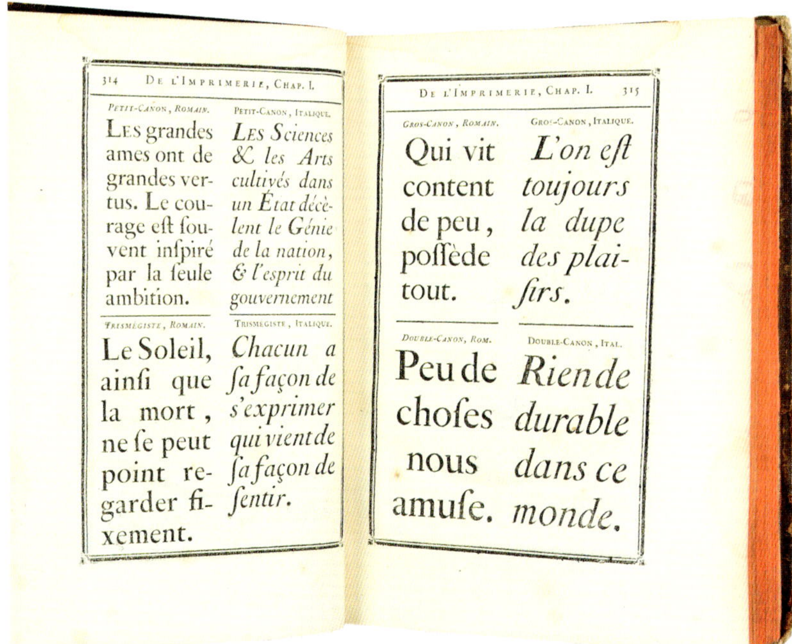

314 De l'Imprimerie, Chap. I.

Petit-Canon, Romain.

Les grandes ames ont de grandes vertus. Le courage eſt ſouvent inſpiré par la ſeule ambition.

Petit-Canon, Italique.

Les Sciences & les Arts cultivés dans un État décélent le Génie de la nation, & l'esprit du gouvernement

Trismégiste, Romain.

Le Soleil, ainſi que la mort, ne ſe peut point regarder fixement.

Trismégiste, Italique.

Chacun a ſa façon de s'exprimer qui vient de ſa façon de ſentir.

De l'Imprimerie, Chap. I. 315

Gros-Canon, Romain.

Qui vit content de peu, poſſède tout.

Gros-Canon, Italique.

L'on eſt toujours la dupe des plaiſirs.

Double-Canon, Rom.

Peu de choſes nous amuſe.

Double-Canon, Ital.

Rien de durable dans ce monde.

Fig 2.8 (left)

Encyclopedie Elementaire **(Jean-Raymond de Petity, Paris, 1767). Petity explained the names and proportions of typefaces according to French convention using types from fellow Parisian Pierre-Simon Fournier's famous 1742 specimen.**

Meanwhile, Petity took a more decorative approach to framing the page than his German forerunners. Small floral motifs decorated the double-rule border. Fleurons and other ornamental material embellished most pages instead of appearing in their own segment. Despite these decorative touches in the French **rococo** style, Petity's treatment of individual typefaces and sizes remained functional. Instead of showing romans and italics on separate pages, like the Breitkopf and Ernesti specimens, Petity featured roman and italic faces of the same size in side-by-side columns, reflecting the increasingly common practice of pairing the two kinds of types.

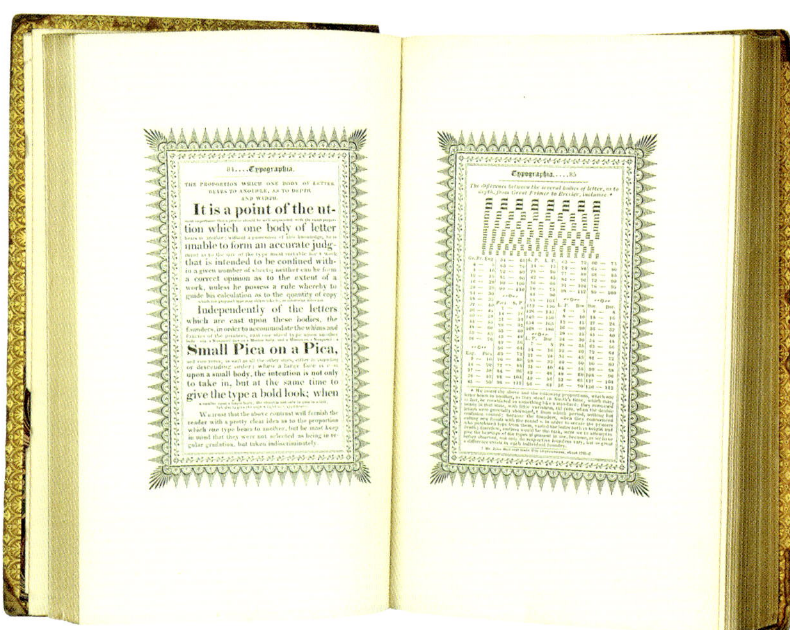

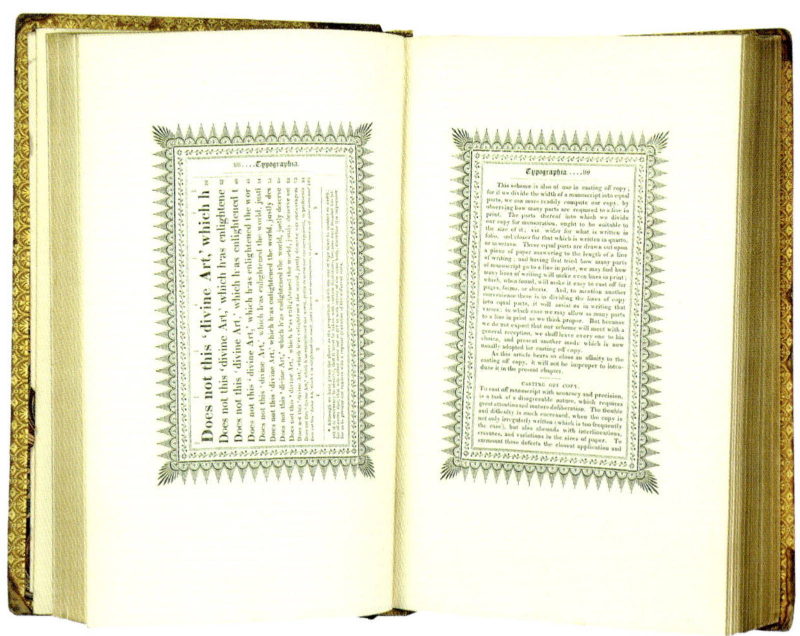

Fig 2.9 (right)

***Typographia* (John Johnson, London, 1824). Johnson's elaborate wood-engraved borders almost entirely obscured the practical information he tried to communicate about typeface styles and sizes.**

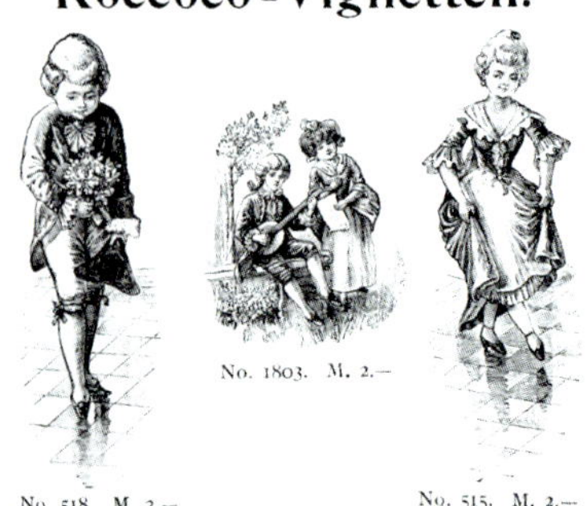

The **rococo** style originated in France in the 1730s and dominated throughout western Europe during the 1740s–70s. Often coded as feminine, the style is characterized by pastel colors, complex decorative details, fine curvilinear lines, and charmingly rendered naturalistic and artistic motifs: shells, leaves, flowers, fruits, birds, elaborately costumed dancers, and musical instruments as seen in these rococo vignettes from Stempel (1920s).

Expressing visual styles

Manuals' title pages often served as vehicles for demonstrating aesthetic conventions particular to regional or national styles. In late eighteenth century France, as both Petity and Fournier demonstrated, the rococo style flourished. Within specimens appended to manuals, however, page design skewed pragmatic, offering typographic appetizer menus. John Johnson's two-volume *Typographia* (1824) stands out because its aesthetic purposefully overshadows its contents as it describes "the Typographic Art."[21] An ornate wood-engraved border frames every page, obscuring the text for the contemporary eye. Even in 1824, *Typographia* garnered unflattering reviews due to its problematic ornament. The *Gentleman's Magazine* opined that:

> Mr. Johnson's meretricious decorations, which have cost him years of frivolous application, may claim a superiority—as gilded gingerbread attracts the notice of children; but we trust the public taste will never be so perverted. Indeed, in his attempts to surpass all his predecessors in ornamental typography he has filled the book with useless matter, and suffered the most glaring errors to escape his notice.[22]

Johnson's engravings surround even the book's few type specimens—not quite rendering them useless, but certainly distracting from their purpose by drawing attention away from the alphabets and their gradations in size [Fig. 2.09]. Though he discussed the different national names by which sizes were known, he overlooked the subtle variations in physical size that might cause difficulties when fonts from multiple foundries were mixed. While flawed as a practical document, though, *Typographia* made an emphatic aesthetic statement.

Evolving tastes

As the landscape of typographic practice evolved, so too did the reception of printers' manuals—such as Hermann Neubürger's *Practical Handbook of Printing* (1841).[23] *A Bibliography of Printing*, written only forty years later, dismissed it an "entirely practical" example of Neubürger's works, which "have not been regarded as of much authority, and are now superseded."[24] Neubürger both reflected the past and offered a glimpse of things to come. Just over 150 years after Moxon's ground-breaking *Mechanick Exercises*, Neubürger's *Praktisches Handbuch* could be criticized as outdated rather than admired for its "entirely practical" approach. Yet Neubürger also offered a preview of Victorian typographic excesses [Fig. 2.10]. While his international predecessors generally demonstrated restraint in the number and variety of types shown on each page or spread, Neubürger observed no such limitations. In only four pages, he displayed twenty-seven separate typefaces. Fanciful ornamented faces, scripts, **fat faces**, and **slab serifs** enlivened a range of workaday romans and blackletters in both **titling** and text sizes. Text faces were set in several lines of body copy, while display faces merited only a single line, often a single word. Quiet design characterized the pages themselves; centered rows of type labeled each face by name and size. Neubürger limited visual variety to the types, not their display on the page. This typographic proliferation within a single spread indicated a growing language of form poised to explode into the exuberance of late nineteenth century type design.

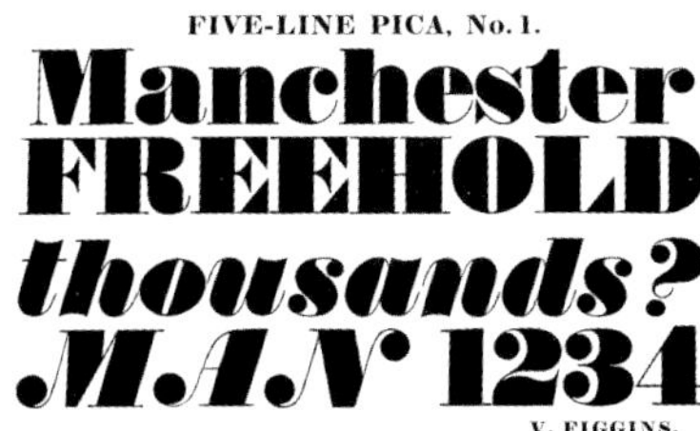

Fat faces appeared in Robert Thorne's 1803 specimen book and remained popular throughout the century. Fat faces exaggerate the characteristic thick/thin contrast of Modern serifs, as this example from Vincent Figgins' 1834 specimen demonstrates.

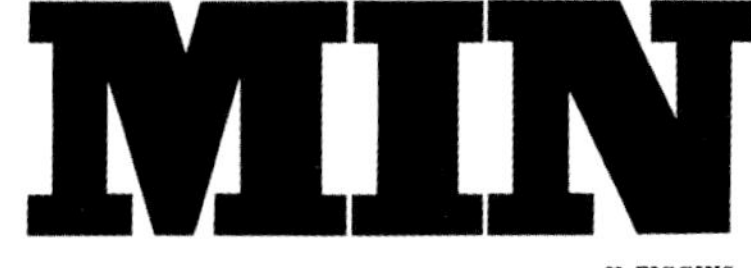

Slab serifs were introduced by Vincent Figgins, first appearing as Antiques, in his *Specimen of Printing Types* (1817). Fann Street founder Robert Thorne, designer of the first known fat face in 1801, first called them Egyptians around 1820. Not to be confused with Caslon's Two-Line English Egyptian of 1816, the first known sans serif in print.

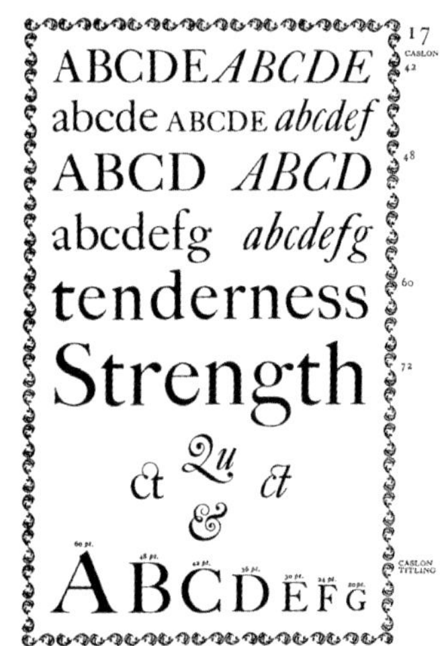

Titling faces are designed for optimal use at larger sizes. Often designed to match book faces, their strokes tend to be lighter than corresponding text sizes of the so that titles don't visually overwhelm the body copy. Here, the Pelican Press (1923) shows Caslon and Caslon Titling.

zu Grunde richten, so muß er einen Preis stellen, welcher die Bestreitung aller dieser Kosten möglich macht. Freilich sieht eine solche Berechnung sehr verwickelt aus; allein die Erfahrung lehrt, daß, wenn man den Setzer- und Druckerlohn addirt und verdoppelt, von dem Übrigen aber den reinen Kostenbetrag berechnet, dies den richtigen Preis für laufende Werke angiebt; bei Accidenzarbeiten kommt man bei dieser Berechnung freilich nicht gut aus, sondern man muß etwas mehr als das Doppelte des Arbeitsbetrages rechnen. Beispielsweise wollen wir ermitteln, was man für den Druck eines Bogens in Oktav, aus der Korpus mit Viertelpetit durchschossen, 37 Zeilen lang und 5 Konkordanzen breit, nehmen muß, um dabei bestehen zu können. Ein solcher Bogen würde 32,000 n enthalten und nach der S. 131. aufgestellten Berechnung 2 Thaler Setzerlohn kosten; der Drucker möge für's Tausend 12 Gr. berechnen, so beträgt dies mithin für Schön- und Widerdruck 1 Thaler. Jetzt rechnet man wie folgt:

Satz	2 Thlr.	= 4 Thlr.	— Gr.
Druck	1 „	= 2 „	— „
Censurgebühren		— „	2 „
Korrekturgebühren		— „	8 „
Summa		6 Thlr.	10 Gr.

Kann nach dieser Berechnung ein rechtlicher Mann einen Theaterzettel in Folio bei 850 Auflage, wobei 25 feine Exemplare, das Papier eingerechnet, für 1 Thlr. 20 Gr. liefern, ohne sein Geld einzubüßen? —

Anhang.

Das Verhältniß der Schriften zu einander.

(Siehe Seite 50 f.)

Fette Missal Fraktur.

Amerika.

Kanon Neugothisch.

Neuhaldensleben.

Kleine Kanon Fraktur.

Konstantinopel.

Fette Doppel-Mittel Fraktur.

Spanien. Portugal.

Text Fraktur.

Blätter aus der Gegenwart.

Tertia Neugothisch.

Neues Conversations-Lexikon.

Fette Mittel Fraktur.

Abenteuer und Naturschilderungen.

Kleine Cicero Fraktur.

Von dem Fuße der hohen Gebirgskette des Hindukusch, welche das Königreich Kabul in Norden begrenzt, dehnt sich bis zu der äußersten Ferne des Horizonts eine unermeßliche Niederung aus.

Corpus Fraktur.

Offenbar war diese Ebene früher vom Meere bedeckt und Alles zeugt von diesem frühern Zustande; bald ist die Ebene von dürrem Flugsande, von Sümpfen mit Rohr und von salzigen Seen bedeckt, bald wird sie von kleinen Hügelketten durchzogen, die sich nach allen Seiten hin verlängern und lange Thäler bilden, in welchen Flüsse strömen.

Petit Fraktur.

Nach dem chinesischen Reiche hin erstreckt sich das Khanat Khokand; die Bucharei begreift den südöstlichen Theil und stößt an Kabul, und mitten in der Ebene, ganz frei, zwischen der Bucharei und den Turkomannen, befindet sich das Khanat Khiwa.

Nonpareille Fraktur.

Dieser Staat ist gar nicht ausgedehnt, weil nach einem orientalischen Schriftsteller „ein Reiter in drei Tagen rund um denselben herum kommen kann.“ aber der Einfluß, den er auf die benachbarten Völker ausübt.

Verzierte Missal Kanzlei.

Buchdruckerei.

Moussirte Missal Antiqua.

HALLE.

Kanon Antiqua.

Die Maschine.

Fette Doppel-Mittel Antiqua.

Konstantinopel.

Text Antiqua.

Russland und Preussen.

Tertia Lapidar.

NEUHALDENSLEBEN.

Mittel Antiqua.

Schriftgiesserei und Buchdruckerei.

Fette Cicero Kursiv.

Bühnen-Repertoir des Auslandes.

Korpus Antiqua.

Das Khanat Khiwa ist eine Oase mitten in der Wüste. Die Verständigkeit, mit welcher die Bewohner das Land bebauen, verdient Bewunderung; sie haben es mit Kanälen und Wasserbehältern durchzogen, die von dem Amu Devia genährt werden.

Throughout Western Europe and North America, specimens captured an ever-growing selection of typefaces. The *Manual de la tipografia Española* (1852), published in Madrid, didn't crowd as many types onto a single spread as Neubürger had [Fig. 2.11]. But it did embrace a similar wide range. Its instructional text followed the well-established sequence of explanatory chapters on typographic printing history and mechanics. Then, its roughly sixty-page specimen displayed scripts, gothic blackletters, slab serifs, grotesques (what we'd now call sans serifs), ornaments, and text types, mostly **Modern** in style.[25] These designs had been selected from Madrid's Petibon foundry, connected to the French foundry of the same name.

Conclusion

Instructional books on typefounding, metal typesetting, and letterpress printing continued to be written and published throughout Western Europe and North America well into the twentieth century, and the format established by early models persisted. The Danish *Typography for [Type] setters: proofreaders, writers and publishers* (1913) attested to changes in production technologies, visual styles, and preferred display methods for typographic specimens [Fig. 2.11]. Yet it followed the template for standard printer's manual fare and narrated how to cut matrices, make molds, cast sorts, and set type on a **composing stick**. It explained nomenclature for **letterform anatomy**, typefounding terminology, classification of type styles, and systems of measurement including Fournier and Didot's point systems as well as the local *leipzigersystemer*.[26] Roughly a decade earlier, the *British Printer* had explained that Germany's "Leipzig system" was "still in vogue in the older printing offices of Denmark, Norway, and Sweden."[27] Images and type samples throughout the manual showed the well-known tools of the trade—from **typestick** to type cabinet to mechanical typesetting machines—and typographic specimens. Despite including the quaint *leipzigersystemer*, the selection of specimens largely reproduced title pages and advertisements. This approach reflected a contemporaneous international trend toward displaying specimen types in their commercial contexts.

Fig 2.10 (opposite)

***The Practical Handbook of Printing* (Leipzig, Hermann Neubürger, 1841). By 1841, "practical" was an insult. Nonetheless, Neubürger's brief 4-page specimen managed to cram in almost 30 different typefaces.**

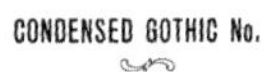

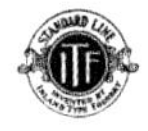

GOTHIC is used

FORMED railroads

What we usually call sans serifs today were often called **Gothics** upon their introduction to western typography in the early nineteenth century. This example is from Inland (USA, 1907).

M M

Modern or Didone typefaces—after Firmin Didot, whose capital M appears on the left—are geometrically constructed with little or no stroke width variation, high contrast between thicks and thins, and hairline serifs which are often unbracketed. Compare to Renaissance typographer Nicolas Jenson's M on the right.

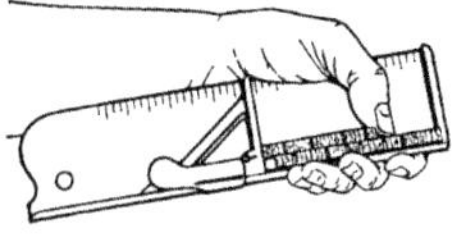

The **composing stick** or **typestick** allowed the typesetter to compose text at the correct line width, one segment at a time.

6 Line No. 2247. O.

Grand Roads!

4 Line No. 2247. Class O.

American Type 365

8 Line No. 2247. O.

Head Line

Letterform anatomy describes specific aspects of typographic characters in a historically rooted vocabulary, for example: 1—bowl, 2—shoulder, 3—leg, sometimes called the *tail* on an uppercase R, 4—counter 5—arm (of the y), 6—descender (of y and p), 7—crossbar, 8—stem and 9—eye (the counter of the lower case e).

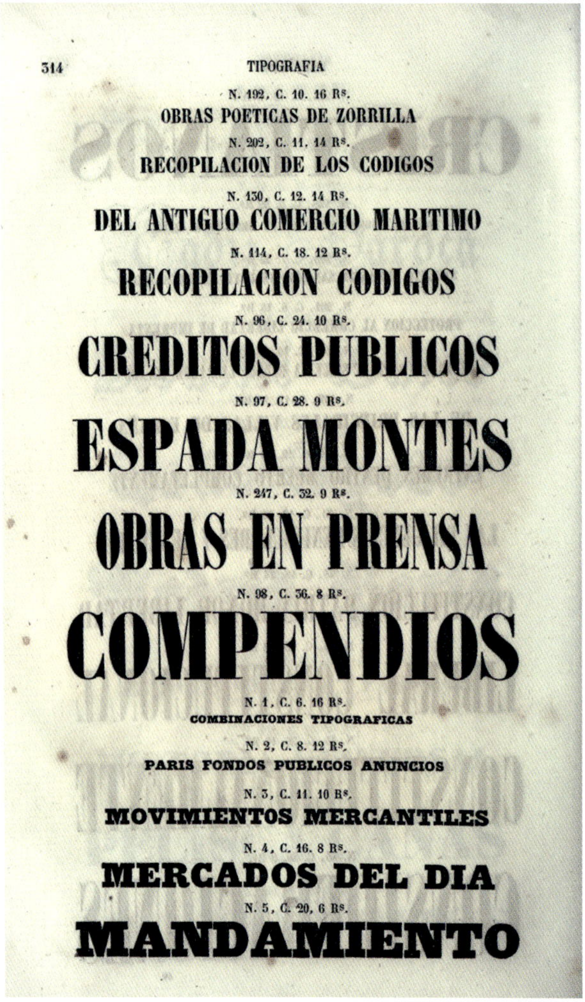

314 TIPOGRAFIA

N. 192, C. 10. 16 Rs.
OBRAS POETICAS DE ZORRILLA
N. 202, C. 11. 14 Rs.
RECOPILACION DE LOS CODIGOS
N. 130, C. 12. 14 Rs.
DEL ANTIGUO COMERCIO MARITIMO
N. 114, C. 18. 12 Rs.
RECOPILACION CODIGOS
N. 96, C. 24. 10 Rs.
CREDITOS PUBLICOS
N. 97, C. 28. 9 Rs.
ESPADA MONTES
N. 247, C. 32. 9 Rs.
OBRAS EN PRENSA
N. 98, C. 36. 8 Rs.
COMPENDIOS
N. 1, C. 6. 16 Rs.
COMBINACIONES TIPOGRAFICAS
N. 2, C. 8. 12 Rs.
PARIS FONDOS PUBLICOS ANUNCIOS
N. 3, C. 11. 10 Rs.
MOVIMIENTOS MERCANTILES
N. 4, C. 16. 8 Rs.
MERCADOS DEL DIA
N. 5, C. 20, 6 Rs.
MANDAMIENTO

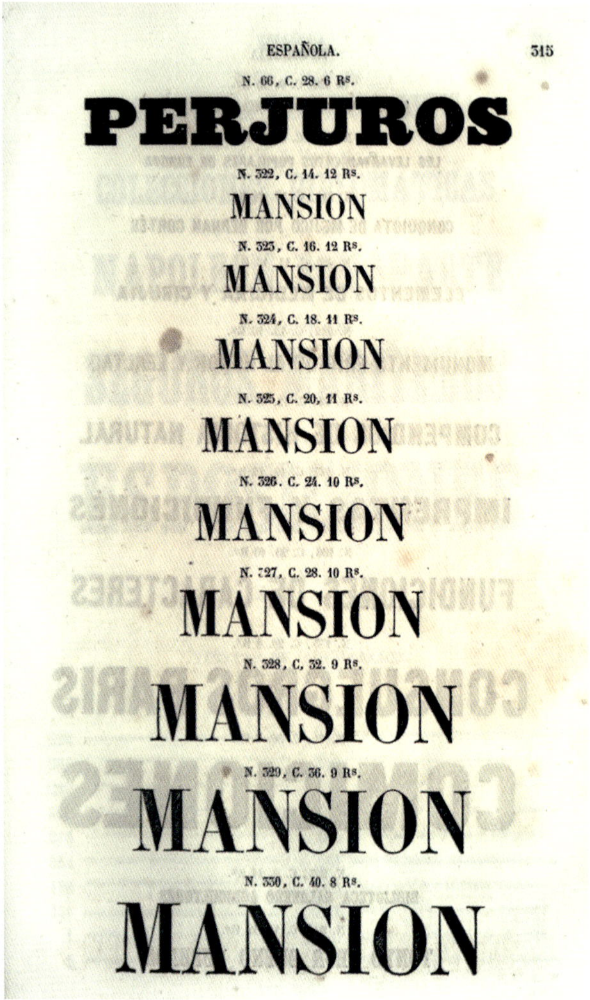

ESPAÑOLA. 315

N. 66, C. 28. 6 Rs.
PERJUROS
N. 322, C. 14. 12 Rs.
MANSION
N. 323, C. 16. 12 Rs.
MANSION
N. 324, C. 18. 11 Rs.
MANSION
N. 325, C. 20. 11 Rs.
MANSION
N. 326. C. 24. 10 Rs.
MANSION
N. 327, C. 28. 10 Rs.
MANSION
N. 328, C. 32. 9 Rs.
MANSION
N. 329, C. 36. 9 Rs.
MANSION
N. 330, C. 40. 8 Rs.
MANSION

Fig 2.11 (above)

Manual de la tipografia Española **(Antonio Serra y Oliveres, Madrid, 1852). As the nineteenth century progressed, typefaces proliferated and even the abbreviated specimens in printers' manuals offered a veritable smorgasbord of stylistic options.**

Fig 2.12 (opposite)

Typografi for Saettere / Typography for Typesetters **(Emil Selmar, Kjøbenhavn [Denmark], 1913). By the early twentieth century, specimens were expected to show not only typefaces, but also how to apply them commercially. Printers' manuals embraced this new function, too.**

INKUNABELTIDENS TYPEFORMER	
Missal- eller *Munkeskrift* (lettres de forme). Benyttet i GUTENBERGS 42-liniede Bibel af 1454.	Et omīs multitudo ppli er rās hora incensi. Apparuit angelus dñi: stans a dext
Semigotisk (lettres de somme). Den øverste type er benyttet af FUST-SCHÖFFER, den nederste er den hyppigst forekommende i det 15-16de aarhundredes tryk.	Johannē fuit aue·et Petrū sch Sz vt arbitror haud multū tibi hec i riā reuocare laborauerī. Solebas em cū blādientē virilibꝰ inceffere vbi s.eā
Den ældste gennemførte *Schwabachertype*. Af LUCAS BRANDIS' plattyske udgave af Saxo. Lübeck 1485.	de Saxo grammaticus de poeta ersl in dat latine vnde daer na in dat du ts Vnde inholt dat van Abrahams marken eyn konninkryke ghewezen v
ALBRECHT DÜRERS *Frakturtype*. Nürnberg 1531; den store linie er forbilledet for den senere kancelliskrift.	domine·Respon·Felix n den cirkel mit dem ein fuß in den puncten ins.d.Darnach setz den cirkel mit dem ein g.durch dz.a.ins.e.so ist das gemacht.D
NICOLAUS JENSONS *Antikvaskrifter*. Venedig 1492. Den øverste er forbilledet for WILLIAM MORRIS' »Golden type«.	NICOLAVS IENSON GA timet. Inde illa ueterū circa occultandā ab hac nostrorum temporū iactatione d meliosi: maligni: supbi: maledici in quē
Den første *Kursivskrift*. Indført i typografien af ALDUS MANUTIUS, Venedig 1501.	*dolebamque, quod non, ut plerique putabat aduersarium, aut obtrectatorem laudum mear sed socium potius, & consortem gloriosi labo amiseram. etenim, si in leuiorum artium stu memoriae proditum est, poetas nobiles poetari*

VORE DAGES GENGIVELSER	
Bogtrykkerkunsten indførtes i Danmark under Kong Hans. A° 1482.	*Psaltergotisk*, en moderne gengivelse af FUST-SCHÖFFERS store psaltertype af 1457. Stemplerne skaarne af FERD. THEINHARDT i Berlin.
Kanniken Hr. Povel Ræff var den første danske Mand, som drev et Bogtrykkeri. Hans største Værk var en katholsk Ritualbog.	*Mediæval Gotisk*, en moderniseret gengivelse af den overfor staaende rundgotisk fra det 15-16de aarh. Stemplerne er formentlig skaarne i Amerika.
Mester Godfred van Ghemen, den første fast bosiddende Bogtrykker i Danmark, virkede i Kjøbenhavn i Tiden fra A° 1490 til 1510.	*Halvfed moderne Schwabacher*. Stemplerne skaarne af skriftstøberfirmaet GENZSCH & HEYSE, Hamburg.
Den første danske Adresseavis stiftedes 1723 af Kancelliraad Joachim Wielandt. Efter dennes Død overtog Ernst Heinrich Berling Privilegiet og Avisen udkommer endnu som Berlingske Morgenavis.	*Renæssance-Fraktur*, tegnet af OTTO HUPP og *Leibniz-Fraktur*, moderniseret gengivelse af det attende aarhundredes frakturtype. — Firmaet GENZSCH & HEYSE, Hamburg.
DEN ÆLDSTE ANNONCE i en dansk Avis findes i HENRIK CLAUSEN GÖDES »Ordinaire Post-Zeitung« af 8de Januar 1665.	*Genzsch-Antikva*. Moderniseret gengivelse af gode latinske tryktyper fra det 15-16de aarhundrede. Stemplerne skaarne af firmaet GENZSCH & HEYSE, Hamburg.
»Det kongelige Bogtrykkeri« i Kjøbenhavn trykte 1788 »Quatuor Evangeliae graece« med græske og latinske Typer fra G. Bodoni i Parma.	*Genzsch-Kursiv* til fremhævning i ovenstaaende antikvaserie. GENZSCH & HEYSE, Hamburg.

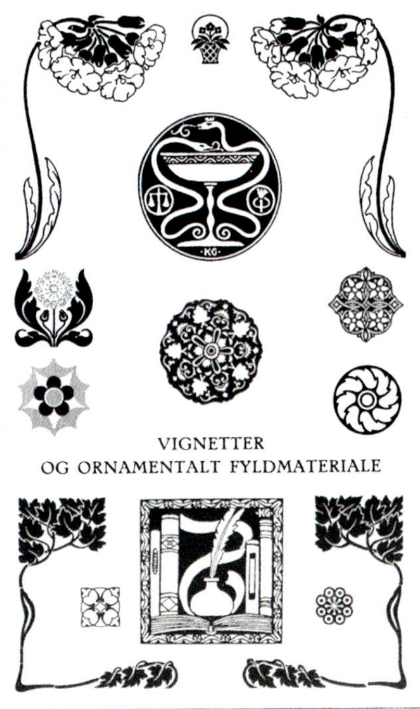

SILKEHUSET
AKTIESELSKAB
J. R. SCHIELDERUPS EFTF.

Hermed tillader vi os at meddele det ærede Publikum, at vi fra dette Aars Begyndelse har indført et

MANDAGS-SALG

af Rester og ukomplette Sortiments af Fløjler og Baand, samt i Silkevarer, forarbejdede som uforarbejdede, til billige Priser.

28 :: VIMMELSKAFTET :: 28
KØBENHAVN

OBSERVER!
HUNDE afhentes til KLIPNING
BORGERGADE
103 STUEN 103

NYHEDER I LETTE OG BILLIGE BRODERIER

IDA COHNS
BRODERI
MAGASIN

HUSK No. 35
PILESTRÆDE
TELEFON 34

HØJESTE UDMÆRKELSE
OG FLERE ÆRESDIPLOMER PAA ALLE NORDISKE FAGUDSTILLINGER

KONGELIG HOF-FOTOGRAF
PETER ELFELT
52 ØSTERGADE 52

Etablissement for smuk og holdbar Udførelse af Enkeltportræter, Gruppebilleder, Interiørs, Exteriørs og Landskabsbilleder til moderate Priser.

GULDMEDAILLE
paa Kunst- og Industriudstillingen i Kjøbenhavn 1888.

1 Alexander S. Lawson, *Printer's Manuals: From Moxon to the PIA* (Kirkwood [MO]: The Printery, 2002); David Pankow, *The Printer's Manual: An Illustrated History: Classical and Unusual Texts on Printing from the Seventeenth, Eighteenth, and Nineteenth Centuries* (Rochester, NY: RIT Cary Graphic Arts Press, 2005).

2 Warren Chappell and Robert Bringhurst, *A Short History of the Printed Word*, 2 Rev Upd edition (Point Roberts, WA: Hartley and Marks Publishers, 2000), 65–67, 93.

3 Lisa Maruca, "Bodies of Type: The Work of Textual Production in English Printers' Manuals," *Eighteenth-Century Studies* 36, no. 3 (2003): 336–37, https://doi.org/10.1353/ecs.2003.0030; Rachel Stenner, *The Typographic Imaginary in Early Modern English Literature* (Taylor & Francis, 2018), 32–55.

4 Moxon and De Vinne, *Moxon's Mechanick Exercises*, 1:1–5.

5 Cornelius S. Van Winkle, *The Printers' Guide: Or, an Introduction to the Art of Printing, Including an Essay on Punctuation, and Remarks on Orthography* (New York: C.S. Van Winkle, 1818), 22–24, https://archive.org/details/printersguideori00vanwuoft..

6 John R. Pannabecker, "Representing Mechanical Arts in Diderot's 'Encyclopédie,'" *Technology and Culture* 39, no. 1 (1998): 44–47, https://doi.org/10.2307/3107003.

7 Graham Hudson, *The Design and Printing of Ephemera in Britain and America 1720-1920* (London: British Library/Oak Knoll, 2008), 26–27.

8 Joseph Moxon, *Regulae Trium Ordinum Literarum Typographicarum, or, The Rules of the Three Orders of Print Letters: Viz. the Roman, Italick, English, Capitals and Small: Shewing How They Are Compounded of Geometrick Figures, and Mostly Made by Rule and Compass. Useful for Writing Masters, Painters, Carvers, Masons, and Others That Are Lovers of Curiosity* (London: Printed for Joseph Moxon on Ludgate Hill at the Sign of the Atlas, 1676).

9 Moxon and De Vinne, Moxon's *Mechanick Exercises*, 1:13.

10 Jocelyn Hargrave, *The Evolution of Editorial Style in Early Modern England* (Springer Nature, 2019), 6–7. Hargrave also notes that Ernesti was concerned with editorial practices, not only printing and typography.

11 Pankow, *The Printer's Manual*, 12.

12 Vervliet, Carter, and Dreyfus, *Type Specimen Facsimiles*, ix.

13 John Smith, *The Printer's Grammar. Containing a Concise History of the Origin of Printing; Also, an Examination of the Superficies, Gradation, and Properties of the Different Sizes of Types ... Tables of Calculations; Models of Letter Cases; Schemes for Casting off Copy, and Imposing; ... with Directions to Authors, Compliers, &c. How to Prepare Copy, and to Correct Their Own Proofs* (London: Wayland & Evans, 1787), 71–72, http://archive.org/details/b2876058x.

14 Pankow, The *Printer's Manual*, 18.

15 Caleb Stower, *The Printer's Grammar; or, Introduction to the Art of Printing: Containing a Concise History of the Art, with the Improvements in the Practice of Printing, for the Last Fifty Years* (London: B. Crosby & Co., 1808), 531; 98.

16 Pankow, *The Printer's Manual*, 24.

17 E.C. Bigmore and C.W.H. Wyman, *A Bibliography of Printing: With Notes and Illustrations*, vol. 1 (London: B. Quaritch, 1880), 87, https://archive.org/details/bibliographyofpr01bigmrich; vol. 3 (London: B. Quaritch, 1886), 80, https://archive.org/details/bibliographyofpr03bigmrich.

18 Van Winkle, *The Printers' Guide*, 232.

19 Pierre-Simon Fournier and Harry Carter, *Fournier on Typefounding: The Text of the Manuel Typographique (1764-1766)*, 468 (New York: Burt Franklin, 1973), xxvi.

20 Jean-Raymond Petity, *Encyclopédie élémentaire ou introduction à l'étude des lettres, des sciences et des arts*, vol. 2 (Paris: Hérissant, 1767), 307–16, https://www.google.com/books/edition/ Encyclop%C3%A9die_%C3%A9l%C3%A9mentaire_ou_introduction/qhdTAAAAcAAJ?hl=en&gbpv=0&kptab=overview..

21 John Johnson, *Typographia, or, the Printers' Instructor: Including an Account of the Origin of Printing, with Biographical Notices of the Printers of England, from Caxton to the Close of the Sixteenth Century: A Series of Ancient and Modern Alphabets, and Domesday Characters: Together with an Elucidation of Every Subject Connected with the Art*, vol. 2 (London: Longman, Hurst, Rees, Orme, Brown & Green, 1824), 1, https://catalog.hathitrust.org/Record/001757401.

22 Bigmore and Wyman, *A Bibliography of Printing*, 1880, 1:372.

23 Hermann Neubürger, *Praktisches Handbuch Der Buchdruckerkunst* (Leipzig: H. Hunger, 1841).

24 E.C. Bigmore and C.W.H. Wyman, *A Bibliography of Printing: With Notes and Illustrations*, vol. 2 (London: B. Quaritch, 1884), 73, https://archive.org/details/bibliographyofpr02bigmrich.

25 Antonio Serra y Oliveres, *Manual de la tipografia Española*; ó sea, el arte de la imprenta (Madrid: Oliveres, 1852), http://archive.org/details/manualdelatipogr00serruoft.

26 Emil Selmar, *Typografi for Saettere: Korrektører, Forfattere Og Forlaeggere*, 2nd ed. (København: Gyldendal, 1913), 21, http://hdl.handle.net/2027/umn.31951002074559i.

27 Hermann Smallian, "Type Systems of To-Day—Part II—the Didot System," *The British Printer* 12, no. 69 (June 1899): 132.

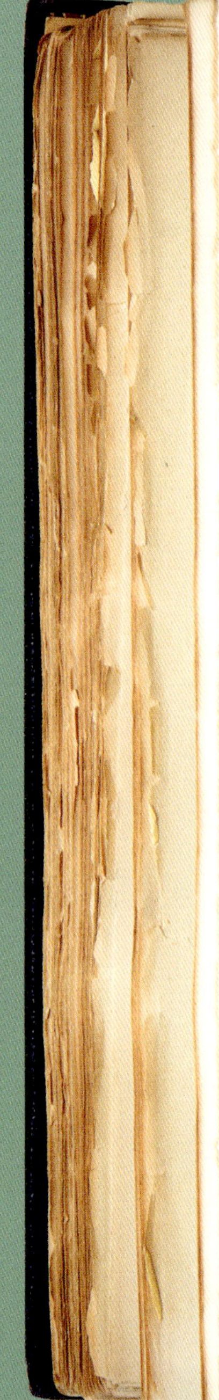

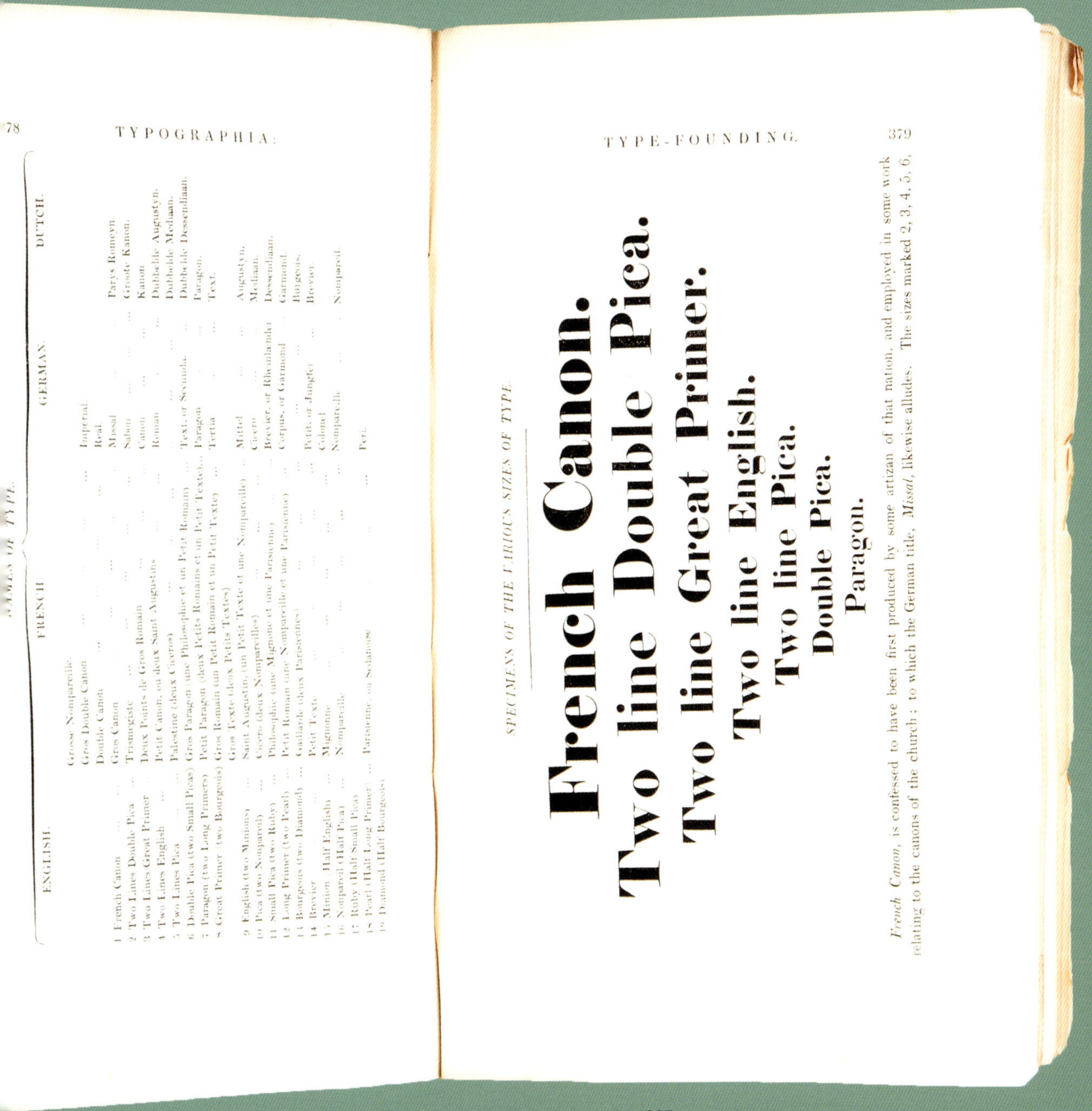

Typographia, Thomas Hansard, 1825

As an English printer-historian, Hansard emphasized mechanical developments as his trade evolved from a guild-based handcraft into an industrial manufacturing process. He wrote barely ten years after the commercial debut of Koenig's steam-powered cylinder press in 1814. At its introduction, the Koenig press produced 1,100 printed sheets per hour; by 1818, it was capable of 2,400. Two of Hansard's chapters were about improvements to presses. For a fairly comprehensive summary of the remaining 24 chapters, standard fare for the genre ever since Joseph Moxon's 1683-4 *Mechanick Exercises*, one need only consult Hansard's subtitle—*An Historical Sketch of the Origin and Progress of the Art of Printing; with Practical Directions for Conducting Every Department of an Office: with a description of Stereotype and Lithography, illustrated by Engravings, Biographical Notices, and Portraits.*

3: FOUNDRY SPECIMEN BOOKS

Probenauszug, Poppelbaum, c.1913

This catalog from the Austrian foundry Hof-Schriftgießerei Poppelbaum blends Germany's visual history from the Incunabula with the contemporary visual culture of Jugendstil. The Incunabula, or first 50 years of Western European typographic printing, originated in Germany, and Germanic printers and type founders took great pride in this heritage. In 1913, blacketter (or fraktur, or gothic) types still served everyday typesetting needs for German-speaking readers. Broadsides, ads, and books frequently treated blackletters as book faces; they were meant not only for headlines or visual interest, but also to be read at length. Adolf Hitler's initial love affair with blackletters associated the style with Nazism, and his eventual rejection of them as un-Aryan didn't alter public perception.

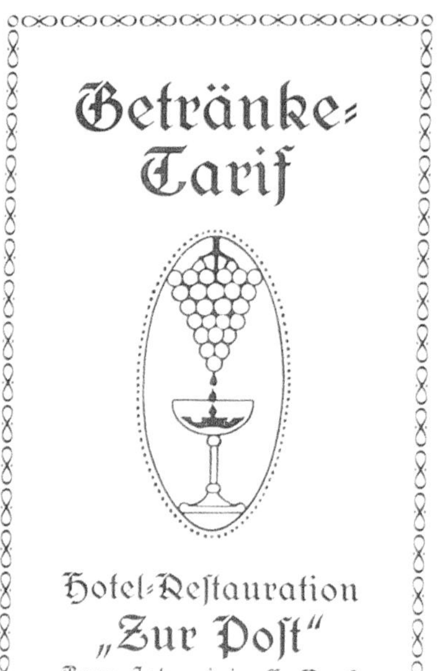

Kaufhaus Reinhold Donat

Straßburg - Ludwigshafen Kaiser - Friedrich - Straße 5

Weiße Woche

vom 21. bis 26. September

Kaffee-Decken, Tisch-Decken	Bettbezüge, Damen-Wäsche
Tisch-Läufer, Taschentücher	Nacht-Hemden, Beinkleider
Servietten, Herren-Wäsche	Korsettschoner, Nachtjacken
Oberhemden, Jägerhemden	Untertaillen, Schürzen usw.
Steh- und Umlege-Kragen	Kinder-Wäsche und Kleider

Nächste Woche Ausnahmetage für

Wirtschaftsartikel, Einrichtungen!

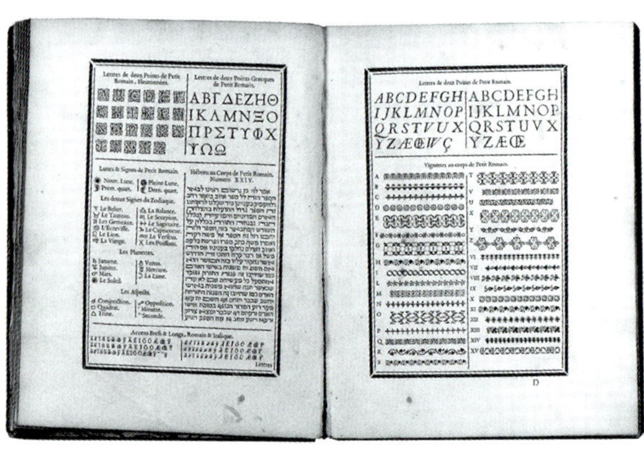

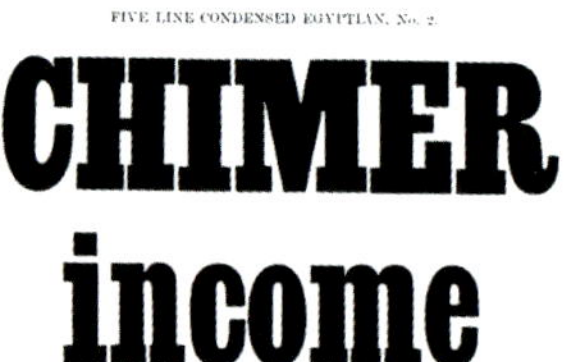

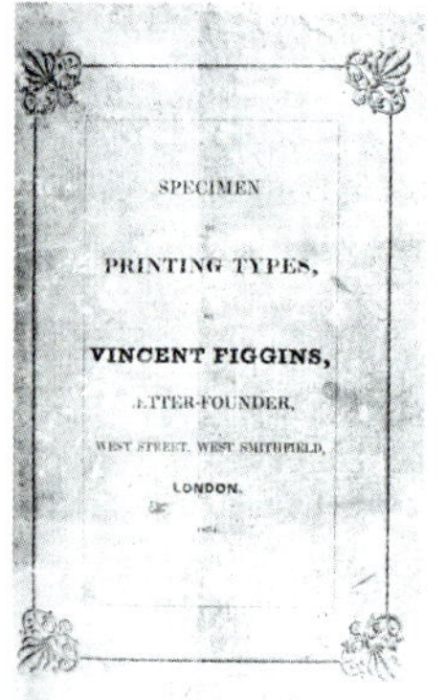
SPECIMEN

PRINTING TYPES,

VINCENT FIGGINS,

LETTER-FOUNDER,

WEST STREET, WEST SMITHFIELD,

LONDON.

TWO-LINE GREAT PRIMER SANS-SERIF.

TO BE SOLD BY AUCTION,
WITHOUT RESERVE;
HOUSEHOLD FURNITURE,
PLATE, GLASS,
AND OTHER EFFECTS.
VINCENT FIGGINS.

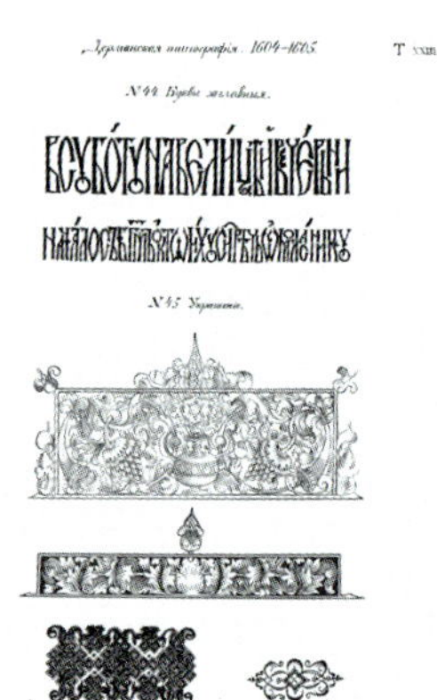

1743 — Netherlands

Enschedé printing house begins type-founding in Haarlem.

c. 1820 — England

Thorne introduces the term *Egyptians* for slab serifs.

1829 — England

Figgins calls his 3 all-caps titling faces *sans serifs*.

1849 — Russia

Specimen of Slavic hands and types issued in St. Petersburg; first printing house in that city est. 1711.

1567 — Belgium

First known type specimen book published.

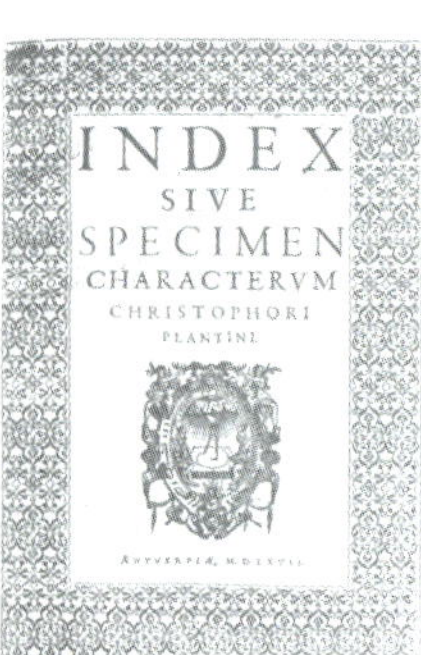

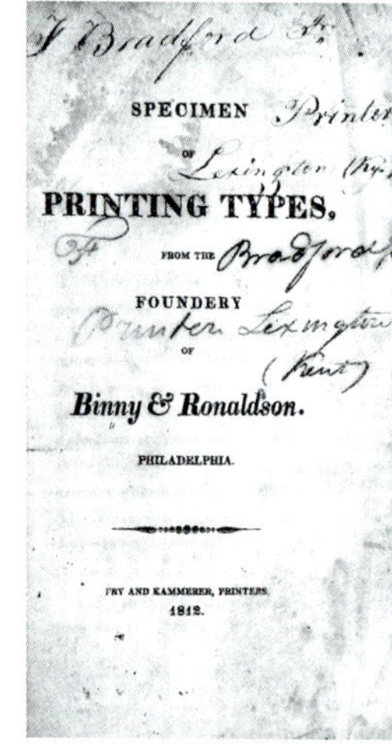
SPECIMEN

OF

PRINTING TYPES,

FROM THE

FOUNDERY

OF

Binny & Ronaldson.

PHILADELPHIA.

FRY AND KAMMERER, PRINTERS.

1812.

1809 — USA

Binny & Ronaldson of Philadelphia print the first type founders' specimen book in the USA.

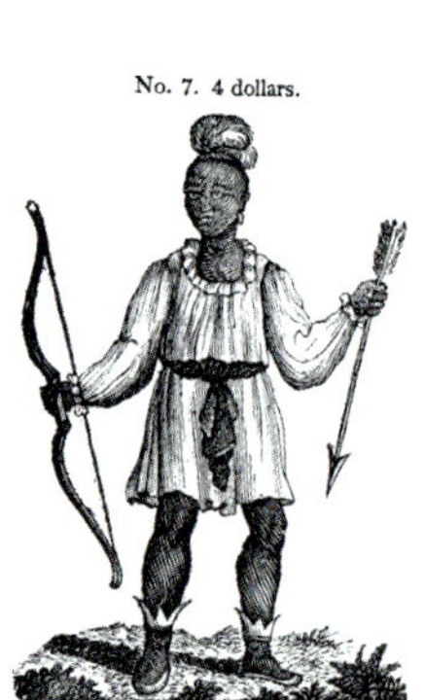

1828 — USA

Cherokee Phoenix, first indigenous language newspaper in the USA, prints first issue.

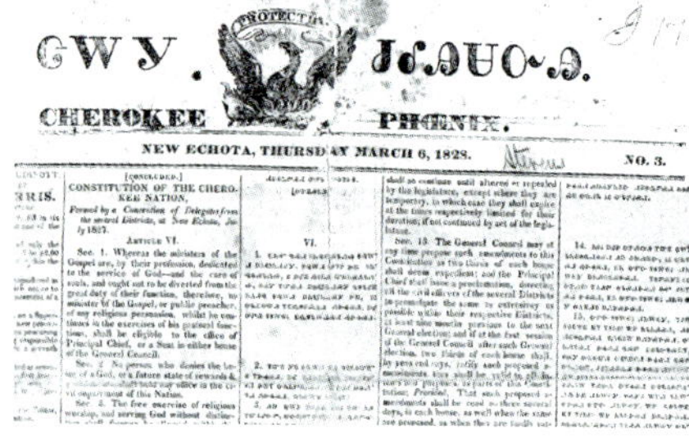
CHEROKEE PHŒNIX.

NEW ECHOTA, THURSDAY MARCH 6, 1828. NO. 3.

CONSTITUTION OF THE CHEROKEE NATION.

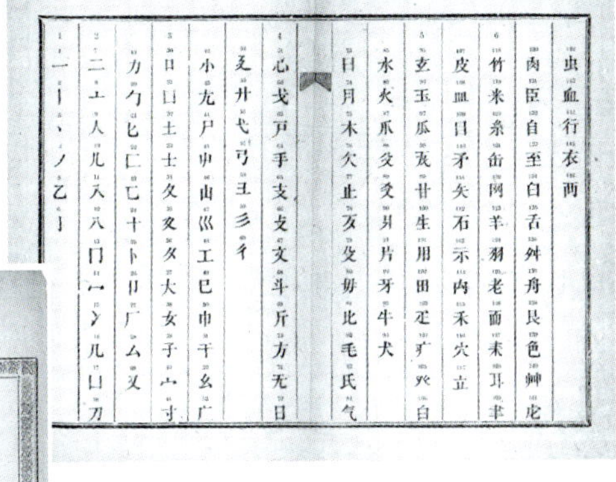

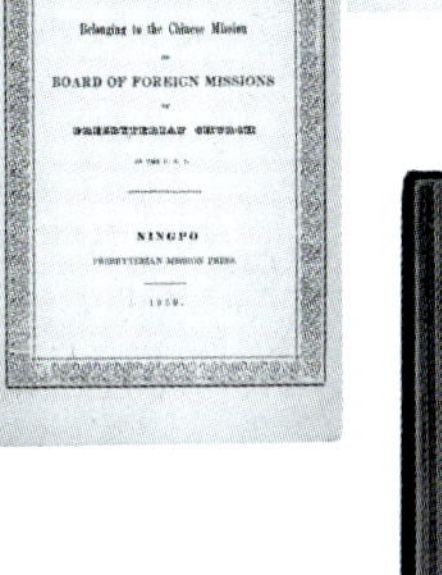

SPECIMENS
OF
CHINESE TYPE
Belonging to the Chinese Mission
OF
BOARD OF FOREIGN MISSIONS
OF
PRESBYTERIAN CHURCH
NINGPO
PRESBYTERIAN MISSION PRESS
1859.

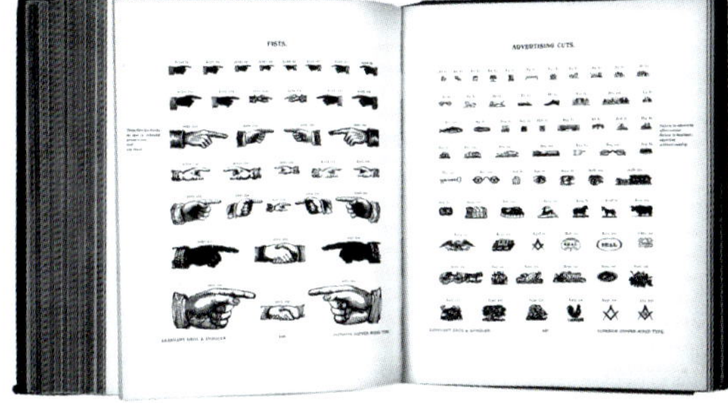

ILLUSTRATED CATALOGUE
AND
PRICE LIST OF PUBLICATIONS
OF THE
American Mission Press,
BEIRUT, SYRIA.
Founded at Malta, 1822, and at Beirut, 1834.
PRICES IN PIASTERS.
The Piaster equal to about four cents, or two pence.
BEIRUT, 1887.

1859 — China

Movable bronze types used in China from the 11–12 c. didn't prevent western missionaries from "introducing" type.

1883 — USA

Great Western Type Foundry, est. 1873, becomes Barnhart Bros. & Spindler.

1887 — Lebanon

American Mission Press est. in Beirut.

1853 — China

First Chinese-language newspaper, the *Chinese Serial*, published in Hong Kong.

1873 — Japan

Tokyo Tsukiji Type Foundry established.

1900 — India

Gujarati Type Foundry, owned and operated by indigenous Indians, est. in Mumbai.

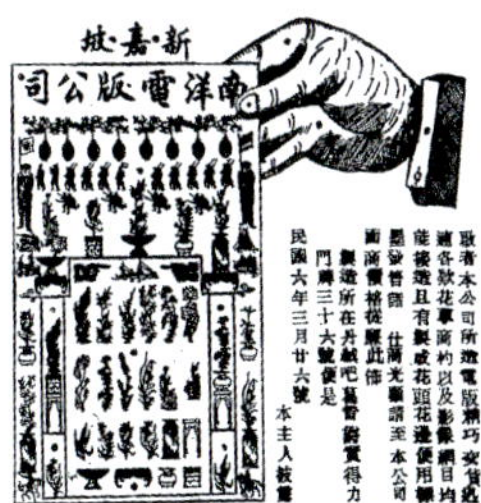

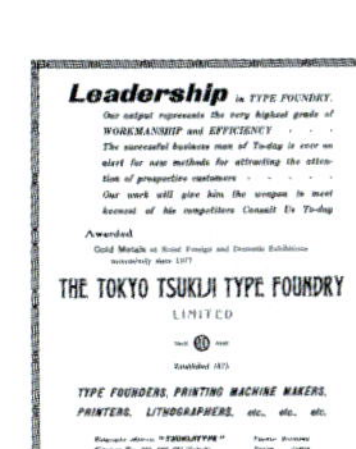

Leadership in TYPE FOUNDRY
THE TOKYO TSUKIJI TYPE FOUNDRY
LIMITED
TYPE FOUNDERS, PRINTING MACHINE MAKERS, PRINTERS, LITHOGRAPHERS, etc., etc., etc.

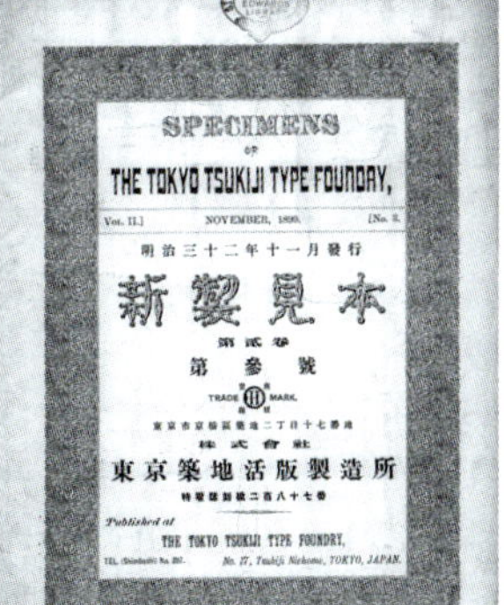

SPECIMENS
OF
THE TOKYO TSUKIJI TYPE FOUNDRY,
Vol. II.] NOVEMBER, 1899. [No. 3.
明治三十二年十一月發行
新製見本
第貳巻
第參號
TRADE MARK.
株式會社
東京築地活版製造所
Published at
THE TOKYO TSUKIJI TYPE FOUNDRY,
No. 17, Tsukiji Nichome, TOKYO, JAPAN.

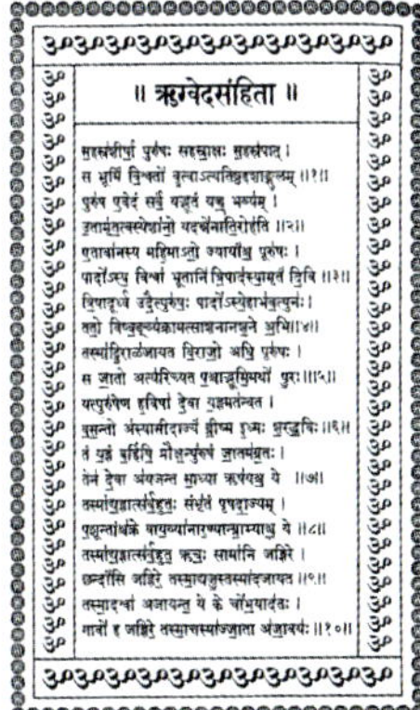

॥ ऋग्वेदसंहिता ॥

During the seventeenth century, specimen books emerged as a distinct genre. Unlike printers' manuals of the same period, they usually avoided lengthy frontmatter. Dedications to patrons, praise for the types, or a cursory note on the foundry's origins might appear, but descriptions of printing mechanics didn't. Instead, founders displayed their own fonts of type for a range of context-dependent purposes including documentation, display, commercial trade, or international circulation. A book's intended purpose informed its design strategy, communicating a range of value-laden concepts attached to typographic practice and consumption.

TWO-LINE GREAT PRIMER SANS-SERIF.

TO BE SOLD BY AUCTION,
WITHOUT RESERVE;
HOUSEHOLD FURNITURE,
PLATE, GLASS,
AND OTHER EFFECTS.
VINCENT FIGGINS.

In 1816, Caslon called his all-caps **sans serif** face Two-Line English Egyptian; it's the first known sans serif printing type. In 1829, Figgins introduced three sans-serifs, calling them by the name we associate with the form. One of these Two-Line Pearl sans serif, was a text face including lowercase letters.

Ornament and composition reflected styles of the day, as popular aesthetics like the rococo or neoclassicism informed typeface and page designs. National tastes played a role; Italian and French specimens throughout the eighteenth and early nineteenth centuries tended to be more decorative than their American, British, and Dutch counterparts. What we now call **sans serif** typefaces appeared—entirely without fanfare—in early nineteenth century Figgins and Caslon specimens, and the nomenclature used to describe them evolved as they grew in popularity within a developing commercial, mass media landscape. By the late nineteenth century, specimens embraced a new purpose: demonstrating what "good type" should look like. They instructed students, novice printers, and those far removed from urban centers of fashion to study their examples of business stationery, calling cards, menus, book pages, railway timetables, ordering forms, and advertisements. From this, readers learned how to apply culturally specific notions of good taste when using the foundry's types for everyday printing tasks. This innovation would become a common feature of specimen books by the early twentieth century.

Majuscules.

(A) (B) (C) (D) (E) (F) (G)
(H) (I ou J) (K) (L) (M) (N) (O) (P) (Q)
(R) (S) (T) (U) (V) (X) (Y) (Z)

Minuscules.

(a) (b) (c) (d) (e) (f) (g) (h) (i) (j) (k) (l) (m) (n) (o) (p)
(q) (r) (s) (t) (u) (v) (x) (y) (z) (et)

Lettres de civilité were meant to duplicate the effect of contemporary French penmanship. Robert Granjon introduced them in 1557, calling his new design *lettres françaises* to indicate his hopes that it would become France's national typestyle.

Formats and functions

As a genre, the specimen book served multiple functions, often rendered visible through design decisions. A utilitarian catalog might make economical use of the space of both the front and back of the page, with minimal marginal allowances. Conversely, small type blocks, expansive pages with generous margins, and recto-only printing might establish or reinforce a foundry's prestige. Specimen books showed how page design and typesetting strategies reflected the varied purposes such books might fulfill. They also documented how type styles evolved over time and across place, recording shifting and culturally specific notions of function and taste.

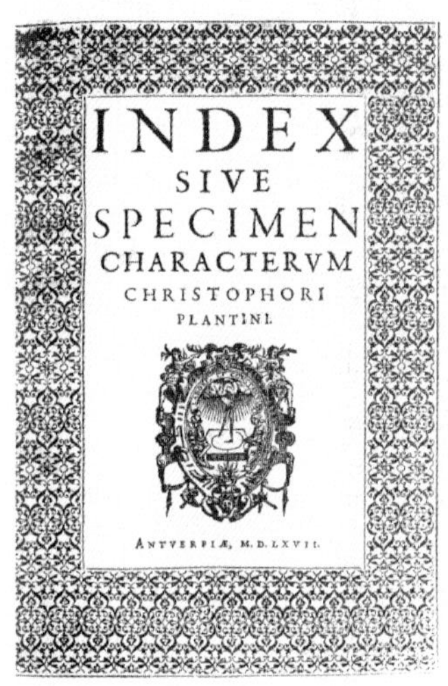
INDEX
SIVE
SPECIMEN
CHARACTERVM
CHRISTOPHORI
PLANTINI.

ANTVERPIÆ, M.D.LXVII.

III. TVSCVL.

Sapienti malum videri nullum videri poteſt, quod vacet turpitudine: aut ita pa rum malum, vt id obruatur ſapientia, vixq́ue appareat: qui nihil opinione affingat, aſſumatq́; ad ægritudinem: neque id putet eſſe rectum: ſed, quammaximè excruciari luctuq́ue confici, quo prauius nihil eſſe poteſt.

B 2

III. TVSCVL.

Sapienti malum videri nullum videri poteſt, quod vacet turpitudine: aut ita pa rum malum, vt id obruatur ſapientia, vixq́ue appareat: qui nihil opinione affingat, aſſumatq́; ad ægritudinem: neque id putet eſſe rectum: ſed, quammaximè excruciari luctuq́ue confici, quo prauius nihil eſſe poteſt.

B 2

Fig 3.1 (above)

Index Characterum **(Christophe Plantin, Antwerp, 1567; Douglas McMurtrie, New York, 1924). McMurtrie's facsimilie edition (pictured) introduced one of the earliest specimen books ever printed to a wider audience, providing access to viewers unable to see the original.**

Comprehensive documentation

The earliest specimen books, printed in Belgium, France, and Italy, established a basic and persistent model for the form. They collected all of a founder or printer's types, organizing them according to size and/or style. Antwerp printer Christophe Plantin issued one of the earliest specimen books [Fig. 3.1], the *Index characterum* (1567). It displayed the Hebrew, Greek, roman, italic, blackletter, and ***lettres de civilité*** faces his press owned, types designed by and purchased directly from what a 1924 facsimile called "the leading punch-cutters of the sixteenth century."[1] Specimen books remained rare for the next half century, until master-printer and type founder Jean Jannon published *Epreuves des caracteres* (1621), the first French type specimen book [Fig. 3.2]. It contained types he'd cast from 1615 onward due to difficulties sourcing type for his then four-year-old press in Sedan.[2] A mere seven years later, in 1628, the Stamperia Vaticana published a specimen book of its forty-nine printing types, including French faces purchased from the foundries of Garamont and Grandjean, as well as Hebrew, Greek, and Syriac alphabets for printing **polyglot** bibles [Fig. 3.3].[3] Jannon's foundry specimen, and the Vatican's and Plantin's printing-house specimens, all displayed individual letters and short words at large sizes, sometimes in landscape format; for smaller text sizes, blocks of sample copy ranged in size from small to large. These might be displayed in one or multiple sizes or styles on a portrait-oriented page, usually in one column, though Plantin deployed two columns for some smaller faces. The pages were recto-only, that is, printed only on the "front" (right-hand) side of the page. These early specimens exude *gravitas*, particularly seen in historical context. Jannon's specimen contained types subsequently purchased by the French royal printing office, the Imprimerie royale, and thereafter frequently misattributed to Claude Garamont; Plantin's contained Garamont's Canon from the Berner sheet of 1592.[4] The Vatican's printing types carried Catholicism around the globe. Even more impactful, though, was the structural model these early specimens provided for visually documenting typeface libraries.

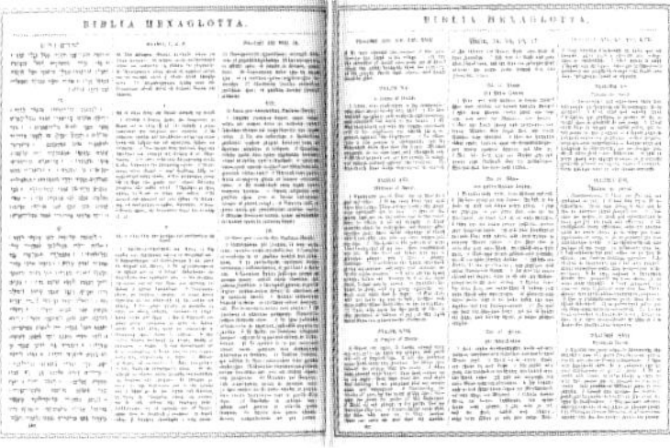

Polyglot printing is multi-lingual. This bible published in New York in 1901 is set in Hebrew, Syriac, and Latin, alongside English, German (blackletter), and French.

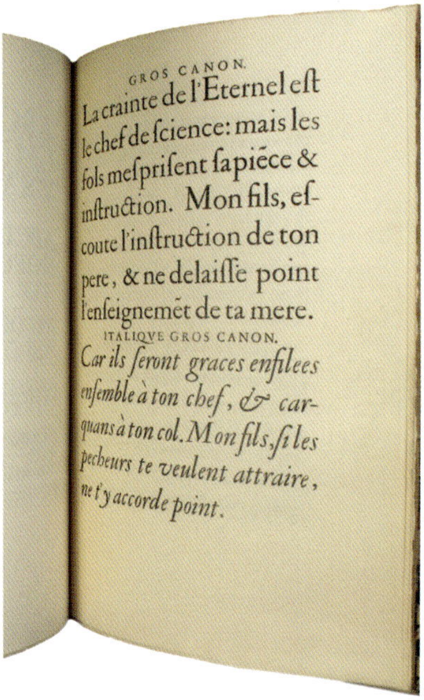

Fig 3.2 (right)

Beatrice Warde, writing as Paul Beaujon, introduced this 1927 facsimilie edition of Jannon's 1621 *Espreuve des Caracteres Nouvellement Taillez*. Shown here, Jannon's Gros Canon and Gros Italique, descriptive names that could be applied to what's now both 44 and 48 point type.

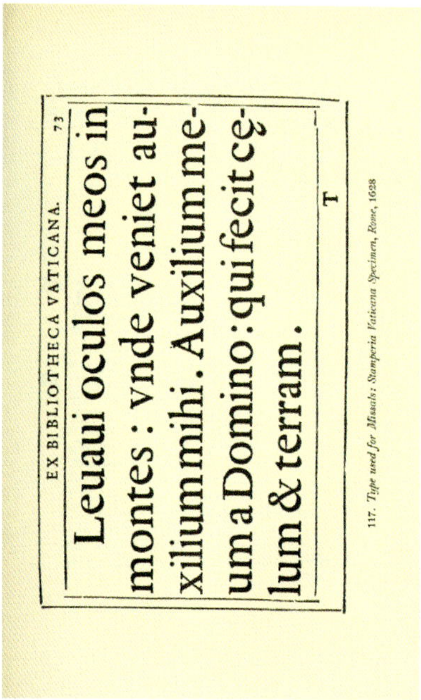

Fig 3.3 (far right)

***Indice de Caratteri* (Stampa Vaticana, 1628). The types at the Vatican Press met the global, multi-script printing needs of the Catholic Church. Egyptian, Latin, and Greek alphabets, shown here, were accompanied by the (sometimes imaginative) Antique Hebrew of Moses, the Chaldaic of Abraham, Cyrillic, Arabic, and an "Alphabetum Indorum," an early attempt at Indian script rendered in woodcut, not metal type. D.B. Updike's 1922 *Printing Types* included reproductions from the famous specimen.**

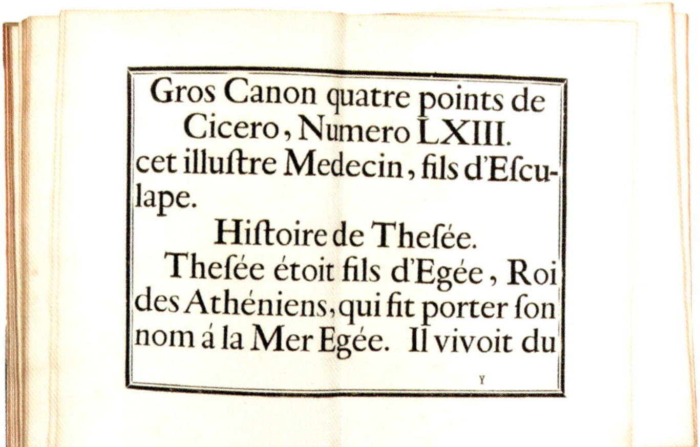

Fig 3.4 (below)

***Epreuves Generales des Caracteres* (Claude Lamesle, Paris, 1742). This specimen reflects Lamesle's organized, logical approach to designing his specimen. Even the display copy reads sequentially.**

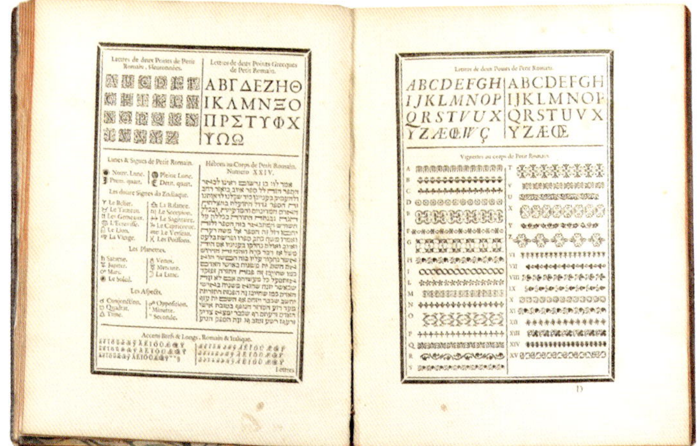

Two French specimen books from the 1740s demonstrated a less visually apparent organizational structure: how typefaces traveled and type foundries grew. Foundries changed hands as type founders died, went bankrupt, passed on the business to a younger generation, or simply sold some or all of their stock for cash. Claude Lamesle's 1742 *Epreuves Generales des Caracteres* (1742) and Nicolas Gando's 1745 *Epreuve des caracteres de la fonderie de Nicolas Gando* (1745) displayed the same physical stock, as Gando purchased Lamesle's Parisian foundry and all of its types. Yet the two founders organized their content very differently. Lamesle planned carefully; the specimen's readable running text continued across typeface and size changes, with types numbered in continuous sequence for easy reference and decorative material interspersed at logical junctures [Fig. 3.4]. Gando's haphazard treatment of the same material showed little forethought [Fig. 3.5].[5] But he displayed his passion for ornaments in a new, spectacular display at the end of the volume; the *piece de resistance*, his fold-out "other ornament in the form of a temple portal," merited its own title page. Ornamental borders and frames built the temple's columns, pediments, and doors; fleurons served as capitals and urns. Lamesle's and Gando's differing treatments of their nearly-identical stock showed how changes in management might impact a foundry's trajectory—and its specimen designs.

Fig. 3.5 (below)
Epreuve des Caracteres de la Fonderie de Nicolas Gando **(Nicolas Gando, Paris, 1745). Gando purchased most of his types from Lamesle. His less organized approach to displaying the material doesn't detract from the impact of his temple constructed of typographic ornaments, an oversized fold-out leaf with its own title page.**

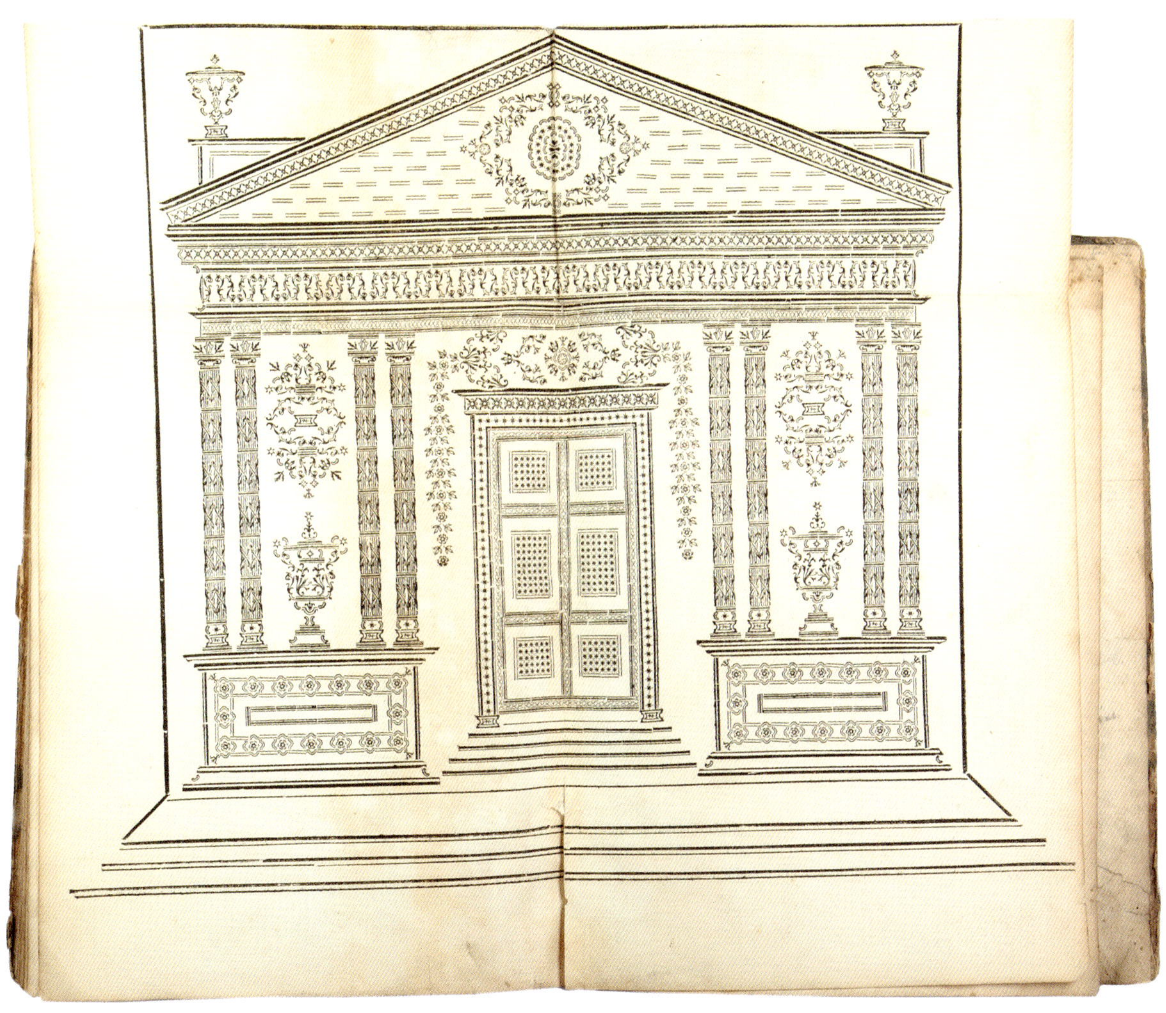

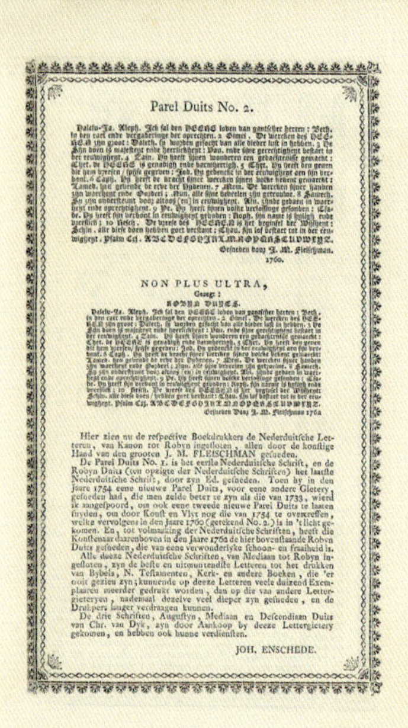

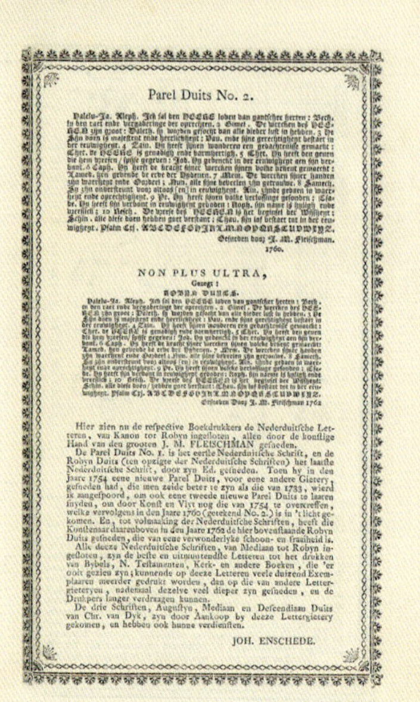

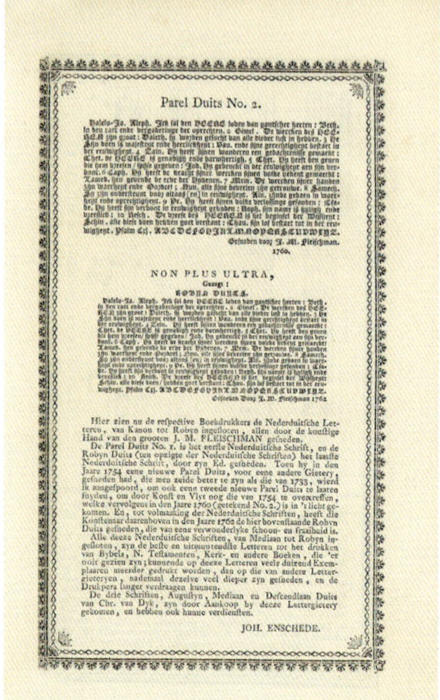

Fig 3.6 (above and right)

Proef van Letteren **(Enschedé, Haarlem, 1768). This comprehensive specimen provided a complete record of the foundry's first quarter-century, including faces that German punch-cutter Johann Fleischmann designed under contract for Enschedé.**

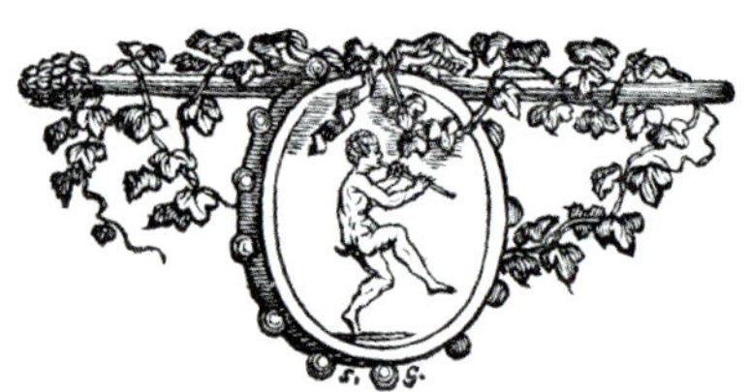

The **Neoclassical** style drew on the visual language of Greek, Roman, and Egyptian architecture and design, inspired by the archeological discoveries at sites like Herculaneum and Pompeii during the eighteenth century.

Comprehensive specimens also documented how contract work circulated evolving typographic styles. The Enschedé printing house (est. 1703 in Haarlem, the Netherlands) opened its type foundry in 1743 and released its first specimen book by the following year. The 1768 edition [Fig. 3.6] contained "all the characters then in the Enschedé foundry," a complete record of the foundry's first quarter century.[6] The presence of noted German punch-cutter Johann Fleischmann's text *romein* evidenced contract design as part of eighteenth century type-founding practice. Fleischmann trained in Nuremberg, worked for Egenolff-Luthersche in Frankfurt am Main, then relocated to Holland, where he eventually opened—and then sold—his own foundry. Afterward, he contracted for Hendrik Floris Wetstein, the founder from whom the Enschedés initially purchased their equipment and typeface matrices, and the Enschedés continued this relationship. Over a twenty-year period, Fleischmann designed about a hundred fonts for Enschedé, doing most but not all of his work for that foundry. He occasionally contracted with other Dutch founders as well. Type designs certainly circulated by way of printed specimens; Caslon, for instance, probably based his typefaces on Dutch models represented in Enschedé's 1744 specimen book.[7] But typographic design features also traveled between foundries through the freelance-like practice of the period's type designers. Fleischmann's significant influence on eighteenth century type design spread through multiple channels—German, English, Dutch, and eventually French and Italian via Fournier and Bodoni, both of whom admired Fleischmann's work.

Most foundry specimens represented a commitment to the design or commission of new typefaces, as with Enschedé and Fleischmann. In contrast, the famous *Type Specimen of Delacolonge* (1773), like the Vatican's 1628 specimen, catalogued only pre-existing typefaces [Fig. 3.7]. Typographic historian Harry Carter called it "the typographical equivalent of a gallery of old masters," explaining that Delacolonge's foundry was "stocked for the most part with matrices whose origins and provenance he is unlikely to have known," including now-famous names like Garamont and Granjon.[8] Delacolonge's page design strategy, however, echoed evolving stylistic preferences popularized first by Fournier in France then modified by Bodoni at the beginning of his career in Italy. The major difference between Delacolonge's specimen and those of Fournier and Bodoni (seen next) isn't presentation strategy or aesthetic but the inherited or newly-invented origin of the type designs themselves. Decorative frames, delicate lines, floral motifs, **neoclassical** ornaments, and generous page margins characterized the page design of all three books.

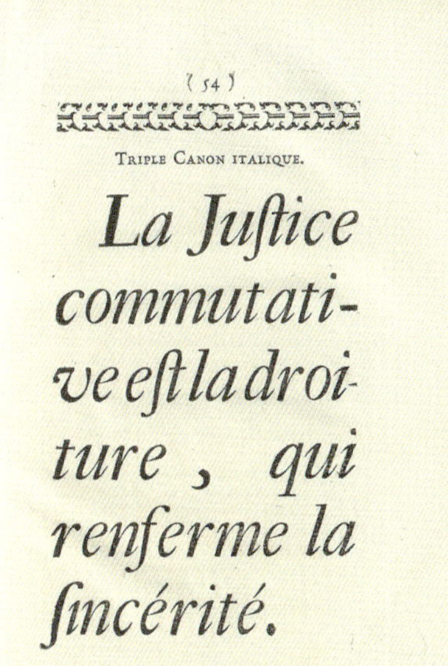

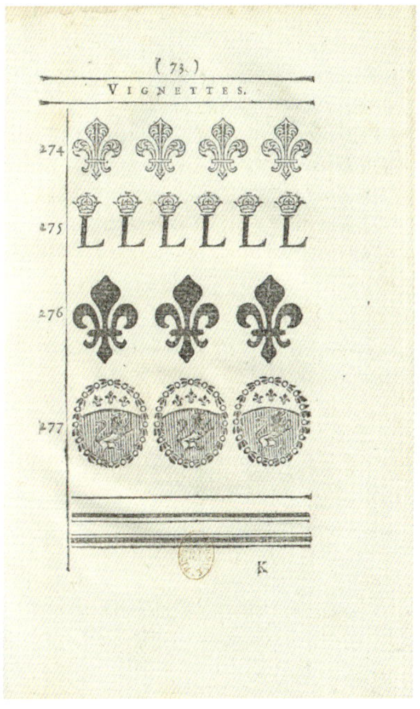

Fig 3.7 (above)

Les Caractères et les Vignettes de la Fonderie du Sieur Delacolonge **(Louis Delacolonge, Lyons, 1773). As a printer's rather than founder's specimen, this book cataloged types purchased by the Delacolonge Foundry, rather than designed by or specifically for the foundry.**

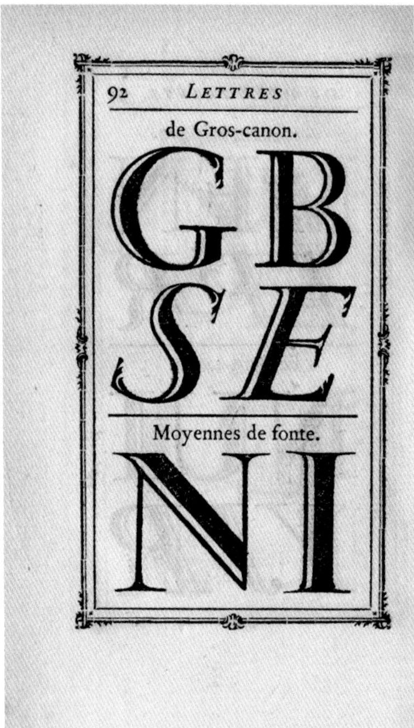

92 *LETTRES*

de Gros-canon.

GB

SE

Moyennes de fonte.

NI

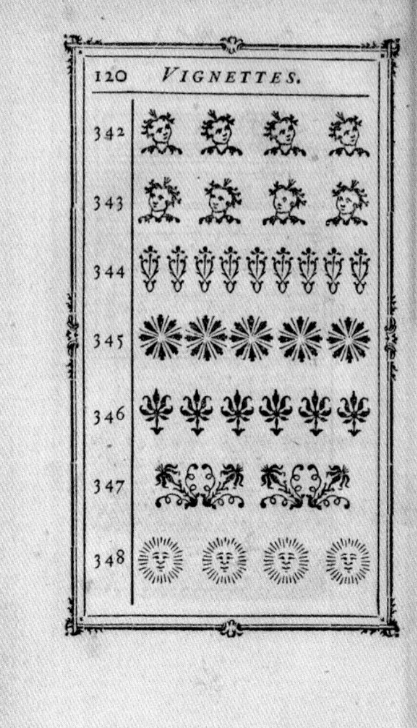

120 *VIGNETTES.*

342

343

344

345

346

347

348

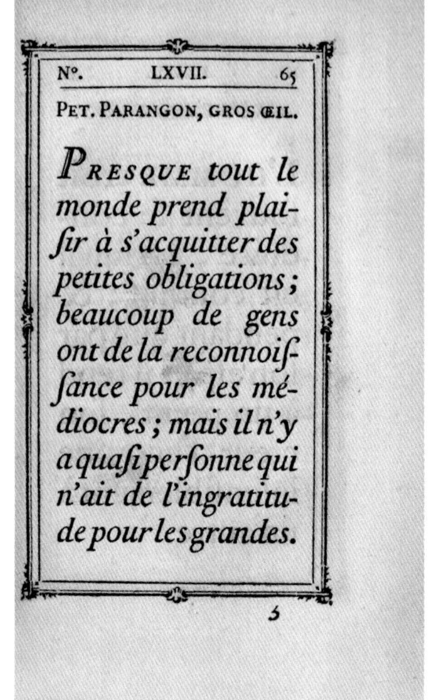

N°. LXVII. 65

PET. PARANGON, GROS ŒIL.

PRESQUE tout le monde prend plai-ſir à s'acquitter des petites obligations; beaucoup de gens ont de la reconnoiſ-ſance pour les mé-diocres; mais il n'y a quaſi perſonne qui n'ait de l'ingratitu-de pour les grandes.

Fig 3.8 (above)

The *Manuel Typographique* (Pierre-Simon Fournier, Paris, 1764). In his specimen, Fournier reprinted his 1737 table about the proportional relationships among type sizes, forerunner to today's point system, along with 101 typeface designs. The page design exemplifies the French rococo style.

Elaborate display

A deluxe edition specimen book signaled its founder's status with luxurious design choices: oversized pages, extravagant margins, and zealous application of contemporary ornamental styles. A well-received book helped cement a foundry or designer's national or international reputation, and some of today's familiar typefaces were initially family names of type founders famous for their early specimen books: Bodoni, Caslon, Didot, Fournier. Official state or religious printing houses produced showpiece specimen books as well. Dedications to wealthy or royal patrons were common; winning the coveted honor of "official letter founder" to a secular or sacred authority figure often prompted the production of an expensive exhibition of a type founder's *oeuvre*, produced for prestige value rather than commercial efficiency.[9]

French founder Pierre Simon Fournier's *Manuel Typographique* (1764) exercised considerable influence as a fashion statement [Fig. 3.8]. Intended as four volumes but truncated by Fournier's death in 1768, its first volume narrated type founding history and technologies. The second showcased Fournier's 101 types in a stunning example of the French rococo, a short-lived artistic style recognizable by its delicacy and high level of decorative detail often coded as "feminine." Fournier's ornaments and compositional strategies reflected these priorities, and he crafted the ultimate demonstration of the rococo book. The *Manuel*'s ornate delicacy didn't prevent its functionality; in it, Fournier codified the typographic **point system**. He illustrated his method of standardized measurement in the "*table generale de la proportion des differens corps de characteres*," first published in 1737, which assigned a standard point size to each typeface.[10] To date, sizes were commonly known by a descriptive name—different depending on country and perhaps even foundry of origin. Fournier popularized a mathematical system in which *Parisienne* became five point, Nompareille became six point, and so forth, and there were always seventy-two points to the Paris-standard inch. Wide

KEGLERNES STØRRELSEFORHOLD

indbyrdes, i typografiske enheder og i millimeter.

DIDOT-BERTHOLDS			LEIPZIGER SYSTEM		
Antal metriske punkter	Keglernes størrelser i millimeter	Keglernes almindelige typografiske betegnelser	Antal kvartpetit	Svarende til metriske punkter	Keglernes størrelser i millimeter
4	1,504	Diamant	2	3,85	1,44
5	1,879	Perle	2,5	4,80	1,80
6	2,256	Nonpareil	3	5,75	2,17
7	2,632	Mignon --- Kolonel	3,5	6,70	2,53
8	3,008	Petit	4	7,65	2,89
9	3,383	Bourgeois	4,5	8,60	3,15
10	3,759	Korpus	5	9,60	3,61
12	4,511	Cicero	6	11,50	4,33
14	5,263	Mittel	7	13,40	5,05
16	6,015	Tertia	8	15,30	5,78
20	7,519	Tekst	10	19,15	7,22
24	9,023	Dobbelcicero	12	23,00	8,66
28	10,526	Dobbelmittel	14	26,80	10,10
32	12,030	Dobbeltertia Lille kanon	16	30,60	11,56
36	13,534	Trecicero --- Kanon	18	34,50	12,99
40	15,038	Dobbelttekst Grov kanon	20	38,30	14,44
48	18,046	Firecicero -- Missal	24	46,00	17,32
60	22,555	Femcicero -- Grov missal	30	57,50	21,66
72	27,066	Sekscicero -- Sabon	36	69,00	25,98

Basis: meteren. 2660 Didot-Bertholdske punkter = 1 meter; 133 nonpareil = 798 metriske punkter = 300 millimeter. Papirhøjde: 62,67 metriske punkter.

Basis: ubekendt, 72 cicerolegemer = 828 metriske punkter = 311,28 millimeter, 231,30 cicerogevierter = 1 meter. Papirhøjde: 5¾ cicerolegemer = 66 metriske punkter.

The Didot and American **point systems** are—as this Danish chart shows—only two of many systems historically deployed to measure type size (*Typografi for Saettere*, Selmar, 1913).

acceptance of this standardization took time, and the system underwent significant evolution along the way. Didot, then the Type Founders Association of the United States, later revised Fournier's system—as did others, whose changes weren't lasting. Yet although Fournier's point isn't our contemporary point, the idea owes much to his 1764 *Manuel*.

Italian printer and type founder Giambattista Bodoni, one of two typographers to characterize Modern serifs in the contemporary imagination, produced many opulent specimens. *Fregi e Majuscole* (1771), his first book, showed only uppercase letters and ornaments; but he published it a mere year after establishing his own foundry [Fig. 3.9]. Fournier's influence permeated the design of both types and book, which demonstrated "Bodoni's weakness for ostentation and large clumsy formats."[11] His approach fit well with public—particularly royal—taste at the time. As printer and letter-founder to Duke Ferdinand of Parma, Bodoni indulged the grandiosity of his patron's taste, and his own specimen books and editions of literary and historical classics participated in the opulence of the royal press over which he presided. Early twentieth century typographer Lewis Gandy observed Bodoni's "fondness for 'grand' printing: this is, books of ample size, set in large type, and with wide margins, his favorite dimension apparently being as large a page as could

Fig 3.9 (below)

***Fregi e Majuscole* (bottom) and *Manuale Tipografico* (Giambattista Bodoni, Parma, 1771 and 1818). As Duke Ferdinand of Parma's official printer and letter-founder, Bodoni was able to indulge his taste for ostentatious design: oversized pages, generous margins, and typefaces that printed best at larger sizes due to their extreme contrast between thick and thin strokes.**

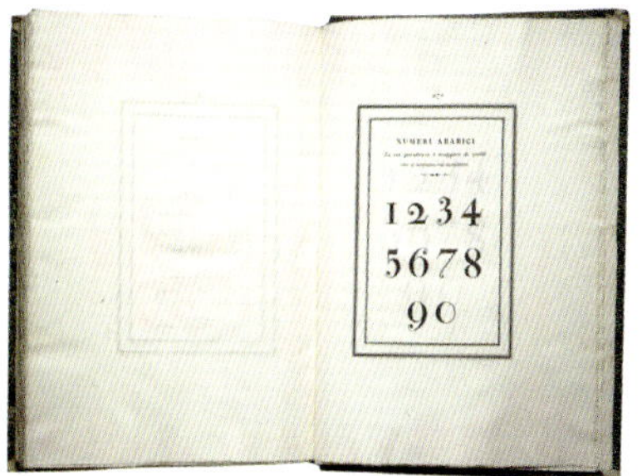

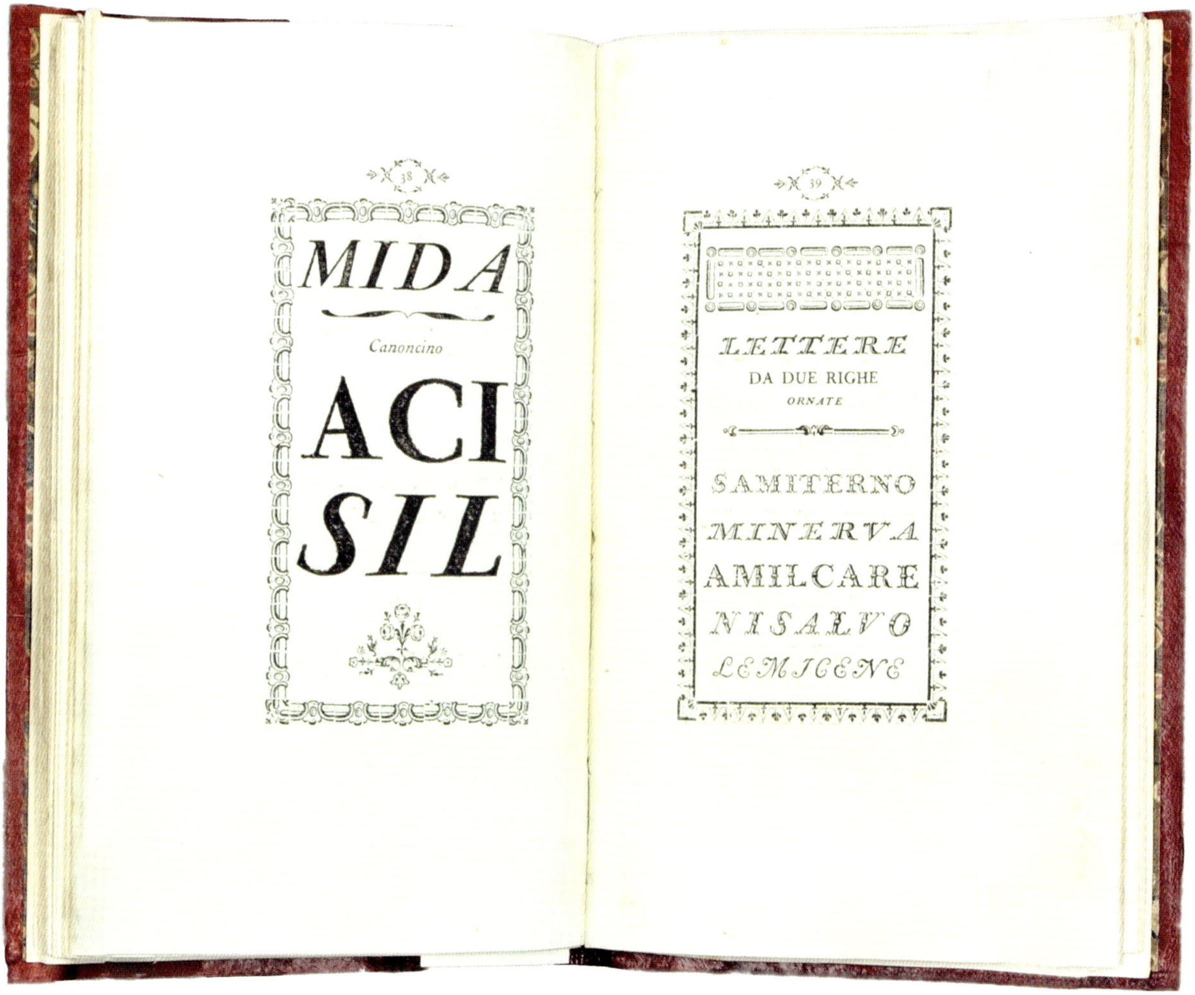

be printed at one time on the hand press then in use.”[12] Bodoni’s *Manuale Tipografico* (1778) offered a more mature expression of his own design aesthetic, eventually known as Modern. In his new types, Bodoni emphasized high contrast and geometric precision, inspired by John Baskerville’s English and Firmin Didot’s French types, rather than Fournier’s.[13] The enlarged 1818 edition, finished by his widow after his death in 1813, showed his roman, italic, and gothic alphabets in a rationally proportioned sequence of sizes and weights; decorative capital initials, borders, ornaments, and symbols; musical notation; and Greek, Syriac, Hebrew, Arabic, **Coptic**, and **Cyrillic** typefaces [Fig. 3.09]. His Latin and Cyrillic types both proved highly influential when exported to Russia, and his range of Cyrillics was extensive.[14] The *Manuale*’s design sympathized with Bodoni’s types, well-known to typographers today for their extraordinarily fine hairline serifs, generous counters, bold contrasts between thick and thin strokes, vertical axis, and rationalist construction.

The other typographic tastemaker of the Modern style was Firmin Didot, whose family dominated French printing for almost two centuries. François Didot opened a Paris bookstore in 1713, then received a royal printing charter in 1754; a second generation of Didots expanded the business, introduced various mechanical and material improvements, and c.1780 adapted Fournier’s point system to contain seventy-two points per French royal (instead of Paris-standard) inch. A third generation memorialized the

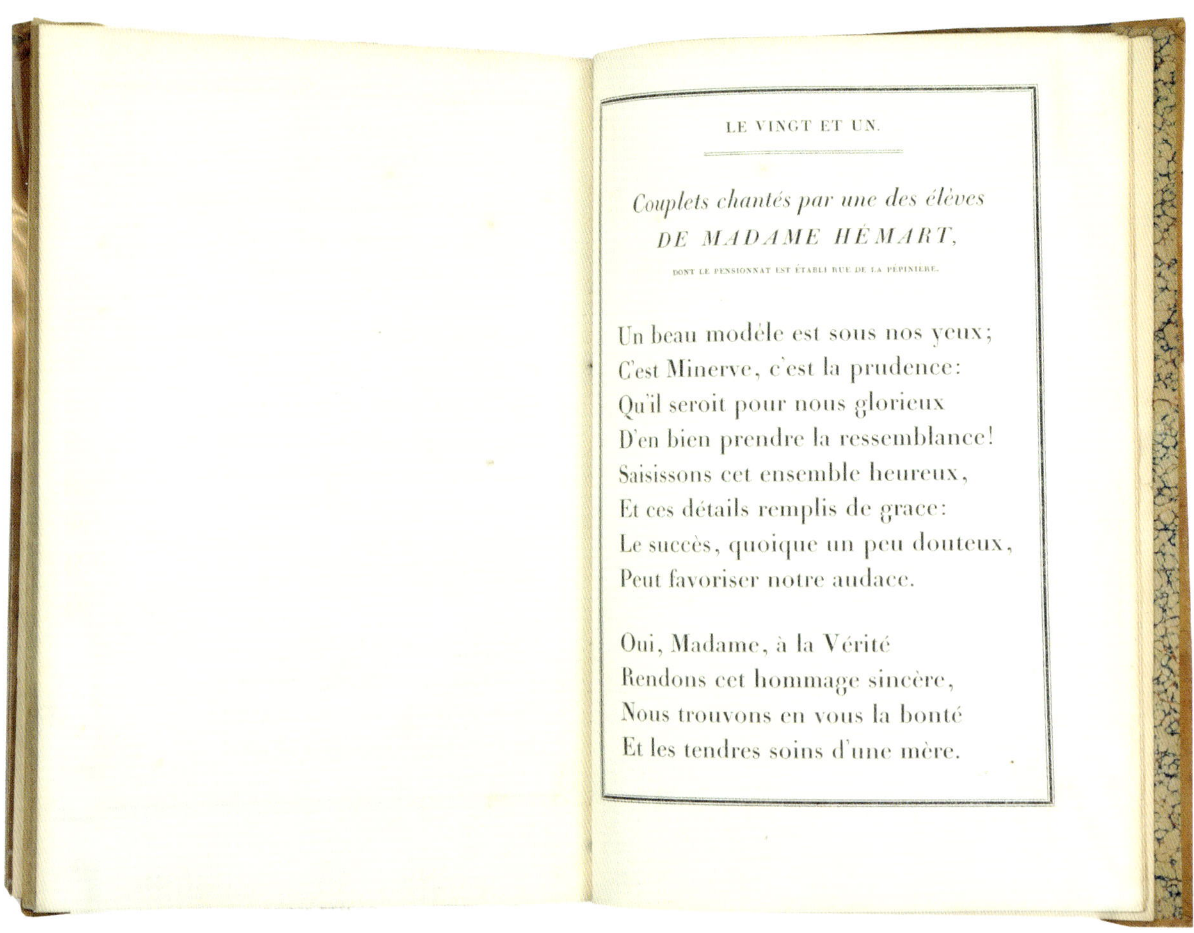
LE VINGT ET UN.

Couplets chantés par une des élèves
DE MADAME HÉMART,
DONT LE PENSIONNAT EST ÉTABLI RUE DE LA PÉPINIÈRE.

Un beau modèle est sous nos yeux;
C’est Minerve, c’est la prudence:
Qu’il seroit pour nous glorieux
D’en bien prendre la ressemblance!
Saisissons cet ensemble heureux,
Et ces détails remplis de grace:
Le succès, quoique un peu douteux,
Peut favoriser notre audace.

Oui, Madame, à la Vérité
Rendons cet hommage sincère,
Nous trouvons en vous la bonté
Et les tendres soins d’une mère.

Fig 3.10 (below)

***Specimen des Nouveaux Caractères* (Pierre Didot, Paris, 1819). Pierre’s poems, set in his brother Firmin’s 1817 typeface, provide the display text for the Didot foundry’s first specimen book.**

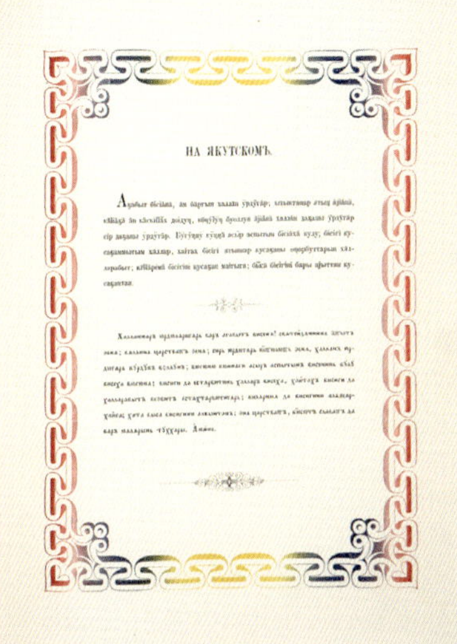

Fig 3.11 (left)
***Specimens of Type of the Printing Office of the Imperial Academy of Sciences* (Russian National Printing House, St. Petersburg, 1870). Designed for display, this specimen showed the Christian Lord's prayer set in 325 languages, as well as a variety of typographic material including a "typeface for the blind" (right).**

firm's history in *Epître sure les Progrès de l'Imprimerie* (1784) and introduced the visual language associated with the Modern typographic style. Firmin designed the now-quintessential Didot typeface, releasing a broadside specimen in 1817; his brother Pierre wrote a series of rhyming poems to display them; and Pierre printed the *Specimen des Nouveaux Caractères* (1819), commonly referenced as the first Didot specimen book [Fig. 3.10]. The venerable digital foundry H&FJ (now H&Co.) consulted it as inspiration for their 1997 Didot revival.[15] Though unusual as specimen texts because of their literary aspirations, Pierre's poems barely rated mention in subsequent typographic histories. In 1921, the *Inland Printer* reported simply that "the wording of all the specimens are poems written by Pierre."[16] The specimen's pioneering use of the Didot point, conversely, elicited significant commentary, publicizing and universalizing that system. Pierre introduced it by writing that he'd "adopted the numerical order for the identification of my types, in place of the meaningless and often absurd names preserved up to the present day in nearly all the printing-offices. These names," he authoritatively stated, "offer no idea of the particular proportions of the letters, nor of their relation to others; in fact, they vary in size in different offices." Thus, he proposed adopting a universal, mathematical system for identifying typefaces. He credited his father with introducing this "numerical order, the only one really convenient," and applied it throughout the specimen.[17] Despite this functional element, the Didot specimen (as with Bodoni and Fournier) was designed for its display value, increasing the visibility and name recognition of the foundry.

It wasn't only individual founders who produced elaborate specimens as status symbols. Royal and religious printing houses did the same with their existing stock, quite apart from promoting the famous type founders they might employ or new types they might commission. This offered a chance to visualize the importance and global reach of the issuing authority. Russia's national printing house undertook this task in 1870 with their *Specimens of Type of the Printing-office of the Imperial Academy of Sciences* [Fig. 3.11].[18] Russia, a relative latecomer to movable metal type, had established its first printing house in Moscow in 1563; in 1711, Peter I sponsored presses in St. Petersburg and printing spread more rapidly thereafter. The printing-office at

The **Coptic** alphabet emerged during the third c. BCE as the Greek alphabet was used to transcribe Demotic Egyptian texts. Most of its 32 letters are adopted directly from Greek, with 7 retained from Demotic Egyptian to represent sounds not found in Greek. This Coptic language Christian New Testament was printed in London (1716).

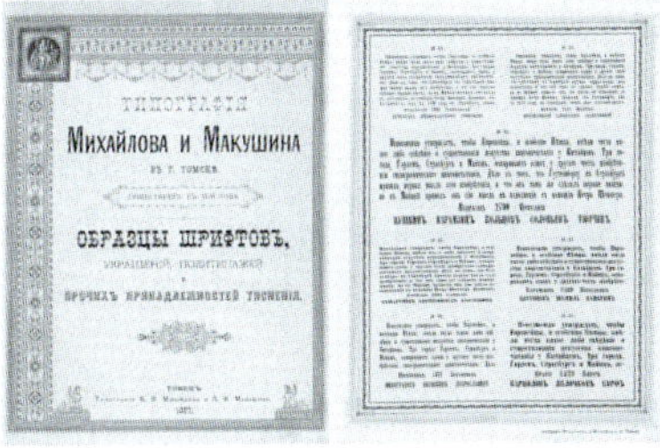

Cyrillic script emerged in the ninth century from Greek roots; it's used today for the Russian (33 letters) and Serbo-Croatian (30 letters) alphabets, among many others. This 1887 specmen was printed in Tomsk, Russia.

RUNICA.

French linguist and printer Jean-Joseph Marcel's 1805 ***Oratio Dominica*** for the newly-crowned Emperor Napoleon's Imperial printing house set the Christian Lord's Prayer in 150 languages, a remarkable display of typographic scope and quality. Pope Pius VII's admiration of this lavish volume prompted his challenge to Bodoni to produce a superior Italian version, an 1806 edition in 155 languages. Bodoni's celebrity status inspired printers throughout Europe and North America to follow suit for over a century—though the tradition hardly originated in the nineteenth century, as shown by this Runic Lord's Prayer from a 1713 book printed in London.

the Imperial Academy of Sciences (est. 1724) traced its family tree to the first presses in that city.[19] At the core of the 1870 specimen was a 325-language ***Oratio Dominica***, following an internationally popular practice. Missionary presses in Asia and Africa often did the same, usually for the benefit of imperialist and colonialist audiences rather than locals.[20]

Yet despite its lavish color printing, much of the material in the 1870 Russian Imperial specimen had a pragmatic origin. That same year, the Imperial printing-office printed the Christian Lord's Prayer for the Russian Evangelical Bible Society in the 108 languages and dialects spoken in Russia. The printing-office incorporated this material, along with the prayer in another 217 languages, into the larger specimen book, adding a color-printed ornamental border to each setting. The volume concluded with borders, cuts, text and jobbing types, and a sample of printing for the blind. These embossed characters were felt instead of seen, though the specimens included color-printed borders and captions for sighted readers. Design choices prioritized display with generous page margins, large point sizes, **chromatic** and polychromatic ornamental borders, and pages printed recto-only. In comparison, Russian foundry Frantz Mark & Co.'s *Illustrated Price List* (1892) read as a workaday catalog [Fig. 3.12]. It offered Cyrillic types, ornaments and **religious iconography**, and printing equipment. Its two-color print job—black for type and images, light coral for linear page borders—added color without significantly increasing cost or complexity. Modest margins framed the tightly-packed pages, printed both recto and verso. All of the text and display types were Cyrillic, none Latin; the ornament's iconography was visually specific to Russia's monarchy and its Orthodox Christian church. The specimen addressed a Russian audience and everyday, utilitarian printing needs rather than cultivating an admiring, international viewership.

Berthold's 1924 specimen of their **Hebrew** types, on the other hand, [Fig. 3.13] leveraged the notion of the elaborate specimen to articulate cultural and community identity. The specimen celebrated Berthold's investment in the design, manufacture, and circulation of new Hebrew types, part of an energetic international movement to reanimate the Hebrew alphabet, and both the Hebrew and Yiddish languages, for contemporary use.[21] Berlin was a flourishing center for Jewish art, literature, and political philosophy between the two world wars.[22] The Berthold foundry's Hebrew specimen benefited both from the cultural and intellectual contributions of a large Jewish émigré community and from Berthold's geographic location in Germany, a printing center since Gutenberg. The catalog was designed for display value, including gilted covers and title pages and vibrant polychromatic interior printing. The latter drew attention to the beauty and complexity of the specimen's extensive collection of borders, frames, decorative initials, and fleurons. Berthold's Hebrew ornaments embraced Egyptian motifs—reflecting the Hebrew flight from Egypt, as well as the current taste for "Egyptian" design—and historical references to Jewish art, culture, religion, and literature. Many pictorial cuts retained traces of the German Jugendstil aesthetic: curling vines, young women with flowing hair, gently abstracted organic motifs, flat fields of color, and curvilinear lines. Berthold displayed the types in a range of contexts, from religious texts to commercial advertisements, as well as on purely pragmatic pages with types arranged by style and size.

ПЕТРОЗАВОДСКЪ

БИРМИНГАМЪ МАНЧЕСТЕРЪ

СѢВЕРНЫЕ ШТАТЫ

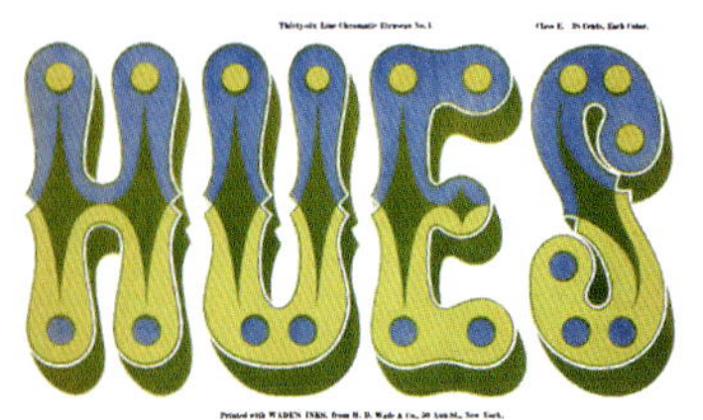

The two overlapping component parts of a **chromatic** wood type letter lent a shadowed effect and/or a third color when printed, as shown in these specimens from Russia (1887) and the USA (1874).

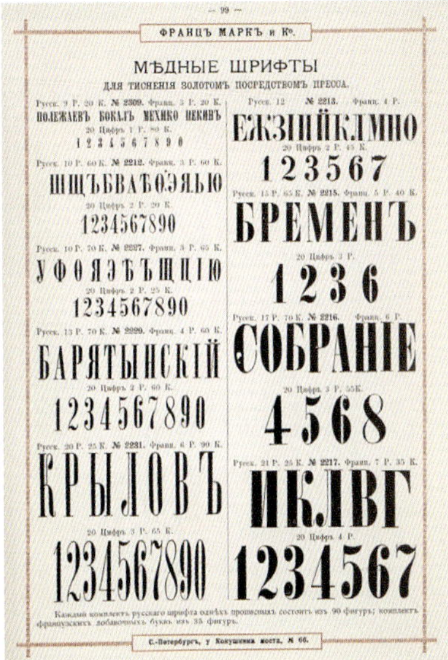

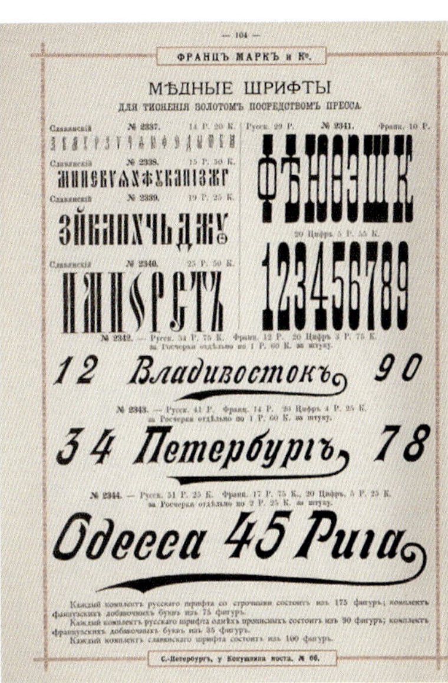

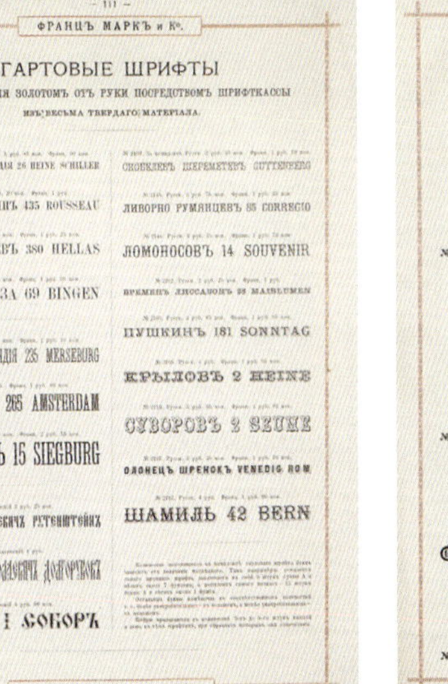

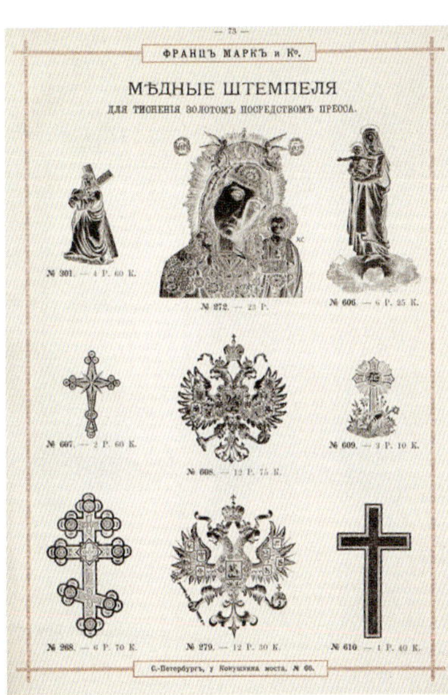

Fig 3.12 (left)

***Illustrated price list* (Frantz Mark & Co., St. Petersburg, 1892). Designed to be practical, this catalog was full of useful, everyday printing material, including Cyrillic types in a variety of styles and ornaments and pictorial cuts specific to Russia's state and religious iconography.**

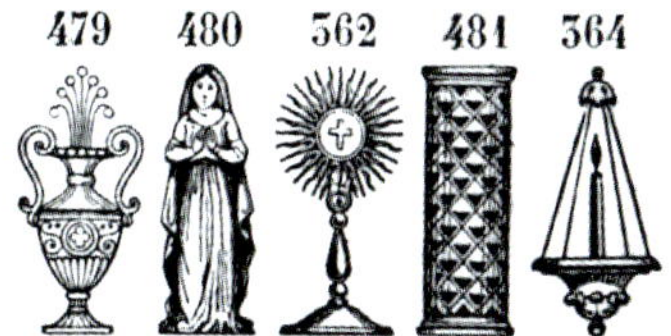

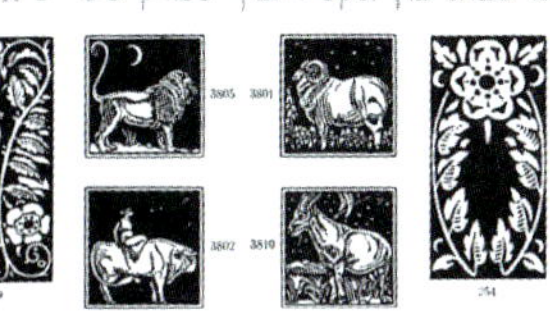

Religious iconography includes ornaments, cuts, and calendar symbols congruent with the audience's religious traditions. Even within a single religion, these vary by place, time, and audience. The Oliveres catalog (Spain, 1852; above) primarily focuses on Roman Catholic iconography, Berthold's Hebrew specimen (Germany, 1924) on Jewish symbolism and motifs.

36

כלמנפצרוץ

48

חטיכלמנ

The **Hebrew** alphabet (or aleph-bet, for its first two letters) has 22 letters, all consonants; some characters have a Final version used when the character appears at the end of a word. Nikkudim (vowel points) indicate the placement of vowels, an accommodation developed as Hebrew-language literacy declined. Yiddish is also written in the Hebrew script. This 1959 Ham Bold specimen in 36 and 48 points is from the Jerusalem Type Foundry.

As a visual statement of purpose, the Berthold specimen and its types influenced future typographers, sometimes in unexpected ways. In 1932, Hugh Schonfield cited Berthold's Hebrew specimens as one of several influences on his type design process; historical manuscript and print sources also informed his mission to "enlarge" Hebrew typography so that it would "cover the whole gamut of modern ideas and activities." In his introduction to a specimen of his types, which also included an analysis of Hebrew typography at large and a foreword by Stanley Morison, he wrote that he was "submitting to the Jewish people and to all who are interested in printing ... my new Hebrew types." His purpose was cultural and political as much as aesthetic; "I have in my mind's eye a vision of Hebrew presses in a free Jewish State turning out volume after volume, vieing [sic] in typographical excellence with the best work of any other country."[23] Modelling Jan Tschichold's *Die Neue Typographie*, Schonfield—a Hebrew Christian living in England—advocated for a new

Fig 3.13 (right)

***H. Berthold: Schriftgiessereien und Messinglinienfabriken Aktien-Gesellschaft* (H. Berthold foundry, Berlin, 1924). Berthold's Hebrew specimen celebrated their foundry's new typefaces designed to meet contemporary printing needs in the Yiddish and Hebrew languages.**

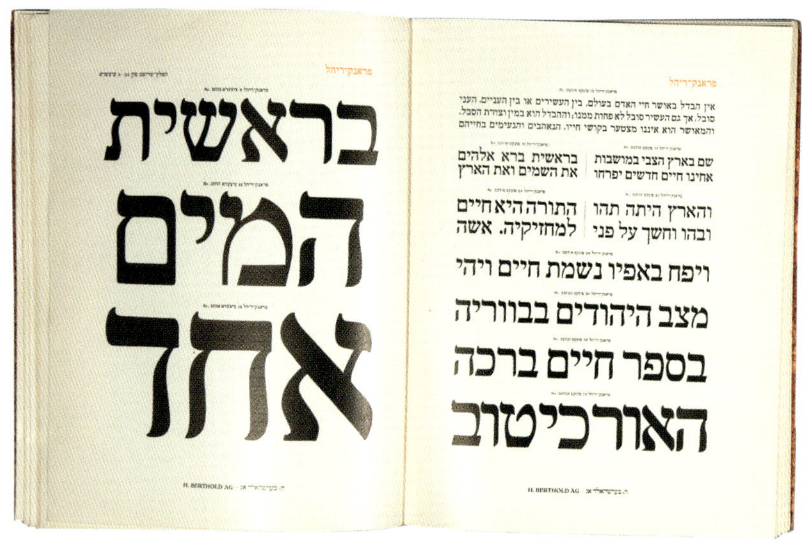

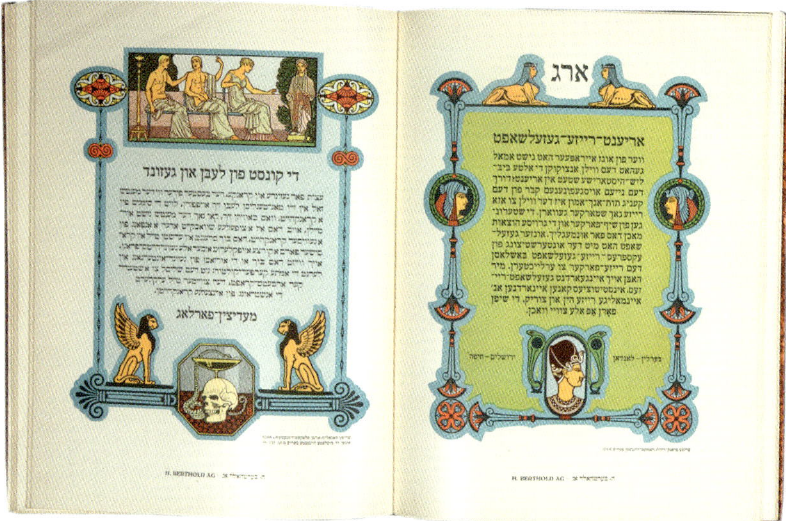

approach in a new era: a simplified and somewhat Latinized Hebrew script with lowercase letters and streamlined diacritical marks. Schonfield argued that existing types were too similar and too historicist, incapable of the aesthetic variation required to attract consumers' attention. His proposed revisions would facilitate Hebrew typographic expression equal to that available to Latin type designers. Because "a people without an adequate typography is gravely handicapped in the economic struggle," a new Hebrew typography would first and foremost be commercially viable—a concern long shared by makers and users of type. Schonfield's proposed reforms were never implemented, but many twentieth century Hebrew type designers grappled with the question of functional contemporary and commercial application.[24]

Commercial utility

As a commercial product, type had to be advertised by makers and ordered by users. After the introduction of movable metal type in Germany, this process first took place physically, initially at the Frankfurt Book Fair.[25] The need for catalogs emerged as typographic printing spread and founders sought customers among printers, then printers sought customers among publishers and advertisers.[26] Though many foundries also had printing offices, most printers ordered their type from a foundry prior to the twentieth century, some over long distances. Specimen books usefully displayed a comprehensive range of type styles and sizes labeled according to the foundry's nomenclature. This utilitarian information facilitated specific and accurate orders, allowed printers to make visual comparisons and estimates of fit, and kept the foundry in a printer's literal line of sight through the book's presence on a desk or shelf.

Unlike their Continental European contemporaries, early specimen books from England and the United States often reflected an emphasis on usefulness. French and Italian typefaces in particular struck British and American typefounders as impractical and over-designed, unsuitable for everyday printing jobs and informational reading. High-contrast strokes interfered with legibility, while the large type size, generous leading, and vast page margins required to show such faces at their best read as ostentatious. Early twentieth century printer and typographic historian Daniel Berkeley Updike concluded that Modern types were "capable of greater vulgarity and degradation than was ever the case with older fonts."[27] Some typographers agreed. In 1836, second-generation type founder Edmund Fry found the "fanciful letters" of Modern faces "rude, pernicious, and unclassical" in their design.[28] English and American specimen books reflected similar sentiments. Caslon and Figgins in England and Binny & Ronaldson and Bruce in the United States designed pragmatic types—and specimens.

William Caslon issued the first English specimen book in 1764 [Fig. 3.14]. Fournier's *Manuel* was published the same year, over 100 years after the first French specimen book. Despite being designed in the second half of the eighteenth century, Caslon's types are now commonly considered the first wholly English typefaces.[29] His approach was certainly less decorative

Fig 3.14 (below)

A Specimen of Printing Types **(William Caslon, London, 1764). Caslon's was the first English specimen book, and unlike its contemporaries in Continental Europe, it spoke an austere visual language. Even the title page was unadorned.**

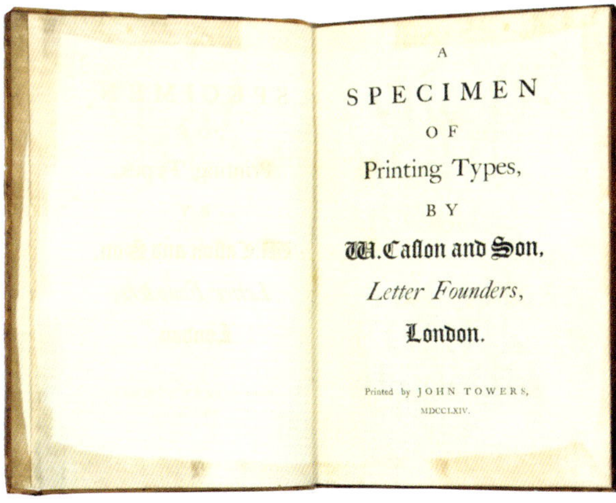

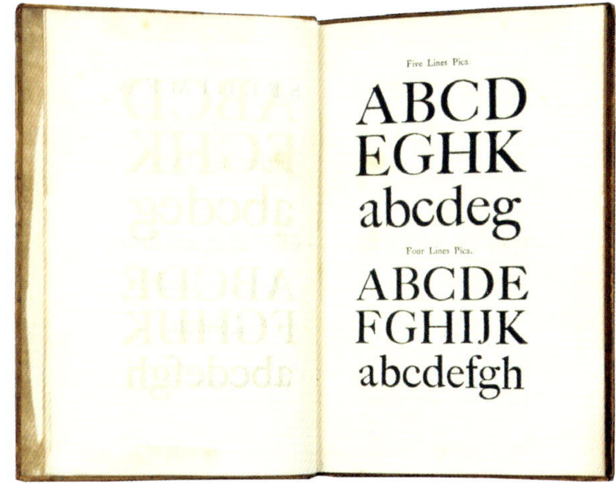

Fig 3.15 (right and below)

Specimen of Printing Types **(Vincent Figgins, London, 1821 and 1829). Figgins' 1829 specimen (right) was the first to employ the term sans-serif. Though Caslon had introduced a type without serifs in 1816, he'd called it English Egyptian. Figgins' 1829 specimen also continued to show a new style he'd been the first to introduce in 1817. Figgins called this style Antique but subsequently it came to be known as Egyptian, or slab serif.**

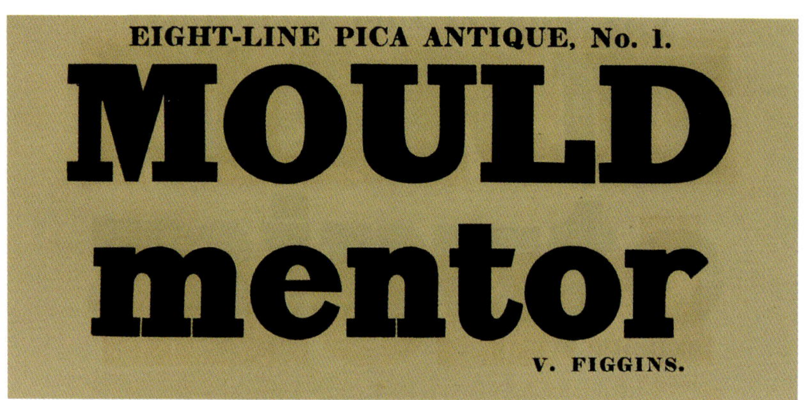

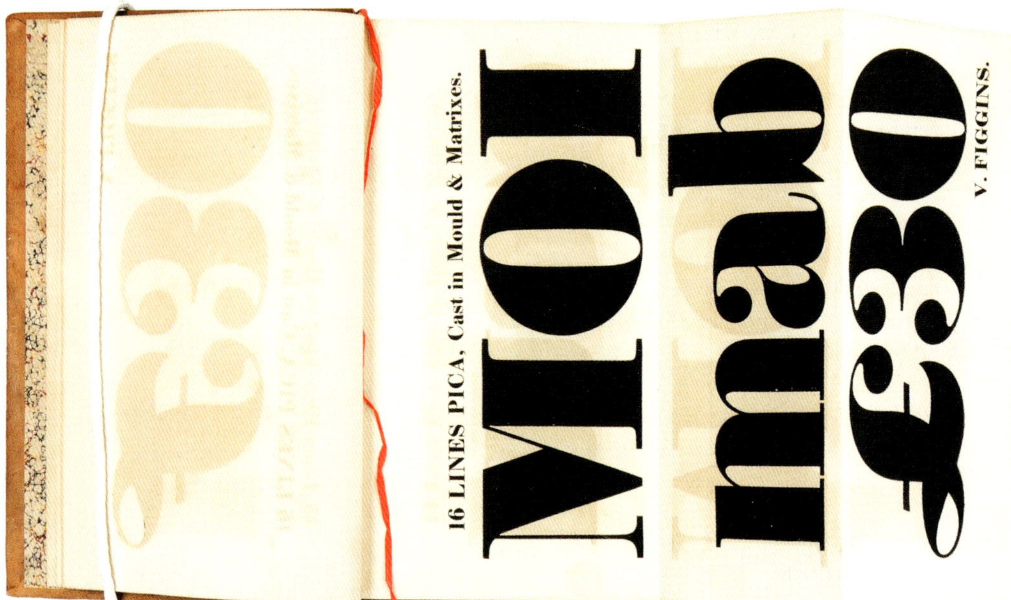

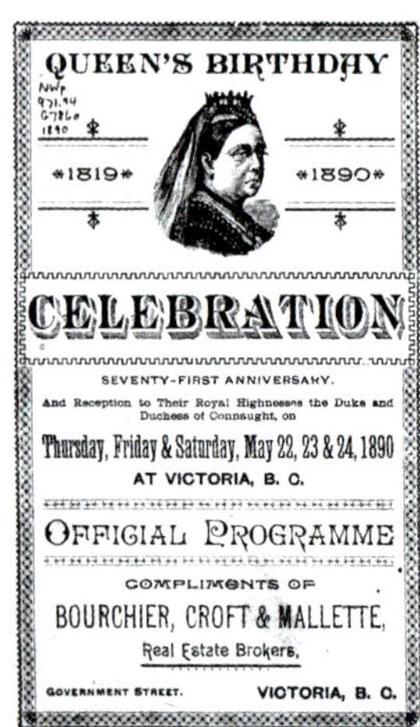

QUEEN'S BIRTHDAY

1819 *1890*

CELEBRATION

SEVENTY-FIRST ANNIVERSARY.

And Reception to Their Royal Highnesses the Duke and Duchess of Connaught, on

Thursday, Friday & Saturday, May 22, 23 & 24, 1890

AT VICTORIA, B. C.

OFFICIAL PROGRAMME

COMPLIMENTS OF

BOURCHIER, CROFT & MALLETTE,

Real Estate Brokers,

GOVERNMENT STREET. VICTORIA, B. C.

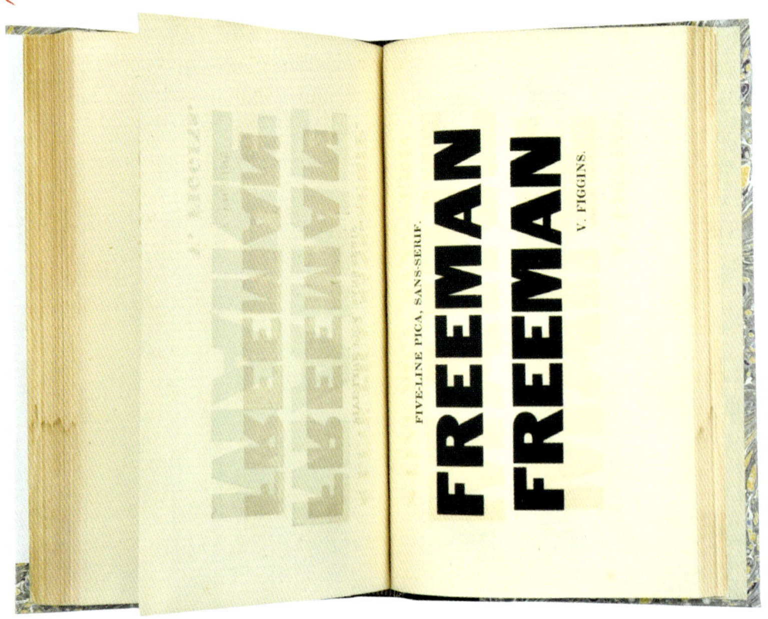

The **Victorian** aesthetic, named for Queen Victoria (reigned 1837-1901), embraced detail and ornament in profuse combinations.

than Fournier's. His title page relied entirely on type for visual interest, mixing roman, italic, and blackletter faces. Some pages contained only one or two sizes of larger display type; others, displaying smaller text sizes, showed up to five. These unadorned blocks of copy lacked borders, frames, or ornaments. The specimen ended with a section of printer's flowers presented in linear rows; typographic gymnastics like Gando's 1745 fold-out temple of ornament had no place in Caslon's functionalist strategy. Caslon's **colophon** summarized the establishment of his foundry; a decorative border with an arrangement of flowers beneath framed the short note. Aside from this single ornamental touch, the specimen—and the typefaces it contained—spoke a highly utilitarian visual language.

Vincent Figgins' new London foundry issued its first specimen book in 1793; new editions followed quickly [Fig. 3.15]. After his apprenticeship with well-known punch-cutter Joseph Jackson ended with Jackson's death, Figgins opened his own foundry and his sons followed him into the family business.[30] Figgins' contemporaries admired the "number and beauty of [the foundry's] founts," which "strayed less into the folly of the fat-faced, preposterous disproportions" of its competitors' faces.[31] Importantly, Figgins' specimens introduced two new varieties of type: slab serifs (or **Egyptians**, as English founder Robert Thorne first called them around 1820) and sans serifs.[32] Slab serifs, which Figgins called **Antiques**, first appeared in his *Specimen of Printing Types* (1817).[33] His 1829 specimen introduced three sans serif faces: Two-Line Pearl sans serif (a text face), and Five-Line and Eight-Line Pica sans serif (larger titling faces). In 1816, the Caslon foundry had introduced one caps-only sans serif face, confusingly named Two-Line English Egyptian.[34] But Figgins coined the term *sans serif* in his 1829 specimen, using it to name his three all-caps types. Figgins introduced both the slab serifs (1817) and the sans serifs (1829) without fanfare or visual differentiation. Despite Figgins' austere compositional approach, influenced by the Neoclassical craze which had given Caslon's and Thorne's Egyptians their names, decorative excesses loomed on the horizon. Figgins' unembellished pages soon contrasted with the ornamental **Victorian** aesthetic.

Binny & Ronaldson, the United States' first successful type foundry, opened in Philadelphia in 1796. "At least seven prior establishments had failed," Ronaldson wrote in 1816.[35] The foundry issued America's first specimen books, a showing of ornaments (1809) followed by a *Specimen of Printing Type* (1812). The 1816 edition announced Archibald Binny's retirement and Ronaldson's sole proprietorship [Fig. 3.16]. In it, Ronaldson articulated his love/hate relationship with European type designs. He acknowledged their market appeal but simultaneously expressed a desire for common-sense and therefore American forms. The foundry copied "specimens of the European improvements as fast as they came to the United States," though Ronaldson disagreed with some of these fashions. He modified his own types, "in some instances, contrary to [his] own judgment," believing recent European models were "suited only for works of fancy." Ronaldson's adjustments sought to unify fashion and function, making changes to Modern faces like Bodoni's and Didot's in order to accommodate American functionalism. The foundry's redesigns of European faces took care to "combine elegance with durability; making the least possible sacrifice of these important properties to each other." Less philosophically, Ronaldson described his specimen's purpose:

Edited by F. S. Ellis, and printed by me, William Morris, at the Kelmscott Press, Upper Mall, Hammersmith, and finished on the 5th day of February, 1896.

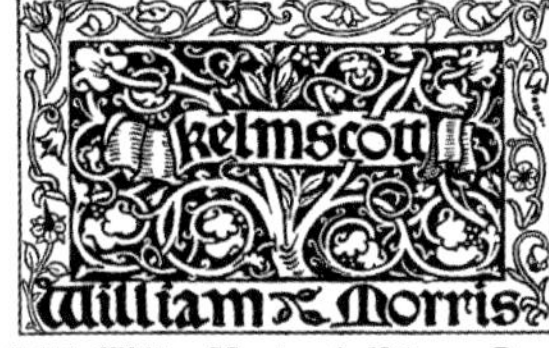

Sold by William Morris at the Kelmscott Press.

The **colophon** appears at the end of a book, usually offering remarks on the editor, contributors, translator, designer, and/or typefaces and images used, as well as the printer's emblem. The emblem itself might also be called a colophon, especially when appearing on the title page or spine of the book.

SIXTEEN-LINE PICA, ANTIQUE.

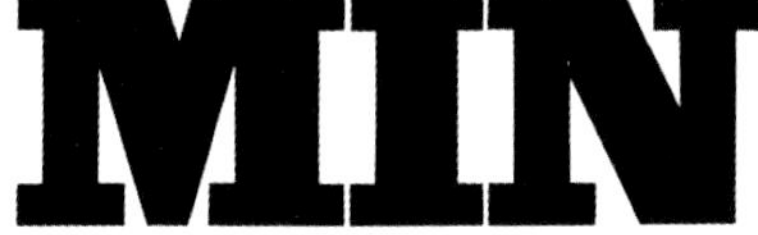

V. FIGGINS.

Egyptian types were originally called Antiques when introduced in Figgins' 1817 specimen book. Their unbracketed slab serifs suggested to audiences following archeological excavations and Napoleanic campaigns in Egypt the monolithic weight of ancient architecture.

AN EARLY ANTIQUE
probably cut before 1820
CAST BY GEORGE BRUCE
as a substitute for the bold-face
THE DORIC ANTIQUE
has features of roman
THE IONIC ANTIQUE
has large face, open counters
THE LIGHT-FACE ANTIQUE
is not much bolder than roman
THE EXPANDED ANTIQUE
has no overhanging descenders

Antiques originally appeared in the early nineteenth century as an alternative to bold romans; their heavier strokes made them useful for advertising and display.

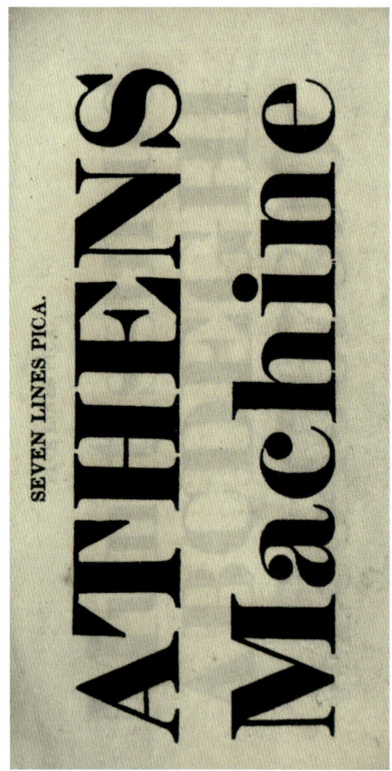

SEVEN LINES PICA.

ATHENS
Machine

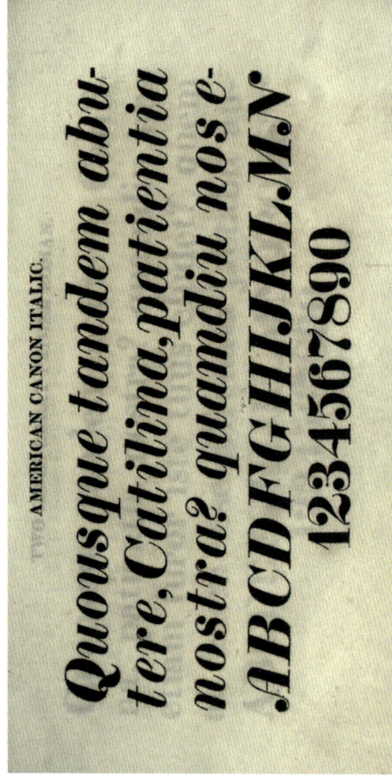

TWO AMERICAN CANON ITALIC.

*Quousque tandem abu-
tere, Catilina, patientia
nostra? quamdiu nos e-
ABCDFGHIJKLMN*
1234567890

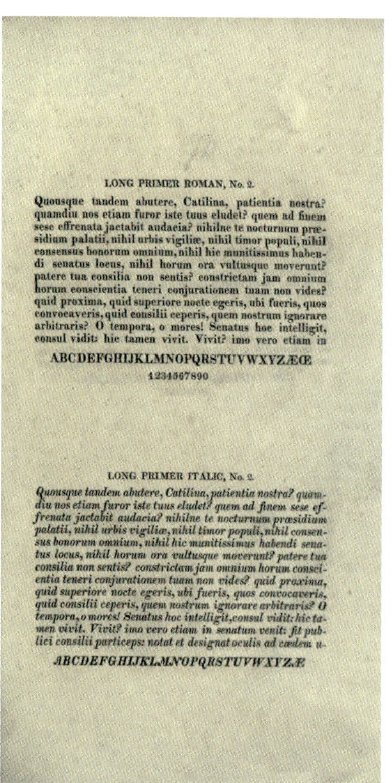

LONG PRIMER ROMAN, No. 2.

Quousque tandem abutere, Catilina, patientia nostra? quamdiu nos etiam furor iste tuus eludet? quem ad finem sese effrenata jactabit audacia? nihilne te nocturnum præsidium palatii, nihil urbis vigiliæ, nihil timor populi, nihil consensus bonorum omnium, nihil hic munitissimus habendi senatus locus, nihil horum ora vultusque moverunt? patere tua consilia non sentis? constrictam jam omnium horum conscientia teneri conjurationem tuam non vides? quid proxima, quid superiore nocte egeris, ubi fueris, quos convocaveris, quid consilii ceperis, quem nostrum ignorare arbitraris? O tempora, o mores! Senatus hoc intelligit, consul vidit: hic tamen vivit. Vivit? imo vero etiam in

ABCDEFGHIJKLMNOPQRSTUVWXYZÆŒ

1234567890

LONG PRIMER ITALIC, No. 2.

Quousque tandem abutere, Catilina, patientia nostra? quamdiu nos etiam furor iste tuus eludet? quem ad finem sese effrenata jactabit audacia? nihilne te nocturnum præsidium palatii, nihil urbis vigiliæ, nihil timor populi, nihil consensus bonorum omnium, nihil hic munitissimus habendi senatus locus, nihil horum ora vultusque moverunt? patere tua consilia non sentis? constrictam jam omnium horum conscientia teneri conjurationem tuam non vides? quid proxima, quid superiore nocte egeris, ubi fueris, quos convocaveris, quid consilii ceperis, quem nostrum ignorare arbitraris? O tempora, o mores! Senatus hoc intelligit, consul vidit: hic tamen vivit. Vivit? imo vero etiam in senatum venit: fit publici consilii particeps: notat et designat oculis ad cædem u-

ABCDEFGHIJKLMNOPQRSTUVWXYZÆ

Fig 3.16 (above)

***Specimen of Printing Type* (James Ronaldson, Philadelphia, 1816). Binny & Ronaldson, the first successful type foundry in the United States, issued specimens in 1809 and 1812. James Ronaldson issued this specimen, the foundry's third, when he assumed sole ownership in 1816.**

"to show the form of the type, and the proportion that one size or number bears to another."[36] His specimen very pragmatically met this goal, unencumbered by any kind of ornamental impulse. In this regard, his European counterparts were English and Dutch rather than Italian and French.

Roughly two decades later, in 1837, New York's Bruce & Company (est. 1806, first specimen 1815) issued *A Specimen of Printing Types* [Fig. 3.17]. It reflected rapid growth not only in American typefounding but also in a new typographic product: **advertising cuts**. These stock illustrations met the needs of businesses and advertisers. Unlike ornaments or printer's flowers, which appeared in the earliest type specimens, cuts filled an illustrative purpose. And unlike **intaglio** printing methods such as copperplate engraving, they printed simultaneously on the same press bed as a galley of type. Most cuts represented a common need or suited multiple purposes. But some were oddly specific; Bruce's figure 621, priced 37 cents, pictured a long-tailed monkey drinking from a champagne flute. Whimsical or not, utilitarianism informed the presentation of these materials. The Bruce specimen numbered its hundreds of ad cuts, not always sequentially, and organized them on a dense grid. Unlike their text and display types, decorative material and cuts were marked with their prices, generally ranging from $0.30 to $1.50. These simplified images, with their everyday people, places, and things, established a shared visual vocabulary among their users. Common categories—not just in New York, but internationally—included domestic and wild plants and animals, dry goods, transportation, landscapes, architecture, people at work and play, and nationalist or religious symbols.

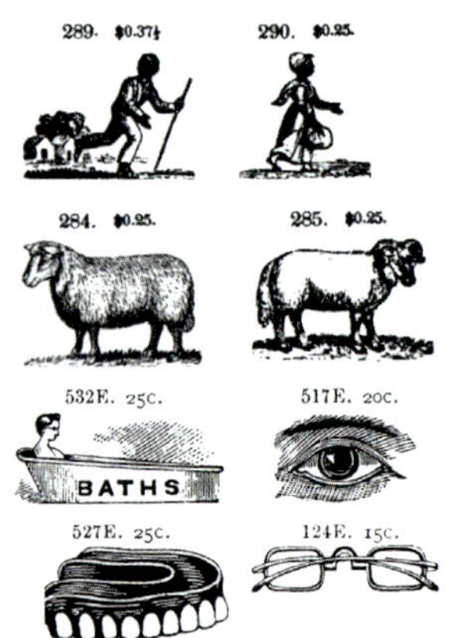

Advertising cuts like these from the Bruce foundry pictured generic people, places and things for use as illustrations in periodical and job printing. But, as the "escaped slaves" show, the images weren't value neutral.

To their American audience, Bruce & Co. offered ad cuts depicting (among hundreds of other things) wheat, corn, hoes, plows, horses, hunting dogs, stage coaches, schoolboys, and sailing ships in a variety of styles and sizes. These might add visual interest to anything from a seed catalog to a coach schedule. But they weren't value-neutral. Star-spangled banners framed flying eagles proclaiming *E Pluribus Unum*; a minister baptised a woman in a river; and a Gutenberg press descended to the Earth on a cloud pierced by a beam of light. With its clear parallels to images of Christ descending from heaven, this image conflates typographic printing and a Eurocentric world view centered in Christianity and global print capitalism.[37] Typically of their place and time, Bruce & Co. also offered cuts of so-called "runaway slaves"—persons of African descent seeking freedom from the institution of slavery. These images facilitated newspaper ads and broadsides on behalf of white customers, who might be perpetrators in the institution of slavery or abolitionists; Black printers or customers controlled these images' uses infrequently.[38] The utilitarian visual language of commercial trade framed all of these images, from the fairly generic to the morally and politically charged, in the same way—with an ordering number and a price tag.

Elaborate **display types**, another emergent trend, appeared in the Bruce specimen as well [Fig. 3.17]. Late eighteenth and early nineteenth century specimens had offered fat faces (often exaggerated versions of Modern serifs) and blackletters; and Figgins had introduced slab serifs and sans serifs. All of these—with the exception of blackletter text for Germanic languages—almost exclusively functioned as display types. Bruce & Co. offered all of these, plus ornamented and **comic faces**, **lottery figures**, and exaggerated slab serifs, early forerunners of a mid- to late-century explosion of display faces. They were elaborate, excessive, even beautiful in their own right; but they were also ephemeral and nonfunctional outside a narrow context. How were printers and their clients supposed to choose among and correctly apply such a dazzling range of typographic options? As the nineteenth century progressed, specimen books began answering that question, as well.

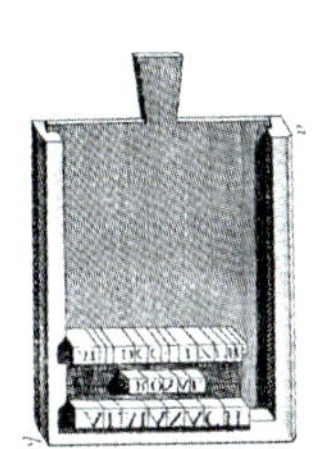

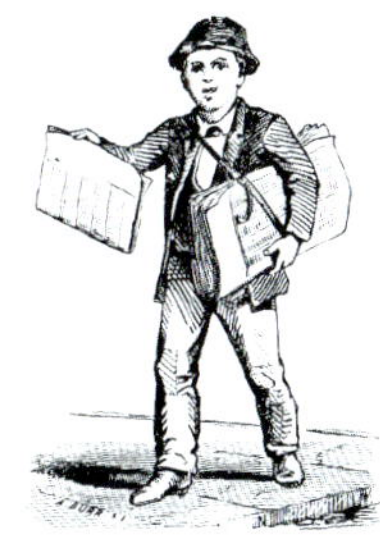

In **Intaglio** processes like copperplate engraving, incised lines fill with ink when the plate is inked, and it's the lines below the surface of the plate which print when the press applies pressure. This results in fine lines and a high level of detail, as seen in the engraving (left) from Diderot's *Encyclopedie*. Typographic sorts are a form of relief printing; the raised surface receives ink and prints. Because intaglio and relief process require separate print runs, relief images (adcuts, like the newsboy above) were quicker and cheaper to print in combination with letterpress typography.

Fig 3.17 (below)

***A Specimen of Printing Types* (George Bruce, New York, 1837). The Bruce foundry offered a wide range of decorative typographic materials, including an Italian face with its characteristic triangular serifs (left) and a comic face with droll humans and animals peering out at the viewer (right).**

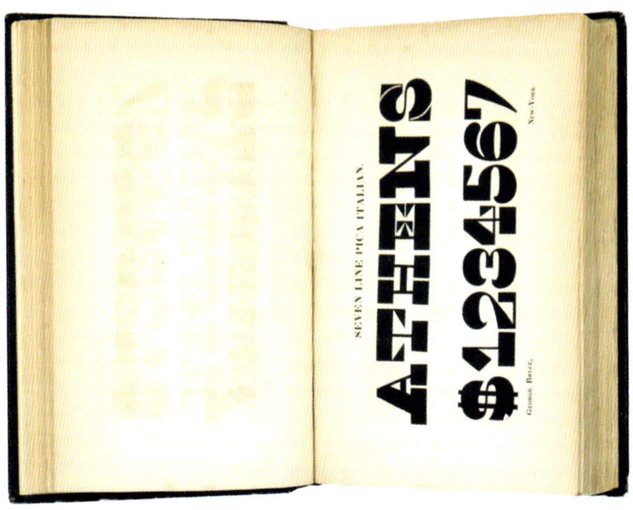

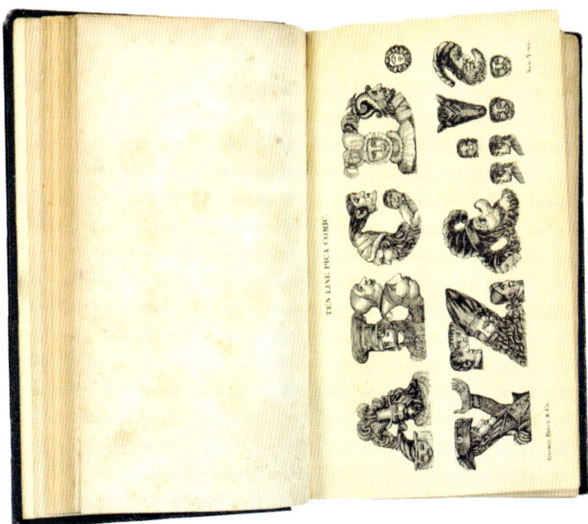

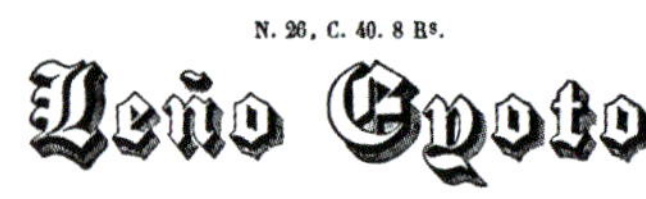

N. 259, C. 36. 10 Rs.

Madrid Paris

N. 85, C. 11. 12 Rs.

MEDICINA CIRUJIA Y FARMACIA

N. 222, C. 16. 10 Rs.

HISTORIA UNIVERSAL

Display types like these sold by Spain's Oliveres foundry in their 1852 catalog did just what their name suggested, displaying important visual information through large size and/or decorative style. They varied based on place, time, and current tastes in fashion.

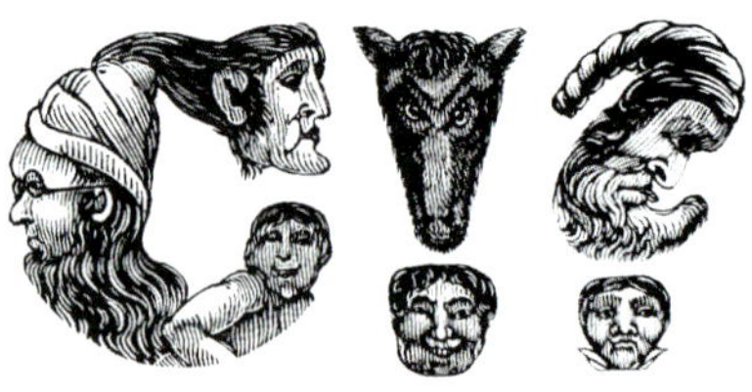

Comic faces like these American examples from the 1837 Bruce foundry catalog provided visual interest in nineteenth century newspapers, advertisements, and broadsides.

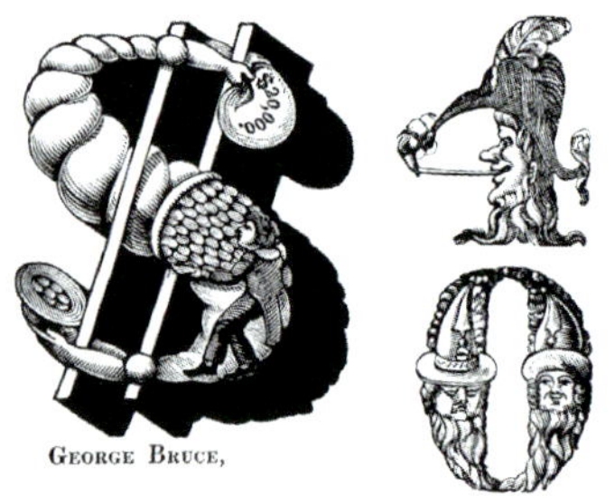

Lottery figures like these American examples were illustrated, often humorous large-scale numerals used for decorative purposes, such as lottery tickets.

Stylistic instruction

Printers positioning themselves within a competitive market needed to stay abreast of current style and taste—whatever that might mean in their own place, time, and cultural context. Foundry specimen books offered an efficient, economical tool for self-education. Foundries produced them, often dedicating significant resources and their best designers to the task, then distributed them free of charge to printers as an advertising method. Before it was known as Barnhart Bros. & Spindler (BB&S), Chicago's Great Western Type Foundry celebrated its opening year in 1873 with a *Specimen Book and Price List* [Fig. 3.18]. It promised to "show, in a concise and convenient form, the most useful and popular styles of letter, omitting such faces as serve neither the purpose of utility nor beauty."[39] The hefty specimen included book, jobbing, and newspaper faces, ornaments, borders, advertising and stock cuts, **catchwords** and **logotypes**, titling faces (a relatively staid range of sans serifs, slab serifs, and fat faces designed to be set at larger sizes), and—overwhelmingly—elaborate display faces. An appended supplement of "late styles of type" brought the specimen up to the moment. Even in 1873, some of these faddish letters must have reeked of gimmickry rather than the promised "utility and beauty." Nonpareil Grotesque, for instance, added a decorative descender or tail to every character, even the O. Though later editions featured more convincing and elaborate commercial examples, the 1873 specimen began to suggest broadsides, book pages, social invitations, and newspaper ads. The foundry's **house organ**, *The Type-founder* (published 1876-c.1908), followed the same trajectory.[40] Earlier issues hinted at common commercial forms, but by the turn of the century, facsimile ads appeared with every display of a new type, and these often found their way into the next bound specimen issued.

The 1907 BB&S catalog claimed to be "a Complete Compendium; the only book of its kind needed in a printing office; a well-rounded, instructive, valuable book." Its almost 1,000 pages demonstrated newspaper sheets, advertisements for everything from footwear to oyster bars, social invitations, business stationery, book pages, theater broadsides, and—for the audience of printers—full-page, visually-rich ads for BB&S types and equipment. The catalogue's introductory note "recommend[ed] it to the careful study of every printer," highlighting its educational value.[41] Stylistically, the commercial

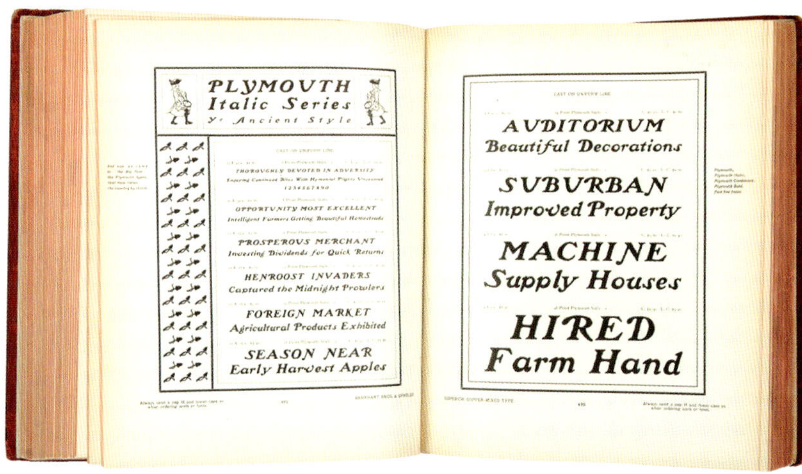

Fig 3.18 (right)

Specimen Book and Price List **(Great Western Type Foundry, Chicago, 1873, top). In the late nineteenth and early twentieth centuries, it was important for specimen books to show printers how the types they displayed should be used in a range of applied commercial contexts.**

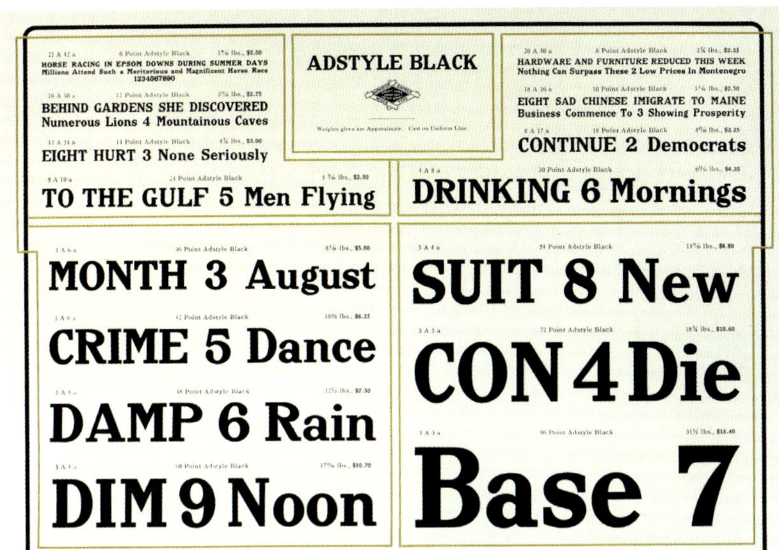

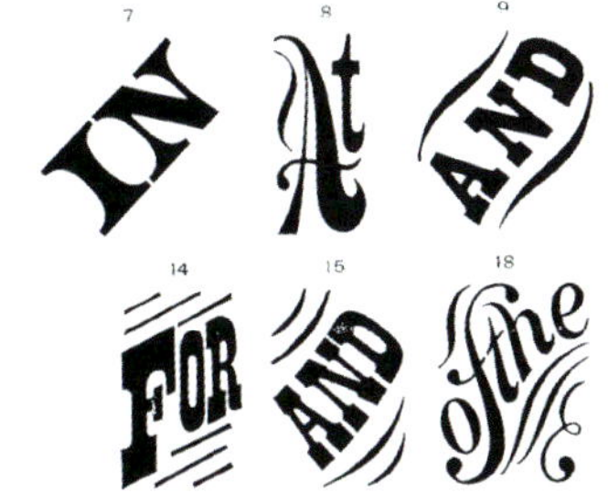

Catchwords are single typographic sorts containing an entire word or phrase, often treated decoratively.

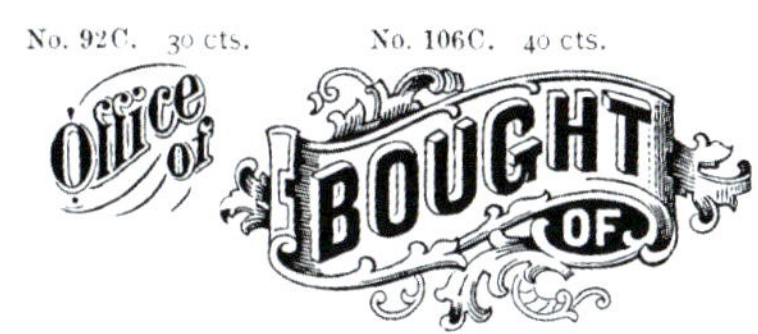

Logotypes are graphic representations of company names (or, more generically, categories of businesses) designed for quick visual recognition. These are from the 1897 ATF catalog.

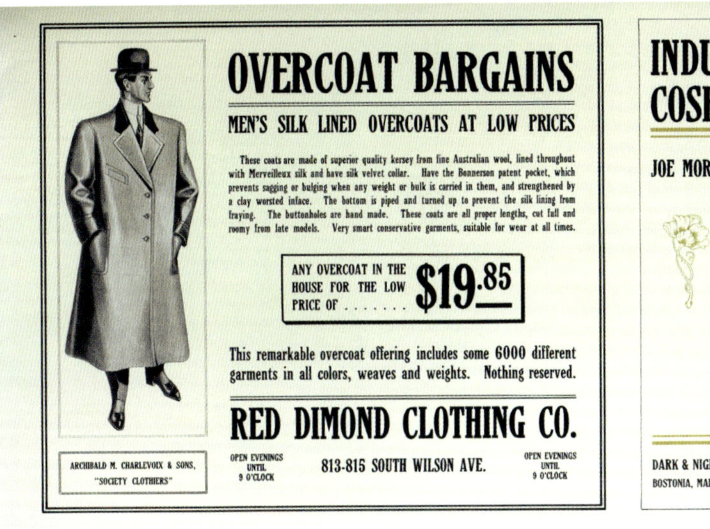

Fig 3.19 (left)

Adstyle Family **(Barnhart Bros. & Spindler, Chicago, 1906-11). Quickly changing fashions and an ever-growing commercial range of packaged goods and branded services meant that specimens needed to include a wide range of type styles. At almost 1,000 pages, the 1907 BB&S catalog had plenty of opportunity to do so; a much smaller booklet specifically for the Adstyle family established a more cohesive aesthetic.**

samples ranged from judiciously simplified late Victorian to American **Art Nouveau**, offering printers a range of inspirational material in currently popular styles. A less-hefty contemporaneous specimen booklet designed to introduce the Adstyle Family was styled in much the same way, mocking up ads for everything from ornamental carpets and men's overcoats to windmills [Fig. 3.19]. A Clarendon in a range of widths and weights, Adstyle was designed for BB&S by Sydney Gaunt between 1906 and 1911.

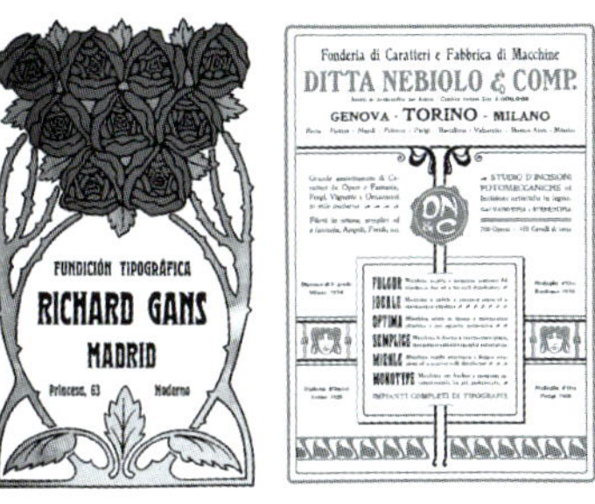

Art Nouveau originated in France at the end of the nineteenth century and soon spread internationally. These Spanish (left) and Italian (right) foundries both used the style to advertise in 1904. Natural motifs, curvilinear lines, and beautiful young women with flowing hair were popular tropes.

N° 2721 Kl. Kanon (28 p.) Min. 10 kilo

cht verwegen, Unglück

BISMARCK BEUST

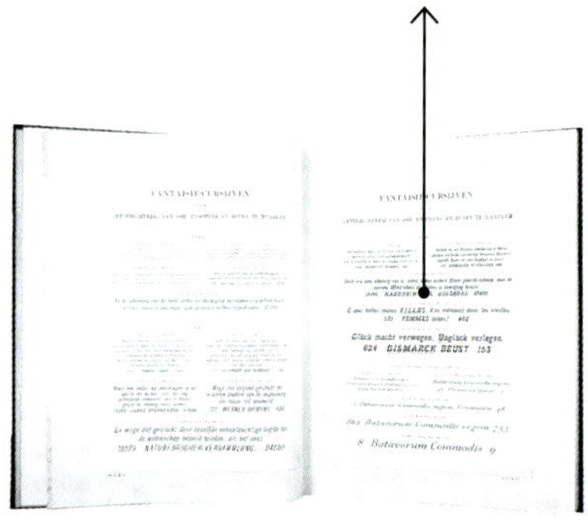

Fantasy letters like these from v.2 of Enschedé's 5-volume 1895 specimen were often decorative variations on otherwise fairly standard typeface designs.

The five-volume *Letterproef* of Enschedé & Zonen (1895–7) stands as a massive monument to the ornamental typographic taste of the latter half of the nineteenth century [Fig. 3.20]. The books measured 30x38cm (about 12x15in), landscape-oriented in the first volume and portrait in the subsequent four. The first volume presented roman and script faces, the second **fantasy letters**, the third ornaments, the fourth vignettes, and the fifth titling faces. The fantastical faces were especially stunning, displayed at large sizes with generous marginal spacing. The filigree embellishments of *fantaisie-cursijven* series four, the hairline strokes and fat stems of *halfvette kapitalen* series two, the elaborately shaded and riveted *fantaisie kapitalen* series seven, the orientalizing *fantaisie kapitalen* series three, the revivalist impulse demonstrated by *Renaissance schriften*—this variety contributed to the late nineteenth century's spirit of typographic excess.

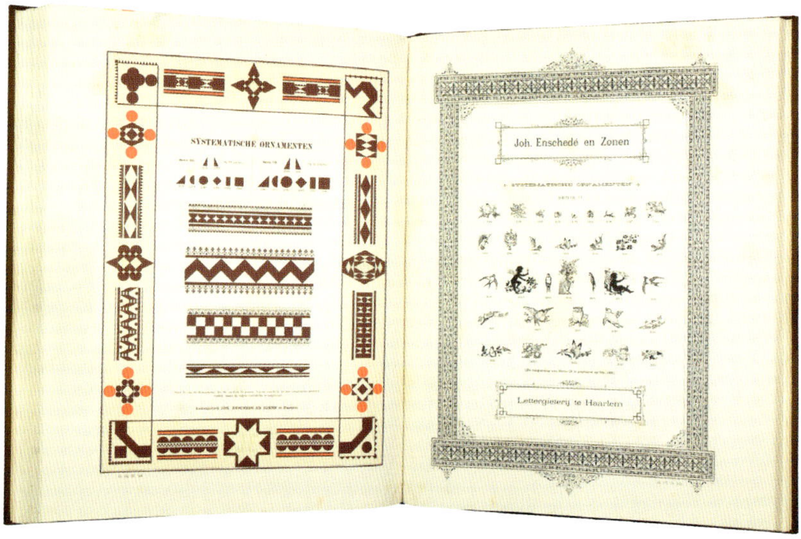

Fig 3.20 (right and below)

***Letterproef* (Enschedé & Zonen, Haarlem, 1895–7). This oversized, five-volume specimen displayed the typographic extravagance of the late nineteenth century with both dignity and enthusiasm.**

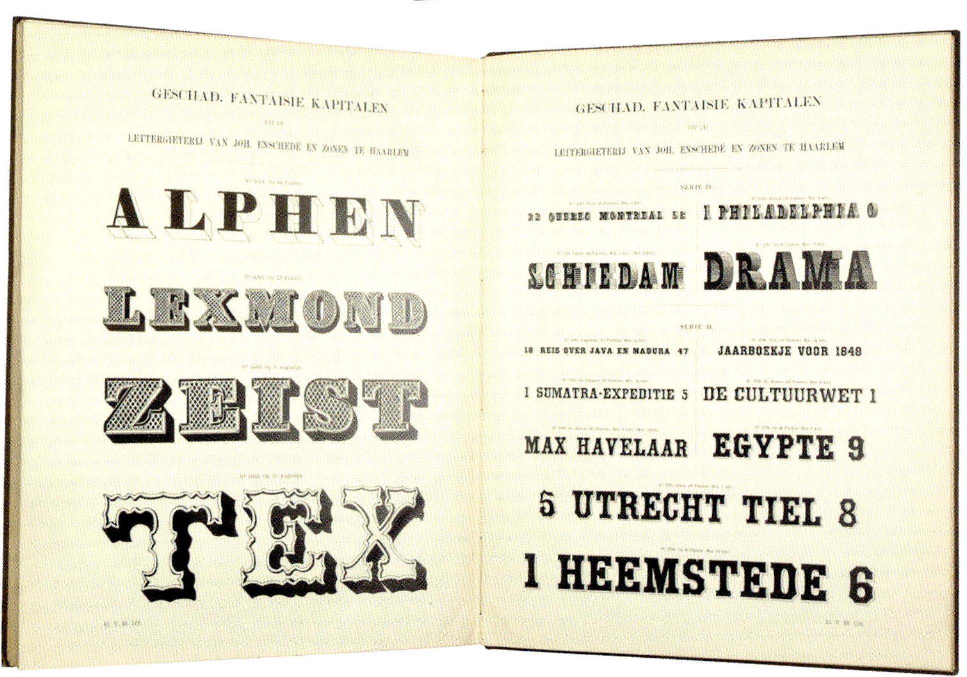

International circulation

Specimen books played a role in spreading technologies, styles, and their associated value systems. Importing or exporting type between European countries, or between Europe and the United States, had long been a philosophically and economically charged question.[42] Early foundry and press specimens from locations outside Western Europe and the United States documented an even more complex situation. Types might be designed from afar or *in situ* by colonizers for local readerships, either indigenous or colonial. Alternatively, types might be designed by local, sometimes novice, typographers for their own culture's use and/or for the use of their colonizers. Finally, printers in colonized locations imported types from abroad via commercial channels.

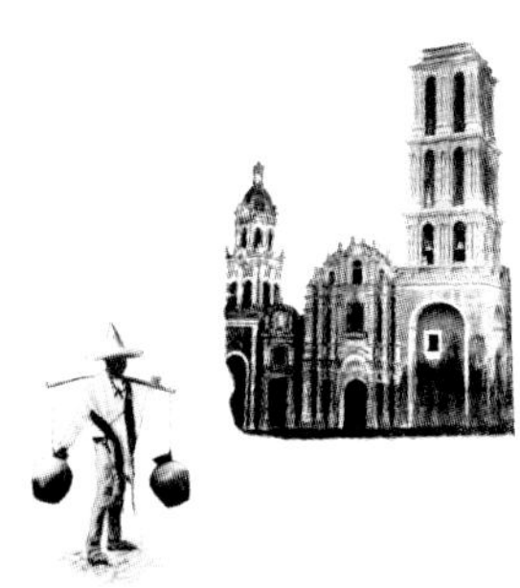

Eurocentric models position Western Europe as the center of technological and cultural progress, imagining the East and Global South as peripheral and backward. Image from *The Señora's Granddaughters* by American Baptist missionary to Mexico, Janie Duggan (1898).

Eurocentric models of taste, quality, and cultural identity usually determined a specimen's reception internationally. Yet local populations found ways to adopt and adapt western printing methods and the typographic specimen to meet their own needs. These needs were often complex and specific. Prolific and influential nineteenth century Mexican printer Ignacio Cumplido, for instance, sourced his press equipment and types from Europe and the United States, using imported fonts and pictorial cuts to develop a recognizable personal style influenced by his own national context. His 1871 sample book included a catalog of his types, which he labeled using European size conventions and arranged according to printing purpose—literary, editorial, or advertising.[43] As a printer, he deployed these elements to craft a culturally specific Mexican **visual language**, most famously in *El Álbum Mexicano* (1849). Within an entirely different geographical and cultural context, Muslim printers deployed Arabic typographic printing to support prostylezation efforts in a range of locations—Iran, India, Turkey, Egypt, China, and eventually the United States—with zeal equal to that of Christian missionaries in their own countries, and with significant success.[44]

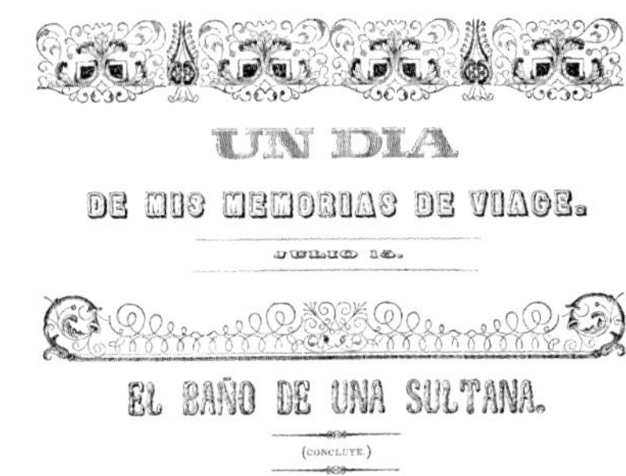

Mexican printer and designer Ignacio Cumplido's **visual language** combined and re-contextualized typographic material imported from Western Europe and North America to craft an aesthetic reflective of his own Mexican culture.

Missionary zeal

Outside of Western Europe and the United States, colonialist and imperialist **proselytization** efforts often undergirded the production of typographic specimens. The American Mission Press of Beirut's catalog (1887) captures the complexity of transcultural, multilingual, multiscript typographic printing in a colonized region with an active mission press [Fig. 3.21]. Locally produced type, rather than European imports, played a role in this process.[45] The AMP (founded 1834 by the Presbyterian Church of the United States) focused on proselytization, publishing, and distributing Arabic translations of the Christian bible not only in Syria but across the region. Because they believed printing "acceptable work in Arabic" demanded "a new and perfect fount of type," three American missionaries to Syria undertook supervision of this process from 1847-60, when the AMP printed its first translation of the New Testament. The contributions of local workers to the design and production process were undocumented but likely profound.[46] Smaller and later mission presses throughout the region acknowledged Beirut's AMP as "a missionary agency of incalculable value" among, as the Nile Mission Press phrased it, "Moslems" and "the Levant."[47]

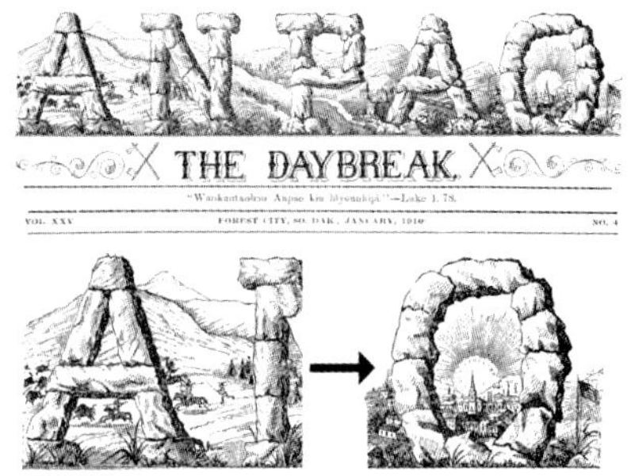

Proselytization seeks to convert people of one faith or belief system into another. Christian missionaries often forcibly assimilated Indiginous North Americans into the Christian religion, for instance.

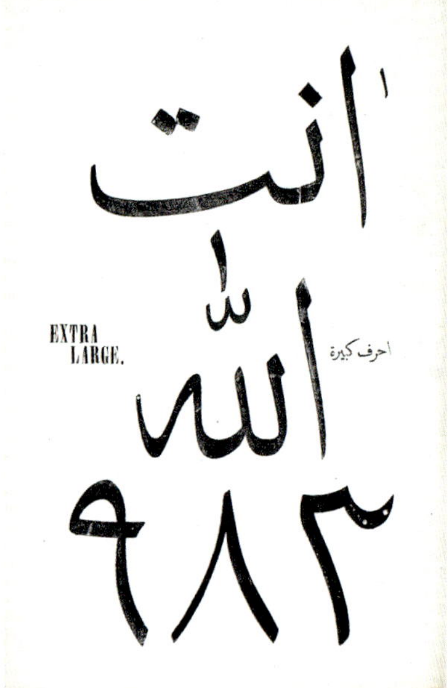

١٠

٢ ثلث كبير

LARGE CAP.

اجناس الاحرف والاعداد

في المطبعة الاميركانية

٠٩٨٧٦٥٤٣٢١

٣ ثلث صغير

SMALL CAP.

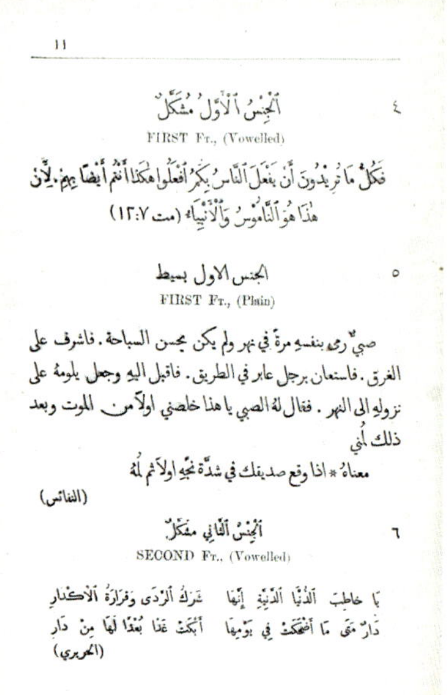

Fig 3.21 (above)

Barnāmaj Al-Matba'at al-Amīrikānīyah / Illustrated Catalogue and Price List **(American Mission Press, Beirut, 1887). Eventually, the types advertised in this catalog came to be known as "American Arabic." Despite heavy-handed colonization efforts in the region, local writers and printers developed a robust printing aesthetic to meet their own needs and preferences.**

Yet the AMP's Arabic readership maintained priorities of its own. The local availability of a carefully and—for its time—accurately designed Arabic typeface, eventually known as "American Arabic," offered opportunities to publish "independent national and literary works" of interest and value to local and regional Arabic-speaking audiences.[48] The type was an economical choice, as it was cut, cast, and sold locally rather than imported. The AMP's 1887 catalog describes "type founders [with] punches and matrices made" on-site, offering "Arabic and English type for sale, according to samples in this catalogue."[49] Local printers and publishers, producing and circulating the historical and contemporary literature and scholarship of their own culture, utilized the typeface in specific ways. They accepted the western printing conventions that aligned with their own needs and attitudes toward what a printed Arabic text should look like and rejected those which didn't. In particular, they avoided attempts to duplicate the effect of **manuscripts** and made the choice to see printing as a different technology of production with its own aesthetic and functional standards.[50]

The 1887 AMP catalog opened with six pages of Arabic type specimens. Display texts in Arabic had captions with English translations denoting size and style. The type was available in plain and thick (i.e., bold) versions, voweled (i.e., including diacritical **vowel points** above and/or below vowels to indicate pronunciation) and not, small and large caps, and a range of sizes for setting body text. The English language captions called these sizes first (the largest), second, and third; an "extra-large" display size was available as well.

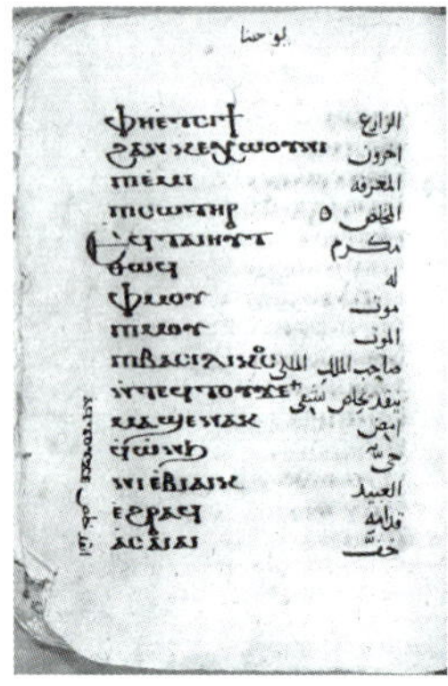

Manuscripts are texts produced by hand. Many cultures reproduced massive numbers of liturgical, scholarly, and commercial texts in this way for centuries. Arabic manuscripts like this page from a Coptic-Arabic glossary (Egypt, c.1400) were particulraly vital to the transmission of linguistic, scientific, medical, mathematical, and historical information throughout the Medieval world.

The various sizes contained different inconsistencies and errors in rendering the Arabic alphabet, and their legibility and availability, not their complete accuracy, led to their wide adoption.[51] An ad within the catalog described the AMP as "[b]ook publishers, book binders, lithographers, electrotypers, [and] stereotypers," offering "**job printing** in many languages ... printed in eastern or western styles."[52] The explicit use of styles, when much of the copy to follow discussed typographic alphabets, suggested attention to the cultural preferences and visual languages of multiple audiences, not simply the language they read. The illustrated science, history, and literature texts for sale demonstrated a markedly colonialist attitude toward picturing knowledge as a Western import, however. Western European and North American titles in translation dominated, as did illustrations of white westerners in pictorial works. Later editions of the catalog, including the 1896 edition, re-used much of this specimen material.[53]

Colonizers tended to read all types, not only those connected to explicit missionary activity, as weapons in the fight to "civilize and christianize" cultures different from their own. In 1875, the American trade journal *Printers' Circular* had reported on the "progress" of printing in Japan.

> In an Oriental country, intensely prejudiced against Western civilization, where neither types, newspapers, nor books existed ten years ago, there are now published thirty-four newspapers ... There has also been erected a type foundry, which is in active operation. Many printing presses have been imported, and more are needed, and will no doubt soon be sent for. A number of Americans and Europeans are ... preparing for the press dictionaries, vocabularies, phrase books, and grammars ... The old time opposition to printing has vanished, and the clinking of types and the clattering of presses will do more in five years to civilize and christianize Japan than would have been accomplished in the same direction by fifty years of bombardment from the combined fleets of Europe and America.[54]

The notion that printing western-style dictionaries and newspapers would "civilize and christianize Japan" overlooked the country's long history of types, printing, books, and **kawaraban** (news sheets). Though manuscript production and **woodblock** printing dominated Japan's textual landscape until the last quarter of the twentieth century, at least in part because of the primarily **logographic** character set of Japanese, the country had a flourishing literary culture. Historically, Japanese printers embraced some printing methods and rejected others, not out of ignorance but through experimentation and choice.[55] Likewise, adopting movable metal type and the steam-powered press was a choice, one that explicitly sought to incorporate not only western technologies but also western formal structures and systems of knowledge.

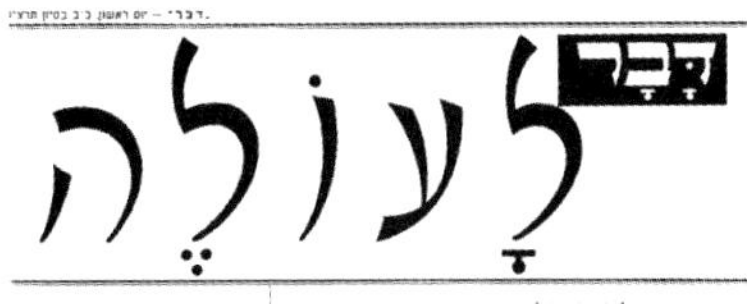

Vowel points are diacritical marks which modify consonats in order to indicate the sounds made by unprinted vowel characters; they're essential to Hebrew, traditionally written and printed without vowels, as seen in this Aharoni specimen (1936).

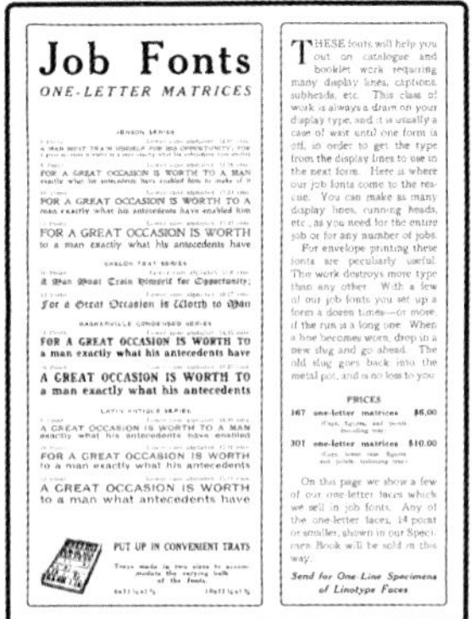

Job printing required **job fonts** this 1911 Linotype specimen put it—You can make as many as you need for the entire job or for any number of jobs.

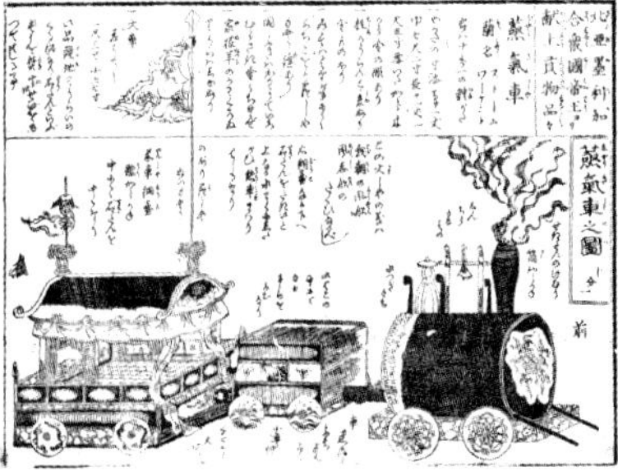

Kawaraban spread news or commemorated significant events from the 17c. forward. Like most Japanese texts, these woodblock-printed broadsides used many **logographic** Chinese characters (one character per word) so **woodblock** printing offered maximum efficiency.

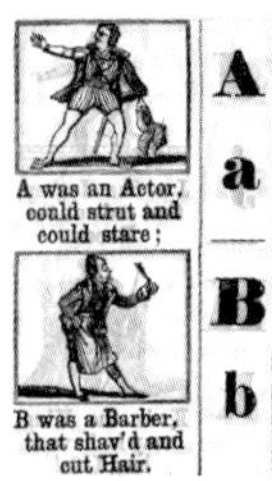

Though its forms are familiar enough to seem universal to readers in Western Europe and North America, the **Latin alphabet** is only one of many scripts in contemporary use; *New London Alphabet* (1847).

The 300-page *Specimens of printing types and ornaments cast at the Insetsu-Kioku* (1885) [Fig 3.22] displayed the transcultural range of Japan's Imperial Printing Office. **Latin-alphabet** text and display types, borders described as "ornamentors [sic] and business bringers," flowers and "wreath's, festoon, scrolls and dingle-dangles," and "combination borders" for labels and logotypes filled most of the specimen.[56] Inaccurate translations occasionally signaled the compositors' unfamiliarity with English and many of the sample texts referenced Japan, but stylistically, the typefaces and ornaments were conventional examples of late nineteenth century Western European and North American design. The text types often deployed an excerpt from Thomas MacKellar's *The American printer* (1866) as display copy. Thirteen pages of Chinese and Japanese text and smaller display types concluded the volume for western readers—and began it for Japanese readers. The complete lack of English captions indicated a Japanese-fluent audience for these pages, as did the sample text selections, excerpts of Japanese poetry and historical literature. Yet regardless of language and audience, the page design throughout the specimen resembled Euroamerican examples printed around the same time. Thus equipped, the Imperial Printing Office printed bank notes, postage stamps, government reports in Japanese and English, a newspaper, and—if its specimen was any indication—quite a lot of commercial jobbing work. Anglophone observers frequently offered the presence of such printing establishments as proof of successful westernization, though they rarely found non-western printing up to their own standards of quality and fashion.

Fig 3.22 (below)

Specimens of Printing Types and Ornaments Cast at the Insetsu-Kioku **(Tokyo, Imperial Printing Office, 1885). Though American and British observers saw western-style printing as a tool to "civilize and christianize" the country, Japanese printers made informed decisions about how to use movable metal type in different contexts—for colonialist Anglophone customers versus local reading publics.**

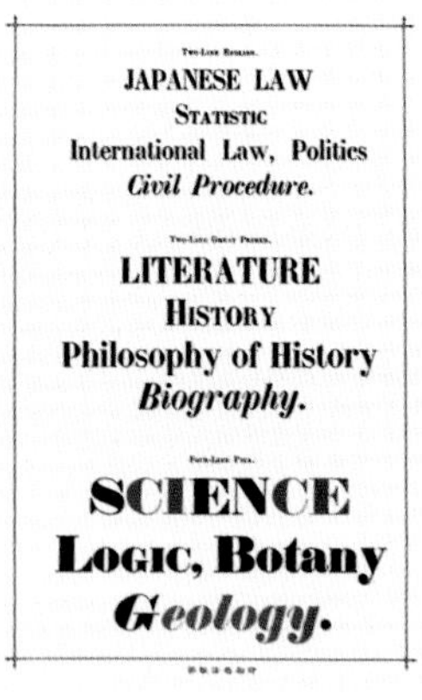

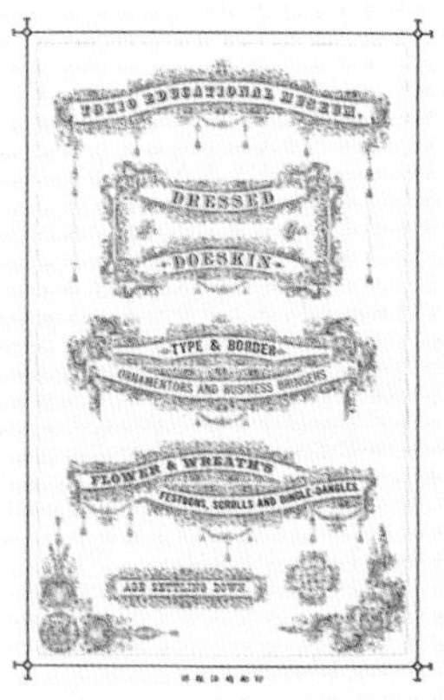

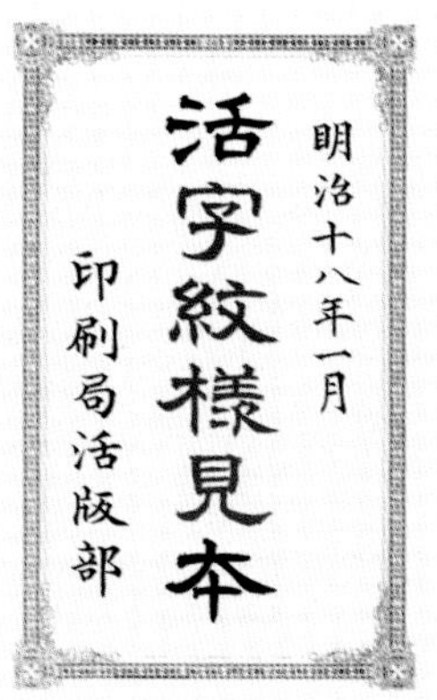

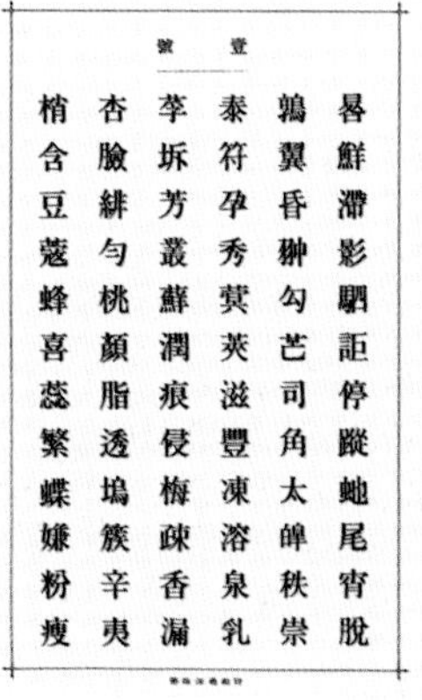

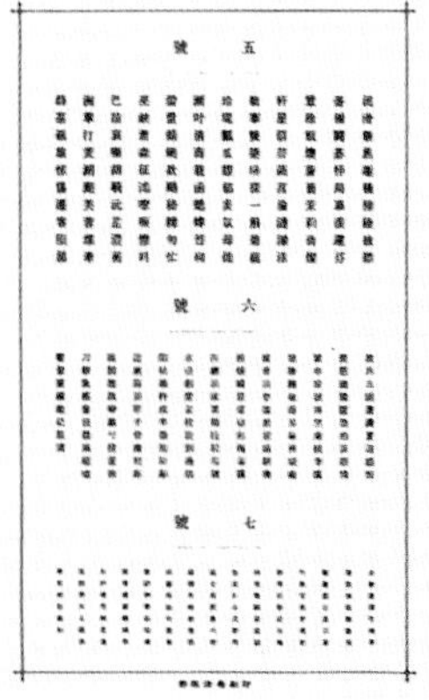

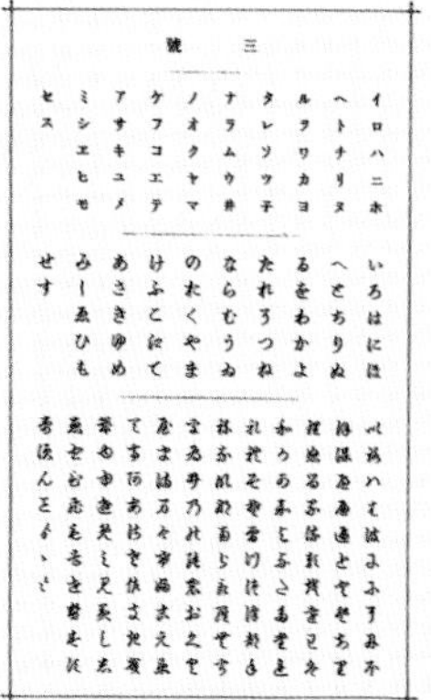

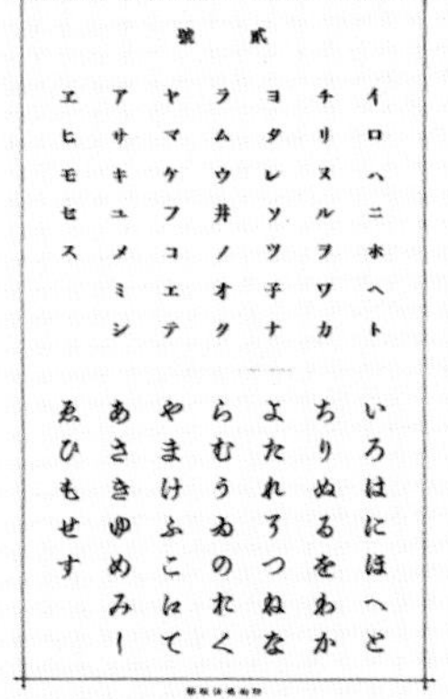

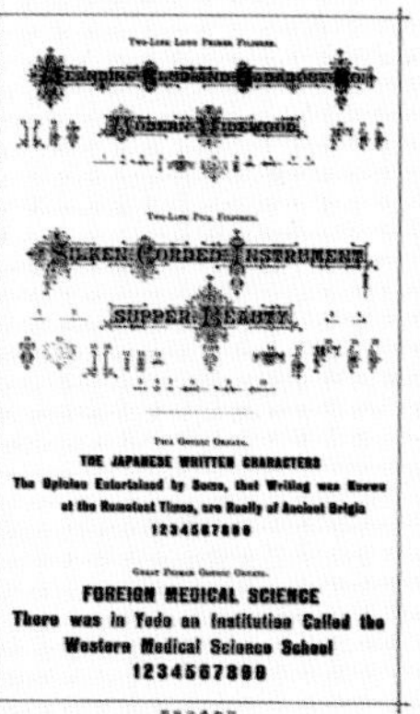

Centers and peripheries

Japan at the turn of the twentieth century offers many insights into the complexities of an international typographic market. In 1894, the New Zealand **trade journal** *Typo* mentioned a specimen received from Tokyo showing "a set of six odd little Japanese ornaments and two borders" but concluded these were "not much to European taste."[57] This brief news item casts Western Europe and the United States as geographic and scientific "centers" of progress, knowledge production, and design, while "peripheral" locations elsewhere lagged behind, producing "primitive" design until indigenous populations began consuming and imitating Euroamerican exports—though often in an "inferior" mode. The center-periphery model remained problematic for design history and criticism throughout the twentieth century, misunderstanding or misrepresenting indigenous design practices as substandard in a wide variety of contexts and geographic locations.[58] Japan is only one example of the center-periphery model at work in typographic practice as documented in type specimens.

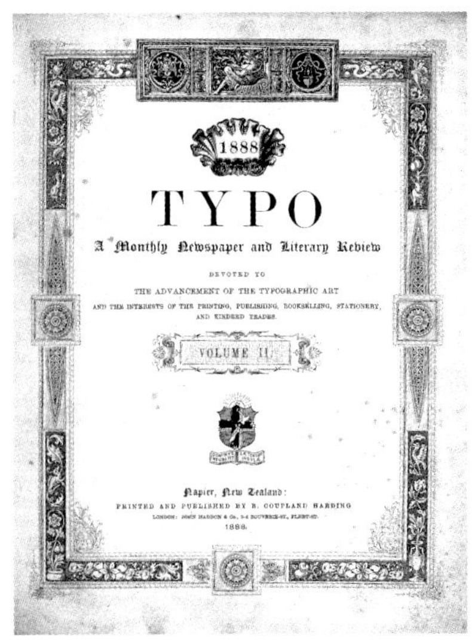

Trade journals are periodical publications for members of a specific trade, like printing. Typically they contain articles, advice columns, and advertisements pertinent to practitioners. Typo addressed the printers of New Zealand (and beyond) around the turn of the twentieth century.

Even leaving aside that Japanese printers chose non-typographic printing and text production methods for a variety of practical and aesthetic reasons,[59] the Japanese adoption of movable metal type had a long historical trajectory. Japanese experiments with movable metal type began in the last decade of the sixteenth century. In Korea, an otherwise unsuccessful Japanese military campaign acquired a set of Korean metal type—pioneered there in the thirteenth century—and brought it back to Japan in 1593. Movable wooden types of Japanese design, inspired by the Korean types, appeared by 1597; small-scale presses for government, private, and commercial printing utilized them.[60] The Jesuit Mission Press in Nagasaki (est. 1585) began printing Japanese-language texts in 1598, using types produced with metal printing dies acquired by a Japanese delegation sent to Europe to learn Western-style printing.[61] But **xylography** dominated the Japanese market until the Dutch East India Company imported Western-style printing presses into Nagasaki in 1848. The first English newspaper printed in Japan followed in 1861, and by the 1870s, a growing number of newspapers circulated in Japanese. During the 1880s, movable metal type subsumed woodblock printing as the dominant publishing technology in Japan.[62] An 1894 biographical sketch in the *British Bookmaker*, written by S. Magata, director of the Tokyo Tsukiji Type Foundry, described Motogi Nagahisa (1824-75) as "the first Japanese printer." Magata mentioned "very coarsely made" wood types "from ancient times" but didn't seem to count these as true printing and didn't mention movable metal types imported from Korea; nor did he mention the flourishing Japanese publishing trade facilitated for centuries by xylography. In 1851-2, Nagahisa used an imported press and movable metal type of his own making to print a narrative account of his own career. He exported the slender book to Holland, thus beginning—in words that Magata ascribed to Nagahisa—a "new era" of printing in Japan.[63] In 1901, the American *Book Lover* called Nagahisa "the Japanese Gutenberg," and this honorific neatly captured the center-periphery dynamic at work in Western European and North American attitudes toward Japanese printing.[64]

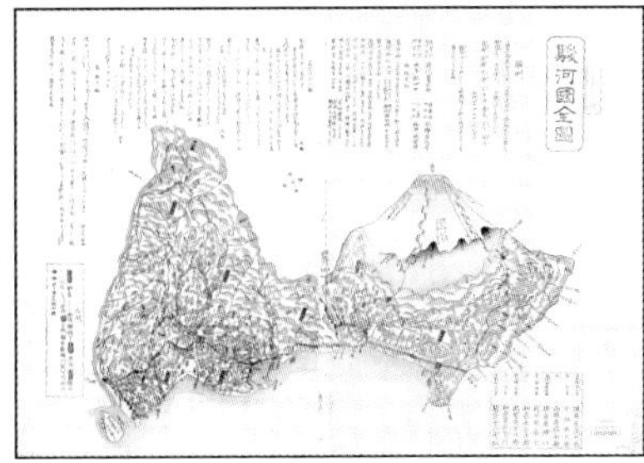

Xylography or woodblock printing was the logical choice for writing systems incorporating logographic or ideographic characters; this 1828 map of Shizuoka Prefecture combines text and image in a single woodblock.

18 DOZ 4-LINE JAPANESE T 29 PER DOZ 1/6

Heroic Men

Orientialized types were Latin types meant to suggest Asian scripts. Pictured: 4-line Japanese (Wimble, 1910)

Motoki Shōzō, the first Japanese letterpress printer to achieve broad commercial success, also appeared in the guise of "the Japanese Gutenberg," forcing Japan's printing history into a familiar—and thus truncated—model for Anglophone readers.[65] Founder of the Tokyo Tsukiji Type Foundry (as it came to be known when Magata assumed directorship), Shōzō cultivated both Western and Japanese customers. In its advertising copy, the foundry (est. 1873) carefully aligned Western expectations of Japanese scenery and culture with Western expectations for typographic printing. As an 1893 ad produced for the World's Columbian Exposition in Chicago claimed, "Our Sunrise Land is noted for the beauty of its scenery, for the matchless perfection of snow-clad Fuji-san and the wonderful temples of Nikkô, but nothing can exceed the perfection, beauty and durability of our types! They are iron-clad and last forever." The ad described Tsukiji as "the oldest and yet the most progressive of type foundries in the East."[66] Other Tsukiji ads promised "the very highest grade of workmanship and efficiency."[67] In 1907, the *Inland Printer* reproduced some of Tsukiji's pictorial cuts, captioning the image "Decorative materials in use by printers of the Far East" and declaring the cuts "quaint and attractive" [Fig. 3.23][68] In imagining Japan as timeless and beautiful, Anglophone typographic literature around the turn of the century joined a wider visual culture of **Orientalism** in which Japanese designers also self-reflexively participated.[69] Yet simultaneously, the Tsukiji foundry designed and produced Japanese types in ***kanji*** (logographic characters adopted from Chinese) and ***kana*** (syllabic characters), facilitating locally and nationally specific book, newspaper, and magazine printing.

魯 遞 籌 魁 乾
戈 攻 箭 柄 坤
蔑 烏 應 昭 闔
駐 兔 鐘 煥 闢
吳 奔 候 蒼 肇
斧 走 序 穹 開

いろはにほへと
ちりぬるをわか
よたれそつねな
らむうゐのおく
やまけふこえて
あさきゆめみし
ゑひもせす

In Japanese, logographic ***kanji*** (one character per word; top 6 rows, above) were primarily adopted from Chinese; schoolchildren learn over 2,000 common kanji. Syllabic ***kana*** (one character per syllable; bottom 7 rows) are further divided into hiragana (used for transcribing native/naturalized words) and katakana (for foreign/loanwords).

TRADE MARK.

THE TOKYO TSUKIJI TYPE FOUNDRY

No. 17, Tsukiji, Nichome, Tokyo, Japan.

ESTABLISHED 1868.

THE oldest and yet the most progressive of TYPE FOUNDRIES in

THE EAST,

AND THE CHEAPEST

The World Over.

Comparison with the prices of American and European Type Foundries shows that our types are *actually cheaper* than those produced in the largest Foundries of the West. Our Works cover an enormous space of ground, and our Workmen are as skilled as they are ready to take hints from their Compeers in the Occident. We can produce every kind of printing, from

Electrotypy, Lithography, Stereography,

up to ARTOTYPE,

COLLOTYPY, AND MEZZOTINT.

WE DEFY COMPETITION!

Our Sunrise Land is noted for the beauty of its scenery, for the matchless perfection of SNOW-CLAD FUJI-SAN and the wonderful temples of Nikkô,

— BUT —

nothing can exceed the perfection, beauty and durability of our types! They are IRON-CLAD and last forever. Chinese, Japanese, Sanskrit, Greek, German, Corean and Arabic fonts, of unrivalled make; Borders in Japanese style, with artistic arrangement of Japan's fairest flowers; Presses of improved make, and all the requisites of the Printer's Art.

For further particulars, catalogues and specimen sheets,

ADDRESS,

S. MAGATA, Director.

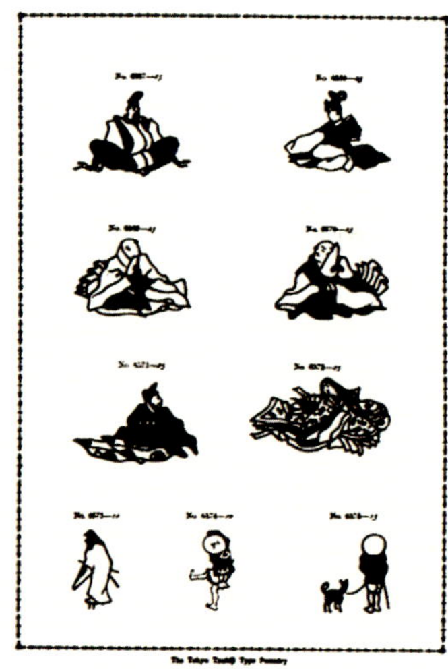

Decorative material in use by printers of the Far East.

Fig 3.23 (right)

Tsukiji Type Foundry ad (*An Itinerary of Hokkaido*, Japan, 1893) and *Inland Printer* illustration (April 1907, p. 91). The Tokyo Tsukiji Type Foundry took care to align its English-language ads with western understandings of both the printing industry and Japanese culture; Anglophone viewers were likely, though, to read all type emerging from locations they deemed peripheral as "quaint."

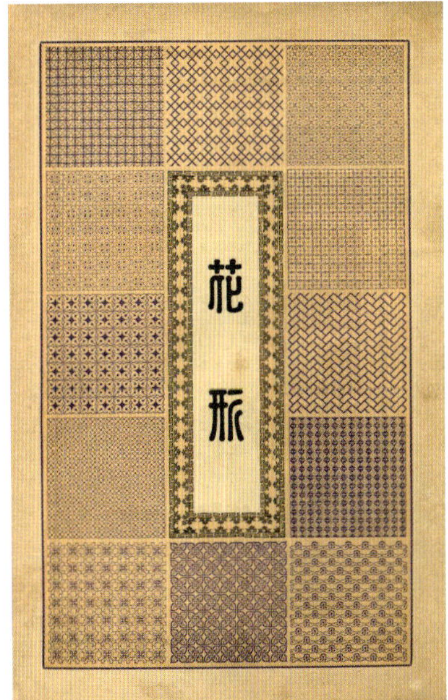

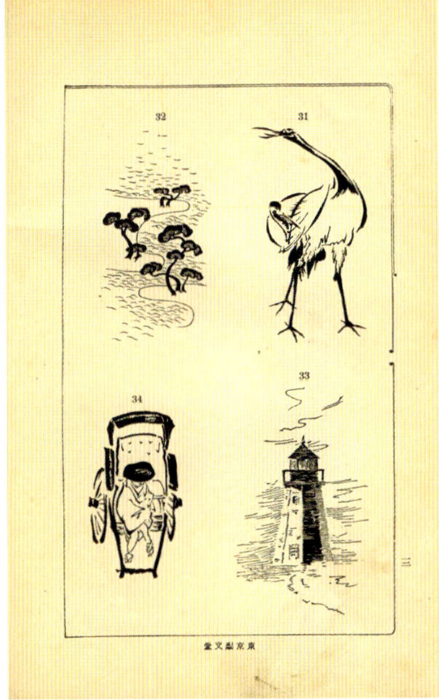

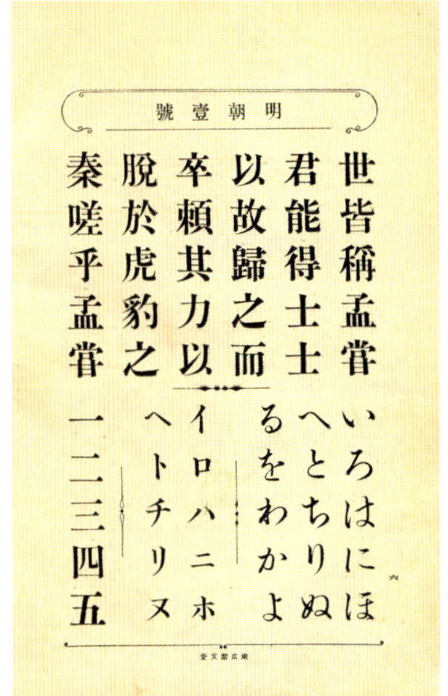

Fig 3.24 (above)

***Seibundo Type Specimens* (Shueisha Seibundo, Tokyo, 1903). Like many Japanese specimen books, this one began at the "front" for Anglophone readers and at the western "back" for Japanese readers—which was actually the beginning, as Japanese codex-style books were customarily bound on the right-hand side.**

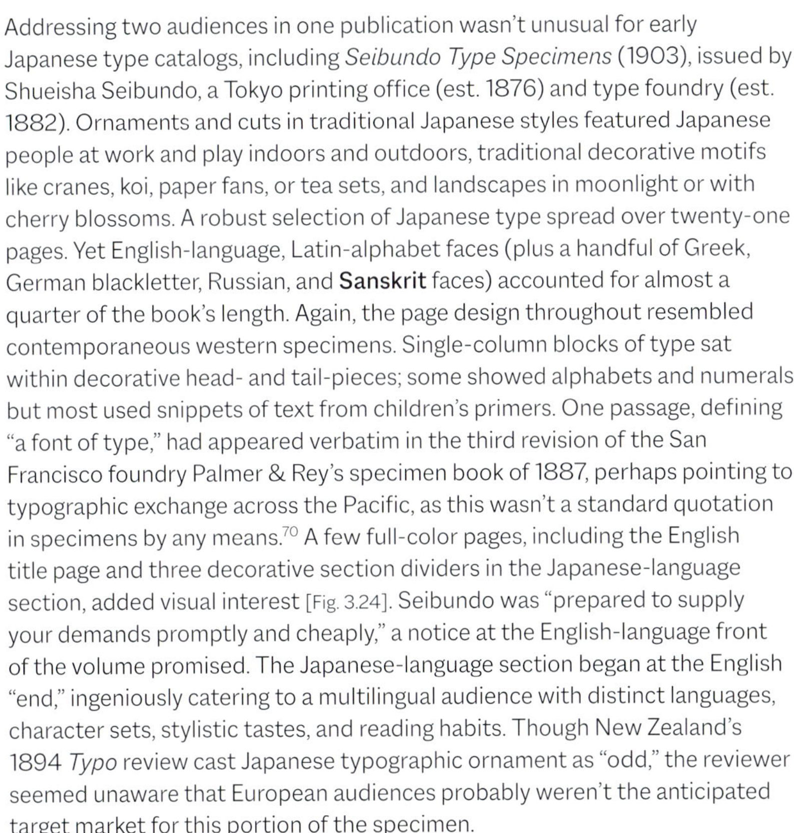

Addressing two audiences in one publication wasn't unusual for early Japanese type catalogs, including *Seibundo Type Specimens* (1903), issued by Shueisha Seibundo, a Tokyo printing office (est. 1876) and type foundry (est. 1882). Ornaments and cuts in traditional Japanese styles featured Japanese people at work and play indoors and outdoors, traditional decorative motifs like cranes, koi, paper fans, or tea sets, and landscapes in moonlight or with cherry blossoms. A robust selection of Japanese type spread over twenty-one pages. Yet English-language, Latin-alphabet faces (plus a handful of Greek, German blackletter, Russian, and **Sanskrit** faces) accounted for almost a quarter of the book's length. Again, the page design throughout resembled contemporaneous western specimens. Single-column blocks of type sat within decorative head- and tail-pieces; some showed alphabets and numerals but most used snippets of text from children's primers. One passage, defining "a font of type," had appeared verbatim in the third revision of the San Francisco foundry Palmer & Rey's specimen book of 1887, perhaps pointing to typographic exchange across the Pacific, as this wasn't a standard quotation in specimens by any means.[70] A few full-color pages, including the English title page and three decorative section dividers in the Japanese-language section, added visual interest [Fig. 3.24]. Seibundo was "prepared to supply your demands promptly and cheaply," a notice at the English-language front of the volume promised. The Japanese-language section began at the English "end," ingeniously catering to a multilingual audience with distinct languages, character sets, stylistic tastes, and reading habits. Though New Zealand's 1894 *Typo* review cast Japanese typographic ornament as "odd," the reviewer seemed unaware that European audiences probably weren't the anticipated target market for this portion of the specimen.

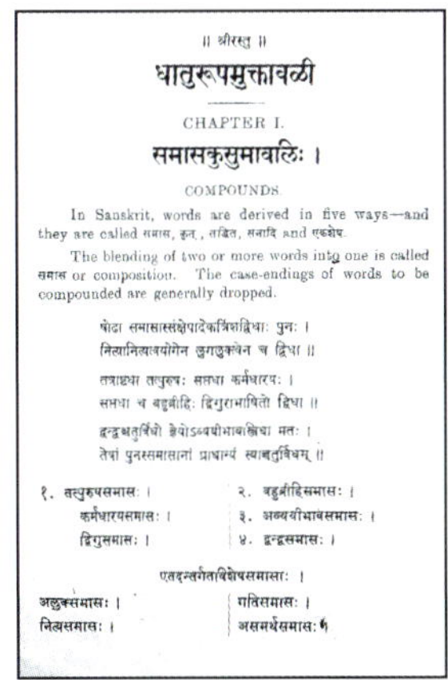

॥ श्रीरस्तु ॥

धातुरूपमुक्तावळी

CHAPTER I.

समासकुसुमावलिः ।

COMPOUNDS

In Sanskrit, words are derived in five ways—and they are called समास, कृत्, तद्धित, सनादि and एकशेष.

The blending of two or more words into one is called समास or composition. The case-endings of words to be compounded are generally dropped.

षोढा समासस्संक्षेपादेकत्रिंशद्विधाः पुनः ।
नित्यानित्यत्वयोगेन लुगलुक्त्वेन च द्विधा ॥
तत्राष्टधा तत्पुरुषः सप्तधा कर्मधारयः ।
सप्तधा च बहुव्रीहिः द्विगुराभाषितो द्विधा ॥
द्वन्द्वश्चतुर्विधो ज्ञेयोऽव्ययीभावस्त्रिधा मतः ।
तेषां पुनस्समासानां प्राधान्यं स्याच्चतुर्विधम् ॥

१. तत्पुरुषसमासः । | २. बहुव्रीहिसमासः ।
कर्मधारयसमासः । | ३. अव्ययीभावसमासः ।
द्विगुसमासः । | ४. द्वन्द्वसमासः ।

एतदन्तर्गतविशेषसमासाः ।

अलुक्समासः । | गतिसमासः ।
नित्यसमासः । | असमर्थसमासः ।

This bilingual **Sanskrit** grammar by P.K. Duraiswami Iyengar was printed in Madras (1915).

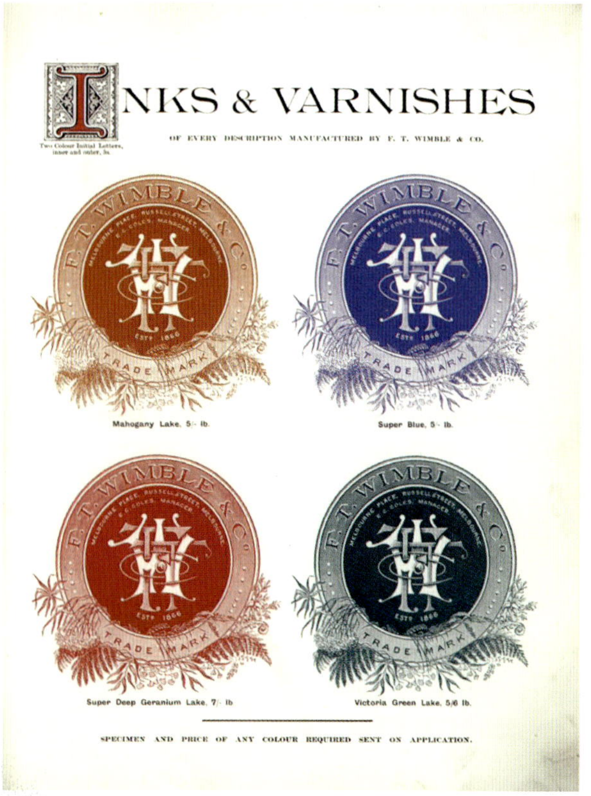

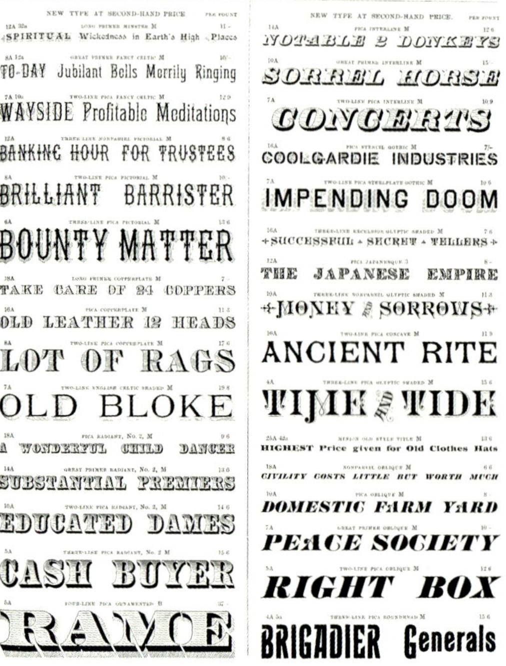

Fig 3.25 (above)

***New and Second-Hand Printing Type* (F.T. Wimble & Co, Melbourne, 1910). Wimble wasn't Australia's only type founder, but he successfully advertised himself as such. He often renamed imported types with Australian names to make them seem local. Miller & Richard's Grotesque No. 6 became Tasmanian Expanded, for instance.**

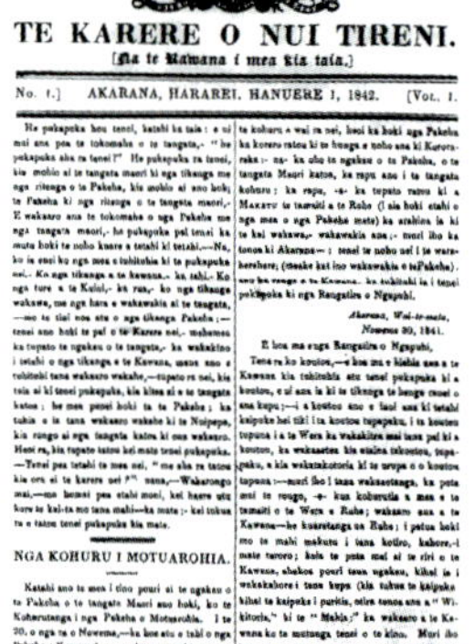
TE KARERE O NUI TIRENI.

Māori newspapers used the Latin alphabet to represent spoken Māori, a language without written form until European colonizers arrived. *Te Karere O Nui Tireni*, 1842.

Meanwhile, Australia and New Zealand were just as much a part of the conceptual and geographic periphery for American and British observers as Japan had been to New Zealand. In 1899, the *Inland Printer* reported a "rapid" rate of "Typographic Progress in Australia"—though they were actually discussing New Zealand, a separate country (and different British colony) entirely. This report measured progress via numbers: of printing establishments, employees, newspapers being published, pounds of imported paper consumed by printers.[71] By applying these metrics, and noting "rapid progress," one of the United States' leading trade journals reinforced established, normative notions of center/periphery and colonizer/colonized relationships. Yet printers in Australasia, particularly those from larger cities, perceived the printing scene in other colonial countries as provincial, adopting the same metrics the *Inland Printer* would apply to Australasia. A Melbourne printer who had relocated to South Africa, for instance, wrote to the *Australasian Typographical Journal* in 1894 that Capetown had a typographical society, "but its influence is of a partial character only" and the town had only one newspaper. He also reported that "the [British South Africa] Chartered Company, having disposed of [the indigenous King] Lobengula, have made Buluwayo [Bulawayo] their headquarters, and civilisation has so far advanced that they have a newspaper."[72] Typographic printing registers as a clear signifier of colonial occupation in this letter, as do the interdependent violences—one figurative, one literal—of the two processes. Colonial settlers dominated New Zealand's market for metal type, though Indiginous **Māori** printers published newspapers. *Te Hokioi* (1862-3), the first of these, was printed on an iron press owned by Māori printers who had learned their trade in Austria. But spoken Māori had no indiginous writing system, and English missionaries transliterated it into the Latin alphabet when they arrived in New Zealand around 1814.[73] Thus, Māori printers relied on imported international type, as did their colonizers, who almost exclusively imported type from abroad for reasons of economy and efficiency.[74]

Australian typefounding was somewhat more robust, and though very few copies survive, trade journals and newspapers record the existence of nineteenth century specimens. The first type founder in Australia arrived in Sydney from Scotland in 1841. Others followed, but the Melbourne foundry F.T. Wimble & Co. (est. 1900) proved so successful at marketing themselves as Australia's only type foundry that a record of these earlier efforts has only recently emerged. Frederick Wimble sold new and secondhand type and printing equipment, much of it imported. Originally a manufacturer of **printing ink**, he expanded into the type business at the turn of the century as the sole Australian agent for McKellar, Smiths & Jordan of the United States and Figgins of England; he soon purchased the Australian Type Founding Company in Sydney and continued to expand his customer base across Australia. He prided himself on importing new, up-to-the moment types and, beginning in 1908, he renamed these with Australian names for national market appeal.[75] Wimble's early catalogs (1900, 1910) hinted at the challenges faced, offering "reduced prices to effect a speedy sale" and accommodate restocking [Fig. 3.25]. A single page displayed discounted "founts of Figgins roman type" in text sizes ranging from Nonpareil no. 15 to Pica no. 11. What the newer, more fashionable English and American text faces would be after restocking, the catalog didn't say. The Figgins text type was followed by a thirty-page selection of jobbing faces advertised as "new type at second-hand price."[76] The section devoted to **wood type**, which Wimble introduced into Australia again via imports, ran even longer. The common practice of imitating imported English and American designs left Australian founders with what Australian type historian Dennis Bryans calls "little incentive to indulge in creative design" and a specimen like Wimble's supports this claim.[77] Positioned by varying stakeholders and observers as both center and periphery, advanced and provincial, Australia and its neighbor, New Zealand, demonstrated the multi-layered, multivocal nature of an international typographic landscape.

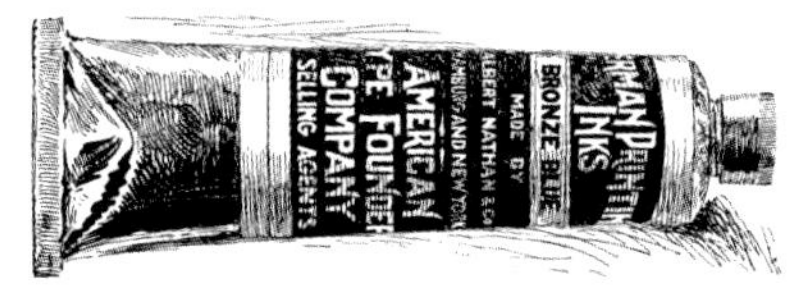

Printing ink was produced industrially beginning in the seventeenth century; prior to this, most printers made their inks out of soot or lampblack and vegetable oil or animal glue.

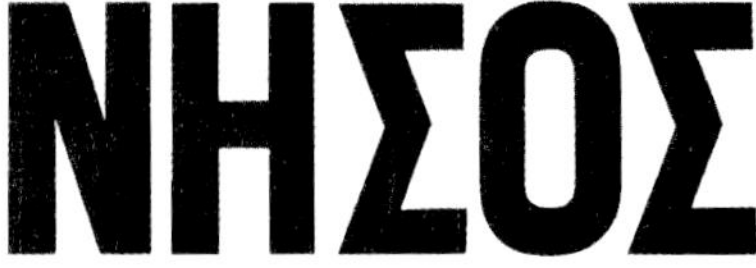

Wood type was lighter, cheaper, and more structurally sound than metal at large sizes—sometimes reaching several feet tall.

Conclusion

Specimen books met many needs, and the types they carried traveled with them in context-dependent ways. Whether establishing a foundry's importance, making a fashion statement, filling utilitarian needs, or providing a visual primer, specimen books still shared a fundamental purpose: the display of types available for purchase or use. Outside of Western Europe and North America, secular and/or religious colonizers typically introduced the practice of producing a typographic specimen shortly after they introduced letterpress printing with movable metal type. Yet despite complex and sometimes violent early engagements with western print culture and its associated value systems, indiginous users of type deployed the form—and the mode of communication it represented—in sophisticated ways that were adaptable and effective. Thus, in addition to providing visually rich records of aesthetic styles, typefounding practices, and foundry histories, specimen books offer a mechanism for understanding global networks of exchange.

1 Christophe Plantin and Douglas C. McMurtrie, *Plantin's Index characterum of 1567* (New York: Douglas C. McMurtrie, 1924), iii–vii.

2 Jean Jannon, *Espreuve des caractères nouvellement taillez*. (Sedan: Jean Jannon, 1621); Pollard, *Catalogue*, 11.

3 Hendrik D. L. Vervliet, Harry Carter, and Gary Schwarz, eds., *The Type Specimen of the Vatican Press, 1628: A Facsimile* (Amsterdam: M. Hertzberger, 1967), 10.

4 Knight, *Historical Types*, 49; Beaujon [Beatrice Warde], "The Garamond Types: Sixteenth and Seventeenth Century Sources Considered."

5 Claude Lamesle, *Epreuves Generales Des Caracters Qui Se Trouvent Chez Claude Lamesle, Fondeur de Caracters d'imprimerie* (Paris: Pres la place Maubert, 1742); Nicolas Gando, ed., *Epreuve Des Caracteres de La Fonderie de Nicolas Gando* (Paris: De l'imprimerie de Jacques Guerin, 1745); A.F. Johnson, "The Type-Specimen Books of Claude Lamesle and Nicolas Gando," *Library* s4-XVIII, no. 2 (September 1937): 207–8, https://doi.org/10.1093/library/s4-XVIII.2.201; John Dreyfus, *Aspects of French Eighteenth Century Typography: A Study of Type Specimens in the Broxbourne Collection at Cambridge University Library* (Cambridge: [John Erhman?], 1982), 83, 92–93.

6 Bigmore and Wyman, *A Bibliography of Printing*, 1880, 1:202–3.

7 Knight, *Historical Types*, 61–63, 67; Neil Macmillan, *An A-Z of Type Designers* (New Haven: Yale University Press, 2006), 83; Middendorp, *Dutch Type*, 27–28.

8 Fonderie du sieur Delacolonge and Harry Graham Carter, *The Type Specimen of Delacolonge: Les Caracters et Les Vignettes de La Fonderie Du Sieur Delacolonge* (Amsterdam, New York: Van Gendt; Abner Schram, 1969), 11.

9 Vervliet, Carter, and Schwarz, *The Type Specimen of the Vatican Press, 1628*, 8.

10 Pierre-Simon Fournier et al., *The Manuel Typographique of Pierre-Simon Fournier le Jeune: Together with Fournier on Typefounding*, vol. 3 (Darmstadt: Lehrdruckeri Technische Hochschule, 1995), xxvi, 13, 49.

11 Giambattista Bodoni, Giovanni Mardersteig, and Herman Cohen, *Manuale Tipografico, 1788*, Editiones Officinae Bodoni (Verona: Officina Bodoni, 1968), ix.

12 Lewis C. Gandy, *Bodoni Type; an Historical Sketch of Its Origin, Together with Suggestions as to Its Proper Use*. (Boston: Pinkham Press, 1920), 14, https//catalog.hathitrust.org/Record/100191615.

13 Allan Haley, *Typographic Milestones* (Wiley & Sons, 1992), 46–49.

14 Bodoni, Mardersteig, and Cohen, *Manuale tipografico*, 1788.

15 Pierre Didot, *Spécimen Des Nouveaux Caractères de La Fonderie et de l'imprimerie de P. Didot, l'ainé: Chevalier de l'ordre Royal de Saint-Michel, Imprimerie Du Roi et de La Chambre Des Pairs, Dédié à Jules Didot, Fils, Chevalier de La Légion d'honneur* (Paris: Didot, 1819), https://catalog.hathitrust.org/Record/011273746; Hoefler & Co., "Didot Fonts: History," Typography.com, 2020, http://www.typography.com/fonts/didot/history/.

16 Fred T. Singleton and Henry Lewis Bullen, "The Didot Dynasty of Printers," *Inland Printer/American Lithographer* 68, no. 1 (October 1921): 59.

17 Bigmore and Wyman, *A Bibliography of Printing*, 1880, 1:175.

18 Bigmore and Wyman, *A Bibliography of Printing*, 1880, 1:355.

19 Robert Hilton, "Introduction of Printing into Russia," *British Printer* 1, no. 5 (October 1888): 15; William E. Burns, *Science in the Enlightenment: An Encyclopedia*, History of Science (Santa Barbara: ABC-CLIO, 2003), 138; Peter Burke and Asa Briggs, *A Social History of the Media: From Gutenberg to the Internet* (Cambridge: Polity, 2005), 13–14.

20 Fiona Ross, "An Approach to Non Latin Type Design," in *Language Culture Type: International Type Design in the Age of Unicode* (New York: ATypI, 2002), 67.

21 Steven Heller, "Berthold's 1924 Hebrew Type Catalogue," *Baseline*, 2006.

22 Naomi Brenner, "Milgroym, Rimon and Interwar Jewish Bilingualism," *Journal of Jewish Identities* 7, no. 1 (February 2, 2014): 23–48, https://doi.org/10.1353/jji.2014.0009.

23 Hugh J. Schonfield, *The New Hebrew Typography* (London: Denis Archer, 1932), 15, 18, 25–30, http://archive.org/details/Schonfield1932TheNewHebrewTypography.

24 Shani Avni, "Ismar David's Quest for Original Hebrew Typographic Signs," *Visible Language* 53, no. 1 (2019): 51–75, http://www.visiblelanguagejournal.com/issue/292.

25 Peter Weidhaas, *A History of the Frankfurt Book Fair*, trans. Carolyn Gossage and Wendy A. Wright (Toronto: Dundurn, 2007)..

26 Dreyfus, *Aspects of French Eighteenth Century Typography*, v.

27 Daniel Berkeley Updike, *Printing Types, Their History, Forms, and Use; a Study in Survivals*, vol. 2 (Cambridge: Harvard University Press, 1922), 197, https://archive.org/details/printingtypesthe02updi.

28 Edmund Fry obituary, *The Gentleman's Magazine*, no. 159 (May 1836): 557–58.

29 For instance, type designer John Downer discussed Caslon's seminal role in forestalling the importation of Dutch types and the "emergence of an English style" in an essay originally printed on the verso of his *Not Caslon* type specimen poster in 1995. "Emigre Essays The Art of Founding Type," *Emigre* Fonts, 1995/2020, https://www.emigre.com/Essays/Type/TheArtofFoundingType.

30 Bigmore and Wyman, *A Bibliography of Printing*, 1880, 1:219–20.

31 T. C. Hansard, *Typographia: An Historical Sketch of the Origin and Progress of the Art of Printing; with Practical Directions for Conducting Every Department in an Office: With a Description of Stereotype and Lithography. Illustrated by Engravings, Biographical Notices, and Portraits* (London: Baldwin, Cradock, and Joy, 1825), 360, https://archive.org/details/typographiaanhi00hansgoog.

32 Slab serifs, frequently called Egyptians when the form emerged, ostensibly originated with Napoleon's Egyptian military campaigns but more probably represented a somewhat random association because they gained popularity around the same time. Alexander S. Lawson, *Anatomy of a Typeface* (Boston: Godine, 1990), 310–11.

33 Fry and Chambers, *Specimen of Modern Printing Types*, 11.

34 Lawson, *Anatomy of a Typeface*, 295.

35 James Ronaldson, *Specimen of Printing Type, from the Letter Foundry of James Ronaldson, Successor to Binny & Ronaldson* (Philadelphia: J. Ronaldson, 1816).

36 Ronaldson, n.p.

37 For a detailed case study of how print capitalism and typography interact, see William Kuskin, *Symbolic Caxton: Literary Culture and Print Capitalism* (Notre Dame: University of Notre Dame Press, 2008).

38 Lara Langer Cohen and Jordan Alexander Stein, *Early African American Print Culture* (Philadelphia: University of Pennsylvania Press, 2012). See particularly chapters 6 by Corey Capers and 16 by Radiclani Clytus.

39 Great Western Type Foundry, *Specimen Book and Price List of the Great Western Type Foundry, Chicago, Barnhart Bros. & Spindler, Proprietors* (Chicago: Great Western Type Foundry, 1873), n.p.

40 Burton Raffel and Ellen Mazur Thomson, *The Origins of Graphic Design in America, 1870-1920* (Yale University Press, 1997), 183.

41 Barnhart Brothers and Spindler, *Book of Type Specimens* (Chicago: Barnhart Bros. & Spindler, 1907), n.p., http://archive.org/details/BBSSpecimenNo9_1907.

42 For instance, Mores placed the question of importing type, typeface designs, and skilled labor at the heart of typefounding's emergence in England. Edward Rowe Mores, Harry Graham Carter, and Christopher B. Ricks, *A Dissertation upon English Typographical Founders and Founderies (1778): With a Catalogue and Specimen of the Type-Foundry of John James (1782)*, Oxford Bibliographical Society Publications, new ser, v.9 (Oxford: Oxford Bibliographical Society, 1961), lxx–lxxi.

43 Marina Garone Gravier, "Nineteenth-Century Mexican Graphic Design: The Case of Ignacio Cumplido," *Design Issues* 18, no. 4 (2002): 59–63, https://www.jstor.org/stable/1511979.

44 Nile Green, *Terrains of Exchange: Religious Economies of Global Islam* (Oxford University Press, 2015), 100.

45 Arabic type was cast in Europe as early as 1514, and increased missionary activity inspired type production in London during the early nineteenth century, with the Figgins foundry in particular known for its "exotic" types. Nile Green, "Persian Print and the Stanhope Revolution: Industrialization, Evangelicalism, and the Birth of Printing in Early Qajar Iran," *Comparative Studies of South Asia, Africa and the Middle East* 30, no. 3 (2010 2010): 478–80, https://www.muse.jhu.edu/article/430311.

46 Hala Auji, *Printing Arab Modernity: Book Culture and The American Press in Nineteenth-Century Beirut* (Leiden: Brill, 2016), 111–15.

47 Nile Mission Press, *Blessed Be Egypt: A Challenge to Faith for the Mohammedan World.* (London & New York: Nile Mission Press, Partridge, and Revell Co., 1906), 94, http://archive.org/details/blessedbeegypta00palegoog.

48 David D. Grafton, *The Contested Origins of the 1865 Arabic Bible: Contributions to the Nineteenth Century Nahda, The Contested Origins of the 1865 Arabic Bible* (Leiden: Brill, 2015), 231, https://brill.com/view/title/32470.

49 American Mission Press, *Barnāmaj Al-Matba'at al-Amīrikānīyah / Illustrated Catalogue and Price List of Publications of the American Mission Press, Beirut* (Beirut: American Mission Press, 1887), http://www.dlir.org/archive/items/show/11122.

50 Auji, *Printing Arab Modernity*, 111–15.

51 Auji, 111–15.

52 American Mission Press, *Illustrated Catalogue of the A.M.P.*, n.p.

53 American Mission Press, *Illustrated Catalogue and Price List of Publications of the American Mission Press, Beirut, Syria* (Beirut: American Mission Press, 1896), http://archive.org/details/illustratedcata00missgoog.

54 [Printer's Circular], "Typography in Japan," *Printers' Circular* 10:5 (July 1 1875): 130.

55 Andrew T. Kamei-Dyche, "The History of Books and Print Culture in Japan: The State of the Discipline," *Book History* 14 (2011): 272–77, https://www.jstor.org/stable/41306539.

56 Insetsu-Kyoku, *Katsuji Mon'yō Mihon [Specimens of Printing Types and Ornaments Cast at the Insetsu-Kioku]* (Tokyo: Insetsu-Kyoku [Imperial Printing Office], 1885), 24–30, 78, http://hdl.handle.net/2027/nnc1.cu13207504.

57 [Typo], "Type Specimens," *Typo* 8, no. 86 (February 1894): 9.

58 D.J. Huppatz, "Globalizing Design History and Global Design History," *Journal of Design History* 28, no. 2 (2015): 182–202, https://doi.org/10.1093/jdh/epv002.

59 Peter Kornicki, *The Book in Japan: A Cultural History from the Beginnings to the Nineteenth Century* (Honolulu: University of Hawaii Press, 2001), 163–65.

60 Edward Mack, *Manufacturing Modern Japanese Literature: Publishing, Prizes, and the Ascription of Literary Value* (Duke University Press, 2010), 21-22.

61 Yoshimi Orii, "The Dispersion of Jesuit Books Printed in Japan: Trends in Bibliographical Research and in Intellectual History," *Journal of Jesuit Studies* 2, no. 2 (April 9, 2015): 125–29, https://doi.org/10.1163/22141332-00202002..

62 Kornicki, *The Book in Japan*, 163–65

63 S. Magata, "Motogi Nagabisa: The First Japanese Printer," *The British Bookmaker* 7, no. 75 (1894): 53-56, https://books.google.com/ books?id=aaA3AQAAMAAJ&dq=tsukiji+type+foundry&source=gbs_navlinks_s.

64 Phillip Johnson, "The Japanese Gutenberg," *The Book Lover: A Magazine of Book Lore* 2, no. 9 (December 1901): 390, https://www.google.com/books/edition/_/jaA5AQAAMAAJ?hl=en&gbpv=0.

65 Mack, *Manufacturing Modern Japanese Literature*, 318–24; Brian Burke-Gaffney, "Information and International Exchange in Meiji-Period Nagasaki," *Journal of Socio-Informatics* 4, no. 1 (2011): 27, http://www.ssi.or.jp/eng/pdf/Vol4No1.pdf; Nathan Shockey, *The Typographic Imagination: Reading and Writing in Japan's Age of Modern Print Media* (Columbia University Press, 2019).

66 Japanese Central Association, *An Itinerary of Hokkaido, Japan* (Tokyo: Hakodate Chamber of Commerce, 1893), 41, https://archive.org/details/itineraryofhokka00batc.

67 Tsukiji Type Foundry, "Tsukiji Type Foundry Ad," *Kokka: The Illustrated Monthly Journal of the Fine and Applied Arts of Japan* 26, no. 304 (1915): 81.

68 Inland Type Foundry, "Specimens," *The Inland Printer* 39, no. 1 (April 1907): 91.

69 Gennifer Weisenfeld, "Japanese Typographic Design and the Art of Letterforms," in *Bridges to Heaven: Essays on East Asian Art in Honor of Professor Wen C. Fong*, ed. Wen Fong and Jerome Silbergeld, vol. 2 (Princeton, N.J.: Princeton University Press, 2011), 827–48.

70 Palmer & Rey, *Third Revised Specimen Book and Price List of Printing Material* (San Francisco: Palmer & Rey, 1887), 23, https://archive.org/details/thirdrevisedspec00palmrich.

71 Inland Type Foundry, "Typographic Progress in Australia," *Inland Printer* 23, no. 4 (July 1899): 451-52.

72 ["Africander"], "[Letter to the Editor]," *Australasian Typographical Journal* 25 (July 1894): 2476.

73 Johnson Witehira, "Mana Mattauhi: A Survey of Maori Engagement with the Written and Printed Word during the 19th Century," *Visible Language* 5, no. 1 (April 2019): 76-109, http://www.visiblelanguagejournal.com/issue/292.

74 Jonty Valentine, *Printing Types: New Zealand Type Design since 1870* (Auckland [N.Z.]: Objectspace Gallery, 2009), 7.

75 Dennis Bryans, *A Survey of Australian Typefounders' Specimens* (Blackburn [Australia]: Golden Point Press, 2014), 3, 53-54; Dennis Bryans, "The Beginnings of Type Founding in Sydney: Alexander Thompson's Type, His Foundry, and His Exports to Inter-Colonial Printers," *Journal of Design History* 9, no. 2 (April 1996): 83-84, https://doi.org/10.1093/jdh/9.2.75.

76 F.T. Wimble & Co, *New and Second-Hand Printing Type, Material and Machinery* (Melbourne, Australia: F.T. Wimble & Co., 1900), https://nla.gov.au/nla.obj-52845999.

77 Bryans, *A Survey of Australian Typefounders' Specimens*, 32.

***Die Hauptprobe*, D. Stempel, c.1920**

As Art Nouveau swept across Europe and North America during the last decade of the nineteenth century and the first decade of the twentieth, Germany developed its own localized response to the French style—Jugendstil, or *youth style*. Flat fields of color, strong black outlines, and geometric simplification joined the sinuous lines, natural motifs, and beautiful young women of French Art Nouveau. Stylistic differences, while more noticable in pictorial illustration, made their way into typographic design as well. F. Schweimanns designed the Jugendstil script face Moderne Reklame for Stempel in 1901, and the blackletter Frankfurt Series in 1905. *Reihen-Einfassungen* means *ornament*; notice, here, the ways in which Stempel suggests blending historically-rooted and entirely modern styles.

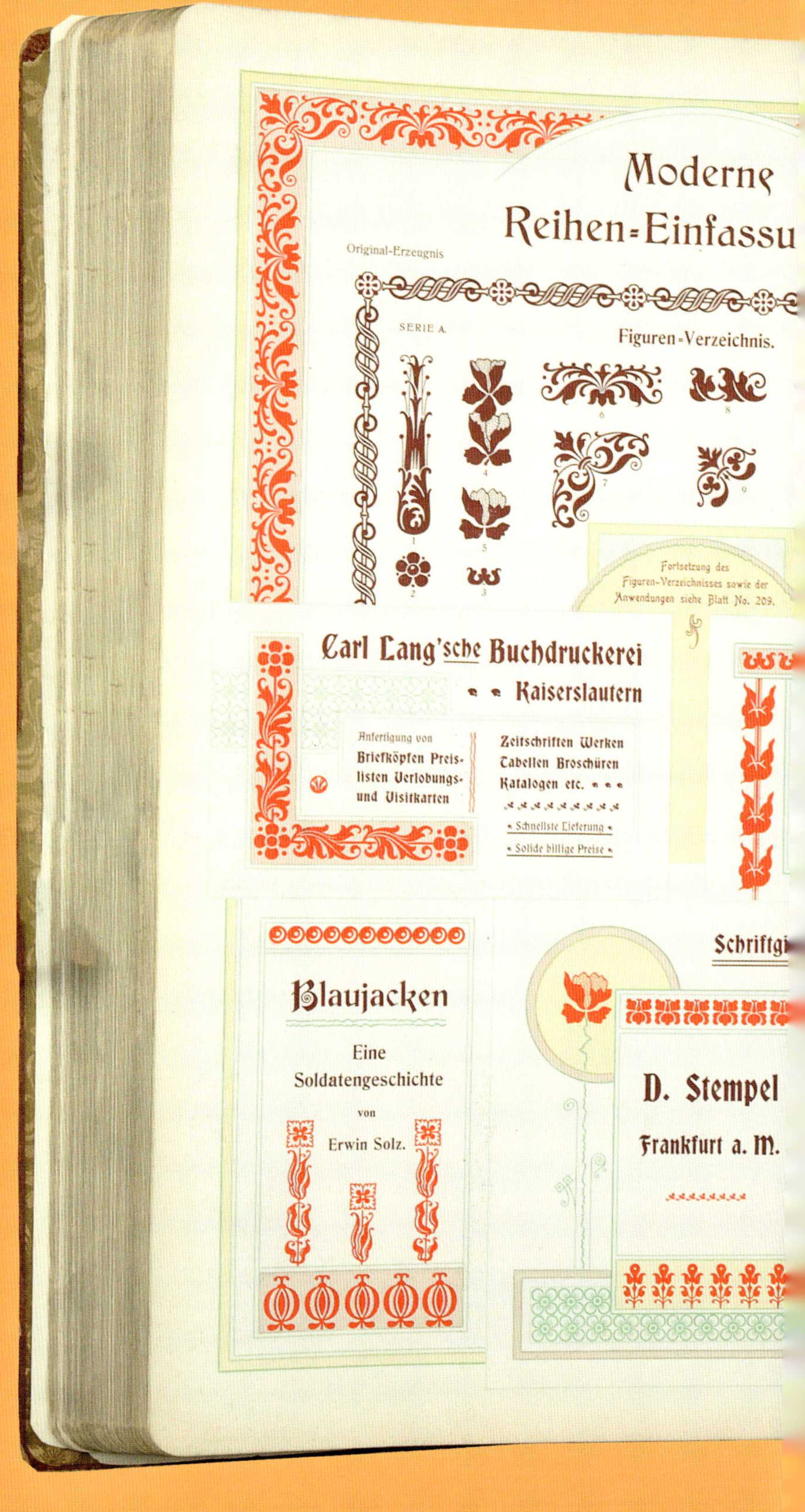

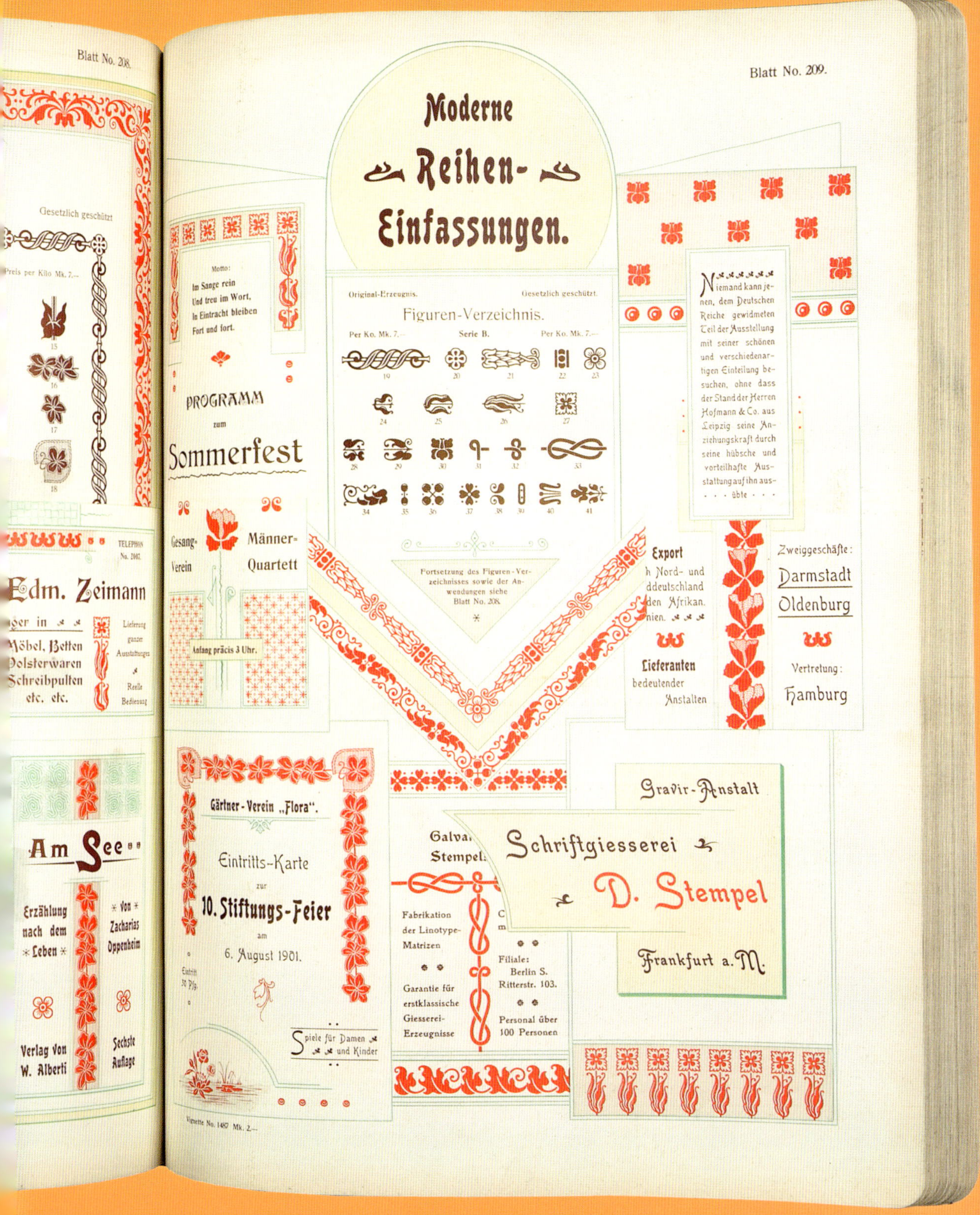
Blatt No. 208.
Gesetzlich geschützt
Edm. Zeimann
Am See
Blatt No. 209.
Moderne Reihen-Einfassungen.
Original-Erzeugnis.
Gesetzlich geschützt.
Figuren-Verzeichnis.
Serie B.
Motto:
Im Sange rein
Und treu im Wort,
In Eintracht bleiben
Fort und fort.
PROGRAMM
zum
Sommerfest
Gesang-Verein
Männer-Quartett
Anfang präcis 3 Uhr.
Niemand kann jenen, dem Deutschen Reiche gewidmeten Teil der Ausstellung mit seiner schönen und verschiedenartigen Einteilung besuchen, ohne dass der Stand der Herren Hofmann & Co. aus Leipzig seine Anziehungskraft durch seine hübsche und vorteilhafte Ausstattung auf ihn ausübte
Fortsetzung des Figuren-Verzeichnisses sowie der Anwendungen siehe Blatt No. 208.
Export
Lieferanten
bedeutender
Anstalten
Zweiggeschäfte:
Darmstadt
Oldenburg
Vertretung:
Hamburg
Gärtner-Verein „Flora".
Eintritts-Karte
zur
10. Stiftungs-Feier
am
6. August 1901.
Spiele für Damen und Kinder
Fabrikation der Linotype-Matrizen
Garantie für erstklassische Giesserei-Erzeugnisse
Filiale:
Berlin S.
Ritterstr. 103.
Personal über 100 Personen
Gravir-Anstalt
Schriftgiesserei
D. Stempel
Frankfurt a. M.

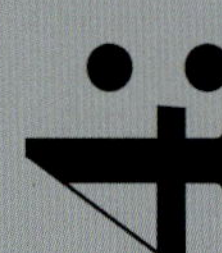

4: INDUSTRIAL METHODS AND MATERIALS

Specimen Book & Catalog, ATF, 1923

American Type Founders (ATF) formed as a corporate trust of 23 of the United States' most notable type foundries in 1892, and continued to grow thereafter. With inventor and type designer Linn Boyd Benton as its first director, ATF reshaped the landscape of foundry type. It popularized the notion of the type family—among many other now-commonplace concepts. With a shared design sensibility at its core, a *type family* offers multiple sizes, weights, and styles; today's superfamilies often offer related serif, sans serif, and slab faces. When the almost 2-pound 1923 ATF specimen debuted, though, suggesting appropriate combinations of sans, slab, and serif faces was more common. Coordinating ornament, like these Della Robbia Initials, played an important role in ATF's corporate programme.

Della Robbia Initials

48 Point

Two colors, p
One color, p

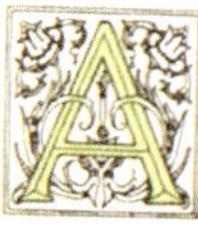

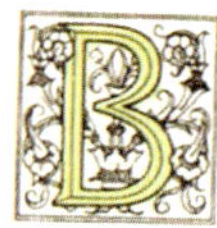

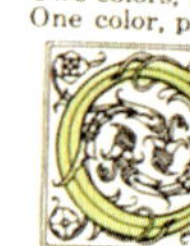

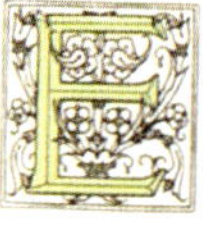

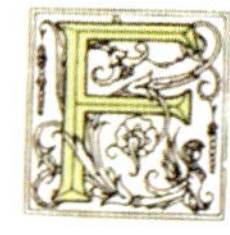

12 Line Two colors, per letter $1 20 One color,

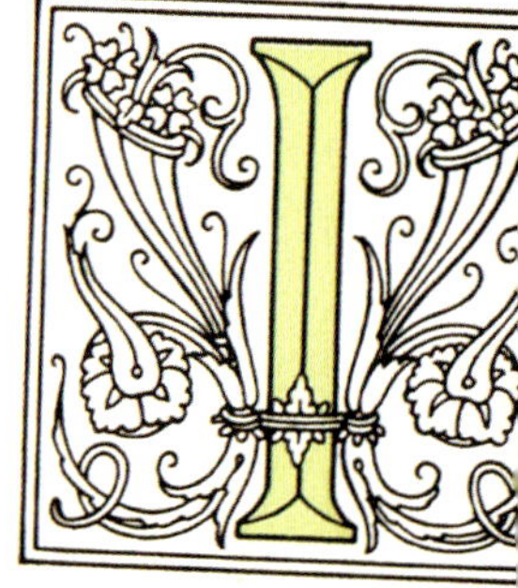

72 Point

Two colors, pe
One color, per

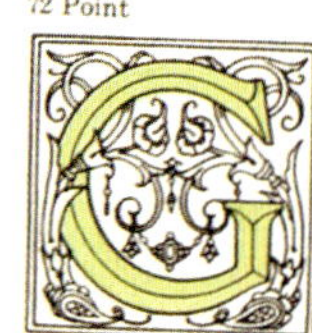

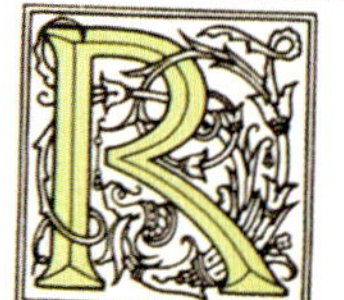

9 Line

Two colors, per letter $1 00

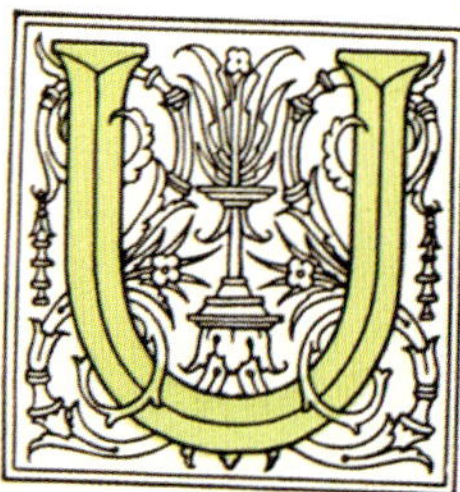

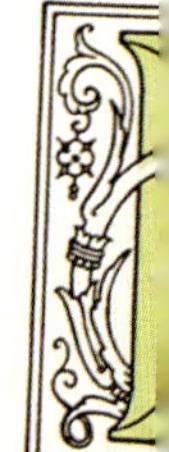

The 48 and 72 Point sizes are cast in type mould. All the
may be obtained in all the sizes

828b

per font $5 00
per font $2 50

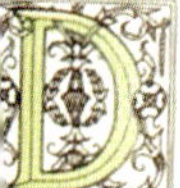

r font $9 00
r font $4 50

etter $0 50

lphabet

Della Robbia Initials—Continued

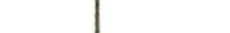

48 Point

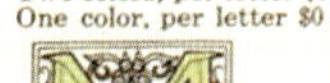

Two colors, per letter $0 40, per font $5 00
One color, per letter $0 20, per font $2 50

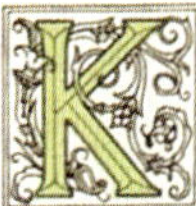 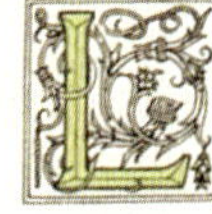  

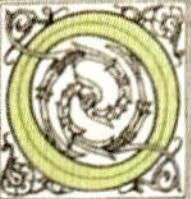 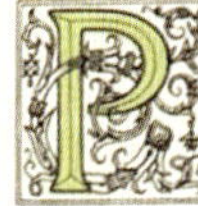  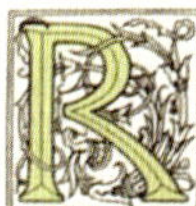

12 Line Two colors, per letter $1 20 One color, per letter $0 60

72 Point

Two colors, per letter $0 50, per font $9 00
One color, per letter $0 25, per font $4 50

 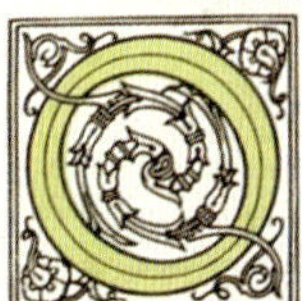 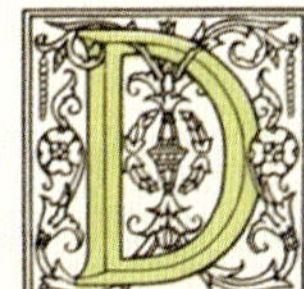

9 Line Two colors, per letter $1 00 One color, per letter $0 50

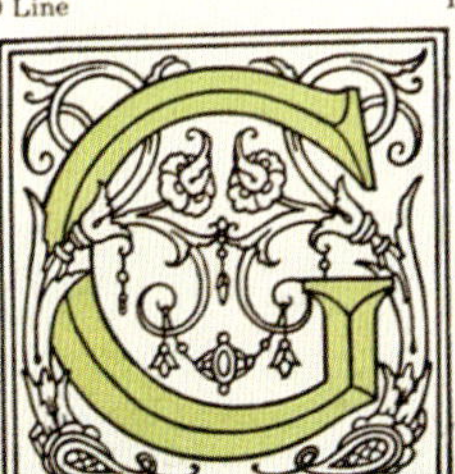 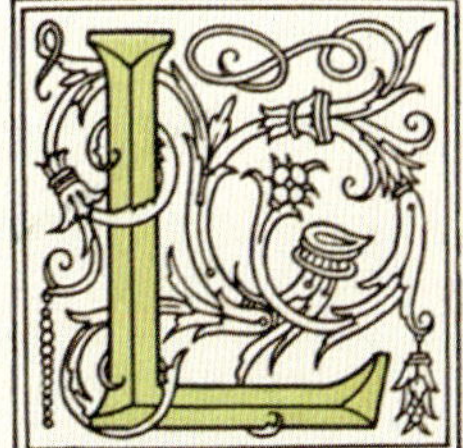

The 48 and 72 Point sizes are cast in type mould. All the letters of the alphabet may be obtained in all the sizes

828c

SPECIMENS
OF
Vanderburgh, Wells & Co's
WOOD TYPE
BORDERS, RULES, &c.
Manufactured at
110 FULTON, 16 & 18 DUTCH Sts.
NEW-YORK.
1872.

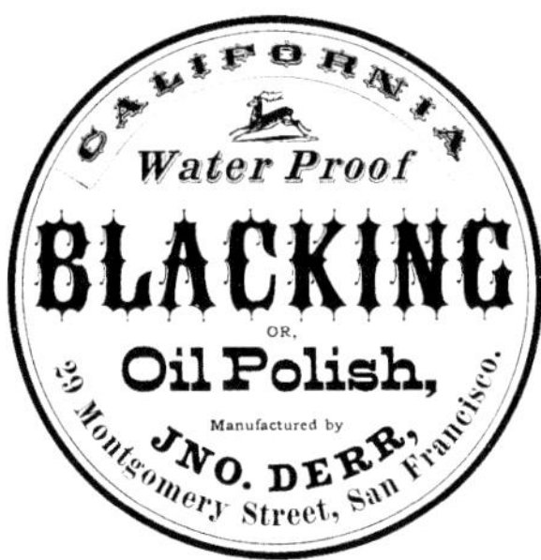

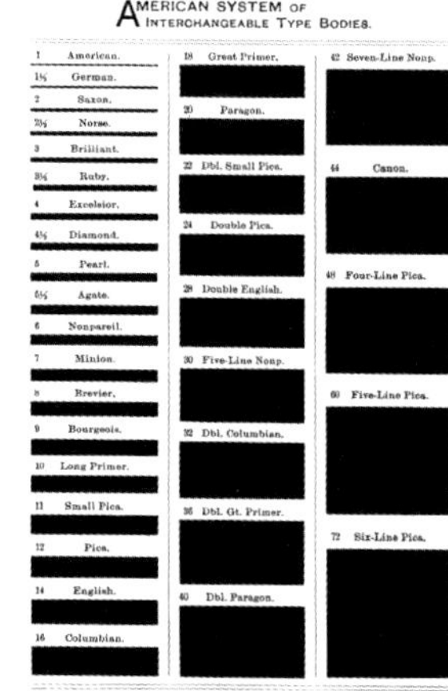
172 MARDER, LUSE & CO.

AMERICAN SYSTEM OF INTERCHANGEABLE TYPE BODIES.

1 American.	18 Great Primer.	42 Seven-Line Nonp.
1½ German.	20 Paragon.	44 Canon.
2 Saxon.	22 Dbl. Small Pica.	48 Four-Line Pica.
2½ Norse.	24 Double Pica.	60 Five-Line Pica.
3 Brilliant.	28 Double English.	72 Six-Line Pica.
3½ Ruby.	30 Five-Line Nonp.	
4 Excelsior.	32 Dbl. Columbian.	
4½ Diamond.	36 Dbl. Gt. Primer.	
5 Pearl.	40 Dbl. Paragon.	
5½ Agate.		
6 Nonpareil.		
7 Minion.		
8 Brevier.		
9 Bourgeois.		
10 Long Primer.		
11 Small Pica.		
12 Pica.		
14 English.		
16 Columbian.		

OR POINT SYSTEM.

12 POINT Unit of measure, 7 to Pica 25 A 38 a

THIS SERIES of Old Style Bold was cut after many inquiries for a Job Face that could be used with Self Spacing to emphasize certain words. All sizes shown on this page will line and justify with the corresponding sizes of our Old Style Self Spacing Series. Repeated experiments with

1827 — USA

Mass-produced wood type first marketed, thanks to Darius Wells' lateral router.

1837 — England

Queen Victoria takes the throne; what we now call Victorian typography is officially underway.

1883 — USA

Linn Boyd Benton introduces self-spacing type.

1890 — USA

American Point System est. by Chicago foundry Marder & Luse.

1814 — England

Steam-powered cylinder printing press, built by Koenig & Bauer, installed at the Times in London.

1820 — USA

Washington press invented.

1826 — USA

Daniel Fanshaw, the first "production printer of the machine age," uses Treadwell presses to fill contracts for the American Bible Society.

1838 — Russia

Moritz von Jacobi invents electrotyping (metal printing plates made via chemicals and electricity).

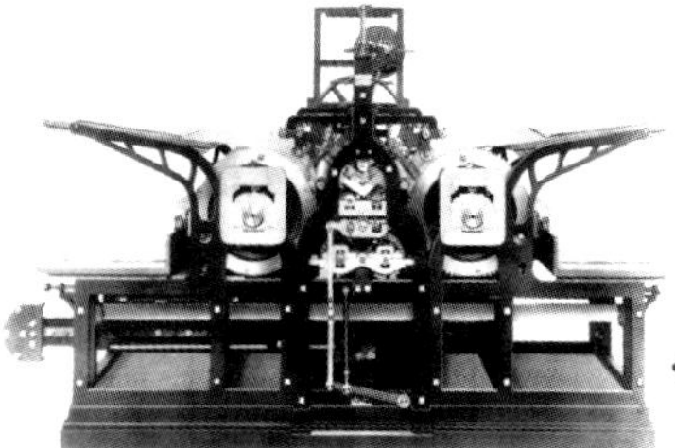

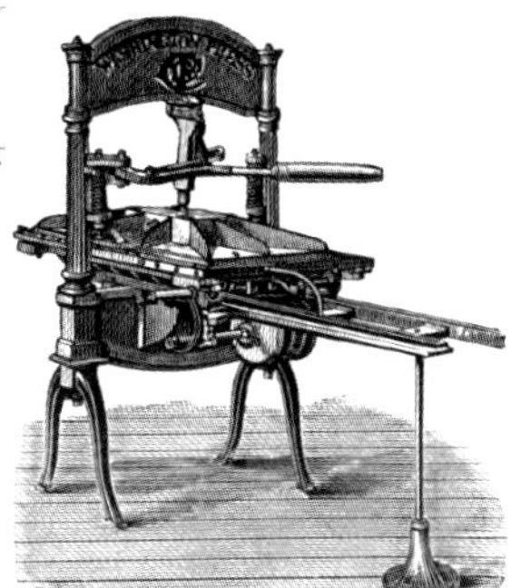

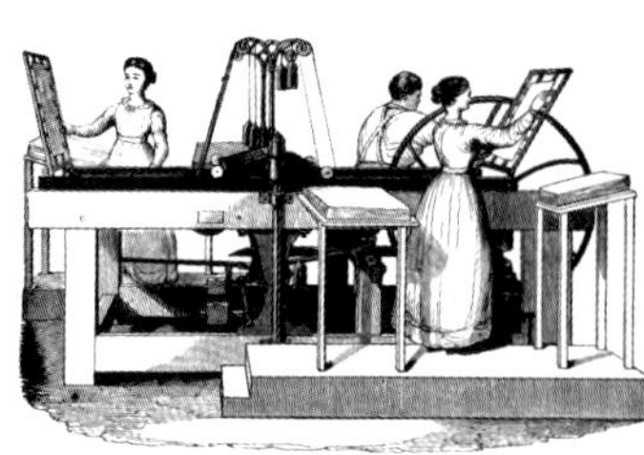

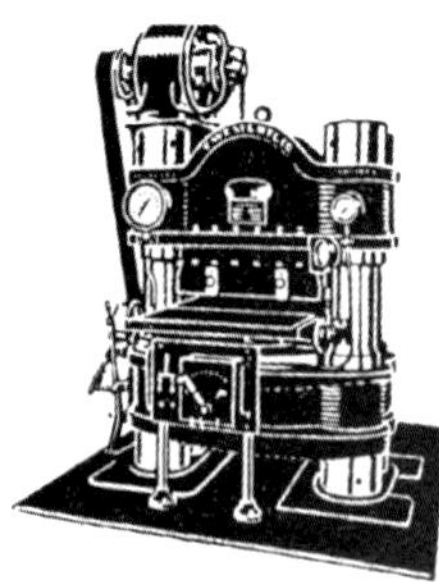

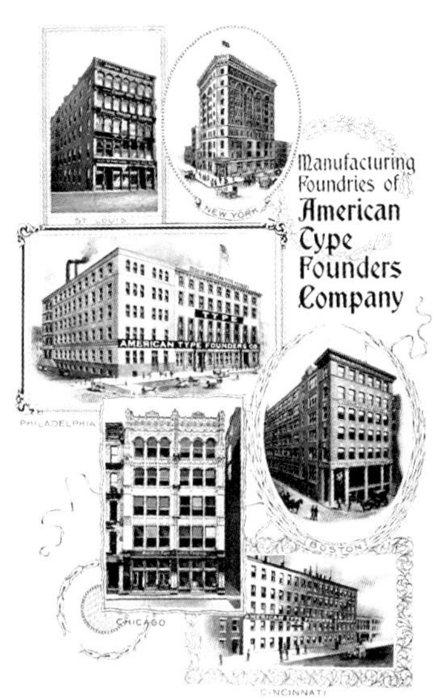

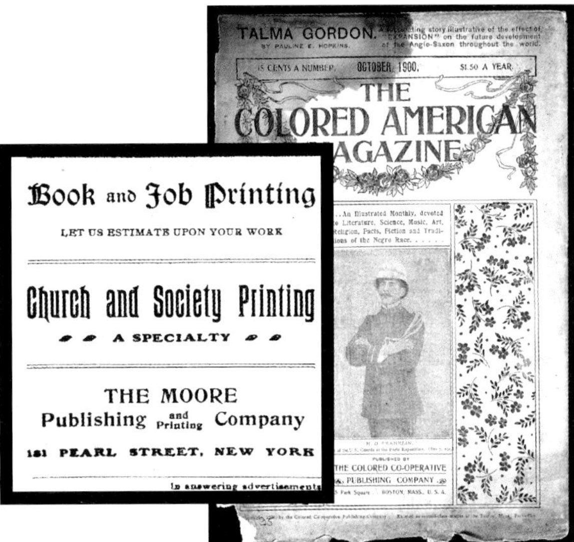

The Parsons Family

With the Parsons types a great many pleasing results may be obtained. The long characters, with swash initials and initial decorators, afford the printer a varied range of display. When using long ascenders or descenders it is advised not to use more than two in any line of display. They should never be used double except where the long strokes come close together and at no time should ascenders or descenders be used for one of a double-letter combination

American Type Founders Company

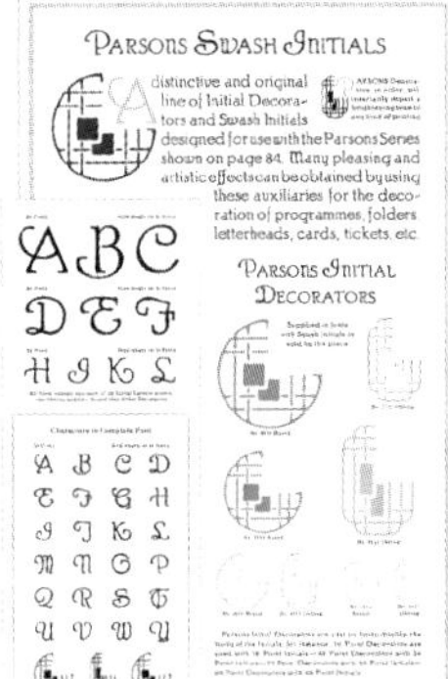

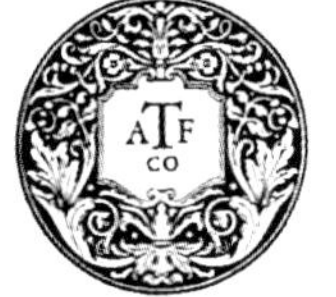

GRAND STANDARD LINE
BEST SYSTEM OF LINING TYPE

1892 — USA

American Type Founders (ATF) forms as a corporate trust of about 85% of the USA's foundries.

1895 — USA

Inland Type Foundry of St. Louis introduces the Standard American Line.

1900 — USA

Colored Co-operative of Boston launches *Colored American* magazine; Black-owned New York business Moore Publishing & Printing assumes control in 1907.

1906 — USA

ATF's new catalog emphasizes the importance of type families.

1838 — USA

First successful type-casting machine, the pivotal typecaster, patented by type founder David Bruce.

1843 — USA

Richard Hoe invents double-cylinder rotary press.

1851 — USA

George Gordon develops platen job press.

1903 — USA

Sextuple press prints 48,000 sheets/hr; each sheet fits up to 12 pages, two can print in two colors.

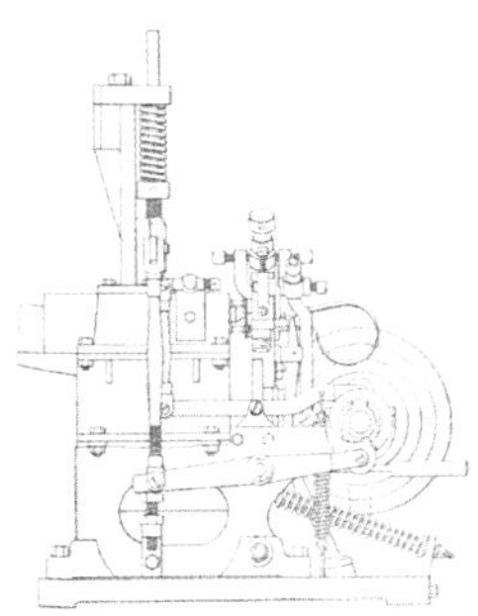

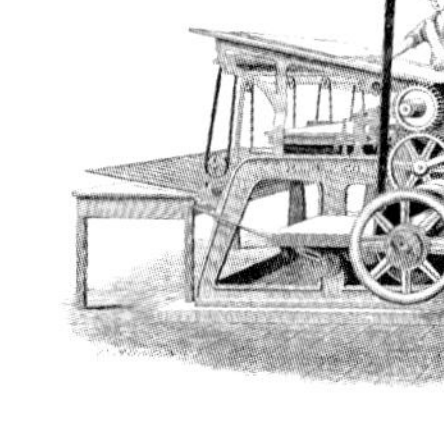

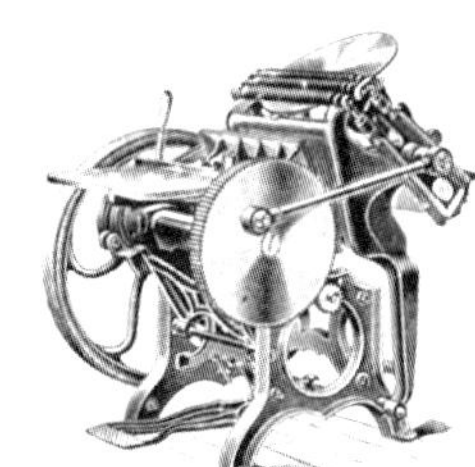

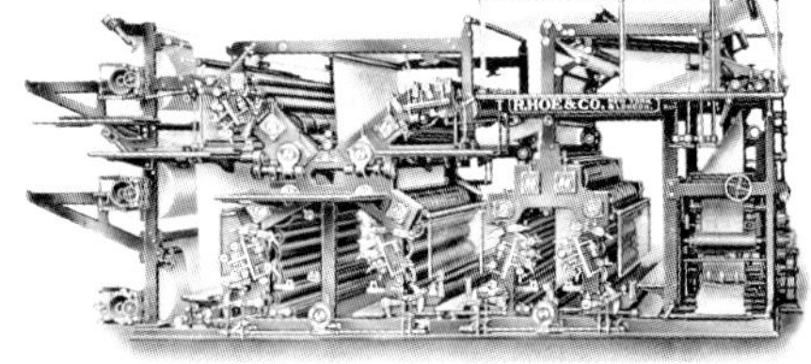

The nineteenth century witnessed significant changes in the form and function of the printing press. Charles Mahon, Earl Stanhope introduced the iron **handpress** in 1800; it increased the geographical range of printing, because it was much smaller, lighter, and sturdier than the screw press, and therefore easier and cheaper to ship.[1] 1814 saw the first newspaper printed on Friedrich Koenig's steam-powered **double-cylinder press**, exponentially increasing printing speed and decreasing cost. These and other developments streamlined *printing*, but casting and setting type remained labor-intensive, leading to experimentation in the *typographic* aspects of the printing process. Eventually, these efforts would result in "hot metal type," the Linotype and Monotype machines first patented in 1884 and 1885, respectively. Hot-metal automation, though, represented only one aspect of late nineteenth and early twentieth century innovation in type-founding. Period specimens promoted new materials, technological innovations, and increasing systemization. Often, foundries designed specimens as teaching tools, guiding printers as they navigated a changing professional environment. Elaborate displays and explanatory texts offered technical and aesthetic advice for printers seeking to economize, expand, and prosper.

Tools for economizing

Nineteenth century trade journals reflected a persistent interest in increased efficiency, measured in saving both time and money. Mechanization offered the obvious solution for economizing typography, though not all typesetters embraced the possibility, as machines stood to replace their jobs. But while the difficult journey toward mechanization took place, inventors and practitioners proposed other economizing strategies. These enjoyed varying levels of success, though few lasted long. Some typographic specimens constructed their entire visual language around the alterations they proposed, while others mentioned the key features of their new products or systems only incidentally.

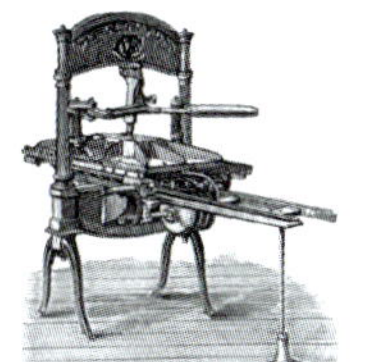

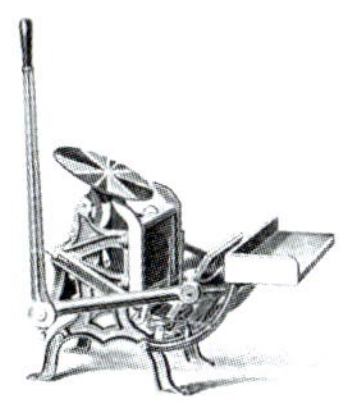

The iron **handpress** operated via a series of levers and required only 10% of the force used to operate a wooden screw press like Gutenberg's. Sturdier and simplier, iron handpresses—introduced in 1899 by Charles Mahon, Earl Stanhope—revolutionized printing and significantly increased its geographic spread. A handpress might be large (Washington press, 1893, left) or small (handlever press, 1903, right).

Saving time, materials, and money

For printers, time had long equaled money. Benton's Self-Spacing Type, introduced in 1883, proposed saving time through the use of a short-lived product designed to simplify justifying lines of type by hand [Fig. 4.1]. Sample copy in an 1886 Benton's specimen lamented "so little progress in four centuries," with "no development" in typesetting to match improvements in the "slow, laborious hand presses of half a century ago." Ads explained how Benton's type imposed a system with only nine possible body widths for any given character, instead of the average 190. A too-short line of type "must lack one or more [of nine] exact units," so filling the empty space was quicker and easier.[2] Throughout the specimen, the compositional simplicity of a single column of fully justified text directed focus to the type's purpose. Annotations included point sizes and traditional descriptive names (e.g., 10-point [Long Primer] Self Spacing No. 17½) and the unit measure according to Benton's system (10-point [Long Primer] is 8 units per **pica**). This reflected the mathematical system governing the type's design, as each of the nine character widths was evenly divisible by a unit into a pica **em**.

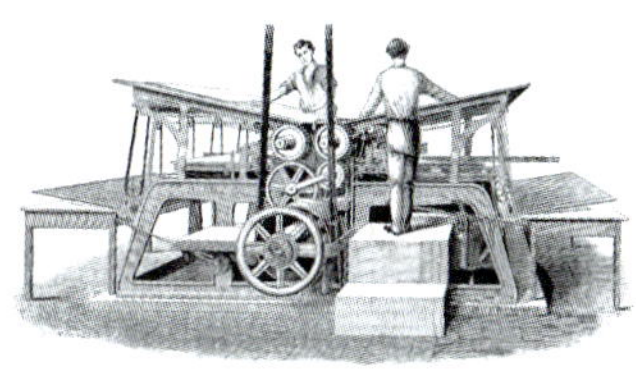

The **double-cylinder press** doubled the number of sheets which could be printed per hour when the first steam-powered model was put into commercial use at the London Times in 1814.

Fig 4.1 (below)

***Benton's Self-spacing Type* (Milwaukee, Linn Boyd Benton, 1886). By making all sorts (individual pieces of metal type) one of only nine standard widths, Benton's time-saving system was intended to speed the process of typesetting.**

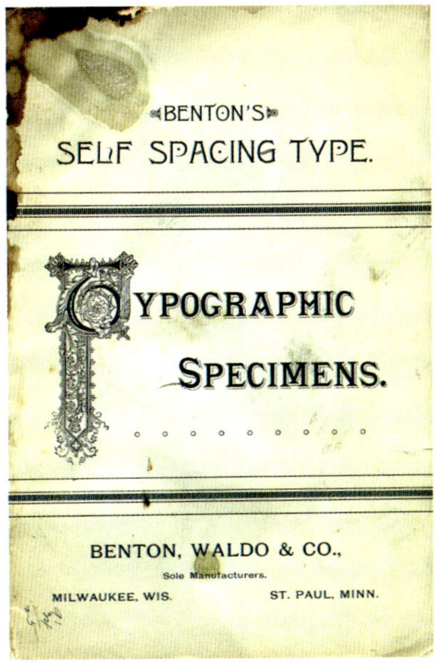

BENTON'S

SELF SPACING TYPE.

TYPOGRAPHIC SPECIMENS.

BENTON, WALDO & CO.,

Sole Manufacturers.

MILWAUKEE, WIS. ST. PAUL, MINN.

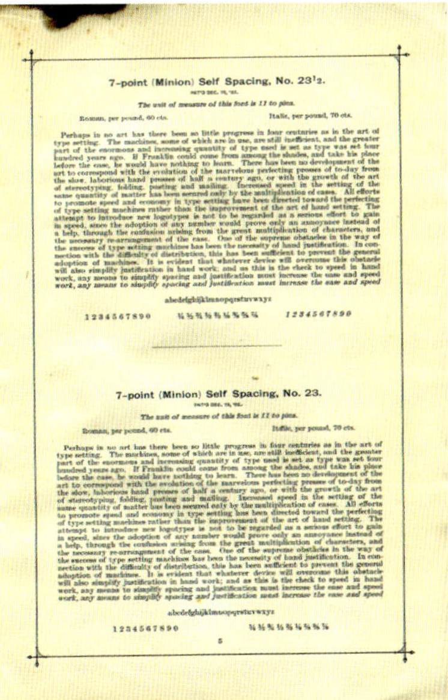

7-point (Minion) Self Spacing, No. 23½.

The unit of measure of this font is 11 to pica.

Roman, per pound, 60 cts. Italic, per pound, 70 cts.

Perhaps in no art has there been so little progress in four centuries as in the art of type setting. The machines, some of which are in use, are still inefficient, and the greater part of the enormous and increasing quantity of type used is set as type was set four hundred years ago. If Franklin could come from among the shades, and take his place before the case, he would have nothing to learn. There has been no development of the art to correspond with the evolution of the marvelous perfecting presses of to-day from the slow, laborious hand presses of half a century ago, or with the growth of the art of stereotyping, folding, pasting and mailing. Increased speed in the setting of the same quantity of matter has been secured only by the multiplication of cases. All efforts to promote speed and economy in type setting have been directed toward the perfecting of type setting machines rather than the improvement of the art of hand setting. The attempt to introduce new logotypes is not to be regarded as a serious effort to gain in speed, since the adoption of any number would prove only an annoyance instead of a help, through the confusion arising from the great multiplication of characters, and the necessary re-arrangement of the case. One of the supreme obstacles in the way of the success of type setting machines has been the necessity of hand justification. In connection with the difficulty of distribution, this has been sufficient to prevent the general adoption of machines. It is evident that whatever device will overcome this obstacle will also simplify justification in hand work; and as this is the check to speed in hand work, any means to simplify spacing and justification must increase the ease and speed *work, any means to simplify spacing and justification must increase the ease and speed*

abcdefghijklmnopqrstuvwxyz

1234567890 *1234567890*

7-point (Minion) Self Spacing, No. 23.

The unit of measure of this font is 11 to pica.

Roman, per pound, 60 cts. Italic, per pound, 70 cts.

Perhaps in no art has there been so little progress in four centuries as in the art of type setting. The machines, some of which are in use, are still inefficient, and the greater part of the enormous and increasing quantity of type used is set as type was set four hundred years ago. If Franklin could come from among the shades, and take his place before the case, he would have nothing to learn. There has been no development of the art to correspond with the evolution of the marvelous perfecting presses of to-day from the slow, laborious hand presses of half a century ago, or with the growth of the art of stereotyping, folding, pasting and mailing. Increased speed in the setting of the same quantity of matter has been secured only by the multiplication of cases. All efforts to promote speed and economy in type setting have been directed toward the perfecting of type setting machines rather than the improvement of the art of hand setting. The attempt to introduce new logotypes is not to be regarded as a serious effort to gain in speed, since the adoption of any number would prove only an annoyance instead of a help, through the confusion arising from the great multiplication of characters, and the necessary re-arrangement of the case. One of the supreme obstacles in the way of the success of type setting machines has been the necessity of hand justification. In connection with the difficulty of distribution, this has been sufficient to prevent the general adoption of machines. It is evident that whatever device will overcome this obstacle will also simplify justification in hand work; and as this is the check to speed in hand work, any means to simplify spacing and justification must increase the ease and speed *work, any means to simplify spacing and justification must increase the ease and speed*

abcdefghijklmnopqrstuvwxyz

1234567890

5

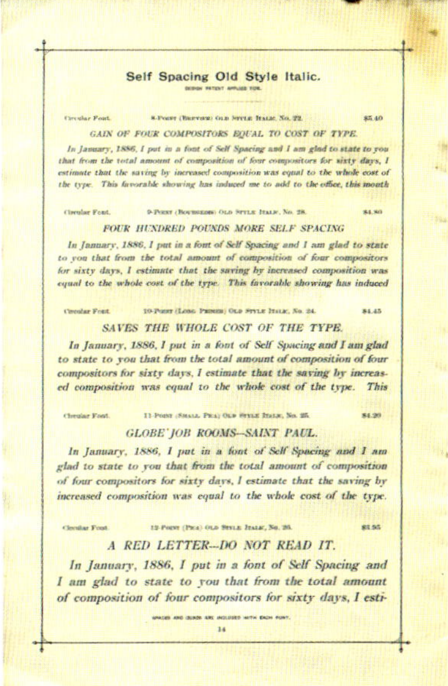

Self Spacing Old Style Italic.

GAIN OF FOUR COMPOSITORS EQUAL TO COST OF TYPE.

In January, 1886, I put in a font of Self Spacing and I am glad to state to you that from the total amount of composition of four compositors for sixty days, I estimate that the saving by increased composition was equal to the whole cost of the type. This favorable showing has induced me to add to the office, this month

FOUR HUNDRED POUNDS MORE SELF SPACING

In January, 1886, I put in a font of Self Spacing and I am glad to state to you that from the total amount of composition of four compositors for sixty days, I estimate that the saving by increased composition was equal to the whole cost of the type. This favorable showing has induced

SAVES THE WHOLE COST OF THE TYPE.

In January, 1886, I put in a font of Self Spacing and I am glad to state to you that from the total amount of composition of four compositors for sixty days, I estimate that the saving by increased composition was equal to the whole cost of the type. This

GLOBE JOB ROOMS—SAINT PAUL.

In January, 1886, I put in a font of Self Spacing and I am glad to state to you that from the total amount of composition of four compositors for sixty days, I estimate that the saving by increased composition was equal to the whole cost of the type.

A RED LETTER—DO NOT READ IT.

In January, 1886, I put in a font of Self Spacing and I am glad to state to you that from the total amount of composition of four compositors for sixty days, I esti-

14

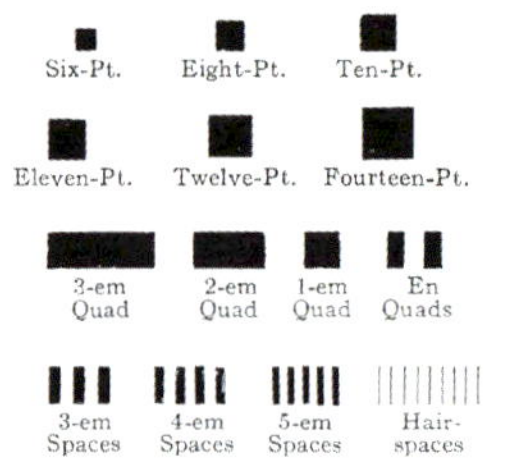

An **em quad** is a unit of measure for typographic spacing equal to the point size of the type in both width and height; a 72-point em quad is 72 points square. Quads, like furniture, don't print.

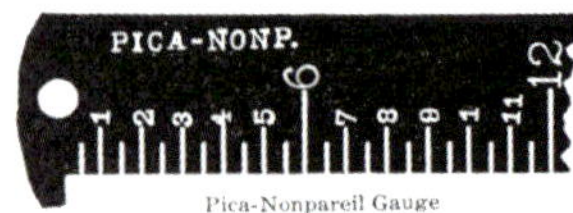

The **pica** is a unit of typographic measurement equal to 12 points or ⅙ inch. Pica rulers or gauges like this one were sometimes called pica poles. The traditional name for 6-point type was nonpareil.

A change in type, to multi-sized italic, signified customer endorsements. After purchasing a font of self-spacing type, the *Globe* of St. Paul, Minnesota, reported that over sixty days, four compositors sped up their work, and "the saving by increased composition was equal to the whole cost of the type." Benton devised his system around the pica because it was the unit of measure for newspaper column widths, and quoting the *Globe* situated Benton's product in its desired environment. The facing page showed a "specimen of table work" with price lists and a railway timetable, further demonstrating how Self-Spacing Type sped up the multiple kinds of typesetting required by a newspaper. The final page described the type's "superiority," claiming that Benton had "made *more* and *greater* improvements in type and type making, in the past four years, than all the type founders of the United States combined, during a period of fifty years."[3] Given that the Linotype had been patented two years before, in 1884, this overstated matters. Ingenious though Benton's self-spacing type may have been as a time-saving economy, it was short-lived, rendered obsolete by mechanical typesetting.

Durability presented another economical roadblock, soon to be extinct. Repeated use and user error damaged metal type, knocking off delicate serifs or squishing the type (making it too short) by applying too much pressure during printing. Type metal mixtures varied among foundries, and founders often claimed their own proprietary **alloy** outperformed all others. In 1885-6, Miller & Richard of Edinburgh innovatively added copper to the traditional mix of lead, tin, and antimony. They subsequently supplied type for the London *Times*, an accomplishment they attributed to this change. Other foundries followed, seeking type metal that was both stronger and lighter. Type's relative strength and durability sparked lively discussion among printers. In 1874, the *Typographic Messenger* reported that recent claims that "American type is as soft as pewter" were entirely false and probably made by someone who "came over with the last importation of type" and had "never set a type in his

Fig 4.2 (below)

***Abridged Specimen Book* (Keystone Type Foundry, Philadelphia, 1906). Keystone promised that its nickel alloy type metal mixture was durable and therefore cost effective.**

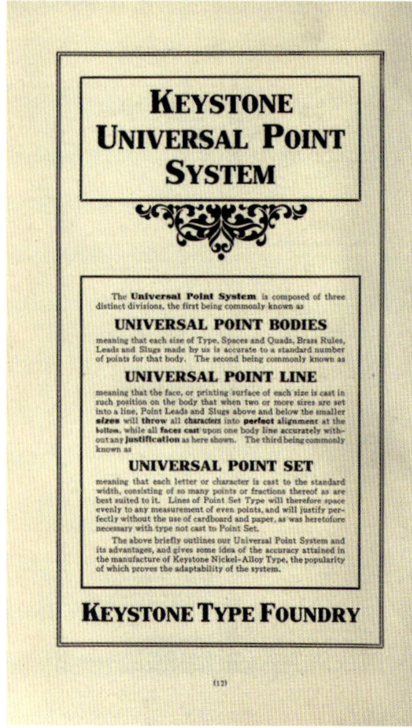
KEYSTONE UNIVERSAL POINT SYSTEM

The **Universal Point System** is composed of three distinct divisions, the first being commonly known as

UNIVERSAL POINT BODIES

meaning that each size of Type, Spaces and Quads, Brass Rules, Leads and Slugs made by us is accurate to a standard number of points for that body. The second being commonly known as

UNIVERSAL POINT LINE

meaning that the face, or printing surface of each size is cast in such position on the body that when two or more sizes are set into a line, Point Leads and Slugs above and below the smaller **sizes** will **throw** all **characters** into **perfect alignment** at the **bottom**, while all **faces cast** upon one body line accurately without any **justification** as here shown. The third being commonly known as

UNIVERSAL POINT SET

meaning that each letter or character is cast to the standard width, consisting of so many points or fractions thereof as are best suited to it. Lines of Point Set Type will therefore space evenly to any measurement of even points, and will justify perfectly without the use of cardboard and paper, as was heretofore necessary with type not cast to Point Set.

The above briefly outlines our Universal Point System and its advantages, and gives some idea of the accuracy attained in the manufacture of Keystone Nickel-Alloy Type, the popularity of which proves the adaptability of the system.

KEYSTONE TYPE FOUNDRY

(12)

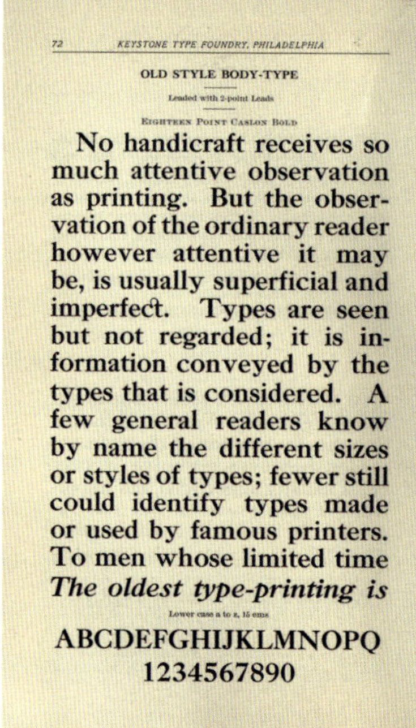
72 KEYSTONE TYPE FOUNDRY, PHILADELPHIA

OLD STYLE BODY-TYPE

Leaded with 2-point Leads

EIGHTEEN POINT CASLON BOLD

No handicraft receives so much attentive observation as printing. But the observation of the ordinary reader however attentive it may be, is usually superficial and imperfect. Types are seen but not regarded; it is information conveyed by the types that is considered. A few general readers know by name the different sizes or styles of types; fewer still could identify types made or used by famous printers. To men whose limited time *The oldest type-printing is*

Lower case a to z, 15 ems

ABCDEFGHIJKLMNOPQ

1234567890

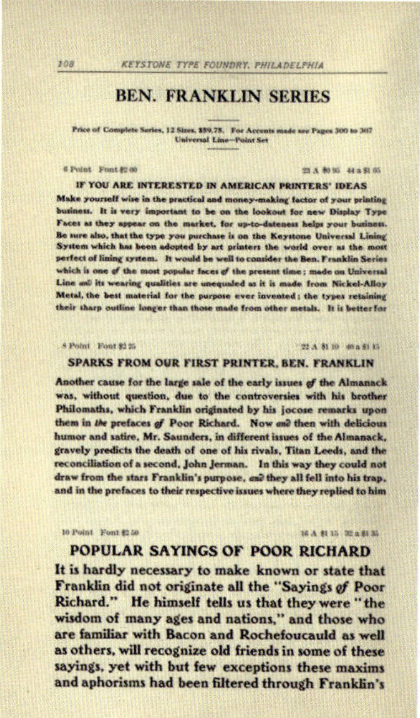
108 KEYSTONE TYPE FOUNDRY, PHILADELPHIA

BEN. FRANKLIN SERIES

Price of Complete Series, 12 Sizes, $59.75. For Accents made see Pages 300 to 307

Universal Line—Point Set

6 Point Font $2 00

IF YOU ARE INTERESTED IN AMERICAN PRINTERS' IDEAS

Make yourself wise in the practical and money-making factor of your printing business. It is very important to be on the lookout for new Display Type Faces as they appear on the market, for up-to-dateness helps your business. Be sure also, that the type you purchase is on the Keystone Universal Lining System which has been adopted by art printers the world over as the most perfect of lining system. It would be well to consider the Ben. Franklin Series which is one of the most popular faces of the present time; made on Universal Line and its wearing qualities are unequaled as it is made from Nickel-Alloy Metal, the best material for the purpose ever invented; the types retaining their sharp outline longer than those made from other metals. It is better for

8 Point Font $2 25

SPARKS FROM OUR FIRST PRINTER, BEN. FRANKLIN

Another cause for the large sale of the early issues of the Almanack was, without question, due to the controversies with his brother Philomaths, which Franklin originated by his jocose remarks upon them in the prefaces of Poor Richard. Now and then with delicious humor and satire, Mr. Saunders, in different issues of the Almanack, gravely predicts the death of one of his rivals, Titan Leeds, and the reconciliation of a second, John Jerman. In this way they could not draw from the stars Franklin's purpose, and they all fell into his trap, and in the prefaces to their respective issues where they replied to him

10 Point Font $2 50

POPULAR SAYINGS OF POOR RICHARD

It is hardly necessary to make known or state that Franklin did not originate all the "Sayings of Poor Richard." He himself tells us that they were "the wisdom of many ages and nations," and those who are familiar with Bacon and Rochefoucauld as well as others, will recognize old friends in some of these sayings, yet with but few exceptions these maxims and aphorisms had been filtered through Franklin's

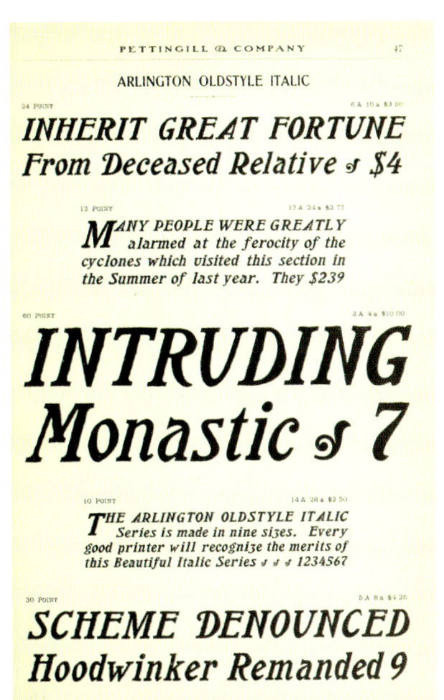
PETTINGILL & COMPANY 47

ARLINGTON OLDSTYLE ITALIC

INHERIT GREAT FORTUNE
From Deceased Relative & $4

MANY PEOPLE WERE GREATLY alarmed at the ferocity of the cyclones which visited this section in the Summer of last year. They $239

INTRUDING
Monastic & 7

THE ARLINGTON OLDSTYLE ITALIC Series is made in nine sizes. Every good printer will recognize the merits of this Beautiful Italic Series & & & 1234567

SCHEME DENOUNCED
Hoodwinker Remanded 9

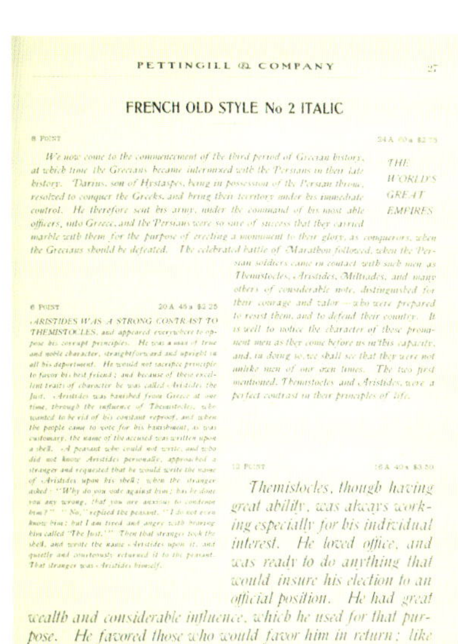
PETTINGILL & COMPANY 27

FRENCH OLD STYLE No 2 ITALIC

Themistocles, though having great ability, was always working especially for his individual interest. He loved office, and was ready to do anything that would insure his election to an official position. He had great wealth and considerable influence, which he used for that purpose. He favored those who would favor him in return; like some men of to-day. About election time there are often those who are ready to grant favors in order to secure the desired object. Their money is made to flow freely, and their affability is most remarkable. This was characteristic of Themistocles. 123456

THE ARMY OF VALOR

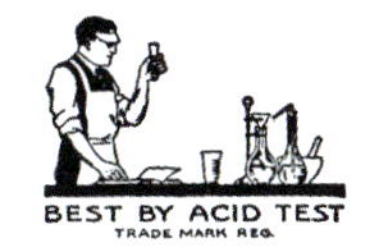

Imperial Type Metal Company

Type metal **alloys** mixed lead, tin or copper, and antimony. Foundries often bragged about the strength of their proprietary alloy.

Fig 4.3 (left)

Copper Alloy Type Book **(Pettingill & Co., Boston, 1901). Pettingill's claimed their copper alloy type was "the lightest and most durable in the world."**

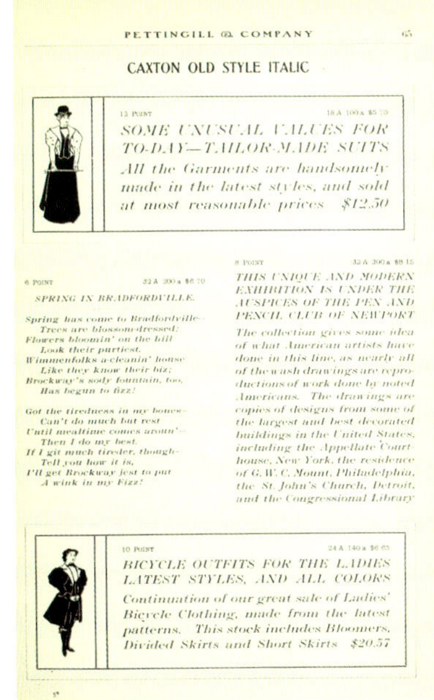
PETTINGILL & COMPANY 65

CAXTON OLD STYLE ITALIC

SOME UNUSUAL VALUES FOR TO-DAY—TAILOR-MADE SUITS
All the Garments are handsomely made in the latest styles, and sold at most reasonable prices $12.50

BICYCLE OUTFITS FOR THE LADIES
LATEST STYLES, AND ALL COLORS
Continuation of our great sale of Ladies' Bicycle Clothing, made from the latest patterns. This stock includes Bloomers, Divided Skirts and Short Skirts $20.57

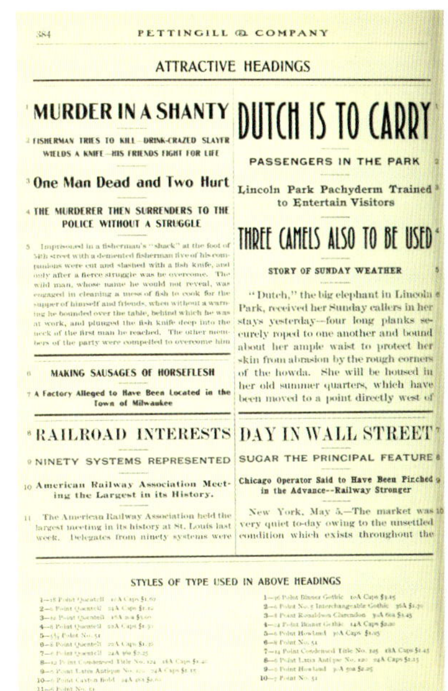
84 PETTINGILL & COMPANY

ATTRACTIVE HEADINGS

MURDER IN A SHANTY

One Man Dead and Two Hurt

THE MURDERER THEN SURRENDERS TO THE POLICE WITHOUT A STRUGGLE

MAKING SAUSAGES OF HORSEFLESH

DUTCH IS TO CARRY

PASSENGERS IN THE PARK

Lincoln Park Pachyderm Trained to Entertain Visitors

THREE CAMELS ALSO TO BE USED

STORY OF SUNDAY WEATHER

RAILROAD INTERESTS

NINETY SYSTEMS REPRESENTED

DAY IN WALL STREET

SUGAR THE PRINCIPAL FEATURE

STYLES OF TYPE USED IN ABOVE HEADINGS

life."[4] Logically, printers cared about the strength and durability of type, and specimens reflected this concern. In its 1906 specimen, the Keystone foundry of Philadelphia advised printers to "use metal of known durability; nickel-alloy [is] famous wherever type is in use"—Keystone types, of course, used nickel alloy, as the specimen indicated [Fig. 4.2].[5]

Pettingill's Copper Alloy Type Book (1901) likewise highlighted a proprietary type metal mixture [Fig. 4.3]. With newspaper publishers as their primary customer base, durability represented a key selling point for Pettingill. The foundry claimed industry-wide superiority, boasting that their types "excel in design, and their durability is assured" by their alloy, "the lightest and most

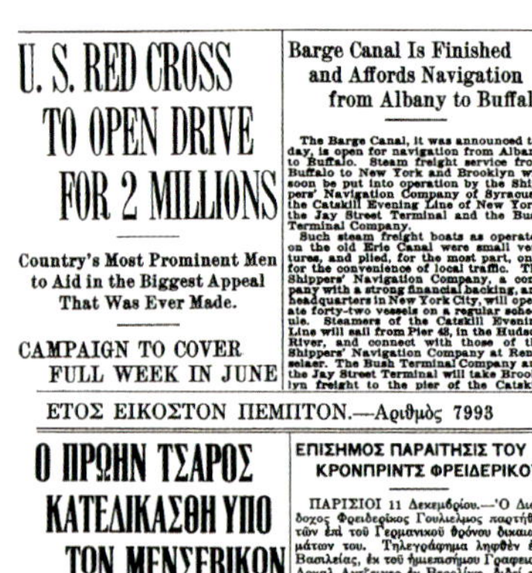

U. S. RED CROSS TO OPEN DRIVE FOR 2 MILLIONS

Country's Most Prominent Men to Aid in the Biggest Appeal That Was Ever Made.

CAMPAIGN TO COVER FULL WEEK IN JUNE

Barge Canal Is Finished and Affords Navigation from Albany to Buffalo

The Barge Canal, it was announced today, is open for navigation from Albany to Buffalo. Steam freight service from Buffalo to New York and Brooklyn will soon be put into operation by the Shippers' Navigation Company of Syracuse, the Catskill Evening Line of New York, the Jay Street Terminal and the Bush Terminal Company.

Such steam freight boats as operated on the old Erie Canal were small ventures, and plied, for the most part, only for the convenience of local traffic. The Shippers' Navigation Company, a company with a strong financial backing, and headquarters in New York City, will operate forty-two vessels on a regular schedule. Steamers of the Catskill Evening Line will sail from Pier 48, in the Hudson River, and connect with those of the Shippers' Navigation Company at Rensselaer. The Bush Terminal Company and the Jay Street Terminal will take Brooklyn freight to the pier of the Catskill

ΕΤΟΣ ΕΙΚΟΣΤΟΝ ΠΕΜΠΤΟΝ.—Αριθμὸς 7993

Ο ΠΡΩΗΝ ΤΣΑΡΟΣ ΚΑΤΕΔΙΚΑΣΘΗ ΥΠΟ ΤΩΝ ΜΕΝΣΕΒΙΚΩΝ

Οἱ Κροᾶται Σλοβένοι, Σέρβοι θὰ ὑπερασπίσουν μὲ ὅλας των τὰς δυνάμεις

ΟΙ ΤΟΥΡΚΟΙ ΕΙΣ ΔΙΚΕΝ

Οἱ Γιουγγοσλαῦοι καὶ Σέρβοι ἀνένδοτοί ἀπέναντι τῶν Ἰταλικῶν ἀξιώσεων

ΕΠΙΣΗΜΟΣ ΠΑΡΑΙΤΗΣΙΣ ΤΟΥ ΚΡΟΝΠΡΙΝΤΣ ΦΡΕΙΔΕΡΙΚΟΥ

ΠΑΡΙΣΙΟΙ 11 Δεκεμβρίου.—Ὁ Διάδοχος Φρειδερίκος Γουλιέλμος παρῃτήθη τῶν ἐπὶ τοῦ Γερμανικοῦ θρόνου δικαιωμάτων του. Τηλεγράφημα ληφθὲν ἐκ Βασιλείας, ἐκ τοῦ ἡμιεπισήμου Γραφείου Λοκαλ Αντζειγερ ἐν Βερολίνῳ, δίδει τὸ κείμενον τῆς παραιτήσεως ὡς ἑξῆς.

«Παραιτοῦμαι τῶν δικαιωμάτων μου ἐπὶ τοῦ Στέμματος τῆς Πρωσσίας ὡς καὶ τοῦ Αὐτοκρατορικοῦ Στέματος, τὰ ὁποῖα ἤθελον περιέλθη εἰς ἐμὲ ὡς ἐκ τῆς παραιτήσεως τοῦ Βασιλέως ἢ ἐξ ἄλλων λόγων. Ἐδόθη κατ' ἐξουσιοδότησίν μου, ὑπεγράφη διὰ τῆς χειρός μου. Ἐγένετο ἐν Γουϊριγκεν. Δ)βρίου 1, 1918, Φρεδερικ.

ΒΕΡΟΛΙΝΟΝ, Ἡ Κυβέρνησις κατήργησεν ἐπισήμως τὸ πρώην προνόμιον τῶν μελῶν τῆς οἰκογενείας Χοεντζόλλερν τοῦ νὰ μὴ καταδιώκονται ὑπὸ τοῦ νόμου.

Εὔσνερ ἐδήλωσεν ἐν χθεσινῷ λόγῳ του ὅτι θὰ δημοσιεύσῃ ἐντὸς ὀλίγων ἡμερῶν τὰ εγγραφα τοῦ ὑπουργείου τῶν Ἐ-

True to form, this Linotype specimen (1919) offered **newspaper headings** that ranged widely in size (6–60 points) and were available in a number of alphabets, including Latin, Greek, Hebrew, and Arabic.

durable in the world." Their specimen should be kept on "the publisher's desk, for daily use and reference" to its 450+ pages of text, jobbing, and titling faces, advertising figures, and ornament.[6] Unlike *Benton's*—which used the display text to describe its product—*Pettingill's* rarely mentioned its defining feature, copper alloy, after the introduction. Instead, display words and phrases mimicked newspaper headlines and ads, or filled space with nonsensical phrases and witticisms, a staple of specimen texts.[7] Most jobbing faces were displayed simply, in centered lines of one or two columns. But some pages included sample commercial jobs like ads, business cards, title pages, invitations, and musical programs. A diverse and extensive **newspaper headings** section prioritized Pettingill's primary audience, and an "attractive headings" section demonstrated how various type sizes and faces could be combined with borders and ornaments to create the organizational hierarchy of a newspaper page. These carefully annotated examples demonstrated Pettingill's suitability for their customers' specific needs, including physical durability in types used daily.

Standardization of form

Individual printers might choose time-saving, innovative typographic products or a particular type of metal alloy in order to economize. But on a systems level, structural changes to typographic form exerted a greater impact, and increasingly, formal consistency supported printers' efforts to economize. At the turn of the twentieth century, type size and height still varied—by continent, country, even foundry. An 1891 New Zealand trade journal ad promised "casting guaranteed accurate to English or other standards," underscoring both the need for precision and the variety of standards in use internationally.[8] As uniform systems evolved, founders often paid their price, particularly if the foundry had to replace their entire inventory to remain

Fig 4.4 (right)

Price List and Printers' Purchasing Guide **(Marder & Luse, Chicago, 1872). After they lost all their stock to Chicago's Great Fire of 1871, Marder & Luse redesigned all their types to a standardized point system. It was so popular that other American foundries were forced to adopt it. Instead of names, types now had numbers; two-line nonpareil became 12pt. and two-line Great Primer became 96pt.**

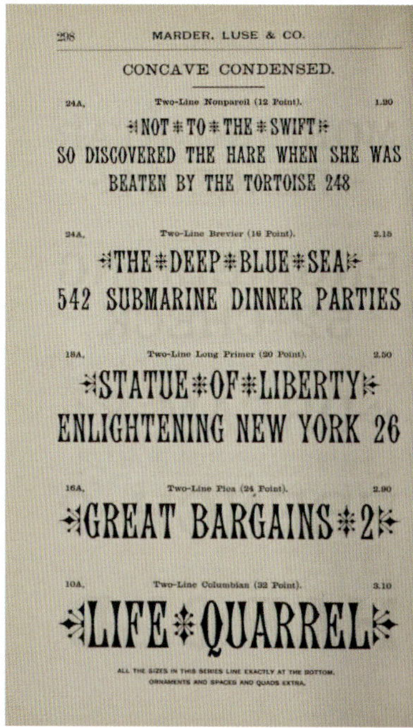

298 MARDER, LUSE & CO.

CONCAVE CONDENSED.

24A. Two-Line Nonpareil (12 Point). 1.90

NOT TO THE SWIFT
SO DISCOVERED THE HARE WHEN SHE WAS BEATEN BY THE TORTOISE 248

24A. Two-Line Brevier (16 Point). 2.15

THE DEEP BLUE SEA
542 SUBMARINE DINNER PARTIES

18A. Two-Line Long Primer (20 Point). 2.50

STATUE OF LIBERTY
ENLIGHTENING NEW YORK 26

16A. Two-Line Pica (24 Point). 2.90

GREAT BARGAINS 2

10A. Two-Line Columbian (32 Point). 3.10

LIFE QUARREL

ALL THE SIZES IN THIS SERIES LINE EXACTLY AT THE BOTTOM.
ORNAMENTS AND SPACES AND QUADS EXTRA.

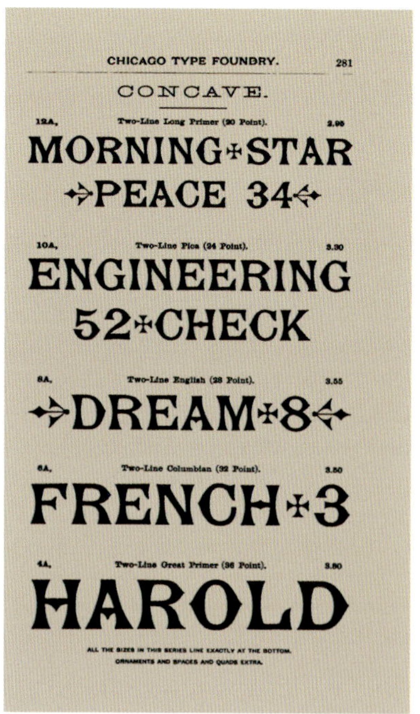

CHICAGO TYPE FOUNDRY. 281

CONCAVE.

12A, Two-Line Long Primer (20 Point). 2.95

MORNING STAR
PEACE 34

10A, Two-Line Pica (24 Point). 3.30

ENGINEERING
52 CHECK

8A, Two-Line English (28 Point). 3.55

DREAM 8

6A, Two-Line Columbian (32 Point). 3.50

FRENCH 3

4A, Two-Line Great Primer (36 Point). 3.80

HAROLD

ALL THE SIZES IN THIS SERIES LINE EXACTLY AT THE BOTTOM.
ORNAMENTS AND SPACES AND QUADS EXTRA.

competitive. During the twentieth century, the United States and Western Europe developed separate standardized systems, widely adopted on their respective continents then exported elsewhere.

The **American point system** standardized typographic measurement in the United States, allowing printers to combine fonts from different foundries. Though others attempted it before them, Marder, Luse & Company achieved the first widely successful standardization effort in 1872, when they reopened after Chicago's Great Fire (1871) decimated their existing stock. They defined a point as 1/12 pica, redesigned their types to correspond, and publicized their "American System of Interchangeable Bodies." Their 1890 catalog's 550+ pages emphasized how interchangeability "insur[ed] perfect accuracy and justification" among "various bodies of type."[9] It educated novice users, labeling every type by both its traditional name and its new point size (e.g., Nonpareil/6pt., Great Primer/8pt.) [Fig. 4.4]. Unremarkable page design displayed text types in single justified columns and display faces in single centered columns. But the specimen offered visual evidence of Marder & Luse's new point system, and its negligible aesthetic impact hid an underlying organizational logic that endures today.

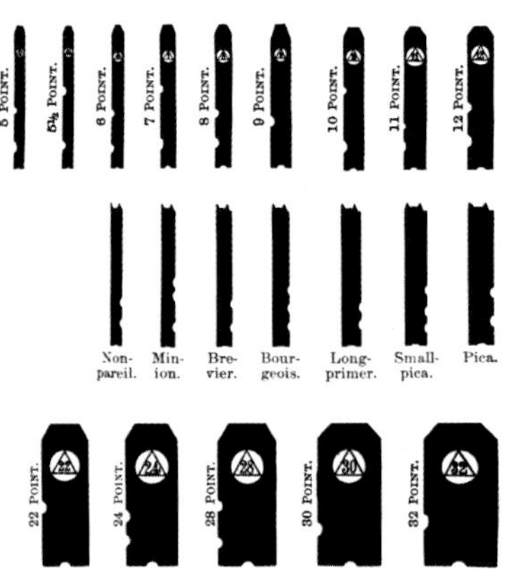

The **American point system**, 72 points to the inch, contrasts with Europe's Didot point system and the traditional naming systems of past centuries; Long Primer becomes 10 point.

Simultaneously, the *Inland Printer* credited Marder & Luse with "work[ing] an entire revolution in the printing trade" by introducing "uniform type bodies," a "genuine sensation" receiving "universal favor among progressive printers" who followed suit.[10] Yet in 1886, the United States Type Founders Association adopted the American point using the McKeller, Smith & Jordan pica (1/12″) since MS&J was the United States' oldest, largest foundry.[11] This decision fully standardized the American point's absolute measurement to today's 1/72″ and gave MS&J bragging rights. They described their "effort to bring about uniformity" as successful, applauded the "intelligent printer" for recognizing its benefits, and decreed "general recognition and approval" for their system.[12] The reality involved more turmoil. Re-designing matrices and recasting type was laborious and expensive, and while some foundries embraced standardization, others complained. In 1890, United Typothetæ's committee on type size uniformity addressed ongoing debates, phlegmatically concluding, "the American point system is here to stay, and we are to make the best we can of it." But they cautioned that "[t]oo much should not be expected of the new system," given imperfect implementation and inevitable human error.[13] Nevertheless, their interviewees reported generalized industry approval.

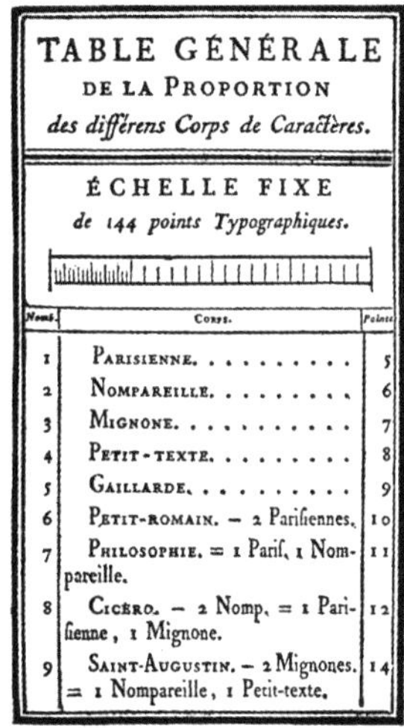

TABLE GÉNÉRALE
DE LA PROPORTION
des différens Corps de Caractères.

ÉCHELLE FIXE
de 144 points Typographiques.

Noms.	Corps.	Points.
1	Parisienne.	5
2	Nompareille.	6
3	Mignone.	7
4	Petit-texte.	8
5	Gaillarde.	9
6	Petit-romain. — 2 Parisiennes.	10
7	Philosophie. = 1 Paris. 1 Nompareille.	11
8	Cicéro. — 2 Nomp. = 1 Parisienne, 1 Mignone.	12
9	Saint-Augustin. — 2 Mignones. = 1 Nompareille, 1 Petit-texte.	14

The **Didot** (or French) point measures ≈0.375mm, representing Firmin Didot's 1783 adjustment of Fournier's 1764 ≈0.345mm point (above); it predates the 1886 ≈0.3515mm American point and continues to be used in Europe to measure metal type.

Across the Atlantic, similar conversations took place while continental Europe slowly adopted France's **Didot point** (12pts/1 cicero, ~67.29 Didot points/American inch). Germany had embraced the Didot point by the mid-nineteenth century, and in 1899 the *British Printer* reported its widespread use throughout much of Europe, including Austria, Denmark, Greece, Hungary, Italy, Norway, Portugal, Spain, and Turkey. An accepted standard type height lagged behind, but contemporary observers acknowledged that "universal adoption of the uniform Didot height is now but a question of time."[14] In 1900, James Figgins offered America as evidence that England *shouldn't* standardize its point size and suffer "the disastrous and costly effect of attempting to carry out a system so thoroughly unnecessary, quite at variance with everything in the plant of a well-equipped office, and possessing no merit whatever" in a practical sense.[15] Eventually, though, the British adopted the American point, criticisms like Figgins' notwithstanding, and exported it to their colonies.

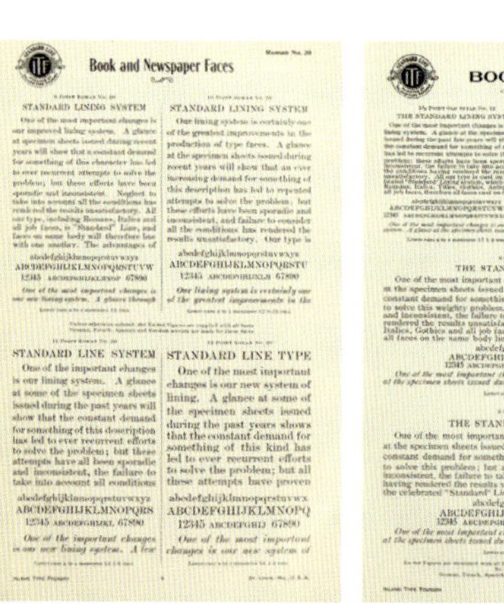

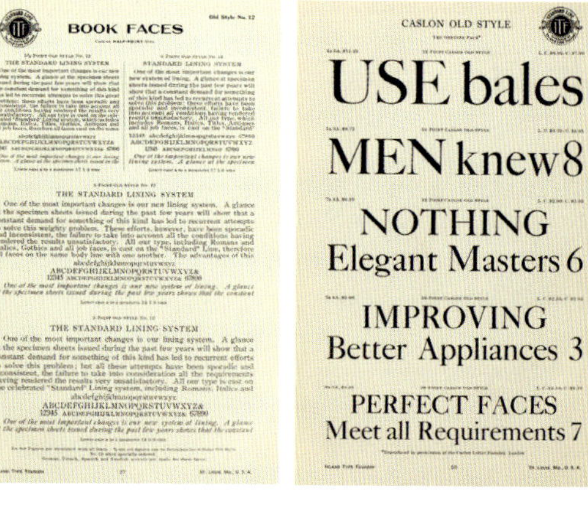

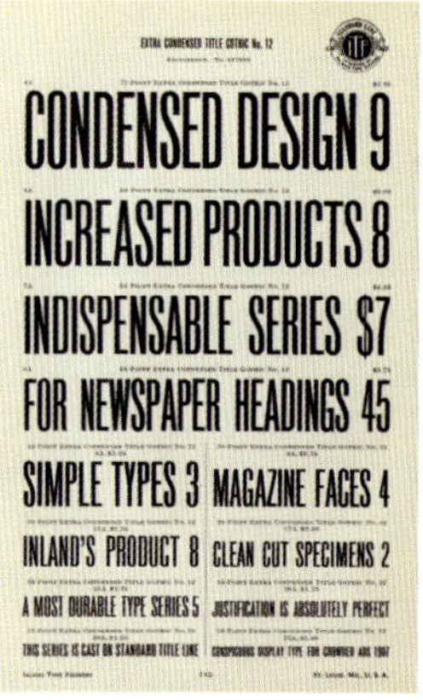

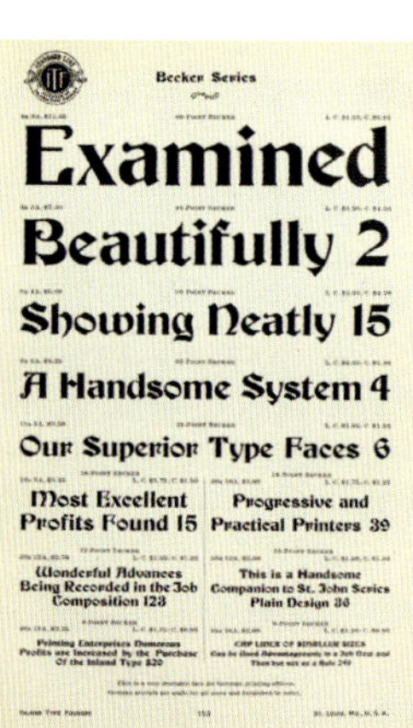

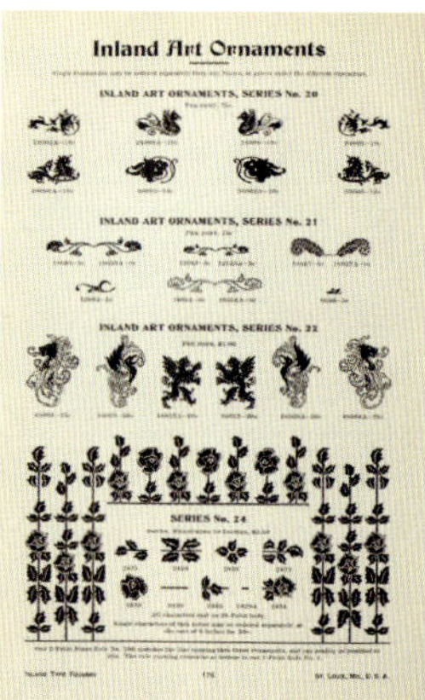

Fig 4.5 (right)

***Specimen Book and Catalog* (Inland Type Foundry, St. Louis, 1907) In 1895, Inland introduced the Standard Line, which imposed a uniform distance between any character's baseline and the bottom of the metal printing sort on which it sat. All the types in its 1907 catalog were cast on the Standard Line.**

Point size wasn't the only standardization project underway at century's close. In 1895, the newly-established Inland Type Foundry of St. Louis introduced the **Standard Line**, a system for locating every type's baseline at precisely the same distance from the bottom of the sort's body, regardless of typeface or size [Fig. 4.5]. While points standardized *size*—all 8-point type bodies measured 8/72"—they didn't lend a shared **baseline**, making it difficult to combine faces and sizes. In 1889, Nicholas Werner had argued in the trade periodical *Artist Printer* that typographic sorts needed a universally shared baseline, because printers needed to be able to create emphasis and variety easily. Inland's first specimen book (1895) contained only Standard Line faces, which evolved from Werner's proposal. Werner supervised its printing at Inland, and the Standard Line endured.[16] Inland advertised their Standard Line extensively in trade periodicals, including their own *Practical Printer*; they also emphasized it in their specimens. Their 1907 Specimen book and catalog showed a variety of faces combined into a single line, then compared lining and non-lining type by showing the "best system of lining type"—theirs, of course. Lining type represented "one of the greatest improvements in the production of type faces," the catalog's sample body copy claimed. Likewise, display faces shouted the benefits of a "modern system," promising that "lining type [is] money saved."[17]

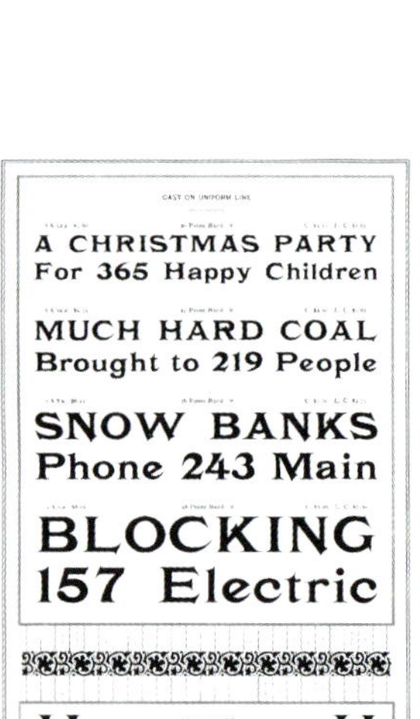

Standard Line types shared a baseline and a uniform distance from the bottom edge of the type metal body, making it easy to combine types across sizes, styles, and eventually foundries. ATF called this the American line, while BB&S called it Uniform Line (above, from the 1902 catalog).

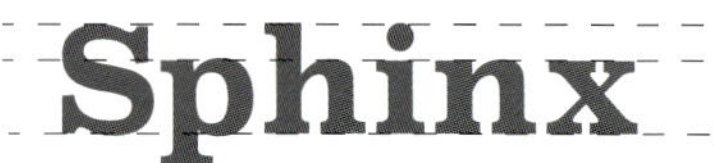

Letters sit on an imaginary **baseline** with descenders falling below; also shown, Superclarendon's capital height and x-height, with ascenders rising above.

Enthusiastic reception from printers forced other foundries to participate in the Standard Line system, if grudgingly [Fig. 4.6]. Keystone adopted the Standard Line in 1901, and ATF followed in 1902, calling their system the American Line but adopting an identical physical measurement.[18] The Standard Line subsequently migrated to Canada, England, and Europe. London foundry Stephenson Blake's Toronto office titled its 1908 catalog *Specimens of Point Line Type*, a decision that bore "witness to the changes which have taken place in the system of typefounding during recent years." The specimen demonstrated the foundry's capacity to "supply our complete collection of Body and Jobbing Types not only on American Point Bodies, but also on a uniform Lining System." Sample texts reiterated this "economic advantage." Lining Etrurian offered "American method, British prices," while Lining Old Style No. 5 promised that the "American method ensures expedition."[19] Uniform systems demanded significant structural changes in the material aspects of metal type, forcing foundries to redesign faces and cast types on bodies of new, standardized sizes and with new, uniformly located baselines. But these changes weren't always immediately observable within the visual language of the specimens themselves. Most of the pages that weren't displaying commercial ads in Stephenson Blake's 1908 specimen *looked* similar to those in their 1868 edition [Fig. 4.7].

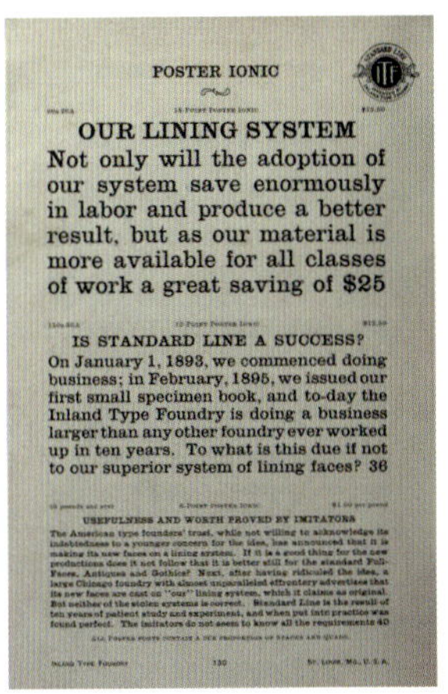

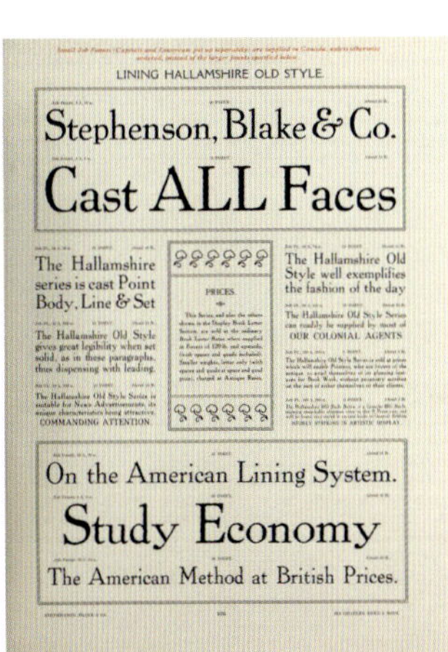

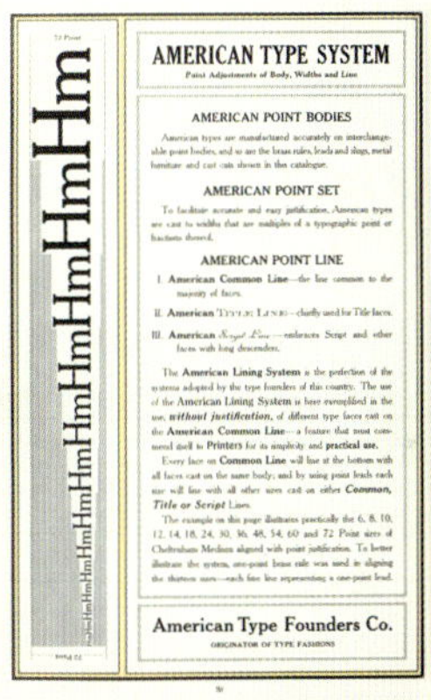

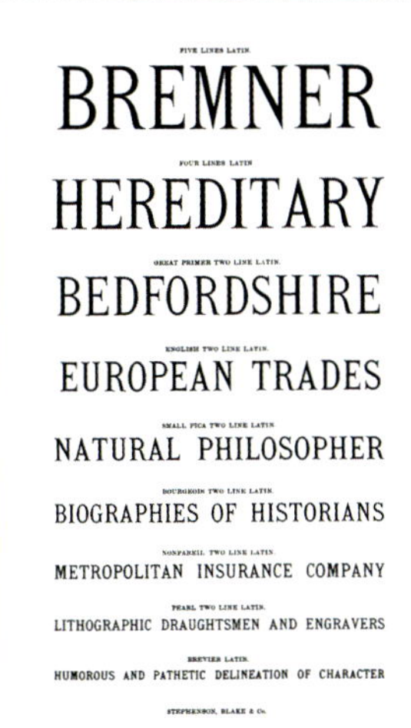

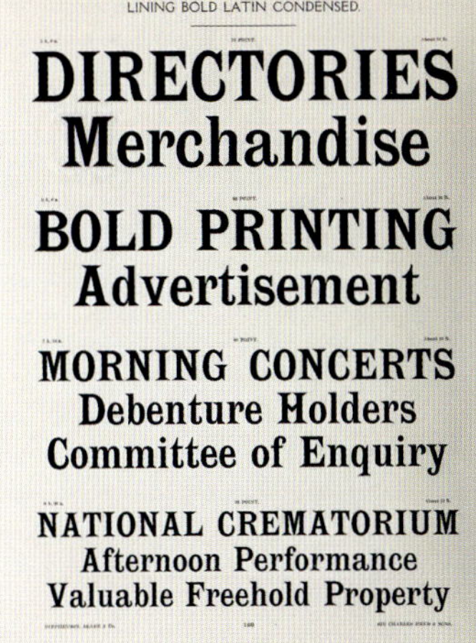

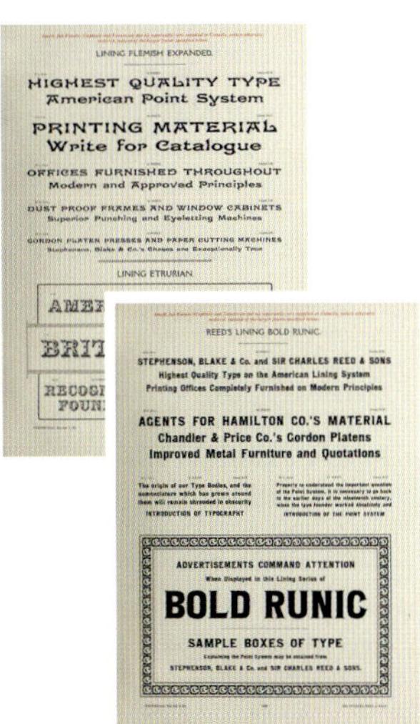

Fig 4.6 (top row)

Advertising the Standard Line in foundry specimens: Inland Type Foundry (St. Louis, 1897), Stephenson Blake (Toronto, 1908), and ATF (Jersey City, 1912). Like the American point, the Standard Line quickly became popular, and type foundries around the country were forced to adopt it. American Type Founders (ATF) called their version the American Line, but its measurements were identical.

Fig 4.7 (bottom row)

Not all developments in typographic technology were visible on the printed page. Though many foundries introduced the standard line (top row) starting in 1895, Stephenson Blake's 1868 catalog (bottom row, left) looked much like its 1908 catalog of lining type (bottom row, right).

A DESK BOOK OF
PRINTING TYPES
TO WHICH IS APPENDED A
CONDENSED CATALOGUE AND
PRICE LIST OF PRINTING
MACHINERY AND
MATERIALS

BOSTON, MASS. U. S. A.
AMERICAN TYPE FOUNDERS CO.
1898

The American Type Founders Company or **ATF** formed when the 23 most prominent type foundries in the USA joined forces in 1892. ATF controlled pricing and streamlined production and distribution of metal type.

Organizational redesign—ATF's example

Historically, type foundries opened, closed, split, merged, changed hands, and otherwise underwent structural reorganization on a frequent basis; corporate histories reveal a complex tangle of name changes.[20] In the United States at the turn of the twentieth century, this phenomenon helped radically reorganize American printing through the formation of the American Type Founders corporate trust (or **ATF**, 1892–1993). Initially formed of twenty-three foundries and spearheaded by typographic pantograph inventor Linn Benton, ATF represented roughly 85% of the type manufactured and sold in the United States in 1892.[21] The consolidation responded to a saturated late nineteenth-century American market which threatened type foundries with steep financial losses. Once limited to a few foundries in large East Coast cities, typefounding grew steadily until foundries in smaller, newer cities across the country supplied local and regional printers with type quickly and affordably. Meanwhile, the mechanized systems of Linotype and Monotype also grew quickly, with newspapers among their most enthusiastic early adopters. These developments meant that traditional foundries competed for customers fiercely, forcing unsustainably low prices on **foundry type**.[22]

Consolidation offered a chance to control cost and ensure market survival, but it proved easier and faster on paper than in physical practice. The Central Type Foundry in St. Louis published the first specimen under ATF's name in 1895, a 727-page book of their own existing stock.[23] On its pages, the foundry's incorporation into ATF remained largely invisible. ATF advertised its first

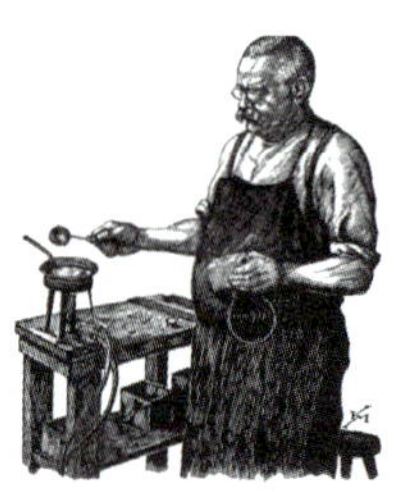

Foundry type is metal type cast as individual sorts from punches cut by hand, then set by hand, rather than through automated processes like those used in Linotype and Monotype machines. In 1937, the Bauer foundry published The Human Touch, lauding the superiority of foundry type (above).

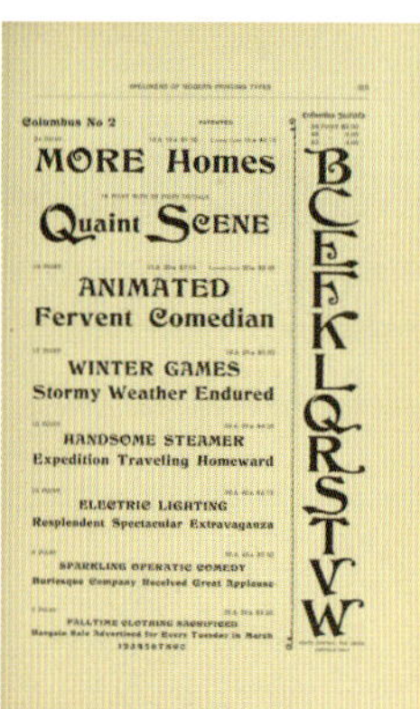

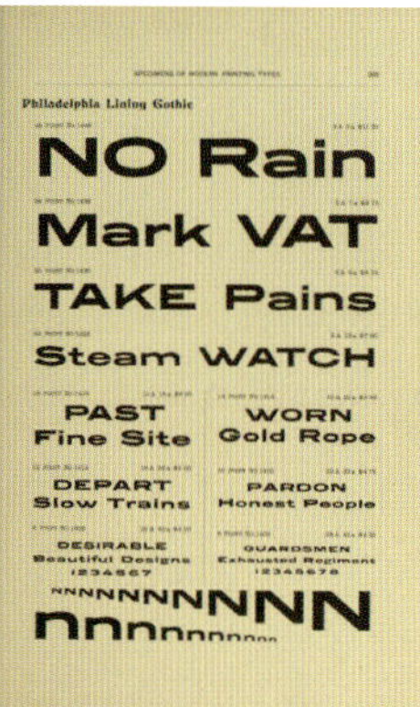

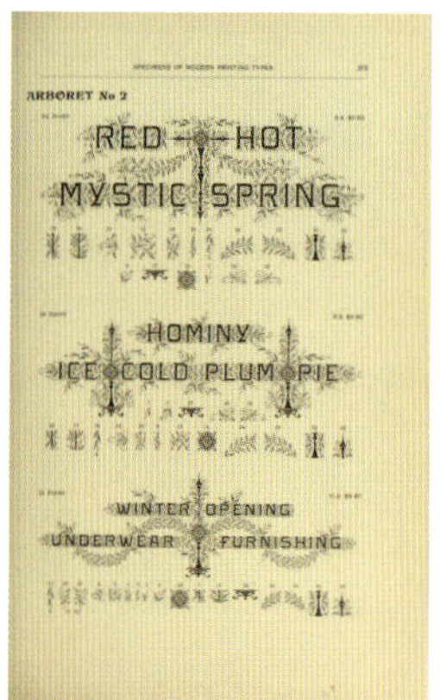

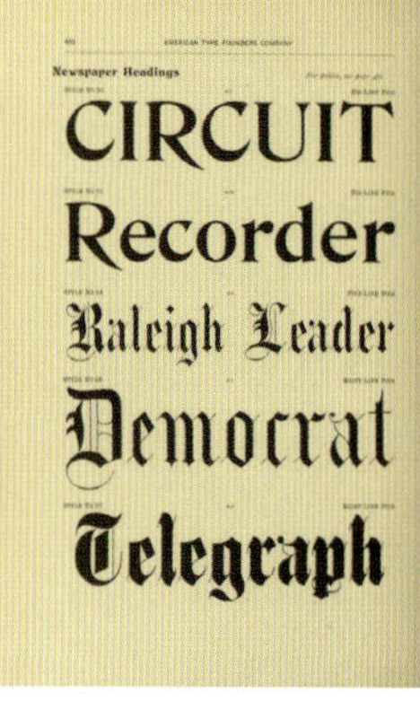

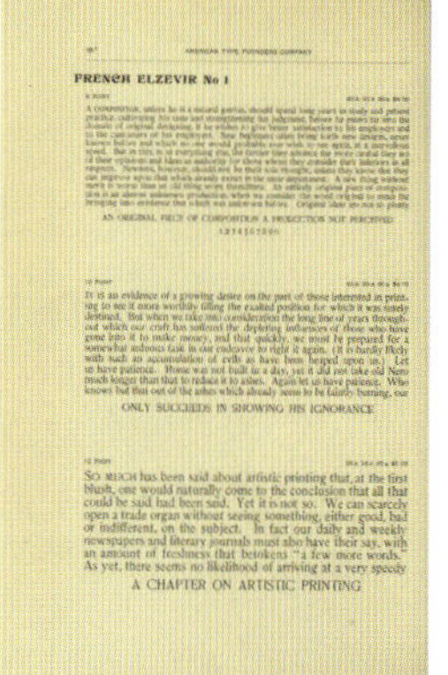

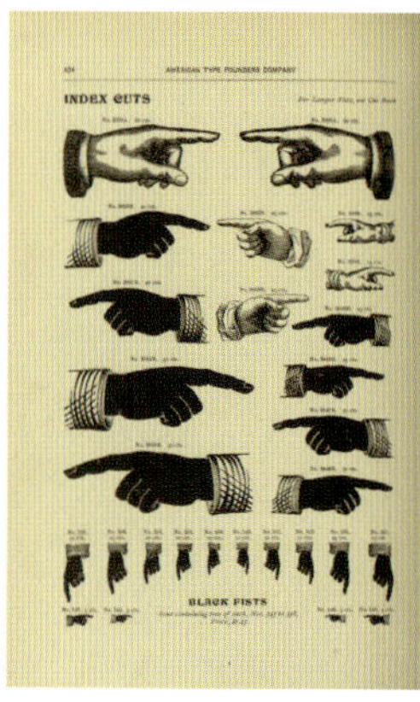

Fig 4.8 (right)

***Specimens of Printing Types* (ATF, New York, 1897). The American Type Founders (or ATF, est. 1892) consolidated 23 foundries into one corporate trust. The earliest ATF specimens concentrated on bringing together a comprehensive set of types from branch locations and eliminating duplicates, sometimes known by different names at different foundries.**

collective specimen (1895–6) by emphasizing that the "Printer is now for the first time enabled to find, collected within one cover, the type faces which have hitherto been found only in local Specimen Books."[24] By dominating the market for foundry type, ATF hoped to meet the needs of both founders and printers.

ATF's slogan, "covering the continent," neatly captured their early intent. The 1897 specimen declared itself "the standard for excellence throughout the world"—both in "design—the chief merit of type" and in durability, due to ATF's copper alloy [Fig. 4.8]. A printing business using their types instead of stock "made up from the productions of incomplete foundries" was therefore more profitable.[25] The specimen's almost 1,000 pages testified to ATF's "completeness." Over time, the foundry introduced new typefaces and retired outdated or unpopular ones, but early specimens concentrated on gathering local branch inventories into a single national catalog. Utilitarian design strategies underscored the corporate goals of collecting, indexing, and streamlining. Display types, decorative material, and all but the smallest text sizes in the 1897 specimen generally appeared in a single column, either centered or justified, and labeled with name, point size, and price. Few variations appeared. A brief section strongly influenced by the fine printing of the **Arts & Crafts** movement included the Bradley Series, ATF's Jenson revivals, (William) Morris initials, and ATF's infamous Satanick Series, which pirated Morris' **Kelmscott Press** types Troy and Chaucer.[26] A few scattered pages deployed idiosyncratic design strategies, stacking type or arranging it into asymmetrical columns. But the majority adhered to a strict system of structural logic regardless of individual type style. The "Chinese Series" and the "French Old Style Extended Series," for instance, received identical compositional treatment despite marked differences as types.[27] The book's stark, pragmatic design strategy included no ornamental page frames, limited use of rules, and monochromatic printing aside from title pages for the two sections, types, and equipment. System-wide standardization, soon to become characteristic of hot metal typography, made an early visual appearance in the organization of ATF's 1897 specimen.

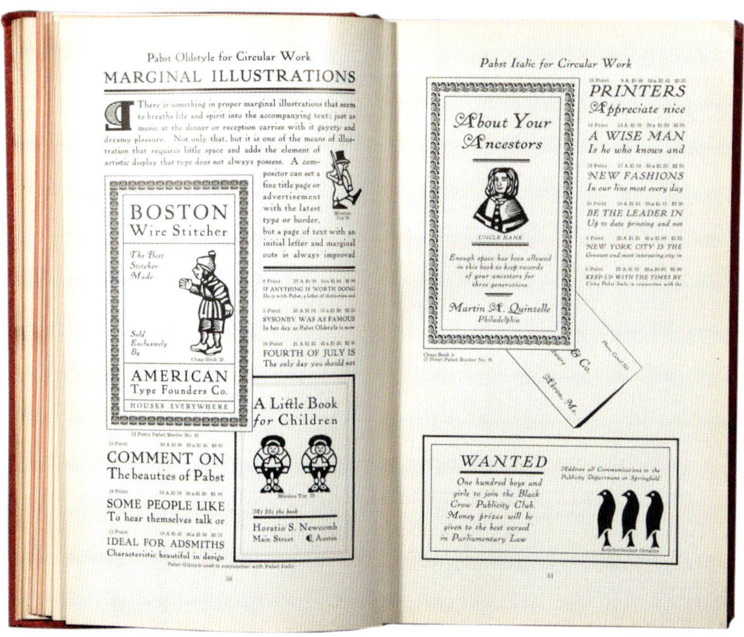
Pabst Oldstyle for Circular Work

MARGINAL ILLUSTRATIONS

BOSTON Wire Stitcher

AMERICAN Type Founders Co.

A Little Book for Children

COMMENT ON The beauties of Pabst

SOME PEOPLE LIKE To hear themselves talk or

IDEAL FOR ADSMITHS

Pabst Italic for Circular Work

PRINTERS Appreciate nice

A WISE MAN Is he who knows and

NEW FASHIONS In our line most every day

BE THE LEADER IN Up to date printing and not

About Your Ancestors

Martin M. Quintelle Philadelphia

WANTED

One hundred boys and girls to join the Black Crow Publicity Club. Money prizes will be given to the best versed in Parliamentary Law

Fig 4.9 (left)

***American Line Type Book* (ATF, Chicago, 1906). Under the direction of Morris Fuller Benton, ATF introduced type series of type families in the way designers understand them now: a set of types sharing essential structural traits across a range of widths, weights, and styles, with matching ornament.**

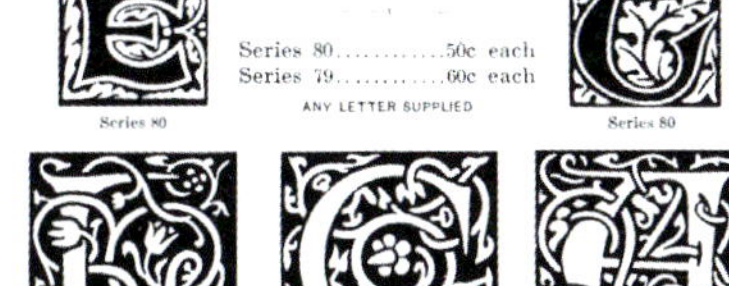

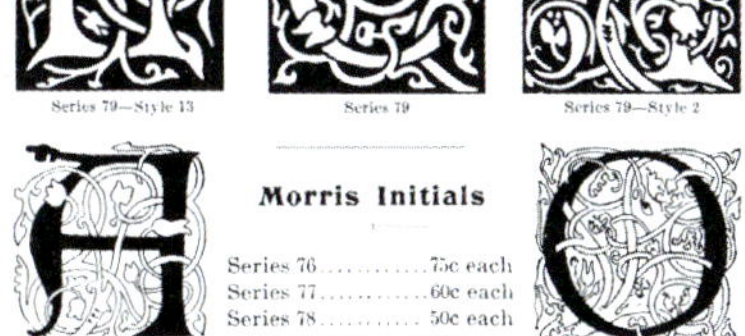

Morris Initials

Series 76 ....75c each
Series 77 ....60c each
Series 78 ....50c each
ANY LETTER SUPPLIED

Series 77

Series 77

The **Arts & Crafts** movement originated in England, where William Morris reimagined Gothic and Renaissance typeface and page layout design for audiences exhausted by the mass production and shoddy materials of industrialization.

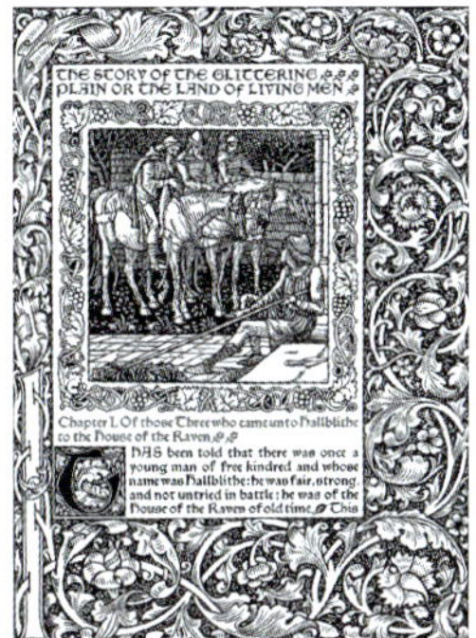

William Morris founded **Kelmscott Press** at Hammersmith, England, in 1891 and it remained one of the most noted Arts & Crafts fine presses even after its closure upon his death in 1898. The press published Morris' own work, like *The Story of the Glittering Plain* (1894, pictured), as well as editions of classic works, like Chaucer's *Canterbury Tales* (1896).

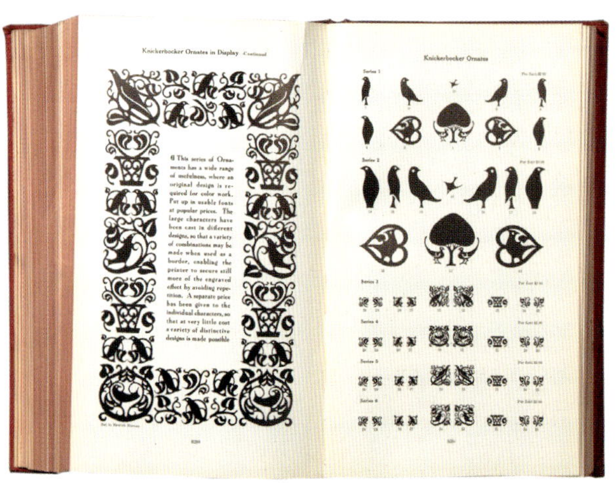

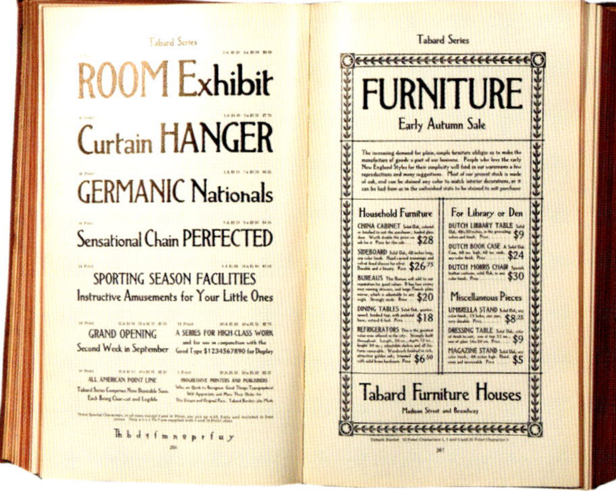

Fig 4.10 (above)

American Line Type Book **(ATF, Chicago, 1906). ATF's 1906 catalog marked not only their switch to lining type, but also a larger shift in the industry. With the advent of hot metal type, foundry type became synonymous with decorative work and fine printing. Commercial samples demonstrated how printers should use ATF's types in this emergent context.**

Specimens for foundry type marked a shift in perception, one that conceptualized foundry type as specific to decorative work and fine printing. ATF's 1,100+ page *American Line Type Book* (1906) coincided with the consolidation of their typecasting operations into one "Central Plant" in New Jersey. The catalog reflected this, discontinuing 436 existing series, redesigning 126 series to conform to the American Line system, and adding 224 entirely new series [Fig. 4.9]. The *Inland Printer* reviewed it as "a landmark in typefounding" and "the first specimen book of a new period in the type trade"—one in which "the field of the typemaker is narrowed to the decorative department, his work to provide style to the body-work of the composing machines." Thus ATF had no need to cast "long familiar plain-job faces ... which twelve years ago were the very bone and sinew of the type-trade" and could concentrate instead on display, jobbing, and specialist types.[28] The specimen offered extensive visual examples of ATF's types in use for advertising and fine printing.

ATF's specimens also emphasized another of their lasting organizational innovations: the **type family** [Fig. 4.10]. Now standard practice, the concept traces its contemporary identity to the prolific type designer Morris Benton (1872–1948). Linn Benton's son and head of ATF's design department, he fueled the widespread popularity of type families—typefaces in varying widths, weights, sizes, and styles which shared core visual traits.[29] His Cheltenham family, for example, originated with a type designed by Bertram Goodhue for New York's Cheltenham Press (1896); Benton's eighteen variations included oldstyle, wide, italic, bold, bold italic, bold condensed, bold condensed italic, and outline, plus matching decorative material.[30] Should more ornament be required, the 1906 catalog suggested pairing Cheltenham with Renaissance and Sectional Initials, and Strathmore Ornaments.[31] Benton and his team designed over 200 typefaces, some historical revivals (Bodoni, Baskerville, Garamond, a Jenson revival named Cloister Old Style) and others new responses to contemporary taste (Clearface, Hobo)[32]. ATF's massive *Specimen Book and Catalogue* (1923) explained that the "first important work of the newly established [ATF] type design department was the creation of type families," through which "the compositor automatically achieves perfect harmony in his work, while using all degrees of emphasis in headings and in display." ATF claimed that "the superiority of the Company's

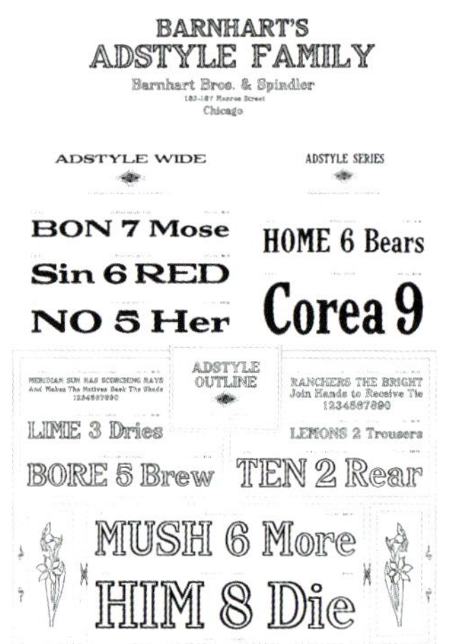

A **type family** (or historically, a series) is a set of faces designed around shared formal principles and often includes a range of widths, weights, and styles—some pragmatic, like companion italics, and others more decorative, like inline or outline versions.

type faces," renamed Publicity Types (instead of job types), facilitated more effective advertising and better printing [Fig. 4.11]. Furthermore, ATF's specimens represented "the most valuable textbooks of typography available to the printers." The 1923 catalog, printed in an edition of 60,000 copies, served as "a guide to many printers," intending its "supremely useful, as well as inspiring" examples to exercise a "beneficial influence on the future prosperity of the printing industry."[33]

The development of type families informed ATF's corporate rationale, sometimes maintained at other type designers' expense. Frederic Goudy, for instance, designed almost 125 typefaces in his lifetime, many during his tenure as Lanston Monotype's art director from 1920–47, and his contemporaries greatly admired his work. His early typeface Goudy Old Style (1915), commissioned by ATF, proved extremely popular and led to an extensive and commercially successful type family of derivative variants. Yet Goudy himself designed only Goudy Old Style, and he earned no royalties, as he'd sold his design outright to ATF.[34] Morris Benton developed the "parent type design," as the 1923 specimen's Goudy segment called it, "into a type family" so "that printing may be kept forceful and lively" through "variety."[35] ATF's advertising copy attributed the family's lasting popularity to the "distinct touch of tomorrow" that "anticipates the future" and makes present-day users seem forward-thinking by association.[36] ATF's programmatic (and

Fig 4.11 (below)

Specimen Book and Catalogue **(ATF, Jersey City, 1923). ATF's Goudy Family was based on Frederic Goudy's 1915 Goudy Old Style, which ATF had commissioned. But Goudy earned no royalties and received no credit for the additional faces Benton designed to round out the family that bore his name.**

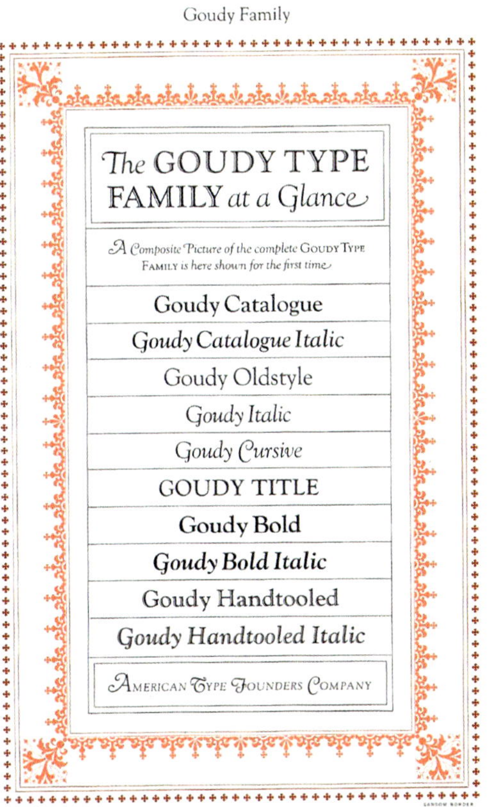

cut-throat) rationale, combined with the sheer size and national scope of its corporate trust, secured the foundry a lucrative market presence until the Great Depression despite continual improvements in mechanical typesetting technologies. Their *Book of American Types* (1934), followed by a new edition and supplement issued in 1941, attest to a long-lasting presence in the American printing trades.[37] Like many ATF innovations, the idea of the type family influenced other foundries. Barnhart Bros. & Spindler of Chicago, purchased by ATF in 1911 but operational under its own name until closing in 1933, also adopted and promoted the idea of the type family. BB&S introduced their Author's Roman family c.1901 and the Adstyle family during that same decade [Fig. 4.12]. Variations in width, weight, and style allowed designers to create variety without sacrificing harmony.

Fig 4.12 (below)

Though purchased by ATF in 1911, BB&S continued issuing specimens under their own name until closing in 1933. But like ATF, they adopted the notion of the type family, as seen here in Author's Roman and Adstyle, both of which debuted in the first decade of the twentieth century, before ATF's purchase.

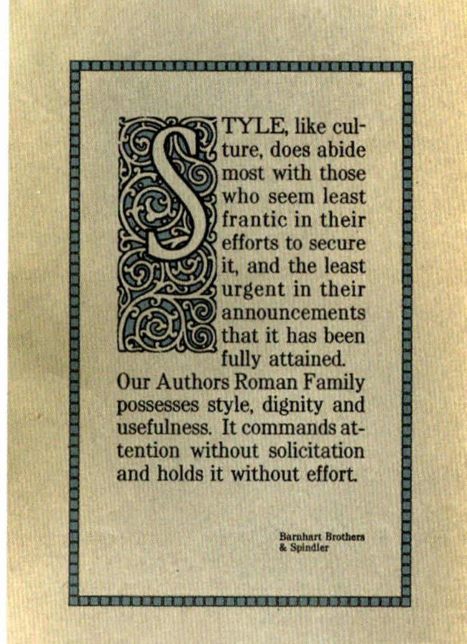

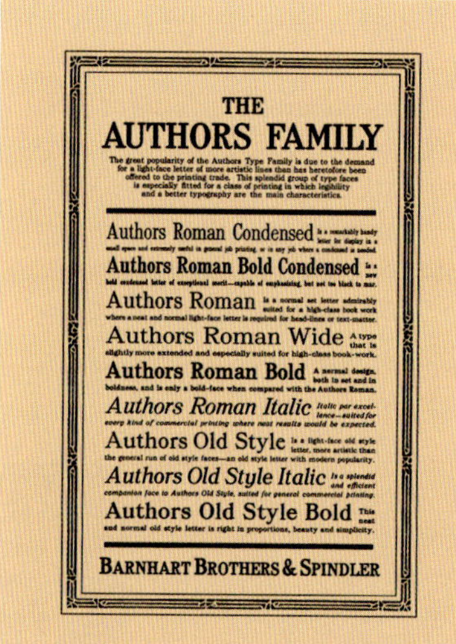

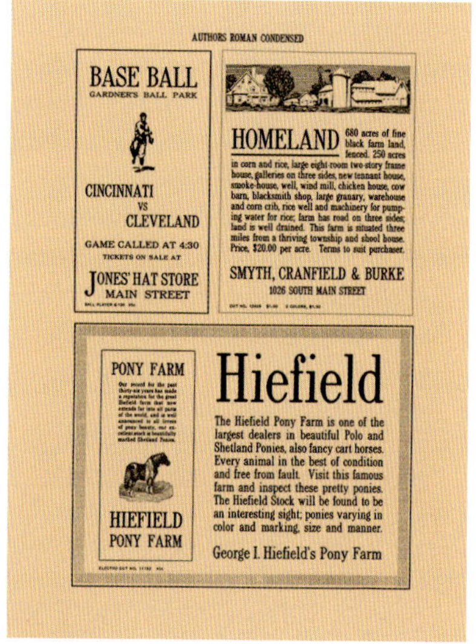

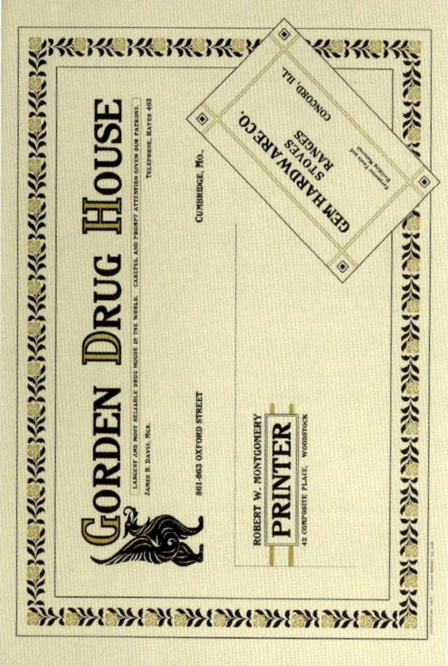

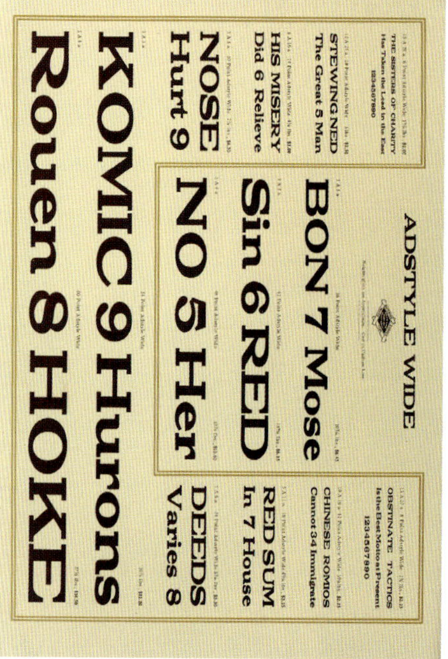

Tools for mechanization

Though automatic typecasting and typesetting dominated efforts to develop new typographic technologies, this wasn't the nineteenth century's only mechanical development. New tools for producing and reproducing letterforms emerged, and type specimens contextualized them for printers.

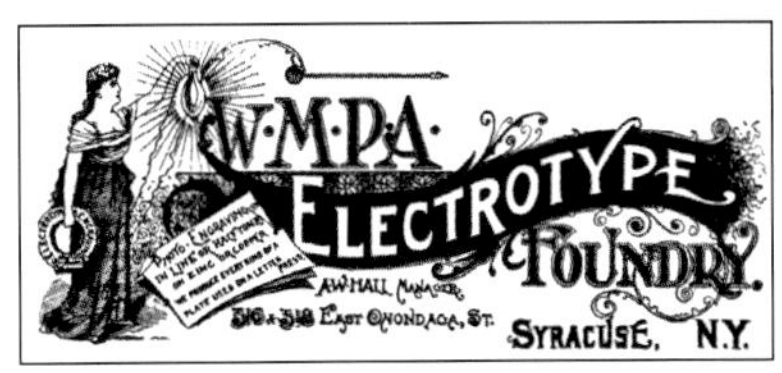

Electrotyping is a chemical method facilitated by electric currents. It produces exact copies of an existing image plate or three-dimensional object.

Reproduction—electrotyping and the pantograph

Electrotyping, a mid-century innovation, used electricity to copy an image onto thin metal deposited into a mold. Used to reproduce images and decorative objects affordably, it also allowed easy duplication of type designs. James Figgins, whose family had been typefounding in London since 1792, wrote in 1900 that "To the Printer it [electrotyping] has been of great advantage ... but to the Type Founder it has been disastrous." The technology was "used against [the type founder] by an unscrupulous and disreputable crew to pirate his productions and appropriate his designs," both for the electrotyper's own use and for "making a trade of selling matrices and duplicates to others." Consequently, the founder was "plundered without a shadow of redress."[38] Printed specimens had always circulated type designs, and copying—either loosely or piratically—wasn't unheard of, as James Figgins' predecessors knew well, having copied Caslon and Baskerville. But mechanically produced copies, which required little skill or training, opened up new avenues for typographic theft.

Electrotyping also facilitated typographic ornamentation, a useful capacity during an intensely decorative aesthetic period. The Tokyo Tsukiji Type Foundry's 72 Line Japonica, a face of illustrated initial letters, utilized electrotyping to cultivate Western European and North American customers.[39] The Latin-alphabet characters of Japonica were framed by what Western viewers would have seen as typically Japanese motifs: cherry blossoms, lotus, koi, monkeys, ocean waves, moonlit trees. The oversized polychromatic print folded out of a slender specimen booklet, part of a regularly-issued series. But Anglophone audiences weren't the foundry's only focus. Equal representation of Japanese types and pictorial electrotypes served local printing needs. Most booklets in the series featured a larger, fold-out, color-printed insert like the one for Japonica, alternating between Japanese and English language decorative material and demonstrating the foundry's investment in cultivating multiple audiences. An 1899 volume, for instance, included a series of color-printed vignettes for Japanese audiences. The images showed scenes of beautiful women holding fans or umbrellas, schoolchildren, traveling tradesmen, and the interior of a printing shop where a crowd of Japanese men and boys learned the typographic craft. The everyday contexts depicted in these images, as well as their Japanese-language labels, indicated a local audience.[40] Throughout the series of specimen booklets, workaday Latin and Japanese types were printed in black ink on pages numbered with Arabic numerals, framed by decorative or linear borders, and labeled with their names. But these audience-specific labels weren't translated from Japanese to English, or vice versa; though languages and alphabets mixed within a single volume, the specimens seemed to assume two distinct audiences for the contents [Fig. 4.13].

Fig 4.13 (right)

***72-Line Japonica* (1897) and *Specimens* (issue 3:11, 1899); Tokyo Tsukiji Type Foundry, Japan. Tsukiji, like most Japanese foundries upon the adoption of Western European letterpress printing in the late nineteenth century, addressed multiple audiences in each specimen produced. Readers might be American, British, or European tourists or colonizers; they might also be local Japanese civic or businesses organizations or individual community members. Ingenious design strategies accommodated not only diverse audiences, but also their multiple scripts: Chinese, Japanese, and the Latin alphabet, at minimum.**

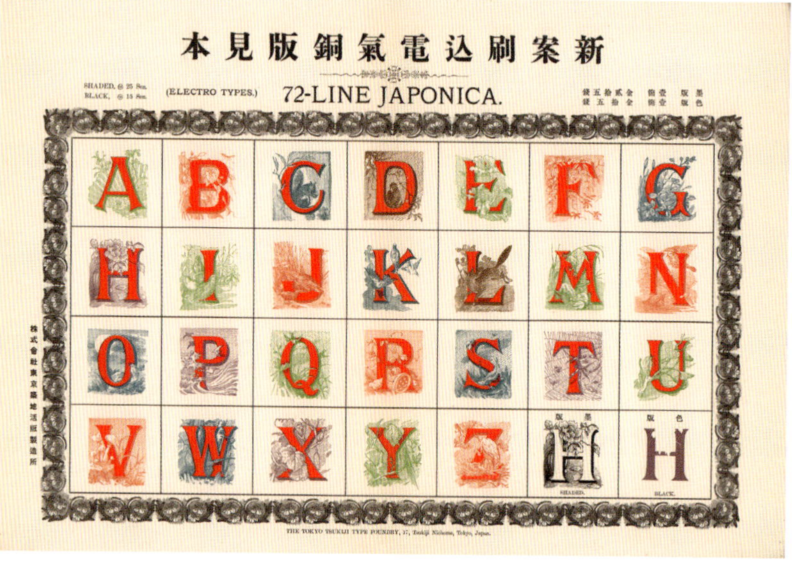

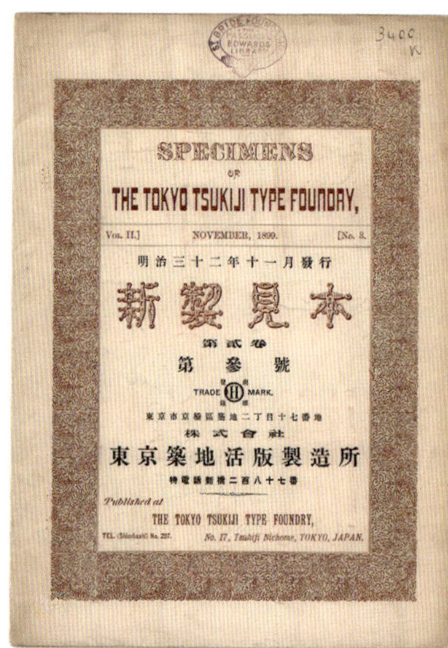
SPECIMENS OF THE TOKYO TSUKIJI TYPE FOUNDRY,

Vol. II.] NOVEMBER, 1899. [No. 3.

明治三十二年十一月發行

新製見本

第貳卷

第參號

TRADE MARK.

株式會社

東京築地活版製造所

Published at THE TOKYO TSUKIJI TYPE FOUNDRY, No. 17, Tsukiji Nichome, TOKYO, JAPAN.

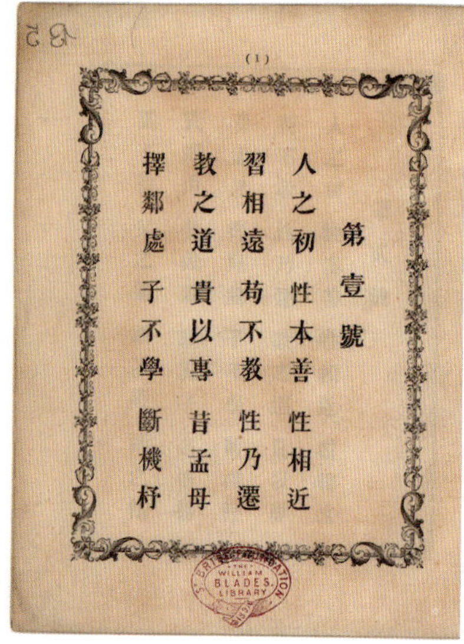
(1)

第壹號

人之初 性本善 性相近
習相遠 苟不教 性乃遷
教之道 貴以專 昔孟母
擇鄰處 子不學 斷機杼

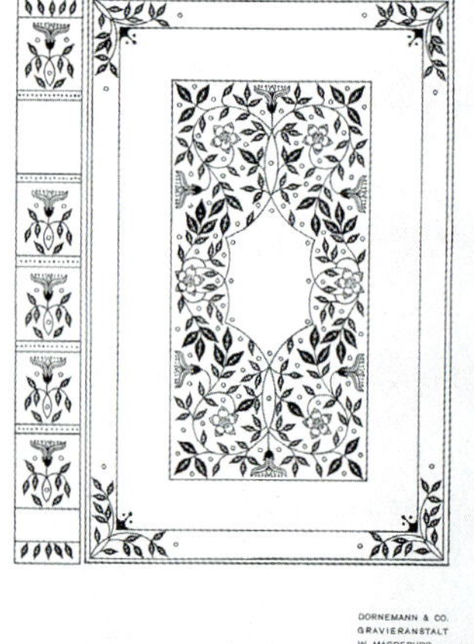

Tintypes, or **ferrotypes**, were high in iron; they printed like copper display types, but were closer in price to wood poster types. The German Dornemann & Co. specialized in ferrotypes, including ornament, often used to emboss book covers.

Tintypes, or **ferrotypes**, achieved the print quality of brass poster type at a price closer to wood type, while being composed primarily of iron and thus stronger than both brass and wood. The German Dornemann & Co. advertised their new product in trade journals and produced specimens; their 1925 catalog specifically showed types intended for the gilding press—used, often, to apply decorative book cover titles.[41] Like specimens of electrotype, Dornemann's for tintype didn't comment extensively on materials or manufacturing processes. Introductory matter in English, French, Italian, and German summarized the technical details of ordering—what punctuation and diacritical marks a font of type included, what information to send in a request, how long filling an order would take ("several weeks"), and how *not* to order types (by mailing a sample cut out of the specimen). Dornemann also offered lengthy commentary on copyright, advising viewers that their letterform designs shouldn't be copied. Unsurprisingly, given their point of origin, the types included a wide selection of blackletter and Jugendstil (German Art

Nouveau) designs. The January 1907 issue of *Archiv für Buchgewerbe* displayed Carola Grotesk (designed by Hermann Hoffman for Berthold, 1896) in tintype, offering a range of display sizes measured in *cicero* [Fig. 4.14].

The **pantograph** and **lateral router**, both American inventions, mechanized wood type production. Like electrotyping and tintyping, these tools facilitated both piracy and aesthetic innovation. Darius Wells introduced the lateral router in 1827, a tool described at the time as "a revolving, verticle spindle, carrying a cutter, by which the surplus wood was speedily and neatly cut away" from the type-high block of wood with the letter outlined on its surface to serve as a guide for cutting.[42] In 1834, William Leavenworth improved this process by combining the lateral router with a pantograph specially adapted for the purpose of making wood type.[43] This allowed the basic letterform on the template to be condensed or **expanded**, made larger or smaller, and reused over and over. It also allowed manufacturers to purchase a competitor's type and modify it into a template.[44] Leavenworth manufactured wood type briefly, but in 1839 he sold his enterprise to J.M. Debow, a New Jersey printer who promptly issued a specimen (c.1840) displaying the aesthetic flights of fancy and the impressive physical sizes made possible with Wells' and Leavenworth's new technologies [Fig. 4.15].

Fig 4.14 (bottom left)
Dornemann & Co. ad in *Archiv für Buchgewerbe* (January 1907). Tintyping, also known as ferrotyping, allowed easy duplication of existing fonts. Dornemann's types for gilding presses were used to imprint decorative gilt titles on book covers, but despite their specialized purpose, the types spoke the visual language of their day. Carola Grotesk, designed for Berthold in 1896, offered a prime example of Jugendstil, or German Art Nouveau.

Fig 4.15 (below)
***Specimen of Leavenworth's Patent Wood Type* (J.M. Debow, Allentown, 1840-9). Mass-produced wood type was facilitated by two American inventions, the pantograph and the lateral router. Wood type was sturdier than metal at large sizes, and it was much cheaper as a material. Wood type, sometimes called poster type, made large-scale environmental advertising possible.**

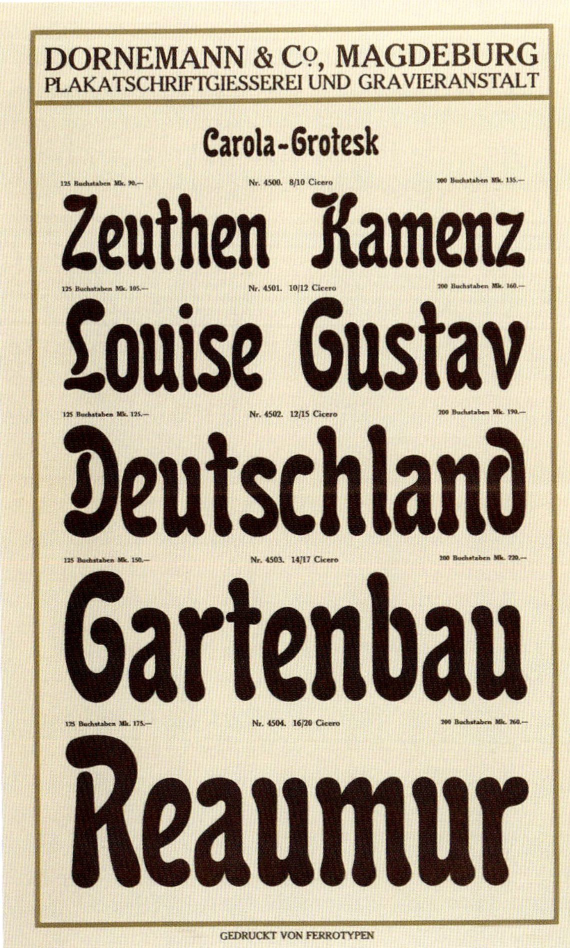

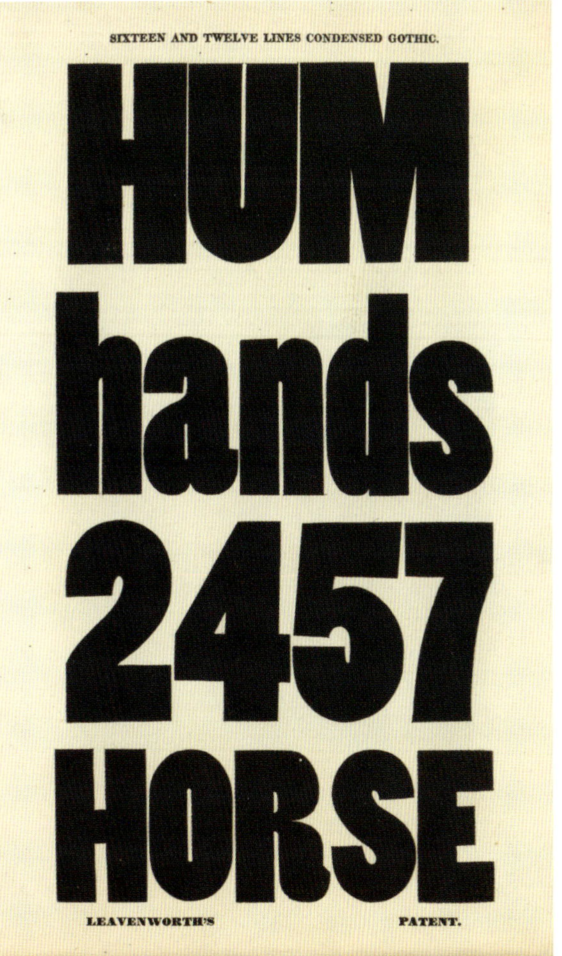

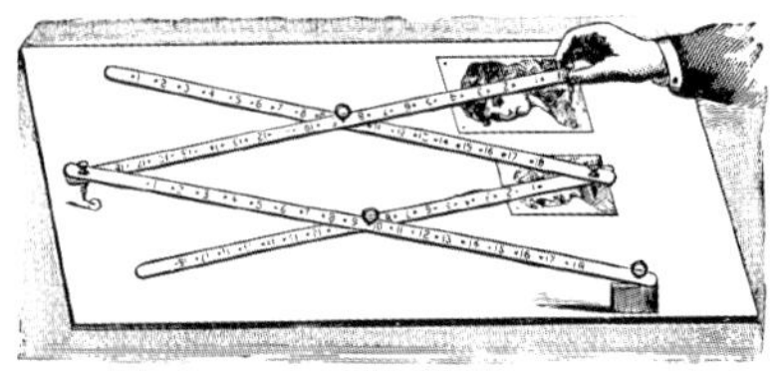

The **pantograph** allowed the operator to mechanically trace an image while adjusting its size and width-height ratio automatically.

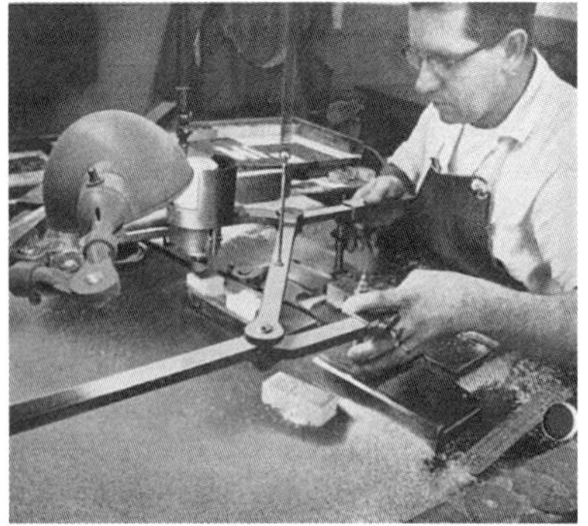

Attaching a **lateral router** to a typographic pantograph let the machine's operator use one arm of the pantograph to trace the outline of the letter from a template, while the lateral router attached to the pantograph's second arm cut the design into wood at the specified size and width/height ratio. Image: Hamilton Wood Type catalog (ND).

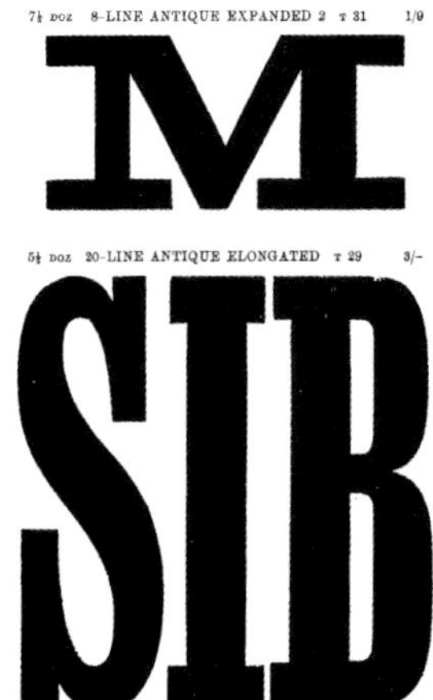

The **elongated** & **expanded** Antiques shown here demonstrate how changing the width-height ratio of a letterform alters its character. These wood faces are from Australian typyefounder Wimble's 1910 catalog, likely imported from Hamilton as were most of the wood fonts he sold.

Experiments with machine casting and composition

Early experiments with **machine casting and composition**, of course, stood to offer printers the largest economical advantage. Widespread mechanization arrived via Linotype (linecasting) and Monotype (sort-casting), as seen in the next chapter. But early experiments with automation sometimes proved successful enough that specimens documented them and their types. *The History of Composing Machines* (1904), initially an *Inland Printer* series, described over fifty British and American patents for automated machines: operational and quasi-operational, automated and semi-automated, capable of casting lines or characters, equipped for either casting or setting, or occasionally for both. William Church patented the first in 1822 but never successfully introduced it to market. In 1871, Charles Westcott's Direct Casting Machine combined casting and setting, though it also failed to capture significant market share.[45] Yet despite the complexities, efforts continued, because the benefits would be so profound. One such functional yet ultimately unsuccessful machine was the Thorne/Simplex/Unitype "one-man type setter"—iterations of the same typesetting machine marketed under different names over time [Fig 4.16]. None cast new type, but promotional materials incorporated type specimens regardless.

An 1894 specimen booklet for the *Thorne Type-Setting and Distributing Machine* described the benefits of the Thorne system, which added a special notch to foundry type to facilitate machine use. Thorne sold this notched type in a handful of standard faces, and type purchased from other foundries could be modified. For Thorne, foundry types represented the "highest perfection of typefounding" because stereotyping and line-casting lent inferior printing results. The booklet's sample copy quoted "a most thorough and exhaustive report" by a committee which had "investigate[d] the methods practised for securing accuracy and perfection in workmanship" at Thorne's Hartford factory. Selected excerpts highlighted how the Thorne's design boosted efficiency and quality. The machine itself was the fastest and cheapest on the market, a "simpler" design which offered "the best result."[46] But the five pages of type specimens were distinctly underwhelming, never varying from a simple page design of two justified columns. A header labeled each type with both point size and traditional name—for example, Thorne 8 point/brevier No. 1. Though the text emphasized quality and efficiency equally, the design speaks a wholly serviceable, economical visual language. This reflected the priorities of Thorne users who, based on the "letters of commendation" reprinted, primarily inhabited the pressrooms of newspapers and periodicals.

The Simplex, a later iteration of the same machine, appeared at the Pan-American Exposition in 1901; a year earlier, the company estimated 300 printing offices used the Simplex. This was a small number compared to the 10,000 Linotype machines that would be in use by 1904, but it was significant enough at the time that the *Inland Printer* noted the figure with some excitement.[47] The final iteration was marketed as the Unitype. A distributor's (rather than manufacturer's) specimen from Wood & Nathan of New York promoted the Unitype with samples from newspapers, advertisements, and trade publications, all set on the Unitype. Their tall, narrow booklet boasted an ornamented green paper cover but otherwise displayed black type on white pages, emphasizing the practicality of machine and types. Some pages noted how the samples were composed. "All the matter on this page was set on the same Ten Point machine, with two fonts of type, one having an eight point face, the other a law brief face, both faces cast on ten point body."[48] The specimen prioritized functionality over artistic merit and performed its job well, demonstrating the utility of the Unitype for newspaper printers. However, the ability to cast and set type simultaneously—by this time already possible via both Linotype and Monotype—soon rendered other early experiments in mechanization obsolete.

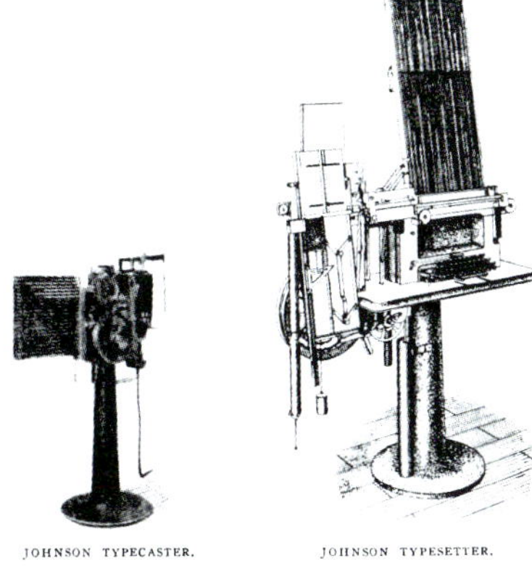

Machine casting & composition required many experiments before mechanical and commercial success. Frank Johnson's typecaster and typesetter (1897) failed, as did most attempts.

Wood types as "new" tools

Metal type—either foundry type or, after Linotype and Monotype, hot metal type—was the primary means by which typographic printing took place until the introduction of phototypesetting in the 1950s. But large-format printing and advertising, as we've seen, inspired the manufacture of a new kind of typographic product: mass-produced wood type. In an increasingly industrialized market flooded with manufactured goods and packaged products, advertising communicated brand identity to customers. Metal type in larger sizes accommodated ads in books and periodicals. But handbills, broadsides, and roadside advertisements required a significant increase in scale, and large-format **chromolithographic** printing didn't emerge until the 1890s. An 1865 ad for the Edinburgh foundry Miller & Richard captures the benefits of "Wood Letter," namely, that "its accuracy in size and height to paper, combined with its superior finish, render it equal to large metal type, while its durability and economy make it more advantageous."[49] Lightweight,

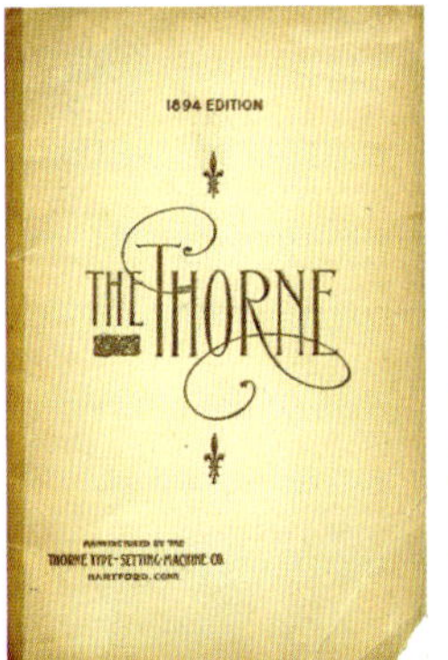

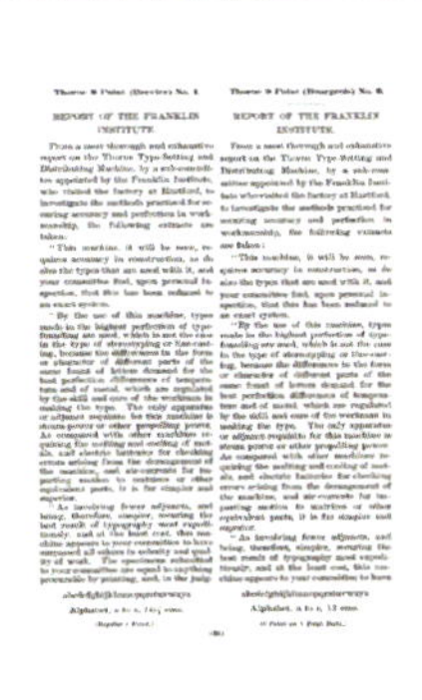

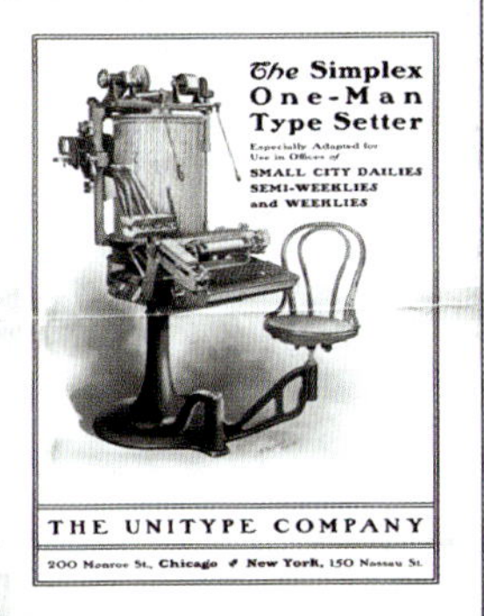

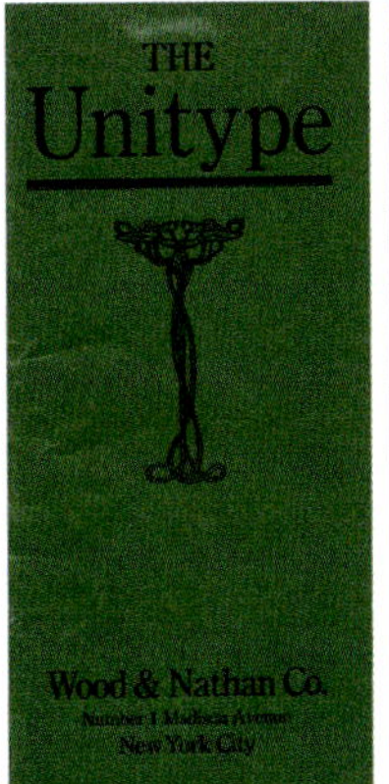

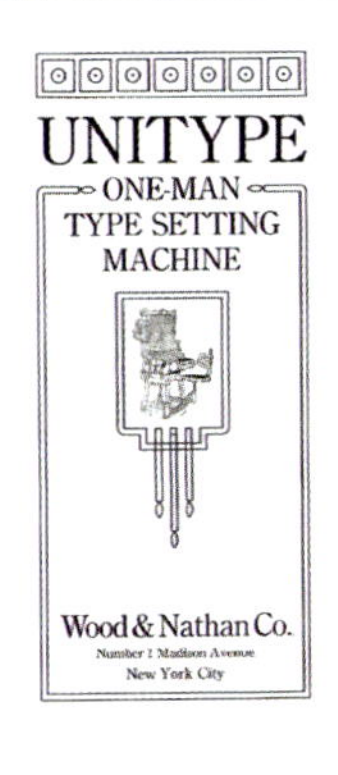

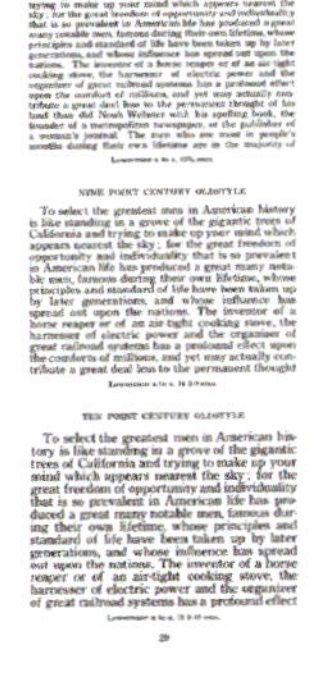

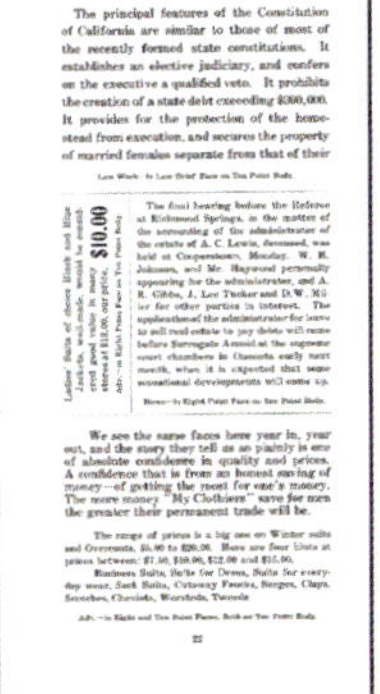

Fig 4.16 (left)

Specimens for the "one-man type setter" show its three different names over its lifespan: the Thorne (Hartford, 1894), the Simplex (Chicago, c.1900), and the Unitype (New York, 1902). The Monotype and Linotype, both of which could mechanically cast and set type, would soon render it and other early mechanization experiments obsolete.

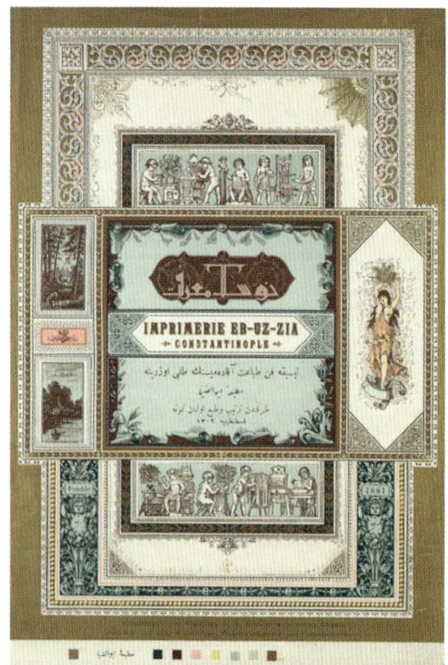

Chromolithographs, like this c.1895 ad for a Turkish printing house, used multiple print runs to build the image. The swatches along the bottom edge of the print indicate its eight ink colors.

sturdy, and cheap in comparison to metal, with no perceived loss of print quality, wood type accommodated sizes up to three feet tall. American manufacturers introduced mass-produced wood type in 1828, and their names—particularly Page (est. 1865) and Hamilton (est. 1880)—have become synonymous with wood type in the contemporary imagination. Wood type specimens, though, document a more complex, global landscape.

An American (?) invention

Wood type, often portrayed as a quintessentially American typographic form, emerged as a mass-produced product in 1828. *Inland Printer*'s 1907 profile of wood type manufacturer Darius Wells told the story of an entirely American invention—technologically, materially, and aesthetically.[50] Seeking a way to automate the laborious process of hand-engraving large letterforms into wooden printing blocks, Wells invented the lateral router in 1827 after collaborative experiments with the Bruce foundry of New York, then released his first specimen book the following year. In 1834, New York based inventor William Leavenworth improved this process by combining the lateral router with a pantograph specially adapted for the purpose.[51] This combination facilitated tracing a letterform template while the machine copied it onto a block of wood at a size/width/height ratio specified by the operator, and America introduced wood type to an eager public. As part of their comprehensive program for "covering the continent," ATF distributed wood type at the height of its popularity. Their 1897 catalog included a fifteen-page introductory selection of ATF's wood types, two pages of borders and rules, and a notice to request the *Complete Specimen Book of Wood Type* [Fig 4.17]. This speciality catalog, "forwarded on application," included "the most up-to-date, and also all the standard, styles of wood type" with full font schemes.[52] The brief sample in the 1897 catalog included blackletters, romans, italics, Egyptians, Tuscans, and grotesques in sizes from 5-line to 15-line.

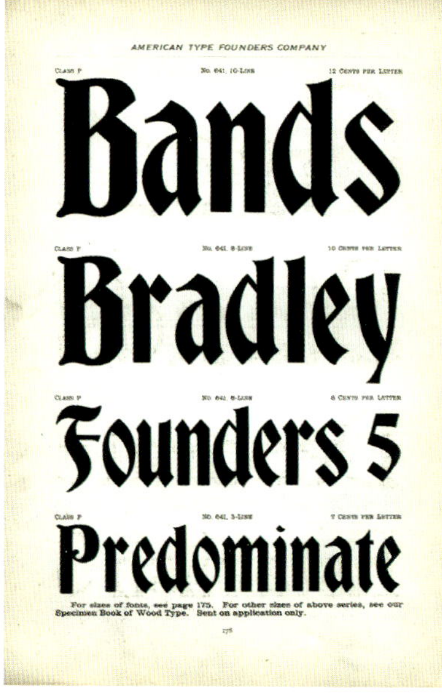

AMERICAN TYPE FOUNDERS COMPANY

Class F　No. 641, 10-Line　12 Cents per Letter

Bands

Bradley

Founders 5

Class F　No. 641, 5-Line　7 Cents per Letter

Predominate

For sizes of fonts, see page 175. For other sizes of above series, see our Specimen Book of Wood Type. Sent on application only.

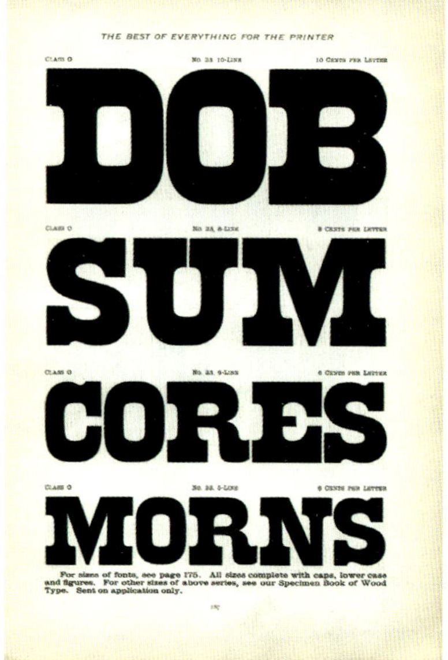

THE BEST OF EVERYTHING FOR THE PRINTER

Class O　No. 38, 10-Line　10 Cents per Letter

DOB

SUM

CORES

MORNS

For sizes of fonts, see page 175. All sizes complete with caps, lower case and figures. For other sizes of above series, see our Specimen Book of Wood Type. Sent on application only.

Fig 4.17 (right)

***Specimens of Printing Types* (ATF, New York, 1897). In their quest to "cover the continent," ATF manufactured and marketed wood type, though in much smaller quantities than their metal types. The wood type section in their 1897 catalog advised printers to write and request a copy of the *Complete specimen book of wood type*.**

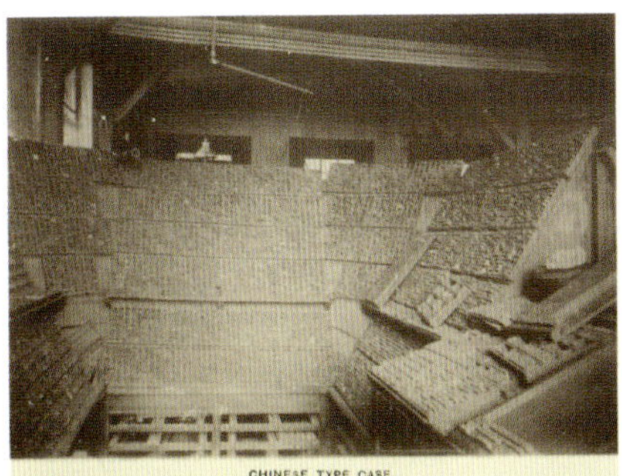

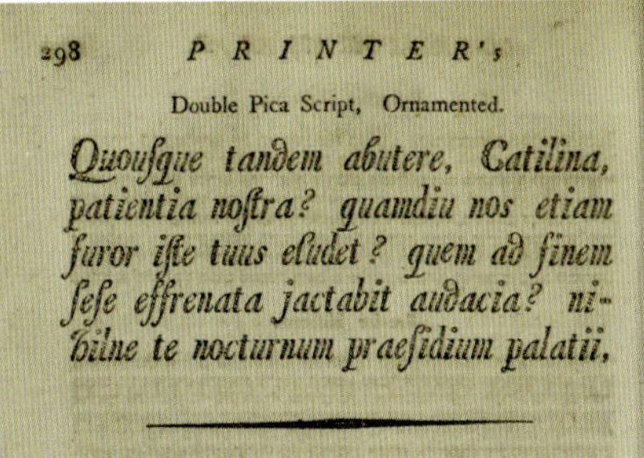

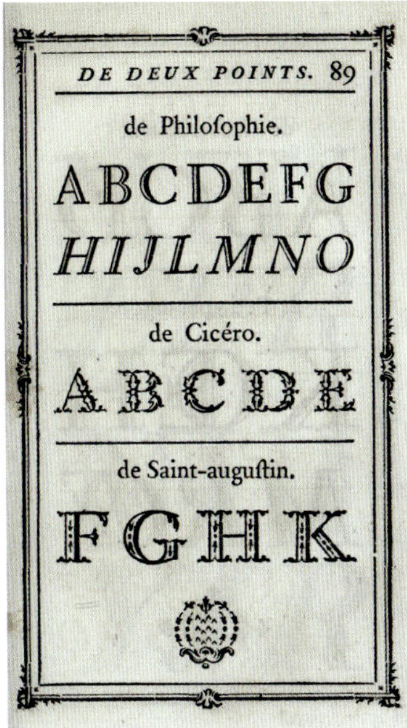

Fig 4.18 (left)

The origins of wood type aren't entirely American. Chinese experiments with movable wooden type began around the turn of the fourteenth century, but the medium wasn't particularly useful given the vast number of Chinese characters, as a photo of a Chinese type case shows (from *The Mission Press in China*, American Presbyterian Mission Press, Shanghai, 1895). Decorative flourishes much like those in American wood type enlivened earlier English and French metal types, too, as seen in the first known English ornamental typeface (Union Pearl, c.1690) and Fournier's display faces (in his *Manuel*, v. 2, 1766).

The history of wood as a type-making material, and of the letterforms most commonly produced in wood, are more complex and less American than the *Inland Printer*'s story asserted [Fig. 4.18]. Wood as a *material* to construct movable type dates to early experiments in mid-eleventh century China; successful early publishing applications of this technology include Wang Zhen's Yuan dynasty text. *A Method of Making Moveable Wooden Types for Printing Books* (1313), which followed his 100-copy print run of *Records of Jingde County* (1298).[53] Movable type proved less useful for the vast character set of **Chinese** than it would for Western European printers of the 26-letter Latin alphabet roughly a century and a half later, and it wasn't widely adopted by Chinese printers. Still, Darius Wells wasn't the first to make printing types out of wood. The aesthetic origins of wood type as we know it today are likewise polyphonic, traced by wood type collector Rob Roy Kelly to the first known ornamented display types in metal. The visual heritage of the English face Union Pearl (London, 1690) and the display faces of French type founder Fournier (1749, 1770) informed the design decisions of wood type manufacturers.[54] Kelly initially proposed three primary stylistic categories for wood type—Roman, Antique, and Gothic; later he added Clarendon, Tuscan, and Script. All of these might be ornamental, semi-ornamental, or plain, based on categories Nicolete Gray laid out in *Nineteenth Century Ornamented Typefaces*.[55] Wood type manufacturers embellished and modified these basic letterform categories with enthusiasm, leaving behind a vast range of playful, ornate, imaginative types.

Complexities of origin aside, many nineteenth-century American manufacturers certainly specialized in large, visually ornate, mass-produced wood types for display purposes. Other manufacturers quickly joined Darius Wells and William Leavenworth: J.G. Cooley (Connecticut, c.1832); George Nesbitt (New York, 1838); William Page (1856, Connecticut) and his employee Charles Tubbs (who pirated Page's designs to form his own company); Morgans & Wilcox and the Celluloid Wood Type Company

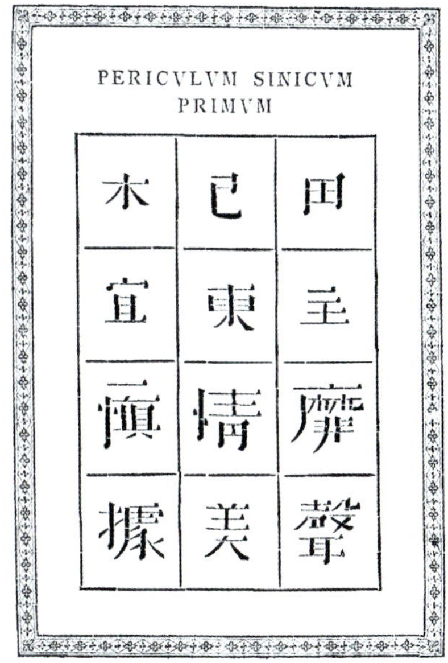

This **Chinese** typeface (Breitkopf, 1789) breaks characters into component strokes, using multiple sorts to build a single logograph (character representing one word). With about 2,200 Chinese logographs in everyday use, a sort for each would be unwieldy; but Breitkopf's proposed system was illegible.

Lines pica, the unit of measurement for wood type in the USA, was often shortened to lines. A pica measures 12 points; there are 6 picas to the inch, so 6 lines pica type is 1″ tall.

(New York); and Hamilton (Wisconsin, 1880). The United States dominated the market for wood type, and surviving specimens skew heavily American; Hamilton, especially, pursued an international market starting in 1889.[56] Naming conventions, however, reflect multiple geographic points of origin. Since larger sizes rendered points an unwieldy unit of measurement, American wood type manufacturers adopted the existing practice of measuring larger metal sizes in **lines pica** instead. "Twelve line pica" type is twelve picas (144 pts., 2″) tall, a nomenclature eventually shortened to "twelve line." In continental Europe, the unit of measurement was usually the **cicero**, abbreviated *cic*. Like the pica, one cicero equaled six points—but six Didot points, a slightly different measurement from the American point. So, as with metal type, small but meaningful differences in size occurred between American and European types, and standardization remained elusive even within a single system of measurement. Kelly's categorization system, though developed from his close study of American wood type, remains in use today for visual analysis of wood type regardless of national origin. Intended for ephemeral use when produced, wood types—physical materials and written records alike—have largely been lost or discarded.[57] However, Kelly's investment in researching, documenting, and printing with American wood types provided a robust foundation upon which scholars and printers continue to build.[58]

Fig 4.19 (below)

Specimens of Holly Wood Type **(Two Rivers WI, Hamilton & Katz, 1880). Hamilton's holly wood types were cost effective, even for wood type, because they were produced by veneering a thin letterform in holly to a cheaper printing block. The largest types in the 1880 catalog required a 5-page fold-out to accommodate their giant size.**

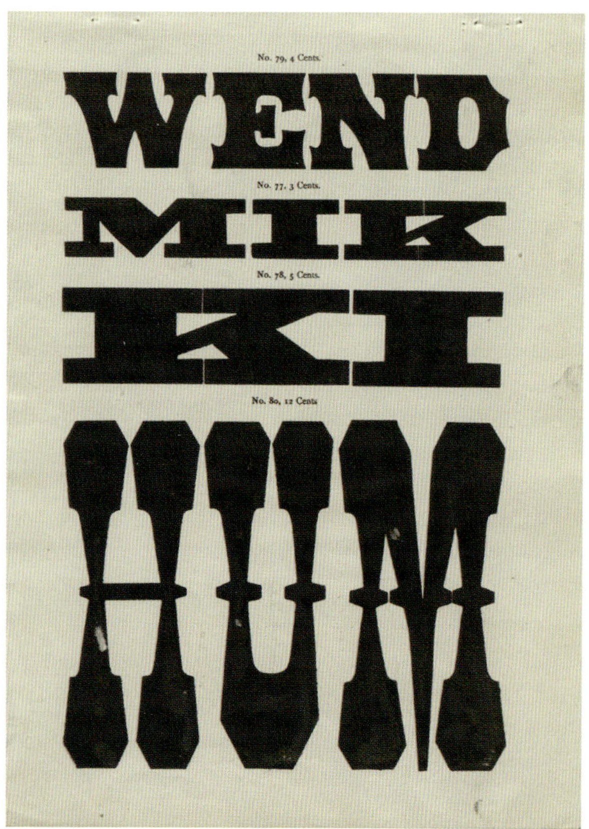

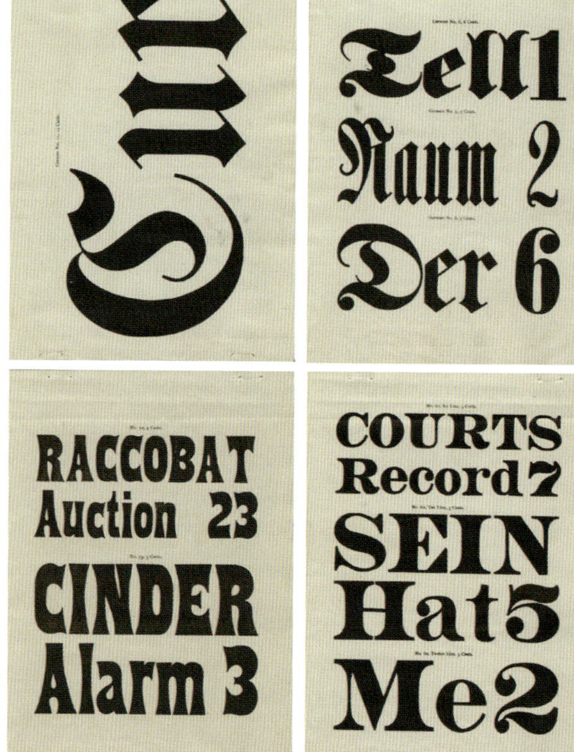

Advantages of wood type

The primary benefits of wood type—that it was cheaper, larger, and easier to alter and embellish than metal type without lessening print quality—informed the design of specimens produced to sell it. The specimens addressed these concerns, describing in words and images why printers should stock wood type and how they should use it most advantageously.

The Hamilton Manufacturing Company's *Specimen of Holly Wood Type* (c.1880) addressed the relationship between size and price [Fig. 4.19]. Hamilton's veneer types—letters cut from a thin sheet of holly wood and glued to the surface of a cheaper block of wood—cut cost by half to three-quarters compared to end-cut types.[59] Hamilton, the only maker of veneer types, marketed them specifically as a money-saving innovation, promising prices "sixty per cent cheaper than any other wood type" and supplying two pages of customer testimonies as evidence. "We pronounce your improvement a decided benefit to the country publishers," gushed one Jewel City, Kansas, newspaper printer. "They can now afford to carry a nice assortment at a trifling cost."[60] The catalog's display text for typeface No. 70 promised a "wood type revolution," and the sheer size of the printed letterforms offered visual proof. To fully demonstrate their size, a fold-out spread five pages wide showed Nos. 81–83, the largest types. This strategy emphasized the type's scale, which was far too large for metal.

Apart from the impressive size achieved by its fold-out pages, though, the *Holly Wood* specimen followed a well-established format for display faces, showing types in single, centered, horizontally-oriented lines. At the end of the specimen, five pages of blackletter types catered to the typographic tastes of German-American audiences, a growing demographic given contemporary patterns of immigration to the United States.[61] The catalog called these types "German" and numbered them to indicate different styles and sizes (e.g. German No. 5). The twenty-page catalog also offered fat faces, **Tuscans**, and gothics, most labeled only with a number—No. 76 was a clarendon, No. 68 a gothic. A few faces came in multiple sizes; No. 62 was shown in both six line and ten line, with size and price included in the numerical label.

Conversely, Palmer & Rey's *New Specimen Book* (1884) described the size range available in its wood types [Fig. 4.20]. It displayed each face at a relatively small size, twelve to fifteen lines, but each page included the header, "Wood Type. Made any size desired." Printers chose a design, named a size, and placed an order. The pantograph and lateral router ensured an identical match to the design seen in the catalog, since types of all sizes were produced from a single template; metal type required separate punches and matrices for every variable. As the west coast agents for William Page & Company, Palmer & Rey's San Francisco foundry sold Page's designs rather than designing their own wood type. Their 150+ page 1884 specimen concluded with some twenty pages of Page wood types, corners, and borders, attesting to Page's wide geographic reach—though not as profoundly as Page's 1879 catalog designed specifically for export to its Australian distributor.[62]

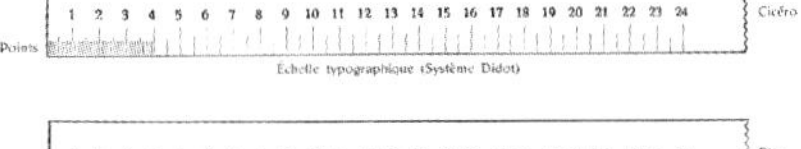

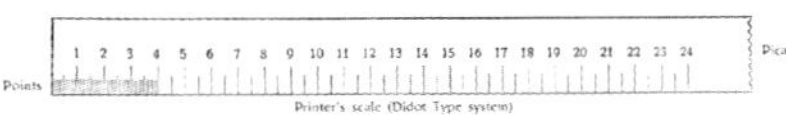

The **cicero** was the unit of measurement for wood type in much of Western Europe, roughly equivalent to the United States' one line pica.

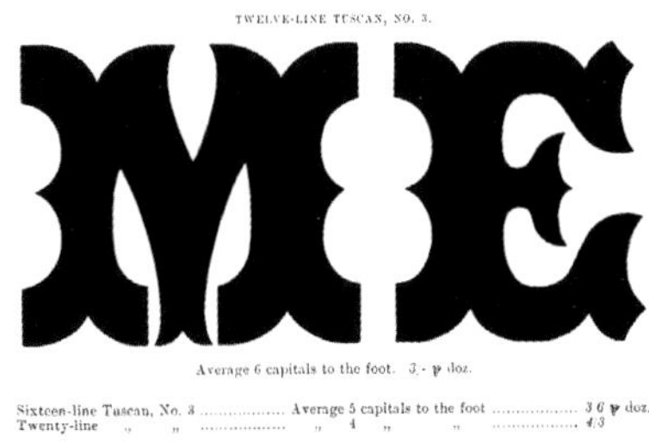

Tuscans are display faces with bifurcated or trifurcated serifs; pointed, wedge-shaped, concave, rounded, or otherwise unusually shaped terminaals, wavy countours, and medial (at the middle of the stroke) or additive (shadows, fills, or patterns within the stroke) ornament.

Wood type also offered exciting aesthetic opportunities, particularly for polychromatic printing. Chromatic wood type reached its pinnacle in Page's *Specimens of Chromatic Types and Borders* (1874), unrivaled in terms of visual complexity [Fig. 4.21]. Every letter was built from interlocking pieces, each piece designed to print in a separate color. In the finished print, the overlapping pieces formed additional colors—a two-part letterform printed in yellow and blue inks had the third color of green. Page wasn't the only manufacturer of **chromatic wood type**, but he was acknowledged as its outstanding designer and producer. "Mr Page was a practical printer ... and a mechanical genius," the *Inland Printer* reported. "His factory produced the most and the best wood type in its day."[63] His 1874 specimen, with 100 colorful pages of decorative types, dizzies the viewer with its aesthetic exuberance. Elaborate ornamental borders frame many pages; often, only one or two letters appear on the page, emphasizing their scale. Page used smaller types to show faces offered in multiple sizes and styles (e.g., solid or outlined). The specimen's overall effect is highly decorative and visually complex—which was, of course, the entire point of printing with chromatic wood type.

Fig 4.20 (below)

Third Revised Specimen Book **(Palmer & Rey, San Francisco, 1887). Palmer & Rey was the west coast distributor for Page & Co., which despite a home office in Connecticut cultivated a geographically diverse customer base. Page reached west not only to California but also across the Pacific to Australia.**

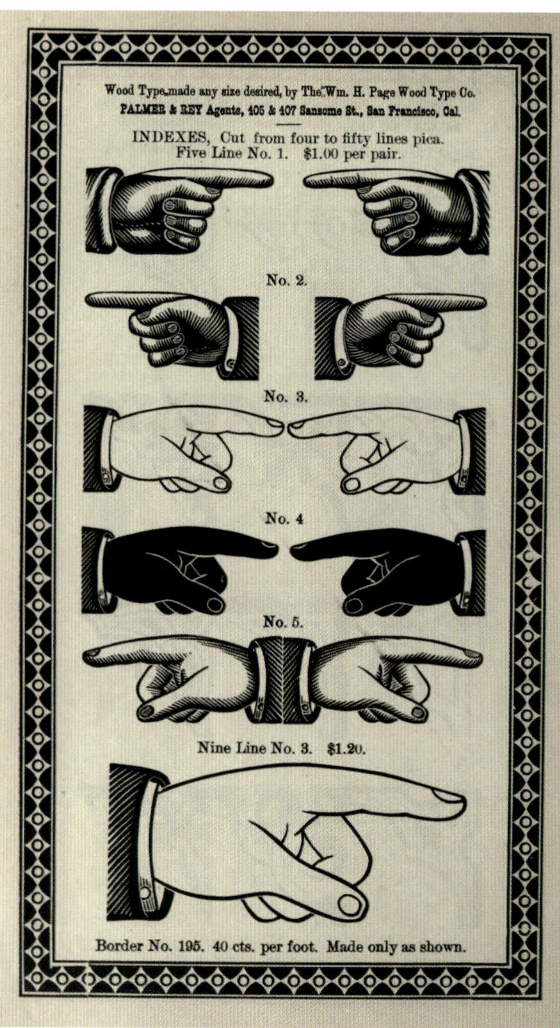

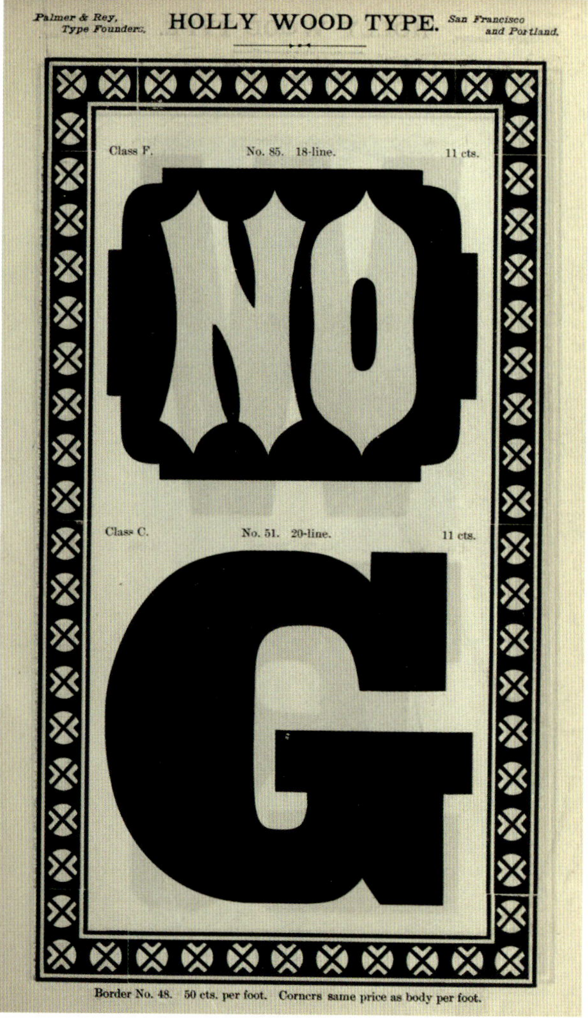

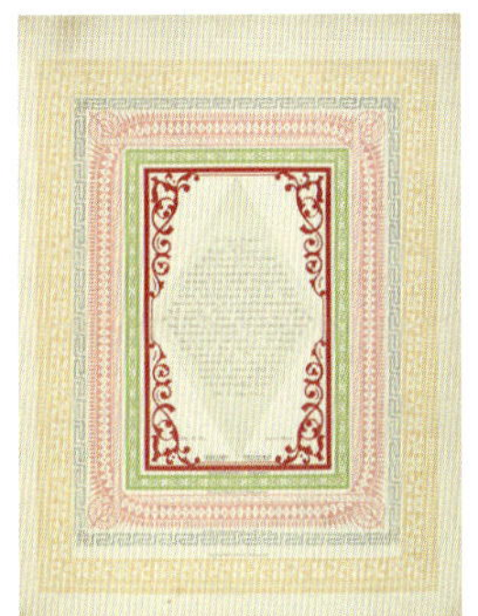

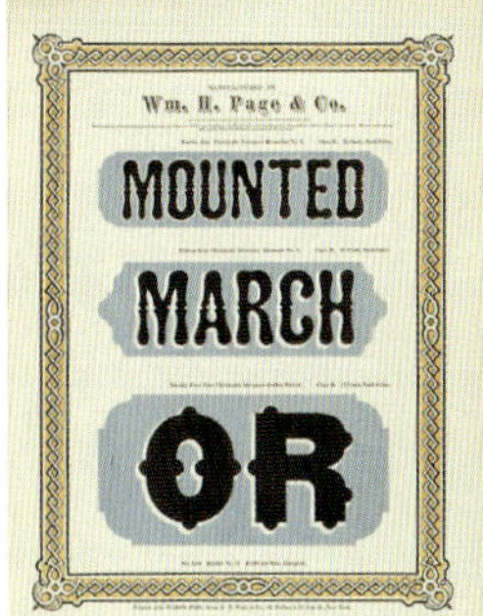

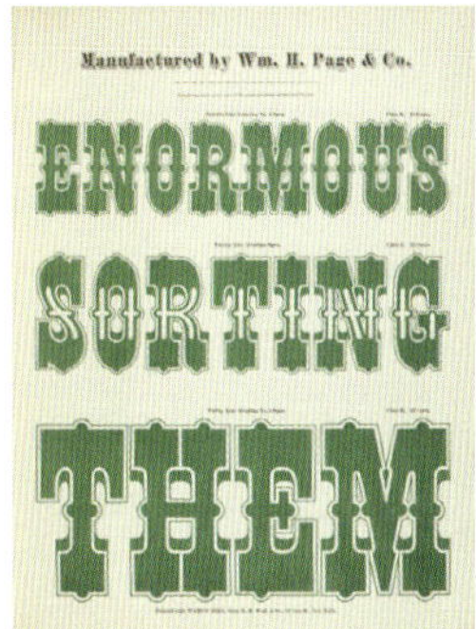

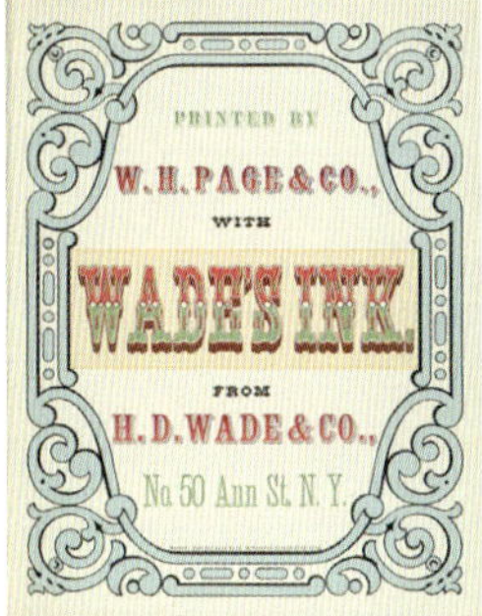

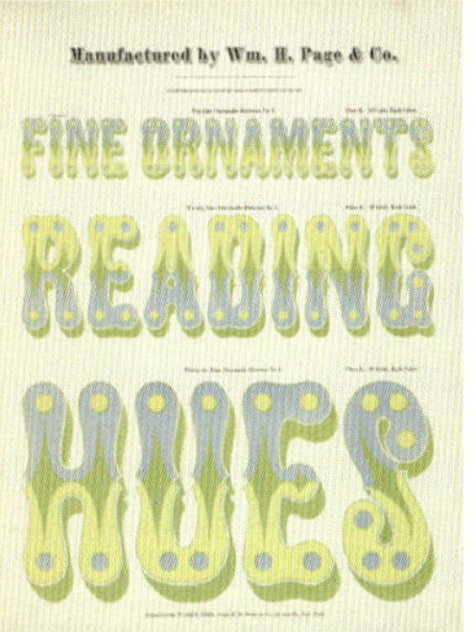

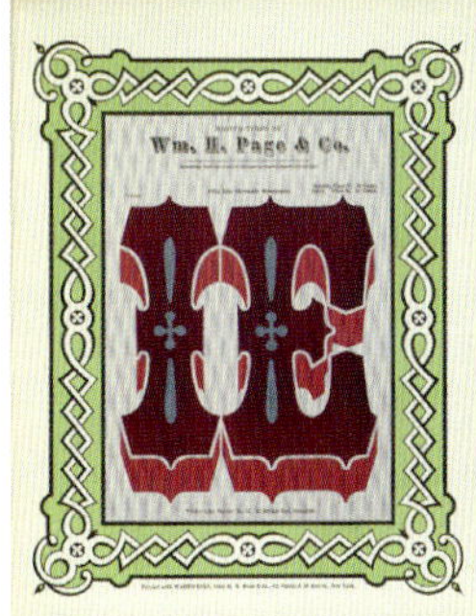

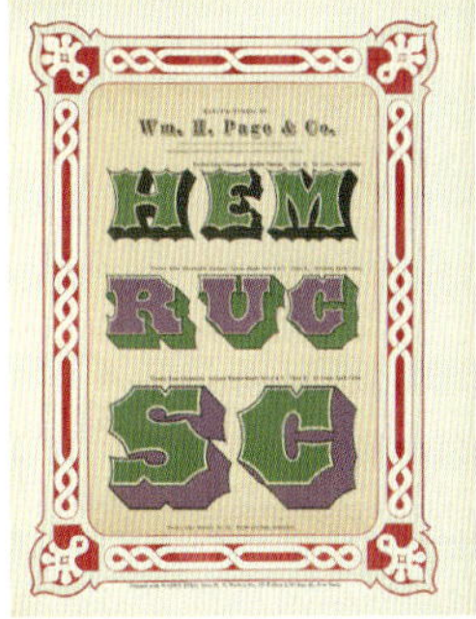

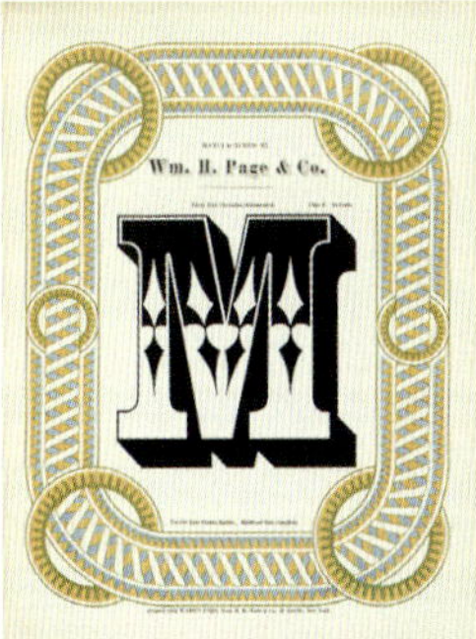

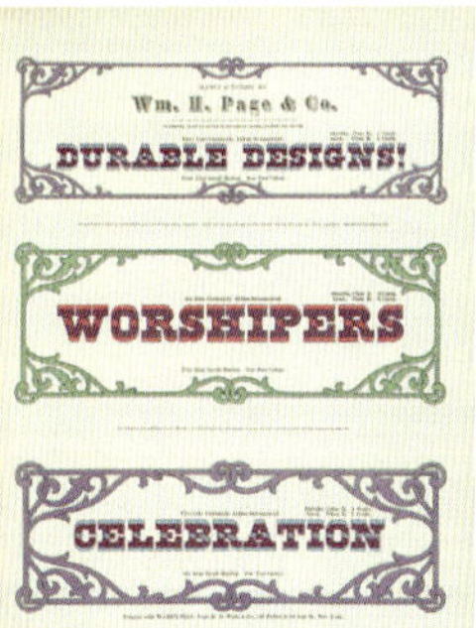

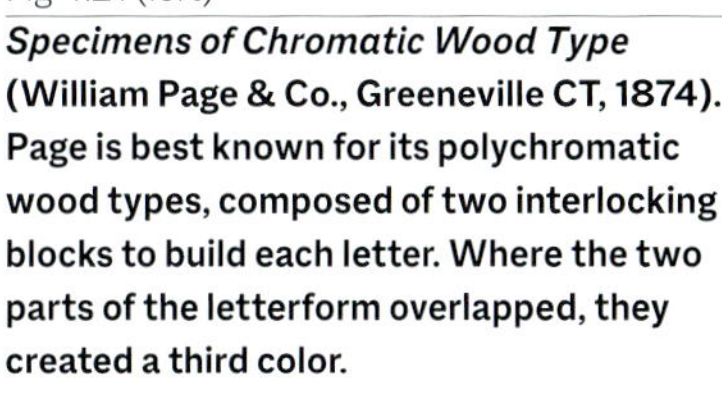

Fig 4.21 (left)

Specimens of Chromatic Wood Type **(William Page & Co., Greeneville CT, 1874). Page is best known for its polychromatic wood types, composed of two interlocking blocks to build each letter. Where the two parts of the letterform overlapped, they created a third color.**

Chromatic wood types often combined two ink colors, creating a third where they overlapped, as seen in the detail from Hamilton's catalog. The Russian sample from 1887 is much less complex, but it too is chromatic wood type.

Though Page's chromatic type is well-known, foundries outside the United States used the technique too. The Caslon foundry, for instance, offered polychromatic wood type to the English market [Fig. 4.22]. The *Specimen of Wood Letter Founts, Plain, Ornamental, and Double-working* (c.1870) offered a wide selection of Gothics, which Caslon by this time called *Sanserifs*, countering the perception that Victorian design always applied heavy decoration. Some of these very practical typefaces were available in a range of sizes; Sanserif Condensed No. 2, for instance, at 16-line and 20-line sizes, with annotations about its 18-, 24-, 30-, and 40-line sizes. At twenty lines, the face averaged seven capital letters to the foot, while at forty it averaged only three. These "plain founts" were no doubt just as useful and flexible to job printers of the 1870s as today's sans serifs are to designers. Decorative letterforms very much aligned with period taste, however, and Caslon's "ornamental" wood types offered printers the novelty they craved with faces like Tuscan No. 3, which boasted **bifurcated** serifs and **concave** stem strokes. Finally, "double-working letters" achieved dazzling color effects. These polychromatic letters translated everything from the plainest Gothic to the most ornamented Tuscan into colorful eye candy.

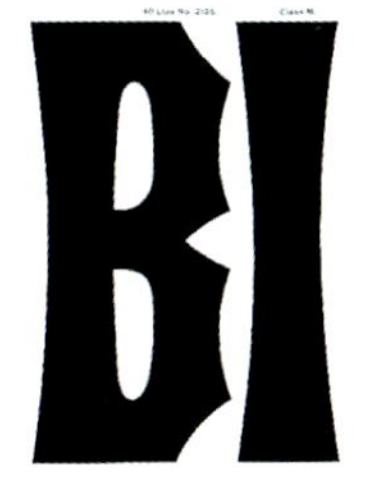

Bifurcated serifs are divided in half, like those seen in the slab serif (right); **concave** strokes curve inward (left) like those seen on the sans serif.

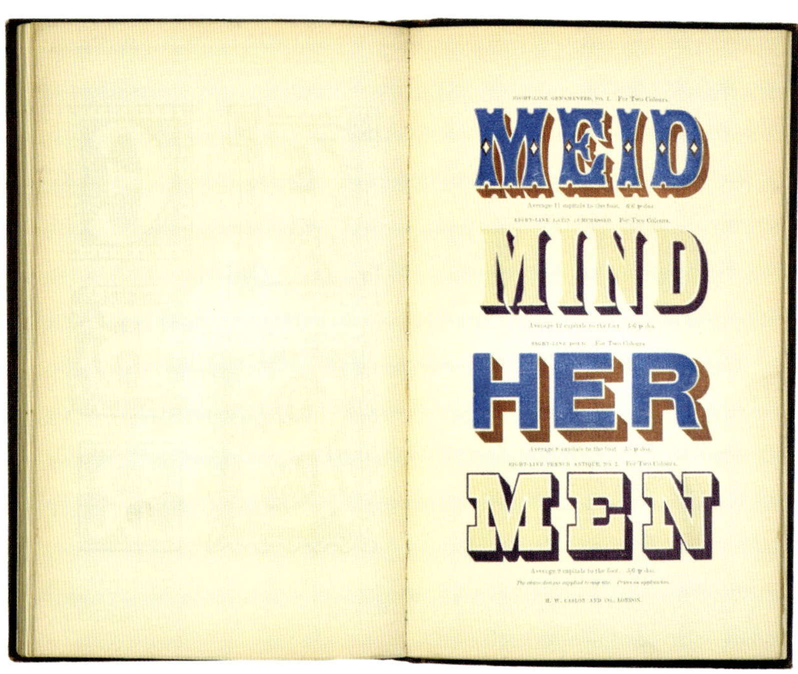

Fig 4.22 (right)
***Specimens of Wood Letter* (Caslon & Co., London, 1900). The Caslon foundry's "double-working" wood types offered designs both "plain and ornamental." While contemporary viewers associate wood type with overwrought Victorian ornament, the original producers intended it for a variety of purposes, some of them requiring very minimal decoration.**

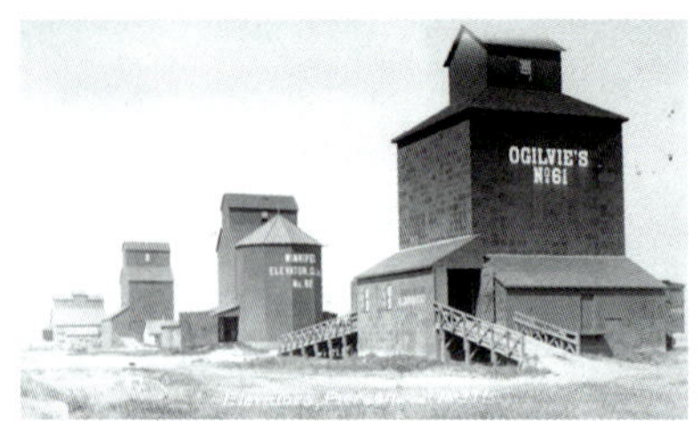

Larger-scale advertising marketed goods and services to passing pedestrians and motorists. Some letters were painted, like those on the grain elevators on this c. 1920 postcard by the Winnipeg Printing Company; others were printed, requiring large type.

Advertising at large scale

Primarily, wood type needed to attract public viewing attention. Printers who used it produced what was perceived as visually engaging poster work, a fact that didn't escape commentators of the day. The *American Encyclopedia of Printing* observed of a firm using wood type that "The great consequent superiority of their posters, soon compelled others to imitate their example, and thus the use of wood type soon became universal" for this kind of job work.[64] Wood type specimens articulated this purpose in both their visual form and descriptive language. Indeed, specimens sometimes presented wood type and **larger-scale advertising** as one and the same. *Tubbs Wood Type*, published in Connecticut in the 1880s, depicts a dialogue between two printers, which opens with one saying to the other, "That's a dandy poster you have put out! Been getting a lot of new wood type, I see." In other words, wood type must be responsible for the visual appeal of the recent poster designs.

The roughly 175-page Tubbs specimen offered printers ample material for aesthetic expression [Fig. 4.23]. It opened with borders, **ornaments**, and manicules; types—most pirated from Page—included fat faces, gothics, slab serifs, and **scripts**, the majority either plain or semi-ornamented. Pictured sizes ranged from four-line pica to 40-line, just over three inches, with larger sizes made upon request.[65] The text introduced wood types as suitable for posters, but the specimen made no further effort to visualize this purpose through displaying actual or simulated ads or phrases of advertising copy. Instead, Tubbs displayed the types very simply, in one or two columns, rotating the baseline vertically to save space at larger sizes. The types were numbered, not named, with sizes indicated in lines (e.g., 15-line No. 2234). How the type was to be used was left to the printer's imagination.

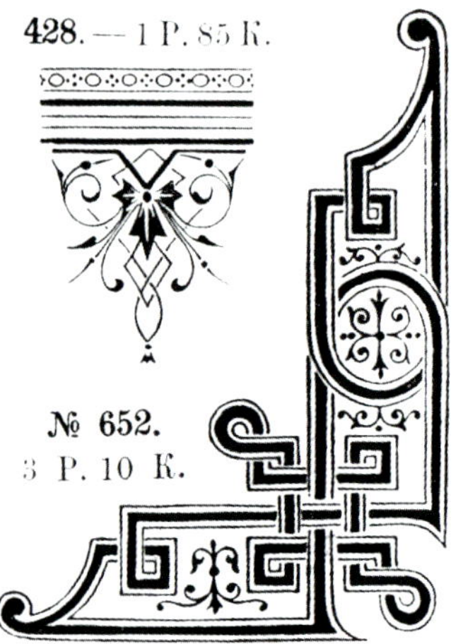

Ornaments might be a generic term encompassing any decorative material, including borders, corners, and manicules, or it might specifically mean fleurons (printer's flowers); examples from an 1887 Russian catalog.

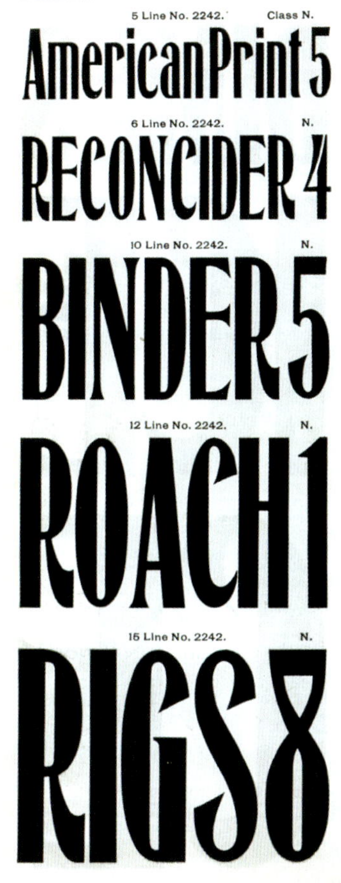

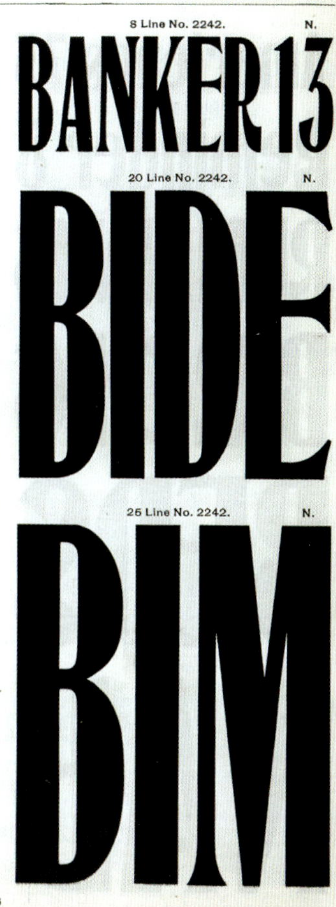

Fig 4.23 (left)

Tubbs Wood Type **(Tubbs & Co., South Windham, 188--). Charles Tubbs, who stole his employer William Page's designs to start Tubbs Wood Type, advertised his wares as particularly suited for printing "dandy" posters.**

In contrast, the cover of *Hamilton's Specimens of Wood Type Faces* (c.1907) spoke directly to the role its wares played in saturating the visual environment with large-scale commercial typography [Fig. 4.24]. The full-bleed image showed a man wheat-pasting a huge broadside to a barn door; its text doubled as the specimen's title. By this time, Hamilton had acquired the Page company, so its stock was extensive. Instead of an elaborate ornamental face, though, the broadside on the cover used a simple gothic face. The image cultivated a decidedly everyday reading: a working man in rolled-up shirtsleeves and suspenders, a barn door, and more posters awaiting wheat-paste stacked near the paste bucket. This normalized the presence of large-scale advertising within the built environment, and the massive scale of the letterforms demonstrated how wood type communicated advertisers' messages to viewers throughout their daily lives.

Cuerpo 36

Andrés Bello

Weir Scott & Co.

Cuerpo 42

Huáscar

Rocamora

Script typefaces mimic handwritten letters, seen here in *Catálogo de los Tipos i Viñetas de la Imprenta i Encuadernación Barcelona* (1895).

Fig 4.24 (right and below)
Hamilton's Specimen of Wood Type faces **(Hamilton Manufacturing Co., Two Rivers WI, 1907). The scale of wood type meant that it was particularly suited for large-format advertising in the everyday environment. It was also used for road signs in the early days of automobile travel.**

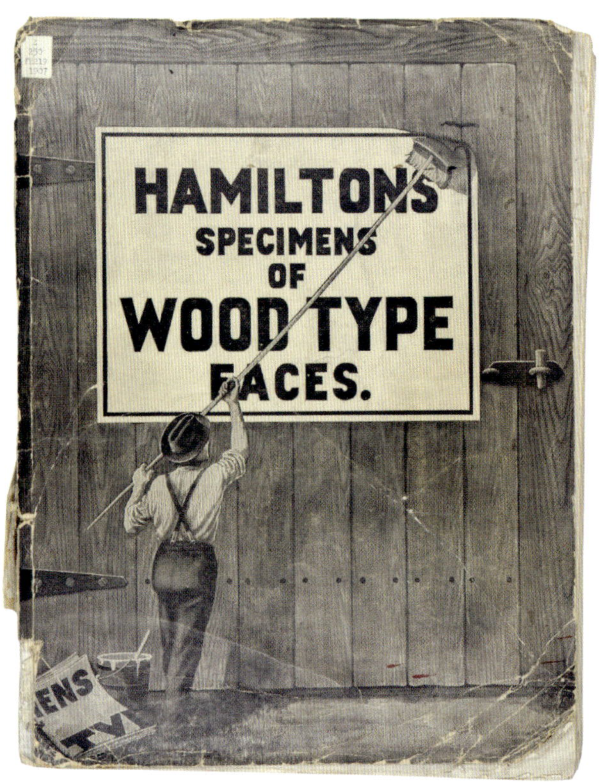

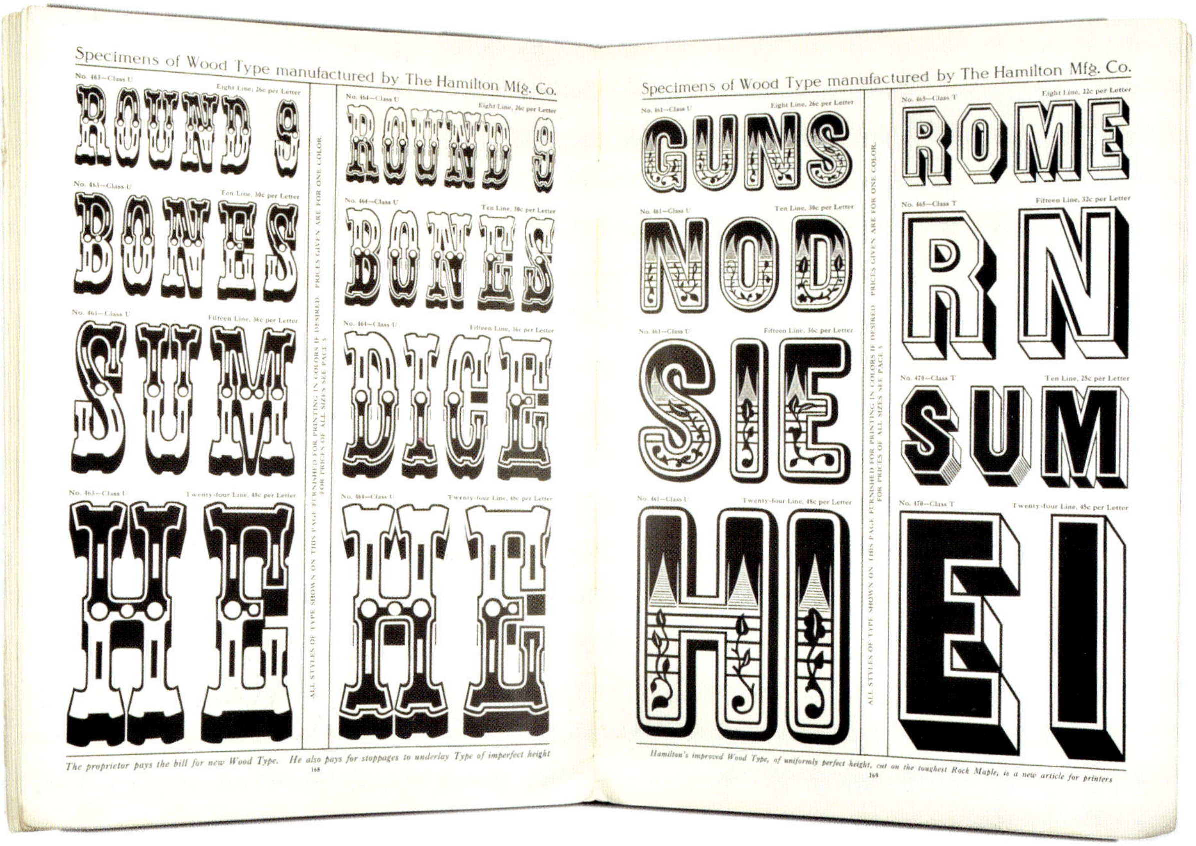

Though most often associated with mid- to late nineteenth century American printing, wood type remained integral to international advertising well into the twentieth century. The German foundry Schelter & Giesecke (est. Leipzig, 1819) produced wood types as a supplement to their traditional metal faces [Fig. 4.25]. *Plakatschriften* (1928) offered wood and metal display types designed specifically for posters and other advertising media. A double rule, printed in a single bright color, framed each page of black type. Throughout, sizes were marked in both Cicero and [Didot] points, numbered, and usually named as well; a table listed typeface names alongside a sample of the type's letterforms. The catalog showed metal display types (*Plakatschriften*) and wood types (*Holzschriften*), as well as calendar numbers, arrows, borders, and rules. It opened with a robust selection of blackletters, still commonly used in Germany at the time. The lingering aesthetic influence of Jugendstil informed Edelgotisch and Schelter-Antiqua, and the catalog included multiple languages and alphabets, including the Cyrillic Nicodemus, the Greek Gräconautilius, and Berthod's Hebrew Meruba.[66] Proportionally, though, Gothics (sans serifs) dominated the stylistic menu. While it might be tempting to think of wood type as a medium that demands ostentatious ornamentation, Schelter & Giesecke's focus on businesslike and functional Gothics offers another reminder that wood type was marketed and used for a wide range of aesthetic objectives. Scale, rather than style, visually differentiated many of the faces.

Zvi Bregman's *Wood Type* (1938) demonstrated the persistent, international market for wood type as well [Fig. 4.26]. Bregman, a Palestine-based manufacturer of Hebrew wood type, offered eight pages of Hebrew faces in his roughly 25-page catalog, some in traditional styles and others, like his outline and inline faces, more contemporary. These highly **geometricized** styles translated Bauhaus and Art Deco aesthetics into the Hebrew alphabet. The 1920s–30s had been a productive period for Hebrew type design, both in Germany where there was an active Zionist movement and in Palestine. Type designers more commonly developed Hebrew types in metal for book

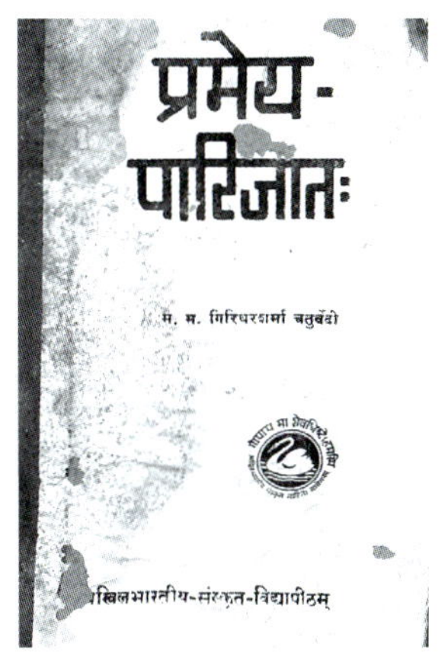

Geometricized typefaces break characters down into straight lines, right angles, and basic component shapes — as seen in the title (compared to the subtitle and imprint) in this mid 20c. Sanskrit publication of The Myth of the Parijat [night-blooming jasmine].

Nr. 4500. 8/10 Cicero 200 Buchstaben Mk. 135.—

Kamenz

Nr. 4501. 10/12 Cicero 200 Buchstaben Mk. 160.—

The **cicero** is the unit of measure for wood type in Europe. One cicero equals roughly 1.066 American pica. One pica equals ⅙ inch, or 72 points.

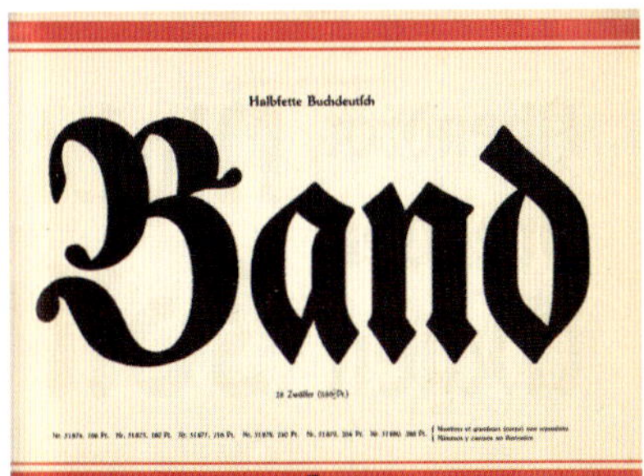

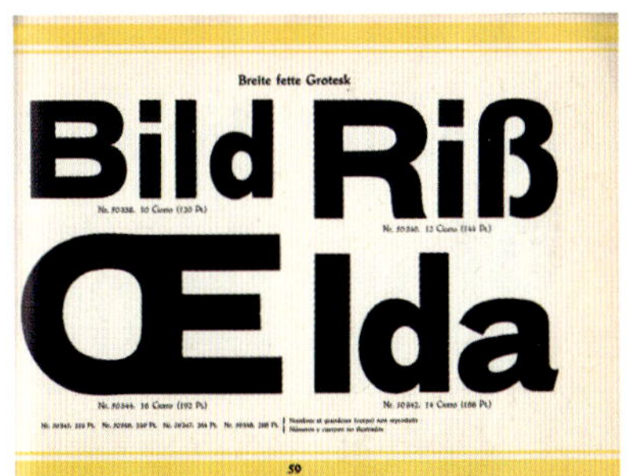

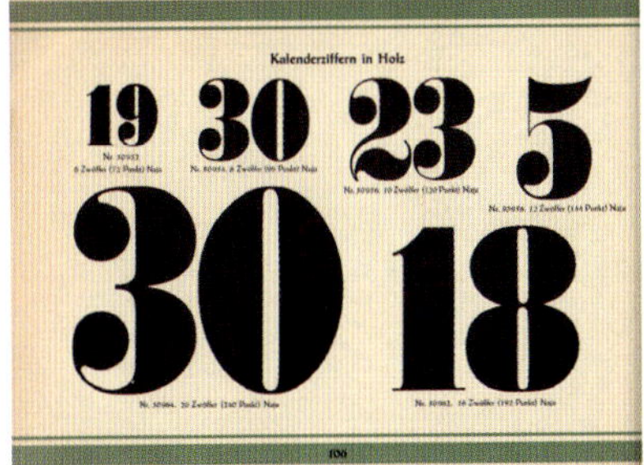

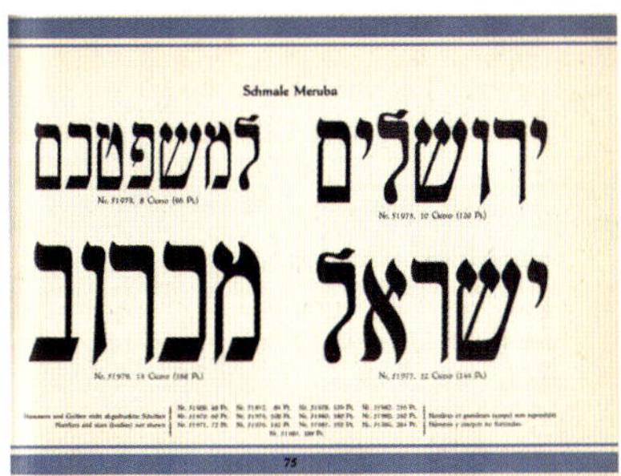

Fig 4.25 (left)

Plakatschriften & Holzschiften / Display Type & Wood Type **(Schelter & Giesecke, Leipzig, 1928). Wood type, though now most often associated with the nineteenth century United States, continued to be useful for large-scale advertising well into the twentieth century and around the world, as this German catalog shows.**

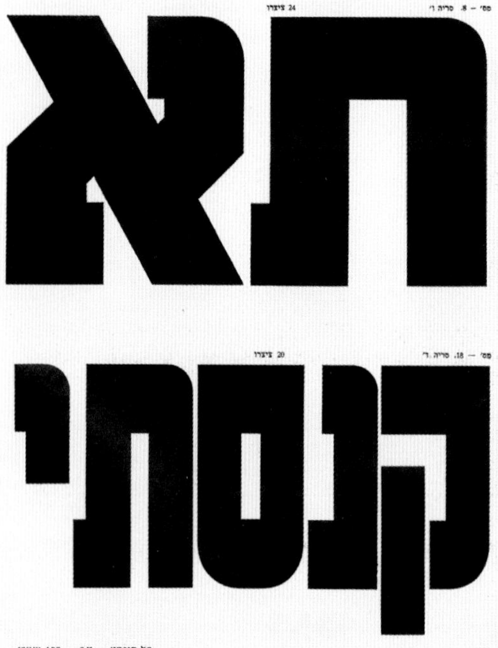

בית חרושת לאותיות עץ צבי ברגמן תל־אביב
חתא
קנסחי
כל דוגמא מ3 — 100 ציצרו

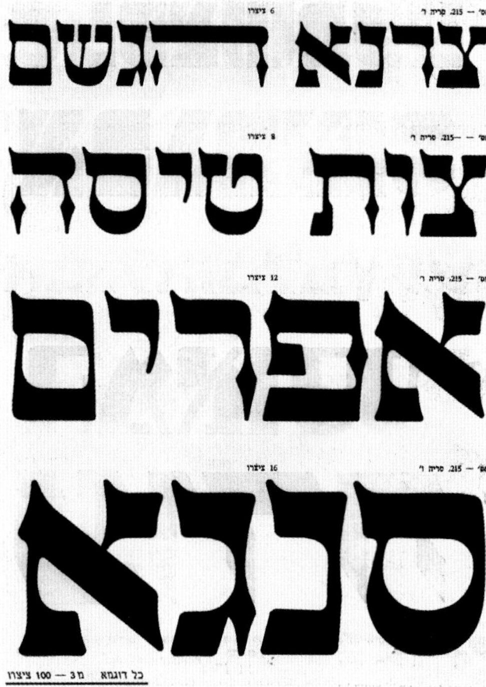

צבי ברגמן בית־חרושת לאותיות עץ תל־אביב
צרנא הגשם
צות טיסה
אפרים
סנגא
כל דוגמא מ3 — 100 ציצרו

and newspaper printing, however.[67] Bregman's wood types extended these existing efforts to develop a distinctly Hebrew visual language of typographic form, one that drew on tradition but also participated in contemporary design movements. They facilitated the use of Hebrew at large scale for printing environmental advertising, signs, and posters.

Throughout his specimen, Bregman highlighted the multilingual nature of his types. In addition to Hebrew, the specimen included one Arabic face (No. 285, class G) and ten pages of Latin alphabets with some sample words in English. Two pages of borders rounded out the selection. Both Hebrew and Latin faces utilized arabic numerals to label type size, but the Latin-alphabet pages had English-language text (*No. 207—Class G—12 Cic*). Following European convention, sizes were marked in *cic.*, or **cicero**. In the Hebrew section, these labels were typeset in Hebrew. In both alphabets, though, printers ordered based on how many of the letter A they needed, a fairly common way to order wood type. A **fonting scheme** chart showed how many of each alphabetic character was included with a given number of A's. Thirty A's, for instance, were accompanied by thirty-eight E's but only six X's. The type sizes displayed in the catalog ranged from 4–40 cic. and a note on each page reminded printers that each style could be ordered in sizes from 3–100 cic. In the Latin-alphabet section, slab serifs and sans serifs dominated. The catalog offered little evidence of wood type's ornate decorative possibilities, focusing instead on contemporary, functional letterforms.

In the twenty-first century, wood type evokes a particular nostalgic aesthetic. Digital revivals and translations facilitate its application to screens and digital printing.[68] At its original time of production, though, wood type met a series of very practical needs, and it accommodated a wide range of aesthetics, including the strictly functional. Yet unlike body types, which above all needed to be serviceable, wood type was almost always display type. This opened up expansive design possibilities, including the ability to embrace up-to-the-moment—and momentary—fashions. Casual twenty-first century viewers might assign generic nostalgia or Victoriana to these styles. But for their original audiences they connoted more specific cultural meanings, connoted by the visual language and physical characteristics of the specimens themselves.

Conclusion

During a period of rapid mechanization around the turn of the twentieth century, typefounders and printers navigated a changing professional landscape. The ultimate goal—the printed page—remained constant, but the methods and machines used to reach this goal were evolving. At times, these changes were invisible on the printed page, as with Pettingill's durable copper-alloy type or Benton's Self-spacing Type. Arguably, such innovations didn't instrumentally change the printing trades. Rather, their existence pointed toward the priorities of founders and printers as they sought typographic innovations equal in impact to changes in printing presses. Other changes were more visible, as with the massive scale of wood type or the language (visual and written) describing standardized point and lining systems. These changes proved less profound than the mechanization introduced by Linotype and Monotype, though, and the automatic typecasting and typesetting machines of these two companies altered the typographic landscape permanently.

Fig 4.26 (opposite)

עץ תויתוא / *Wood Type* (Zvi Bregman, Tel Aviv, 1938). This catalog of Hebrew wood types shows twentieth century styles like Art Deco applied to alphabets and materials not usually associated with Modernism or the Moderne.

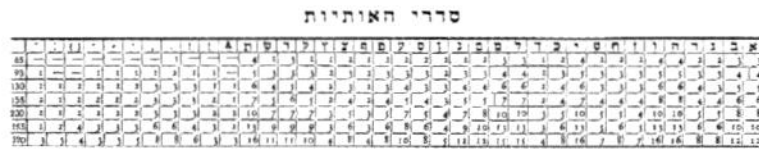

A **fonting scheme** shows the quantity of each character in one font of type. Smaller sizes included more sorts than larger ones, and common characters (A, S) appeared more frequently than uncommon ones (Q, Z).

1 Green, "Persian Print and the Stanhope Revolution."

2 Advertisement, *Inland Printer* 4, no. 3 (December 1886): 180.

3 Linn Boyd Benton, *Benton's Self Spacing Type* [Typographic Specimens] (Benton, Waldo and Company, 1886), 14, 16, http://archive.org/details/BentonWaldoSpecimenBooklet1886.

4 Typographic Messenger, "News to American Type-Founders," *Typographic Messenger* 9, no. 1 (January 1, 1894): 2.

5 Keystone Type Foundry, *Abridged Specimen Book, Type: Nickel-Alloy on Universal Line Comprising a Price List of Types, Borders, Leads and Slugs, Brass Rule, Brass Galleys; Miscellaneous Cuts and General Supplies for Printers* (Philadelphia: Keystone Type Foundry, 1906), 230, http://archive.org/details/abridgedspecimen00keysrich.

6 Pettingill & Co, *Copper Alloy Type Book, Comprising Newspaper, Book, and Display Types, Borders and Ornaments : Also Brass Rules, Dashes, Etc* (Boston: Pettingill, 1901), http://archive.org/details/copperalloytypeb00pett.

7 Alastair Johnston, *Alphabets to Order: The Literature of Nineteenth-Century Typefounders' Specimens*, 1st ed. (New Castle, DE: Oak Knoll, 2000).

8 Advertisement, *Typo* 49, no. 4 (January 31, 1891): front cover.

9 Marder, Luse & Company, *Price List and Printers' Purchasing Guide, Showing Specimens of Printing Type Manufactured by Marder, Luse & Co., Chicago, Illinois, U. S. A.* (Chicago: Marder, Luse & Company, 1890), https://catalog.hathitrust.org/Record/000772993. Marder, Luse & Company, *Price List and Printers' Purchasing Guide, Showing Specimens of Printing Type Manufactured by Marder, Luse & Co., Chicago, Illinois, U. S. A.* (Chicago: Marder, Luse & Company, 1890), https://catalog.hathitrust.org/Record/000772993.

10 [Inland Printer], "Type Foundries of the United States," *Inland Printer* 8, no. 2 (November 1890): 153-4.

11 Walter Tracy, *Letters of Credit: A View of Type Design* (Boston: David R. Godine, 2003), 23–24.

12 McKeller, Smith & Jordan, *1796-1896: One Hundred Years* (Philadelphia: McKeller, Smith & Jordan, 1896), 65, http://hdl.handle.net/2027/pst.000015538079.

13 United Typothetæ, "Report of the Committee on the Uniformity in the Bodies of Type," *The American Bookmaker* 11, no. 3 (September 1890): 88.

14 Smallian, "Type Systems of To-Day—Part II—the Didot System."

15 James Figgins, *Type Founding and Printing During the 19th Century* (London: Figgins, 1900), 18, https://archive.org/details/Figgins1900TypeFoundingPrinting..

16 Robert A. Mullen, *Recasting a Craft: St. Louis Typefounders Respond to Industrialization* (Carbondale: SIU Press, 2005), 39-41.

17 Inland Type Foundry, *Specimen Book and Catalog: A Price List of Printers' Supplies* (St. Louis: Inland Type Foundry, 1907), 114, 142, http://archive.org/details/specimenbookcata00inla.

18 Mullen, *Recasting a Craft*, 41.

19 Stephenson, Blake and Company and Sir Charles Reed & Sons, *Specimens of Point Line Type : Borders Ornaments Brass Rules &c. &c* (Toronto: Stephenson, Blake & Co., 1908), 3, 233, http://archive.org/details/specimensofpoint00step..

20 One example: during its first quarter-century, what became Sweden's Royal Printing Office (in 1879) experienced six changes in management, name, or corporate composition; Christian Axel-Nilsson, *Type Studies: The Norstedt Collection of Matrices in the Typefoundry of the Royal Printing Office: A History and Catalogue* (Stockholm: Norstedts Tryckeri, 1983), 39–46.

21 [Inland Printer], "American Typefounder's Company," *Inland Printer* 10, no. 2 (November 1892): 150-1.

22 Patricia Cost, *The Bentons: How an American Father and Son Changed the Printing Industry* (Rochester, N.Y: RIT Cary Graphic Arts Press, 2010), 70–86.

23 Maurice Annenberg, *Type Foundries of America and Their Catalogs* (New Castle [DE]: Oak Knoll Books, 1994), 41–42.

24 Alexander S. Lawson, John Bidwell, and American Type Founders Co., *Specimens of Type, Brass Rules and Dashes, Ornaments and Borders, Society Emblems, Check Lines, Cuts, Initials and Other Productions of the American Type Founders Co [1896]*, Nineteenth-Century Book Arts and Printing History (New York: Garland Pub, 1981), ix–xi; Annenberg, *Type Foundries of America and Their Catalogs*, 45.

25 American Type Founders Company, *Specimens of Printing Types* (New York: American Type Founders Co., 1897), 7, http://archive.org/details/specimensofprint00amerrich.

26 American Type Founders Company, 507–26.

27 American Type Founders Company, 949, 168–69.

28 Quadrat [Henry Lewis Bullen], "An Ideal American Citizen—the Inventor of Wood Types and the Routing Machine, and His Successors and Competitors," *Inland Printer* 35, no. 5 (August 1907): 513–14.

29 Cost, *The Bentons*. See particularly the chapter on "Morris Benton's Type Designs."

30 W.P. Jaspert, A.F. Johnson, and W.T. Berry, *Encyclopaedia of Typefaces*, 5th ed. (London: Cassell Illustrated, 2008), 44..

31 American Type Founders, *American Line Type Book, Borders, Ornaments: Price List Printing Material and Machinery 1906* (Chicago: American Type Founders Co., 1906), 139-61.

32 Jaspert, Johnson, and Berry, *Encyclopaedia of Typefaces*, 50, 295.

33 American Type Founders Co., *Specimen Book and Catalogue 1923* (Jersey City: American Type Founders Co., 1923), 7–8, http://archive.org/details/1923AmericanTypeFoundersSpecimenBookCatalogue-Hi-resolution.

34 Lawson, *Anatomy of a Typeface*, 114–16.

35 American Type Founders Co., *Specimen Book and Catalogue 1923*, 43a.

36 American Type Founders Co., *Specimen Book and Catalogue 1923*, 42.

37 David Pankow, "The Rise and Fall of ATF [editor's introduction]," *Printing History* 22, no. 1 & 2 (2002): 13-14.

38 James Figgins, *Type Founding and Printing*, 14–15.

39 *Specimens of the Tokyo Tsukiji Type Foundry* 1, no. 6 (July 1897), n.p.

40 *Specimens of the Tokyo Tsukiji Type Foundry* 2, no. 3 (Nov 1899), n.p.

41 Dornemann & Co, *Schriften in Glockenmetall Für Die Vergoldepresse [a Catalog of Bell Metal Types for the Gilding Press]* (Marderburg: Dornemann & Co, 1925), i-vii, http://objects.library.uu.nl/reader/index.php?obj=1874-284602&lan=en#page//15/03/71/1503715233329036119724221933 24083907218.jpg/mode/1up.

42 John Luther Ringwalt, *American Encyclopaedia of Printing* (Menamin & Ringwalt, 1871), 503.

43 Rob Roy Kelly, "American Wood Type," *Design Quarterly*, no. 56 (1963): 4, https://doi.org/10.2307/4047285.

44 David Shields, "Considering Rob Roy Kelly's American Wood Type Collection," *Printing History* 7 (January 1, 2010): 4.

45 John Smith Thompson, *History of Composing Machines* (Chicago: Inland Printer Company, 1904), 5, 70, 74, https://books.google.com/books?id=vIQsAAAAYAAJ&dq=history+of+the+linotype&source=gbs_navlinks_s.

46 The Thorne Type-Setting Machine Company, *The Thorne Type-Setting Machine* (Hartford: Thorne, 1894), 34, http://archive.org/details/ThorneTypeSettingMachine1894.

47 "The Simplex one-man typesetter," *Inland Printer* 28, no. 3 (Dec 1901): 398; Alessio Leonardi and Jan Middendorp, *A Line Of Type*, Mergenthaler Edition (Bad Homburg [Germany]: Linotype, 2006), 36.

48 Wood & Nathan Co., *Unitype One-Man Type Setting Machine* (New York: Wood & Nathan, 1902), 23, http://archive.org/details/UnitypeOneManTypeSettingMachineWoodNathan.

49 Miller & Richard ad in *Bookseller: The organ of the book trade* (December 12, 1865): 1090.

50 Quadrat [Henry Lewis Bullen], "Ideal American Citizen."

51 Kelly, "American Wood Type," 4; Shields, "Considering Rob Roy Kelly's American Wood Type Collection," 24.

52 American Type Founders Company, *Specimens of Printing Types*, 175.

53 Michela Bussotti and Han Qi, "Typography for a Modern World?: The Ways of Chinese Movable Types," *East Asian Science, Technology, and Medicine*, no. 40 (2014): 18, https://www.jstor.org/stable/eastasiascietech.40.9..

54 Kelly, "American Wood Type," 1; David Consuegra, *American Type: Design & Designers* (New York: Allworth Press, 2004).

55 Stephen O. Saxe and Rob Roy Kelly, *Specimen Book of Wood Type* (Madison [WI]: Silver Buckle Press, 1999), 12; Kelly, "American Wood Type," 11–17; Nicolete Gray and Ray Nasher, *Nineteenth Century Ornamented Typefaces* (London: Faber and Faber, 1976). In Gray, see particularly Nasher's chapter on "Ornamented typefaces in America."

56 Quadrat [Henry Lewis Bullen], "Ideal American Citizen," 681–82.

57 Kelly, "American Wood Type," 39–40.

58 Kelly's collection is archived—and used—at the University of Texas at Austin. "Rob Roy Kelly Collection of American Wood Type," Rob Roy Kelly Collection, 2017, https://rrk.finearts.utexas.edu/.

59 Kelly, "American Wood Type," 5; Shields, "Considering Rob Roy Kelly's American Wood Type Collection," 24.

60 Hamilton Manufacturing Co., *Specimens of Holly Wood Type* (Two Rivers [WI]: Hamilton & Katz, 1880), http://archive.org/details/ldpd_12465515_000.

61 Kelly, "American Wood Type," 22.

62 Kelly, "American Wood Type," 22.

63 Quadrat [Henry Lewis Bullen], "Ideal American Citizen," 681.

64 Ringwalt, *American Encyclopaedia of Printing*, 503.

65 Tubbs & Co., *Tubbs Wood Type* (South Windham: Tubbs & Co., 188--), http://archive.org/details/case_wing_Z250_t884.

66 J.G. Schelter & Giesecke, *Plakatschriften & Holzschiften [Display Type & Wood Type]* (Leipzig: Schelter & Giesecke, 1928), 20, 30, 70, 72, 74, http://archive.org/details/PlakatschriftenJ.G.SchelterGiesecke.

67 Ada Wardi, ed., *New Types: Three Pioneers of Hebrew Graphic Design*, (Jerusalem: The Israel Museum, 2016). In particular, see Phillip Messner's essay "Hebrew type design in the context of the book art movement and new typography," 33–67.

68 Arden Stern, "Freaks of Fancy, Revisited: Nineteenth-Century Ornamented Typography in the Twenty-First Century," *Design Issues* 32, no. 4 (October 2016): 76–90, https://doi.org/10.1162/DESI_a_00418; Paul Shaw and Jonathan Hoefler, *Revival Type: Digital Typefaces Inspired by the Past* (New Haven: Yale University Press, 2017).

Specimen Caracterès d'Affiches,
Deberney & Peignot, 1937

Today, wood type often calls to mind elaborate Victorian designs, not simple and serviceable sans serifs. Wood type was introduced in 1827 and became much less common by the turn of the twentieth century. Yet this French specimen of wood poster letters reminds us that wood fonts were designed to serve a particular function and not necessarily to promote a specific aesthetic. In an environment increasingly dominated by commercial goods and services, and travel at ever-higher speeds, large-scale advertising demanded oversized letters to catch viewers' attention, and these were too heavy and expensive in metal. Wood type is measured in picas (exactly 6 to the inch) or cicéros (roughly 6 to the inch). The United States was a leading manufacturer of mass-produced wood type, but other countries produced it too—including Australia, England, France, Germany, and Israel.

BOIS

CARACTÈRES D'AFFICHES

ANTIQUES N° I Série A

D D D D D De

6 cicéros

8 cicéros

10 cicéros

15 cicéros

20 cicéros

30 cicéros

Série A **ANTIQUES N° 3**

Biens

6 cicéros

Bien

10 cicéros

Série C **ANTIQUES N° 5**

École

15 cicéros

École

20 cicéros

SE FONT DE 6 A 60 CICÉROS

S

***Specimen Book of Type Styles*, Linotype, 1915**

Linotype's 1915 specimen, a hefty 12-pound volume of over 1,000 pages, included 768 complete fonts in sizes 5-14 points, inclusive. Eighty more were "foreign language fonts requiring their own characters," such as the Greek types shown here. Additional partial fonts, display faces, ornament, borders, numerals and fractions, and newspaper headings rounded out the catalog's "astounding" selection of typographic material. Perhaps nowhere else was Linotype's corporate mission—of mechanization, standardization, globalization, and efficiency—quite so clearly demonstrated. All styles of type, from elaborate display scripts to workaday text serifs, received the same visual treatment; all global scripts were adapted to be cast on the same machines; and all alphabets except Latin were conceptualized as "foreign."

GREEK MATRICES

10 Point Greek Bold Face No. 1

WILL RUN IN ALL MACHINES EXCEPT MODELS 1 AND

(Two Point Leaded)

Στοιχειοθεσία εἰς πλείονας τῶν τριάκον διαφόρων γλωσσῶν, ἐν οἷς ἡ Γερμανικὴ κ ἡ Ρωσσικὴ γίνεται σήμερον διὰ τῆς στοιχει θετικῆς μηχανῆς Λαϊνοτάϊπ, εἰς τὸ ὁσημέρ δὲ εὐρυνόμενον στάδιον δράσεως τῆς μηχαν ταύτης ΠΡΟΣΕΤΕΘΗ ἌΡΤΙΟΣ καὶ γλῶσσα τῶν Ἑλλήνων. Καίτοι ἡ Λαϊν τάϊπ λειτουργεῖ διὰ χειριστηρίου περιέχοντ μόνον ἐννενήκοντα κλεῖδας τὰ 160 καὶ πλέ στοιχεῖα ἅτινα ὑπάρχουσιν ἐν τῇ Ἑλληνι γλώσσῃ τίθενται εἰς χρῆσιν δι' ἁπλουστάτ

Lower case alphabet, 14.8 ems, 148 points.
Special Set Table Characters. Figures and em quad, .1483; comma, per and en quad, .0742; thin space, .0371.
This face aligns with all 10 point one- and two-letter faces except German

Characters Included in Font

ΑΒΓΔΕΗΙΚΛΜΝΞΟΠΡΣΤΥΩ
Θ Ζφφ Χ Ψ Φ
αβγδεζηθικλμνοπρσςτυφχω 13579
24680

Special Characters—Must be Ordered Extra, if Desired

Code Word: SPALCOSIMO

For other characters that may be used with this face, see "Special Characters"

MERGENTHALER LINOTYPE COMPANY, NEW YORK, U. S. A.

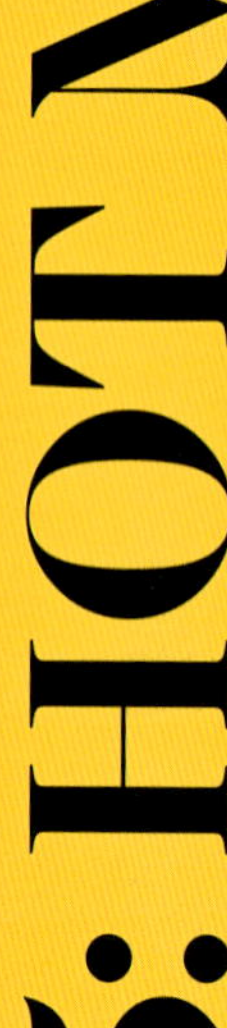

9 Point Greek Elzevir

WILL RUN IN ALL MODELS

(Solid)

Στοιχειοθεσία εἰς πλείονας τῶν τριάκοντα διαφόρων γλωσσῶν, ἐν αἷς ἡ Γερμανική, ἡ Ἑβραϊκή καὶ ἡ Ρωσσική, γίνεται σήμερον διὰ τῆς στοιχειοθετικῆς μηχανῆς Λαϊνοτάϋπ, εἰς τὸ ὁσημέραι δὲ εὐρυνόμενον στάδιον δράσεως τῆς μηχανῆς ταύτης προσετέθη ἀρτίως καὶ ἡ κλασικὴ γλῶσσα τῶν Ἑλλήνων. Καίτοι ἡ Λαϊνοτάϋπ λειτουργεῖ διὰ χειριστηρίου περιέχοντος μόνον ἐννενήκοντα κλεῖδας, τὰ 160 καὶ ΠΛΕΟΝ ΣΤΟΙΧΕΙΑ ἅτινα ὑπάρχουσιν ἐν τῇ Ἑλληνικῇ γλώσσῃ τίθενται εἰς χρῆσιν δι' ἁπλουστάτου μηχανήματος, καθιστῶντος τὴν διὰ τῆς Μηχανῆς ταύτης στοιχειοθεσίαν Ἑλληνικοῦ κειμένου ταχυτέραν ἢ δι' οἱασδήποτε ἄλλης μεθόδου. Ἀκριβῶς δὲ εἰπεῖν, ἡ αὐτὴ κατ' ἀναλογίαν ταχύτης, ἥτις ἐπιτυγχάνεται ἐν Ἀγγλικῇ στοιχειοθεσίᾳ, ταχύτης ἴση πρὸς τὴν ἐργασίαν τεσσάρων ἢ πέντε στοιχειοθετῶν διὰ τῆς χειρός, δύναται νὰ ἐπιτευχθῇ καὶ ἐν Ἑλληνικῇ στοιχειοθεσίᾳ. Ἐν ἄλ-

Lower case alphabet, 11.08 ems, 99.72 points.

Special Set Table Characters. Figures and figure space, .0667; period, comma, and thin space, .0334.

This face aligns with all 9 point one- and two-letter faces except German.

Characters Included in Font

ΑΒΓΔΕΗΙΚΛΜΝΞΟΠΡΣΤΥΩ

Θ Ζῳῷ ϋ ΧΡ Φ

αβγδεζηθικλμνοπρσςτυφχψω 13579

24680

:!—–§†'[]ΑΗΩϛ

Special Characters—Must be Ordered Extra, if Desired

Code Word: SOUTIROD

11 Point Greek Elzevir

WILL RUN IN ALL MODELS

(Solid)

Στοιχειοθεσία εἰς πλείονας τῶν τριάκοντα διαφόρων γλωσσῶν, ἐν αἷς ἡ Ἑβραϊκή ἡ Ρωσσική, γίνεται σήμερον διὰ τῆς στοιχειοθετικῆς μηχανῆς Λαϊνοτάϋπ, εἰς τὸ ὁσημέραι δὲ εὐρυνόμενον στάδιον δράσεως τῆς μηχανῆς ταύτης προσετέθη ΑΡΤΙΟΣ καὶ γλῶσσα τῶν Ἑλλήνων. Καίτοι ἡ Λαϊνοτάϋπ λειτουργεῖ διὰ χειριστηρίου περιέχοντος μόνον ἐννενήκοντα κλεῖδας, τὰ 160 καὶ πλέον στοιχεῖα ἅτινα ὑπάρχουσιν ἐν Ἑλληνικῇ γλώσσῃ τίθενται εἰς χρῆσιν δι' ἁπλουστάτου μηχανήματος, καθιστῶντος τὴν διὰ τῆς Μηχανῆς ταύτης στοιχειοθεσίαν Ἑλληνικοῦ

Lower case alphabet, 10.37 ems, 114.07 points.

Special Set Table Characters. Figures and figure space, .0816; period, comma, and thin space, .0408.

This face aligns with all 11 point one- and two-letter faces except German.

Characters Included in Font

ΑΒΓΔΕΗΙΚΛΜΝΞΟΠΡΣΤΥΩ

Θ Ζῳῷ ϋ ΧΡ Φ

αβγδεζηθικλμνοπρσςτυφχψω 13579

24680

:!—–§†'[]ΑΗΩϛ

Special Characters—Must be Ordered Extra, if Desired

Code Word: SPANKALB

For other characters that may be used with this face, see "Special Characters"

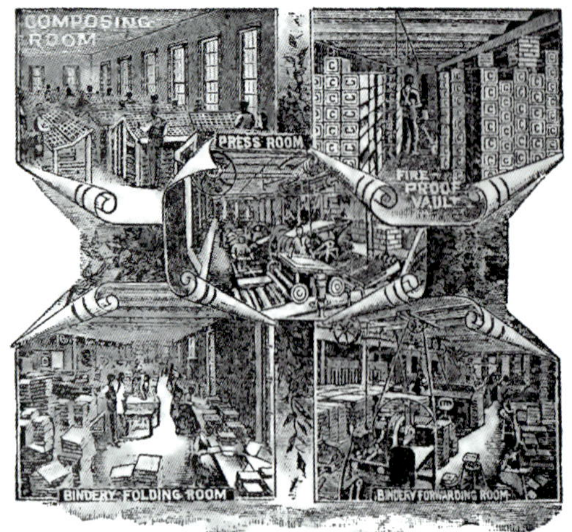

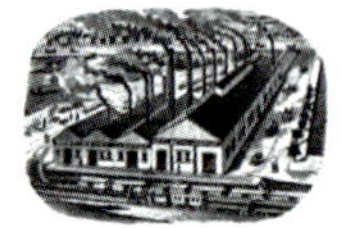

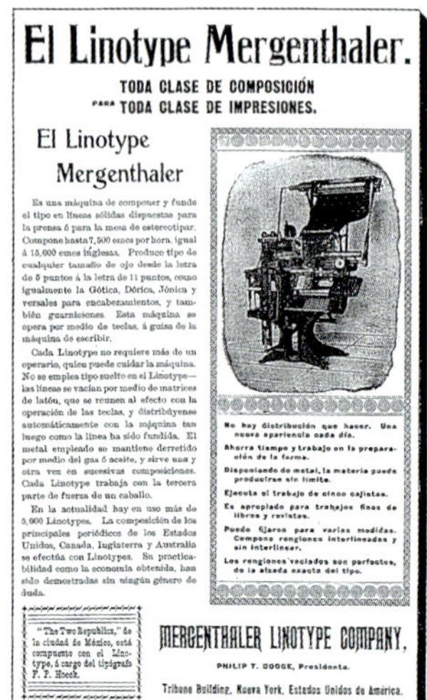

1871 — USA

R. Hoe patents the web-perfecting newspaper press; printed 800 ft/minute, or 18,000 printed & folded newspapers/hr.

1891 — USA

The Afro-American Press & Its Editors by Irvine Garland Penn documents African-American periodicals published 1827-91; pictured, its frontispiece.

1898 — Mexico

Linotype advertises globally, as in this ad; first Linotype arrives to England in 1889, to Europe in 1894.

c.1900 — [internationally]

"Hot metal" typesetting proliferates, generating new tools & products but replacing many human printing trade workers.

1882 — Austria

The setzmachine, one of many failed experiments in mechanized typesetting.

1886 — USA

Ottmar Mergenthaler patents Linotype, first successful automatic typesetting and line-casting machine.

1887 — USA

Tolbert Lanston patents Monotype, which sets and casts sorts.

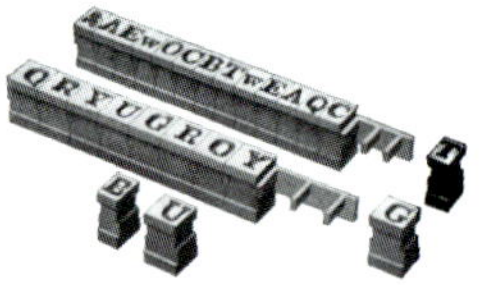

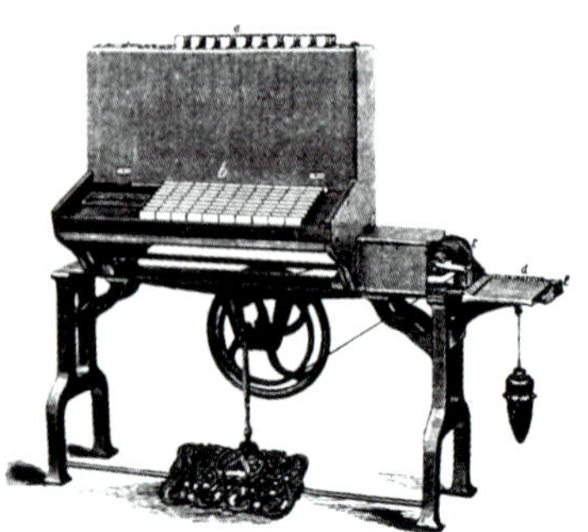

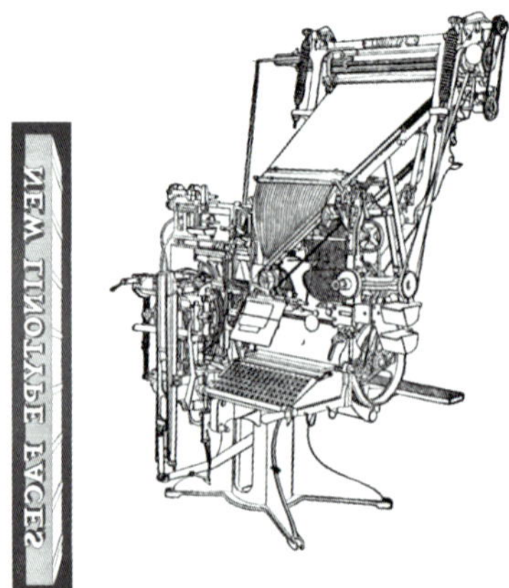

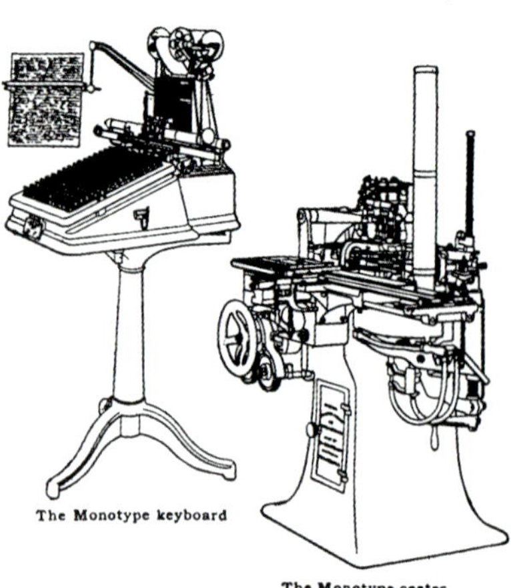

The Monotype keyboard

The Monotype caster

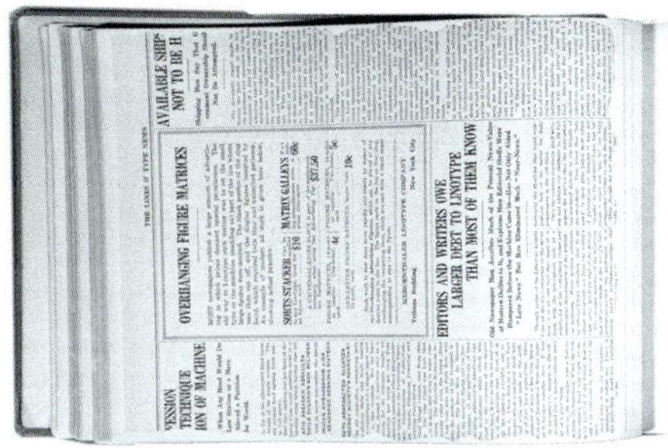

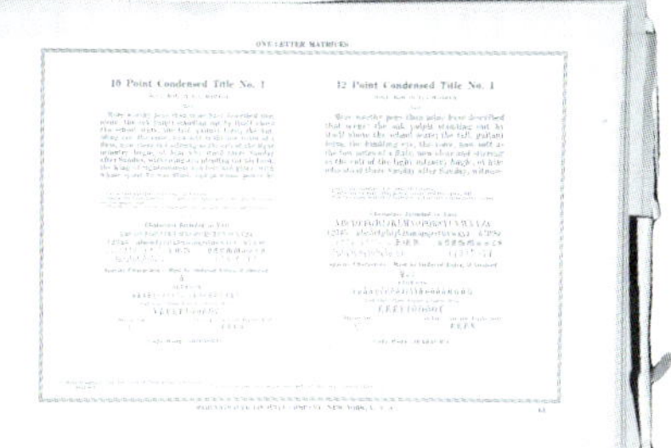

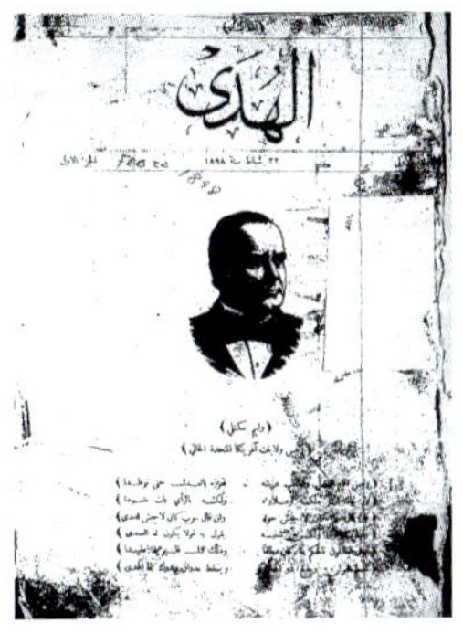

THE NEW PHONETIC ALPHABET

THE NEW HINDI ALPHABET
as adopted March 14, 1937
by the Revision Committee of the Indian Congres

1937 — India

New, simplified Hindi alphabet adopted by the Reivision Committee, Indian Congress.

1911 — USA

Linotype debuts Arabic 22, designed for *al Hoda* newspaper in New York City.

1915 — USA

Linotype releases the 1,000+ page *Specimen Book of Type Styles*; it weighs 12 lbs.

1921 — China

New phonetic Chinese alphabet, primarily a Linotype project, proves unsuccessful.

1927 — USA

Hebrew Monotype Press of New York releases its first specimen book.

1906 — USA

Ludlow Typograph system developed, hand-set matrices (a) are used to cast sorts (b).

(a)

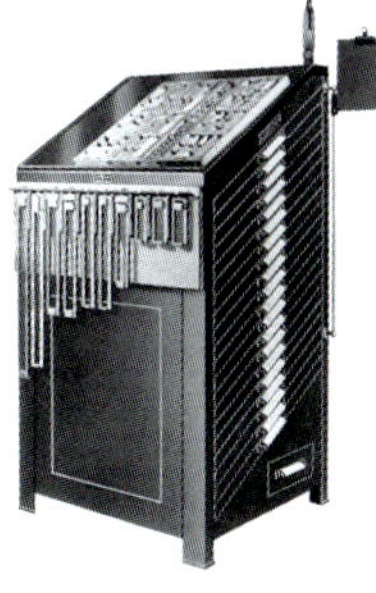

(b)

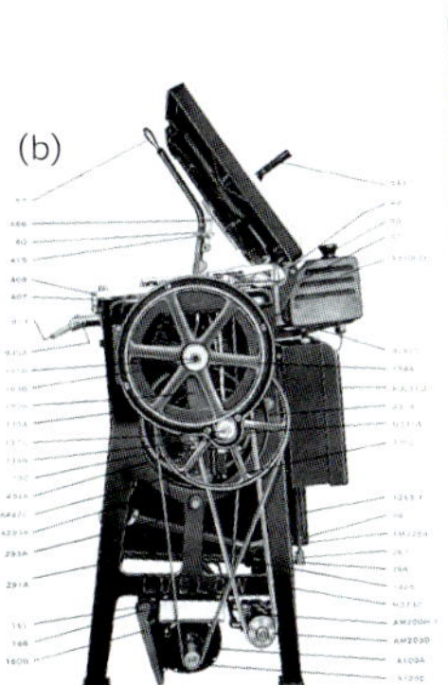

1917 — USA

Intertype no longer refurbishes Linotypes but manufactures its own machines, offering three models.

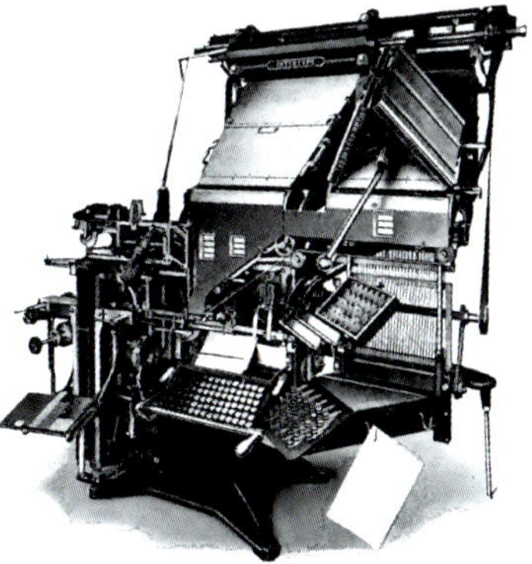

1940s — [internationally]

The Linotype (pictured) dominates newspaper publishing, the Monotype display printing.

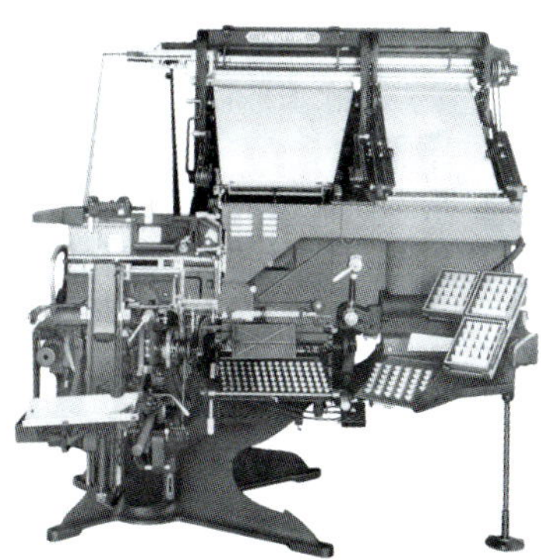

Type-founding and typesetting changed very little during the first four centuries of European printing. Improvements in paper, ink, and printing press design played a role in evolving styles and improved printing efficiency.[1] But casting and setting type remained labor-intensive. At the turn of the sixteenth century, type-founding shifted from—in the words of Stanley Morison—"an individual artistic handicraft to an item of manufacture."[2] During industrialization, the specialization of labor at type-foundries increased even further. Cutting punches, making matrices, and casting type became discrete jobs held by highly trained craftsmen.[3] Each job, however, was still performed manually. The options available from any given foundry were determined by the punches and matrices they owned, and printers in turn ordered specific faces and sizes of type individually. Typesetting took place in the printer's composing room, where a compositor selected individual sorts one at a time from a type case, placed them in reverse reading order on the composing stick, gathered all of the type needed for a page into a form, placed the form on the press for printing, then distributed the type back into its case once the print run was completed. These jobs might be divided among multiple employees, but regardless of their skill, the process consumed significant time. Mechanized typecasting and typesetting, introduced in the late nineteenth century and widely adopted by the early twentieth, caused a seismic shift in the printing industry.

Hot metal: how and why

The premise of mechanized typography was simple: replace the specialized individual labor of multiple humans with a machine that did these jobs automatically. But making this happen required a vexing number of moving parts and more than a half-century of active experimentation. Finally, the Linotype proved mechanically and commercially successful. In 1886, German immigrant Ottmar Mergenthaler cast the first typographic slug from hot metal, legendarily declaring this a "line o' type!"[4] In 1890, he founded the Mergenthaler Linotype Company in Brooklyn and introduced a model operating on the same basic mechanical principles that would inform production for decades to come. By 1895, Linotypes had been shipped to Australia, the Hawaiian Islands, and South Africa.[5] By 1915, there were some 30,000 in North American use with another 3,000 abroad.[6] The Linotype, though mechanically complex, offered unparalleled efficiency. An operator controlled a keyboard which dropped individual character matrices from a storage magazine, down chutes, and into place to set the text. Once a line was composed, molten type metal filled the matrices and created a **slug**, a solid line of finished type. After use, the Linotype automatically redistributed matrices to the magazine, sorting them based on tiny teeth cut into each matrix's upper edge. Used slugs were melted for reuse, eliminating the purchase and storage of individual foundry fonts.[7] This process reduced human hours spent composing; early Linotype models replaced the work of four humans. By the late 1940s, one machine replaced eighteen humans, and Linotype's entrenchment in the printing industry led to psychology research about "Improving the selection of Linotype trainees" based on their psychological attributes and other cost-effective new employee training strategies.[8]

Though efficient, the Linotype didn't facilitate single-character corrections; a misspelled word required recasting the entire line of type. The Monotype, Linotype's primary competitor, solved this problem by casting individual **sorts**. Another American, Tolbert Lanston, patented his invention and opened the Lanston Monotype Company in 1887; a British offshoot, Lanston Monotype Corporation Ltd., opened in 1897.[9] The Monotype's keyboard controlled the perforation of a paper tape, which the operator then fed into the separate casting machine, or caster. Within, a die case held the matrices for a specific font—for instance, 10pt. Times New Roman italic. The punched tape controlled the mechanized alignment of the desired **matrix** over the mold. Molten type metal filled the mold to cast the character, which was then delivered to a runway. When the entire line was complete, a human worker moved it to the galley and printing proceeded in the normal fashion. The Monotype offered detailed typographic control, assigning each character a proportional width unit and automatically spacing characters and words according to a mathematical model, which the keyboard operator could adjust manually. The Linotype simply inserted equally-sized spaces between the words on a line. Thus the Monotype offered distinct advantages for precision work like railway timetables, math and science textbooks, and fine book printing. The Linotype Company was larger, and it developed but never marketed the competing Logotype single-character caster.[10] But Monotype first answered the needs of a specific portion of the market, and they dominated this niche.

Line-casting machines such as the Linotype cast **slugs**, entire lines of type cast as a solid typographic unit.

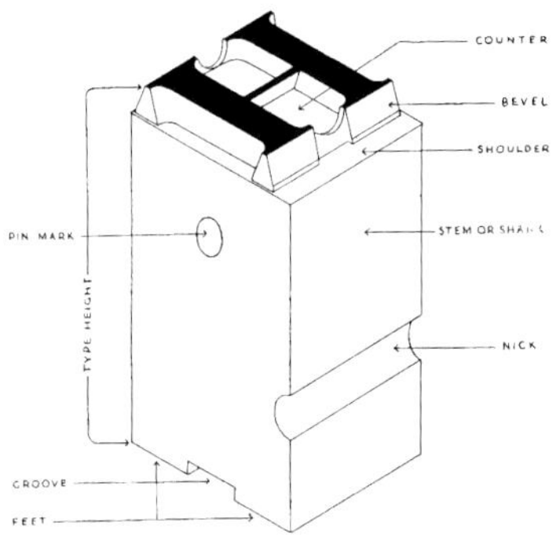

Sorts are individual pieces of metal type containing a single character, which might be one alphabetic letter, an ornament, or a typographic unit such as a catchword or a ligature.

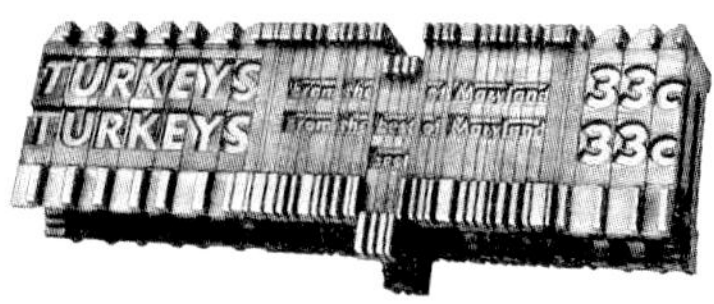

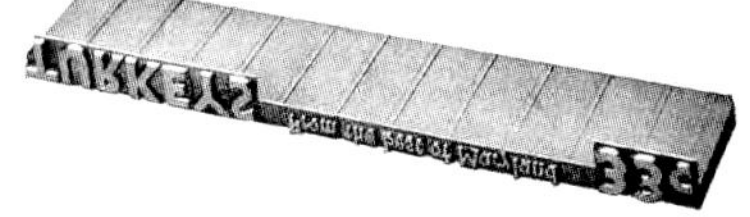

TURKEYS From the best of Maryland Fancy Grade—*Special lb.* **33c**

The **matrix** (top) is the mold into which the character is cast; some matrices held one character, others two (pictured, roman and oblique). Monotype cast individual sorts, while Linotype cast slugs.

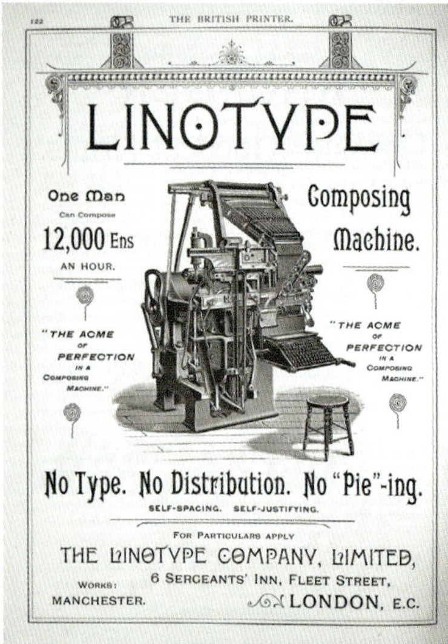

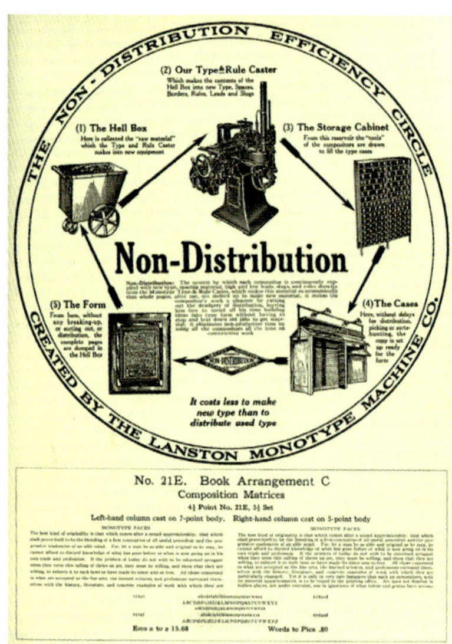

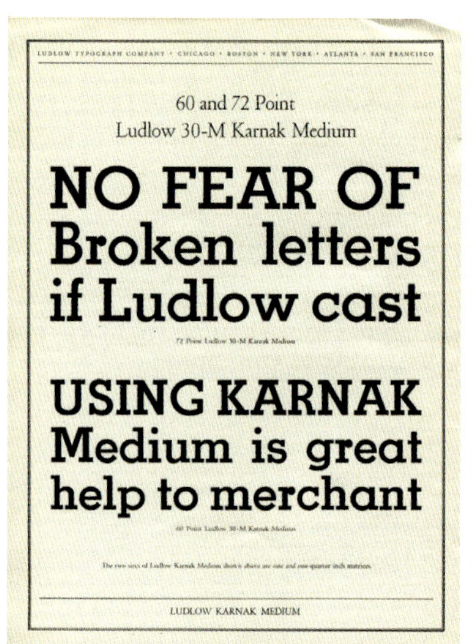

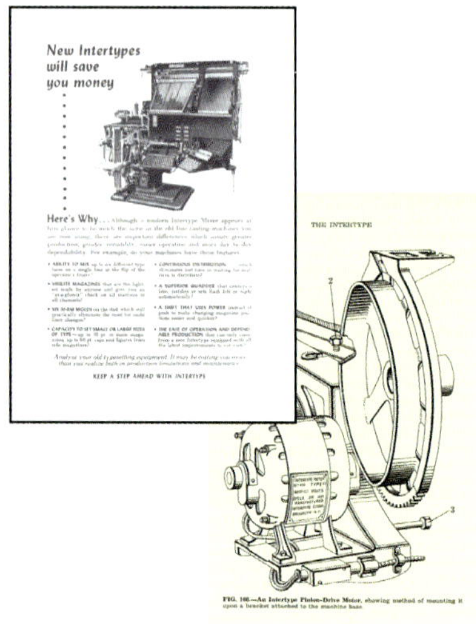

Fig 5.1 (above)

"Hot metal" type changed printing fundamentally, saving storage space, time spent typesetting, and above all money. Intertype illustrations in *Intertype Parts and Accessory Manual* (1968) and *The Intertype* (1929); Linotype ad in the *British Printer* (8:3, 1895); Monotype ad in the *Monotype Book of Typefaces* (1916), Karnak specimen in *Ludlow Typefaces Supplement* (November 1933).

A handful of other fully functional automated systems competed with industry giants Linotype and Monotype, including the Ludlow Typograph and the Intertype, seen in more detail below. These systems advertised in trade publications and released specimen books for their own typefaces. Like the publicity materials produced by their larger counterparts, these showed both types and the machines that produced them. Many included an illustrated introduction to the technology, explaining the machine's parts and operation. Regardless of manufacturer, ads and specimens for "hot metal type" extolled its benefits compared to "foundry type." Chiefly, they emphasized efficiency, economy, and improved print quality when using newly-cast type.

Benefits

The interconnected concerns of efficiency and economy permeated discussions about—and advertisements for—hot metal type. Manufacturers emphasized that saving time meant saving money [Fig. 5.1]. Eager to convince printers they could increase speed without decreasing quality, an early Linotype ad touted "cheap composition" for "body work, job work, [and] newspapers"—that is, all the jobs average shops handled.[11] Display type and fine typography merited hand-setting and optical adjustment, a distinction ATF capitalized on by marketing foundry type. Yet in 1922, the *Linotype Bulletin* advised that "Hand display wastes money—Linotype display earns money."[12] Nor was Linotype the sole proprietor of cost-saving efficiency. Another 1922 ad explained that "Monotype means much more than the name of a machine—it includes a complete system of composing room efficiency."[13] As the November/December 1928 *Monotype Recorder* cover summarized it, "The Monotype is a money-saver." Meanwhile, the Prompt Printing and Publishing Company of Cleveland found the competing "Ludlow Typograph practically indispensable," according to a 1923 Ludlow ad. "We can produce composition faster in slugs by the Ludlow system than we can set type by hand, and in addition we save the time of distribution."[14] Intertype made similar claims in a 1933 ad boasting that "36% of this composition was done *automatically* ... sav[ing] five of the six operations now necessary to center lines by hand."[15]

Besides saving time and money, hot metal type offered the possibility of printing from new type at any time. Repeated use damages type; serifs chip off, thin strokes crack, or the type itself might be squished through the application of too much pressure from the press. This introduces time-consuming corrections or low print quality—problems mechanized typecasting solved, though at a significant start-up cost. Mechanically casting type on-site, using it once, and melting it down for future reuse rendered the problem of worn-out type obsolete.

Drawbacks

As typographic technologies evolved, letterform design responded dialogically. Not everything about mechanization was positive; both letterform design and print quality suffered from the compromises required, particularly in the eyes of typographic purists. A 1900 trade journal article on current composing machine technologies damned the Linotype with faint praise: "Considering the means, however, and that a linotype slug is not true in its proportions as are [foundry] types, it is a matter of admiration that such good work is turned out."[16] American typographer and historian Douglas McMurtrie criticized **lining Caslon**, which redesigned "the original Caslon with shortened ascenders and descenders to make it cast on the so-called American Line." The system accommodated mixing type sizes and styles—and, once broadly adopted, mixing types from different foundries. But fitting the type to the system often required a redesign of the letterforms themselves, and McMurtrie's description left no doubt about his views on this subject. He called the American Line "a pernicious invention useful perhaps to newspaper and catalogue compositors, which did much to deform American

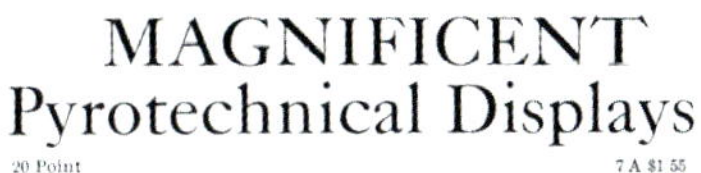

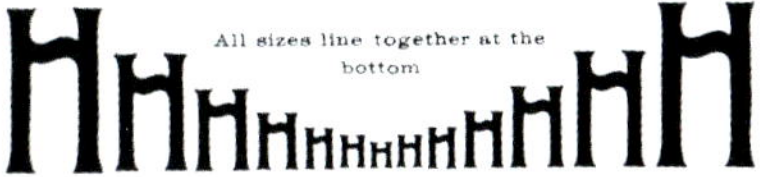

Lining Caslon, like many typefaces designed to accommodate the American Line and later the Linotype, had stubby ascenders and descenders compared to the original. But multiple sizes and styles could share a single baseline.

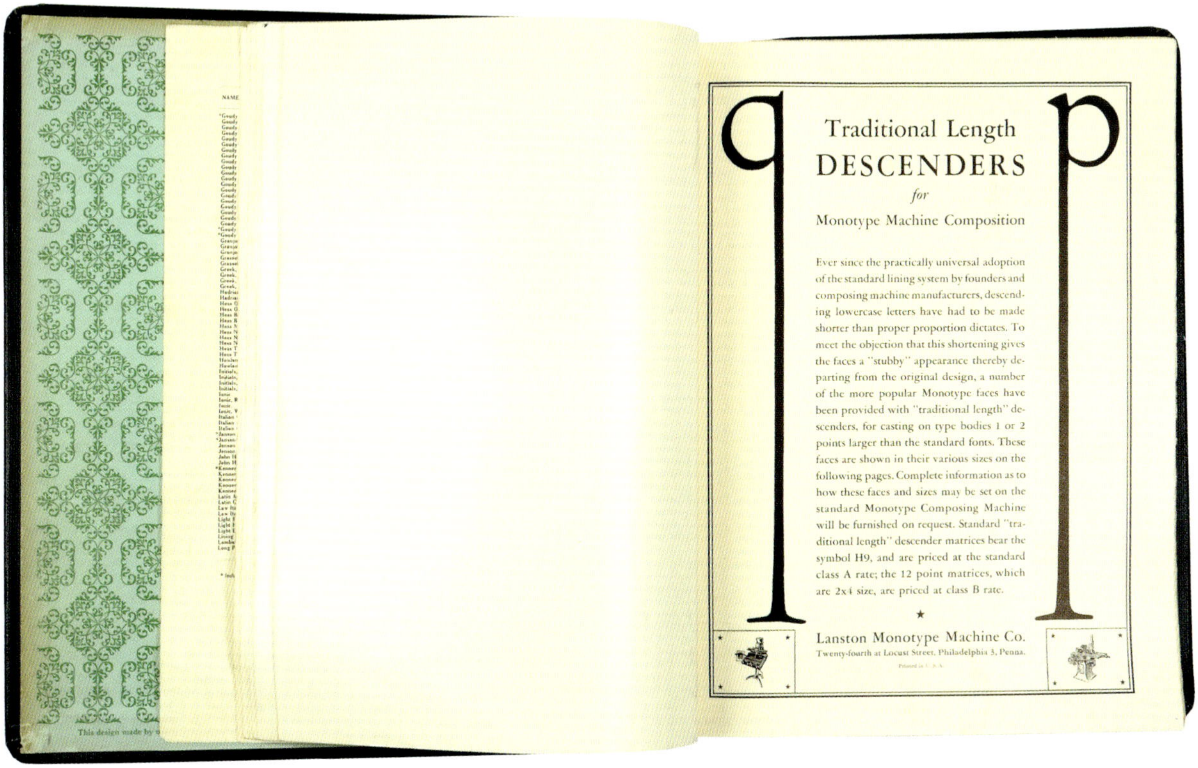

Fig 5.2 (below and following page)
***Monotype Type Faces* (Lanston Monotype, Philadelphia, 1904, below) and *Monotype Pony Specimen Book of Type Faces* (1921, following page). Monotype criticized Linotype's "stubby" descenders and marketed their "traditional length descenders" as a solution to the "defilement" of modern redesigns.**

Traditional Length
DESCENDERS
for
Monotype Machine Composition

Ever since the practically universal adoption of the standard lining system by founders and composing machine manufacturers, descending lowercase letters have had to be made shorter than proper proportion dictates. To meet the objection that this shortening gives the faces a "stubby" appearance thereby departing from the original design, a number of the more popular Monotype faces have been provided with "traditional length" descenders, for casting on type bodies 1 or 2 points larger than the standard fonts. These faces are shown in their various sizes on the following pages. Complete information as to how these faces and sizes may be set on the standard Monotype Composing Machine will be furnished on request. Standard "traditional length" descender matrices bear the symbol H9, and are priced at the standard class A rate; the 12 point matrices, which are 2x4 size, are priced at class B rate.

★

Lanston Monotype Machine Co.
Twenty-fourth at Locust Street, Philadelphia 3, Penna.

THE ORIGINAL OLD CASLON ON THE MONOTYPE

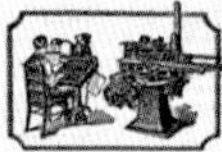

THIS NEW MONOTYPE CASLON (the No. 337 Series) is a faithful reproduction of a face that has steadfastly maintained its popularity in spite of defilement by designers who have distorted this beautiful old face to suit the so-called "standard line" and in other ways endeavored to "modernize" a classic.

WE confidently rest our typographic reputation upon this real Caslon, for, although these matrices have been made in the cellular sizes from 7 to 12 point, for use on a composing machine, surely there is nothing "machinery" about the face here shown; all the charm of the original hand-cut letters has been preserved.

CASLON should be set leaded, and therefore we have made the face with its distinctive long descenders; for those who must set this face solid, almost a desecration, we have provided, in the cellular point sizes, matrices for the shortened descenders, but these are much less stubby than the descenders of most of the modern adaptations of this face.

ONE other point should be noted; Caslon was made to be printed upon hand-made paper—there was no machine-finish in those good old days. We have not attempted the impossible, to make a face that would be Caslon under totally different printing conditions.

WE have two other Caslons, the Nos. 37 and 137E Series; therefore we have made this new-old Caslon for our own satisfaction and to delight those who love to mix type, paper and brains. To show the great difference that paper makes in this face we here print it both on antique and on coated paper. *In ordering, please be sure to specify whether you wish the long or the short descenders.*

A faithful reproduction of the real old Caslon Series cut in the year 1720, by William Caslon, the first, of London

Fonts of Matrices of the No. 337 Series shown on these pages are sold at Class A prices
NOT INCLUDED IN MATRIX LIBRARY AND WILL NOT BE LEASED

59

No. 337E. Book Arrangement C

Composition Matrices

7 Point No. 337E, 7½ Set
Monotype Standard Line

The best kind of originality is that which comes after a sound apprenticeship; that which shall prove itself to be the blending of a firm conception of useful precedent and the progressive tendencies of an able mind. For, let a man be as able and original as he may, he cannot afford to discard knowledge of what has gone before or what is now going on in his own trade and profession. If the printers of today do not wish to be esteemed arrogant when they term this calling of theirs an art, they must be willing, and show that they are willing, to subject it to such laws as have made its sister arts so free. All those concerned in what are accepted as the fine arts, the learned sciences, and professions surround themselves with the history, literature, and concrete examples of work with which they are particularly engaged. *Yet it is only in very rare instances that such an atmosphere, with its material appurtenances, is to be found in the printing office.*

12345 abcdefghijklmnopqrstuvwxyzæœfiffflffiffl 67890$
ABCDEFGHIJKLMNOPQQRSTUVWXYZ&ÆŒ
ABCDEFGHIJKLMNOPQQRSTUVWXYZ&ÆŒ
12345 abcdefghijklmnopqrstuvwxyzæœfiffflffiffl 67890$
ABCDEFGHIJKLMNOPQRSTTUVWXYYZ&ÆŒ

7 Point No. 337E, 7½ Set
With Long Descenders for 8-Point Body, Line Standard .075"

The best kind of originality is that which comes after a sound apprenticeship; that which shall prove itself to be the blending of a firm conception of useful precedent and the progressive tendencies of an able mind. For, let a man be as able and original as he may, he cannot afford to discard knowledge of what has gone before or what is now going on in his own trade and profession. If the printers of today do not wish to be esteemed arrogant when they term this calling of theirs an art, they must be willing, and show that they are willing, to subject it to such laws as have made its sister arts so free. All those concerned in what are accepted as the fine arts, the learned sciences, and professions surround themselves with the history, literature, and concrete examples of work with which they are particularly engaged. Yet it is only in very rare instances that such an atmosphere, with its material appurtenances, is to be found in a printing office. Art does not flourish in hidden places, nor under restraint, *nor in ignorance of what talent and genius have accomplished and are accomplishing throughout the world. For to follow precedent wisely*

JQgjpqy35797Q/gjpqyfiffflffiffl34579

These characters take the place of those in font at left

8 Point No. 337E, 8 Set
Monotype Standard Line

The best kind of originality is that which comes after a sound apprenticeship; that which shall prove itself to be the blending of a firm conception of useful precedent and the progressive tendencies of an able mind. For, let a man be as able and original as he may, he cannot afford to discard knowledge of what has gone before or what is now going on in his own trade and profession. If the printers of today do not wish to be esteemed arrogant when they term this calling of theirs an art they must be willing, and show that they are willing, to subject it to such laws as have made its sister arts so free. All those *concerned in what are accepted as the fine arts, the learned sciences, and professions surround themselves with the history, literature,*

12345 abcdefghijklmnopqrstuvwxyzæœfiffflffiffl 67890$
ABCDEFGHIJKLMNOPQQRSTUVWXYZ&ÆŒ
ABCDEFGHIJKLMNOPQQRSTUVWXYZ&ÆŒ
12345 abcdefghijklmnopqrstuvwxyzæœfiffflffiffl 67890$
ABCDEFGHIJKLMNOPQRSTTUVWXYYZ&ÆŒ

8 Point No. 337E, 8 Set
With Long Descenders for 9-Point Body, Line Standard .085"

The best kind of originality is that which comes after a sound apprenticeship; that which shall prove itself to be the blending of a firm conception of useful precedent and the progressive tendencies of an able mind. For, let a man be as able and original as he may, he cannot afford to discard knowledge of what has gone before or what is now going on in his own trade and profession. If the printers of today do not wish to be esteemed arrogant when they term this calling of theirs an art, they must be willing, and show that they are willing, to subject it to such laws as have made its sister arts so free. All those concerned in what are accepted as the fine arts, the learned sciences, and professions surround themselves with the history, literature, and concrete examples of the work with which they *are particularly engaged. Yet it is only in rare instances that such an atmosphere, with its material appurtenances, is to be*

JQgjpqy35797Q/gjpqyfiffflffiffl34579

These characters take the place of those in font at left

9 Point No. 337E, 9 Set
Monotype Standard Line

The best kind of originality is that which comes after a sound apprenticeship; that which shall prove itself to be the blending of a firm conception of useful precedent and the progressive tendencies of an able mind. For, let a man be as able and original as he may, he cannot afford to discard knowledge of what has gone before or what is now going on in his own trade and profession. If the printers of today do not wish to be esteemed arro*gant when they term this calling of theirs an art, they must be willing, and show that they are willing, to subject it to*

12345 abcdefghijklmnopqrstuvwxyzæœ 67890$
ABCDEFGHIJKLMNOPQQRSTUVWXYZ&ÆŒ
ABCDEFGHIJKLMNOPQQRSTUVWXYZ&ÆŒ
12345 abcdefghijklmnopqrstuvwxyzæœfiffflffiffl 67890$
ABCDEFGHIJKLMNOPQRSTTUVWXYYZ&ÆŒ

9 Point No. 337E, 9 Set
With Long Descenders for 10-Point Body, Line Standard .095"

The best kind of originality is that which comes after a sound apprenticeship; that which shall prove itself to be the blending of a firm conception of useful precedent and the progressive tendencies of an able mind. For, let a man be as able and original as he may, he cannot afford to discard knowledge of what has gone before or what is now going on in his own trade and profession. If the printers of today do not wish to be esteemed arrogant when they term this calling of theirs an art, they must be willing, and show that they are willing, to subject it to such laws as have made its sister arts so free. All those concerned in what are accepted as the fine *arts, the learned sciences, and professions surround themselves with the history, literature, and concrete examples*

JQgjpqy35797Q/gjpqyfiffflffiffl34579

These characters take the place of those in font at left

The left column shows this face with slightly shortened descenders on Standard Monotype Line. The right column, directly opposite, shows the same sizes with long descenders, conforming to the Original Caslon, cast on a body that is one point size larger, the body being lengthened below the Monotype line

Page six

60

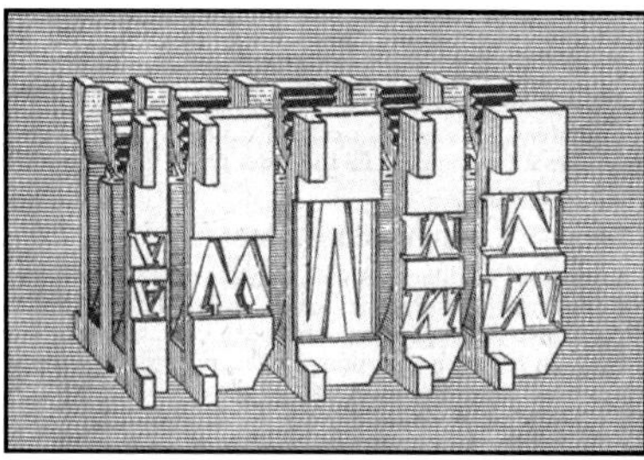

14-POINT

Caslon (Modernized)
Figure size, .0968.
1234567890
VBCDEFGRTJ

Original Old Style (Modernized)
Figure size, .0968.
1234567890
VBCDEFGRTJ

Linotype's **two-face matrices** included not one but two typefaces: roman and matching italic, serif and contrasting sans serif, or display numerals and small caps. Shown here, two **old style** (or humanist serif) typefaces, Caslon and Original Old Style. Both show the lingering influence of manuscript hands.

type designs which might otherwise have been most satisfactory. ... No types with descenders of normal length were shown in the specimen books" of the twentieth century's first quarter.[17]

Monotype, meanwhile, slammed Linotype for its **two-face matrices**, an efficiency that came at the expense of type design principles. "Two letters [were] never carried on the same matrix in the Monotype system" as they were in Linotype; rather, "typographic beauty and commercial utility" resulted from single-sort casting.[18] Monotype criticized the "stubby appearance" of ascending and descending characters on the American Line. So, in 1904, *Monotype Type Faces* introduced the "more popular faces" redesigned "with 'traditional length' descenders" on a display page emphasizing the q and p characters [Fig. 5.2]. These were cast "on type bodies 1 or 2 points larger than the standard fonts"—the *sorts* for an entire face were taller, but the type size wasn't. The sample texts in this section advised printers that "Good typography embraces good design, fitness, good taste and unity. Good printers judge the products of the Monotype sufficient [to meet] these requirements."[19] In the *Monotype Pony Book* (1921), a direct comparison of the "stubby" versus "traditional length" descenders appeared with every font, demonstrating the aesthetic advantages of the latter [Fig. 5.02]. Finally, Monotype emphasized the historical accuracy of its longer descenders, particularly for **old-style** faces like Caslon, which had survived "defilement by designers who have distorted this beautiful old face to suit the so-called 'standard line' and in other ways endeavored to 'modernize' a classic

… almost a desecration." The use of phrases like "satisfactory, good taste, good design"—and conversely, "pernicious, abnormal, deformed, distorted, desecration"[20]—made clear the ways in which mechanized type could be considered a drawback.

New formats for the specimen

New hot metal technologies led to new physical formats for the typographic specimen. Comprehensive specimen books were massive, and frequently elaborate and expensive to produce. Binder systems and supplements offered more efficiency, though they posed problems of their own. The one-line specimen sought a balance between size and completeness. During the first quarter of the twentieth century, these formats coexisted, each with its own benefits and drawbacks.

Mega-books

As typefaces proliferated, comprehensive specimens grew ever larger. *Linotype's Specimen Book of Type Styles* (1915) displayed typeface matrices alone and in exhaustive combinations, an extensive collection of borders and ornaments, and elaborate examples of the Linotype in use [Fig 5.3]. Eighty "specimens"—polychromatic pages produced to a high level of artistry—demonstrated the Linotype's capacity for fine printing, not just newspaper or cheap advertising work. Specimen number one displayed 14pt. Old Roman

Fig 5.3 (below)

***Specimen Book of Type Styles* (Mergenthaler Linotype, Brooklyn, 1915) and *Book of the matrix* (1916). A 12-pound colossus, this specimen captured both the extensive scope of Linotype's typographic program and its capacity to support fine printing.**

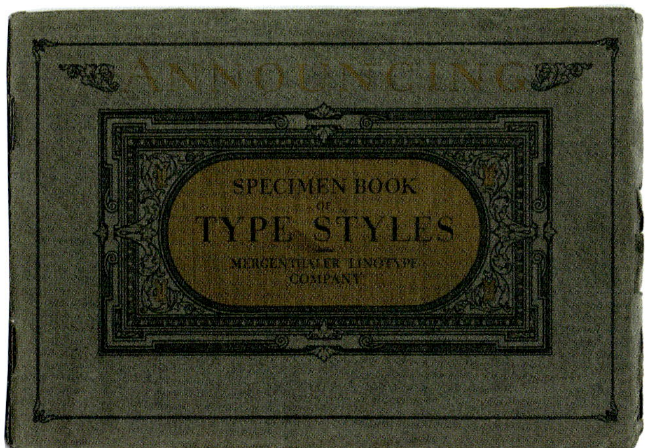

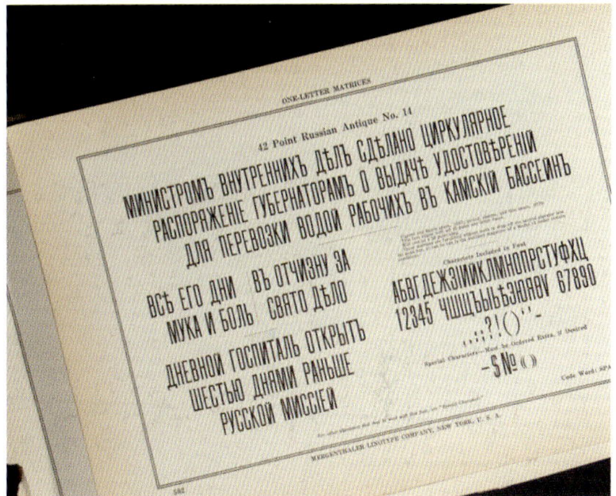

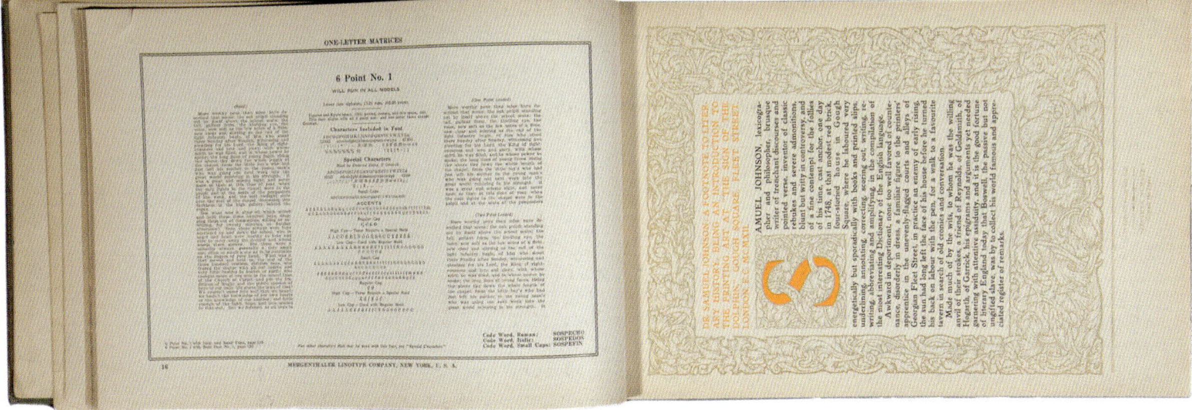

Fig 5.4 (opposite)
***The Monotype Specimen Book of Type-faces* (Lanston Monotype, Philadelphia, 1916). This post-bound book with tabbed dividers allowed individual printers to update their own comprehensive specimen with newly issued supplements.**

with italic, printed in three colors with a decorative initial and elaborate border. The text, an introduction to eighteenth century English author Dr. Samuel Johnson, was taken from a privately printed booklet by British fine printer George W. Jones at the Sign of the Dolphin—as was the design. Reproduced at reduced size in the American trade journal *The Printing Art* in 1912, the page was already in circulation as an exemplar of fine printing.[21] Its recreation on the Linotype signalled to printers that mechanical methods could accommodate aspirational professional and aesthetic standards. Meanwhile, the sixteen-page *Book of the Matrix* (1916) narrated the *Specimen Book*'s physical extravagance, opening—like a birth announcement—with the new arrival's weight:

> The finished book weighs 12 pounds. It is 13¾ x 9 inches, and 3 inches thick. It contains over 1,000 pages. More than 115,920 lbs. of paper were consumed, requiring over 500 lbs. of ink. There are listed more than 768 complete fonts ... We have cut eighty fonts of foreign languages requiring their own characters. ... The eighty specimens were given over 1,000 hours of shop time alone. ... The binding of the book was an undertaking in itself.[22]

The "colossal affair" that was Linotype's 1915 specimen certainly wasn't the only hefty tome of its day, but its landscape format gave it a particularly substantial physical presence.

Loose-leaf binders and supplements

Updating a bound specimen required the foundry to produce a new book or the printer to improvise a system for organizing loose supplements. Binders provided a built-in physical structure for this process. The massive *Monotype Specimen Book of Type-faces* (1916) allowed updating the specimen without replacing it; users added loose-leaf specimens between its expandable, post-bound covers. "The attached sheets should be inserted in your specimen book immediately to avoid soiling or losing them and to keep your book up-to-date," advised a 1921 supplement. Monotype stressed the commercial value of careful maintenance: "Your solicitors have to be up-to-the-minute in these days of keen competition—why employ a back-number Specimen Book?" Printers who didn't "want to be bothered with bringing [the] book up-to-date" could return it to corporate headquarters in Philadelphia, where the task was done for them and Monotype paid return postage.[23] In most supplements, detailed instructions described where and how to file the new specimens in the printer's binder, which was held together by screw posts while index tabs grouped faces by classification—moderns, old styles, antiques, gothics, "foreign" faces, **initials**, borders and ornaments [Fig. 5.4]. Most sheets were full-sized, matching the dimensions of the original book, but some were half-sized or quarter-sized. Once in use, any given copy of the book quickly became entirely unique—updated (or not) at the discretion of the individual printer and organized according to whatever system that printer imposed (or didn't). The copies in twenty-first century archives bear signs of their use as working documents, with pages or text blocks missing. Though specimen books discouraged cutting out the samples, printers seeking clear communication might attach such extractions to a specifications sheet, a proof, or an order form for matrices.

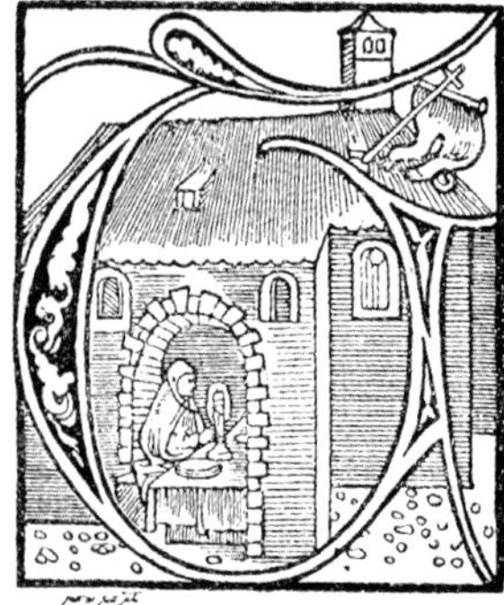

Historiated **initials** like this 16c. German example tell stories through the people, places, and objects depicted within them. Like versals, usually they visually indicate the beginning of a text or text segment.

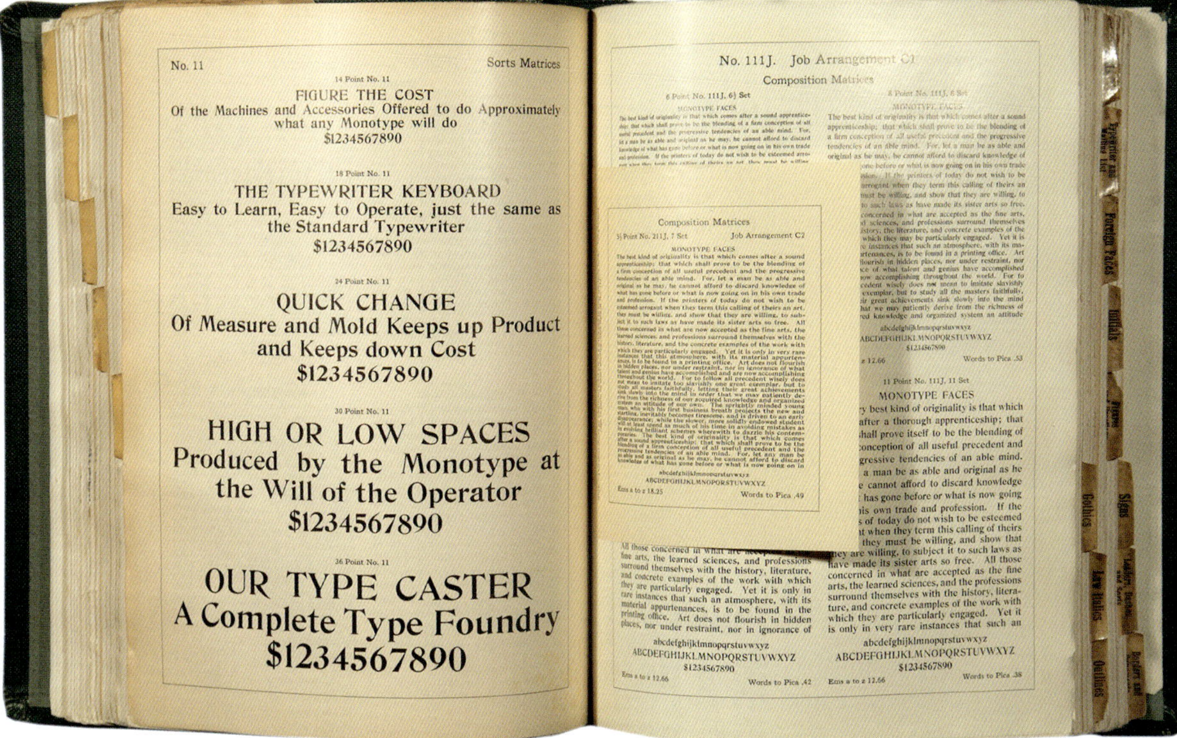

No. 11 Sorts Matrices

14 Point No. 11

FIGURE THE COST
Of the Machines and Accessories Offered to do Approximately what any Monotype will do
$1234567890

18 Point No. 11

THE TYPEWRITER KEYBOARD
Easy to Learn, Easy to Operate, just the same as the Standard Typewriter
$1234567890

24 Point No. 11

QUICK CHANGE
Of Measure and Mold Keeps up Product and Keeps down Cost
$1234567890

30 Point No. 11

HIGH OR LOW SPACES
Produced by the Monotype at the Will of the Operator
$1234567890

36 Point No. 11

OUR TYPE CASTER
A Complete Type Foundry
$1234567890

No. 111J. Job Arrangement C1

Composition Matrices

Composition Matrices

Job Arrangement C2

MONOTYPE FACES

11 Point No. 111J, 11 Set

MONOTYPE FACES

abcdefghijklmnopqrstuvwxyz
ABCDEFGHIJKLMNOPQRSTUVWXYZ
$1234567890

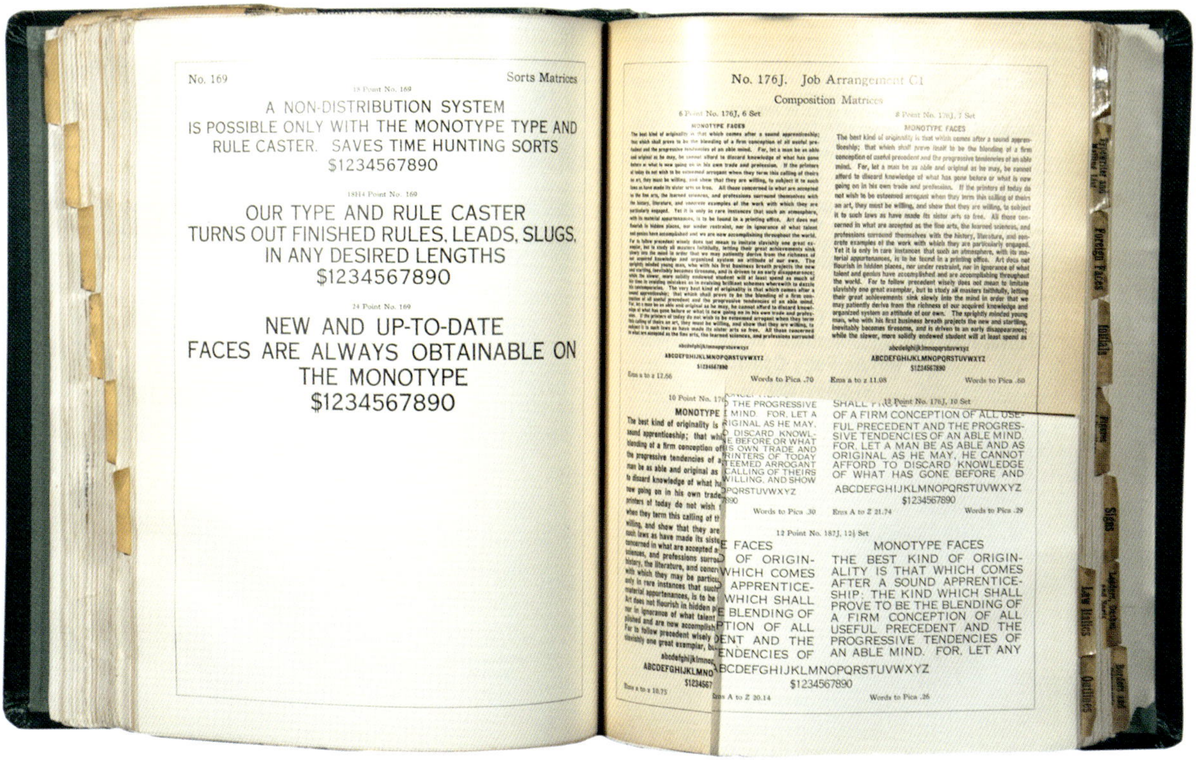

No. 169 Sorts Matrices

A NON-DISTRIBUTION SYSTEM
IS POSSIBLE ONLY WITH THE MONOTYPE TYPE AND RULE CASTER. SAVES TIME HUNTING SORTS
$1234567890

OUR TYPE AND RULE CASTER
TURNS OUT FINISHED RULES, LEADS, SLUGS, IN ANY DESIRED LENGTHS
$1234567890

24 Point No. 169

NEW AND UP-TO-DATE
FACES ARE ALWAYS OBTAINABLE ON THE MONOTYPE
$1234567890

No. 176J. Job Arrangement C1

Composition Matrices

MONOTYPE FACES

OF A FIRM CONCEPTION OF ALL USEFUL PRECEDENT AND THE PROGRESSIVE TENDENCIES OF AN ABLE MIND. FOR, LET A MAN BE AS ABLE AND AS ORIGINAL AS HE MAY, HE CANNOT AFFORD TO DISCARD KNOWLEDGE OF WHAT HAS GONE BEFORE AND
ABCDEFGHIJKLMNOPQRSTUVWXYZ
$1234567890

MONOTYPE FACES
THE BEST KIND OF ORIGINALITY IS THAT WHICH COMES AFTER A SOUND APPRENTICESHIP; THE KIND WHICH SHALL PROVE TO BE THE BLENDING OF A FIRM CONCEPTION OF ALL USEFUL PRECEDENT AND THE PROGRESSIVE TENDENCIES OF AN ABLE MIND. FOR, LET ANY
ABCDEFGHIJKLMNOPQRSTUVWXYZ
$1234567890

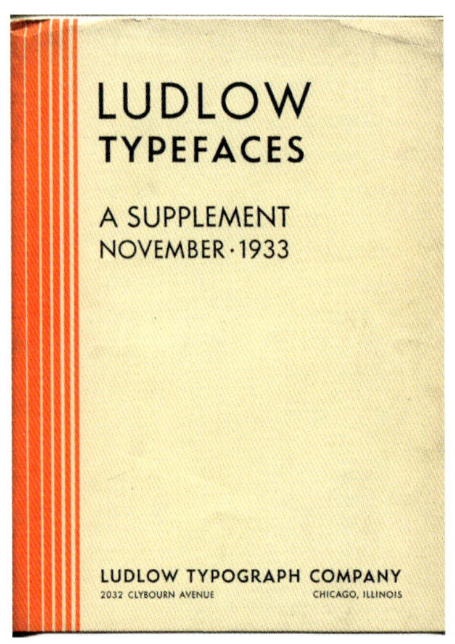

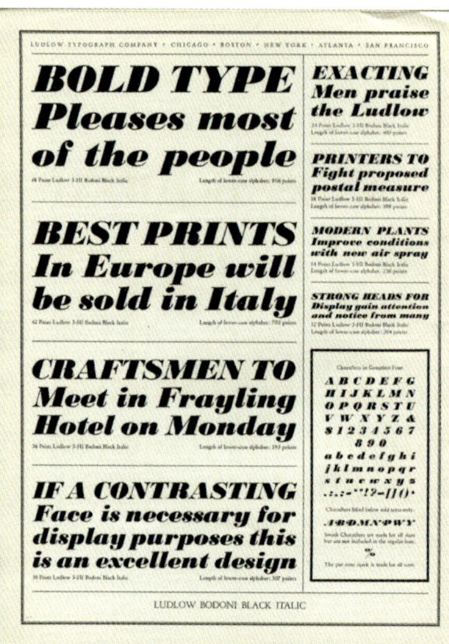

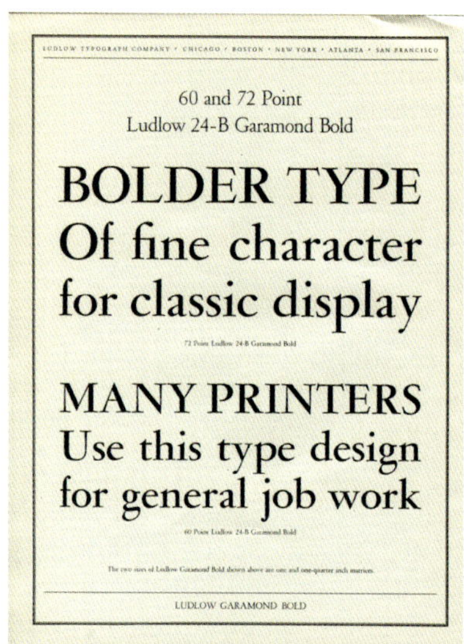

Fig 5.5 (above)

***Ludlow Typefaces* (Ludlow, Chicago, 1933) and *Supplement to the Typeface Book* (ND, c.1943). Though the original specimen was hardbound, Ludlow consistently applied its format to a series of supplements, all of which spoke the same visual language as the book they continually updated.**

Not all supplements were designed for insertion into the manufacturer's book, however. Ludlow's first comprehensive specimen, *Ludlow Typefaces: A Specimen Book of Matrix Fonts* (1930), was a hardbound book with a cloth cover. Yet Ludlow published supplements beginning the following year, announcing types designed since the release of the most recent large specimen book. In their design, Ludlow's supplements echoed the aesthetic language and compositional strategies established by their hardbound predecessor [Fig. 5.5]. These slender, paper-covered booklets arrived in a mailing envelope; printers presumably shelved supplements adjacent to the hardbound book, perhaps (given that many envelopes survive in archives) still in their protective wrappers. Clearly, Ludlow intended printers to collate the specimens as they were released, maintaining a comprehensive record. February 1934's supplement proclaimed on its cover that it, "together with the supplements dated March, 1931, and April, 1932, and the blue cloth-bound book, constitute[d] a complete showing to date of available Ludlow typefaces." Yet the supplements themselves suggested the availability of additional, specialized specimens. The March 1931 supplement informed printers of Ludlow's "three new Hebrew type designs," Hebrew Modern, Bold, and Bold Condensed, available in 48–84pts. "Specimen sheets showing these typefaces will be gladly sent to you upon request," **Ludlow** promised. Maintaining a comprehensive library of specimens required significant effort for printers, and as Ludlow's Hebrew supplement suggested, most printers probably focused on the types they used in their day to day work.

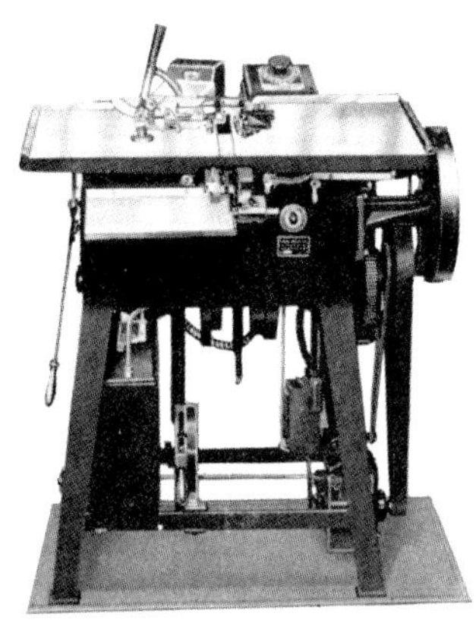

The **Ludlow** utilized a mechanically simple but manually labor-intensive process compared to the Linotype or Monotype; shown here, the Ludlow caster.

1-line specimens

Massive, elaborate specimens were impressive but prohibitively expensive; binder systems and supplements fell victim to sloppy maintenance. Linotype's first comprehensive *One Line Specimen* (1910) sought an efficient mix of completeness and thrift. In it, a single line of type represented each one-letter matrix and its corresponding typeface, a tiny individual sample within a vast network of related typographic material. Two-letter matrices displayed one line for each of their two types. Despite this severe visual economy, showing every available matrix resulted in a substantial, repetitive book quickly rendered incomplete as Linotype expanded its library. Some reviewers found individual types easy to overlook amidst the sheer volume. "Besides the remarkably large number of faces available for Linotype users, one is attracted by many novel accessories," wrote one reviewer, saying nothing else about the types but offering matrix gauges—among several other gadgets—as an example of handy tools printers may not have known they needed. For other reviewers, the most notable feature was the specimen's "condensed" form, making it possible to consult a comprehensive reference volume of a manageable size.[24] Thereafter, the *Linotype Bulletin* consistently advised readers to request a copy of the one-line specimen if they hadn't yet received one. The *Bulletin* often included a sample of new one-line specimens to whet the typographic appetite; June 1913 drew from the Caslon family in

Fig 5.6 (below)

One-Line Specimens **(Mergenthaler Linotype, Brooklyn, 1914). Like its 1910 predecessor, this efficient specimen showed a single line of every matrix in Linotype's library; two-letter matrices (far right) required two lines, one for each typeface on the matrix.**

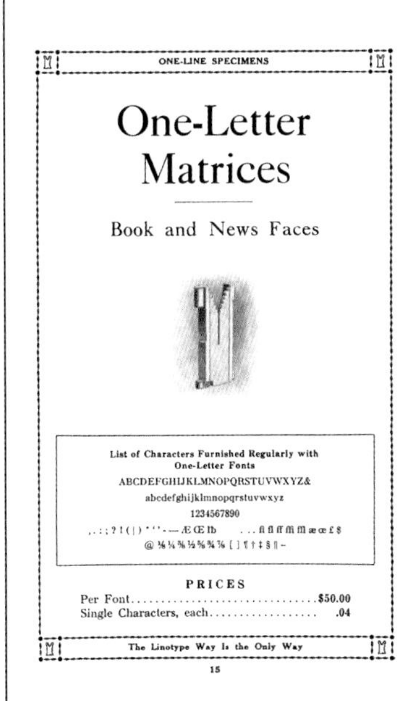

ONE-LINE SPECIMENS

One-Letter Matrices

Book and News Faces

List of Characters Furnished Regularly with One-Letter Fonts

ABCDEFGHIJKLMNOPQRSTUVWXYZ&

abcdefghijklmnopqrstuvwxyz

1234567890

PRICES

Per Font $50.00

Single Characters, each .... .04

The Linotype Way Is the Only Way

15

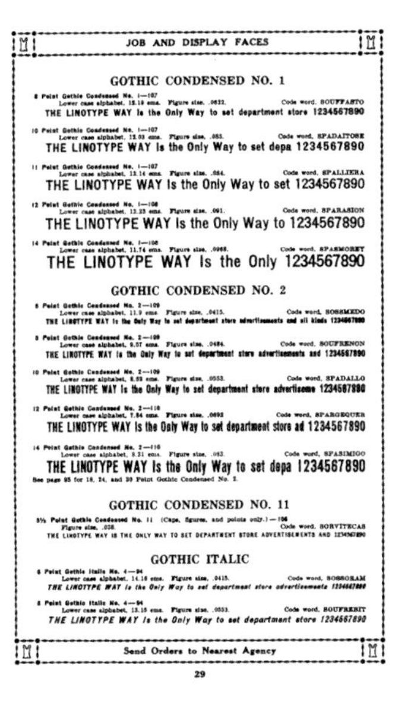

JOB AND DISPLAY FACES

GOTHIC CONDENSED NO. 1

THE LINOTYPE WAY Is the Only Way to set department store 1234567890

THE LINOTYPE WAY Is the Only Way to set depa 1234567890

THE LINOTYPE WAY Is the Only Way to set 1234567890

THE LINOTYPE WAY Is the Only Way to 1234567890

THE LINOTYPE WAY Is the Only 1234567890

GOTHIC CONDENSED NO. 2

THE LINOTYPE WAY Is the Only Way to set department store advertisements and 1234567890

THE LINOTYPE WAY Is the Only Way to set department store advertiseme 1234567890

THE LINOTYPE WAY Is the Only Way to set department store ad 1234567890

THE LINOTYPE WAY Is the Only Way to set depa 1234567890

GOTHIC CONDENSED NO. 11

GOTHIC ITALIC

THE LINOTYPE WAY Is the Only Way to set department store 1234567890

Send Orders to Nearest Agency

29

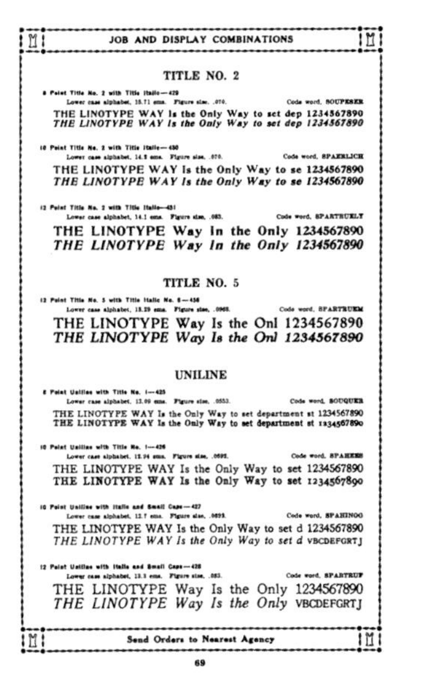

JOB AND DISPLAY COMBINATIONS

TITLE NO. 2

THE LINOTYPE WAY Is the Only Way to set dep 1234567890

THE LINOTYPE WAY Is the Only Way to set dep 1234567890

THE LINOTYPE WAY Is the Only Way to se 1234567890

THE LINOTYPE WAY Is the Only Way to se 1234567890

THE LINOTYPE Way In the Only 1234567890

THE LINOTYPE Way In the Only 1234567890

TITLE NO. 5

THE LINOTYPE Way Is the Onl 1234567890

THE LINOTYPE Way Is the Onl 1234567890

UNILINE

THE LINOTYPE WAY Is the Only Way to set department st 1234567890

THE LINOTYPE WAY Is the Only Way to set department st 1234567890

THE LINOTYPE WAY Is the Only Way to set 1234567890

THE LINOTYPE WAY Is the Only Way to set 1234567890

THE LINOTYPE WAY Is the Only Way to set d 1234567890

THE LINOTYPE WAY Is the Only Way to set d VBCDEFGRTJ

THE LINOTYPE Way Is the Only 1234567890

THE LINOTYPE Way Is the Only VBCDEFGRTJ

Send Orders to Nearest Agency

69

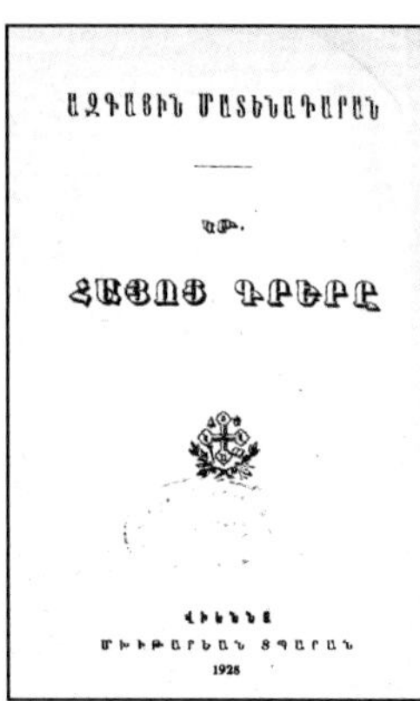

Introduced around 405 CE, the **Armenian** alphabet originally had 36 letters, then grew to 39; it reads left to right. The Ottoman Empire used Armenian widely during the 18–19c. Shown, *The Armenian Letters* (Hracheay Acharean, 1928).

anticipation of a new face, Caslon no. 3 with Italic.[25] This practice provided quick access, mitigating lag time between the release of a face and the publication of a new specimen book or supplement.

By 1914, the 700 **matrices** of 1910 increased to almost 1,000, and it was time for Linotype to issue a new edition of its *One-Line Specimens* [Fig. 5.6]. As with its 1910 predecessor, concise individual specimens comprised the entire design strategy of the 200-page 1914 update. The contents were again divided into one-letter and two-letter matrices and within those categories sorted into "book and news faces," often named after historical type founders such as Ronaldson and Elzevir, and "job and display faces," including antiques and gothics, which we'd now call slab serifs and sans serifs. "The Linotype way is the only way to set department store advertisements," the display copy read, over and over again. If the line wasn't long enough to accommodate the whole sentence, the text simply stopped, mid-word. Foreign-language faces were segregated into their own section; the 1914 specimen showed Arabic (only 22 pt. was available), **Armenian**, German (blackletters, with the sample sentence set in the German language), Greek, Hebrew, and Russian. The book concluded with head letters (large sizes for headlines), advertising figures (large numerals and fractions), tabular matrices (for setting figures in charts and tables), and a four-page index. What one-line specimens lacked in visual appeal, they made up for in efficiency, one of Linotype's guiding principles. The release of one-line specimens continued throughout Linotype's decades-long engagement with the production of hot metal type. The 1958 edition, for instance, ran for 291 pages—as efficient as possible, but still a sizable book.

Roles of the specimen

Regardless of their physical format, specimens for hot metal type performed a variety of pragmatic and philosophical functions. Some of these echoed historical precedents, but others emphasized new technologies or concepts. Specimens continued to serve as commercial catalogs, facilitating the selection and ordering of matrices. They explained how mechanical typesetting worked, and how it impacted typographic and page design. They modeled how typefaces should be selected and used in everyday practice. They differentiated each manufacturer's product from its competitors. And they communicated each company's programmatic world view.

Commercial catalogs

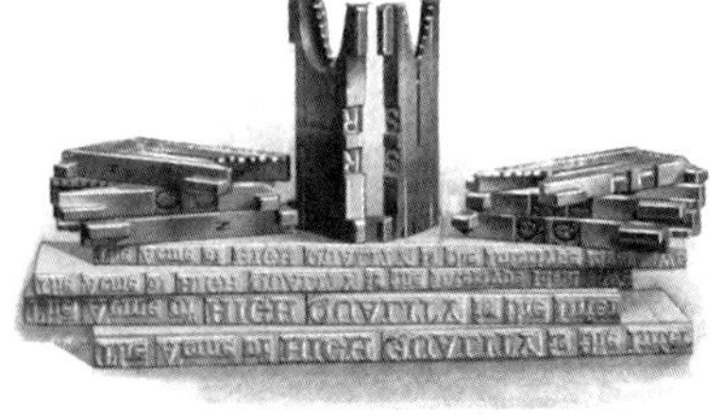

The **matrix** is the mold from which individual characters are cast. In linecasting machines, these are aligned into an entire line of type before being filled with hot metal; in sortcasters, they're filled individually. Here, matrices from Intertype's 1920 catalog sit atop slugs, or finished lines of type.

The type specimen's primary job remained unchanged despite significant technological innovation. Ordering—foundry sorts or matrices—required printers to see the typefaces, sizes, and styles available. *Linotype Faces* (1905) embraced commercial functionality over noteworthy design; the first 400 of its 500 pages followed a single design formula [Fig. 5.7]. Framed by a hairline rule, the recto page displayed a captioned image of the **matrix** and its special characters, the verso page sample paragraphs of text in a single column. A running header reminded readers they were consulting the *Mergenthaler Linotype Co. Specimens of Linotype Faces*. The sample paragraph repeated throughout, describing "ancient materials used for recording events." Footnotes offered comments on special characters, alignment, and which Linotype models were compatible with the pictured matrices. Sections

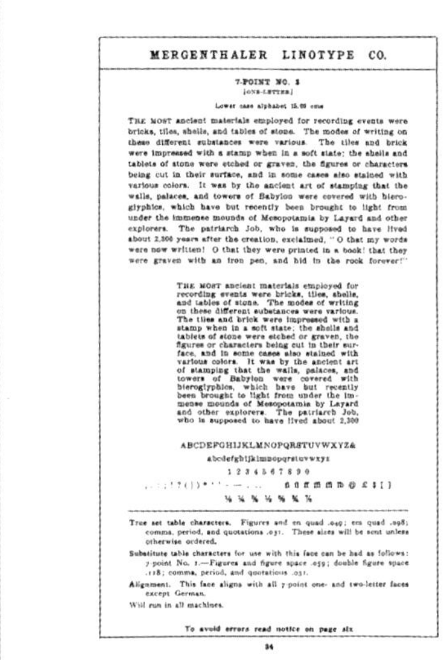

MERGENTHALER LINOTYPE CO.

7-POINT NO. 1
[ONE-LETTER]

Lower case alphabet 15.69 ems

THE MOST ancient materials employed for recording events were bricks, tiles, shells, and tables of stone. The modes of writing on these different substances were various. The tiles and brick were impressed with a stamp when in a soft state; the shells and tablets of stone were etched or graven, the figures or characters being cut in their surface, and in some cases also stained with various colors. It was by the ancient art of stamping that the walls, palaces, and towers of Babylon were covered with hieroglyphics, which have but recently been brought to light from under the immense mounds of Mesopotamia by Layard and other explorers. The patriarch Job, who is supposed to have lived about 2,300 years after the creation, exclaimed, "O that my words were now written! O that they were printed in a book! that they were graven with an iron pen, and hid in the rock forever!"

THE MOST ancient materials employed for recording events were bricks, tiles, shells, and tables of stone. The modes of writing on these different substances were various. The tiles and brick were impressed with a stamp when in a soft state; the shells and tablets of stone were etched or graven, the figures or characters being cut in their surface, and in some cases also stained with various colors. It was by the ancient art of stamping that the walls, palaces, and towers of Babylon were covered with hieroglyphics, which have but recently been brought to light from under the immense mounds of Mesopotamia by Layard and other explorers. The patriarch Job, who is supposed to have lived about 2,300

ABCDEFGHIJKLMNOPQRSTUVWXYZ&

abcdefghijklmnopqrstuvwxyz

1 2 3 4 5 6 7 8 9 0

⅛ ¼ ⅜ ½ ⅝ ¾ ⅞

True set table characters. Figures and en quad .049; em quad .098; comma, period, and quotations .031. These sizes will be sent unless otherwise ordered.

Substitute table characters for use with this face can be had as follows: 7-point No. 1.—Figures and figure space .059; double figure space .118; comma, period, and quotations .031.

Alignment. This face aligns with all 7-point one- and two-letter faces except German.

Will run in all machines.

To avoid errors read notice on page six

34

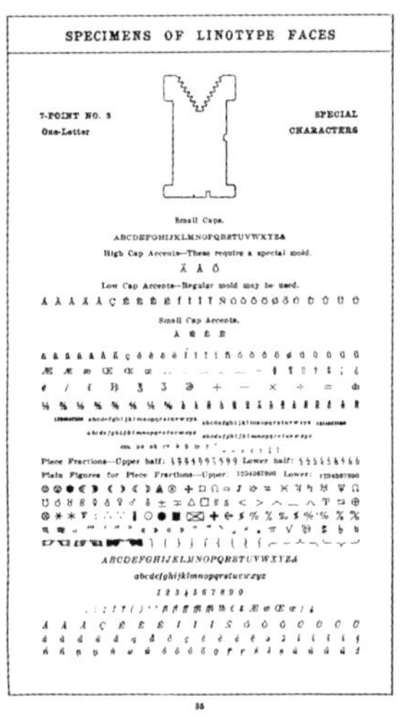

SPECIMENS OF LINOTYPE FACES

7-POINT NO. 1
One-Letter

SPECIAL
CHARACTERS

Small Caps.

ABCDEFGHIJKLMNOPQRSTUVWXYZ&

High Cap Accents—These require a special mold.

Low Cap Accents—Regular mold may be used.

Small Cap Accents.

Piece Fractions—Upper half: … Lower half: …

Plain Figures for Piece Fractions—Upper: 1234567890 Lower: 1234567890

ABCDEFGHIJKLMNOPQRSTUVWXYZ&

abcdefghijklmnopqrstuvwxyz

1 2 3 4 5 6 7 8 9 0

35

Fig 5.7 (left)

Linotype Faces **(Mergenthaler Linotype, Brooklyn, 1905). Pragmatism, not visual appeal, dictated the repetitive page design of many specimens. As a working catalog, this Linotype book performed its job effectively and without fuss, even if it wasn't very exciting.**

organized the material into one- and two-letter matrices for book, news, and job face, plus miscellaneous material like borders, ornaments, and rules. The specimen expressed its purpose clearly, with design decisions supporting its practical, commercial use as a printers' catalog.

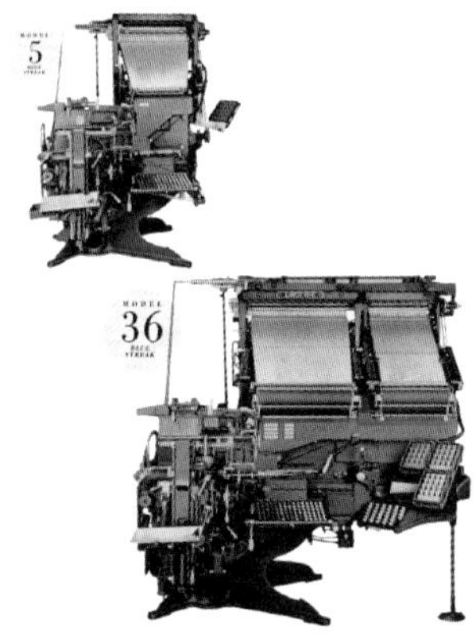

The **machine model** — with new releases as technology improved or production methods changed — determined many parameters, from how many magazines a Linotype could hold (Model 5 holds one, Mixer Model 35 up to eight) to how many pages and of what size a printer could produce per hour.

Instruction manuals

Specimen books didn't only display types; frequently, they instructed printers in how (and why) to use the machinery that produced them. Like earlier printers' manuals, hot metal specimens often described the production process. This practical, educational content explained, for instance, which accessories and matrices were compatible with which **machine models**, or how to maintain equipment. This provided opportunities for competitive comparisons; companies described their machines as the most advanced, fastest, simplest, sturdiest, or most economical option in order to differentiate themselves and attract customers. Often, an illustrated description of how the machine in question worked served as the introduction to a specimen book.

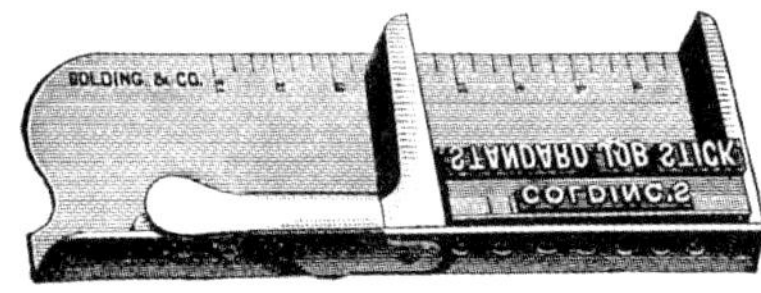

Typesetters used composing **sticks** to arrange individual sorts into lines of a set width, measured in picas.

Monotype's 1916 specimen had opened with some forty pages of introductory material, most of it a detailed explanation of the matrix system for casting individual typographic sorts. In contrast, the fourth edition of *Ludlow Typefaces* (undated, c.1940-58) opened with a modest four-page introduction [Fig. 5.8]. "Both in mechanism and operation the Ludlow system is characterized by extreme simplicity," it promised. "Individual matrices are set from the matrix case by hand in a special **stick**, which is then inserted in the casting machine to produce the corresponding line of type in slug form." Four photographs summarized the process: a casting machine and matrix cabinets, a close-up of 6-point and 48-point matrices, a matrix stick ready for casting, and a print-ready Ludlow **form**. Further detail couldn't "be discussed in this book of typefaces," but technical literature was mailed upon request.[26] The next 250 pages showed Ludlow's types, often formatted into commercial ads.

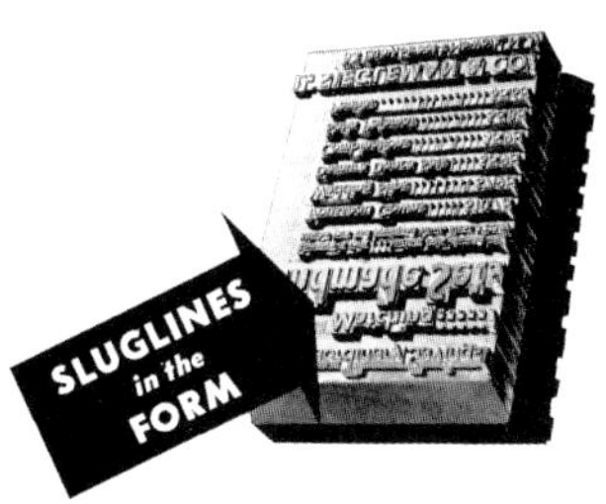

This Ludlow **form** is ready to be locked down on the press bed and printed.

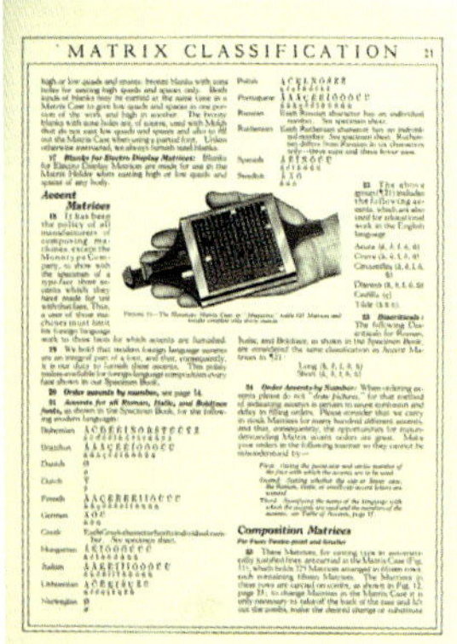

MATRIX CLASSIFICATION 21

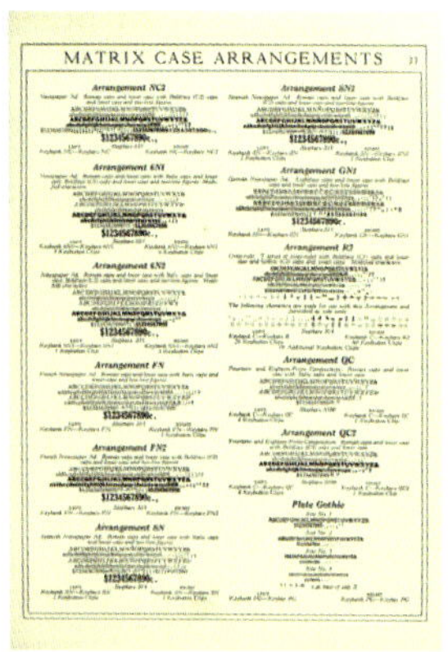

MATRIX CASE ARRANGEMENTS 33

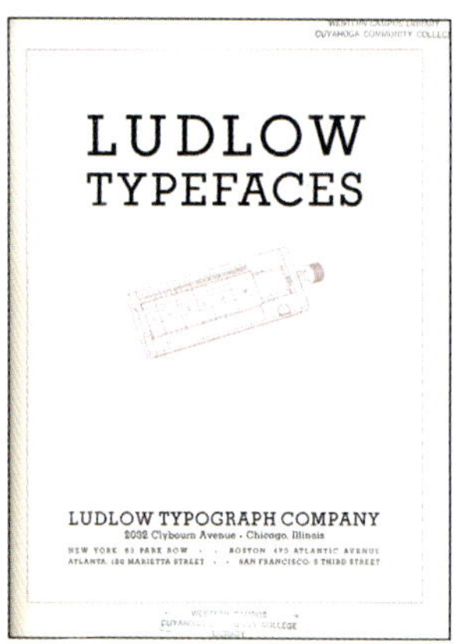

LUDLOW TYPEFACES

LUDLOW TYPOGRAPH COMPANY

2032 Clybourn Avenue · Chicago, Illinois

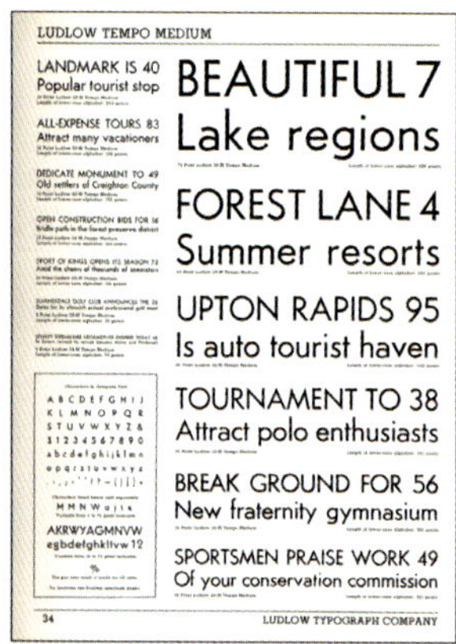

LUDLOW TEMPO MEDIUM

LANDMARK IS 40
Popular tourist stop

BEAUTIFUL 7
Lake regions

FOREST LANE 4
Summer resorts

UPTON RAPIDS 95
Is auto tourist haven

TOURNAMENT TO 38
Attract polo enthusiasts

BREAK GROUND FOR 56
New fraternity gymnasium

SPORTSMEN PRAISE WORK 49
Of your conservation commission

34 LUDLOW TYPOGRAPH COMPANY

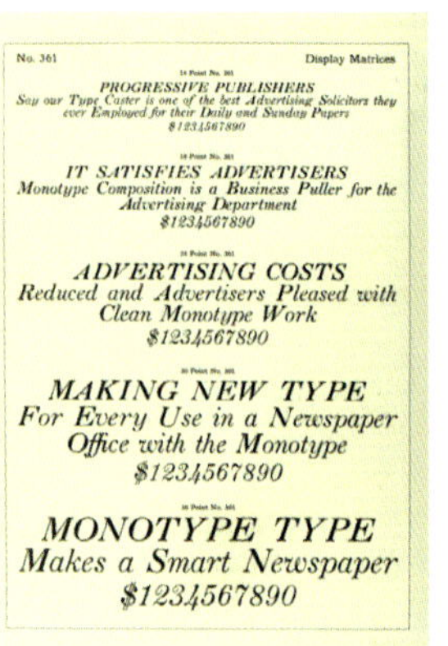

No. 361 Display Matrices

PROGRESSIVE PUBLISHERS
Say our Type Caster is one of the best Advertising Solicitors they ever Employed for their Daily and Sunday Papers
$1234567890

IT SATISFIES ADVERTISERS
Monotype Composition is a Business Puller for the Advertising Department
$1234567890

ADVERTISING COSTS
Reduced and Advertisers Pleased with Clean Monotype Work
$1234567890

MAKING NEW TYPE
For Every Use in a Newspaper Office with the Monotype
$1234567890

MONOTYPE TYPE
Makes a Smart Newspaper
$1234567890

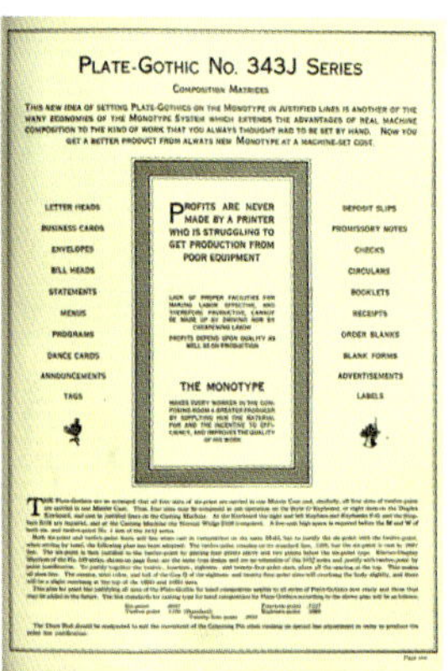

PLATE-GOTHIC No. 343J SERIES

COMPOSITION MATRICES

PROFITS ARE NEVER MADE BY A PRINTER WHO IS STRUGGLING TO GET PRODUCTION FROM POOR EQUIPMENT

THE MONOTYPE

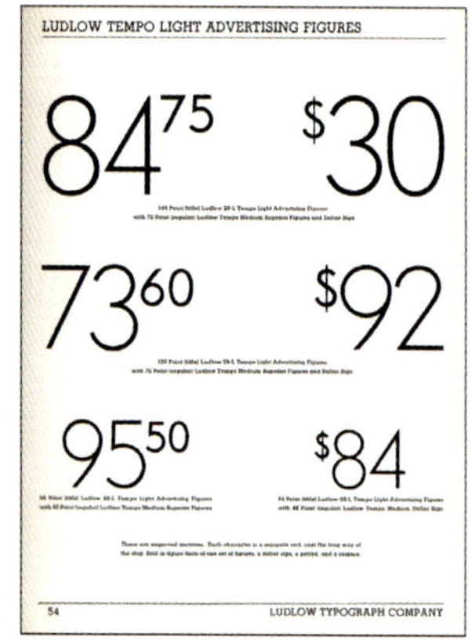

LUDLOW TEMPO LIGHT ADVERTISING FIGURES

84[75] $30

73[60] $92

95[50] $84

54 LUDLOW TYPOGRAPH COMPANY

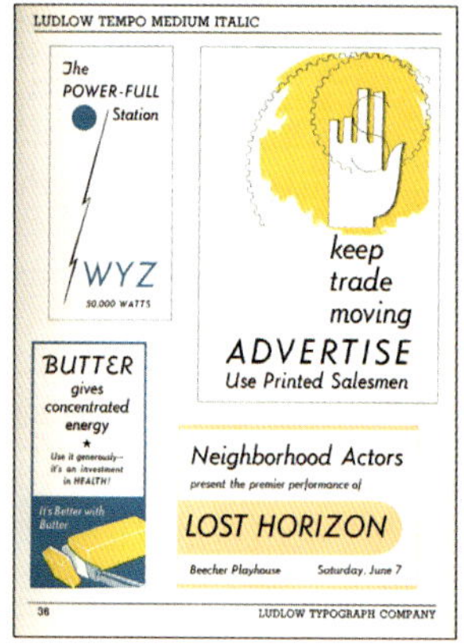

LUDLOW TEMPO MEDIUM ITALIC

The POWER-FULL Station

WYZ

50,000 WATTS

keep trade moving

ADVERTISE

Use Printed Salesmen

BUTTER gives concentrated energy

Neighborhood Actors

LOST HORIZON

Beecher Playhouse Saturday, June 7

36 LUDLOW TYPOGRAPH COMPANY

Fig 5.8 (above)

The Monotype Specimen Book of Typefaces **(Lanston Monotype, Philadelphia, 1916; left) and *Ludlow Typefaces* (Ludlow, Chicago, c.1940-58). While some hot metal specimens devoted chunky sections to how and why their machines should be used, others said little about technologies of production, as these contrasting specimens from Monotype and Ludlow demonstrate.**

Display devices for “good” mechanical type

Specimens frequently articulated their own value as reference books. Linotype’s 1915 book emphasized its use in “assisting the Linotype user to a proper selection and use of Linotype matrices,” allowing the printer “to select from it a style of type not only best suited to his particular need, but which will, as well, meet that most critical of all standards: ‘Type was made to read’.”[27] Likewise, Monotype’s 1916 specimen offered a rationale for how printers should select appropriate types. The sample copy, used repeatedly for all text faces, outlined a philosophy focused on understanding historical models and engaging with a flourishing contemporary professional culture. It suggested “blending” together “useful precedent” and “progressive” ideas, which would help young printers avoid “becom[ing] tiresome” through overwrought innovation. The “solidly endowed student” studied historical and contemporary exemplars—ideally, from a large stock handily located in the print shop. This cultivated the nascent printer’s balance between “avoiding mistakes” and “evolving brilliant schemes to dazzle his contemporaries.”[28] The 700+ page 1916 specimen offered few visuals in this educational vein, though other contemporaneous Monotype materials explicated historical examples, emergent or noteworthy typographic strategies, and the work of printing “masters” past and present.

In a quickly evolving professional and cultural context, type manufacturers assumed viewers would appreciate firm guidance and visual models. This specific, explicit goal characterized many hot metal specimens—and, for that matter, many foundry specimens from roughly the same period. For novice printers and those practicing far from fashionable urban centers, specimens offered useful demonstrations of current aesthetic trends, tastefully applied and competently printed. Clients, too, might benefit from seeing examples of what specimens always described as the "latest" and the "best" in typographic fashion. The *Manual of Linotype Typography* (1923), for instance, related via its subtitle that it was "prepared to aid users and producers of printing in securing greater unity and real beauty in the printed page." Though educational text was one aspect of the book, most of its work was visual. Some 250 pages showed ads, social and business stationery, title pages, textbook layouts, **timetables**, and catalog listings, along with more abstract displays of different Linotype series. For every job, there was an example to be consulted [Fig. 5.9].

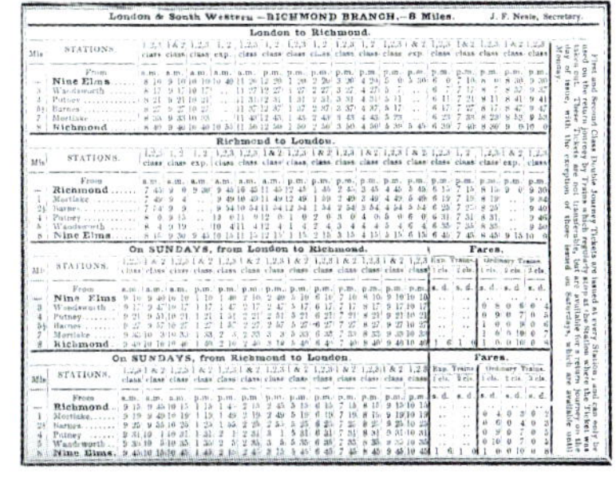
London & South Western.—RICHMOND BRANCH.—8 Miles.

London to Richmond.

Richmond to London.

On SUNDAYS, from London to Richmond.

On SUNDAYS, from Richmond to London.

Timetables, like this 1847 guide to railway and steam-ship schedules in Great Britain and the European continent, often required specialized typographic sorts because of their complicated design.

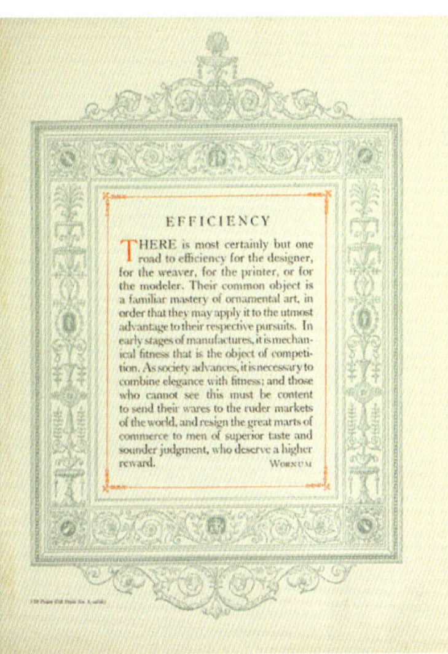
EFFICIENCY

THERE is most certainly but one road to efficiency for the designer, for the weaver, for the printer, or for the modeler. Their common object is a familiar mastery of ornamental art, in order that they may apply it to the utmost advantage to their respective pursuits. In early stages of manufactures, it is mechanical fitness that is the object of competition. As society advances, it is necessary to combine elegance with fitness; and those who cannot see this must be content to send their wares to the ruder markets of the world, and resign the great marts of commerce to men of superior taste and sounder judgment, who deserve a higher reward. WORNUM

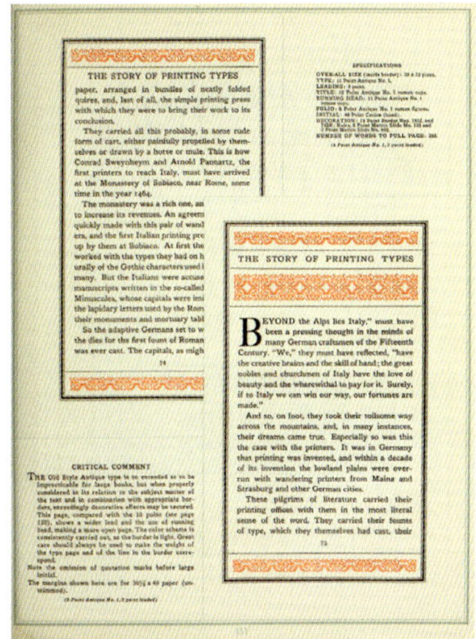
THE STORY OF PRINTING TYPES

paper, arranged in bundles of neatly folded quires, and, last of all, the simple printing press with which they were to bring their work to its conclusion.

They carried all this probably, in some rude form of cart, either painfully propelled by themselves or drawn by a horse or mule. This is how Conrad Sweynheym and Arnold Pannartz, the first printers to reach Italy, must have arrived at the Monastery of Subiaco, near Rome, some time in the year 1464.

The monastery was a rich one, an to increase its revenues. An agreem quickly made with this pair of wand ers, and the first Italian printing pre up by them at Subiaco. At first the worked with the types they had on h urally of the Gothic characters used i many. But the Italians were accuse manuscripts written in the so-called Minuscules, whose capitals were imi the lapidary letters used by the Rom their monuments and mortuary tabl

So the adaptive Germans set to w the dies for the first fount of Roman was ever cast. The capitals, as migh

74

THE STORY OF PRINTING TYPES

BEYOND the Alps lies Italy," must have been a pressing thought in the minds of many German craftsmen of the Fifteenth Century. "We," they must have reflected, "have the creative brains and the skill of hand; the great nobles and churchmen of Italy have the love of beauty and the wherewithal to pay for it. Surely, if to Italy we can win our way, our fortunes are made."

And so, on foot, they took their toilsome way across the mountains, and, in many instances, their dreams came true. Especially so was this the case with the printers. It was in Germany that printing was invented, and within a decade of its invention the lowland plains were overrun with wandering printers from Mainz and Strasburg and other German cities.

These pilgrims of literature carried their printing offices with them in the most literal sense of the word. They carried their founts of type, which they themselves had cast, their

75

SPECIFICATIONS

CRITICAL COMMENT

THE Old Style Antique type is so extended as to be impracticable for large books, but when properly considered in its relation to the subject matter of the text and in combination with appropriate borders, exceedingly decorative effects may be secured. This page, compared with the 10 point (see page 120), shows a wider lead and the use of running head, making a more open page. The color scheme is consistently carried out, as the border is light. Great care should always be used to make the weight of the type page and of the line in the border correspond.

Note the omission of quotation marks before large initial.

The margins shown here are for 30½ x 40 paper (untrimmed).

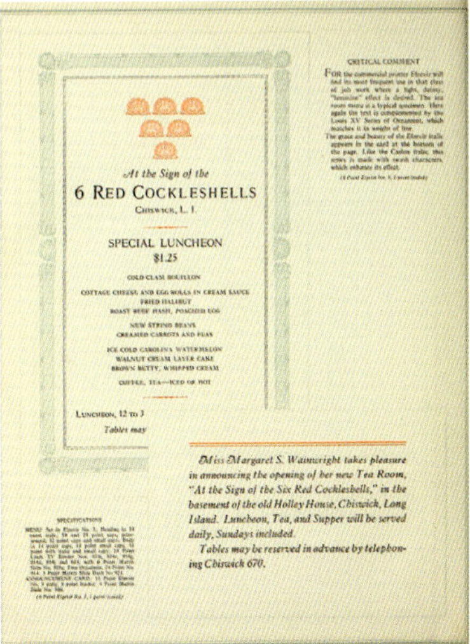
At the Sign of the

6 RED COCKLESHELLS

CHISWICK, L. I.

SPECIAL LUNCHEON

$1.25

COLD CLAM BOUILLON

COTTAGE CHEESE AND EGG ROLLS IN CREAM SAUCE

FRIED HALIBUT

ROAST BEEF HASH, POACHED EGG

NEW STRING BEANS

CREAMED CARROTS AND PEAS

ICE COLD CAROLINA WATERMELON

WALNUT CREAM LAYER CAKE

BROWN BETTY, WHIPPED CREAM

COFFEE, TEA—ICED OR HOT

LUNCHEON, 12 TO 3

Tables may

CRITICAL COMMENT

SPECIFICATIONS

Miss Margaret S. Wainwright takes pleasure in announcing the opening of her new Tea Room, "At the Sign of the Six Red Cockleshells," in the basement of the old Holley House, Chiswick, Long Island. Luncheon, Tea, and Supper will be served daily, Sundays included.

Tables may be reserved in advance by telephoning Chiswick 670.

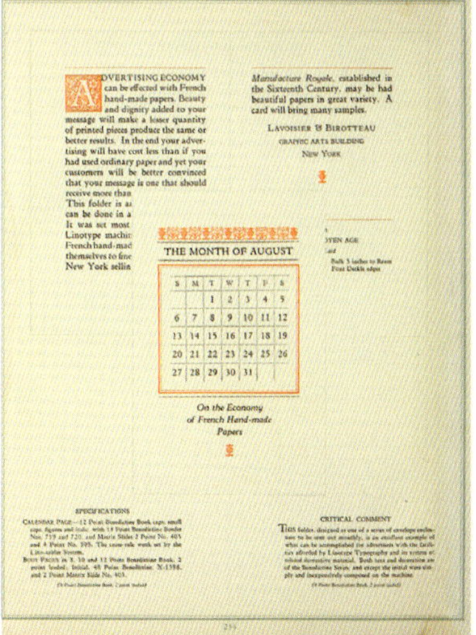
ADVERTISING ECONOMY can be effected with French hand-made papers. Beauty and dignity added to your message will make a lesser quantity of printed pieces produce the same or better results. In the end your advertising will have cost less than if you had used ordinary paper and yet your customers will be better convinced that your message is one that should receive more than

This folder is a can be done in a It was set most Linotype machi French hand-mad themselves to fine New York sellin

Manufacture Royale, established in the Sixteenth Century, may be had beautiful papers in great variety. A card will bring many samples.

LAVOISIER & BIROTTEAU

GRAPHIC ARTS BUILDING

NEW YORK

THE MONTH OF AUGUST

S	M	T	W	T	F	S
		1	2	3	4	5
6	7	8	9	10	11	12
13	14	15	16	17	18	19
20	21	22	23	24	25	26
27	28	29	30	31		

On the Economy of French Hand-made Papers

SPECIFICATIONS

CRITICAL COMMENT

Fig 5.9 (left)

***Manual of Linotype Typography* (Merganthaler, Brooklyn, 1923). Printers seeking design advice might consult specimens offering practical examples of types in everyday use.**

Ludlow, too, excelled at demonstrating the applied, everyday use of their types. Their specimens provided printers with explicit visual instructions, either through the hypothetical approximation of advertisements or the duplication of printed documents. The 1931 supplement displayed the Garamond (1929-30) and Tempo (1930) families designed by R. Hunter Middleton [Fig. 5.10]. These contrasting types were represented with equally contrasting design strategies. Garamond's history dates to sixteenth century France; Middleton's redesign for Ludlow closely consulted the types on the Egenolff-Berner sheet (1592), which Beatrice Warde had recently called to typographers' attention.[29] The Garamond specimens—bookplate, menu, announcement—always centered the type within the page-frame, suggesting classical references. The sample copy explained that Garamond small caps add "charm" to printing jobs and that the sixteenth century saw Europe "casting off her shackles of the Middle Ages under the leadership of scholars fired with a Renaissance ideal," with the implication that Garamont's (and Grandjean's) types reflected this zeitgeist. In contrast, the **Art Deco** aesthetic inspired Tempo, a geometric sans serif with a range of styles,

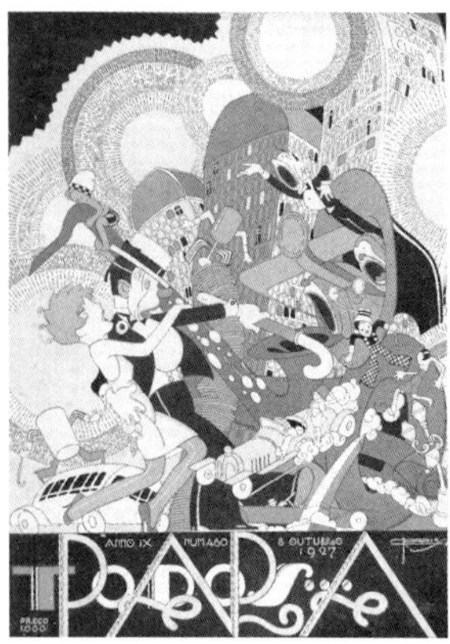

The streamlined forms, soaring skyscrapers, and geometric letterforms of **Art Deco** traveled internationally; in Brazil, the magazine *Para Todos* embraced the style.

Fig 5.10 (right)
***Ludlow Typefaces* (Ludlow, Chicago, 1931). The "oldstyle" Garamond and "contemporary" Tempo demonstrated the contrasting design strategies appropriate to each face.**

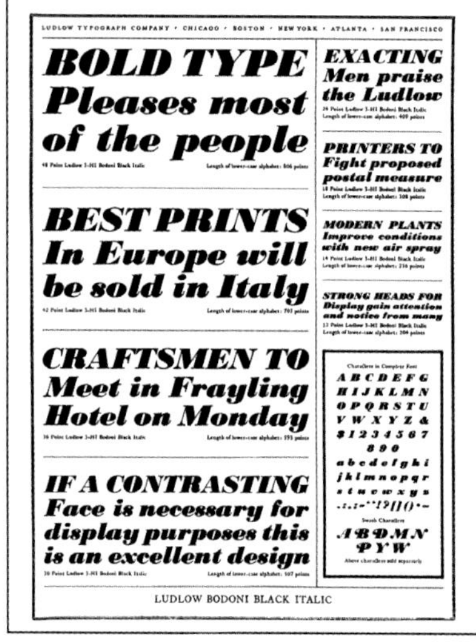

LUDLOW TYPOGRAPH COMPANY · CHICAGO · BOSTON · NEW YORK · ATLANTA · SAN FRANCISCO

BOLD TYPE Pleases most of the people

BEST PRINTS In Europe will be sold in Italy

CRAFTSMEN TO Meet in Frayling Hotel on Monday

IF A CONTRASTING Face is necessary for display purposes this is an excellent design

EXACTING Men praise the Ludlow

PRINTERS TO Fight proposed postal measure

MODERN PLANTS Improve conditions with new air spray

STRONG HEADS FOR Display gain attention and notice from many

A B C D E F G H I J K L M N O P Q R S T U V W X Y Z & $ 1 2 3 4 5 6 7 8 9 0 a b c d e f g h i j k l m n o p q r s t u v w x y z

LUDLOW BODONI BLACK ITALIC

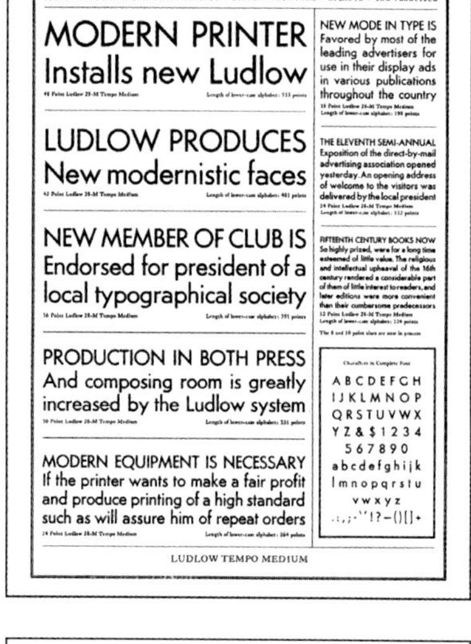

LUDLOW TYPOGRAPH COMPANY · CHICAGO · BOSTON · NEW YORK · ATLANTA · SAN FRANCISCO

MODERN PRINTER
Installs new Ludlow

LUDLOW PRODUCES
New modernistic faces

NEW MEMBER OF CLUB IS
Endorsed for president of a local typographical society

PRODUCTION IN BOTH PRESS
And composing room is greatly increased by the Ludlow system

MODERN EQUIPMENT IS NECESSARY
If the printer wants to make a fair profit and produce printing of a high standard such as will assure him of repeat orders

NEW MODE IN TYPE IS
Favored by most of the leading advertisers for use in their display ads in various publications throughout the country

THE ELEVENTH SEMI-ANNUAL
Exposition of the direct-by-mail advertising association opened yesterday. An opening address of welcome to the visitors was delivered by the local president

FIFTEENTH CENTURY BOOKS NOW
So highly prized, were for a long time esteemed of little value. The religious and intellectual upheaval of the 16th century rendered a considerable part of them of little interest to readers, and later editions were more convenient than their cumbersome predecessors

A B C D E F G H I J K L M N O P Q R S T U V W X Y Z & $ 1 2 3 4 5 6 7 8 9 0 a b c d e f g h i j k l m n o p q r s t u v w x y z

LUDLOW TEMPO MEDIUM

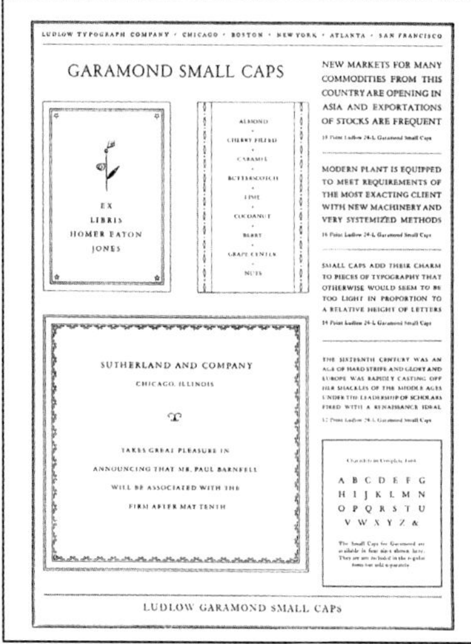

LUDLOW TYPOGRAPH COMPANY · CHICAGO · BOSTON · NEW YORK · ATLANTA · SAN FRANCISCO

GARAMOND SMALL CAPS

EX LIBRIS HOMER EATON JONES

SUTHERLAND AND COMPANY
CHICAGO, ILLINOIS
TAKES GREAT PLEASURE IN ANNOUNCING THAT MR. PAUL BARNFELL WILL BE ASSOCIATED WITH THE FIRM AFTER MAY TENTH

NEW MARKETS FOR MANY COMMODITIES FROM THIS COUNTRY ARE OPENING IN ASIA AND EXPORTATIONS OF STOCKS ARE FREQUENT

MODERN PLANT IS EQUIPPED TO MEET REQUIREMENTS OF THE MOST EXACTING CLIENT WITH NEW MACHINERY AND VERY SYSTEMIZED METHODS

SMALL CAPS ADD THEIR CHARM TO PIECES OF TYPOGRAPHY THAT OTHERWISE WOULD SEEM TO BE TOO LIGHT IN PROPORTION TO A RELATIVE HEIGHT OF LETTERS

THE SIXTEENTH CENTURY WAS AN AGE OF HARD STRIFE AND GLORY AND EUROPE WAS RAPIDLY CASTING OFF HER SHACKLES OF THE MIDDLE AGES UNDER THE LEADERSHIP OF SCHOLARS FIRED WITH A RENAISSANCE IDEAL

A B C D E F G H I J K L M N O P Q R S T U V W X Y Z &

LUDLOW GARAMOND SMALL CAPS

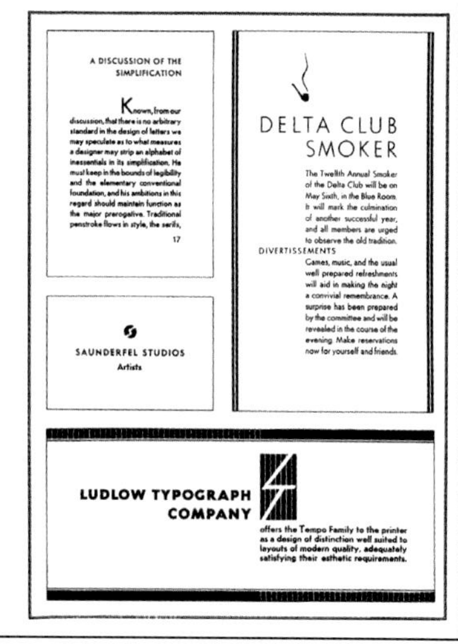

A DISCUSSION OF THE SIMPLIFICATION

Known, from our discussion, that there is no arbitrary standard in the design of letters we may speculate as to what measures a designer may strip an alphabet of inessentials in its simplification. He must keep in the bounds of legibility and the elementary conventional foundation, and his ambitions in this regard should maintain function as the major prerogative. Traditional penstroke flows in style, the serifs,

17

SAUNDERFEL STUDIOS
Artists

DELTA CLUB SMOKER

The Twelfth Annual Smoker of the Delta Club will be on May Sixth, in the Blue Room. It will mark the culmination of another successful year, and all members are urged to observe the old tradition.

DIVERTISSEMENTS

Games, music, and the usual well prepared refreshments will aid in making the night a convivial remembrance. A surprise has been prepared by the committee and will be revealed in the course of the evening. Make reservations now for yourself and friends.

LUDLOW TYPOGRAPH COMPANY

offers the Tempo Family to the printer as a design of distinction well suited to layouts of modern quality, adequately satisfying their esthetic requirements.

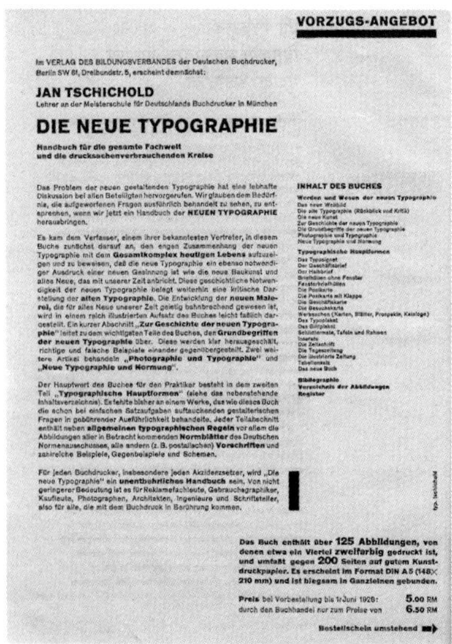

VORZUGS-ANGEBOT

Im VERLAG DES BILDUNGSVERBANDES der Deutschen Buchdrucker, Berlin SW 61, Dreibundstr. 5, erscheint demnächst:

JAN TSCHICHOLD
Lehrer an der Meisterschule für Deutschlands Buchdrucker in München

DIE NEUE TYPOGRAPHIE

Handbuch für die gesamte Fachwelt und die drucksachenverbrauchenden Kreise

Das Problem der neuen gestaltenden Typographie hat eine lebhafte Diskussion bei allen Beteiligten hervorgerufen. Wir glauben dem Bedürfnis, die aufgeworfenen Fragen ausführlich behandelt zu sehen, zu entsprechen, wenn wir jetzt ein Handbuch der **NEUEN TYPOGRAPHIE** herausbringen.

Es kam dem Verfasser, einem ihrer bekanntesten Vertreter, in diesem Buche zunächst darauf an, den engen Zusammenhang der neuen Typographie mit dem **Gesamtkomplex heutigen Lebens** aufzuzeigen und zu beweisen, daß die neue Typographie ein ebenso notwendiger Ausdruck einer neuen Gesinnung ist wie die neue Baukunst und alles Neue, das mit unserer Zeit anbricht. Diese geschichtliche Notwendigkeit der neuen Typographie belegt weiterhin eine kritische Darstellung der **alten Typographie**. Die Entwicklung der **neuen Malerei**, die für alles Neue unserer Zeit geistig bahnbrechend gewesen ist, wird in einem reich illustrierten Aufsatz des Buches leicht faßlich dargestellt. Ein kurzer Abschnitt „**Zur Geschichte der neuen Typographie**" leitet zu dem wichtigsten Teile des Buches, den **Grundbegriffen der neuen Typographie** über. Diese werden klar herausgeschält, richtige und falsche Beispiele einander gegenübergestellt. Zwei weitere Artikel behandeln „**Photographie und Typographie**" und „**Neue Typographie und Normung**".

Der Hauptwert des Buches für den Praktiker besteht in dem zweiten Teil „**Typographische Hauptformen**" (siehe das nebenstehende Inhaltsverzeichnis). Es fehlte bisher an einem Werke, das wie dieses Buch die schon bei einfachen Satzaufgaben auftauchenden gestalterischen Fragen in gebührender Ausführlichkeit behandelte. Jeder Teilabschnitt enthält neben **allgemeinen typographischen Regeln** vor allem die Abbildungen aller in Betracht kommenden **Normblätter** des Deutschen Normenausschusses, alle andern (z. B. postalischen) **Vorschriften** und zahlreiche Beispiele, Gegenbeispiele und Schemen.

Für jeden Buchdrucker, insbesondere jeden Akzidenzsetzer, wird „Die neue Typographie" ein **unentbehrliches Handbuch** sein. Von nicht geringerer Bedeutung ist es für Reklamefachleute, Gebrauchsgraphiker, Kaufleute, Photographen, Architekten, Ingenieure und Schriftsteller, also für alle, die mit dem Buchdruck in Berührung kommen.

INHALT DES BUCHES

Werden und Wesen der neuen Typographie
Das neue Weltbild
Die alte Typographie (Rückblick und Kritik)
Die neue Kunst
Zur Geschichte der neuen Typographie
Die Grundbegriffe der neuen Typographie
Photographie und Typographie
Neue Typographie und Normung

Typographische Hauptformen
Das Typosignet
Der Geschäftsbrief
Der Halbbrief
Briefhüllen ohne Fenster
Fensterbriefhüllen
Die Postkarte
Die Postkarte mit Klappe
Die Geschäftskarte
Die Besuchskarte
Werbsachen (Karten, Blätter, Prospekte, Kataloge)
Das Typoplakat
Das Bildplakat
Schildformate, Tafeln und Rahmen
Inserate
Die Zeitschrift
Die Tageszeitung
Die illustrierte Zeitung
Tabellensatz
Das neue Buch

Bibliographie
Verzeichnis der Abbildungen
Register

typ. tschichold

Das Buch enthält über 125 Abbildungen, von denen etwa ein Viertel zweifarbig gedruckt ist, und umfaßt gegen 200 Seiten auf gutem Kunstdruckpapier. Es erscheint im Format DIN A 5 (148×210 mm) und ist biegsam in Ganzleinen gebunden.

Preis bei Vorbestellung bis 1. Juni 1928: 5.00 RM
durch den Buchhandel nur zum Preise von 6.50 RM

Bestellschein umstehend

The New Typography, a phrase coined by László Moholy-Nagy in 1923, was adopted by Jan Tschichold as the title of his now-canonical 1928 book on the principles of typography reimagined for the Modern age: sans serif typography, assymetrical page layout, geometric form, an absence of ornament, and the use of photography when image information is absolutely required.

widths, and weights. Tempo competed with Bauer's Futura and Klingspor's Kabel (both 1927). The Tempo specimens—advertisement, invitation, book page—established asymmetrical design as the norm. Indicative of modern page layout, asymmetry signalled an awareness of design practice as codified by Jan Tschichold's ***The New Typography*** (1928).[30] Tempo's sample copy described it as "well suited to layouts of modern quality," emphasizing the contemporary nature of the family's design and suggesting to novice printers how the type should—and shouldn't—be used.

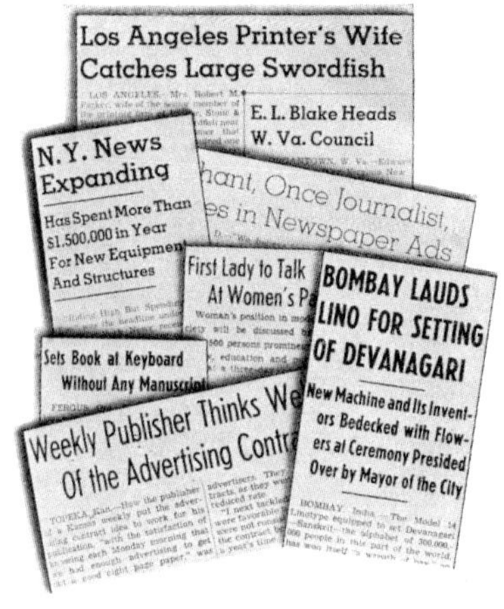

Display type grabbed viewers' attention through size, style, and placement.

Differentiation and cooperation

In their efforts to distinguish themselves from Monotype and Linotype, smaller manufacturers often claimed a simpler machine or superior printed result, or both. Their specimens communicated difference, explaining how their machines worked and highlighting unique user-friendly or mechanically-sturdy features. Superlatives like *best* or *most* regularly implied a direct comparison between (usually unnamed) competing systems. Introductory notes and sample texts praised features like easy machine repairs, high-quality type metal, the visual design of proprietary types, and the superior printing results achieved with type made to the highest standards.

Intertype claimed superiority because of its "distinctive typography in text, headletter and **display composition**, modern border designs and border matrices." Their *Specimen Book of Intertype Faces* (1920) described the "greatest achievement in the mechanical typographical art," realized "through the concentrated efforts of Intertype engineers and designers exclusively" [Fig. 5.11] This simplified redesign replaced "complicated mechanical line casting equipment in use in newspaper and job printing offices"—clearly addressing Linotype users, though Intertype's machines operated similarly. Intertype's uncomplicated, carefully engineered equipment ostensibly offered maximum efficiency at minimum cost, with all the benefits of Linotype but none of its drawbacks.

The Ludlow Typograph came closest to achieving the wide success enjoyed by Linotype and Monotype.[31] Founded in 1906 by William Ludlow and William Reade, the Chicago-based company designed machines for a workflow that combined hand-setting and slug casting. The Ludlow neither used a keyboard

Fig 5.11 (below)

Specimen Book of Intertype Faces **(Intertype, New York, 1920). To differentiate themselves from their larger competitors, smaller companies like Intertype stressed their "distinctive" type designs or their increased simplicity.**

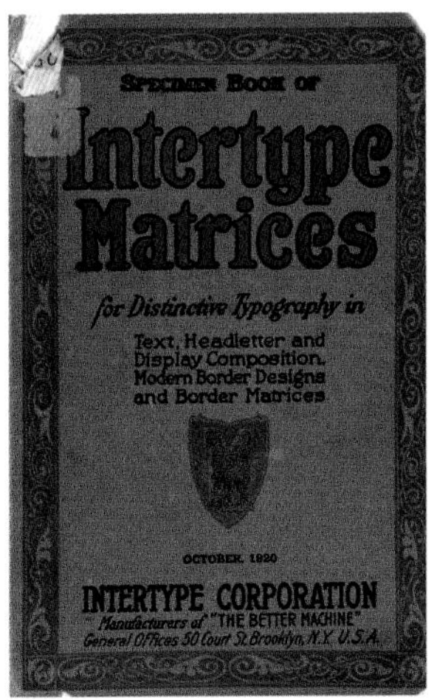

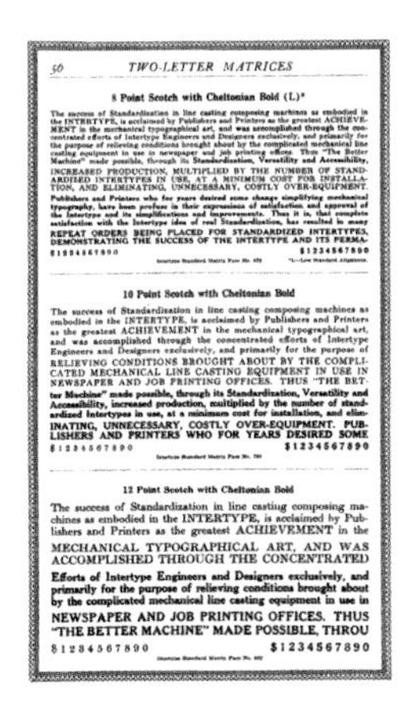

50 TWO-LETTER MATRICES

8 Point Scotch with Cheltonian Bold (L)*

The success of Standardization in line casting composing machines as embodied in the INTERTYPE, is acclaimed by Publishers and Printers as the greatest ACHIEVEMENT in the mechanical typographical art, and was accomplished through the concentrated efforts of Intertype Engineers and Designers exclusively, and primarily for the purpose of relieving conditions brought about by the complicated mechanical line casting equipment in use in newspaper and job printing offices. Thus "The Better Machine" made possible, through its Standardization, Versatility and Accessibility, INCREASED PRODUCTION, MULTIPLIED BY THE NUMBER OF STANDARDIZED INTERTYPES IN USE, AT A MINIMUM COST FOR INSTALLATION, AND ELIMINATING UNNECESSARY, COSTLY OVER-EQUIPMENT. Publishers and Printers who for years desired some change simplifying mechanical typography, have been profuse in their expressions of satisfaction and approval of the Intertype and its simplifications and improvements. Thus it is, that complete satisfaction with the Intertype idea of real Standardization, has resulted in many REPEAT ORDERS BEING PLACED FOR STANDARDIZED INTERTYPES, DEMONSTRATING THE SUCCESS OF THE INTERTYPE AND ITS PERMA-

$1234567890 $1234567890

10 Point Scotch with Cheltonian Bold

The success of Standardization in line casting composing machines as embodied in the INTERTYPE, is acclaimed by Publishers and Printers as the greatest ACHIEVEMENT in the mechanical typographical art, and was accomplished through the concentrated efforts of Intertype Engineers and Designers exclusively, and primarily for the purpose of RELIEVING CONDITIONS BROUGHT ABOUT BY THE COMPLICATED MECHANICAL LINE CASTING EQUIPMENT IN USE IN NEWSPAPER AND JOB PRINTING OFFICES. THUS "THE BETter Machine" made possible, through its Standardization, Versatility and Accessibility, increased production, multiplied by the number of standardized Intertypes in use, at a minimum cost for installation, and eliminating, UNNECESSARY, COSTLY OVER-EQUIPMENT. PUBLISHERS AND PRINTERS WHO FOR YEARS DESIRED SOME

$1234567890 $1234567890

12 Point Scotch with Cheltonian Bold

The success of Standardization in line casting composing machines as embodied in the INTERTYPE, is acclaimed by Publishers and Printers as the greatest ACHIEVEMENT in the MECHANICAL TYPOGRAPHICAL ART, AND WAS ACCOMPLISHED THROUGH THE CONCENTRATED Efforts of Intertype Engineers and Designers exclusively, and primarily for the purpose of relieving conditions brought about by the complicated mechanical line casting equipment in use in NEWSPAPER AND JOB PRINTING OFFICES. THUS "THE BETTER MACHINE" MADE POSSIBLE, THROU

$1234567890 $1234567890

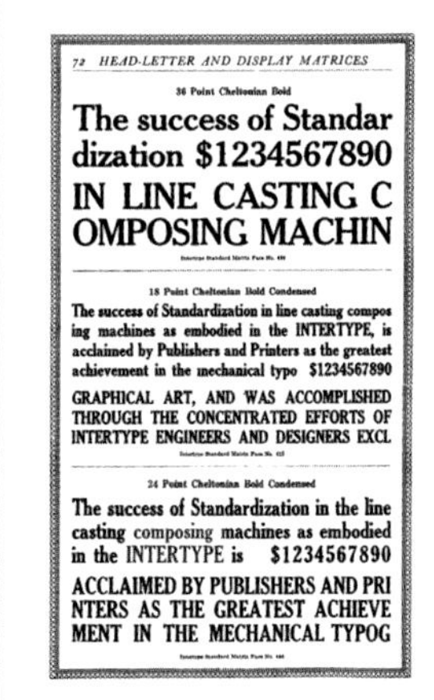

72 HEAD-LETTER AND DISPLAY MATRICES

36 Point Cheltonian Bold

The success of Standar
dization $1234567890
IN LINE CASTING C
OMPOSING MACHIN

18 Point Cheltonian Bold Condensed

The success of Standardization in line casting composing machines as embodied in the INTERTYPE, is acclaimed by Publishers and Printers as the greatest achievement in the mechanical typo $1234567890 GRAPHICAL ART, AND WAS ACCOMPLISHED THROUGH THE CONCENTRATED EFFORTS OF INTERTYPE ENGINEERS AND DESIGNERS EXCL

24 Point Cheltonian Bold Condensed

The success of Standardization in the line casting composing machines as embodied in the INTERTYPE is $1234567890 ACCLAIMED BY PUBLISHERS AND PRINTERS AS THE GREATEST ACHIEVEMENT IN THE MECHANICAL TYPOG

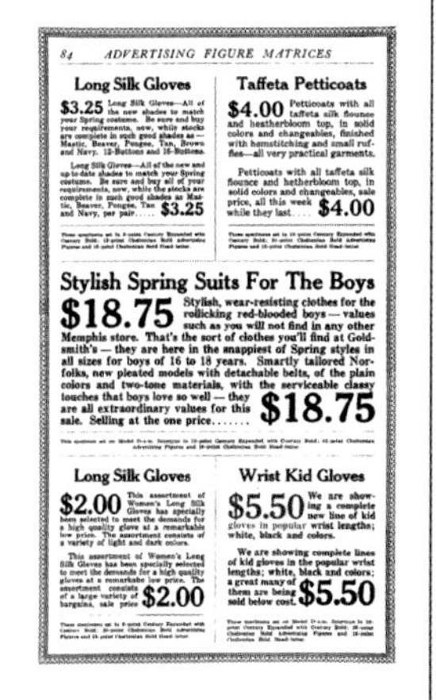

84 ADVERTISING FIGURE MATRICES

Long Silk Gloves

$3.25 Long Silk Gloves—All of the new shades to match your Spring costume. Be sure and buy your requirements, now, while stocks are complete in such good shades as—Mastic, Beaver, Pongee, Tan, Brown and Navy. 12-Buttons and 16-Buttons.

Long Silk Gloves—All of the new and up-to-date shades to match your Spring costume. Be sure and buy all of your requirements, now, while the stocks are complete in such good shades as Mastic, Beaver, Pongee, Tan and Navy, per pair..... $3.25

Taffeta Petticoats

$4.00 Petticoats with all taffeta silk flounce and heatherbloom top, in solid colors and changeables, finished with hemstitching and small ruffles—all very practical garments.

Petticoats with all taffeta silk flounce and hetherbloom top, in solid colors and changeables, sale price, all this week while they last.... $4.00

Stylish Spring Suits For The Boys

$18.75 Stylish, wear-resisting clothes for the rollicking red-blooded boys — values such as you will not find in any other Memphis store. That's the sort of clothes you'll find at Goldsmith's — they are here in the snappiest of Spring styles in all sizes for boys of 16 to 18 years. Smartly tailored Norfolks, new pleated models with detachable belts, of the plain colors and two-tone materials, with the serviceable classy touches that boys love so well — they are all extraordinary values for this sale. Selling at the one price....... $18.75

Long Silk Gloves

$2.00 This assortment of Women's Long Silk Gloves has specially been selected to meet the demands for a high quality glove at a remarkable low price. The assortment consists of a variety of light and dark colors.

This assortment of Women's Long Silk Gloves has been specially selected to meet the demands for a high quality gloves at a remarkabe low price. The assortment consists of a large variety of bargains, sale price $2.00

Wrist Kid Gloves

$5.50 We are showing a complete new line of kid gloves in popular wrist lengths; white, black and colors.

We are showing complete lines of kid gloves in the popular wrist lengths; white, black and colors; a great many of them are being sold below cost. $5.50

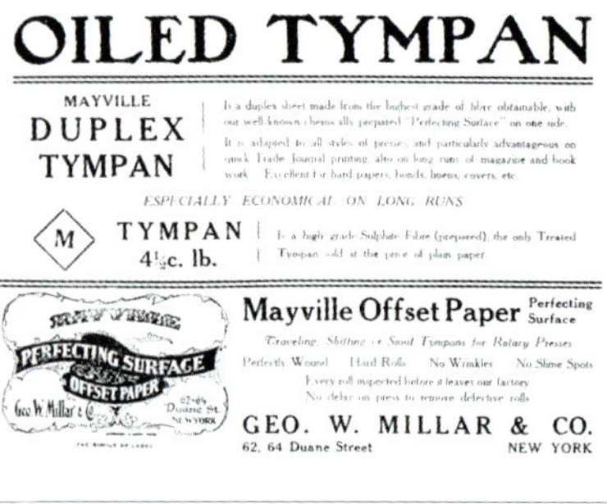

Display composition used complex structural arrangements and larger types, both text and decorative faces, to catch viewers' attention. This 1912 example from the Canadian Printer offers various printing supplies to its trade-based audience.

to set matrices nor automatically redistributed used matrices. Rather, a human compositor manually set the matrices for a line of type, cast a slug, redistributed the matrices, then printed from the slug(s). Unlike the Linotype or Monotype, the Ludlow cast a 12–60pt. size range without changing the **magazine** which stored the matrices, and this single magazine could combine a face's romans and italics. Thus, Ludlow multiplied the range of possible size and style combinations without increasing the complexity of their machine or the number of matrices printers must purchase. And the Ludlow, like its larger competitors, cast new type for every printing job. The Ludlow's workflow meant that mechanical efficiency was a different equation for its users. A 1919 advertisement quoted a pleased customer about increased speed: "We get 20% more work through the press room since we put in the Ludlow Typograph."[32] Fewer components meant fewer opportunities for mechanical failures and broken parts, perhaps more appealing to Ludlow's users than the speed of full automation.

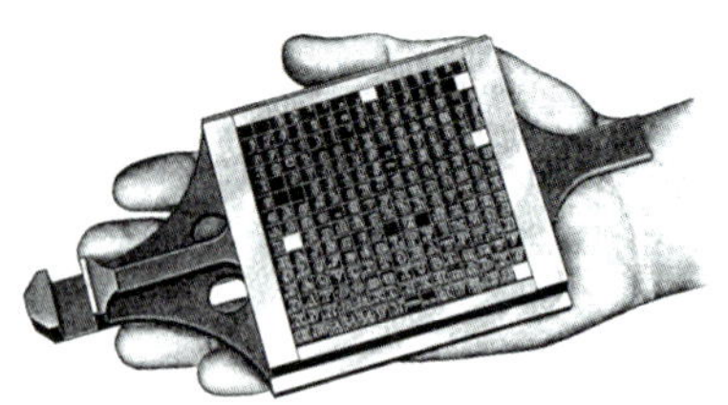

A **magazine** or matrix case stores matrices (molds for casting individual sorts) within the typecasting machine.

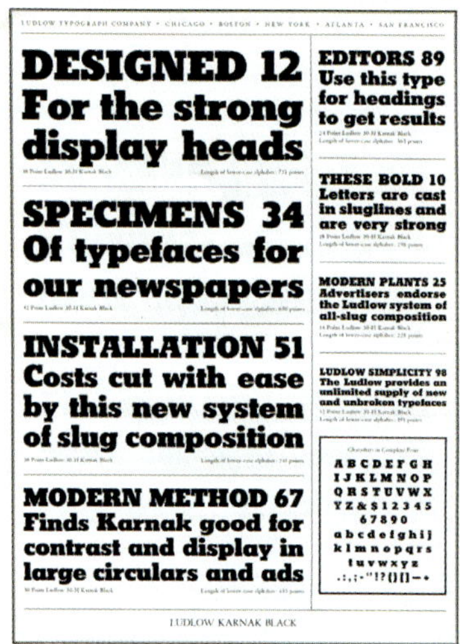

DESIGNED 12
For the strong
display heads

SPECIMENS 34
Of typefaces for
our newspapers

INSTALLATION 51
Costs cut with ease
by this new system
of slug composition

MODERN METHOD 67
Finds Karnak good for
contrast and display in
large circulars and ads

EDITORS 89
Use this type
for headings
to get results

THESE BOLD 10
Letters are cast
in sluglines and
are very strong

MODERN PLANTS 25
Advertisers endorse
the Ludlow system of
all-slug composition

LUDLOW SIMPLICITY 98
The Ludlow provides an
unlimited supply of new
and unbroken typefaces

ABCDEFGH
IJKLMNOP
QRSTUVWX
YZ&$12345
67890
abcdefghij
klmnopqrs
tuvwxyz

LUDLOW KARNAK BLACK

9

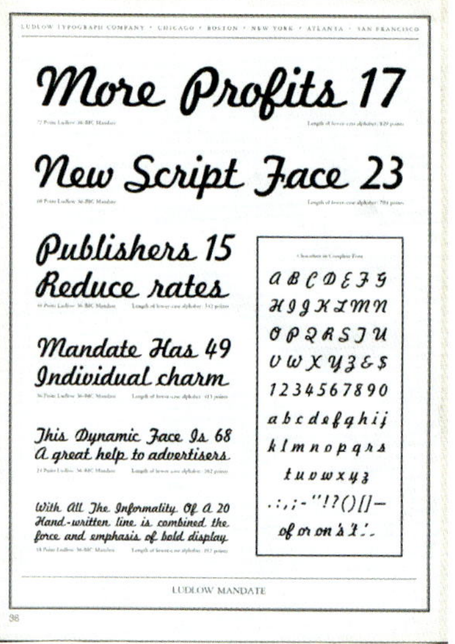

More Profits 17

New Script Face 23

Publishers 15
Reduce rates

Mandate Has 49
Individual charm

This Dynamic Face Is 68
A great help to advertisers

With All The Informality Of A 20
Hand-written line is combined the
force and emphasis of bold display

LUDLOW MANDATE

36

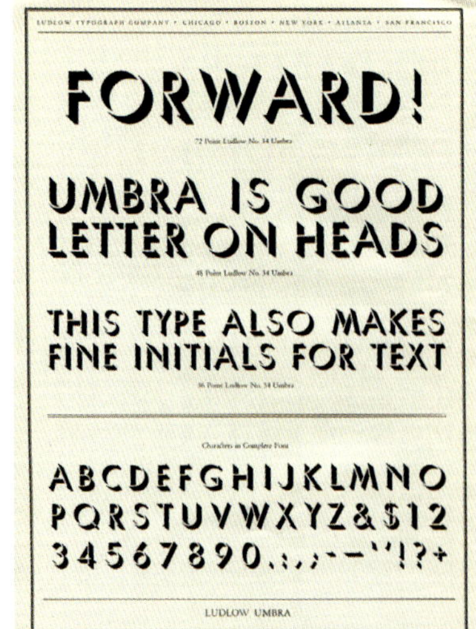

FORWARD!

UMBRA IS GOOD
LETTER ON HEADS

THIS TYPE ALSO MAKES
FINE INITIALS FOR TEXT

ABCDEFGHIJKLMNO
PQRSTUVWXYZ&$12
34567890.:,;-—''!?+

LUDLOW UMBRA

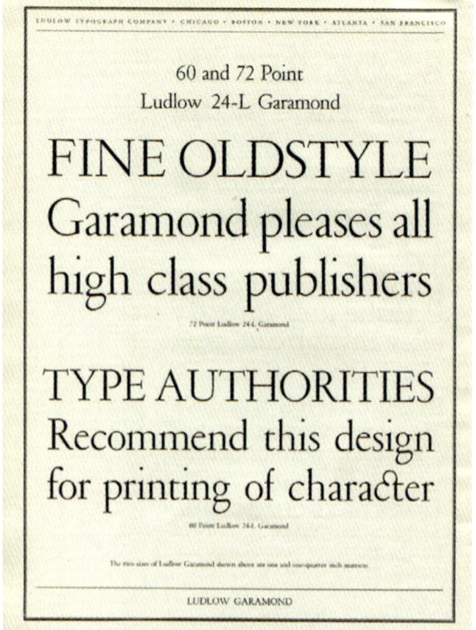

60 and 72 Point
Ludlow 24-L Garamond

FINE OLDSTYLE
Garamond pleases all
high class publishers

TYPE AUTHORITIES
Recommend this design
for printing of character

LUDLOW GARAMOND

Fig 5.12 (right)

***Ludlow Typefaces, A Supplement* (Ludlow, Chicago, 1933) and *Ludlow Typefaces Recently Produced* (1936, bottom). Though Ludlow's machines didn't automatically set and distribute matrices, Ludlow claimed their workflow was more efficient because of its simplicity, and printers still got to use new type for every job.**

While Ludlow addressed saving time and money, the company's printed materials also took care to articulate the attractiveness of its types to printers, clients, and reading audiences, each with specific requirements [Fig. 5.12]. "Printers like the new typefaces that Ludlow is designing," the March 1931 supplement promised. Echoing the syntax of newspaper headlines, the April 1932 supplement expressed typography's value for advertisers: "Using Karnak Medium is great help to merchant." Ludlow stressed the relationship between their product, rapidly changing public tastes, and increased profit margins. The February 1934 supplement claimed that "Great progress is now being made in type designing of modern letters; [the] Ludlow system will help to increase the profits of any printer who will inquire about its merits." Though "any printer" might benefit, Ludlow filled a niche in a cross-platform mechanized **system**. Some of Ludlow's printed materials emphasized its suitability for setting display and advertising type, articulating its advantages in combination with "keyboard slug material for body matter"— that is, Linotype.[33] Perhaps oddly, given that they also advertised their own capacity for setting display type, Linotype similarly acknowledged Ludlow, describing the modern printer of 1918 as someone capable of

> bringing [matrix units] together quickly *for a definite purpose* ... to cast what is needed at the time it is needed—the all-slug way. Modern tactics are not the tactics of a few years ago. ... The massed-matrices tactician brings up the *multiple-magazine Linotype batteries* and the large-calibered *Ludlow* and with *solid all-slug lines* annihilates ... waste and worry.[34]

By articulating the collaborative relationship among technologies in the modern pressroom, Linotype positioned itself as the industry standard for efficient body copy, while Ludlow focused on display type.

In describing their machines as cooperative forces for modern printing, Linotype and Ludlow shared an emphasis on efficiency and suitability to purpose. Driven by applied use, this pragmatic combination made its way into printers'—rather than manufacturers'—books. The small, spiral-bound *Specimens of Linotype and Ludlow Type Faces* (1940) displayed the types used to print the Consolidated Press of Sydney's *Daily Telegraph*, *Sunday Telegraph*, and *Australian Women's Weekly* [Fig. 5.13]. Linotype machines reached Australia in the mid-1890s and saw widespread use by the turn of the century.[35] The Consolidated specimen's display copy describes Ludlow's types as "bright and interesting display" faces and advises that with Linotype, "matter of all kinds can be set more quickly" and the method is "suitable for every class of printing." The sizes shown for the corresponding types reinforced this message, with smaller Linotype faces and larger Ludlow faces. Most specimens distributed by newspaper printers addressed advertisers, though nothing explicitly indicates this purpose in the Consolidated Press specimen. The combination of Ludlow and Linotype, however, demonstrates how even the most universalizing machines might be adapted, combined, and applied to local purposes.

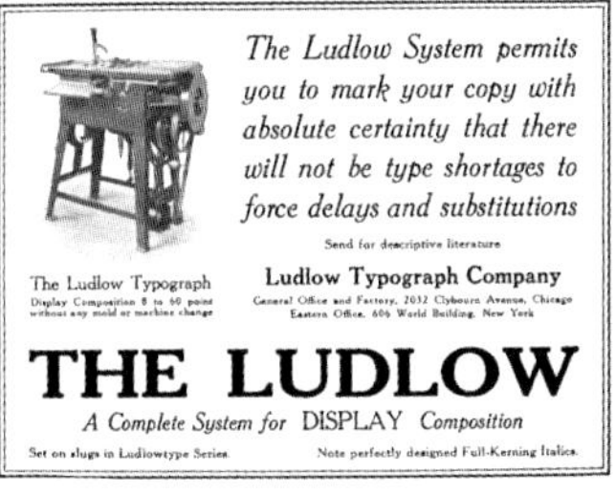

The logical, efficient **system** of mechanical typesetting permeated discussions about the medium at every level.

Fig 5.13 (right)

***Specimens of Linotype and Ludlow Type Faces* (Consolidated Press, Sydney, 1940). Large printing offices often used Linotype for body copy and Ludlow for display and jobbing type. Both Linotype and Ludlow referenced this common practice in some of their advertising materials.**

ULTRA MODERN UM

14 POINT
LUDLOW TYPES HAVE MANY BRIGHT DIS
ludlow types have many bright display faces of

18 POINT
LUDLOW FACES HAVE MANY BRI
ludlow faces have many bright display

24 POINT
LUDLOW FACES HAVE MA
ludlow types have many bright

30 POINT
LUDLOW TYPES HAV
ludlow types have many

36 POINT
LUDLOW TYPES H
ludlow types have m

42 POINT
LUDLOW TYPES
ludlow types have

48 POINT
LUDLOW TYP
ludlow types ha

Page Thirty-three

FAIRFIELD

8 POINT
LINOTYPE MATTER OF ALL KINDS CAN BE SET MORE QUICKLY TH
Linotype matter of all kinds can be set more quickly than by any other method

8 POINT ITALIC
LINOTYPE MATTER OF ALL KINDS CAN BE SET MORE QUICKLY TH
Linotype matter of all kinds can be set more quickly than by any other method

9 POINT
LINOTYPE MATTER OF ALL KINDS CAN BE SET MORE QUICKLY
Linotype matter of all kinds can be set more quickly than by any other method

9 POINT ITALIC
LINOTYPE MATTER OF ALL KINDS CAN BE SET MORE QUICKLY
Linotype matter of all kinds can be set more quickly than by any other method

10 POINT
LINOTYPE MATTER OF ALL KINDS CAN BE SET MORE QUI
Linotype matter of all kinds can be set more quickly than by any other

10 POINT ITALIC
LINOTYPE MATTER OF ALL KINDS CAN BE SET MORE QUI
Linotype matter of all kinds can be set more quickly than by any other

BASKERVILLE

8 POINT
LINOTYPE MATTER OF ALL KINDS CAN BE SET MORE QUICKLY TH
Linotype matter of all kinds can be set more quickly than by any other method

8 POINT BOLD
LINOTYPE MATTER OF ALL KINDS CAN BE SET MORE QUICKLY TH
Linotype matter of all kinds can be set more quickly than by any other method

9 POINT
LINOTYPE MATTER OF ALL KINDS CAN BE SET MORE QUICKLY
Linotype matter of all kinds can be set more quickly than by any other meth

9 POINT BOLD
LINOTYPE MATTER OF ALL KINDS CAN BE SET MORE QUICKLY
Linotype matter of all kinds can be set more quickly than by any other meth

9 POINT ITALIC
LINOTYPE MATTER OF ALL KINDS CAN BE SET MORE QUICKLY
Linotype matter of all kinds can be set more quickly than by any other means

11 POINT
LINOTYPE MATTER OF ALL KINDS CAN BE SET MORE
Linotype matter of all kinds can be set more quickly than any oth

11 POINT ITALIC
LINOTYPE MATTER OF ALL KINDS CAN BE SET MORE
Linotype matter of all kinds can be set more quickly than any oth

12 POINT
LINOTYPE MATTER OF ALL KINDS CAN BE SET
linotype matter of all kinds can be set more quickly than by

12 POINT ITALIC
LINOTYPE MATTER OF ALL KINDS CAN BE SET
linotype matter of all kinds can be set more quickly than by

TYPEWRITER T

10 POINT
LINOTYPE MATTER OF ALL KINDS CAN BE SET MORE QUICKLY T
linotype matter of all kinds can be set more quickly
LINOTYPE MATTER OF ALL KINDS CAN BE SET MORE QUICKLY T
linotype matter of all kinds can be set more quickly t

Page Thirty-five

Arabic

Arabic Bold

Arabic Old Style

Arabic Bold Old Style

Arabic 22 (third line from top) was Linotype's first Arabic face, shown here with later size and style additions.

Programmatic world views

In addition to their multiple pragmatic functions, specimens communicated the manufacturer's broader philosophy. Hot metal typesetting prioritized mechanization, economy, and universality. Despite local practices of use, adoption of mechanized type exerted a strong standardizing effect. Linotype explicitly declared itself "the standard composing machine of the world, unmatched in speed, versatility, [and] durability."[36] The 1915 specimen visualized Linotype's systemization, applying a Eurocentric, universalizing rationale to its eighty "fonts of foreign languages," including Armenian, Cyrillic, Greek, Hewbrew, and Linotype's first Arabic face, **Arabic 22**pt. Because it was modeled on successful foundry types, which had in turn adapted existing manuscript hands to metal, Arabic 22pt. was one of Linotype's more successful Arabic translation efforts. However, Linotype faced challenges in developing Arabic faces compatible with its machines, and these were evident in even its most successful fonts. The lack of control over kerning, primarily an aesthetic issue for the Latin alphabet, significantly impacted legibility for Arabic. Correctly placing diacritical marks above and below characters was likewise impossible, forcing their displacement to either side of the character and impacting meaning and legibility. Finally, Arabic's extensive character set required two magazines per font (i.e., for a single face in one size and style).[37] Yet addressing Arabic typographic requirements wasn't primarily a process of adapting the mechanical system to the language; rather, designers attempted to change the language to fit the system.

In 1911, facilitated by a reduced character set, the Linotype set Arabic type for the first time.[38] In 1912, the *Inland Printer* offered the imperialist observation that Arabic printers "are much interested in the new linotype machine for setting Arabic. As the alphabet of this language contains some four hundred characters, it was considered doubtful if mechanical arrangement could be possible." After imposing the structure of the Linotype machine onto the language, in "the new Arabic linotype the number of characters has been reduced to 180," and with this reductivist system in place, "it is believed that Arabian literature will make notable advances."[39] Exactly how this exchange of "excess" characters for "advanced" literature was to work, Inland's foreign correspondent didn't say.

Arabic, Armenian (which followed it alphabetically in the 1915 specimen), and indeed all character sets followed the design schema established by Linotype's treatment of the Latin alphabet [Fig. 5.14]. Unsurprisingly, printers working in places with a local Arabic readership adopted the two-magazine character sets, which more closely approximated the conventional Arabic alphabet. Linotype's 1903 Model 2, their first double magazine machine, facilitated this choice; Model 4, less complicated and more reliable, followed in 1906. Though two-magazine machines cost more, and even the best Arabic types produced for them remained imperfect, they did allow functional mechanical typesetting in Arabic. "Notwithstanding its shortcomings and the marked quality difference to foundry type, vivacity and proximity to conventional letterforms made the 22pt. fount a viable proposition," observes Arabic type historian Titus Nemeth. In tandem with its efficiency, its design "must have been considered satisfactory for its intended use in [the New York City Arabic-language newspaper] *al-Hoda*."[40] Indeed, observers credited *al-Hoda* with influencing the adoption of the Linotype for increased "use of the Arabic font" more generally.[41]

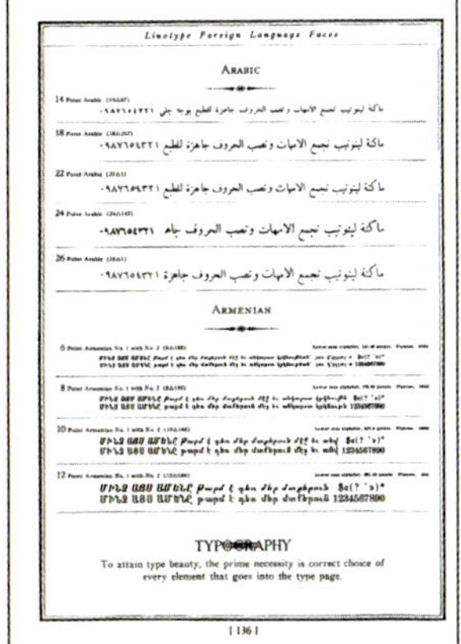

Linotype Foreign Language Faces

ARABIC

ARMENIAN

TYPOGRAPHY

To attain type beauty, the prime necessity is correct choice of every element that goes into the type page.

[136]

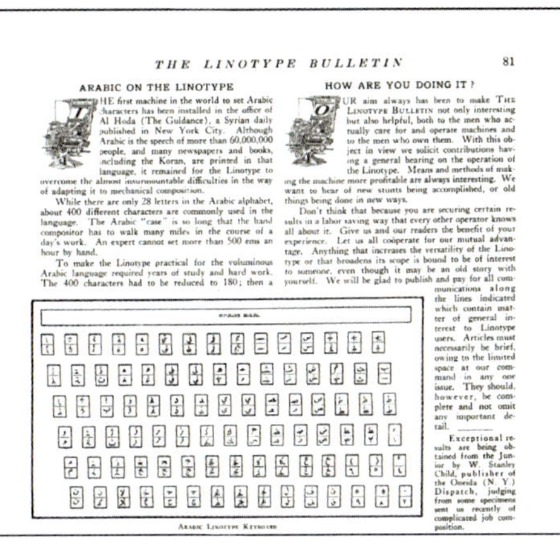

THE LINOTYPE BULLETIN 81

ARABIC ON THE LINOTYPE

THE first machine in the world to set Arabic characters has been installed in the office of Al Hoda (The Guidance), a Syrian daily published in New York City. Although Arabic is the speech of more than 60,000,000 people, and many newspapers and books, including the Koran, are printed in that language, it remained for the Linotype to overcome the almost insurmountable difficulties in the way of adapting it to mechanical composition.

While there are only 28 letters in the Arabic alphabet, about 400 different characters are commonly used in the language. The Arabic "case" is so long that the hand compositor has to walk many miles in the course of a day's work. An expert cannot set more than 500 ems an hour by hand.

To make the Linotype practical for the voluminous Arabic language required years of study and hard work. The 400 characters had to be reduced to 180; then a

HOW ARE YOU DOING IT ?

OUR aim always has been to make THE LINOTYPE BULLETIN not only interesting but also helpful, both to the men who actually care for and operate machines and to the men who own them. With this object in view we solicit contributions having a general bearing on the operation of the Linotype. Means and methods of making the machine more profitable are always interesting. We want to hear of new stunts being accomplished, or old things being done in new ways.

Don't think that because you are securing certain results in a labor saving way that every other operator knows all about it. Give us and our readers the benefit of your experience. Let us all coöperate for our mutual advantage. Anything that increases the versatility of the Linotype or that broadens its scope is bound to be of interest to someone, even though it may be an old story with yourself. We will be glad to publish and pay for all communications along the lines indicated which contain matter of general interest to Linotype users. Articles must necessarily be brief, owing to the limited space at our command in any one issue. They should, however, be complete and not omit any important detail.

Exceptional results are being obtained from the Junior by W. Stanley Child, publisher of the Oneida (N. Y.) Dispatch, judging from some specimens sent us recently of complicated job composition.

Fig 5.14 (left and below)

Specimen Book of Type Styles **(Mergenthaler Linotype, Brooklyn, 1915). As part of its programmatic world view, Linotype applied a universal rationale to the design of all its types and specimens. Rooted in the Latin alphabet, this approach prioritized efficiency over responsiveness to local, script-specific norms, as seen in Linotype's approach to the Arabic alphabet.**

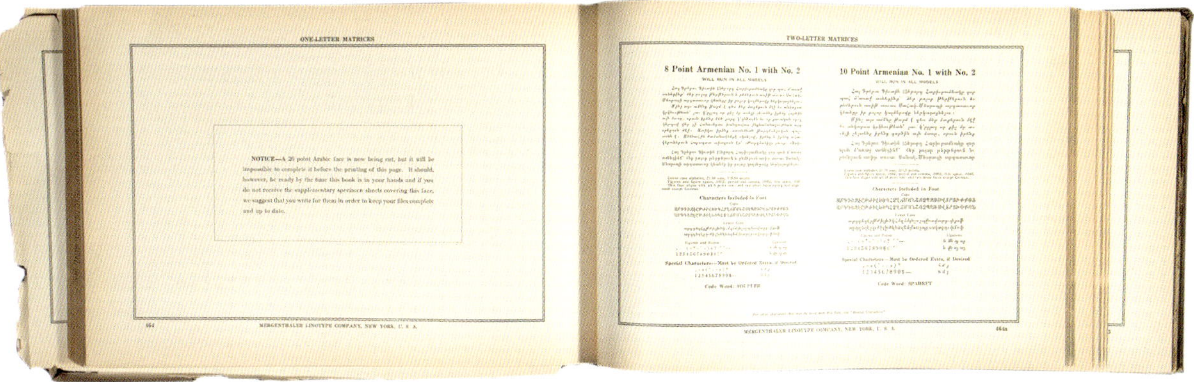

ONE-LETTER MATRICES

NOTICE—A 26 point Arabic face is now being cut, but it will be impossible to complete it before the printing of this page. It should, however, be ready by the time this book is in your hands and if you do not receive the supplementary specimen sheets covering this face, we suggest that you write for them in order to keep your files complete and up to date.

TWO-LETTER MATRICES

8 Point Armenian No. 1 with No. 2

10 Point Armenian No. 1 with No. 2

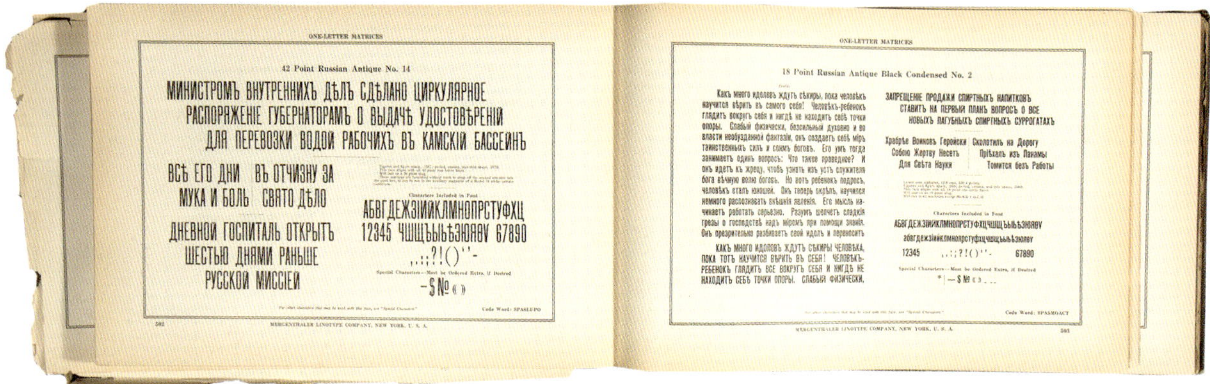
ONE-LETTER MATRICES

42 Point Russian Antique No. 14

МИНИСТРОМЪ ВНУТРЕННИХЪ ДѢЛЪ СДѢЛАНО ЦИРКУЛЯРНОЕ
РАСПОРЯЖЕНІЕ ГУБЕРНАТОРАМЪ О ВЫДАЧѢ УДОСТОВѢРЕНІЙ
ДЛЯ ПЕРЕВОЗКИ ВОДОЙ РАБОЧИХЪ ВЪ КАМСКІЙ БАССЕЙНЪ

ВСѢ ЕГО ДНИ | ВЪ ОТЧИЗНУ ЗА
МУКА И БОЛЬ | СВЯТО ДѢЛО

ДНЕВНОЙ ГОСПИТАЛЬ ОТКРЫТЪ
ШЕСТЬЮ ДНЯМИ РАНЬШЕ
РУССКОЙ МИССІЕЙ

Characters Included in Font

АБВГДЕЖЗІИЙКЛМНОПРСТУФХЦ
12345 ЧШЩЪЫЬѢЭЮЯѲѴ 67890
,.:;?!()''-

Special Characters—Must be Ordered Extra, if Desired

–$№()

Code Word: SPASLUPO

502 MERGENTHALER LINOTYPE COMPANY, NEW YORK, U. S. A.

ONE-LETTER MATRICES

18 Point Russian Antique Black Condensed No. 2

Какъ много идоловъ ждутъ сѣкиры, пока человѣкъ научится вѣрить въ самого себя! Человѣкъ-ребенокъ гладитъ вокругъ себя и нигдѣ не находитъ себѣ точки опоры. Слабый физически, безсильный духовно и во власти необузданной фантазіи, онъ создаетъ себѣ міръ таинственныхъ силъ и сонмъ боговъ. Его умъ тогда занимаетъ одинъ вопросъ: Что такое праведное? И онъ идетъ къ жрецу, чтобъ узнать изъ устъ служителя бога вѣчную волю боговъ. Но вотъ ребенокъ подросъ, человѣкъ сталъ юношей. Онъ теперь окрѣлъ, научился немного распознавать внѣшнія явленія. Его мысль начинаетъ работать серьезно. Разумъ шепчетъ сладкія грезы о господствѣ надъ міромъ при помощи знанія. Онъ презрительно разбиваетъ свой идолъ и переноситъ

КАКЪ МНОГО ИДОЛОВЪ ЖДУТЪ СѢКИРЫ ЧЕЛОВѢКА, ПОКА ТОТЪ НАУЧИТСЯ ВѢРИТЬ ВЪ СЕБЯ! ЧЕЛОВѢКЪ-РЕБЕНОКЪ ГЛАДИТЪ ВСЕ ВОКРУГЪ СЕБЯ И НИГДѢ НЕ НАХОДИТЪ СЕБѢ ТОЧКИ ОПОРЫ. СЛАБЫЙ ФИЗИЧЕСКИ,

ЗАПРЕЩЕНІЕ ПРОДАЖИ СПИРТНЫХЪ НАПИТКОВЪ
СТАВИТЪ НА ПЕРВЫЙ ПЛАНЪ ВОПРОСЪ О ВСЕ
НОВЫХЪ ПАГУБНЫХЪ СПИРТНЫХЪ СУРРОГАТАХЪ

Храбрѣе Воиновъ Геройски | Сколотилъ на Дорогу
Собою Жертву Несетъ | Пріѣхалъ изъ Панамы
Для Свѣта Науки | Томится безъ Работы

Characters Included in Font

АБВГДЕЖЗІИЙКЛМНОПРСТУФХЦЧШЩЪЫЬѢЭЮЯѲѴ
абвгдежзіийклмнопрстуфхцчшщъыьѣэюяѳѵ
12345 ,.:;?!()''- 67890

Special Characters—Must be Ordered Extra, if Desired

*|—$№()...

Code Word: SPASMOACT

MERGENTHALER LINOTYPE COMPANY, NEW YORK, U. S. A. 503

Fig 5.15 (above)

Specimen Book of Type Styles **(Mergenthaler Linotype, Brooklyn, 1915). With only thirty-three letters, the Cyrillic alphabet proved more easily adaptable to mechanized typesetting systems than scripts with large character sets.**

The thirty-three letters of the Cyrillic alphabet, another of Linotype's 1915 "foreign" faces, proved less problematic in terms of mechanization [Fig. 5.15]. As with the Arabic and Armenian pages, the Cyrillic specimens conformed to the Latin model. Larger display sizes appeared on the left hand side of the page spread, text sizes on the right. **Justified** text samples and centered or offset headline-sized words and phrases accompanied a full showing of the upper and lower case alphabet and numerals, centered. The consistent page design reflected the systematic nature of the technology itself. In many ways this was logical; a full showing of the font's characters and range of sizes provided vital information for printers. Even so, the seemingly obvious visual logic of the specimen obscures a deeper and more complex history of cultural erasure and Western hegemony.

As they had with Arabic, Western reformers proposed simplification of India's many and diverse **scripts**, or the unilateral adoption of the Latin alphabet to replace India's mother tongues.[42] Mechanized typecasting and typesetting complicated matters for India's scripts, as it did for many alphabets, and the technologies of hot metal typesetting had to be adjusted to accommodate Indian languages and their character sets.[43] Such adjustments often prioritized alignment with the Latin alphabet over faithfulness to the original language. In this, they echoed modifications made to Indian scripts as they were translated into foundry type first in sixteenth century experiments, and then more successfully in the eighteenth century with the publication of a *Grammar* (1778) which used the first functional metal **Bengali** typeface.[44] Primarily, these machine modifications were the work of Brooklyn-based Indian-American inventor Hari Govil, who worked with Linotype (then Intertype and Monotype) to mechanize **Devanagari** typecasting and typesetting.[45] The patent illustrations for Govil's Devanagari matrices show mechanized letterforms organized into patterns of use accommodated by existing Linotype machines and parts [Fig. 5.16].

What the Automatic Justifier will do for Your Composing Room

IT WILL	IT HAS
¶ Cut the cost of display composition 25% to 75%. ¶ Stop the purchase of additional leads, slugs or metal furniture. ¶ Justify the output of one or twenty-five compositors. ¶ Minimize the use of leads, slugs and quads, thus saving hundreds of dollars of compositors' time. ¶ Give you an unlimited supply of metal furniture, any length. ¶ Save time on the lockup and eliminate workup. ¶ Reduce distribution time 75%. ¶ More than pay for itself the first year.	¶ Made it possible for one compositor to handle a large job individually. ¶ Often paid for itself on one job alone. ¶ Been used to great advantage on blank book work, circulars, posters, tailor books, all kinds of catalogs and commercial work. ¶ Proved itself an absolute necessity in the composing room by oftentimes doubling the compositor's output. ¶ Enabled firms to give low estimates and realize large profits. ¶ Saved hundreds of hours of pressman's time in giving *rigid, solid* forms to pressroom.

SEND FOR OUR LITERATURE

Justified text stretches from one end of the typographic line (or, in hot metal type, the slug) to the other, filling the entire column width. Automatic processes tended to be sloppy, leaving "rivers" of white space through the copy; hand-justification was tedious and time consuming, even for experienced type-setters.

Linotype wasn't alone in its quest to globalize its reach by applying its technology to so-called non-Latin scripts. Intertype claimed the capacity to cast type in twenty-eight languages, though most of these used the Latin alphabet. The three exceptions in Intertype's 1920 specimen [Fig. 5.17] were five two-face Russian matrices; seven single-face Hebrew matrices, each of which required two magazines for Hebrew's extensive character set; and **Korean** in 11 and 14pts.[46] Described as "the better machine" in the display copy, the Intertype demonstrated "the success of standardization." The section

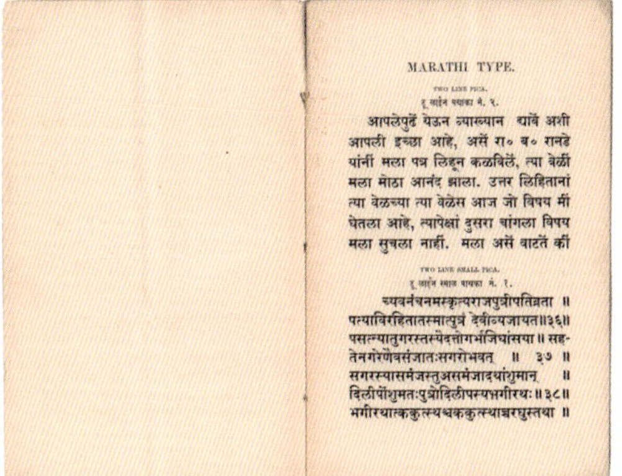

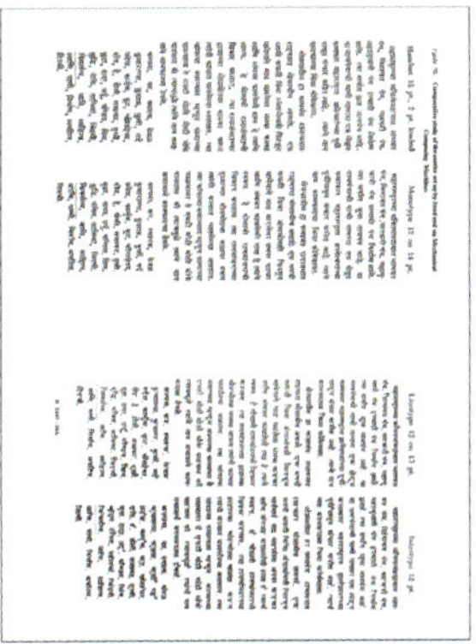

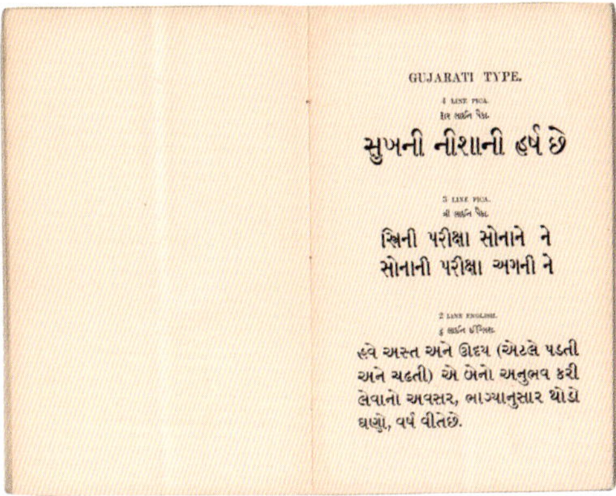

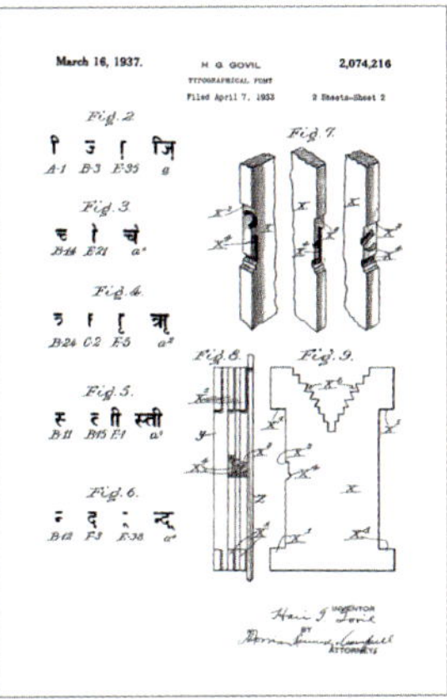

Fig 5.16 (left)

Patent for Devanagari matrices (Hari Govil, 1937, right) and Marathi and Gujarati types from *Kikabhai Harivallubhdas & Co.'s Specimens of Ornamental and Jobbing Type* (Bombay, 1890). Adapting foundry faces to hot metal technologies required formal adaptations in any script, but the technology was designed around the Latin alphabet so other scripts required additional skill.

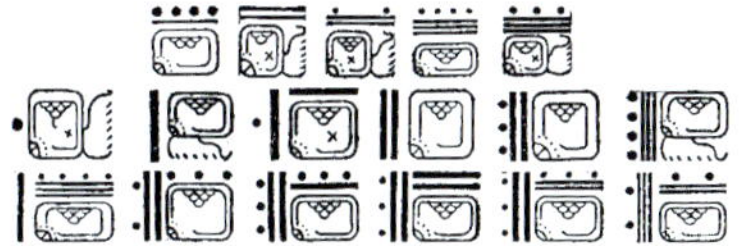

Section *c* consists of 16 glyphs in two rows, above the ce picture. Glyphs 15 and 16 on each page are erased. Tl f general characteristic is the frequent repetition of tl i-compound, ; the repetition on each page of ac-sign with single or double numerals as ion *b*; and of Tun-compounds, with subfix and wi ying prefixes (frequently faces), as especially see page 5.

A languge's **script** is the visual representation of its spoken form. A script might be an alphabet, such as Latin or Korean; a syllabary, such as Cherokee or Japanese kana; or logographic character sets, such as Chinese or classic Maya. Both writing systems shown in William Gates' 1910 *Commentary upon the Maya-Tzental Perez Codex*, above, are scripts.

devoted to "foreign language matrices" looked identical to the Latin-alphabet section. Simple borders framed single columns of text. Headers above each passage indicated the typeface, size, and style. The same brief block of copy about Intertype's advantages demonstrated each matrix, highlighting its "standardization, versatility, and accessibility." Even more than the roman types, the "foreign language" types clearly operationalized this philosophy.

Monotype also worked to globalize mechanized typesetting and adapt all scripts, not just the Latin, to its technological framework. New York's Hebrew Monotype Press, founded by Cyrus Adler, commissioned two custom-built Monotype machines to cast Hebrew sorts with attached **vowel points**; this protected the points from breaking off during use.[47] Thus equipped, the Press issued its *Specimen Book of Hebrew, Yiddish, English, Arabic & Greek Type Faces* (1927), placing its English-language title on the "front" cover and its Hebrew title on the "back" [Fig. 5.18]. The introduction articulated the Monotype's offered Hebrew texts "mechanical advantages" which were lacking before its invention. The Monotype facilitated local publishing in "Hebrew and other Semitic languages"—which, until its introduction, "was done Abroad" and usually by hand, increasing the time and cost of each project. The Monotype combined the "mechanical perfection and speed" of the Linotype with the flexibility of single-character composition. Hebrew typography demanded this capacity, given the alphabet's diacritical marks and vowel-points. Monotype offered several Hebrew faces, an improvement over Linotype's "one old-fashioned type face for the Hebrew language," giving printers and their clients "the choice of various types of printing to suit the

স্থির স্থানে সোমদত্ত পাইয়া এই বর ।
আনন্দিত হইয়া গেল আপনার ঘর ॥

শিব বরে ভূরিশ্রবা সাত্যেকি জিনিন ।
তার উপাক্ষ্যান এই তোমারে কহিন ॥

An Episode from the Mohaabhaarot.

The **Bengali** script generally indicates its 9 vowels via diacritics above or below consonants. This excerpt from the Mahābhārata, a mythological Sanskrit epic written in the 4th c. BCE, appears in Nathaniel Brassey Halhed's 1778 Grammar.

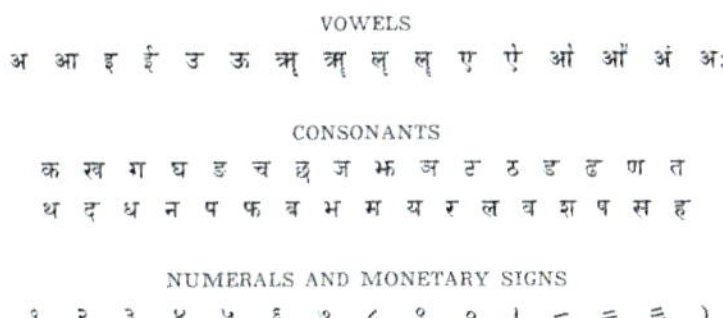

Devanagari was originally known as Sanskrit. Its 16 vowels and 33 consonants informed the development of contemporary Indian languages and scripts including Hindi, Marathi, Gujarati, and Bengali—as Linotype's c. 1933 *Keyboard Operation Manual*, shown here, explained.

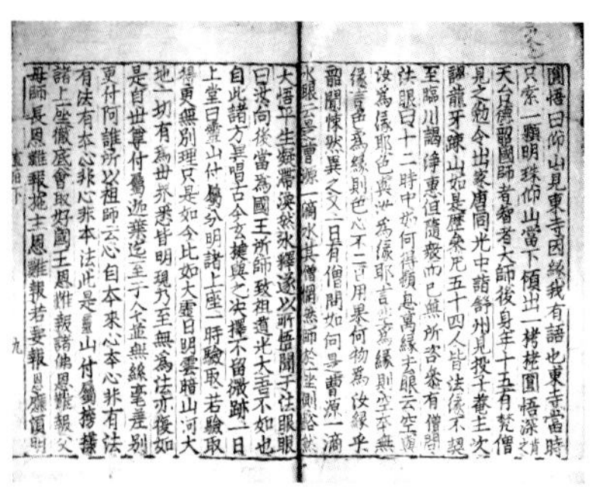

Korean is the language of the world's oldest surviving book set in movable metal type, the Jijki (Zen Buddhist teachings), printed in Korea in 1377. Hangul, the "great script" or Korean alphabet, has 24 characters: 10 vowels, 14 consonants.

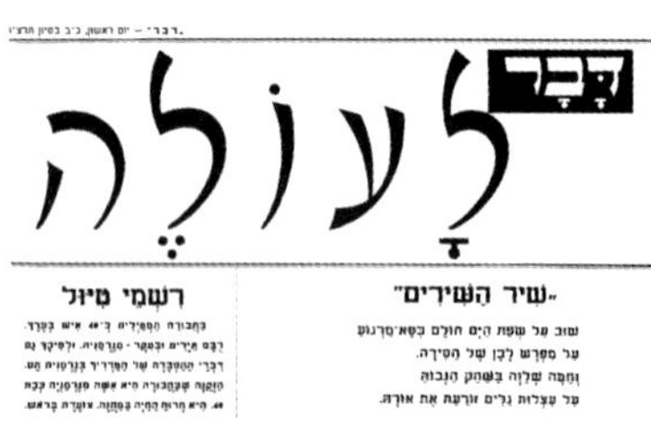

Vowel points are diacritical marks which modify consonats in order to indicate the sounds made by unprinted vowel characters; they're essential to Hebrew, traditionally written and printed without vowels, as seen in this Aharoni specimen (1936).

individual need." Now "free from the handicaps of antiquated methods," printers could meet contemporary demands.[48] The specimen's pages demonstrated this capacity through their design and content choices. Display texts included religious and secular passages, juxtaposing selections from the Talmud with passages from John Ruskin's *Sesame and Lilies*. Most pages included pictorial cuts or decorative borders, many but not all with religious themes. All of the typefaces included English labels for reference (e.g. Ruhl 36pt., Rashi 10pt.). Though mostly dedicated to Hebrew faces, the specimen included three pages of Roman types and one page each of Greek and Arabic types, as well as examples of bilingual English/Hebrew excerpts from scholarly editions of the Torah. This variety emphasized the flexibility, modernity, and multivocality of the press, all facilitated within the strictly inscribed limits of Monotype's program of mechanization and standardization.

Conclusion

Mechanization profoundly altered the typographic landscape at the turn of the twentieth century. Professional practices and aesthetic conventions evolved in relationship to new technologies of production, and type specimen books of the period offered visual evidence of these changes. The era's fat specimen books demonstrated Monotype's "non-distribution efficiency circle," Ludlow's "modern letters," and Linotype's "remarkably large number of faces." In the texts and images on the books' pages, pragmatic concerns like saving time and money co-existed with programmatic corporate philosophies seeking to standardize typographic communication across cultures and places. Mechanization quickly redesigned processes that had been consistent for roughly four centuries. Further changes loomed on the near horizon, however, in the form of photomechanical and then digital type.

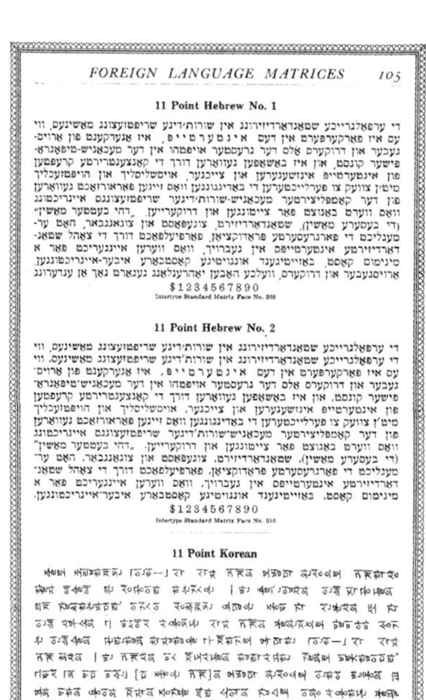

FOREIGN LANGUAGE MATRICES 105

11 Point Hebrew No. 1

$1234567890

11 Point Hebrew No. 2

$1234567890

11 Point Korean

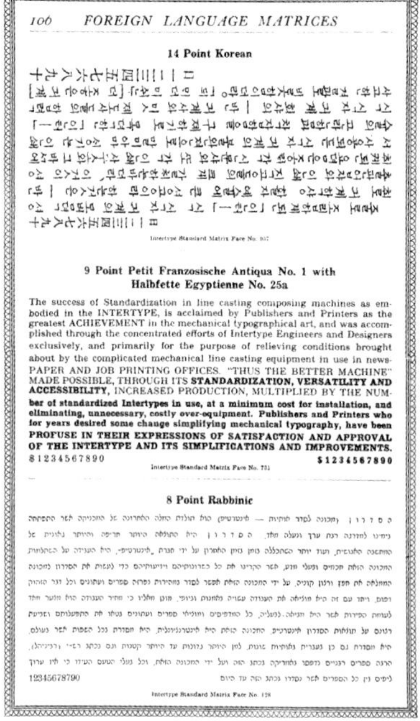

106 FOREIGN LANGUAGE MATRICES

14 Point Korean

9 Point Petit Franzosische Antiqua No. 1 with Halbfette Egyptienne No. 25a

The success of Standardization in line casting composing machines as embodied in the INTERTYPE, is acclaimed by Publishers and Printers as the greatest ACHIEVEMENT in the mechanical typographical art, and was accomplished through the concentrated efforts of Intertype Engineers and Designers exclusively, and primarily for the purpose of relieving conditions brought about by the complicated mechanical line casting equipment in use in newsPAPER AND JOB PRINTING OFFICES. "THUS THE BETTER MACHINE" MADE POSSIBLE, THROUGH ITS **STANDARDIZATION, VERSATILITY AND ACCESSIBILITY**, INCREASED PRODUCTION, MULTIPLIED BY THE NUM**ber of standardized Intertypes in use, at a minimum cost for installation, and eliminating, unnecessary, costly over-equipment. Publishers and Printers who for years desired some change simplifying mechanical typography, have been PROFUSE IN THEIR EXPRESSIONS OF SATISFACTION AND APPROVAL OF THE INTERTYPE AND ITS SIMPLIFICATIONS AND IMPROVEMENTS.**
$1234567890 **$1234567890**

Intertype Standard Matrix Face No. 731

8 Point Rabbinic

12345678790

Fig 5.17 (right)

***Intertype Matrices* (Intertype, New York, 1920). The quest to universalize typesetting practices and technologies was shared by all the major producers of hot metal type, as seen in Intertype's treatment of Hangual, the 24-letter Korean alphabet.**

Fig 5.18 (opposite)

***Specimen Book of Hebrew, Yiddish, English, Arabic & Greek Type Faces* (Hebrew Monotypye Press, New York, 1927). Though Hebrew is written in a 22-letter alphabet, vowel points and other diacritical marks complicated the translation into hot metal. The Hebrew Monotype Press used machines specially made for them.**

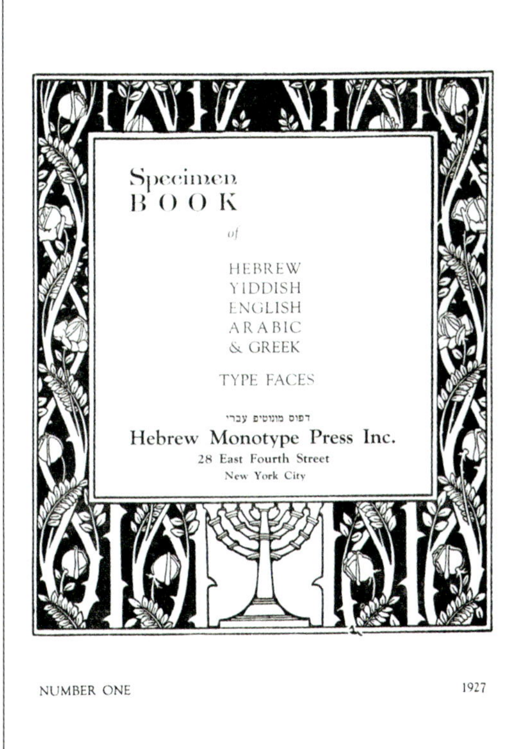
Specimen
BOOK
of
HEBREW
YIDDISH
ENGLISH
ARABIC
& GREEK
TYPE FACES
דפוס מונוטיפ עברי
Hebrew Monotype Press Inc.
28 East Fourth Street
New York City

NUMBER ONE 1927

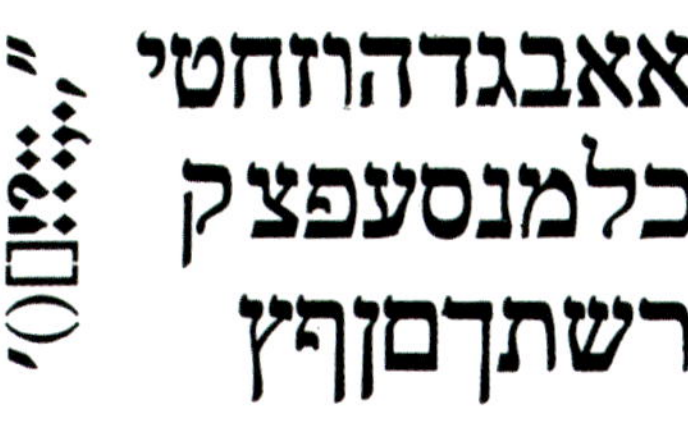

אָאבגדהוזחטיכלמנס
עפצקרשתךםןףץ

אָאבגדהוזחטיכלמנס
עפצקרשתךםןףץ

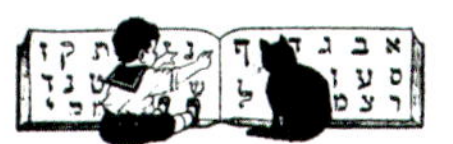

[Ruhl 36 point]
[Ruhl 24 point]
[Ruhl 18 point]

Page Twenty Four

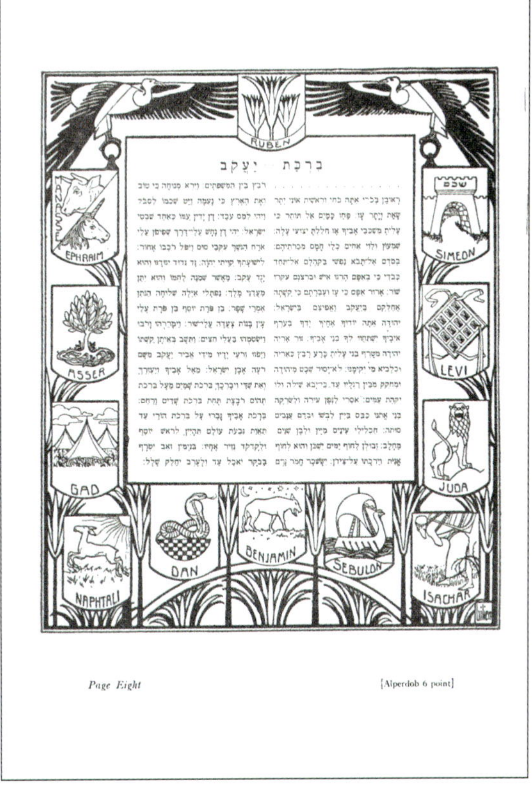

Page Eight [Alperdob 6 point]

1 Aileen Fyyfe, *Steam-Powered Knowledge* (Chicago: University Of Chicago Press, 2012). The introduction offers a good overview.

2 Vervliet, Carter, and Dreyfus, *Type Specimen Facsimiles*, ix.

3 Mores, Carter, and Ricks, *A Dissertation upon English Typographical Founders and Founderies (1778)*. As Carter's introduction discusses, specialization characterized the workflow even at early foundries, and it increased as time progressed.

4 Leonardi and Middendorp, *A Line Of Type*, 23.

5 Frank Romano, *History of the Linotype Company* (Rochester: RIT Press, 2014), 309.

6 John Smith Thompson, *The Mechanism of the Linotype: A Complete and Practical Treatise on the Installation, Operation and Care of the Linotype, for the Novice as Well as the Experienced Operator* (Chicago: Inland Printer Company, 1916), ii–vi.

7 Jeffrey Mifflin, "History of the Linotype Company," *Printing History*, no. 19 (January 2016): 107–8.

8 Bernard Stern, "Upper versus Lower Case Copy as a Factor in Typesetting Speed for Linotype Trainees," *Journal of Applied Psychology* 34, no. 5 (October 1950): 351–54, https://doi.org/10.1037/h0054885; George C. Beamer, Lawrence D. Edmonson, and George B. Strother, "Improving the Selection of Linotype Trainees," *Journal of Applied Psychology* 32, no. 2 (April 1948): 130–34, https://doi.org/10.1037/h0056649; Leonardi and Middendorp, *A Line Of Type*, 27.

9 [Eye magazine], "Deep in the Monotype Archive," *Eye* 21, no. 84 (Autumn 2012): 67.

10 Mifflin, "History of the Linotype Company," 37.

11 Linotype ad, *Inland Printer* 16, no. 1 (October 1895): 15.

12 Linotype ad, *Linotype Bulletin* 17, no. 8 (December 1922): inside cover.

13 Monotype ad, *The Pacific Printer* 37, no. 2 (February 1922): 141.

14 Linotype ad, *Inland Printer* 71, no. 6 (September 1923): 785.

15 Intertype ad, *American Printer* (March 1933): back cover

16 Chas. H. Cochrane, "Composing Machines of Today," *American Printer and Bookmaker*, 256.

17 Douglas C. McMurtrie, *Type Design: An Essay on American Type Design with Specimens of the Outstanding Types* (Pelham [NY]: Bridgman, 1927), 23.

18 Lanston Monotype Machine Company, *The Monotype Specimen Book of Type Faces. A Complete Catalog of Matrices Made for Use with the Monotype Composing Machine and with Type & Rule Caster*, 15.

19 Lanston Monotype Machine Company, ed., *Monotype Type Faces* (Philadelphia: Lanston Monotype Machine Co, 1904), 4.

20 Lanston Monotype Machine Company, *The Monotype Pony Specimen Book of Type Faces, Rules, Ornaments & Borders.* (Philadelphia: Lanston Monotype Machine Co., 1921), xiv, 59, https://catalog.hathitrust.org/Record/008609414.

21 George Mortimer, "English Typography and Design," *The Printing Art* 20, no. 1 (September 1912): 35.

22 Mergenthaler Linotype Company, *The Book of the Matrix Announcing Specimen Book of Type Styles* (Brooklyn: Mergenthaler Linotype Company, 1916), 6–7, http://archive.org/details/MergenthalerSpecimenAnnouncement1916.

23 Lanston Monotype Machine Company, *The Monotype Specimen Book of Type-Faces* (Philadelphia: Lanston Monotype Machine Company, 1916), 3, https://catalog.hathitrust.org/Record/004689420.

24 Editorial reviews of *One Line Specimens, American Printer and Lithographer* 56, no. 4 (June 1913): 516; *The Printing Art* 16, no. 1 (Sept 1910): 50.

25 *Linotype Bulletin* 9, no. 6 (June 1913): 95.

26 Ludlow Typograph Company, *Ludlow Typefaces [Edition D, Copy 1140]* (Chicago: Ludlow Typograph Company, 1940), http://archive.org/details/LudlowTypefacesEditionD1140.

27 Mergenthaler Linotype Company, *Book of the Matrix*, 3.

28 Lanston Monotype Machine Company, *The Monotype Specimen Book of Type-Faces*, n.p.

29 Haley, *Typographic Milestones*, 20; Beaujon [Warde], "The Garamond Types: Sixteenth and Seventeenth Century Sources Considered."

30 Jan Tschichold et al., *The New Typography: A Handbook for Modern Designers* (Berkeley: University of California Press, 2006).

31 John Labovitz, "The Electric Typesetter: The Origins of Computing in Typography," *Printing History*, no. 22 (Winter 2017): 51.

32 Ludlow ad, *American Printer* 69, no. 1 (July 1919): 77.

33 Ludlow Typograph Company, *Newspaper Experience with the Ludlow: A Record of Achievement* (Chicago: Ludlow Typograph Company, 1930), n.p., http://hdl.handle.net/2027/mdp.39015034743461.

34 Linotype ad, *Linotype Bulletin* 14, no. 6 (February 1918): 88-9.

35 Martyn Lyons and John Arnold, *A History of the Book in Australia, 1891-1945: A National Culture in a Colonised Market* (Macmillan, 2001). See particularly the chapter "Printing Technology."

36 Mergenthaler Linotype Company, *Book of the Matrix*, 6.

37 Titus Nemeth, *Arabic Type-Making in the Machine Age: The Influence of Technology on the Form of Arabic Type, 1908–1993* (Leiden: Brill, 2017), 61, 64–65.

38 Romano, *History of the Linotype Company*, 312.

39 [Correspondent], "Incidents in Foreign Graphic Circles by Our Special Correspondent," *Inland Printer* 49, no. 3 (June 1912): 377.

40 Nemeth, *Arabic Type-Making in the Machine Age*, 65.

41 H.I. Katibah, *Arabic-Speaking Americans.* (New York: Institute of Arab American Affairs, 1946), 12, http://hdl.handle.net/2027/uva.x001897252.

42 Frank C. Laubach, *India Shall Be Literate* (Ann Arbor: Jubbulpore/Mission Press, 1940), 182–88, http://archive.org/details/in.ernet.dli.2015.202272. The "New Hindi Alphabet" chart, which the Revision Committee of the Indian Congress adopted in 1937, shows the simplified character set.

43 Nayak S. Baurao, *Epigraphy, Typography Of Devanagari*, vol. 2 (Bombay: Directorate of Languages, 1971), 393–423, https://archive.org/details/epigraphytypographyofdevanagaribauraonayaks.volume2_927_x. Ch. 15, "Mechanical Composing in Devanagari," explains the necessary machine modifications and includes a specimen comparing hand-set, Monotype, Linotype, and Intertype Devanagari texts.

44 Fiona Ross, *The Printed Bengali Character: Its Evolution* (Richmond: Routledge/Curzon, 1999); Ross, "An Approach to Non Latin Type Design," 65; Nathaniel Brassey Halhed, *Grammar Of The Bengali Language* (Hoogly [Bengal]: Halhed, 1778), https://archive.org/details/in.ernet.dli.2015.43675.

45 Sarah Fedirka, "Reorienting Modernism: Transnational Exchange in the Modernist Little Magazine Orient," *English Language Notes* 49, no. 1 (2011): 77–90, https://doi.org/10.1215/00138282-49.1.77.

46 Intertype Corporation, *Intertype Matrices: Specimens of Two-Letter, One-Letter, Head-Letter and Display Matrices, Border Slides and Border Matrices, Font Schemes and Keyboard Layouts, Classified by Series* (New York: Intertype Corporation, 1920), 99, 104–7, 112–13.

48 George Alexander Kohut, "The Contributions of Cyrus Adler to American Jewish History," *Publications of the American Jewish Historical Society*, no. 33 (1934): 25, https://www.jstor.org/stable/43058413.

48 Hebrew Monotype Press, *Specimen Book of Hebrew, Yiddish, English, Arabic & Greek Type Faces* (New York: Hebrew Monotype Press Inc., 1927), 3, https://catalog.hathitrust.org/Record/003005325.

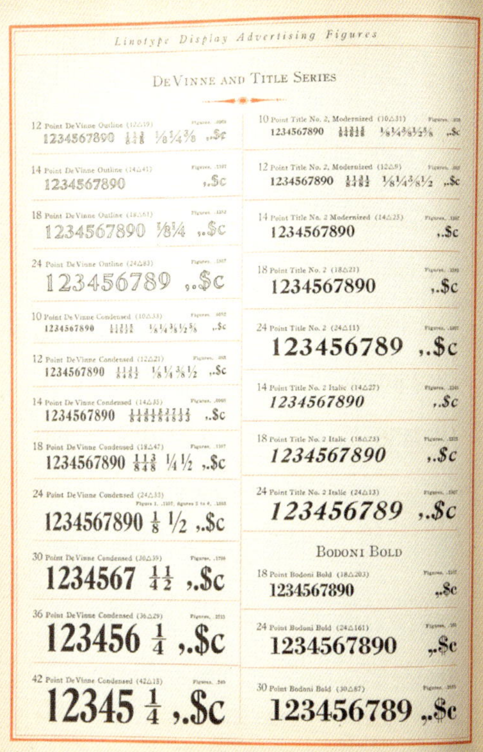

One Line Specimens, Linotype, 1920

Even with just one line for each available matrix, a comprehensive specimen represented a major undertaking for a large distributor like Linotype or its competitors Monotype, Ludlow, and Intertype. While hot metal type setting meant that sizes and styles of an individual face needn't be stored on-site indefinitely, each permutation required a different set of matrices. 10 point De Vinne Condensed and 10 point De Vinne Outline, as two different typefaces, each had their own matrices. Text, display, and jobbing faces, as well as ornament, newspaper headings, numerals, ad cuts, rules, borders, and symbols all required their own segment within the book. Comprehensive specimen books quickly grew into unwieldy beasts—expensive to produce, bulky to store, and quickly outdated. By the mid-1930s, the format's cost-benefit ratio skewed heavily toward cost.

Reklame Reform-Grotesk,
Stempel, 1914

Designed by Karl Matthies for D. Stempel in 1913, this publicity face means to capture the contemporary, urban consumer's visual attention; *reklame* translates to *advertising*. Like most grotesques of its time, its boldness and rectilinear simplicity contrast with stereotypically Victorian or Art Nouveau aesthetics. Its decorative touches tend toward the early Art Deco; notice especially the A, K, and M. The full series has 10 widths and weights. The visual language of the 8-page specimen combines geometric ornament with a modular, blocky structure. Inside the specimen, sample texts feature words like *duplex* and *urbin*, with architectural overtones, or *Mundwasser* [mouthwash], a commercial product first produced around 1890.

REKLAME

REFORM-GROTESK

In der vorliegenden Schrift legen wir der verehrlichen Fachwelt eine neuartige Reklametype von höchster Originalität und auffälliger, dabei malerischer Wirkung vor. Die Schrift betritt einen ganz neuen Weg, sie ist sowohl zur Heraushebung einzelner Zeilen wie auch zur Dekorierung ganzer Flächen geeignet. Die Reklame-Reform-Grotesk, in viereinhalb und sechs Cicero geschnitten, wurde im Grundmaß auf dem Cicero-Viertelgeviert aufgebaut, wodurch ein systematisches Ausschließen möglich ist. Mit dieser Schrift ist das Problem, eine zweifarbige Wirkung durch einen Druckgang zu erreichen, auf eine ideale Weise gelöst worden

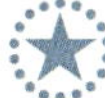

D. STEMPEL AKT.-GES. FRANKFURT A. MAIN

Heft 28

Satz und Druck der Hausdruckerei

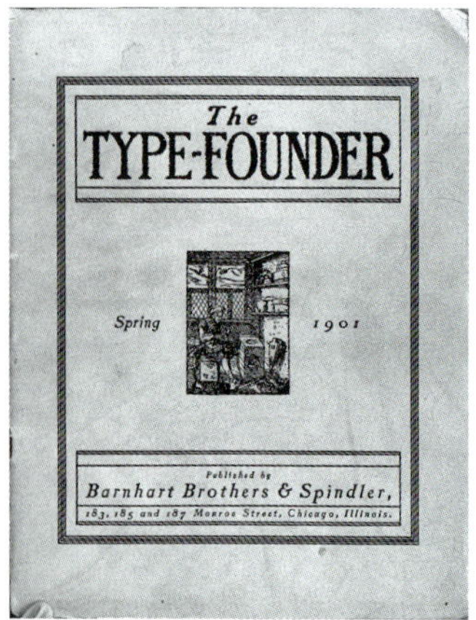

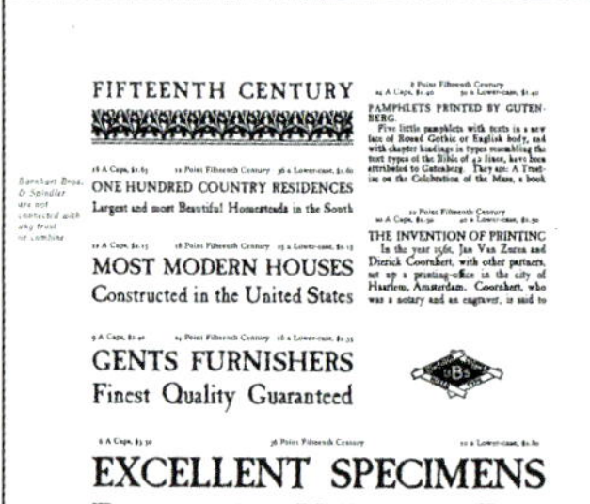

ESSAIS
DE
CARACTERES
D'IMPRIMERIE

A PARIS, 1707.

ΔΦΞΓΠΦΧΣ
ΛΩΛΘΣΦΞ
ΣΔΓΨ
ΘΦΥΞΔΣΔΠΛΥΓΩ

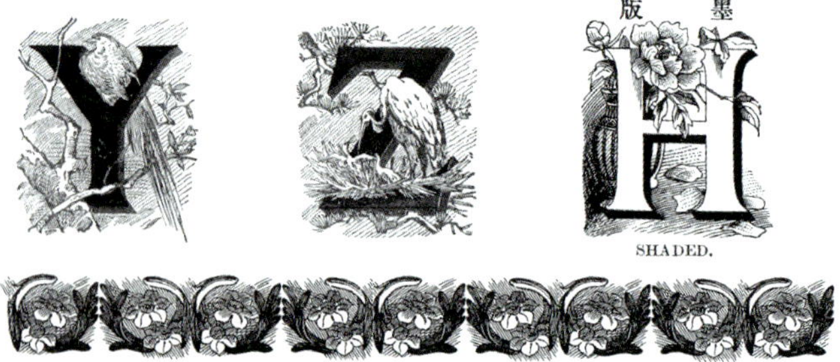

1876 – USA

BB&S issues first *Type-Founder*; it runs until 1908, delivering new specimens to subscribers.

1897 – Japan

Tokyo Tsukiji's house organ includes broadside showing of polychrome electrotype face 72-line Japonica.

1924 – USA

Douglas McMurtrie issues a facsimile of Pierre Cot's 8-leaf specimen (1707) of Hebrew and Greek types.

1886 – USA

Ottmar Mergenthaler patents Linotype, first successful automatic typesetting and line-casting machine.

1887 – USA

Tolbert Lanston patents Monotype, a 2-part machine (keyboard and caster) that casts and sets individual sorts.

1926 – England

The *Fleuron* publishes Beatrice Warde's research on Garamond, under male pseudonym Paul Beaujon.

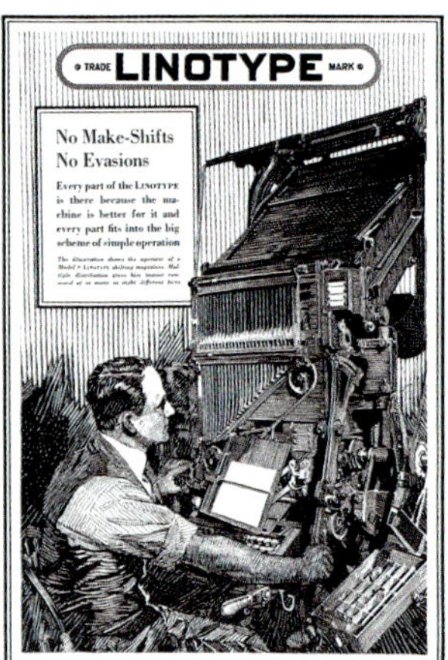

THE LANSTON TYPE-MACHINE.
A MACHINE THAT READS COPY AND AUTOMATICALLY RE-WRITES IT IN TYPE METAL.

THE FLEURON
A JOURNAL OF TYPOGRAPHY

NUMBER ONE
LONDON
At the Office of THE FLEURON
1923

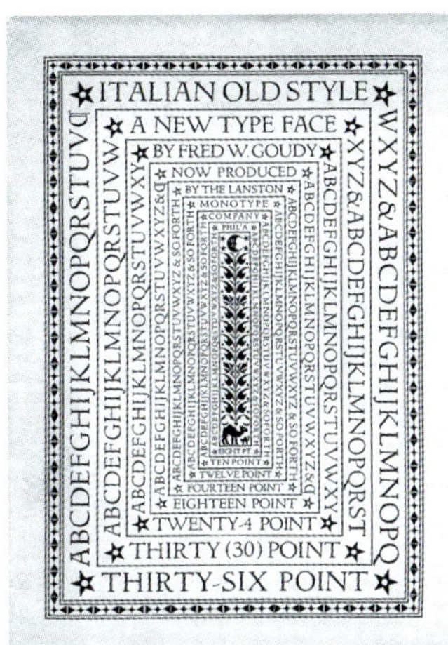

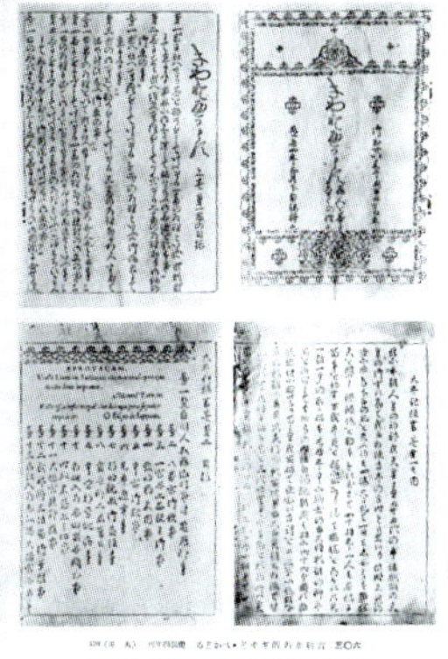

1924 — USA

Bruce Rogers designs specimens for Goudy's Italian Oldstyle, a new yet historicist typeface.

c. 1926 — Germany

At the Bauhaus, Josef Albers designs his Schabloneneschrift [stencil] typeface.

1939 — Japan

Kazuma Kawase's *Kokatsujihan no kenkyu* [A brief history of early Japanese typography].

1973 — USA

U&lc, ITC's house organ, advertises its phototype specimens.

1929-30 — internationally

"Modernistic" type styles saturate urban visual language.

c.1939 — USA

Linotype's "Big Red" is the last major comprehensive foundry specimen book issued.

1944 — USA

ATF introduces Alpha-Blox modular display type system.

1958 — USA

ATF introduces its first phototype machine; but foundry type (shown) remains their strength.

What are Alpha-blox?

Alpha-blox may be used interchangeably

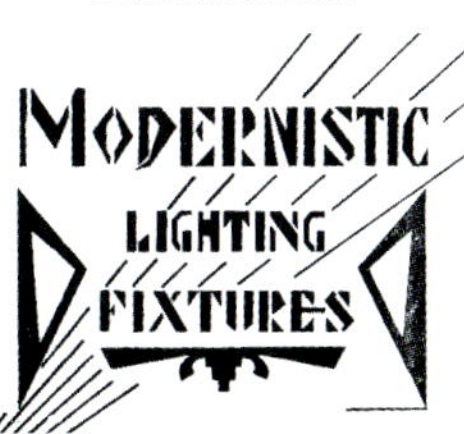

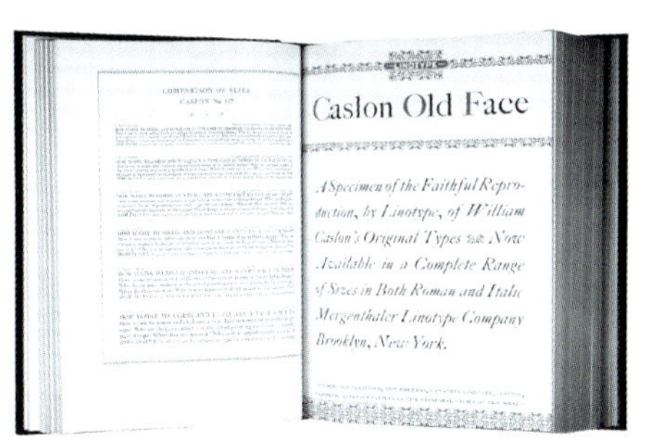

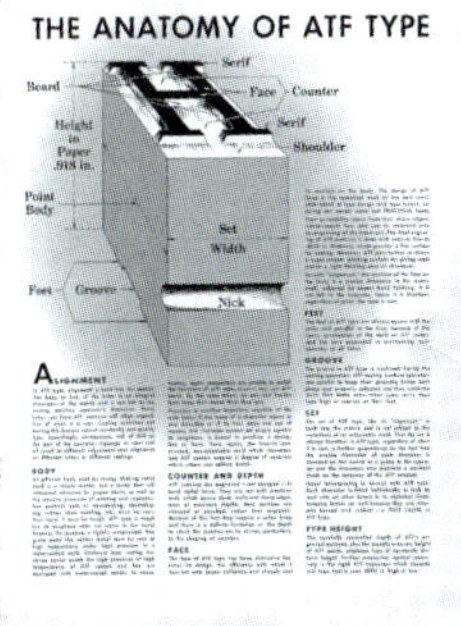

Oversized, comprehensive specimen books attained their dazzling pinnacle in the early twentieth century. But their size, cost, and rapid obsolescence rendered them increasingly unsustainable. MacKeller Smiths & Jordan's centennial souvenir (1896) described their forerunner Johnson & Co.'s 1854 *Minor Specimen Book* (1854) as "too large for forwarding through the mail, and printers were requested to direct how it might be transmitted to them." At the same time, MS&J, ATF's primary office, touted ATF's first *Collective Specimen* book (1896) as "the most extensive ever produced by any type foundry in the world" and boasted that printing it required "over seventy tons of paper."[1] But as the twentieth century progressed, smaller formats overtook the genre. Though lacking a book's impressive physical presence, they offered clear advantages in terms of speed and economy—two longstanding priorities for printers. Booklets, bifolds, small broadsides, and other intentionally **ephemeral formats** facilitated conversations not only about saving time and money, but also about evolving conceptions of visual style and professional identity.[2] Ephemeral formats proved ideal for exploring questions of typographic history, valorizing modern technology, and circulating type and type styles internationally. They also changed the physical structure of specimen books, reflecting the formalization of a longstanding practice: specimens collated by individual printers to meet their own needs and preferences.

New formats

By the 1930s, a hardbound book like the Mergenthaler Linotype Company's *Specimen Book of Linotype Faces* represented the last of a vanishing breed. Undated at publication and over 1,200 pages long, printers nicknamed it "Big Red" for its size and cover [Fig. 6.1]. Three supplements (1939–41) added 50-70 pages each, followed by the 200-page *Supplement Linotype Specimen Book* (1948). "Constant additions to Linotype's extensive resources are inevitable," Big Red had cautioned. Despite "every effort" for a "volume as complete and comprehensive as possible, even before its distribution new developments were in process."[3] The continual, fast-paced release of new type designs facilitated a printing industry centered around notions of contemporary styles and evolving technologies but meant comprehensive specimens became outdated quickly. One solution? Retain the idea of a comprehensive specimen book but shift its physical production into discrete phases, transferring the responsibility for compiling it onto individual printers.

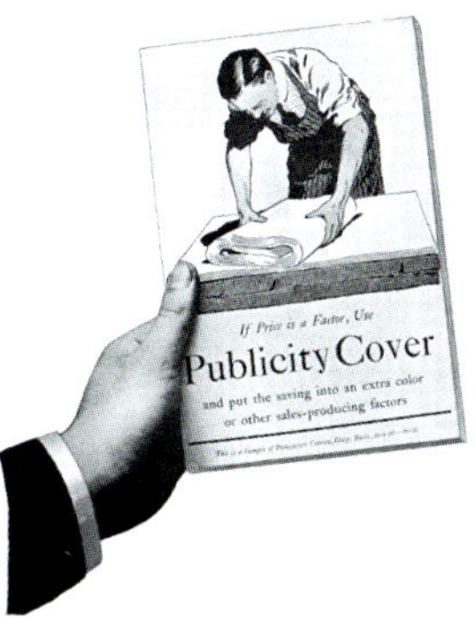

Ephemeral formats were designed and produced for easy, temporary use, as pictorialized by this paper ad from 1920.

Supplements to binder systems

Linotype, Monotype, and their smaller competitors introduced **binder systems** during the early nineteenth century to streamline their specimen production efforts, as seen previously with Monotype's 1916 book. The practice of designing small specimens for insertion into larger binders continued, essentially until printed specimens themselves became less common, and most large foundries utilized the format throughout the majority of the twentieth century. In the 1930s, Intertype hole-punched

Fig 6.1 (below)

***Specimen Book of Linotype Faces*, Linotype, 1930s. Linotype's "Big Red" represented the last of a vanishing breed: the comprehensive, hard-bound, and usually very large specimen book.**

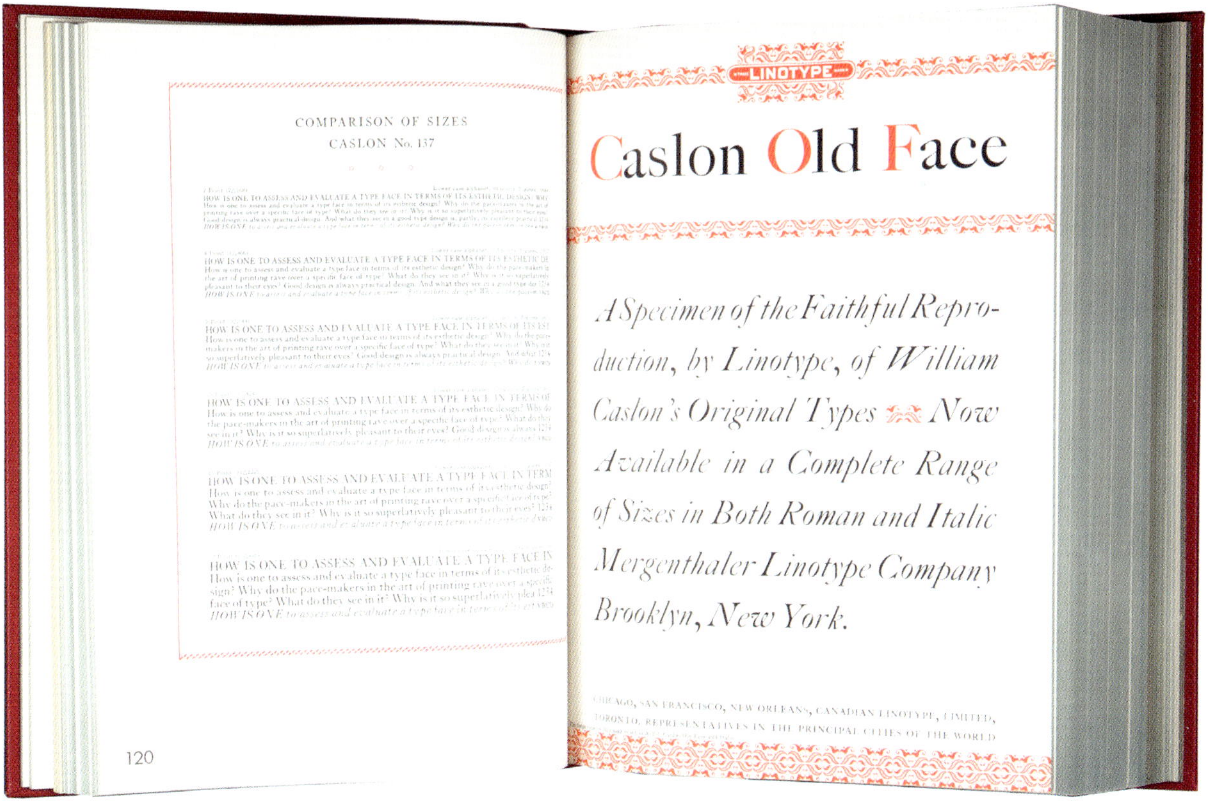

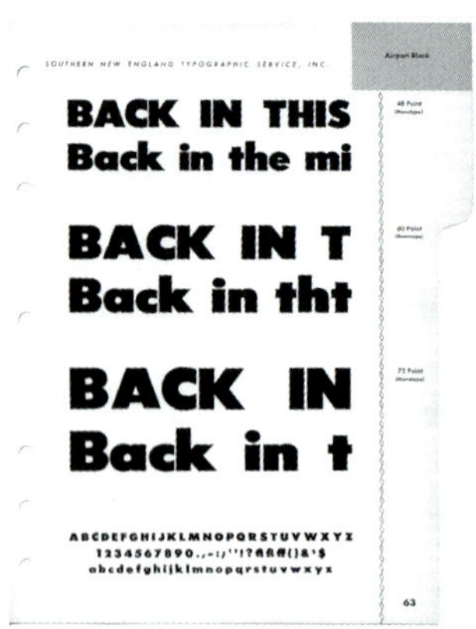

Binder systems allowed foundries to save money; printers collated their own specimens using pages designed to be hole-punched or comb-bound. (Creative Commons 2.0 image by James Puckett.)

individual sheets for insertion into a two-ring binder [Fig. 6.2]. Even the types displayed in the specimens reflected the embrace of modularity. ATF's spiral-bound specimen (1944) included AlphaBlox—a typographic construction system out of which printers built their own display texts and decorative material, much like they used the binder system to construct their own specimen. Page designs worked both as inserts and as stand-alone leaflets [Fig. 6.3]. A quarter century later, ATF's distribution of D&P's Univers (1968) was likewise intended for collation into a larger volume, with index tabs at the edge for easy reference; and Monotype's two-volume *Specimen Book of Monotype Printing Types* (1977) operated on the sample principle [Fig. 6.4]. Printers who skipped specimen maintenance suffered wasted time, effort, and money. Foundries, however, improved efficiency through the binder system. They issued supplements instead of producing new books and released these supplements in multiple forms: for incorporation into binders, as full-page or multi-page ads in trade journals and house organs, or as stand-alone brochures.

Fig 6.2 (right)

The Book of Intertype Faces **(New York: Intertype Corporation, 1930s). One solution to the problem of a quickly outdated bound book was the binder system, which all the major hot metal producers embraced. Here, Intertype 2-hole-punched supplement sheets for insertion into a binder maintained by the individual printer.**

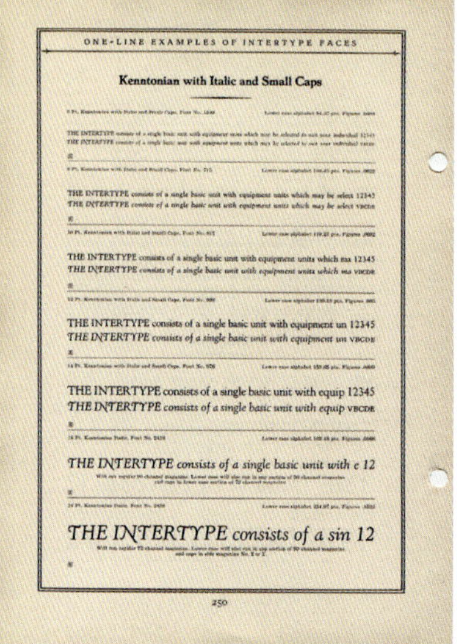
ONE-LINE EXAMPLES OF INTERTYPE FACES

Kenntonian with Italic and Small Caps

THE INTERTYPE consists of a single basic unit with equipment un 12345
THE INTERTYPE consists of a single basic unit with equipment UN VBCDE

THE INTERTYPE consists of a single basic unit with equip 12345
THE INTERTYPE consists of a single basic unit with equip VBCDE

THE INTERTYPE consists of a single basic unit with e 12

THE INTERTYPE consists of a sin 12

250

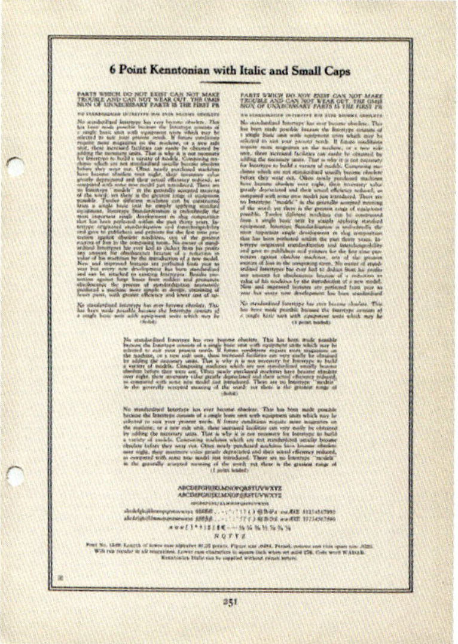
6 Point Kenntonian with Italic and Small Caps

251

Fig 6.3 (below)

Alphablox: A Typographic Novelty **(ATF, Elizabeth NJ, 1944; top) and** ***Design with Type Planning Book*** **(ATF, 1955). Issued both as stand-alone leaflets and as sheets punched for insertion into ATF's binder, AlphaBlox specimens demonstrated modularity at every level—even in the typeface itself, a system of ornament and display type designed to be combined into on-demand decorative material in the print shop.**

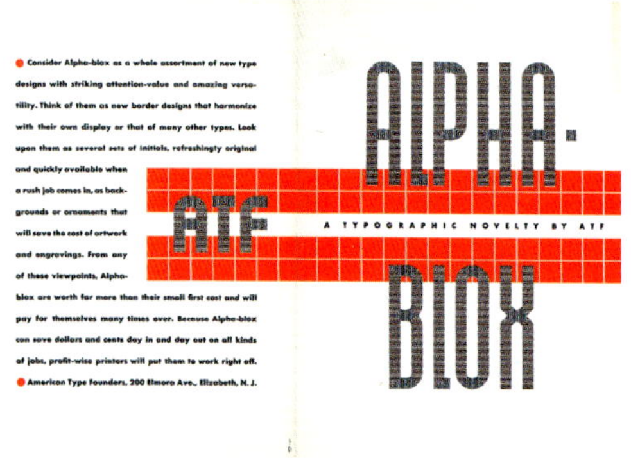

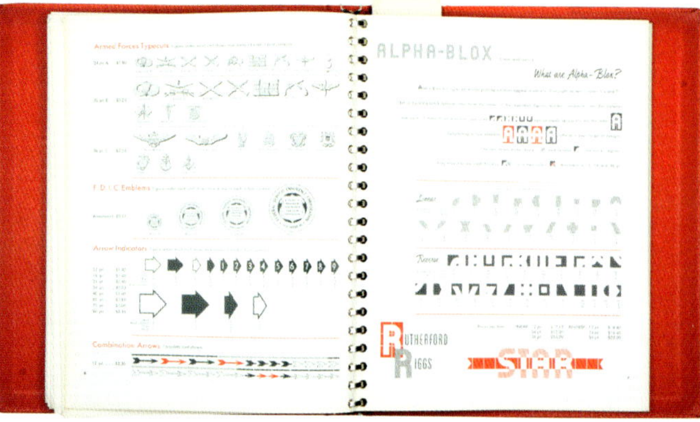

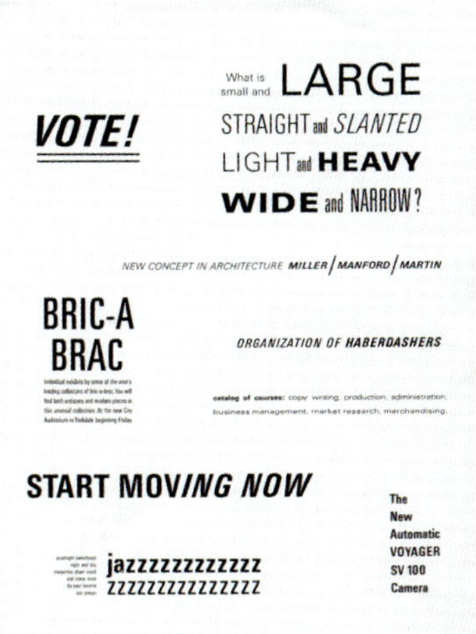

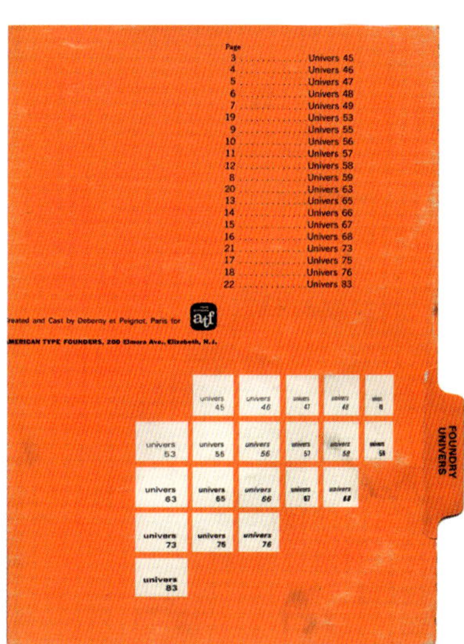

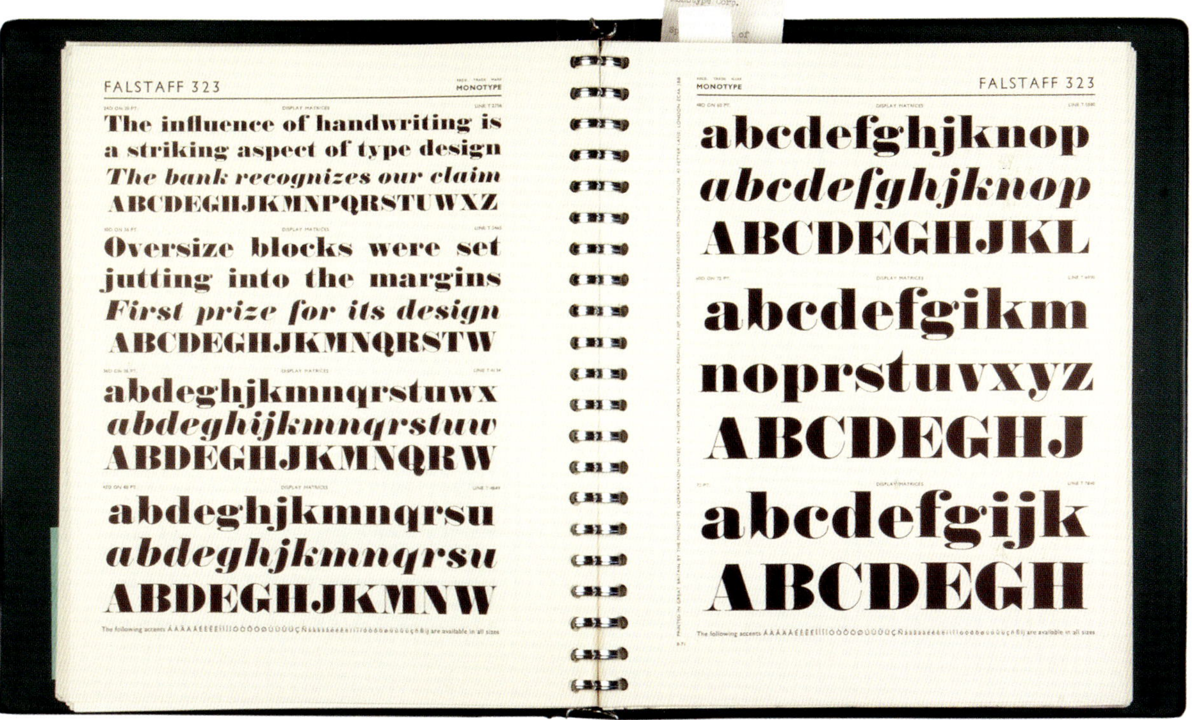

Fig 6.4 (above)

Foundry Univers **(ATF, Elizabeth NJ, 1968; top) and** ***Specimen Book of 'Monotype' Printing Types*** **(Monotype Corporation Ltd, Redhill, England, 1977). Because the strategy was so efficient, foundries continued to issue binder systems with supplements throughout most of the twentieth century.**

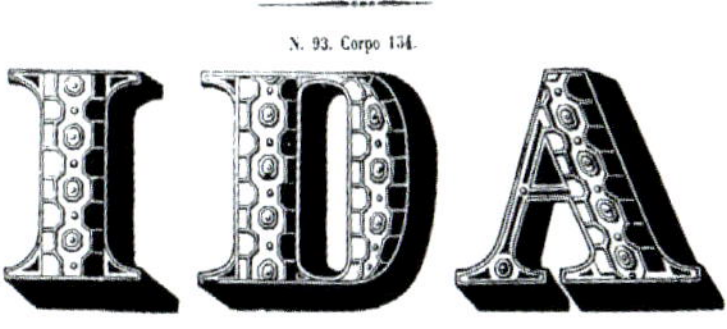

Ornamental or ornamented typefaces, like this Italian example from the Federigo Cappelli foundry's 1870 specimen, have decorative elements added within or onto the strokes.

Many Ludlow supplements pulled exactly this double duty, functioning equally well by themselves, as ads, or bound into the larger book they were designed to update [Fig. 6.5]. Their colorful covers sometimes belied the formulaic, monochromatic pages inside—most of the specimens took the same standardized approach to one, two, and three-column layouts as Ludlow's large specimen books. **Ornamental** supplements could be lavish and colorful, though. *Ludlow Christmas Ornaments* (c. 1940) included trees, carolers, and creches alongside specimens of the blackletter face Old English at a range of sizes, printed in red, green, and black throughout. In *Ludlow Ornament*

Fig 6.5 (below)
***Ludlow Christmas Ornaments* (Ludlow, Chicago, 1940s), *Ludlow Ornament* (1930s), and pages from *Ludlow Supplements* (1933/ right, 1936/left). Ludlow's consistent use of a stable grid system meant that their specimens were equally at home as independent publications or collated into larger, bound volumes.**

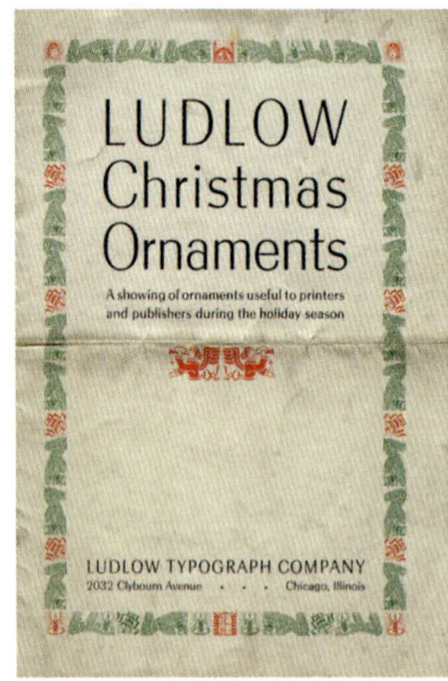

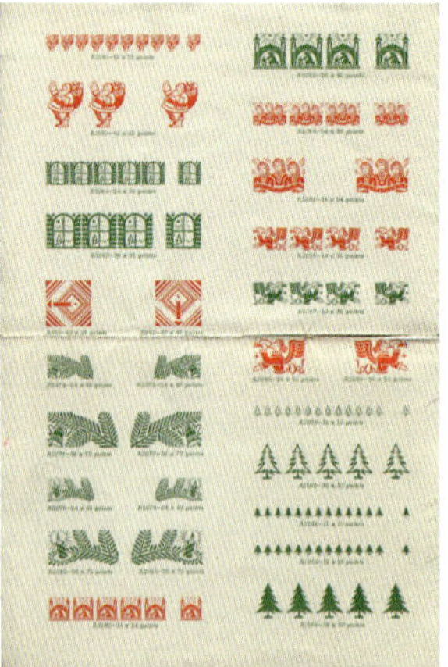

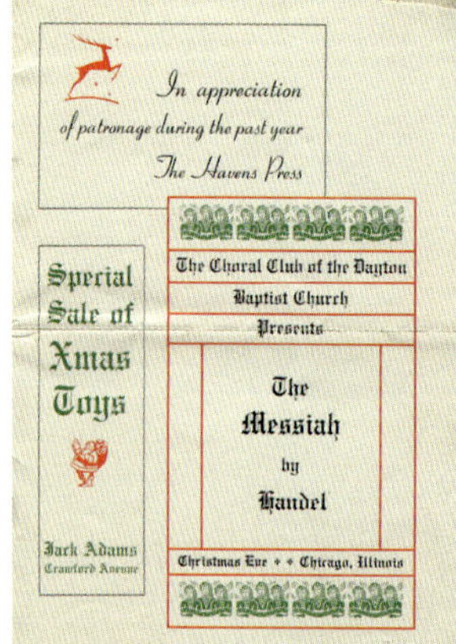

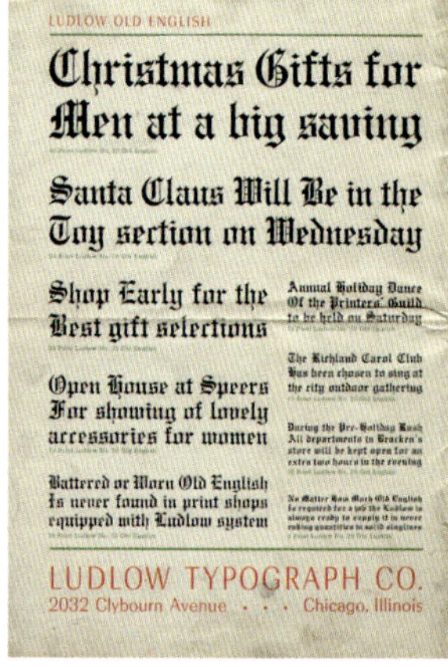

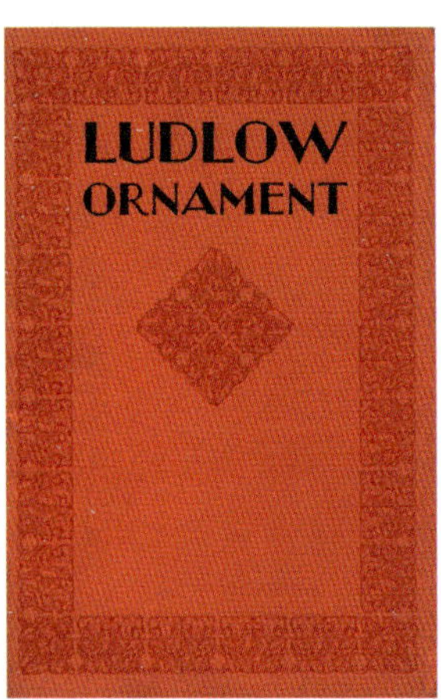

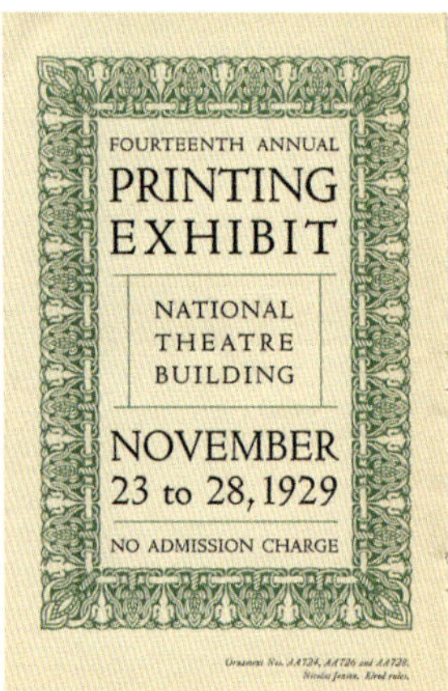

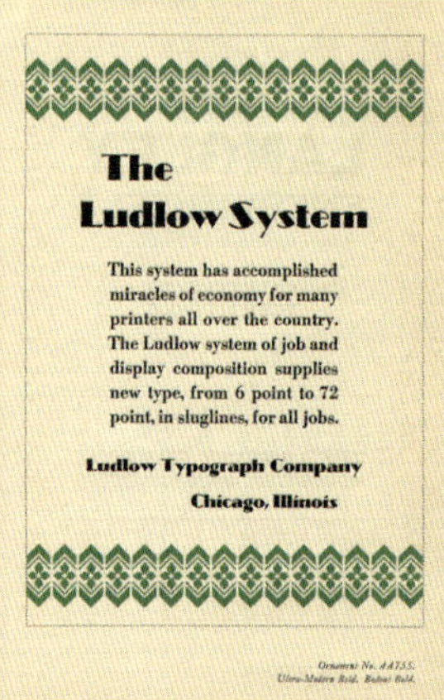

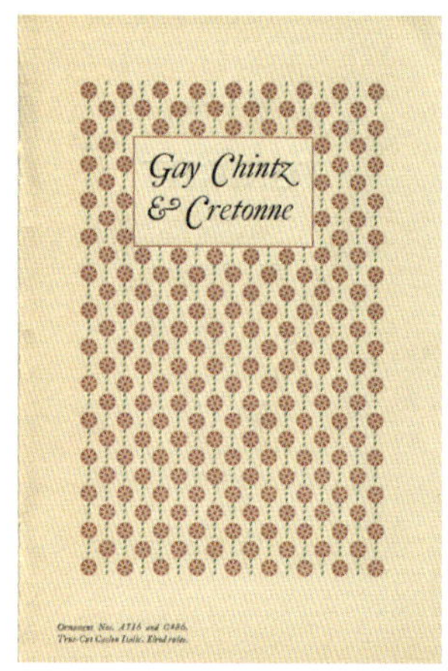

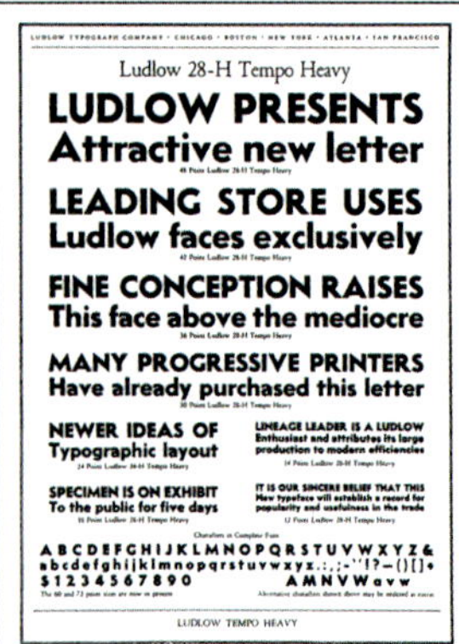

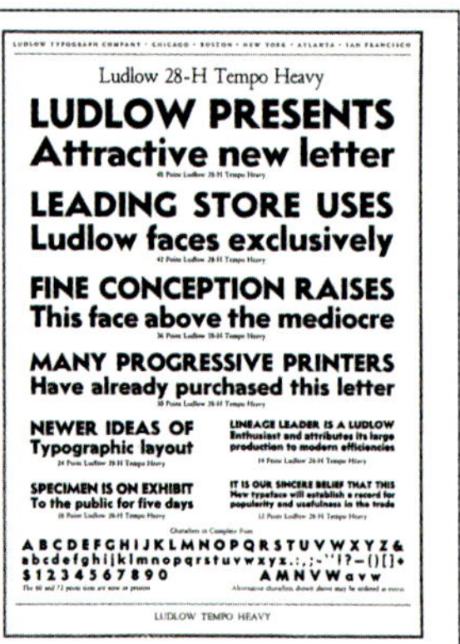

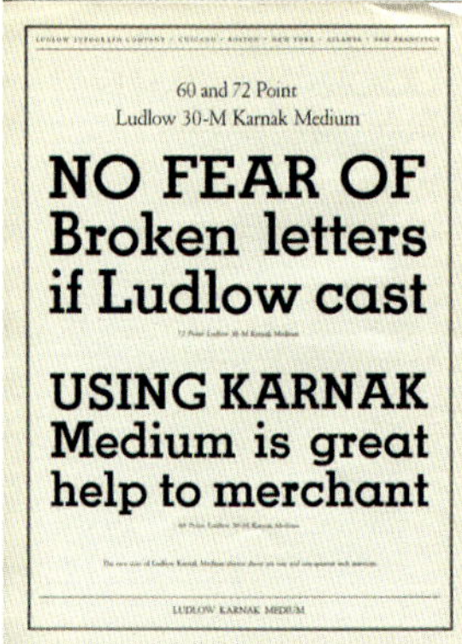

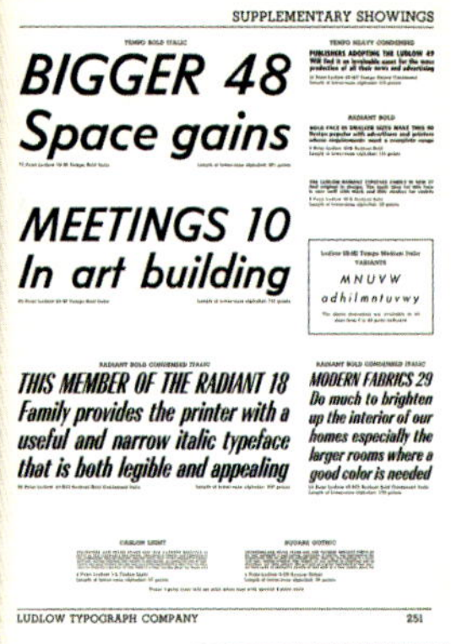

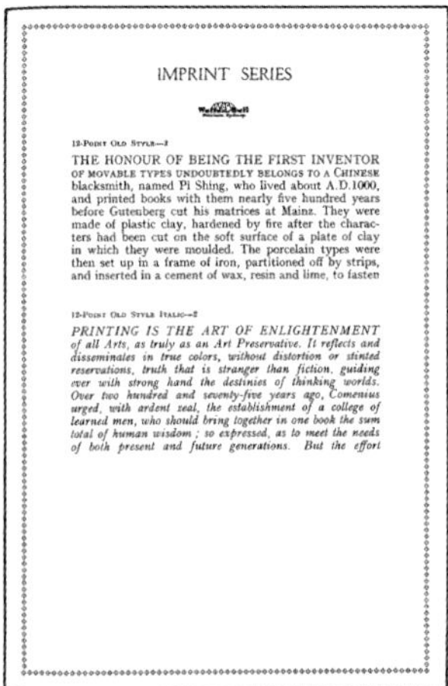

IMPRINT SERIES

18-Point Old Style—3

THE HONOUR OF BEING THE FIRST INVENTOR OF MOVABLE TYPES UNDOUBTEDLY BELONGS TO A CHINESE blacksmith, named Pi Shing, who lived about A.D. 1000, and printed books with them nearly five hundred years before Gutenberg cut his matrices at Mainz. They were made of plastic clay, hardened by fire after the characters had been cut on the soft surface of a plate of clay in which they were moulded. The porcelain types were then set up in a frame of iron, partitioned off by strips, and inserted in a cement of wax, resin and lime, to fasten

18-Point Old Style Italic—3

PRINTING IS THE ART OF ENLIGHTENMENT of all Arts, as truly as an Art Preservative. It reflects and disseminates in true colors, without distortion or stinted reservations, truth that is stranger than fiction, guiding ever with strong hand the destinies of thinking worlds. Over two hundred and seventy-five years ago, Comenius urged, with ardent zeal, the establishment of a college of learned men, who should bring together in one book the sum total of human wisdom; so expressed, as to meet the needs of both present and future generations. But the effort

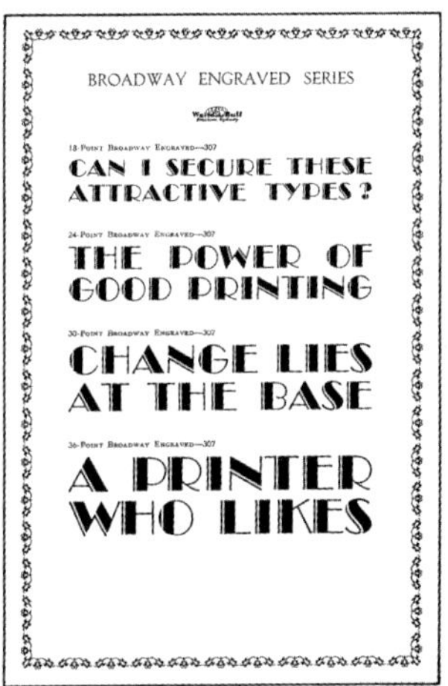

BROADWAY ENGRAVED SERIES

18-Point Broadway Engraved—307

CAN I SECURE THESE ATTRACTIVE TYPES?

24-Point Broadway Engraved—307

THE POWER OF GOOD PRINTING

30-Point Broadway Engraved—307

CHANGE LIES AT THE BASE

36-Point Broadway Engraved—307

A PRINTER WHO LIKES

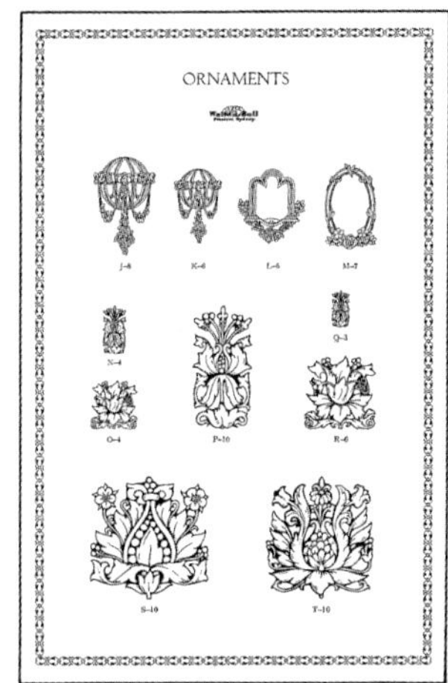

ORNAMENTS

N-4 O-4 P-10 R-6 S-10 T-10

(c. 1929), foliate and geometric borders framed types based on those originally cut by Caslon, Bodoni, and Jenson. Though not strictly **historicist**, the visual language referenced classical sources. By designing supplements that could be collated into their bound predecessor or circulated independently from it, Ludlow—like its competitors—exploited the economy of the ephemeral format yet maintained the idea of a comprehensive specimen.

In Sydney, Australia, the printers Waite & Bull released *Modern Type Design* (c.1930), a specimen book displaying "a selection of the most beautiful of modern type design suitable for all classes of printed matter." The forward articulated the purpose—"to assist the users of printing in the selection of the best faces"—and promised that as new typefaces were released, "specimen pages will be sent to you punched ready for insertion in this book." By placing responsibility for an updated specimen with end users, Waite & Bull extended the model that foundries and typesetting machine manufacturers had introduced to printers. But instead of describing the foundry's or manufacturer's equipment, a fairly lengthy preface introduced customers to "printing trade customs" so they'd know what to expect and how to behave when ordering [Fig 6.06]. The catalog primarily offered everyday printing staples—Garamond, Bodoni, and the popular new Gills Sans (Eric Gill for Monotype, 1928). The conservative, repetitive page design featured a single column of type framed by a double border. Decorative **inline** faces—Broadway Engraved, Modernistic, and Gallia—nodded to contemporary taste inspired by Art Deco. "Modern types displayed," 24-point Gallia proclaimed, reinforcing the association with a contemporary aesthetic.

Fig 6.6 (above)

***Modern Type Design* (Waite & Bull, Sydney NSW, 193-?). Though many binder systems were issued by type foundries, some printing offices adopted the practice, too. In Australia, printers Waite & Bull asked customers to update their own individual copies of the specimen. The preface explained how to be a good customer—how to estimate copy per column, place an order, and so on.**

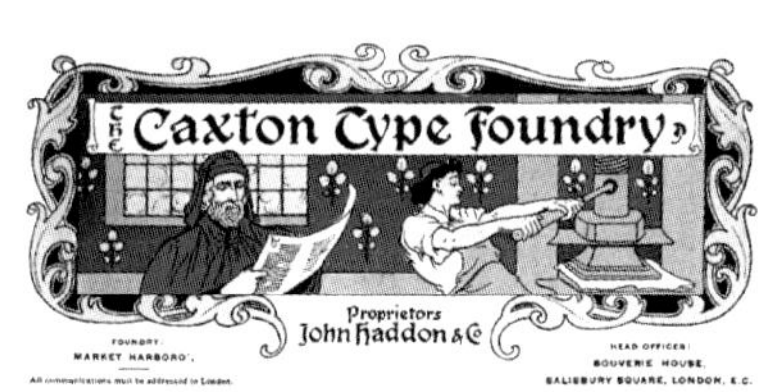

Historicist typefaces and designs evoked the visual language of the past, either through direct quotation or via modernized or otherwise translated versions of historical printing. This 1889 *British Printer* ad for the Caxton Type Foundry uses both type and image to evoke William Caxton's c.1476–92 printing shop, England's first, located near Westminster Cathedral.

MENDELSSOHN
KÜNSTLERKONZERTE

Inline typefaces, like Oskar Kress' 1926 Kress-Versalien for Schriftguss AG (pictured), have a line inside the stroke of each letterform.

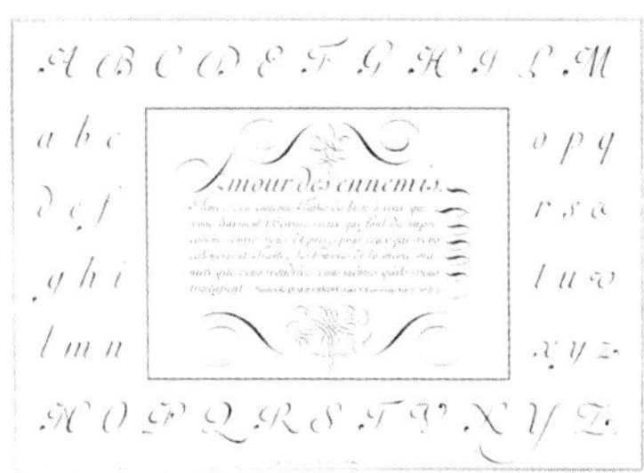

GONG - AN EASY
READING DISPLAY
HAND SCRIPT FACE

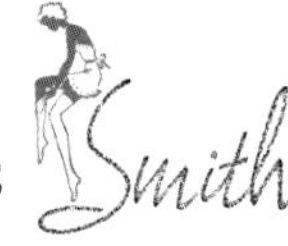

Stylists for Milady

Script typefaces traditionally attempted to duplicate the effects of cursive manuscript hands, like the example shown in Julius Hoffman's *Schriften Atlas* (1889). Later script types might instead suggest neon signs, like Gong from Chicago's Neon Type Foundry (1962).

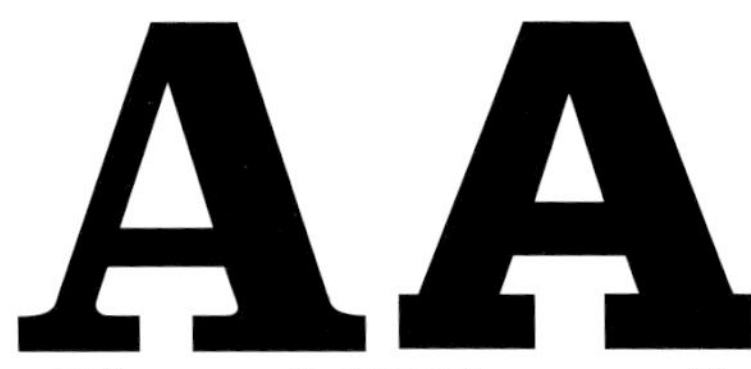

15 A 10 a PICA CLARENDON. L. $4.00
CLARENDON IS SERVICEABLE.
£3.657 was the Amount paid for a Great

Clarendons are bracketed slab serifs, first developed in the early 1830s and very popular by the 1840s. The A on the left is a Clarendon; on the right is an unbracketed slab serif.

Leaflets and brochures

Small, single-sheet, bi-fold, tri-fold, or quarter-fold brochures were an economical, and therefore popular, format. Foundries used them both to provide a succinct overview of their wares and to highlight specific faces, a tradition stretching back centuries [Fig 6.7]. Early eighteenth century French founder Pierre Cot's 1707 8-leaf specimen of Hebrew and Greek faces, reproduced in facsimile by Douglas McMurtrie in 1924, was a well-known example. In the mid-twentieth century, a quarter-fold from England's Stephenson Blake foundry filled printing needs of a different kind. Their *Typographical Frolic* (c. 1960) through display faces, ranging from formal **scripts** to businesslike sans serifs, suggested that the foundry was well-equipped for all the printer's display needs. Alternatively, the small format could direct focus to a single face, cultivating a specific mood in connection to the type's design and suggesting appropriate contexts for use. A Bauer foundry tri-fold offered *Fortune: For When You Want to Stretch a Point* (c.1965). Walter Baum and K.F. Bauer designed Fortune in 1955, one of several **Clarendon** revivals released in the United States and Europe that decade.[4] Like slab serifs, Clarendons were described as ideal for modern advertising. *Fortune* positioned the face as especially capable of getting a message across to viewers. Adjacent to an illustration of a pica stick, the cover title grew in size from twelve to thirty-six points, and the brochure unfolded into a small poster with lines of type ranging from 8pt. Fortune Light to 30pt. Fortune Extra Bold. The copy indicated that all weights were available in sizes up to sixty points. The metaphor—a voice growing louder, a message growing larger—was communicated optically rather than linguistically: In an era of increasing market-driven specialization and analytically targeted advertising, Fortune got the point across.

Many foundries released small brochures in series, encouraging printers to collect the entire set for filing in specially-sized boxes. Much like an entry in a library's card catalog, the individual brochures indexed specific types within a larger network of resources. Consistent design emphasized the serial relationship between parts and the whole. Stempel's Typorello series was an iconic example of this strategy, played out in the **Swiss style** during the 1960s–70s [Fig. 6.8]. Minimalist, brightly-colored covers showed a single sort from the relevant typeface, framed by a uniform series identity. A strictly functionalist interior displayed the face in progressively larger sizes. Every typeface, from businesslike sans serif to elaborate copperplate script, received the same graphic treatment. And thanks to the brochure format, an always-complete library of Typorello specimens was possible for printers and efficient for Stempel.

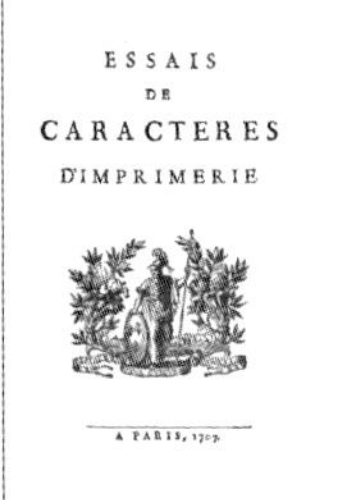

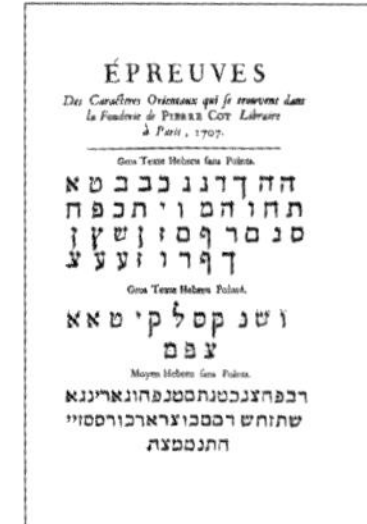

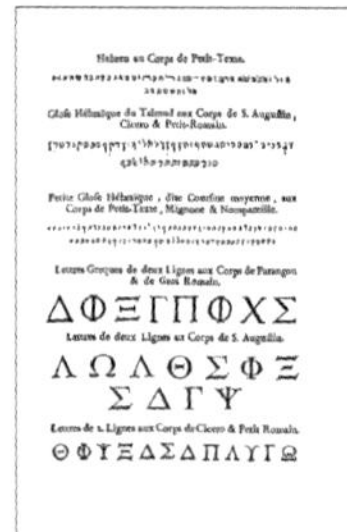

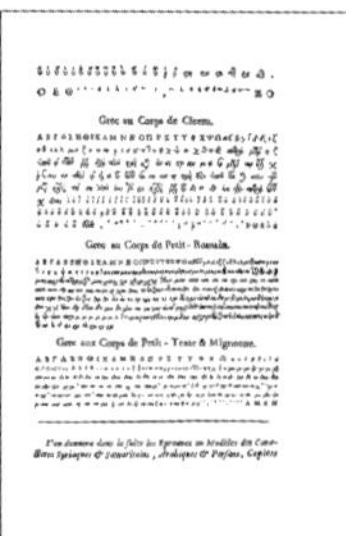

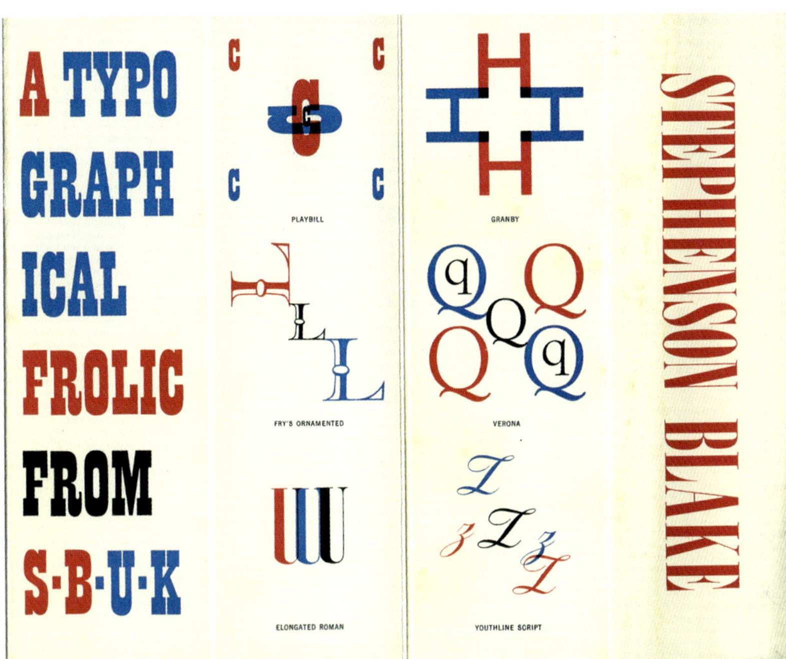

Fig 6.7

***The Pierre Cot Type Specimen of 1707: with a reproduction in facsimile of the original specimen*, (Chicago: R.O. Ballou, 1924, opposite page). *A Typographical Frolic* (Stephenson Blake, London, c.1960). *Fortune: for when you want to stretch a point* (Bauer, New York, c.1965). Small-format specimens for types to meet specific needs had deep historical roots, as seen in French founder Cot's selection of Hebrew and Greek types, useful for printing religious and historical texts. To meet aesthetic rather than linguistic needs, small brochures might be dedicated to an idea, like a whimsical frolic through typographic history, or to a single typeface, like the popular slab serif Fortune.**

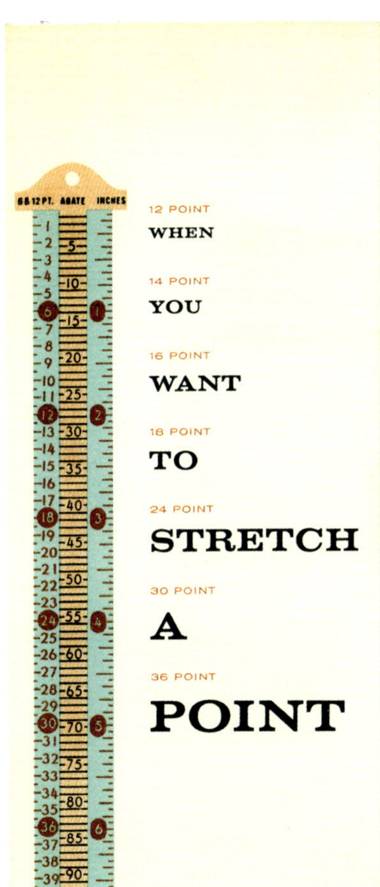

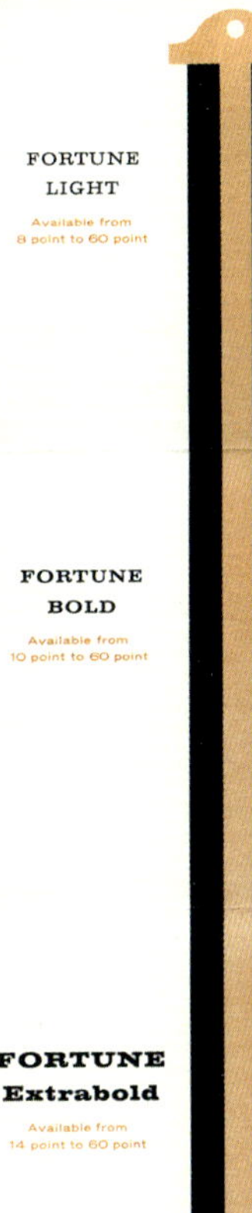

Fig 6.8 (right)

***Typorello 1: Helvetica* and *Typorello 8: Kunstler Schreibschrift [Artist's Script]* (Stempel, Frankfurt am Main, ND). Stempel's Typorello series, issued throughout the 1960s and 70s, applied the same logic to every typeface in Stempel's library. Helvetica, the quintessentially Swiss Modernist typeface, received the same treatment as Artist's Script, originally designed in-house at Stempel, 1901-3.**

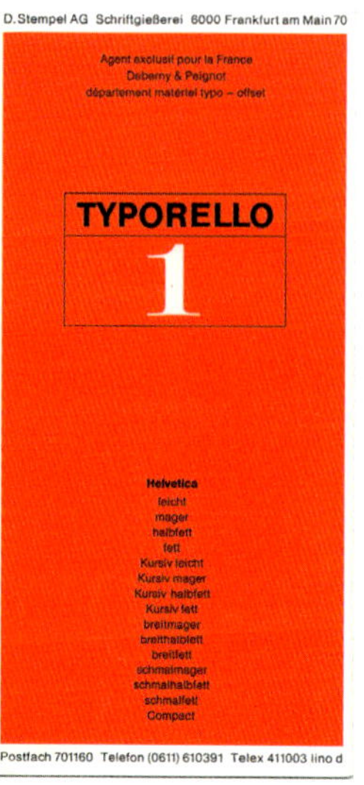

Helvetica leicht

Eine totale Sonnenfinsternis wurde in den Ländern Süd- und Mittelamerikas beobachtet
Düsseldorf, die Modestadt des Westens, im Zeichen der Internationalen Ausstellung
Die technischen Angaben sind auf der ersten und zweiten Seite zu finden
Vacances dans la Provence avec excursions à Bordeaux et Arles
Reise-Erlebnisse und Abenteuer eines Globetrotters in Afrika
Modern methods and appliances for the production
Rad-Weltmeisterschaften in Deutschland
Maison destinée à une seule famille
Gemäldeausstellung in Bonn
Handbook for textile mills
Dortmunder Hemden
Musikinstrument
Straßenbahn

Helvetica mager

Ausscheidungskämpfe zur internationalen Kunstflugmeisterschaft in Hamburg
Das Hansaviertel in Berlin wurde von bekannten Architekten geschaffen
Souvenirs historiques du pays et de la principauté de Liège
Anerkannte Fachleute begutachten die neuesten Modelle
Deutschland und seine alten historischen Bauten
Neuzeitliche französische Damenmoden
Eine Studienreise durch Schweden
Machine dynamo-electrique
Handbuch der Mechanik
Moderne Architektur
Pneumatic post
Handelsblatt
Phantasie

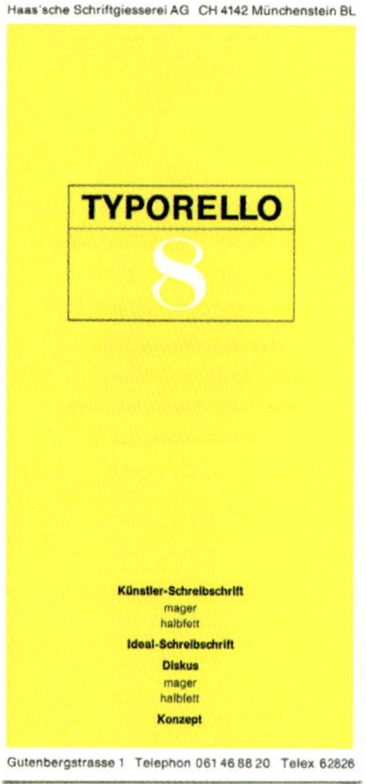

Künstler-Schreibschrift mager

Vacances dans la Provence avec excursions à Bordeaux
Internationale Modenschau in London
New Television and Radio Station
Schwarzwälder Bauernhäuser
Lettre de recommandation
Der Rosenkavalier

Künstler-Schreibschrift halbfett

Bedeutende Premiere im Berliner Residenz-Theater
Världsbekanta universitetsstaden Bonn
Kunstwerke niederländischer Maler
Settimana della moda maschile
Hessisches Landesmuseum
Letter to the Editors
Eine Rundreise

HELVETICA with HELVETICA BOLD (Linotron—Photocomposition)

Case 144Lt12 with Case 145Lt12 12 point Helvetica with 12 point Helvetica Bold—Lt

ABCDEFGHIJKLMNOPQRSTUVWXYZ abcdefghijklm
ABCDEFGHIJKLMNOPQRSTUVWXYZ abcdefghijklm
ABCDEFGHIJKLMNOPQRSTUVWXYZ abcdefghijkln

12 point solid

If time be of all things the most precious, wasting time must be, as Poor Richard says, the greatest prodigality; since, as he elsewhere tells us, lost time is never found again; and what we call time

12 point leaded

If time be of all things t must be, as Poor Richar since, as he elsewhere t again; and what we call tle enough: Let us then the purpose; so by dilige

Case 144Lt14 with Case 145Lt14 14 point Helvetica with 14 point Helvetica Bold—Lt

ABCDEFGHIJKLMNOPQRSTUVWXYZ
abcdefghijklmnopqrstuvwxyz
ABCDEFGHIJKLMNOPQRSTUVWXYZ

The **Swiss style** emerged mid-century from Armin Hofmann and Emil Ruder's Schule für Gestaltung (School of Design, est. 1947 in Basel, Switzerland), Max Bill and Otl Aicher's Ulm School of Design (est. 1953 in Ulm, Germanay), and the tri-lingual *Neue Grafik* journal, founded by Josef Müller-Brockmann and published 1958-65. Helvetica, designed by Maax Miedinger and Eduard Hofmann (1957), is perhaps its most lasting legacy apart from the typographic grid.

Emerging aesthetic trends

In addition to shifting the specimen's physical structure, ephemeral formats contributed to the rapid circulation of ideas and styles. They displayed sometimes-competing notions of the roles history and modernity should play in typographic practice, contextualizing through visual examples how each type cultivated an identity and offered particular associations for viewers.

Revisiting history

The last quarter of the nineteenth century and the first quarter of the twentieth saw not only rapid technological change but also energetic, prolific research from printing historians, bibliographers, and librarians, many originally printers by trade. The period also witnessed a spate of facsimile editions of early works, sometimes with introductions to offer historical context or correct misinformation within the original text. New scholarship and facsimiles alike encouraged an interest in the history of printing practices and technologies, the biographies of typefounders and type designers, and the origins of individual typefaces.[5]

In this environment, **revivals** flourished. At ATF, Morris Fuller Benton's programmatic approach to type design made frequent use of historical models.[6] His "conscientious reproductions" based on historical "masterpieces" drew praise from typographic superstars Henry Lewis Bullen and Douglas McMurtrie, who called Benton's designs faithful "reproductions of historic type by the masters."[7] ATF "makes the Caslon Oldstyle Romans and Italics precisely as Mr Caslon left them in 1766, crafting letters from the original matrices," ATF assured printers [Fig 6.9].[8] Though time-tested quality and historical accuracy played a much-discussed role in the market for revivals, so did financial success. In 1923, Henry Lewis Bullen boasted that "in 1897 I took an obscure, slow-selling type series" and "made it a best-seller." The names for English "Old Face" and American "Old Style No. 1" weren't catchy enough, Bullen related, so "the name I gave it is Caslon Old Style!" With this new

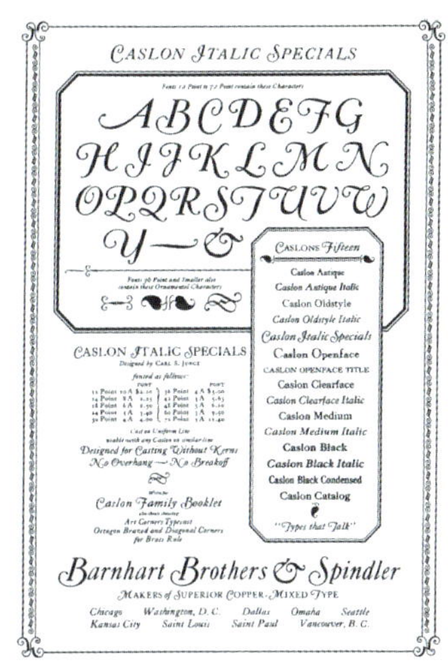

Revivals based on historical typefaces were sometimes faithful, with an emphasis on consulting originals sources, and sometimes less faithful—perhaps through lack of attention to detail, or perhaps to adjust the historical face for use with new technologies.

Fig 6.9 (below)

***Specimen Book & Catalogue* (ATF, Elizabeth NJ, 1923). ATF's Caslon revival was "crafted from the original matrices" and included "all the ancient quaint double and long letters and ligatures used during the lifetime of Mr. Caslon."**

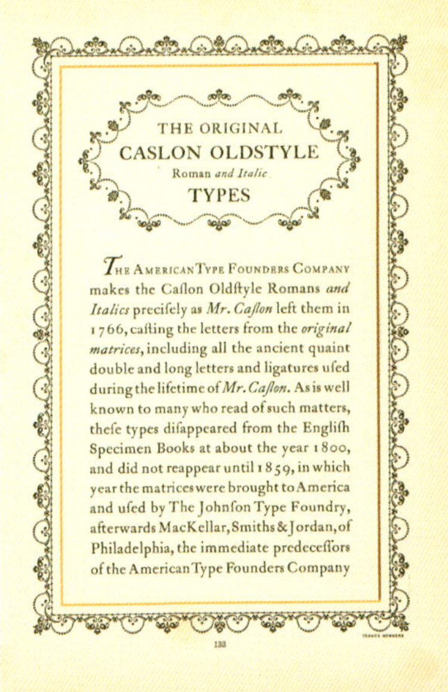

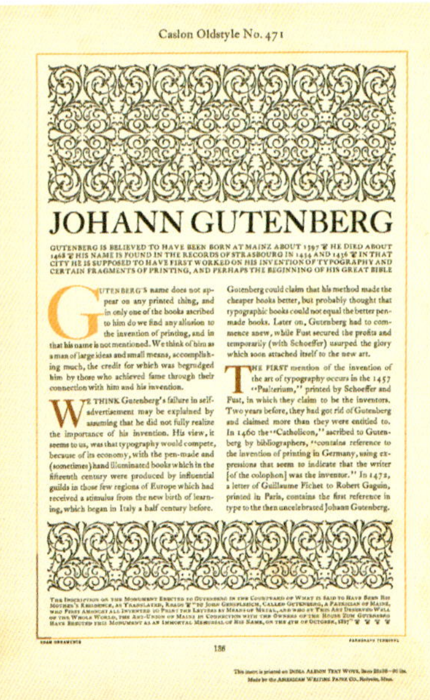

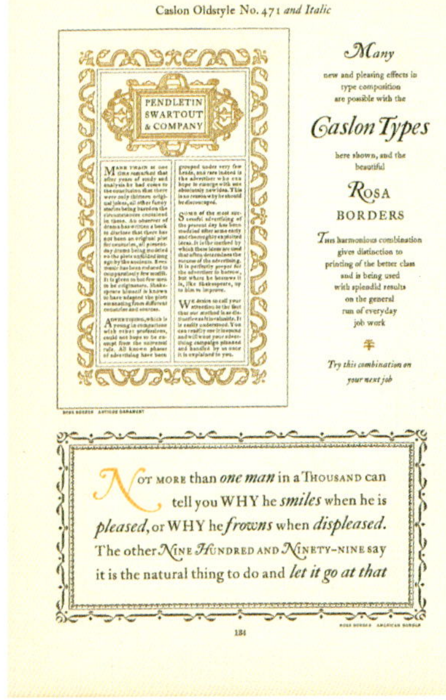

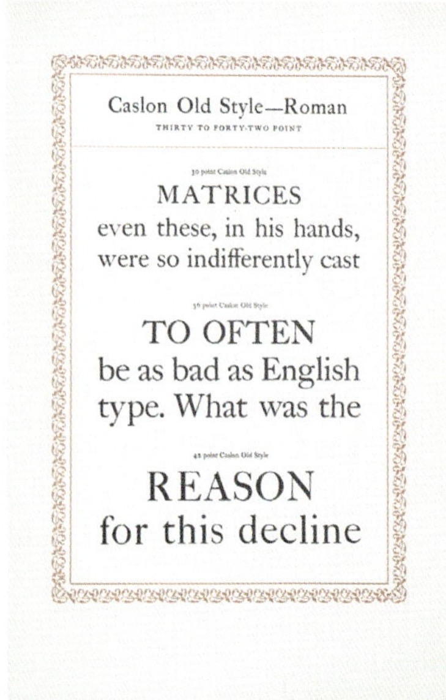

Caslon Old Style—Roman

THIRTY TO FORTY-TWO POINT

MATRICES

even these, in his hands, were so indifferently cast

TO OFTEN

be as bad as English type. What was the

REASON

for this decline

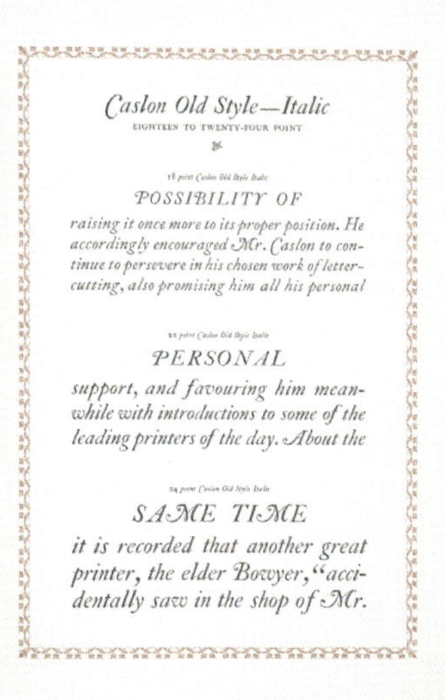

Caslon Old Style—Italic

EIGHTEEN TO TWENTY-FOUR POINT

POSSIBILITY OF

raising it once more to its proper position. He accordingly encouraged Mr. Caslon to continue to persevere in his chosen work of letter-cutting, also promising him all his personal

PERSONAL

support, and favouring him meanwhile with introductions to some of the leading printers of the day. About the

SAME TIME

it is recorded that another great printer, the elder Bowyer, "accidentally saw in the shop of Mr.

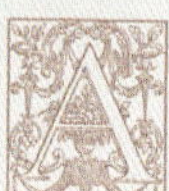

T PRESENT the theory and practice of letter-founding are not, as in his time, an 'art and mystery,' and efficient workmen in every branch are easily procured. He had not only to excel his competitors in his own particular branch of engraving the punches, which to him was probably the easiest part of his task, but to raise an establishment and cause his plans to be executed by ignorant and unpractised workmen. He had also to acquire for himself a knowledge of the practical and mechanical branches of the art, which require, indeed, little genius, but the most minute and painful attention to conduct successfully. The wishes and expectations of his patrons were fulfilled and exceeded by his decided superiority over his domestic rivals and Batavian competitors. The importation of foreign types ceased; his founts were, in fact, in such estimation as to be frequently, in their turn, exported to the Continent.

In 1728 Mr. Caslon narrowly escaped committing an error which might seriously have

18 POINT CASLON OLD STYLE

Fig 6.10 (above)

***A Printed Specimen of Caslon Old Style Type, with Appropriate Ornaments* (Redfield-Kendrick-Odell, New York, 1921). This printer's specimen contextualized Caslon as a typeface suited to everyday use, stressing both its historical origins and its application to the contemporary commercial environment.**

name, and with Bullen's "specimens [made] to demonstrate its adaptability to publicity uses," Caslon Old Style became a commercial success.[9] Bullen explicitly described specimens as a critical tool in the marketing strategy for Caslon Old Style, demonstrating the role specimens played in popularizing historical revivals for contemporary use.

In their forty-page booklet displaying Caslon Old Style [Fig. 6.10], the New York printer Redfield-Kendrick-Odell described how Caslon "suffered an almost total eclipse by the modern Roman letter" of Didot and Bodoni [Fig. 6.10]. Caslon was "[h]appily resurrected in 1843" and "today no printer would seriously attempt to do business without being plentifully supplied with" it.[10] Their Caslon specimen was one of a series "showing the many beautiful types in the composing room of Redfield-Kendrick-Odell," including Bodoni (1923) and Garamond (1927). These, too, were contextualized in the specimen booklets as flexible, fashionable types with historical pedigrees.

Specimens devoted to historical revivals took care to emphasize research, accuracy, and original documents. Design strategies played a role in this contextualization. Bauer's *Bodoni Schriften* (1926) opened with an engraved portrait of Giambattista **Bodoni** and a biographical sketch written by Bauer Bodoni's designer, Heinrich Jost. Subsequent pages reproduced the compositional strategy of Bodoni's 1818 *Manuale Tipografico*, replicating the double and triple hairline frames and floriated borders of the original. Then came a series of title pages, advertisements, and sample texts unrelated to Bodoni's original text [Fig 6.11]. By copying Bodoni's original specimen designs and juxtaposing them with modern compositions, Jost as the designer and Bauer as the foundry established both the historical pedigree and the contemporary utility of the type [Fig. 6.11].

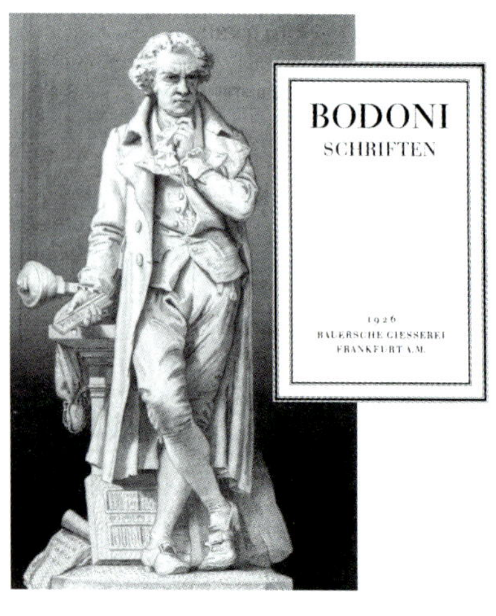

Bodoni left behind many types we now know by his family name, though it was his son Firmin who in 1817 designed the Modern serif face most commonly known as Bodoni today.

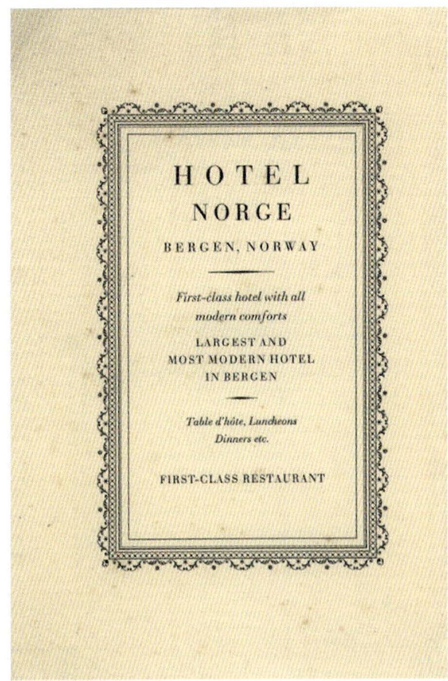

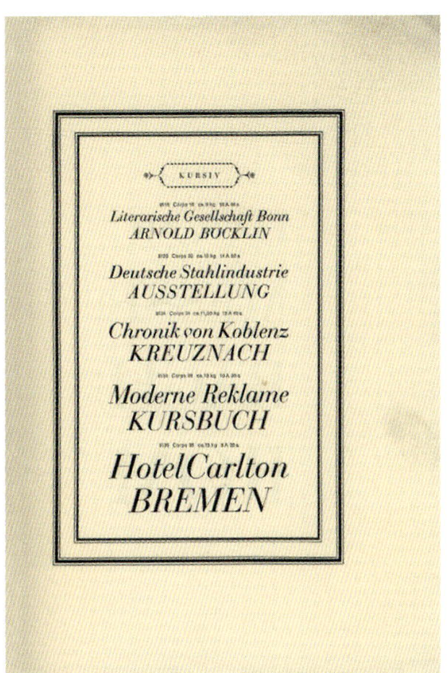

Fig 6.11 (left)

***Bodoni: Schriften* (Bauersche Giesserel, Frankfurt am Main, 1926). In their booklet advertising Heinrich Jost's Bodoni revival, Bauer duplicated the design strategy of Bodoni's original *Manuale Tipografico* on some pages, while others deployed Bodoni for twentieth century purposes, like advertising the Hotel Norge, with all its "modern comforts."**

In addition to strict revivals, typographers produced new types inspired by historical models—and introduced them to printers via ephemeral specimens. A twelve-page pamphlet by well-known book designer Bruce Rogers announced Frederic Goudy's Italian Oldstyle (1924) for Lanston Monotype [Fig. 6.12]. Its detailed colophon identified the printer as W.E. Rudge of Mount Vernon, New York, and the text as an excerpt from T.F. Dibdin's 1817 *Bibliographical Decameron*, a "pleasant discourse" on historical manuscripts, engraving, typography, and bibliography. A print run of 11,600 enabled wide circulation, and an accompanying poster quickly became a familiar visual motif which subsequent designers quoted. Goudy and Rogers shared a love of historically inspired typefaces and compositional strategies, and both were meticulous craftsmen and avid visual researchers. ""If we obey tradition," Goudy advised—by which he meant following historical models of letterform design—"even though our efforts at first are crude and archaic, our work will rest upon a firm foundation."[11] Goudy and Rogers collaborated frequently; in 1923, Rogers designed Monotype's specimens for Goudy's Garamont typeface, another historical revival based on careful research. **Garamond** was revived first, to a warm reception, by the Imprimerie Nationale in 1898; in the United States, ATF released a revival in 1918. Goudy's Garamont relied on a type reproduced in Anatole Claudin's turn-of-the-century *Histoire de l'Imprimerie en France*.[12] Thus, by 1924, the specimens for Italian Oldstyle participated in an established visual dialogue of revivalism with well-known parameters and a familiar set of historical sources. The letterforms themselves, their centered composition on the page, and the framing devices surrounding them—all of these elements contributed to an understanding of Goudy's Italian Oldstyle as an historicist Latin type. In turn, the cover of Monotype's 1941 *XII Typefaces from England* echoed Roger's treatment of Goudy's Italian Old Style, referencing both a proud moment in American book design and a long historical tradition of English type design. The booklet showed types "cut by the Monotype Corporation [of] England [and] offered to discriminating printers in America."

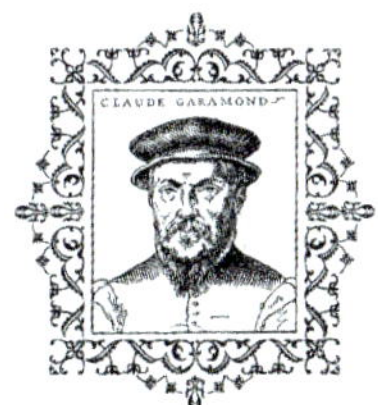

A NOTE ON CLAUDE GARAMOND

PUNCH-CUTTER & TYPE-FOUNDER

By W. M. Ivins, Jr.

F Claude Garamond, the great type designer and punch-cutter, curiously little seems to be known, the scant statements found in the various biographical dictionaries and in the encyclopaedias merely repeating one another with such slight changes in phraseology as may be necessary to escape the penalties of the laws in regard to literary property. Mr. D. B. Updike in his recent book *Printing Types* has brought together more information than is to be found elsewhere in English. The following notes contain what little it has been possible to bring together from material available in New York.

Garamond, the common spelling for the name of French typographer Claude Garamont (1499-1561), was a seemingly endless source of inspiration for early twentieth century typographers.

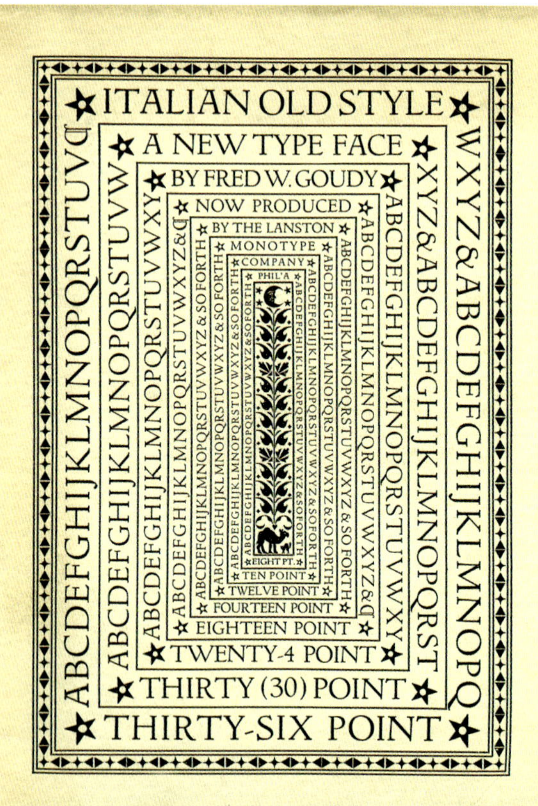

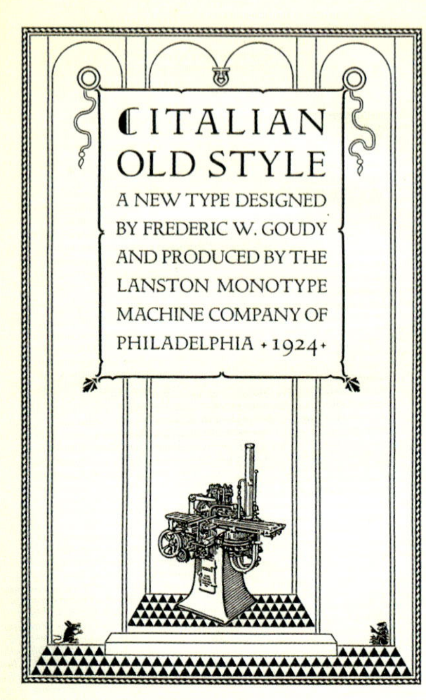

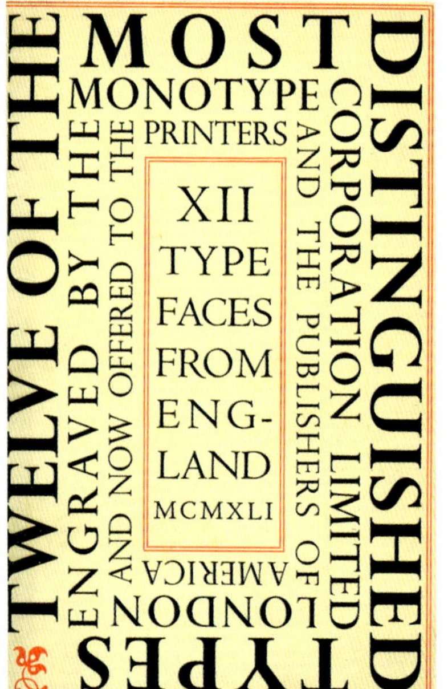

LONDON, ENGLAND: THE MONOTYPE CORPORATION LIMITED

PERPETUA 239

72 We Are
60 Firstly to
48 Provide For
42 Our Security
36 but This is not to
30 Close the Efforts of
24 Our Exertions. Amid the
18 Wreck and Misery of Nations, It

PHILADELPHIA: THE LANSTON MONOTYPE MACHINE COMPANY

26

PHILADELPHIA: THE LANSTON MONOTYPE MACHINE COMPANY

PERPETUA 239, ITALIC & BOLD

is OUR *Just Exultation* that We Have Continued Superior to ALL that **ambition** or that **Despotism** could effect; and that Our Still Higher Exultation ought to be 14

that WE Provide not only for *Our Own Safety*, but Hold Out a **Prospect** to Nations who are Now Bending under the *Iron Yoke of Tyranny* 13

of What the **Exertions** of a Free People can effect, and that, at least *in this Corner of the World*, the Name of LIBERTY is Still Revered, Cherished, and Sanctified. So said *William Pitt in 1804*. 12

THERE IS NO BETTER WAY of perceiving what Printing Stands for than by contrasting it with the Other Kind of *Broadcasting*, the Audible Kind. **Wireless** started as Morse-code signalling: in Other Words, Anyone who 11

10 WANTED TO USE or Enjoy it had first to make himself **Morse-literate.** Up to a point, *History repeated itself*: the Morse-users were mainly in One

WERE studying the Code. If the News-Bulletins of this War were transmitted *only in Morse*, more and **more people** would 6

9 PROFESSIONAL CLASS, just as the Alphabet-Users were in 1440, but *more and more* Amateurs

BE DRIVEN TO de-code it just as their **Forefathers** learnt to *decode* and read the alphabet. 8

LONDON, ENGLAND: THE MONOTYPE CORPORATION LIMITED

27

Franzisca Baruch's Hebrew typeface Stam (c. 1925) drew on historical models as well. Its general categorization—a new design inspired by careful study of historical types—registers as similar to a face like Goudy's Italian Oldstyle, but its cultural context differed. The Berthold foundry released Baruch's Stam, a typeface she'd originally designed for the Hebrew journal *Rimon*, along with Rambam and Rachel, derived without Baruch's permission from Stam.[13] As one of several new Hebrew typefaces heavily marketed by Berthold in the 1920s and early 1930s, Stam participated in a revival of Hebrew and **Yiddish** literary culture in Central and Eastern Europe, particularly Germany.[14] Berthold's specimen for the three faces demonstrated their application to book work and advertising [Fig. 6.13]. Baruch believed that new Hebrew types required appropriate historical models; the Jewish national movement and the Society of Friends of the Jewish Book, both active in Germany at the

Fig 6.12 (opposite)
***Italian Old Style* (Monotype, Philadelphia, 1924) and *XII Typefaces from England* (1941). Bruce Rogers designed Monotype's promotional materials for Frederic Goudy's Italian Old Style, visually articulating the sympathy between Renaissance architecture and letterforms and Goudy's "new type." Monotype quoted this visual language again in 1941, advertising imported British Monotype faces to "discriminating" American printers.**

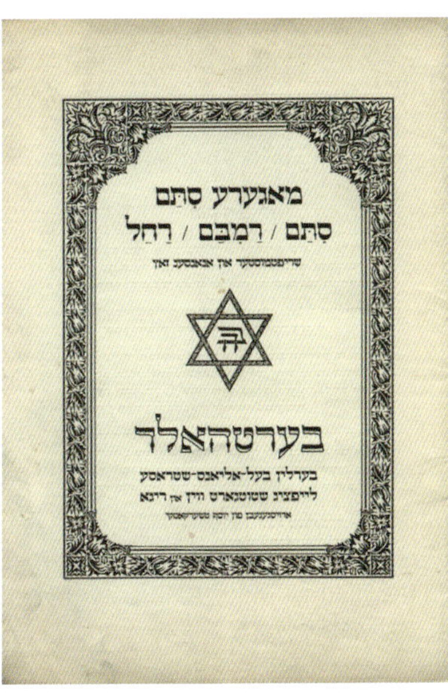

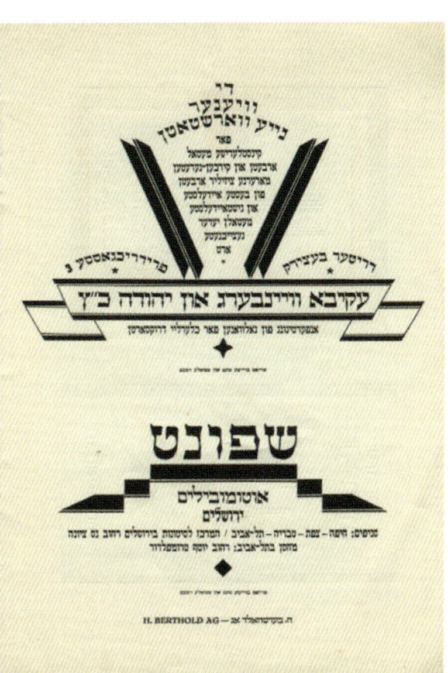

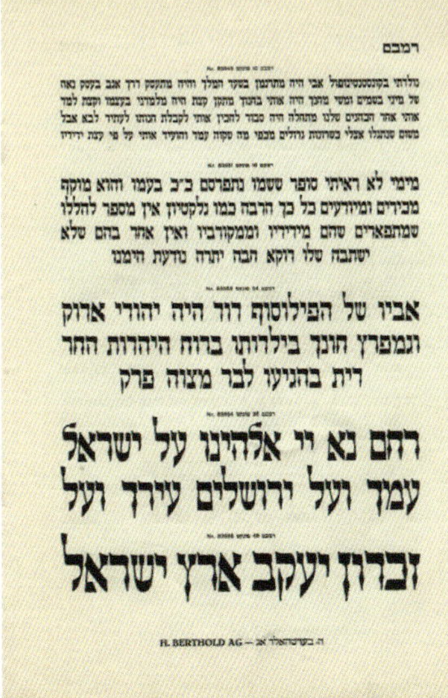

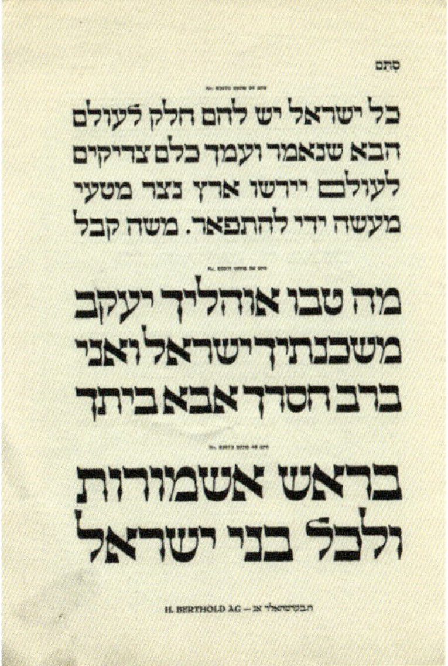

Fig 6.13 (left)
***Stam Specimen* (Berthold, Berlin, c. 1930). Franzisca Baruch designed new Hebrew types based on historical models. She studied an early sixteenth century haggadah as she designed Stam, and Berthold's specimen for Stam, Rambam and Rachel made use of historicist ornament originally found in their lavish 1924 Hebrew specimen.**

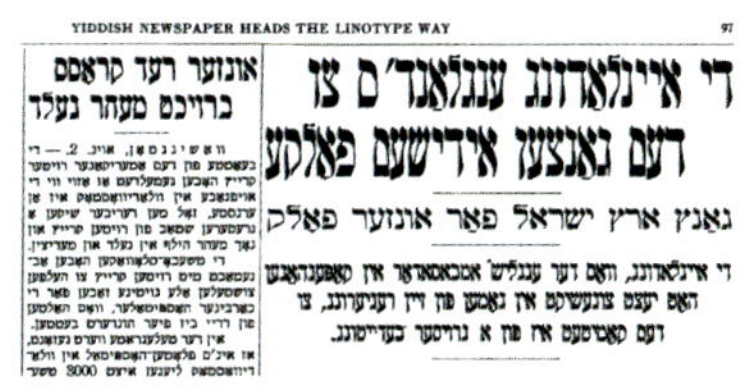

Yiddish uses the Hebrew alphabet. Originally a German dialect, it adopts words from Hebrew, Aramaic, and several Romance and Slavic languages. It was spoken by Jewish people across central and eastern Europe before the Holocaust and continues to be spoken today, largely in the USA, Israel, and Russia.

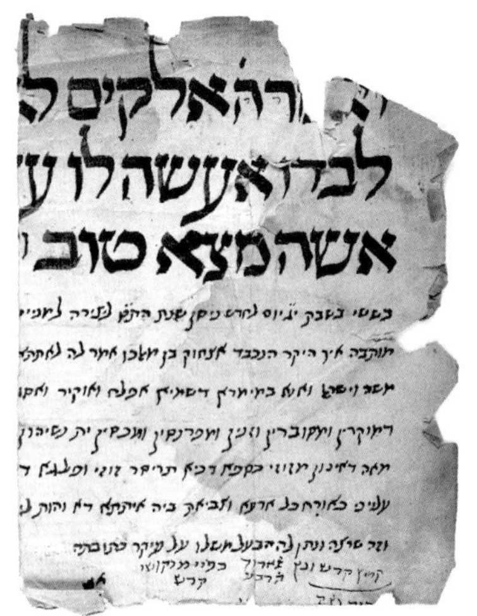

Calligraphic Hebrew texts provided the basis for many 20 c. typographic Hebrew revivals. This fragment of ketubah, a hand-written Jewish marriage contract, dates from 1649.

same time, shared this philosophy. By revitalizing the visual language of the printed page, Hebrew scholarship and culture would be enlivened as well. As a designer, most of Baruch's **calligraphic** and typographic designs, both Latin and Hebrew, drew inspiration from medieval and early printed letterforms. She modeled Stam, her first printing type, on the typeface used in Prague printer Gershon Kohen's 1526 Passover haggadah.

Berthold publicized Baruch's Stam, alongside their variants Rambam and Rachel, in a twenty-page specimen booklet.[15] Its title page suggests Baruch's research process. A woodcut-style foliated border evokes the visual language of the woodcuts for Kohen's haggadah, the first printed copy of that text to survive in its entirety.[16] More directly, it referenced Berthold's own 1924 Hebrew type specimen book, which used the same border on its title page. Stam is displayed at a range of text sizes in double columns across one spread, but most of the specimen contextualizes all three types as display faces—their intended function, for which they were well-suited.[17] Single columns set in large point sizes and sample advertisements with Art Deco style ad cuts reiterate the message. Though set entirely in Hebrew, the specimen retains some non-Hebrew printing conventions. Bound on the left side, rather than the right, it reads from front to back in the conventional sense, with the title page appearing where Latin-alphabet readers would expect to find it. Berthold's elaborate, full-color 1924 Hebrew catalog emphasized the wide scope and diverse application of its types. In comparison, this brief, monochromatic booklet collected three of Baruch's types in an affordable, efficient format. It visually suggested historical origins via the title page, then demonstrated contemporary applications through the sample ad designs.

Defining modernity

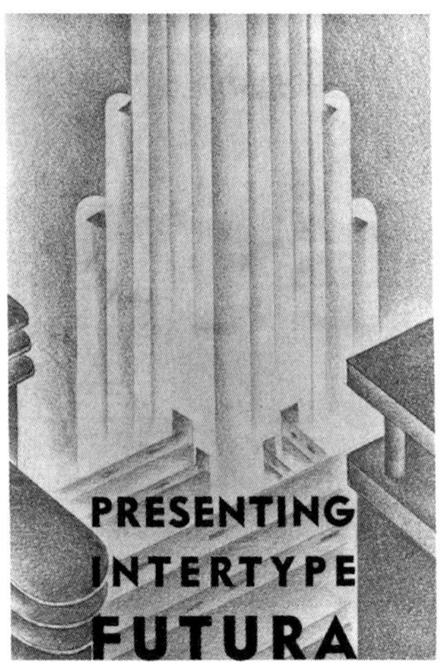

Geometric sans serifs are constructed around circles, triangles, and squares, with little or no stroke weight variation. Paul Renner's 1927 Futura is perhaps the most famous example.

Within the early twentieth century visual language of typography, historicism and revivalism co-existed with ideas about modernity and progress. Smaller, ephemeral formats supported a professional culture in which multiple approaches to typographic form flourished. *Fashions in American Typography* (1931), introduced by Frederic Goudy, argued against revivals as unsuited to the spirit of contemporary times, even though Goudy himself designed many revivals.[18] Across design disciplines, a mechanized, streamlined, geometric aesthetic suggested progress and contemporaneity as hallmarks of "contemporary times." Typefaces were no exception, and specimens framed newly designed **geometric sans serif** and slab serif faces as distinctly Modern typographic products.

Metropolis (1928), designed by Willy Schwerdtner for Stempel in Germany, framed type as a participant in the broader language of Modern design [Fig. 6.14]. Like Heinz Schulz-Neudamm's posters for Fritz Lang's 1927 film *Metropolis*, the specimen centered its visual identity on a **streamlined** skyscraper which dominates an urban skyline. The sleek, geometric architectural forms, and the high contrast between the illustration's thick and thin strokes, echoed the formal characteristics of the Art Deco typeface: heavy stems, hairline serifs, small counters, and rectilinear capital letters. Inside the specimen, geometric borders framed justified headlines displaying Metropolis Bold. A version with long ascenders offered an exaggerated sense of height, visually referencing the skyscrapers so popular in the period's architecture.[19] Both visual and verbal cues established Metropolis' modernity.

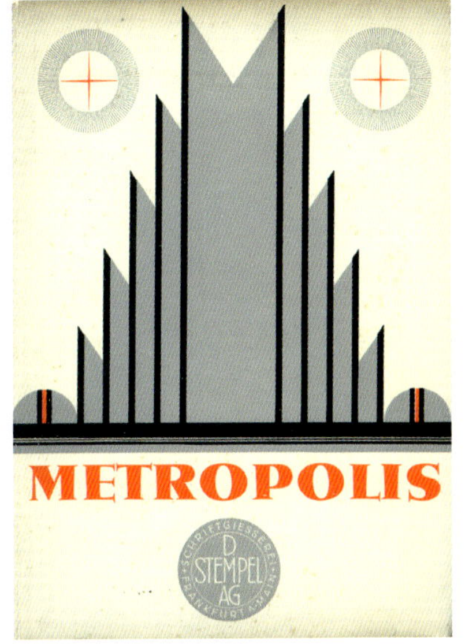

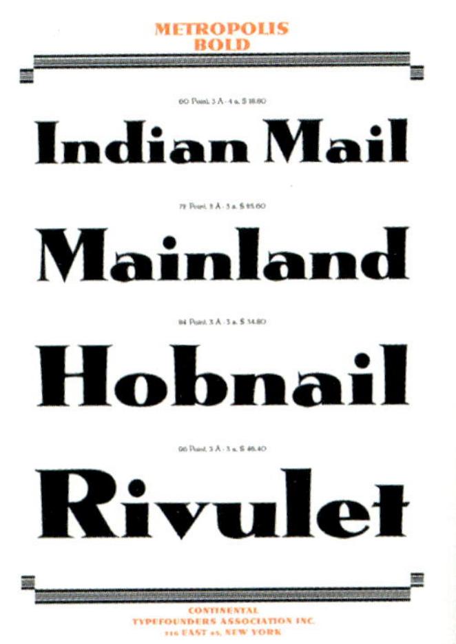

Fig 6.14 (left)

Metropolis (Stempel/Continental Typefounders, Frankfurt and New York, c.1928). In contrast to historical source material, contemporary sans serifs and slab serifs often referenced modern engineering, urban skyscrapers, and the speed of technological developments. Stempel's Metropolis even included a version with longer ascenders to emphasize this relationship.

A 1928 German trade journal ad for Metropolis deployed a recognizably modernist compositional strategy of asymmetry, strong angles, and significant negative space. A subsequent Berthold ad used Metropolis to label the foundry as the source of "Die moderne Typographie," but the layout of both that ad and the 1928 English-language Metropolis specimen were centered and symmetrical, relying on the type itself to connote a modern aesthetic.[20] Significantly, Stempel released the Metropolis specimen in German and English versions, anticipating audiences at home and abroad and indicating the international scope of visual ideas about modernity.

In the United States, Barnhart Brothers & Spindler's inline **Art Deco** typeface Boul Mich (1927) catered to the contemporary taste for the **Moderne**. Named for Michigan Boulevard, it was designed for BB&S by Oz Cooper. In a bifold specimen devoted entirely to the "first showing of a chic display type according to the new mode," BB&S touted the new arrival as evidence of a "spirit of change" and described Boul Mich as a "superb stimulant" for advertising. The following year, BB&S deployed it on the cover of its sixteen-page specimen *Modernism in Advertising*, highlighting an operational definition of Modernism as a visual style suited to the contemporary commercial environment [Fig 6.15].

In France, the two well-known foundries Deberny and Peignot merged into a single foundry in 1923. Deberny & Peignot quickly released Charles Peignot's typeface Sphinx (1924) to counter both the ornate curvilinearity of Art Nouveau and the recent plethora of historical revivals. Rather than organic forms or Renaissance typefaces, Peignot turned to recent archeological excavations in Egypt and South America as his inspiration. Alfred Latour's 1926 French-language Sphinx specimen [Fig. 6.16] described "caractéres nouveaux," while the similarly-designed English-language specimen emphasized the foundry's focus on "up-to-date, modern types" for the publicity needs of contemporary advertisers. Peignot's sources—pyramids and ziggurats—may have originated in **antiquity**, but the language used to describe Sphinx situated it firmly within a modern sensibility. Its geometric attributes and associations with Art Deco architecture lent it a contemporary character.

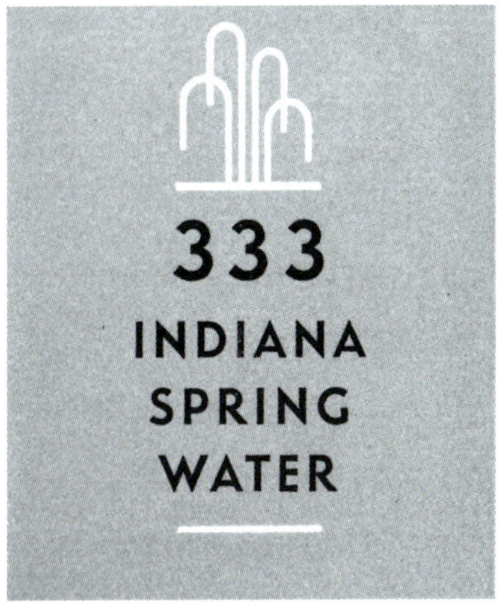

Streamlined forms typified much Modernist and Moderne design of the first half of the twentieth century: the Bauhaus and Futurist movements, the Art Deco style, and their mass-culture counterparts all embraced the implication of speed and technological advances. This Tempo ad (Ludlow, 1931) demonstrates Tempo's suitability for "Modernistic" advertising.

BARNHART BROTHERS
& SPINDLER
BOUL MICH
CUBIST
BOLD

Art Deco and its mass-market counterpart Art **Moderne** drew on the streamlined, geometric visual language of the skyscraper and the automobile to imply speed, modernity, and sophistication.

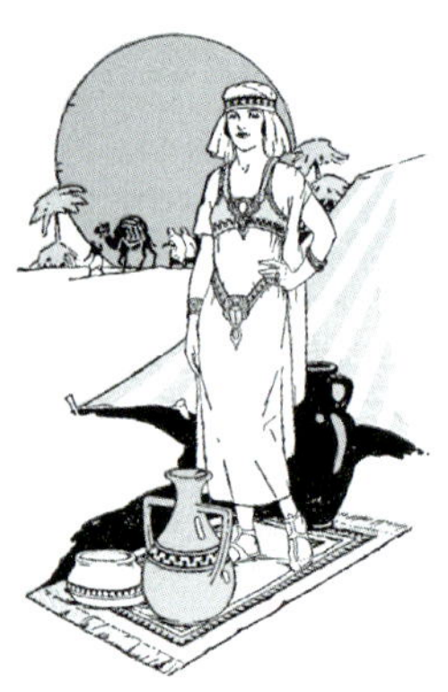

Since the Neoclassical period, artists and designers had been reimagining the visual culture of **antiquity**—ancient Egypt, Greece, and Rome—based on emerging archeological discoveries. Ancient Egypt's bold geometric forms were particularly inspiring for Art Deco designers.

Typographic ornament followed suit. In a catalog published in 1925, BB&S displayed their Cubist Colorettes and Tint Tile Borders—modular systems for designing ornaments in the composing room. The Cubist Colorettes, particularly, reflected the Modernist emphasis on geometric construction. The catalog described the circles, triangles, and squares used to "build up the design" as "the 'makings' for striking and highly effective ornaments."[21] Referencing Cubism further indicated a modern sensibility. The Modernist interest in geometric modularity informed pattern, ornament, and letterforms. ATF's Alpha-Blox (1942) offered a modular system for constructing letters, patterns, and ornaments out of component parts. ATF advertised Alpha-Blox as "a valuable tool for the composing room," a "completely flexible" system for the "artist-printer" with "ingenuity," "good taste," and "imagination." Like Josef Albers' *Schabloneneschrift* [stencil] typeface (c.1926), these systems reduced typography to its basic geometric shapes—circles, triangles, squares, rectangles, and lines.

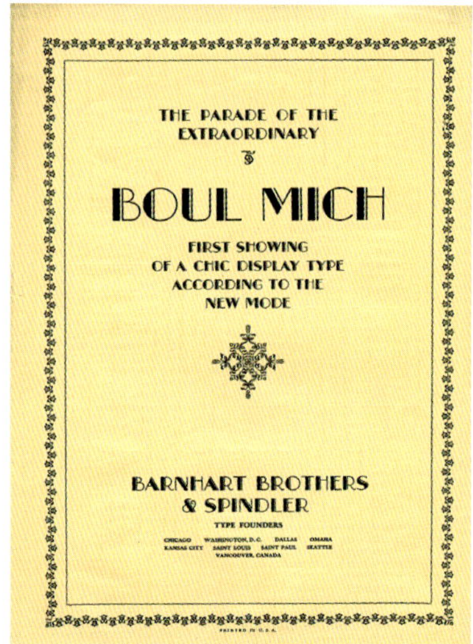

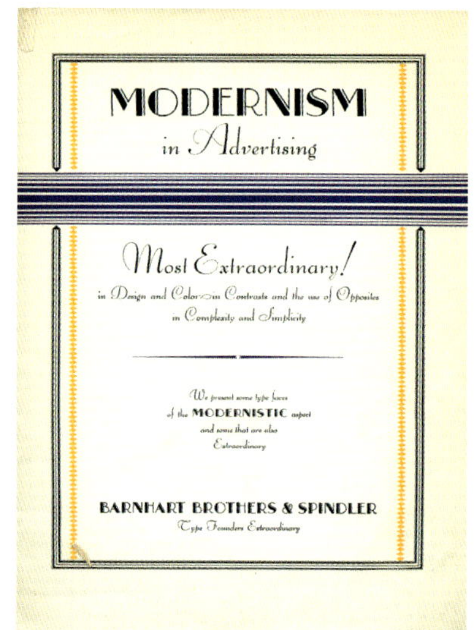

Fig 6.15 (right)

Boul Mich: The Parade of the Extraordinary **(BB&S, Chicago, 1927; left) and *Modernism in Advertising* (1928). The "Moderne" style imparted sleek curves, streamlined geometry, and a sense of urban elegance onto everything from typographic to architectural form.**

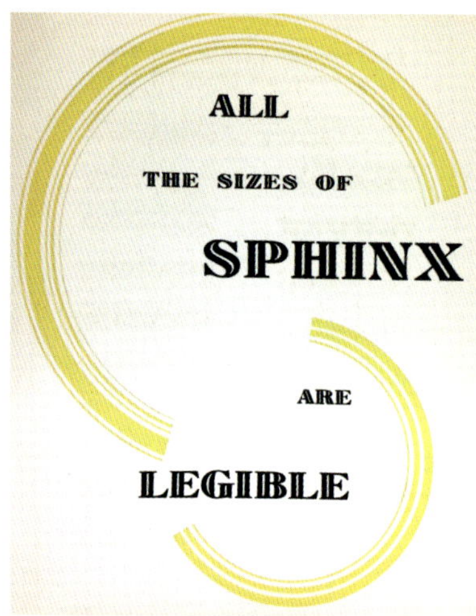

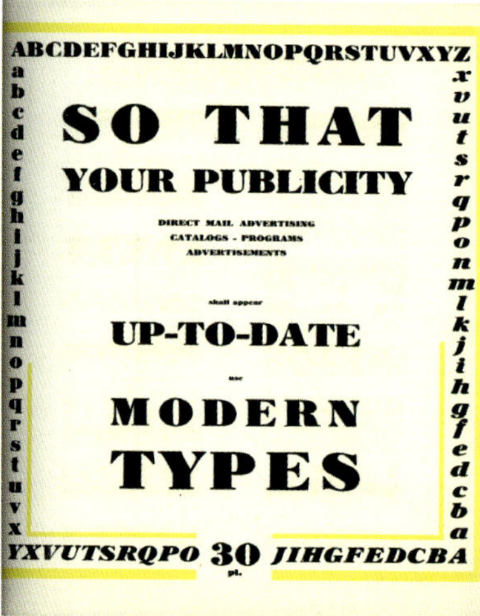

Fig 6.16 (right)

Sphinx (Deberny & Peignot, Paris, c.1926). While Charles Peignot's first typeface for the newly-merged Deberny & Peignot foundry took antique tombs rather than modern skyscrapers as its architectural inspiration, it was framed as an "up-to-date" typeface because of its geometric construction.

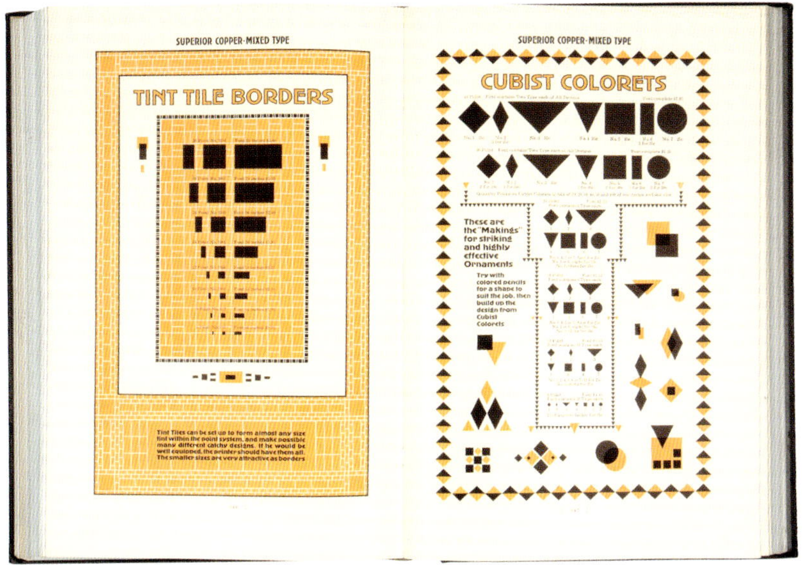

Fig 6.17 (left and below)

Type Faces, Border Designs, Typecast Ornaments.... **(BB&S, Chicago, 1925) and AlphaBlox specimen (ATF, Elizabeth NJ, 1944). BB&S's Cubist Colorettes and Tint Tile Borders, like ATF's AlphaBlox, equipped printers for modular construction of display type and typographic ornament in the pressroom.**

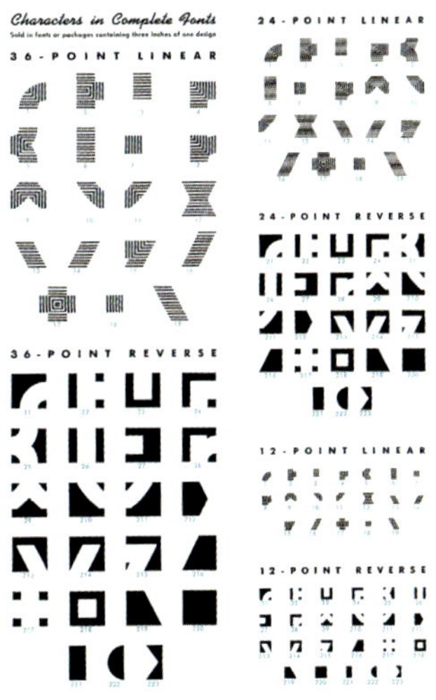

What are Alpha-blox? As their name implies, Alpha-blox are types on whose printing surfaces appear a variety of straight sections, curves, L's and T's. Set in building-block fashion, they form the letters of the alphabet, figures, borders, ornaments and innumerable other typographic devices ● For example, two each of three carefully designed, precision cast units can be made up quickly into the letter Two more of a fourth design serve to elongate the while two more of these latter units will make the same taller ● Because of the complete flexibility of Alpha-blox, the variations in a single letter are limited only by the good taste of the designer or printer using them. For example, the cross-bar on this same A can ride high or low Substituting a few elements affords a new range of designs, while a different approach will produce a variety of lowercase letters *How are Alpha-blox made?* They are made in two styles: linear and reverse and are cut and cast to register. Thus, they may be used interchangeably or for two-color work There are nineteen linear characters and twenty-three reverse characters. All are available in 12, 24 and 36 point sizes as shown on page 7.

In Italy, Microgramma and Eurostile, two of the foundry Società Nebiolo's most successful faces, likewise capitalized on geometry as a signifier of modernity [Fig. 6.17]. The caps-only titling face Microgramma (1952), designed by Alessandro Butti and Aldo Novarese, gave "any printing job a stylish and contemporary look."[22] Its squared-off letterforms echoed the rectilinearity of Modernist architecture and its sans serif structure evidenced a no-nonsense approach to visual communication. Eurostile (1962) followed, designed by Aldo Novarese. Though its capitals came from Microgramma, it included lowercase letters and additional widths and weights, offering designers a wider range of options [Fig 6.18]. Its design responded to what its English-language specimen described as a "tendency towards **functionalism** in graphic arts design." Other specimens described the face as "the first square-letter Gothic fully articulated in capitals and lower case" and "a new type expressing, through its novel design, the dynamic style of our age."[23] This emphasis on newness, dynamism, and functionalism characterized many conversations about Modernist design throughout the twentieth century.

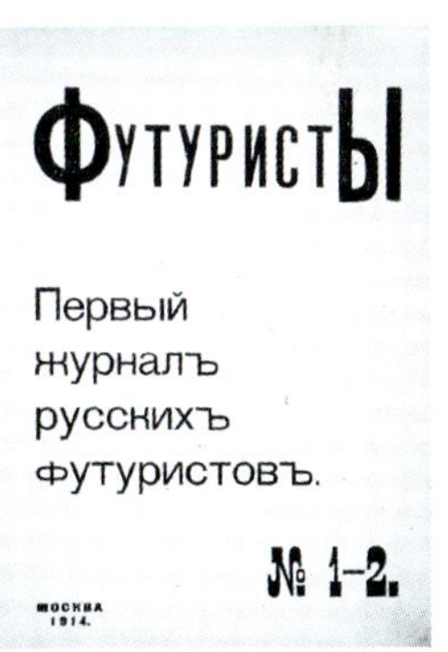

Functionalism asks the typographer to focus on the text's job: communicating information to the reader. What this looks like varies by place and time. This 1914 cover of the Avant Garde Modernist magazine *Futuristy* defines functionalism through a very specific aesthetic, like most Modernist texts

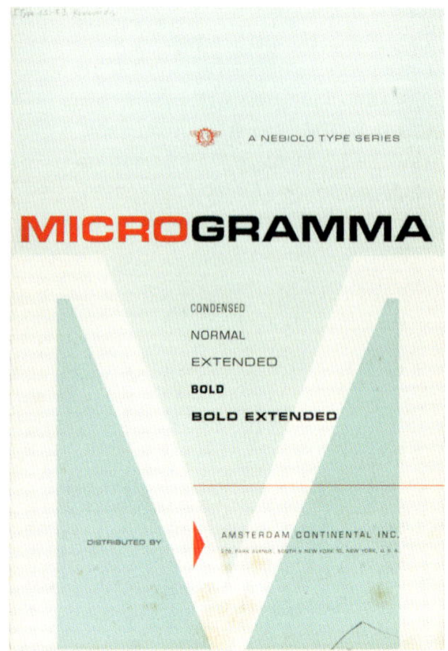

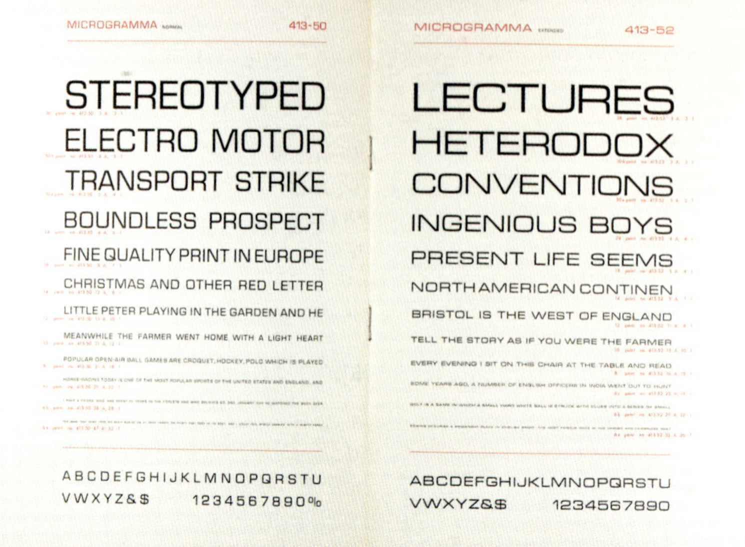

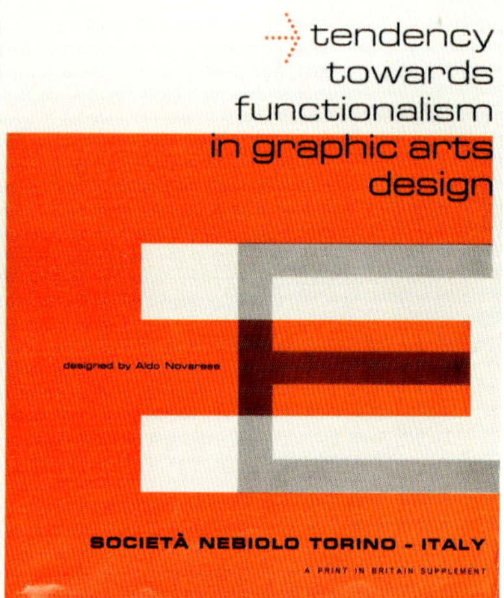

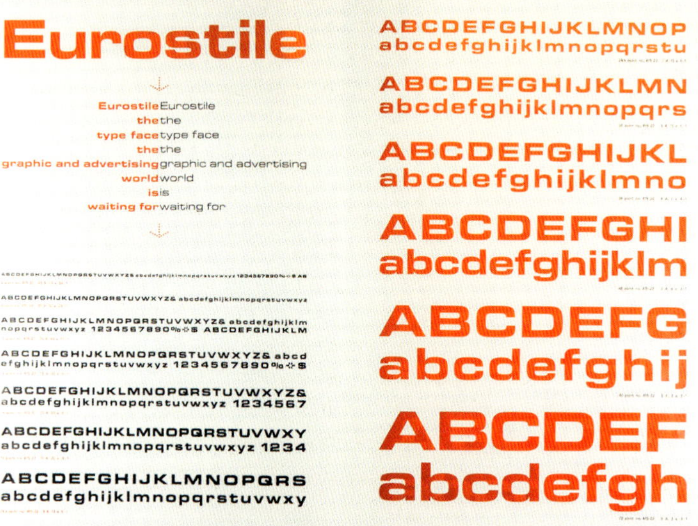

Fig 6.18 (above)

***Microgramma* (Società Nebiolo, Torino, 1962; top) and *Eurostile* (1965). Geometric Modernism influenced the squared-off, sans-serif letterforms of caps-only Microgramma and Eurostile, which offered not only lowercase letters but also a range of styles and widths.**

Networks of circulation

Since their introduction as a form and practice, typographic specimens have carried ideas and styles across time and geographical space. Ephemeral formats didn't alter this fundamental capacity. However, their economy and ease of circulation accelerated existing formal and informal networks of exchange. These might include official distribution agreements for imported matrices or metal sorts, the adaptation of existing technologies for new geographic or linguistic contexts, pirating existing type designs through electrotyping or pantographic methods, or stylistic homages based on work seen in international printers' specimen exchanges.

Imports, exports, and adaptations

Lightweight and easily mailed, ephemeral specimens facilitated the international circulation of typefaces and styles. A steady stream of imports into the United States introduced European designs to American audiences, popularizing a developing **international** visual language of typographic form. For some American printers, using imported European type indicated high standards of trade knowledge and applied craft. At the turn of the nineteenth century, American founders had been keen to advertise high-quality types produced at home rather than abroad. In 1792, an apologetic printer's preface to a copy of New York's state laws admitted that "The Types are not so perfectly Regular as those from the London Foundries, which have been improving for Centuries," but at least they were manufactured in the United States.[24] By the early to mid-twentieth century, however, choosing imported types signaled sophisticated taste and a commitment to either a fine printing aesthetic or a modern typographic style. Both "fine printing" and "modern style" were phrases defined in very specific ways. MoMA's *Exhibition of European Commercial Printing of Today* in May 1935 presented "modern typography" as a European style and offered examples from England, France, Italy, Russia, Germany, Switzerland, Czechoslovakia, and Sweden.[25] In contrast, Frederic Goudy and William Ransom's 1903 Village Press edition of William Morris' essay on *Printing* typified **fine printing**, a genre which prioritized high-quality materials and a carefully controlled aesthetic governed by

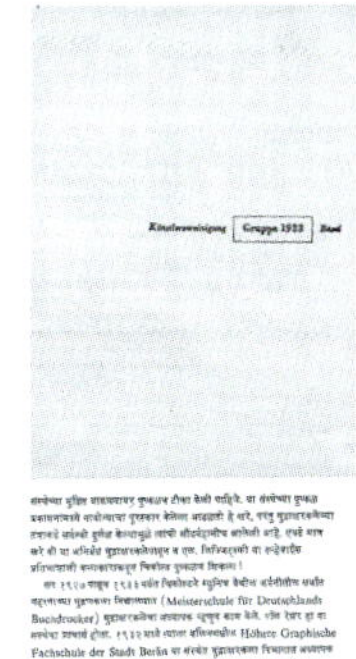

The **International Style**, more accurately the Swiss Style, originated in Switzerland and quickly spread from the School of Design in Basel (est. 1947) around the world, as evidenced by its appearance in the Indian textbook Modern Typesetting Art. The style emphasized "universal" design: relentlessly legible, grid-based compositions using sans serif typefaces like Akzidenz-Grotesk (1896), Univers (1954), and Helvetica (1957).

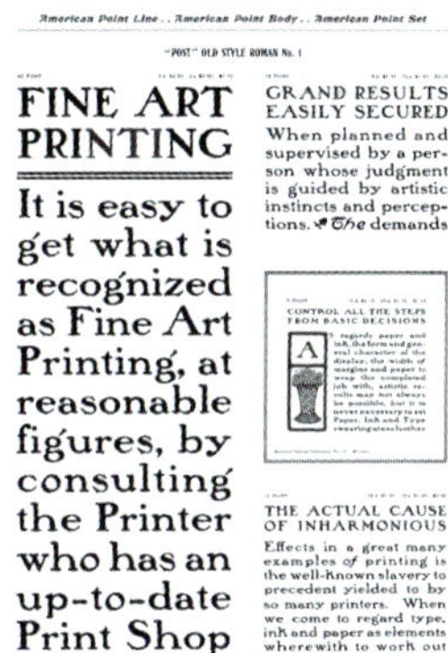

The **Fine Printing** movement, sparked in large part by William Morris' Kelmscott Press issue of Chaucer's *Canterbury Tales* (1896), emphasized the quality of type, materials, and craft in reaction to the low standards and cheap materials of mass-market commercial printing.

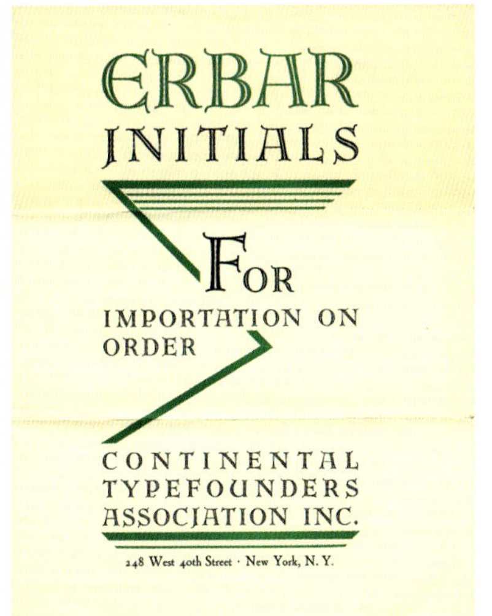

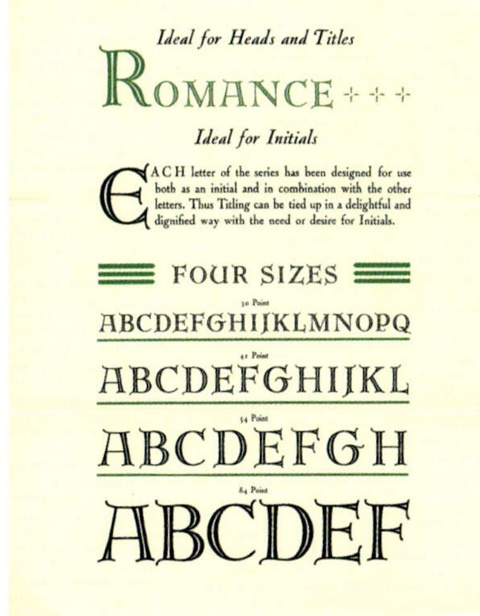

Fig 6.19 (lleft)

***Erbar Initials* (Continental Typefounders Association, New York, c.1926). Importers like the Continental Typefounders Association specialized in playing an intermediary role between American printers and European typefounders, importing faces like Ludwig & Mayer's 1913-14 Erbar Initials.**

Fig 6.20 (right)

Sapphire / Ornata / American Uncial specimen (Amsterdam Continental, New York, 1960s). Amsterdam Continental self-identified as the "sole importer" of many of the typefaces it sold, carving out a niche market among American printers who saw themselves as sophisticated typographic purists.

The titling face **Sapphire,** designed by Hermann Zapf, is spiritually linked to the decorative 18th Century faces. Calendars, jubilee pamphlets and diplomas demand impressive and festive typography, for which Sapphire is especially devised. It fits well with most body faces. The figures can be used independently for calendars, seasonal greeting cards, etc. Sapphire is available in 24, 36 and 42 pt.

SAPPHIRE

A gay friendly decoration
of eye-catching strength,
welcome at all festive occasions

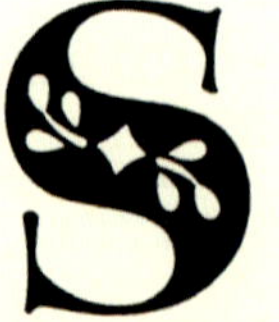

Ornata ranks with the most charming decorative faces existing. It can be used with all typography seeking charm and nobility rather than the merely noisy or gaudy. Designed by the famous German graphic artist O. H. W. Hadank. Ornata is available in sizes 8-72 pt.

ORNATA

Crystal droplets of a shower
of rain . . . a strand
of diamonds, sparkling
in a fair lady's hair . . .
a row of tinsel-dressed
fir trees at Rockefeller Center's
Christmas decoration

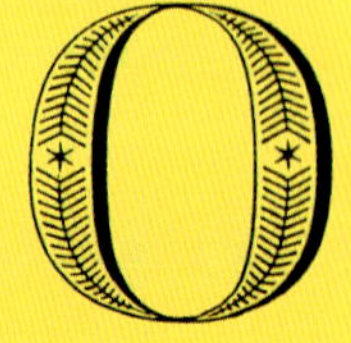

American Uncial uses the forms of caps and lower case freely intermixed, while ascenders and descenders have been shortened. The lines run across the page as beautifully as decorative ribbons. Victor Hammer, famous calligrapher, has created it as a souvenir of the high culture of the last Roman centuries in Italy. American Uncial is available in 14, 18 and 30 pt.

AMERICAN UNCIAL

Reminiscent of the beautiful
handwritten bibles
of the early Middle Ages

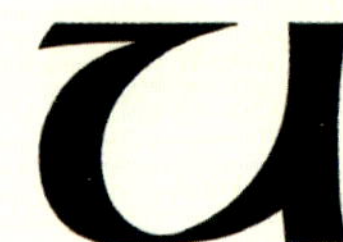

Sole importers:
Amsterdam Continental Types and Graphic Equipment Inc.
276 Park Avenue South, New York 10, N.Y., SPring 7-4980

Printed in Germany

D. STEMPEL AG · TYPEFOUNDRY · FRANKFURT/MAIN

contemporary translation of historical models. The slender book embodied the ideals of fine printing in its text and materials. Printed in an edition of 231, it was set in Goudy's own **Village Type**, which was hand-cast, and printed in the traditional two-color pairing of black and red. Goudy and Ransom bound the book by hand at Goudy's Village Press.[26] That its model was William Morris, a British Arts & Crafts printer and type designer, was significant; the American fine printing movement relied heavily on its British forerunners, often quoting them as a sign of high culture and good taste.[27]

Specimens from type *distributors* further reveal how American printers conceptualized European type as a status symbol. Distributors differentiated themselves from foundries, which produced type, or printers, who used it; instead, they imported and sold type from well-known European foundries, sometimes self-identifying as the only American source of a particular European type to carve out a niche market. Distributors' specimens framed metal type as a commercial product in unique ways, emphasizing quality and taste as central to typeface selection. The Continental Typefounders Association of New York (est. 1925) imported type from historied foundries Caslon & Stephenson Blake in England; Stempel and Klingspor in Germany; Enschedé in Holland; Deberny & Peignot in France; and Società Nebiolo in Italy. Continental's 1929 specimen offered typefaces "imported exclusively" by Continental, a sole point of access to both famous historical types and new fashions in vogue abroad.[28] Continental's smaller, ephemeral publications often highlighted single typefaces or type families. Their four-page Erbar Initials leaflet (c.1926) showcased a decorative inline face in four display sizes, designed by Jakob Erbar to accompany his 1913-14 Erbar-Mediaeval for

This edition of Elisha Brown Bird, His Book-Plates, printed for Winfred Porter Truesdell, Arlington, Massachusetts, consists of one hundred and ten copies on Van Gelder handmade paper, and forty copies on Japan vellum. The text has been composed by Bertha M. Goudy, in Village type designed by Frederic W. Goudy, and printed by them at the Village Press, New York, in September, 1907.

Goudy often used his own **Village Type** (a Venetian face designed in 1903) to print limited edition runs at his fine press, Village Press.

the Frankfurt foundry Ludwig & Mayer [Fig. 6.19]. Continental described the type as "ideal for heads and titles, ideal for initials." Erbar Initials, available "for importation on order" from Ludwig & Mayer, demonstrate Continental's role as an intermediary between American printers and European foundries. Meanwhile, Amsterdam Continental (New York, Chicago, Burbank) imported from Stempel, Berthold, Ludwig & Mayer, and Haas in Germany; Nebiolo in Italy; Lettergieteij Amsterdam; and Mouldtype in England [Fig. 6.20]. "The Distinguished Europeans," as they phrased it in the 1960s, offered type "produced by craftsmen," cast in "Europe's most distinguished foundries," and "reproduced for Amsterdam Continental from original matrices to maintain absolute integrity of design."[29] They described themselves as the "sole importers" of Stempel's Sapphire, Ornata, and American Uncial. An undated flier showcased these three typefaces and emphasized the distributor's place in their network of circulation.

American importers described European types as authentic, but also as vehicles of transferable sophistication. A Klingspor circular (1945) distributed from New Jersey promised that "Klingspor foundry types bring new distinction to your printing," being "outstanding both in design and craftsmanship" [Fig. 6.21]. The copy advised printers to "ask for genuine original Klingspor Foundry types; reject inferior copies." Brads in each corner facilitated hanging the trifold as a poster (22.5x16"). Meanwhile, a bifold advertising Continental Types of San Francisco promised that "New types from Europe lend enchantment to modern typography" and showed Kabel (Rudolf Koch for Klingspor, 1927), Lutetia (Jan van Krimpen for Enschedé, 1925), and Poliphilus (Stanley Morison reviving a fifteenth-century Italian face for Monotype, 1923)—new types from Germany, Holland, and England, respectively [Fig. 6.22]. Descriptions emphasized the types' European origins

Fig 6.21 (bottom left)

Klingspor Foundry Types **(Klingspor, Morristown NJ & Offenbach, 1945). 22.5x16". As WWII concluded and trade between Germany and the United States resumed, the idea that European foundry types would lend "distinction" to American printing required careful contextualization in the case of Klingspor, a German foundry.**

Fig 6.22 (below)

New Types from Europe **(Continental Types, San Francisco, c.1927-30). This bifold proclaimed the "enthusiastic reception" of select European types cast on the American point system. The importer described the faces shown on this specimen as modern, refined, graceful, original, new, and brilliant.**

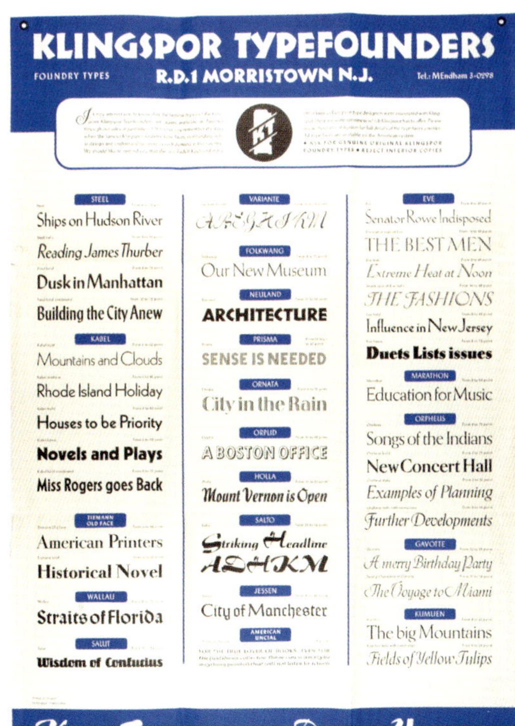

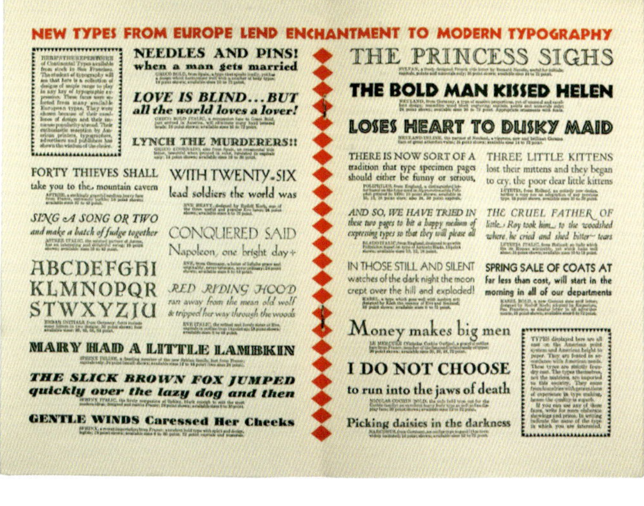

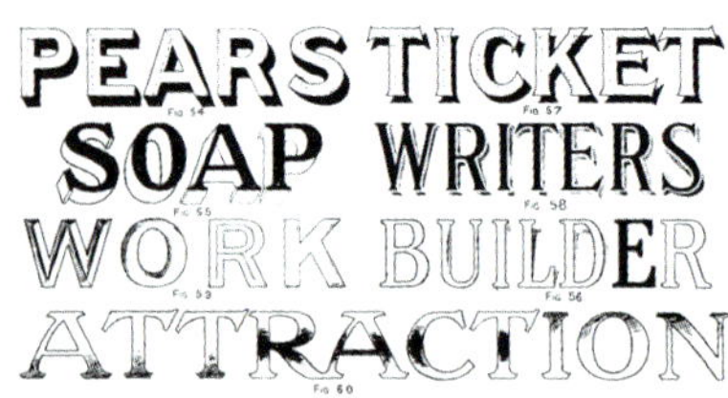

Vernacular letterforms are often handmade and/or specific to a local or regional visual tradition. Though often used to mean amature rather than professional, kitschy rather than tasteful, or rural rather than urban, most places and cultures have a vernacular. This example is from Ticket-writing and sign-painting (London: Cassel, 1916).

and the associated qualities they lent to American printing. Kabel "goes well with modern art" and Kabel Bold was recently "adopted by Emporium, San Francisco, as a display letter in all advertisements." Lutetia represented "an entirely new design, neither a copy nor an adaptation of any previous type." Finally, Poliphilus offered historical credibility, "a distinguished letter based on the type used in *Hypnerotomachia Poliphili* printed in 1499" by Venetian printer Aldus Manutius. Continental Types selected faces for import based on their "excellence of design and their immense popularity abroad," and they imported the types themselves, not the matrices, claiming this ensured quality. Yet the imported types were manufactured on the American point system and conformed to American standards for type height, making them not only authentic and visually sophisticated but also easy to use.

Demonstrations of international reach traveled in many directions. An 1892 Barnhart Bros. & Spindler ad in the Wellington, New Zealand, trade journal *Typo* advertised "Complete outfits furnished to printers and publishers all over the world. Presses, Cutters, Type, Materials. Send for specimen books."[30] Clearly, type circulated from the typographic "centers" of Western Europe and North America to the "peripheries" elsewhere. But it also traveled from seemingly peripheral locations back into typographic centers. Bombay's Gujarati Type Foundry's 1937 specimen highlighted their many contributions to typography for Indian languages and dialects.[31] But a contemporaenous English-language ad described how the locally owned and operated foundry "upheld the best traditions of English as well as **Vernacular** type design in India" and claimed the foundry "steadily maintained a reputation equal to that of the best typefoundries of Europe and America."[32] This important aspiration supported the foundry's aim to distribute their type "not only in India but [in] all parts of the world." The booklet *Type Styles of 1924 by the Gujarati Type Foundry*, for instance, had cultivated an entirely Anglophone audience, displaying only roman types with a marked emphasis on Caslon [Fig. 6.23]. High production standards and careful page design, embellished with ornaments printed in color, addressed "a modern practical printer" concerned with setting "modern typography."[33] Such a printer might be an English or American expatriate living in India, or—so the Gujarati Foundry hoped—might import the type into their own country.

Fig 6.23 (below)

Type Styles of 1924 **(Gujarati, Bombay, 1924). The Gujarati Foundry designed and sold a variety of types in multiple Indian scripts including Sanskrit, Gurmuhki, Gujarati, and Devanagari. But they also catered to the Anglophone market in India, as shown in this booklet featuring Caslon Old Face.**

TYPE STYLES
OF 1924
BY
THE GUJARATI TYPE FOUNDRY
Gaiwadi – Girgaon
BOMBAY No. 4

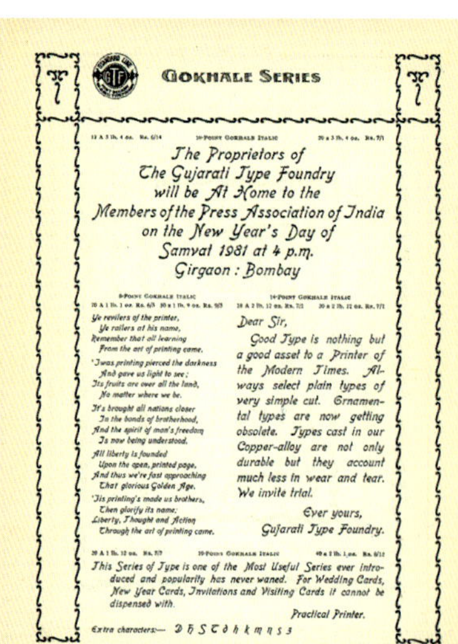

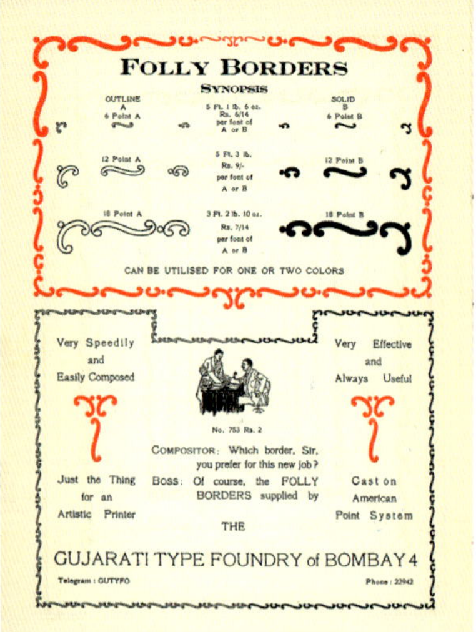

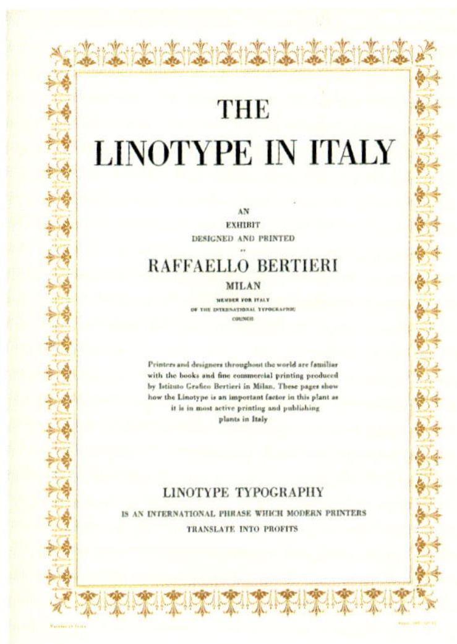

THE
LINOTYPE IN ITALY

AN
EXHIBIT
DESIGNED AND PRINTED
BY
RAFFAELLO BERTIERI
MILAN
MEMBER FOR ITALY
OF THE INTERNATIONAL TYPOGRAPHIC
COUNCIL

Printers and designers throughout the world are familiar with the books and fine commercial printing produced by Istituto Grafico Bertieri in Milan. These pages show how the Linotype is an important factor in this plant as it is in most active printing and publishing plants in Italy

LINOTYPE TYPOGRAPHY
IS AN INTERNATIONAL PHRASE WHICH MODERN PRINTERS
TRANSLATE INTO PROFITS

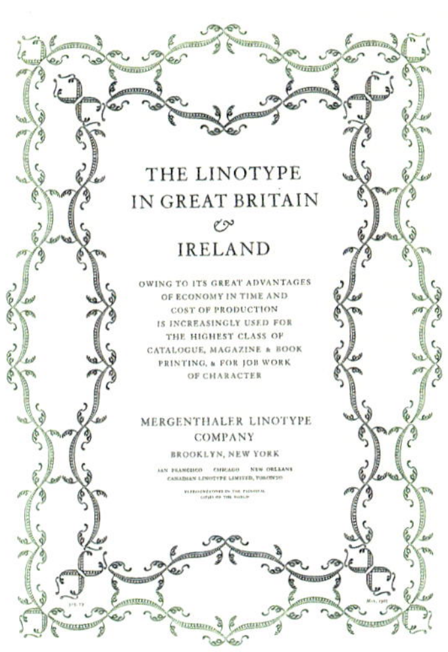

THE LINOTYPE
IN GREAT BRITAIN
&
IRELAND

OWING TO ITS GREAT ADVANTAGES
OF ECONOMY IN TIME AND
COST OF PRODUCTION
IS INCREASINGLY USED FOR
THE HIGHEST CLASS OF
CATALOGUE, MAGAZINE & BOOK
PRINTING, & FOR JOB WORK
OF CHARACTER

MERGENTHALER LINOTYPE
COMPANY
BROOKLYN, NEW YORK
SAN FRANCISCO CHICAGO NEW ORLEANS
CANADIAN LINOTYPE LIMITED, TORONTO

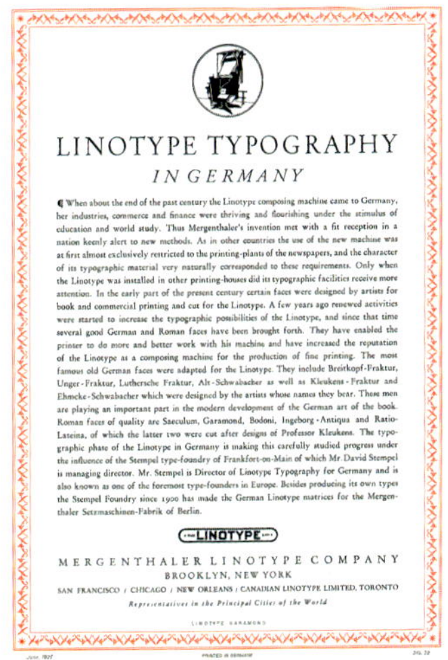

LINOTYPE TYPOGRAPHY
IN GERMANY

¶ When about the end of the past century the Linotype composing machine came to Germany, her industries, commerce and finance were thriving and flourishing under the stimulus of education and world study. Thus Mergenthaler's invention met with a fit reception in a nation keenly alert to new methods. As in other countries the use of the new machine was at first almost exclusively restricted to the printing-plants of the newspapers, and the character of its typographic material very naturally corresponded to these requirements. Only when the Linotype was installed in other printing-houses did its typographic facilities receive more attention. In the early part of the present century certain faces were designed by artists for book and commercial printing and cut for the Linotype. A few years ago renewed activities were started to increase the typographic possibilities of the Linotype, and since that time several good German and Roman faces have been brought forth. They have enabled the printer to do more and better work with his machine and have increased the reputation of the Linotype as a composing machine for the production of fine printing. The most famous old German faces were adapted for the Linotype. They include Breitkopf-Fraktur, Unger-Fraktur, Luthersche Fraktur, Alt-Schwabacher as well as Kleukens-Fraktur and Ehmcke-Schwabacher which were designed by the artists whose names they bear. These men are playing an important part in the modern development of the German art of the book. Roman faces of quality are Saeculum, Garamond, Bodoni, Ingeborg-Antiqua and Ratio-Lateina, of which the latter two were cut after designs of Professor Kleukens. The typographic phase of the Linotype in Germany is making this carefully studied progress under the influence of the Stempel type-foundry of Frankfort-on-Main of which Mr David Stempel is managing director. Mr. Stempel is Director of Linotype Typography for Germany and is also known as one of the foremost type-founders in Europe. Besides producing its own types the Stempel Foundry since 1900 has made the German Linotype matrices for the Mergenthaler Setzmaschinen-Fabrik of Berlin.

LINOTYPE

MERGENTHALER LINOTYPE COMPANY
BROOKLYN, NEW YORK
SAN FRANCISCO / CHICAGO / NEW ORLEANS / CANADIAN LINOTYPE LIMITED, TORONTO
Representatives in the Principal Cities of the World

Fig 6.24 (above)

Booklets from the series *Distinguished Composition on the Linotype* (New York, Linotype, 1927). Linotype emphasized its standardized system and its global reach with a series of booklets devoted to "the Linotype in" a variety of European countries.

While ephemera promoting foundry types stressed authenticity and craftsmanship, hot metal type offered opportunities to emphasize modern, universalizing production methods. Linotype's programmatic investment in dominating a **global**, multilingual market informed the design of their *Distinguished Composition on the Linotype series* (1927). Designed to be stored in a portfolio imprinted with the title, the series of bifolds included *The Linotype in Italy* (April 1927), *The Linotype in Great Britain and Ireland* (May 1927), and *Linotype Typography in Germany* (June 1927). Individually, they did work common to the small-format specimen; each leaflet spoke to its own point of origin and articulated its own message [Fig. 6.24]. In *Italy*, viewers saw "an exhibit designed and printed by Raffaelo Bertieri," whose type designs were released by Neibolo. *Germany*'s cover referenced book page design, text-heavy with a red ornamental border, a nod to the country's identity as the birthplace of (Western European) typographic printing. Even so, Germany was "a nation keenly alert to new methods" in printing. In contrast, *Great Britain and Ireland* focused on the Linotype's "economy in time and cost of production" for a comprehensive range of print matter. Taken together, though, these modest publications demonstrated Linotype's commitment to internationality and geographic reach. As the cover of *Italy* phrased it, "Linotype Typography is an international phrase which modern printers translate into profits." This language connected Linotype to the globalizing ideas expressed in each leaflet and through the series as a whole.

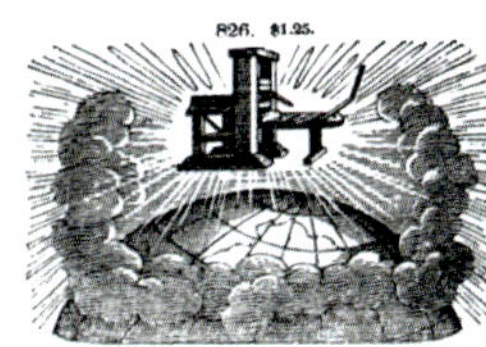

Letterpress printing had long been conceptualized as a **global** technology, as demonstrated by this early nineteenth century adcut from George Bruce.

Linotype's multiscript design program likewise operationalized their universalizing philosophy; the *Linotype* **Syriac** specimen (c.1914-1920) described "reviving a famous ancient language" in its script's three forms. The *One-line Specimen* (1920) explained their different purposes: Estrangela for display, Jacobite for scholarly or historical texts, and Nestorian for contemporary usage. First printed in Rome in 1539, Syriac—a dialect of Aramaic—shares its roots with Hebrew. Linotype's 1914 revival began as a project to facilitate a newspaper for Persian immigrants to the United States.[34] But the value of mechanical typesetting extended beyond the needs of a single client, and the Syriac specimen booklet contextualized the new fonts within a much broader typographic landscape [Fig. 6.25]. "An ancient language,

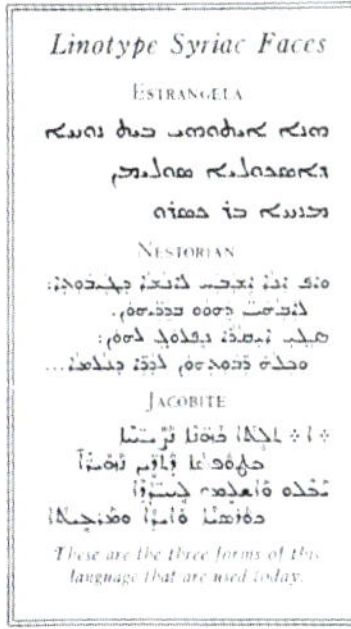

Linotype developed three styles of **Syriac**: the display face Estrangela, the historicist face Jacobite, and the contemporary face Nestorian.

Fig 6.25 (right)

Linotype Syriac **(Linotype, New York, c.1914-20). While its pictorial imagery emphasizes the "ancient" origins of Syriac's three script forms, the specimen takes care to situate the language within a contemporary commercial and scholarly context, showing it used for purposes ranging from newspaper ads to poetry collections.**

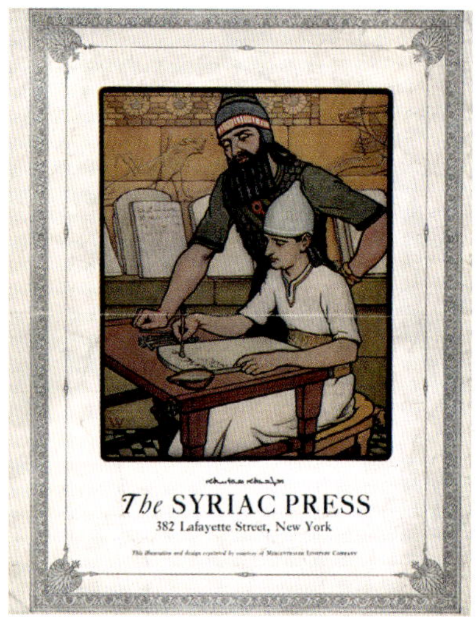

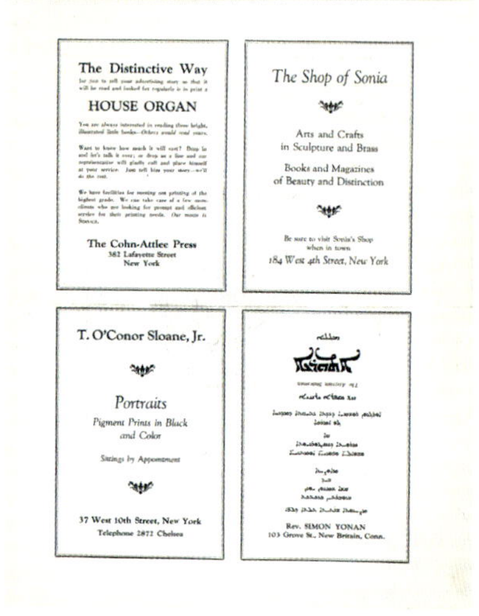

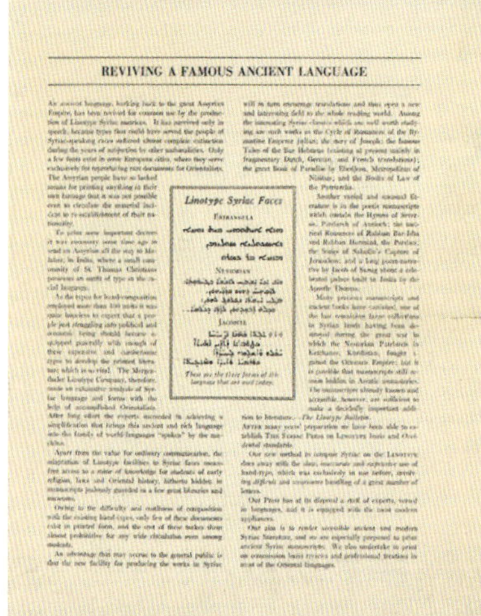

REVIVING A FAMOUS ANCIENT LANGUAGE

Linotype Syriac Faces

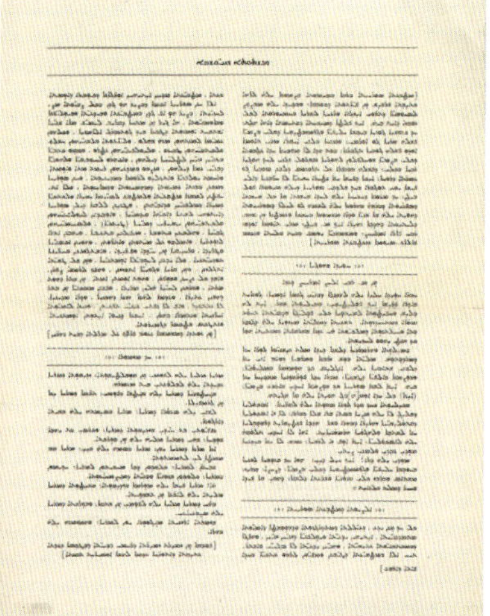

harking back to the great Assyrian Empire, has been revived for common use by the production of Linotype Syriac matrices," the introductory note explained. "After long effort the experts succeeded in achieving a simplification that brings this ancient and rich language into the family of world-languages 'spoken' by the machine." The advantages of this translation were the same for Syriac as for languages using the Latin alphabet; the Linotype did "away with the slow, *inaccurate* and *expensive* use of hand-type."[35]

Linotype's Syriac types addressed a dual audience: scholars of "Oriental studies" and "the Assyrian people," who in the early twentieth century were working to re-establish a national identity and a culture rooted in the **Aramaic** language. Thus the specimen opened with a bilingual advertisement, allowing readers to make a direct visual comparison between the Latin and Syriac types. The choice of an ad, not a historical religious text, underscored the type's contemporary functionality; the original European foundry types of the Syriac alphabet had been designed for scholarly rather than everyday use. Next came six pages of specimens—two columns of type on each page, centered for poetry, justified for prose. Even for viewers unable to read the language, this highlighted the Linotype's capacity to set right-to-left

אִילָן m. *tree.*
אֵימָא f. *terror; fear.*
אֵימָתַי, אֵימַת adv. *when.*
אִין conj. *if.*
אִיקָר, אִיקַר m. *glory.*

Aramaic is a Semetic language that originated in the ancient Syrian region during the middle to late Bronze Age.

reading texts, since paragraphs "end" on the opposite side of the column. Mechanically, reading direction didn't complicate the process of setting slugs, but it remained difficult to accommodate a script face with multiple forms of single letters (depending on if they connect to the characters on their left or their right), tightly-fitting characters (as a matter of legibility rather than aesthetics), and complex **diacritical marks**. As with many of its global projects, Linotype's early efforts with Syriac drew on established models of western European foundry type.[36] But Linotype's "simplification" process imposed even more constraints on translating the alphabet from a manuscript hand into lead type.

Linotype Syriac's covers comment on the process of mechanization, visualizing the purpose of Linotype's "universal machine, adapted to the use of thirty-five different languages." The front cover pictures a Linotype machine with a Latin-alphabet keyboard, a familiar image used across instruction manuals, equipment catalogues, type specimens, and trade journal ads. The monochromatic steel engraving deploys a linear, mechanized visual language. The back cover reproduces an illustration advertising the Syriac Press of New York. The polychromatic, halftone-printed image shows two Assyrian men in traditional dress, at work producing an ancient text. The Syriac caption roughly translates to "Introducing the Syriac printing press." Yet the older man supervises the younger as he inscribes text onto a stone tablet in preparation for carving the letters by hand. The image historicizes its subjects, placing them at an unspecified moment in ancient history. Their **text-production** process further obfuscates the chronology, conflating three distinct processes: manuscript production, stone carving, and typographic printing. The image juxtaposes the historical, exoticized human hand with the precision, mechanization, and standardization of the Linotype. This pictorialized Linotype's rationale, which argued that non-mechanized production methods were historically significant but misaligned with contemporary needs; therefore, they must be replaced.

Cultural specificity and stereotyping

As the Syriac Press specimen demonstrates, metal types in national or regional scripts provided opportunities for both colonizers and indigenous users to exploit the power of mass-producing printed texts. Orientalist gentleman-scholars and Aramaic-speaking immigrants, for instance, almost certainly saw different possibilities in a press equipped with Syriac type. Capitalist advertising culture offered yet another route to constructing a sense of international typographic culture, seen in ephemera promoting **culturally specific typefaces**.[37] Exotic typefaces, as they were known then, weren't new. But ephemeral formats offered a chance for foundries to play up their distinctive features and their role within printing and commercial design.

Barnhart Brothers & Spindler's *Modernism in Advertising* (c.1928) curated a selection of typefaces "of the modernistic aspect." Many fed the contemporary taste for Art Deco, but interspersed among faces like Boul Mich and Cubist Bold were a selection of "extraordinary" faces intended to read as exotic or global [Fig. 6.26]. Chief among these were Japanet, Bamboo, and Peking (a historical, westernized spelling of Beijing). The sample copy explicitly addressed the role such typefaces played in advertising. Japanet "bestow[s] charm" while the "romance and adventure of the East catches the imagination

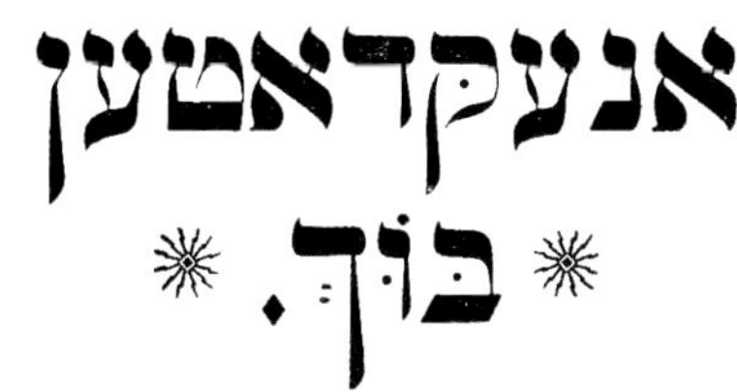

عدّ الاقدمون الجوّ عنصرًا بسيطًا من العناصر الاربعة التي زعموا العالم كلهُ مركبًا منها وظنّ بعضهم الروح جزءًا منهُ ولعلّ ابا الطيب المتنبي اراد ذلك بقولهِ

Many languages rely on **diacritical marks** above, below, or adjacent to alphabetic characters for word meaning and legibility, among them Hebrew and Arabic. Because the Latin alphabet uses diacritical marks differently, Western European typographic design principles and technologies have historically struggled to adapt to languages requiring their frequent use. Hebrew title from *Anecdote Book* (M. Ḳuḳilshteyn, 1920) and passage from Arabic Mission Press specimen (1887).

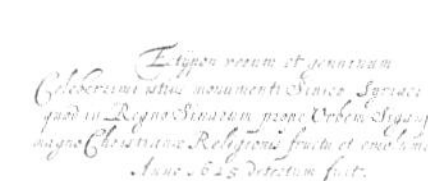

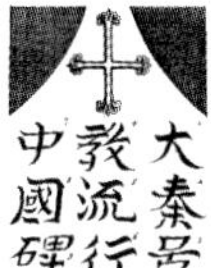

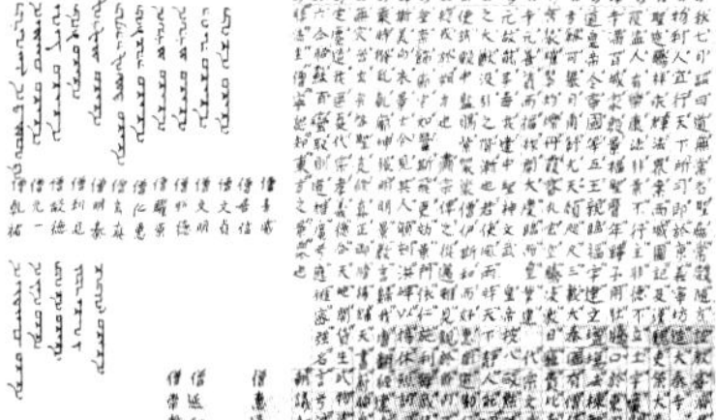

Text-production takes many forms: stone carvings, hand-copied manuscripts, woodblock printing, copperplate engraving, lithography, and typographic printing. This plate from a treatise on the Chinese language, printed by the Dutch printer Johannes Janssonius van Waesberge for Holy Roman Emperor Leopold I (1667), solves the problem of Chinese typography by employing copperplatae engraving instead. In China at this time, xylography (woodblock printing) was the common means of commercial text production.

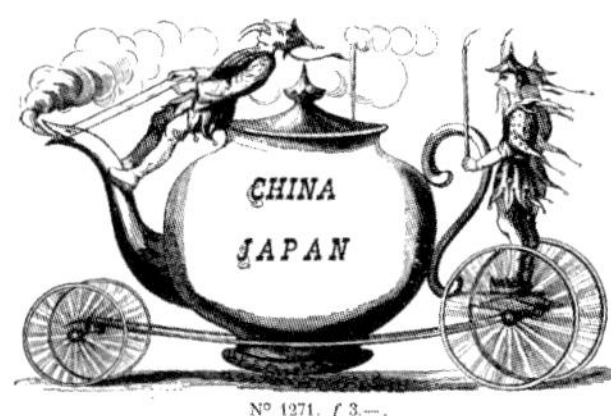

Bamboo
Aa Bb Cc Dd Ee Ff Gg Hh Ii
Jj Kk Ll Mm Nn Oo Pp Qq
Rr Ss Tt Uu Vv Ww Xx Yy
Zz & $1234567890 .-:;'!?

Mandarin 18 pt Caps
ABCDEFGHIJKLMNO'
PQRSTUVWXYZ.,:;'!?
ABCDEFGHIJKLMNOPQRSTUV
WXYZ&.,;'!? 12 pt Caps

Pekin-Dormer—18 pt
Aa Bb Cc Dd Ee Ff Gg Hhh Ii Jj k Ll
Mmm Nn Oo p Qq Rr Ss Tt Uu Vv Ww
Xx Yy Zz & $1234567890 .,-:;'!?

Culturally specific typefaces play on stereotypes to connote cultural identity exoticism, or otherness. Sojin Kim and Sumi Kim coined the term in their 1993 essay "Typecast" for the Lubalin Center's *Lift & Seperate* catalog, though such typefaces have been popular since the nineteenth century.

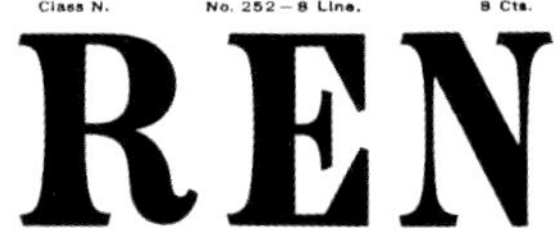

Latins are slab serifs with triangular serifs; this example is from Hamilton Wood Type.

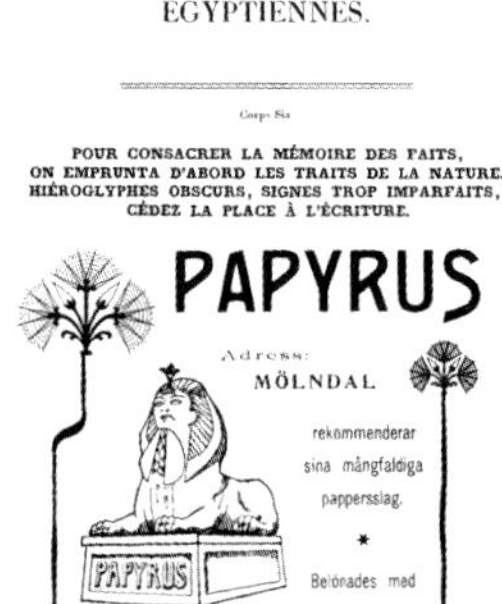

Egyptians, or slab serifs, have thick serifs and no bracketing between stem and serif. The example above was acquired by the Enschedé foundry from Didot. Period ads often referenced ancient Egypt (above).

and creates interest" in the customer. The sample ad demonstrated how Japanet could be used to sell "toys for good little boys" from a company specializing in "Oriental" imports. Stephenson Blake drew on a different visual language to sell their stencil face Tea Chest (c.1950). The brochure's cover deployed an advertising cut of a Chinese man in a conical hat, selling tea in a pagoda-framed Chinese port with a sailing ship in the distance. Robert Harling's 1939 stencil face wasn't inherently "Oriental," but the image explained the typeface's name by drawing a connection between the typeface and the stencils used to label crates of tea for international export. Loose association to stereotypes carried more weight than accuracy or cultural sensitivity.

Cultural stereotyping played an important role in Stephenson Blake's *Rich Fruity Latins* (1962), as well. **Latin** typefaces, identifiable by their triangular serifs, were popular internationally during the 1860s–80s.[38] The Rich Fruity Latins cover illustration showed a Latino man holding a sombrero, a bunch of grapes, and a drawstring money bag full of typographic sorts spilling across the top of the page [Fig 6.27]. The loose connection to Latin America as a center for fruit-growing provided the visual logic for the entire specimen, and the cheerful Latino character appeared throughout, peddling his typographic goods. For instance, Chisel (1935), an engravers' face designed by Robert Harling,[39] showed the illustrated character holding a freshly-picked apple alongside the headline "Pick Where You Will."

Egyptian (slab serif) typefaces drew on imagined histories, establishing connections between Egyptian archeological discoveries and modern, geometric typeface design. A 1916 design manual advised students that when "the Egyptian style is adapted to modern designs" the result is "[d]irectness, simplicity, and severity. "The "vast difference between" cultural conditions rendered Egyptian decorative motifs suitable for limited contemporary use.[40] But Egyptian typefaces suffered from no such limitations. Rather, they had a reputation for legibility and a strong visual presence in a crowded and fast-paced advertising environment. "Modern method finds Karnak good for contrast and display in large circulars and ads," Ludlow explained in a 1933 supplement. Their geometric construction suggested modernity. Despite an origin story connected to Napoleon's nineteenth century military campaigns in Egypt, some specimens emphasized a direct connection to ancient Egypt. Intertype advertised Cairo (1933) as "a modern type face" that "interprets the newest thought in present-day typography" in copy framed by Egyptian obelisks and pharaohs' funeral masks.[41] Similarly, Deberny & Peignot consistently advertised Pharaon (1933) with a flat, graphic image of ancient Egyptians carrying a canopic chest [Fig. 6.28]. Other ads leveraged photographic images of discoveries at archeological digs. While the images suggested historical origins, accompanying texts cast the typeface itself as inherently modern. Both Cairo and Pharon responded to Rudolf Weiss' successful slab serif Memphis (1929) for Stempel.[42] All three faces' specimens demonstrate the consistency of the visual language used to connect these popular faces to ancient Egypt.

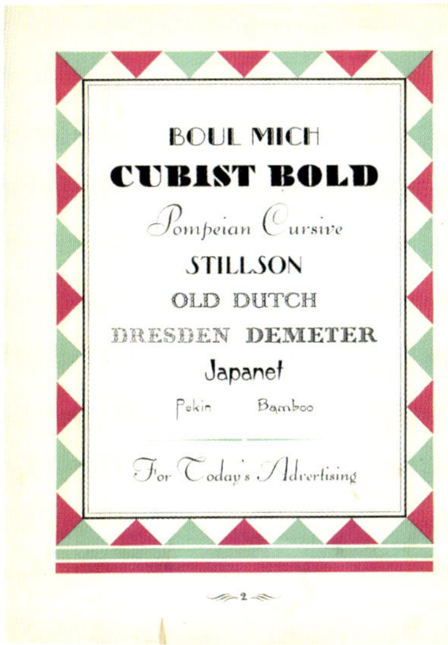

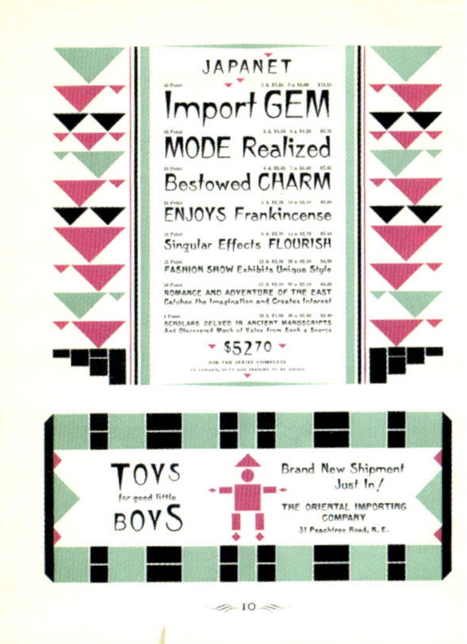

Fig 6.26 (left)

Modernism in Advertising **(BB&S, Chicago, 1928). The BB&S typeface Japanet was one face among many designed and circulated by Western European and North American founders to meet a demand for so-called "Oriental" types in the wake of art movements like Art Nouveau and Aestheticism, both of which embraced *chinoiserie*.**

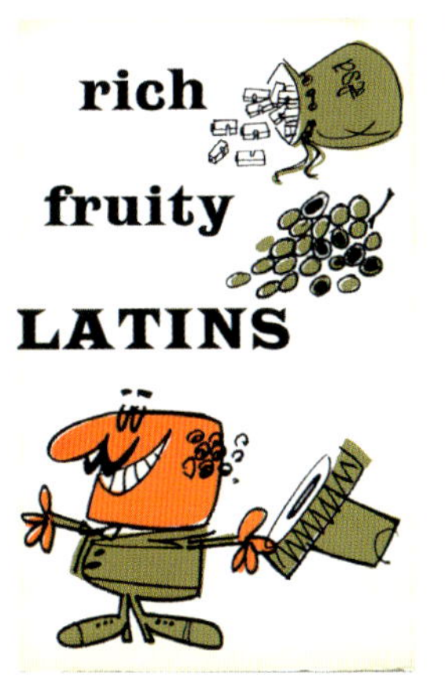

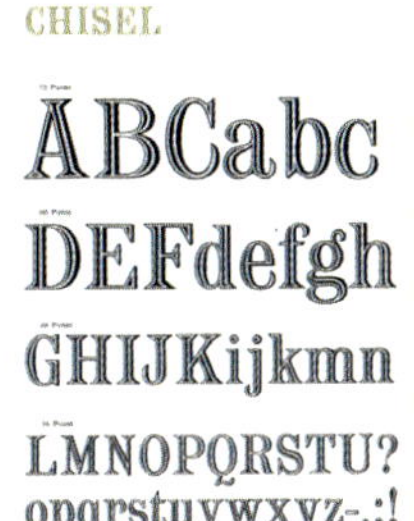

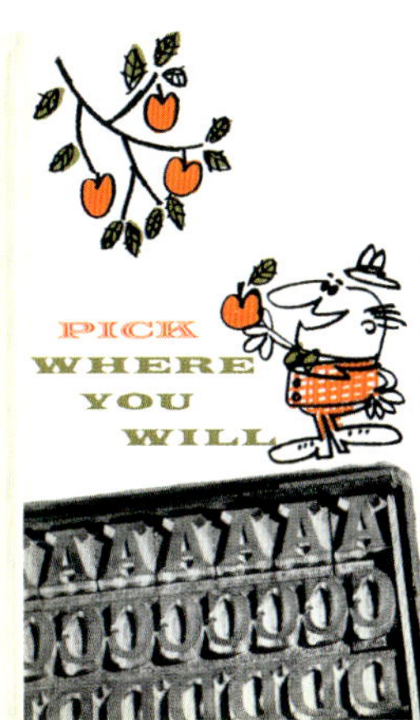

Fig 6.27 (left)

Rich Fruity Latins **(Stephenson Blake, London, 1962). Though Stephenson Blake was instrumental in introducing what came to be known as Latin typefaces to the English market during the latter half of the nineteenth century, Latin types had nothing to do with Latin American visual culture. Rather, the name describes lettter-forms with terminals, including serifs, that are often triangular and sometimes concave.**

Fig 6.28 (below)

Pharaon (Deberney & Peignot, Paris, 1933; top) and Cairo (Intertype, New York, c.1950). Slab serifs were known as Egyptians because of their mostly imagined ties to Egyptian archeological discoveries, and this association provided context for a wide range of promotional campaigns in the 1920s and 30s.

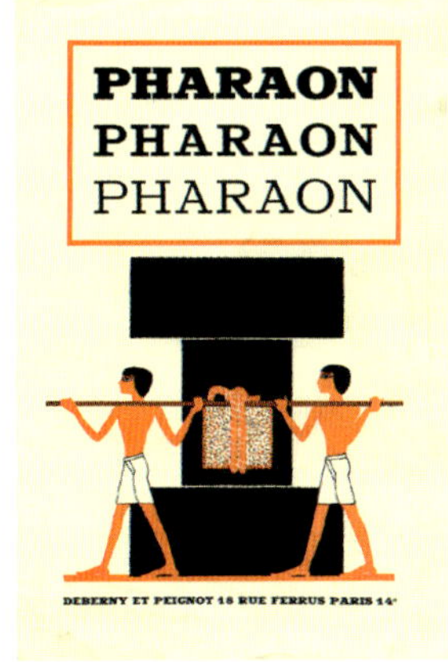

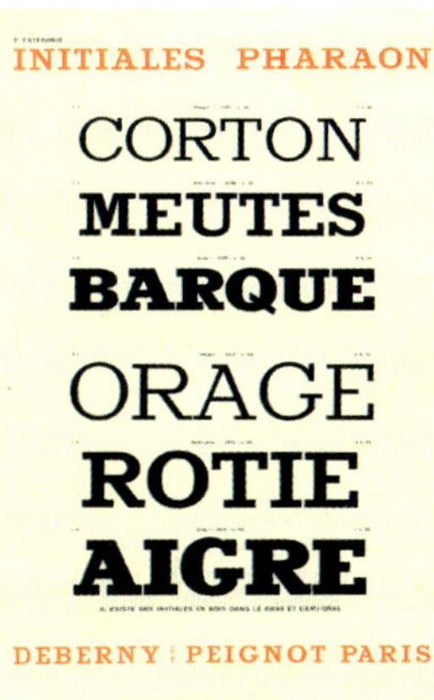

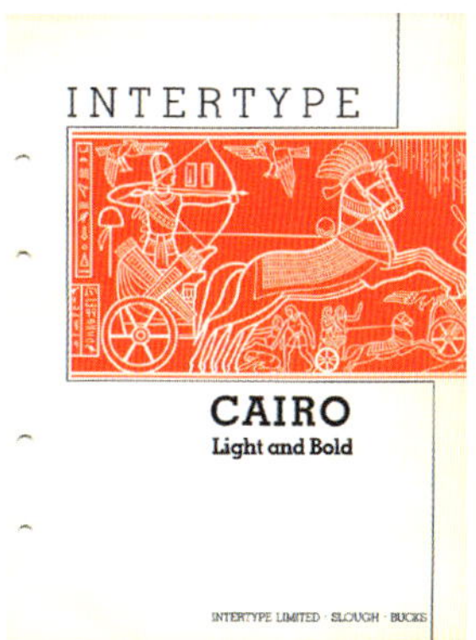

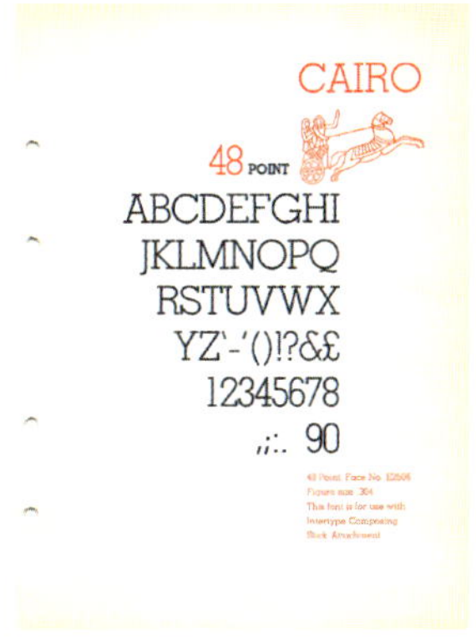

Local, specific, and vernacular forms—Cyrillic and Hebrew

Ephemeral formats were also useful for displaying infrequently used or specialist typefaces. This included scripts marketed to North American or Western European printers whose work demanded them. The caveat "available upon request" reflected the specificity of their target market. Linotype's *Cyrillic* specimen (c.1934) was bi-lingual; German played a minor role, captioning typefaces with name and size [Fig. 6.29]. The remainder of the text was Russian, set in the Cyrillic alphabet. The sample copy recounted Ottmar Mergenthaler's life and described the mechanical properties of his Linotype, as well as displaying full alphabets at different sizes. The booklet's object qualities imparted a sophisticated, loosely historicist air: heavy paper, generous page margins, red headers and footers, and a rich chocolate-brown cover foil-stamped with an image of a Linotype matrix. Inside the booklet, a restrained aesthetic prevailed, featuring one- and two-column display texts set in black type with a hairline divider between columns. Linotype's universalizing corporate program remains in evidence; the page design diverges very little from the Cyrillic specimen in the 1915 *Book of Type Styles*.

Ideological attitudes reflected in specimen design extended beyond those directly connected to printing. Another Cyrillic specimen printed in Germany, *Russische Schriften* (1940), included the *Buch und Tiefdruck* [Book & Gravure Company Ltd.] logotype in blackletter on its cover [Fig. 6.30]. At the time, this typographic decision aligned with the values of the Berlin printing firm, which worked with the Nazi party consistently; the blackletter face signaled Germanic cultural heritage.[43] Yet the Cyrillic body copy throughout repeated descriptions of the company's printing equipment, specific in its technical vocabulary but neutral in its political language. Latin-alphabet captions labeled faces by size and style. The Cyrillic types embraced a variety of aesthetics. *Mediaeval nonpareille* is a small, lightweight text face with Arabic numerals; *Halbfette Hermes-grotesk 5 cicero* is a semi-bold sans-serif that registers as contemporary and geometric. Formulaic page design organized all of the type samples into one or two columns, with red headers and display text, black body copy, and hairline rules to divide the space of the page. The specimen offered no explanatory preface, and its page design differed little from contemporaries in Germany and abroad. So it's difficult

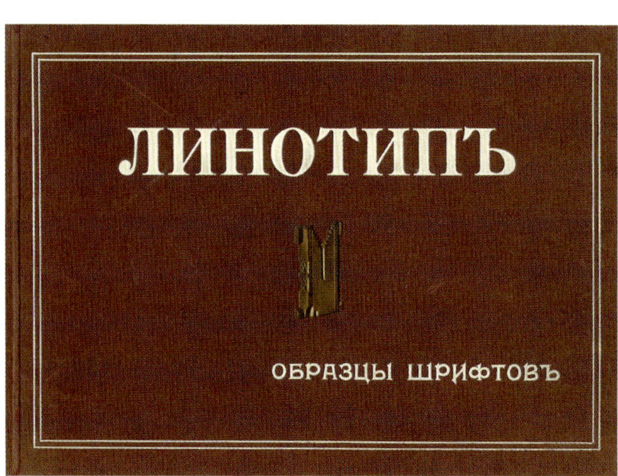

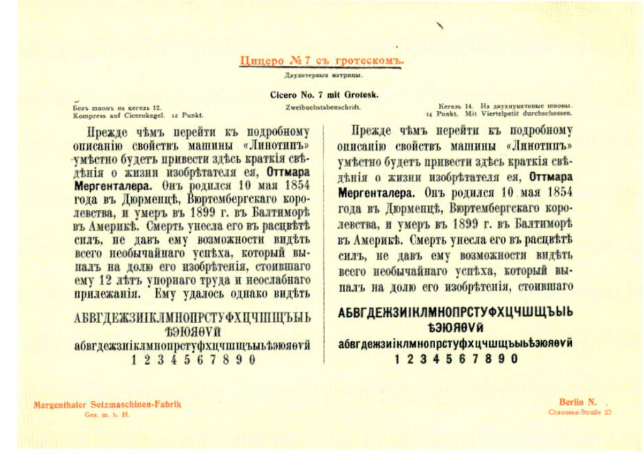
Цицеро № 7 съ гротескомъ.
Двухлитерныя матрицы.

Cicero No. 7 mit Grotesk.
Zweibuchstabenschrift.

Безъ шпонъ на кегель 12.
Kompress auf Cicerokegel. 12 Punkt.

Прежде чѣмъ перейти къ подробному описанію свойствъ машины «Линотипъ» умѣстно будетъ привести здѣсь краткія свѣдѣнія о жизни изобрѣтателя ея, **Оттмара Мергенталера.** Онъ родился 10 мая 1854 года въ Дюрменцѣ, Вюртембергскаго королевства, и умеръ въ 1899 г. въ Балтиморѣ въ Америкѣ. Смерть унесла его въ расцвѣтѣ силъ, не давъ ему возможности видѣть всего необычайнаго успѣха, который выпалъ на долю его изобрѣтенія, стоившаго ему 12 лѣтъ упорнаго труда и неослабнаго прилежанія. Ему удалось однако видѣть

АБВГДЕЖЗИIКЛМНОПРСТУФХЦЧШЩЪЫЬ
ѢЭЮЯѲѴЙ
абвгдежзиiклмнопрстуфхцчшщъыьѣэюяѳѵй
1 2 3 4 5 6 7 8 9 0

Кегель 14. На двухпунктовые шпоны.
14 Punkt. Mit Viertelpetit durchschossen.

Прежде чѣмъ перейти къ подробному описанію свойствъ машины «Линотипъ» умѣстно будетъ привести здѣсь краткія свѣдѣнія о жизни изобрѣтателя ея, **Оттмара Мергенталера.** Онъ родился 10 мая 1854 года въ Дюрменцѣ, Вюртембергскаго королевства, и умеръ въ 1899 г. въ Балтиморѣ въ Америкѣ. Смерть унесла его въ расцвѣтѣ силъ, не давъ ему возможности видѣть всего необычайнаго успѣха, который выпалъ на долю его изобрѣтенія, стоившаго

АБВГДЕЖЗИIКЛМНОПРСТУФХЦЧШЩЪЫЬ
ѢЭЮЯѲѴЙ
абвгдежзиiклмнопрстуфхцчшщъыьѣэюяѳѵй
1 2 3 4 5 6 7 8 9 0

Mergenthaler Setzmaschinen-Fabrik
Ges. m. b. H.

Berlin N.
Chaussee-Straße 23

Fig 6.29 (below)

Linotype Cyrillic **(Linotype, Berlin office, c.1934). Ephemeral formats accommodated the production of specimens devoted to a specific language or alphabet infrequently used in the average Western European or North American print shop. This mid-1930s Linotype Cyrillic specimen is beautifully produced, but otherwise aligns with the generic visual treatment offered global scripts in Linotype's 1915 comprehensive specimen.**

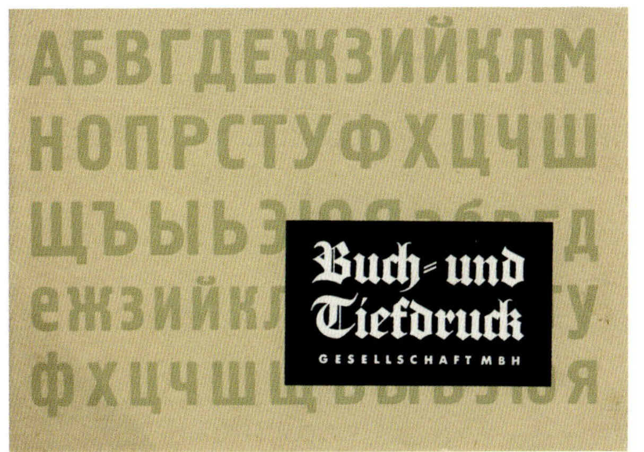

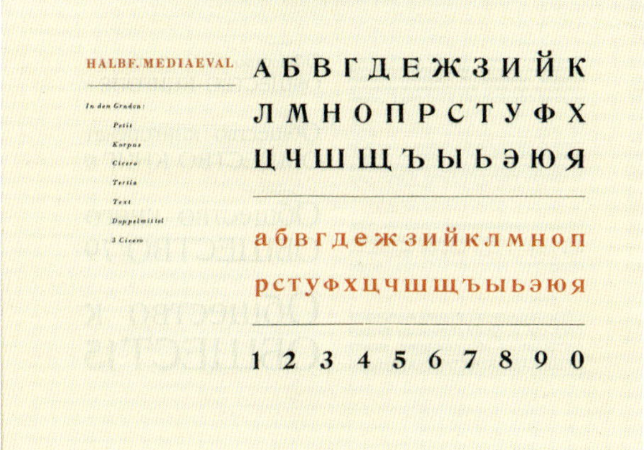

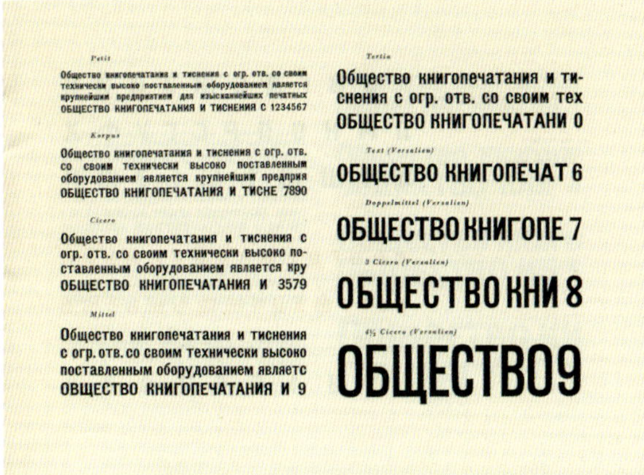

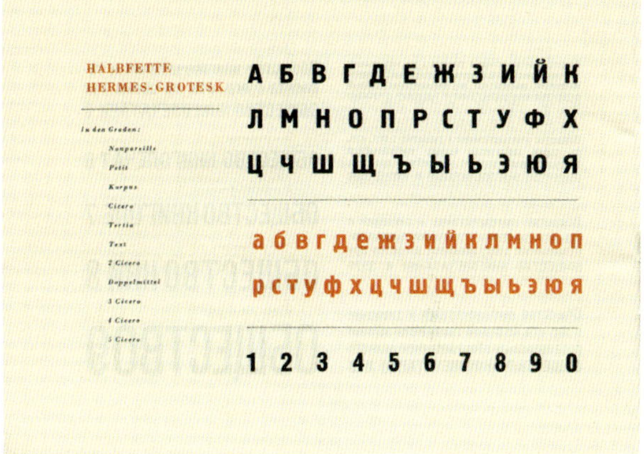

to identify the intended audience. Perhaps the type addressed the émigré community which arrived in Germany after the Russian Revolution of 1917, or perhaps it was intended for Nazi **propaganda** to be distributed in Russia, where historically Germans were a large ethnic minority. Or, possibly, it was meant as a display of the international reach and wide stylistic and linguistic selection of the printing company.

At the same time it fostered the Nazi party's growth, interwar Germany was also a center for Hebrew typography, with multiple foundries releasing newly-designed Hebrew types. A flourishing interwar Hebrew scholarly community and active Zionist organizations prioritized the revival of the Hebrew alphabet and its application to contemporary uses, including publications in vernacular Yiddish.[44] Ludwig & Mayer's specimen for *Aharoni* (1936), a typeface designed by Tuvia Aharoni (1935), deployed traditional motifs of Jewish cultural heritage, like the olive branch and ewer. But it also emphasized present-day, commercial use, showing a Frigidaire ad, business stationery suites, and a children's book. By combining traditional and contemporary uses within a single, small specimen, these ephemeral publications highlighted the adaptability of Hebrew types to diverse printing needs [Fig. 6.31].

Fig 6.30 (above)

***Russische Schriften* (Buch und Tiefdruck, Berlin, 1940). Type specimens encapsulated their makers' worldviews and ideologies, as with this specimen produced by a printing firm closely associated with Germany's Nazi party. The blackletter title on the front cover frames the Cyrillic types within as part of a Germanic visual language.**

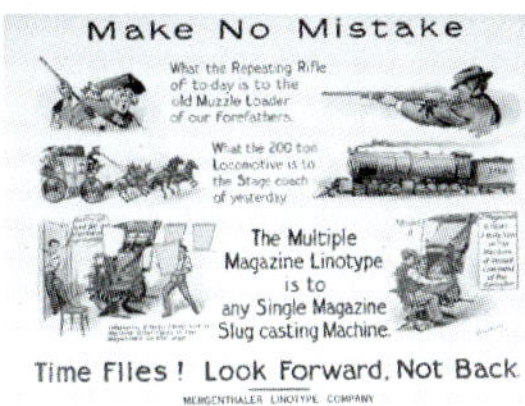

Propaganda at its most basic level is information design to convince viewers of a specific ideology. This 1914 Linotype ad associates mechanical progress in typesetting with the American military's global impact, for instance.

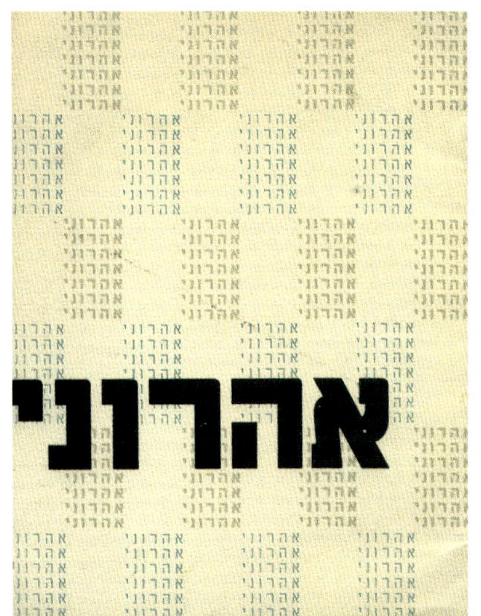

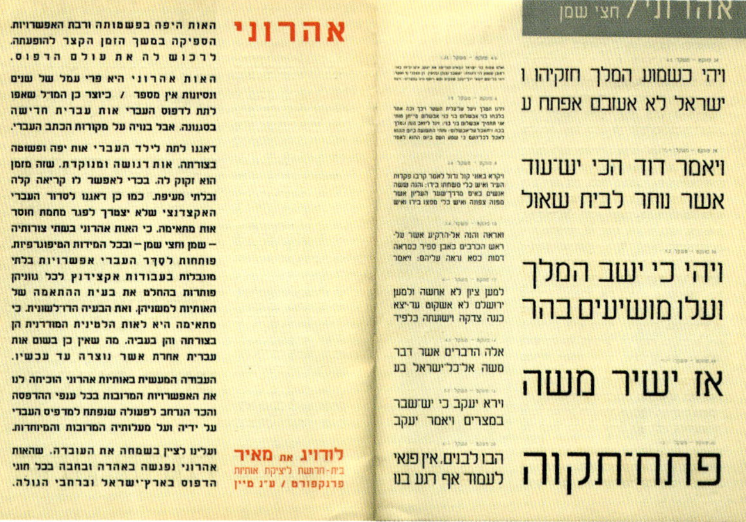

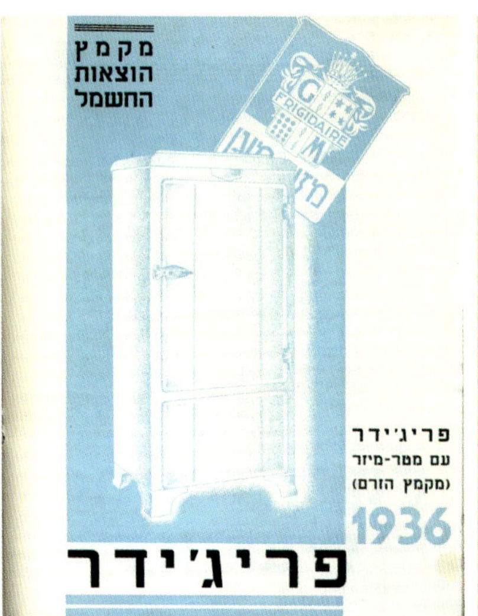

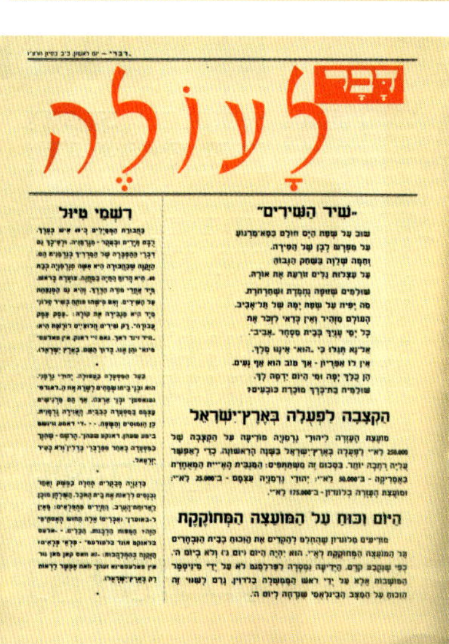

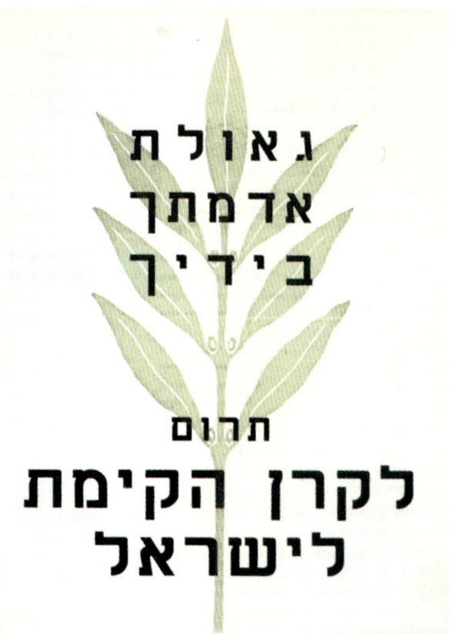

Fig 6.31 (above)

***Aharoni* (Ludwig & Mayer, Frankfurt, 1936). This leaflet publicizing Tuvia Aharoni's Aharoni typeface (1935) contextualizes Hebrew as a language at once historical and contemporary. Traditional motifs associated with Judaism mingle with refrigerator ads.**

Post-war, many surviving Jewish type designers emigrated to Palestine/Israel, where the Bezalel School of Art and the Hadassah Apprentice School of Printing taught calligraphy, typography, and design. The Hadassah school in Jerusalem, where émigré type designer Henri Friedlaender taught a new generation of Hebrew printers, produced a specimen of the Jerusalem Type Foundry's types (1959). Throughout, the simple page design consisted of single columns of type, divided by horizontal rules and labeled with the types' names and point sizes in both Hebrew and English [Fig. 6.32]. Friedlaender's own Hadassah Hebrew (1958), released by Lettergieterij Amsterdam after decades of research and development, wasn't represented in the specimen.[45] Instead, it cataloged earlier faces like Aharoni (Tuvia Aharoni for Ludwig & Mayer, 1935), Frank-Rüehl (Rafael Frank for C.F. Rühl, 1910), and Haim (Jan Le Witt for Jan Idźkowski i S-ka in Warsaw, 1929). It also included Gill Hebrew, a typeface that's since developed a reputation for showing how Hebrew types *shouldn't* be designed. Created by Eric Gill after his visit to Palestine in 1934, it was cast in the 1950s by Gill aficionado Moshe Spitzer, who established the Jerusalem Type Foundry (1951).[46] A spread including Arabic numerals

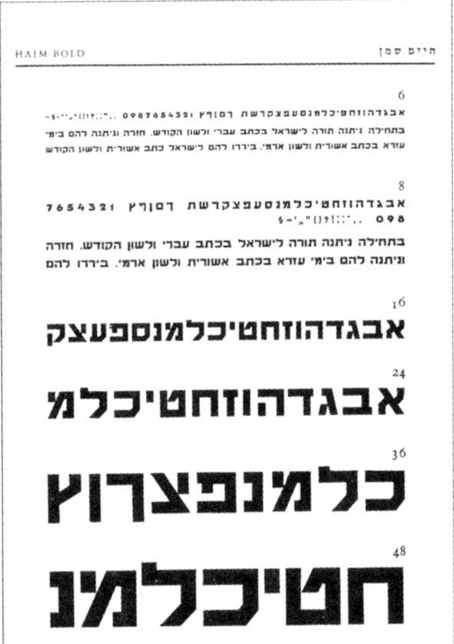

hints at one challenge of Hebrew typography: **Latinization** of the letterforms significantly distorts their shapes relative to Hebrew calligraphy, but renders them more visually compatible with Latin texts and Arabic numerals on the printed page. Gill Hebrew resolved this tension unsuccessfully, prioritizing Latinization at the expense of legibility. Regardless of the relative merits of each of the types it included, the Jerusalem specimen carried Hebrew types to their users efficiently and cost-effectively.

Conclusion

Small, ephemeral specimens circulated separately from larger, bound books. Ephemera traveled more easily, cultivated more specific messages, and perhaps most importantly cost less than bound books. Ephemeral publications served multiple purposes. They taught typographic history, crafted identities for individual types, advertised to specialized audiences, revitalized historical languages for contemporary use, and highlighted the flexibility and modernity of a foundry's wares. Ephemeral formats allowed the makers of type to respond to market changes quickly, a helpful capacity given the rapidly changing typographic technologies of the twentieth century.

Fig 6.32 (above)

רשימת אותיות עבריות / *Catalogue of Hebrew Types* (Jerusalem Type Foundry, Jerusalem, 1959). Printed by students at the Hadassah school, the Jerusalem Type Foundry's specimen displayed Hebrew types crafted, for the most part, in Europe. Combining Arabic numerals with Hebrew words demonstrates the tension between Latinization (for compatible multilingual printing) and traditional Hebrew lettering conventions.

The New Phonetic Alphabet

Latinization is the process by which writing sytems are altered to conform more closely to the Latin alphabet and its design conventions and technologies. The New Phonetic Chinese Alphabet (1921), introduced as a tool to facilite more efficient typographic printing and thus Christian proselytization, is a prime example.

1 McKeller, Smith & Jordan, *1796-1896*, 93, 95.

2 David Pankow's introduction to twentieth century ephemeral specimens shouldn't be missed. David Pankow and John Dreyfus, *The Art of the Type Specimen in the Twentieth Century* (New York: Typophiles, 1993).

3 Mergenthaler Linotype Company, *Specimen Book of Linotype Faces* (New York: Linotype, c.1939), n.p..

4 Philip B. Meggs and Rob Carter, *Typographic Specimens: The Great Typefaces* (John Wiley & Sons, 1993), 118.

5 Theodore Low De Vinne, *Historic Printing Types* (New York: De Vinne & Co., 1886), https://archive.org/details/historicprinting00devirich; Bigmore and Wyman, *A Bibliography of Printing* v.1-3, 1880; Talbot Baines Reed, *A History of the Old English Letter Foundries* (London: E. Stock, 1887); Duff, *Early English Printing*; Updike, Printing Types, 1922; Morison, *A Brief Survey of Printing*; Douglas C. McMurtrie, Le Moreau-Le-Jeune; *A Typographical Specimen with an Introduction* (New York: McMurtrie, 1919), http://hdl.handle.net/2027/uiug.30112046998057; Pierre Cot and Douglas C. McMurtrie, *The Pierre Cot Type Specimen of 1707: With a Reproduction in Facsimile of the Original Specimen* (Chicago: R.O. Ballou, 1924), https://catalog.hathitrust.org/Record/001161141; Christophe Plantin and Douglas C. McMurtrie, *Plantin's Index Characterum of 1567: Facsimile Reprint with an Introduction by Douglas C. McMurtrie* (New York: McMurtrie, 1924), https://books.google.com/books?id=catCAQAAMAAJ&source=gbs_navlinks_s; Jean Jannon, *The 1621 specimen of Jean Jannon, with an introduction by Paul Beaujon [Beatrice Warde]* (Paris, 1927); Edward Rowe Mores et al., *A Dissertation upon English Typographical Founders and Foundries* (New York: Grolier Club, 1924).

6 Cost, *The Bentons*, 185-256.

7 Henry Lewis Bullen, "Observations on Type Designs," *Inland Printer* 71, no. 6 (September 1923): 833; McMurtrie, *Type Design*, 12.

8 American Type Founders Co., *Specimen Book and Catalogue 1923*, n.p.

9 Bullen, "Observations on Type Designs," 833.

10 Redfield-Kendrick-Odell Co., *A Printed Specimen of Caslon Old Style Type, with Appropriate Ornaments* (New York: Redfield-Kendrick-Odell, 1921), n.p., http://archive.org/details/printedspecimeno00redf.

11 Frederic W. Goudy, *Typologia : Studies in Type Design & Type Making, with Comments on the Invention of Typography, the First Types, Legibility, and Fine Printing* (Berkeley: University of California Press, 1977), 34, http://archive.org/details/bub_gb_s5Js_NPRflwC.

12 Tracy, *Letters of Credit*, 143.

13 Einat Adi, *New Types: Three Pioneers of Hebrew Graphic Design*, ed. Ada Wardi (Jerusalem: Israel Museum, 2016), 175-76.

14 Heller, "Berthold's 1924 Hebrew Type Catalogue," 14.

15 Phillip Messner, "Hebrew Type Design in the Context of the Book Art Movement and New Typograph," in *New Types*, ed. Ada Wardi (Jerusalem: Israel Museum, 2016), 26-27. See also Messner's biographical account of Baruch, *New Types*, 308.

16 This book is digitized for online viewing at the Israeli National Library. Gershom Cohen, *The Prague Haggadah of Passover* (1527); https://rosetta.nli.org.il/delivery/DeliveryManagerServlet?dps_pid=IE25975202.

17 Messner, "Hebrew Type Design," 27.

18 Edmund Geiger Gress, *Fashions in American Typography, 1780 to 1930: With Brief Illustrated Stories of the Life and Environment of the American People in Seven Periods, and Demonstrations of E.G.G.'s Fresh Note American Period Typography* (New York: Harper & Bros, 1931), v.

19 Virginia Smith, "Chapter 4: Native and Imported Forms," in *Forms in Modernism: The Unity of Typography, Architecture & the Design Arts 1920s-1970s*, 2005, 84-86.

20 *Typographische Mitteilungen* [Typographical News] 25, no. 12 (December 1928), n.p.; *Typographische Mitteilungen* 27, no. 6 (June 1930), n.p.

21 Barnhart Brothers & Spindler, *Type Faces, Border Designs, Typecast Ornaments, Brass Rule, Superior Specialties, Machines and Materials, Cabinet Equipment* (Chicago: Barnhart Bros. & Spindler, 1925), 347.

22 *Microgramma: A Neibolo Type Series* (Torino: Neibolo, 1952).

23 *Eurostile* [specimens], (Torino: Neibolo, 1962) and (Torino: Neibolo, 1965).

24 Binny & Ronaldson and Rollins, *The Specimen Books of Binny and Ronaldson*, 13-14.

25 MoMA's digital archive contains their 1935 press release: https://www.moma.org/momaorg/shared/pdfs/docs/press_archives/238/releases/MOMA_1934-35_0053_1935-05-15_16-5-15-35.pdf

26 *Printing: An Essay by William Morris & Emery Walker* (Park Ridge [IL]: Village Press, 1903), 17, https://archive.org/details/printing.essayby00morrrich.

27 Megan L. Benton, *Beauty and the Book: Fine Editions and Cultural Distinction in America* (New Haven: Yale University Press, 2000). Megan L. Benton, *Beauty and the Book: Fine Editions and Cultural Distinction in America* (New Haven: Yale University Press, 2000).

28 Continental Typefounders Association, *Specimen Book of Continental Types* (New York: [Continental Typefounders], 1929), https://catalog.hathitrust.org/Record/100952584..

29 Amsterdam Continental Types, *A Handbook of Types* (New York: Amsterdam Continental Types, 1960), 2..

30 Barnhart Bros. & Spindler ad, *Typo* 6, no. 61 (30 Jan 1892): 6.

31 Gujarati Type Foundry, *Book of Type Faces and Printers' Auxiliaries* (Bombay: Gujurati Type Foundry, 1937).

32 The online archive Advertisements in India has digitized this ad; http://www.advertisementsindia.com/2011/04/gujarati-type-foundry/.

33 Gujarati Type Foundry, *New Faces in Types & Borders; Cast in Copper Alloy on the American Point System* ... (Bombay: Gujurati Type Foundry, 1924).

34 J. F. Coakley, *The Typography of Syriac: A Historical Catalogue of Printing Types, 1537-1958* (New Castle [DE]: Oak Knoll Press, 2006), 4, 41-43, 135, 251-57.

35 Mergenthaler Linotype Company and Samuel A. Jacobs, *Reviving a Famous Ancient Language Linotype Syriac Faces: Estrangela, Nestorian, Jacobite*. (New York: Syriac Press, 1914), 1, http://www.columbia.edu/cgi-bin/cul/resolve?clio12719865.

36 J. F. Coakley, *The Typography of Syriac: A Historical Catalogue of Printing Types, 1537-1958* (New Castle [DE]: Oak Knoll Press, 2006), 43-44, 202-6.

37 This term originates with Sojin Kim and Somi Kim, "Typecast: Meaning, Culture, and Identity in the Alphabet Omelet," in *Lift and Separate: Graphic Design and the Quote Vernacular Unqote*, ed. Barbara Glauber (New York: Herb Lubalin Study Center of Design and Typography, 1993), 30-37.

38 Gray and Nasher, *Nineteenth Century Ornamented Typefaces*, 80-84, 197.

39 Roy Millington, *Stephenson Blake: The Last of the Old English Typefounders* (New Castle [DE]: Oak Knoll Press, 2002), 174.

40 International Correspondence Schools, *Design Motifs: Design Composition ; Space Filling ; Color in Design ; Historic Styles* (International Textbook Company, 1916), 13-15.

41 Intertype advertisement, *Typographical Journal* no. 82 (1933), 408.

42 Ron Eason and Sarah Rookledge, *Rookledge's International Directory of Type Designers: A Biographical Handbook* (Surrey: Sarema Press, 1991), 166.

43 Jeremy Aynsley, "Politics and Design: Reaction and Consolidation, 1933-45," in *Designing Modern Germany*, 2009, 121-23.

44 Brenner, "Milgroym, Rimon and Interwar Jewish Bilingualism."

45 Henri Friedlaender, *The Making of Hadassah Hebrew* (Jerusalem: [Typophiles], 1975).

46 Liron Lavi-Turkenich, "Lettering: Drawing Letters for a Variety of Purposes," in *New Types* (Jerusalem: Israel Museum, 2016), 223; Adi Stern, "The Design of Hebrew Type in the First Decade of Israeli Statehood," in *New Types* (Jerusalem: Israel Museum, 2016), 50-51.

ДЪРЖАВНА ПЕЧАТНИЦА „ДЕЧО СТЕФАНОВ"

ЛАТИНЕ СВЕТЪЛ ФРЕНСКИ

20 points
ABCDEFGHIJKLMNOPQRSTU
abcdefghijklmnopqrstuvwxyzáàâäéè

Est-ce à dire, par exemple, que les résultats de l'action des lois de la nature, des forces de la nature soient, en général, inéluctables; que l'action destructive des forces de la nature se produit toujours et partout avec une spontanéité inexorable, qui ne se prête pas à l'action des hommes? Evidemment non. Si l'on fait abstraction des processus astronomiques, géolo-

28 points
ABCDEFGHIJKLMNO
PQRSTUVWXYZABC

36 points
ABCDEFGHIJKL
MNOPQRSTUVZ
abcdefghijklmnopq

ДА ВНЕДРИМ ПОЧИНА НА КОВАЛЬОВ

ДЪРЖАВНА ПЕЧАТНИЦА „ДЕЧО СТЕФАНОВ"

ЛАТИНЕ ПОЛУЧЕР БЪЛГАРСКИ

8 пункта
АБВГДЕЖЗИЙКЛМНОПРСТУФХЦЧШЩЪЬЮЯЫЫ АБВГДЕЖЗИКЛП
абвгдежзийклмнопрстуфхцчшщъьюяаабгдежзи ыэ 1234567890 , . ; : ! ?

да било нарушаване, изменяне или унищожаване на законите на науката, без създаване на нови закони на науката. Обратно, цялата тази процедура се осъществява върху точно основаване на законите на природата, на законите на науката, защото каквото и да било нарушаване на законите на природата, най-малкото им нарушаване би довело само до разстройство на работата, до проваляне на процедурата.

10 пункта
АБВДЕЖЗИГЙКЛМНОПРСТУФХЦЧШЩЪЬЮЯЭЫАБВГД
абвгдежзийклмнопрстуфчцшщъьюя э ы 1234567890 , . ; : ! ?

Същото трябва да се каже за законите на икономическото развитие, за законите на политическата икономия — все едно дали става дума за периода на капитализма или за периода на социализма. Тук също така, както и в естествознанието, законите на икономическото развитие са обективни закони, които отразяват процесите на икономическото развитие, из-

12 пункта
АБВГДЕЖЗИЙКЛМНОПРСТУФХЦЧШЩЪЬЮЯЭ
абвгдежзийклмнопрстуфхцчшщъьюяэ1234567990

вършващи се независимо от волята на хората. Хората могат да открият тези закони, да ги опознаят и опирайки се на тях, да ги използуват в интерес на обществото, да дадат друго направление на разрушителните действия на някои закони, да ограничат сферата на тяхното

16 пункта
АБВДЕЖЗИГЙКЛМНОПРСТУФХЦЧ
абвгдежзийклмнопрстуфхцчшщъья

действие, да дадат простор на други закони, които си пробиват път, но те не могат да ги унищожат или да създадат нови икономически закони.

ЧРЕЗ БЛАГОРОДНО СЪРЕВНОВАНИЕ, КЪМ

***Образци от печатарските букви по шрифт и кегъл*, 1957**

This 40-page booklet shows *Samples of Printed Letters in Font and Size* from the Decho Stefanov State Printing House in Sofia, Bulgaria. One page spread shows the Latin alphabet, offering Garamond in 6 to 36 points. All other sample texts are printed in Bulgarian, Czech, Russian, and Serbian; the specimen shows no ornament, but includes a wide range of mathematical symbols. Foundry type dominates, with a limited range of machine-set type available from Monotype. Notice how the imprint of the metal type on the back of the page "bites" into the front—this is most noticeable in the typeface names below the main header on each page. This indicates significant pressure on the type as it's run through the press, perhaps enough to eventually squish the type over time.

7: PHOTOGRAPHIC AND BINARY PROCESSES

Penrose Annual,
Arthur Dutton's Photoline, 1924

The London trade publication Penrose Annual ran from 1895 to 1982; William Gamble, its initiator, edited from 1895-1933. This 1924 article—more of an advertisement, really—by Photoline inventor Arthur Dutton describes how photo-typographic technology will soon render metal type entirely obsolete. After an early patent on phototype technology in 1856, an initial prototype was built in 1894, and Dutton's Photoline appeared in 1915. While ultimately unsuccessful, it was available commercially for over a decade. The Photoline produced thin, flat plates of metal photographically engraved with a reverse image of a typographic page. These plates were mounted to type-high blocks of wood for letterpress printing. It took the elimination of metal plates and type-high printing blocks, replaced with entirely photographic technology, for phototype to achieve wide success beginning around 1950.

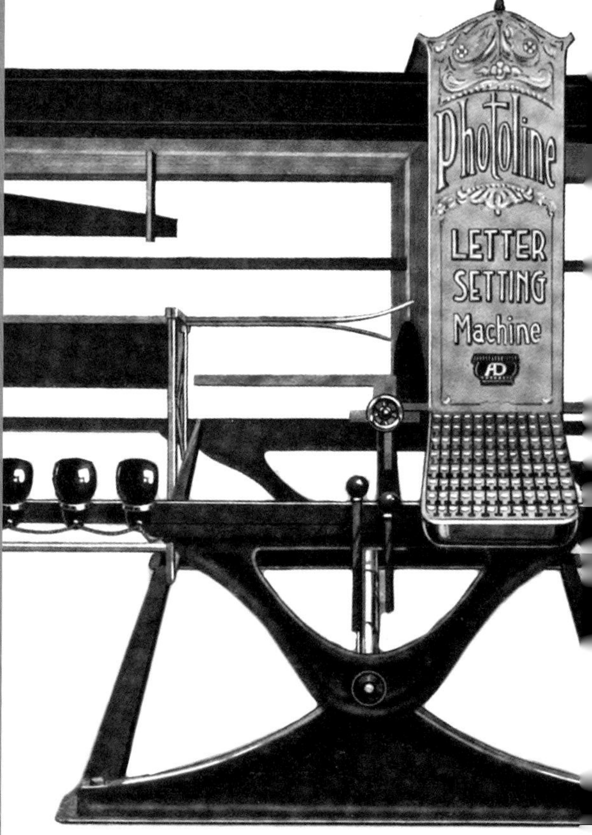

PHOTOLINE LETTER-SETTING MACHINE

(*See article " Photoline," page 67*)

A SPECIMEN OF

PHOTOLINE

A NEW PROCESS OF

TYPELESS PRINTING

TYPELESS PRINTING

TYPELESS PRINTING

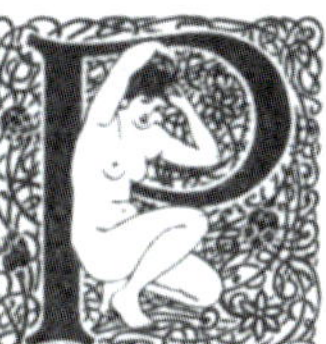

HOTOGRAPHY takes another step forward in the science of printing by the introduction of "Photoline." Without type being used, it accomplishes everything for the letterpress printer, and gives equal facilities to all other printers. "Photoline" deals with solid, displayed, or tabular matter, initials, borders, designs, etc., all photographed line by line; variety of size being secured by regulating camera distances. The product, a "Photoline" negative, may be used in the place of types, for printing by Zincotype, Lithotype, Gravotype, Collotype, or any other of the photo-process methods. "Photoline" inaugurates a new era for printers. Inventor of "PHOTOLINE," Arthur Dutton.

Offset Printing by
FOSH & CROSS Ltd.,
Paul Street, E.C.2

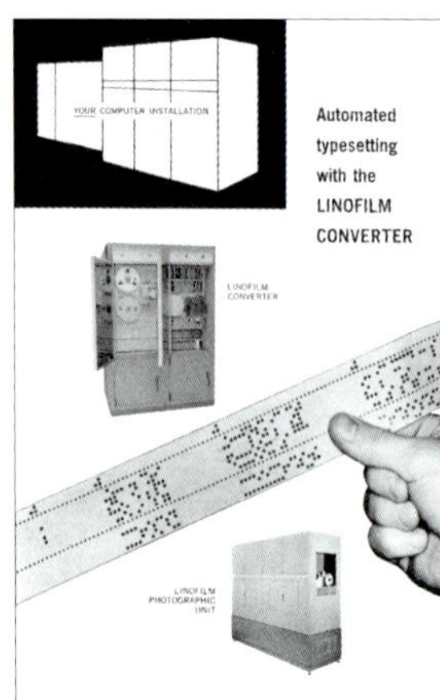

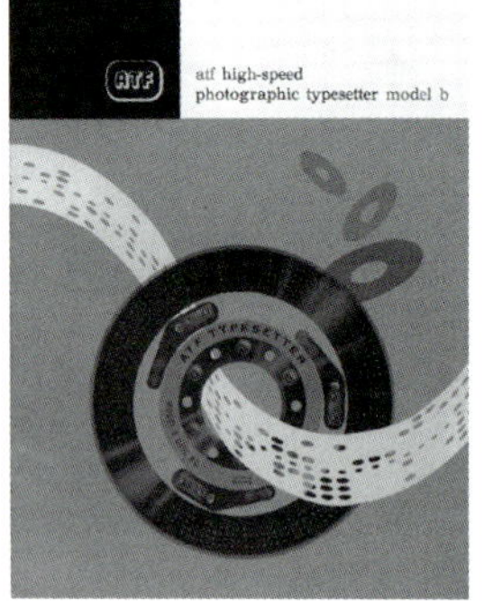

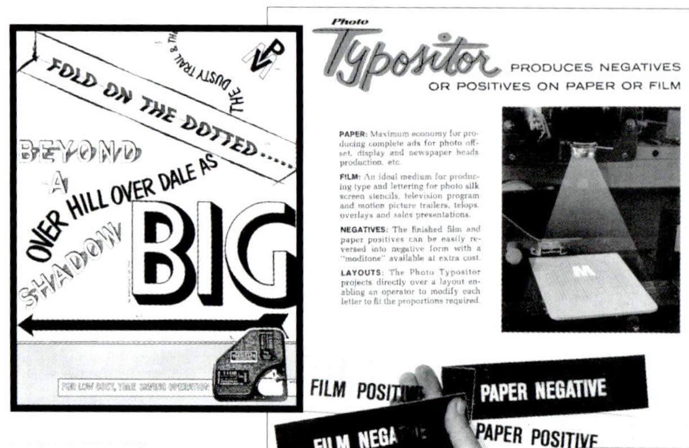

1950 — USA

Linofilm Phototypesetting system introduced.

1958 — USA

ATF introduces its first phototype system, with limited success.

1959 — USA

Photo Typositor offers a simple system exclusively for display type.

1959 — USA

Foundry, hot metal, & photo types co-exist; the *Practical Handbook* (Butler Typo-Design Research Center) shows how to use all three.

1946 — USA

Intertype Fotosetter, first-generation phototype system, invented.

1949 — France & USA

Photon-Lumitype, first commercially successful phototype system, introduces "second generation" phototype.

1957 — USA

Monophoto phototypesetting system introduced.

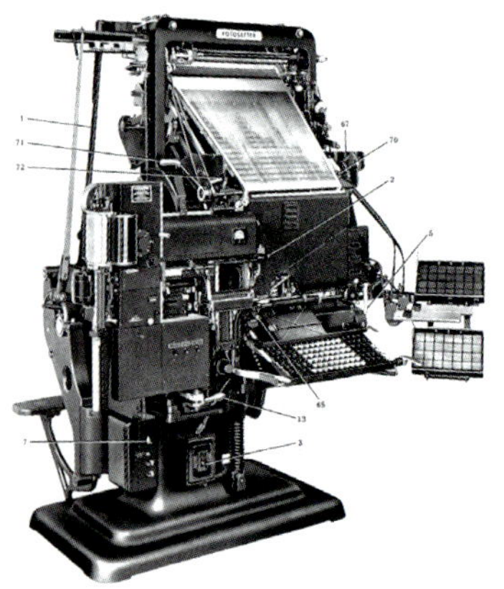

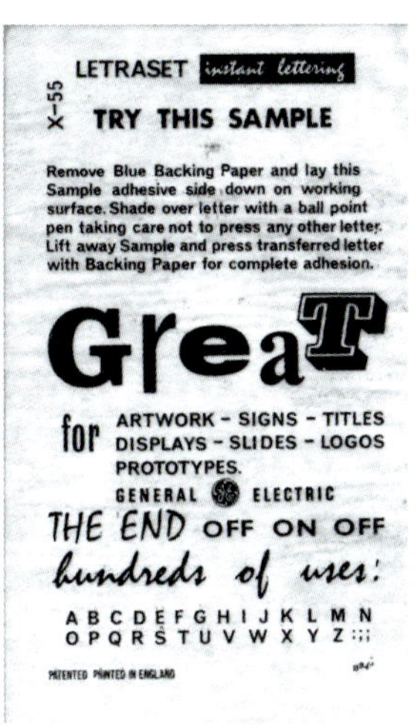

Digi-Grotesk

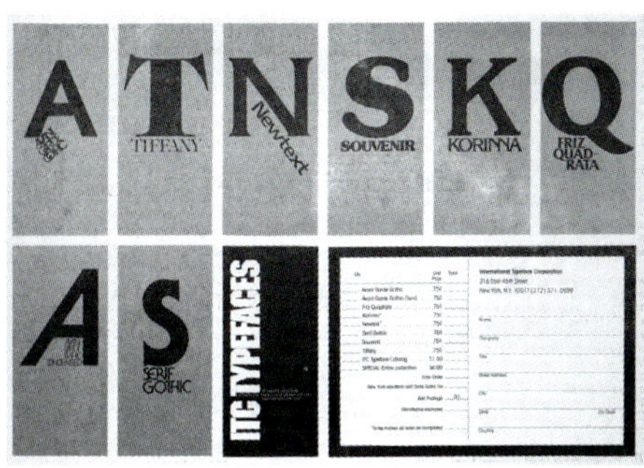

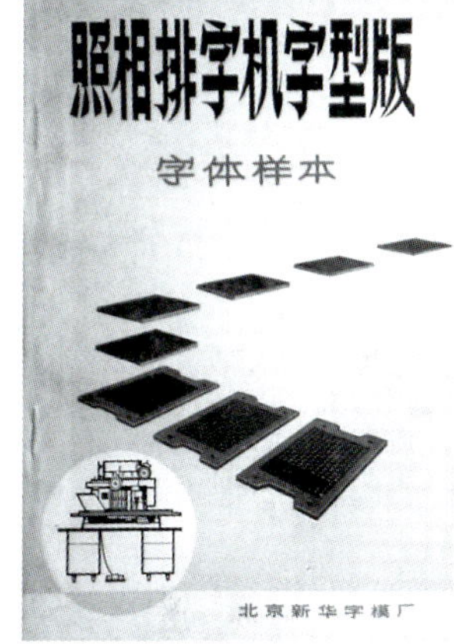

1961 — USA

Letraset (dry rub-down instant lettering) introduced.

1961 — Germany

Digi-Grotesk S, first digital typeface, released for Rudolf Hell's Digiset machine.

1961 — USA

International Typeface Corporation (ITC), first phototype-only foundry.

1985 — China

Newspapers adopt photo-typesetting.

1963 — [internationally]

Phototype overtakes hot metal as most common type-setting method; sets 3,600 words per minute vs. hot metal's 30.

c. 1970 — USA

Graphic Developments Inc. markets FOTOMAGIC optical overlay units to warp phototype.

1978 — USA

New York Times retires its last Linotype.

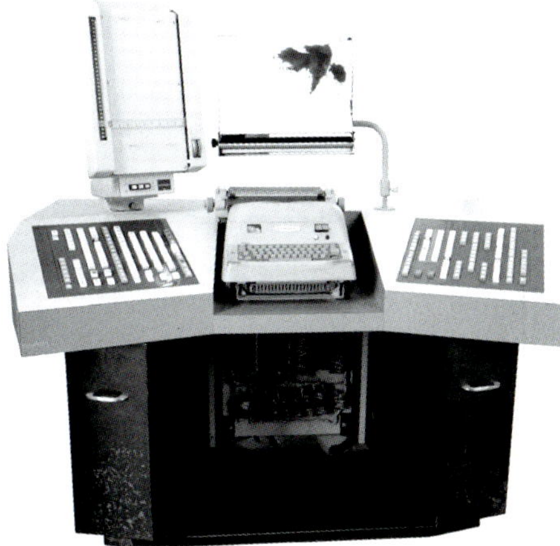

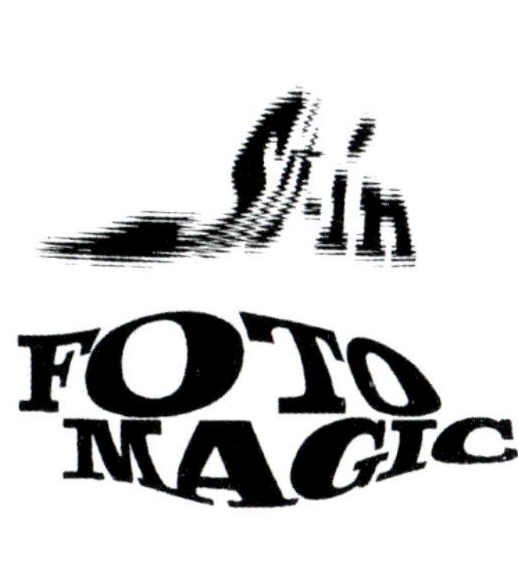

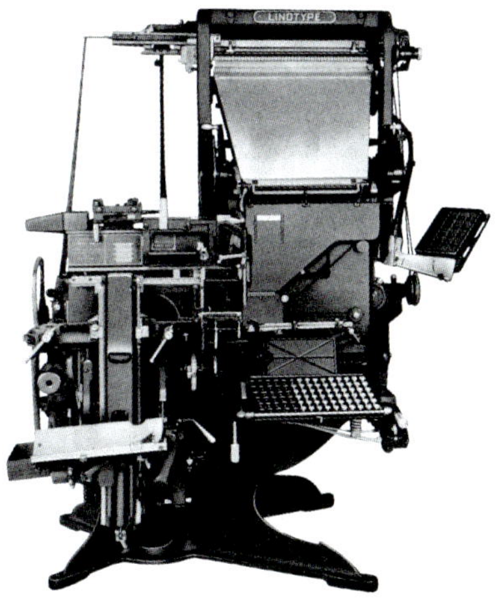

For almost as long as typographers and printers had experimented with mechanized metal type, they'd also explored photographic typesetting processes. **Phototype** machines, like hot metal machines, underwent significant development before a viable commercial model entered the market in 1949. Sometimes called "cold type," in contrast to hot metal type, phototype penetrated the market quickly. Barely a decade after its introduction, early experiments with digital type opened the way for the digital type foundries of the late twentieth and early twenty-first centuries. The 1960s-70s witnessed increasing interest in combining the dematerialization inherent to phototype with emergent computing technologies. In 1987, computer software giant Adobe acquired a digital license for the entire Linotype library and hastened the shift from physical to digital type. During the twentieth century, three separate typographic technologies—hot metal, cold or photographic, and digital—subsequently displaced the foundry/handsetting model of over four centuries. The specimens designed and circulated by foundries, distributors, and printers reflected these rapid shifts in technology in a variety of ways ... or, sometimes, not at all.

Phototype: "inherently superior"

Almost a century of intermittent development preceded the release of the first commercial phototype machine in 1949. An English inventor filed a patent on early phototype technology in 1856, building initial prototypes in 1894 and 1898.[1] A 1915 machine, the Photoline, proved successful enough that trade periodicals advertised it for at least a decade. Widely reprinted *Penrose's Annual* ads, quoting Photoline's inventor Arthur Dutton, predicted that photographic methods would soon "eliminate the use of metal types for printing purposes."[2] However, before phototype became commercially successful, Photoline's engraved plates mounted to type-high blocks of wood were replaced by entirely photographic processes.

A so-called "first-generation" of phototypesetters produced **negatives** for offset printing. But existing industry leaders developed these machines, and a failure to imagine entirely new systems limited them. The Intertype Fotosetter

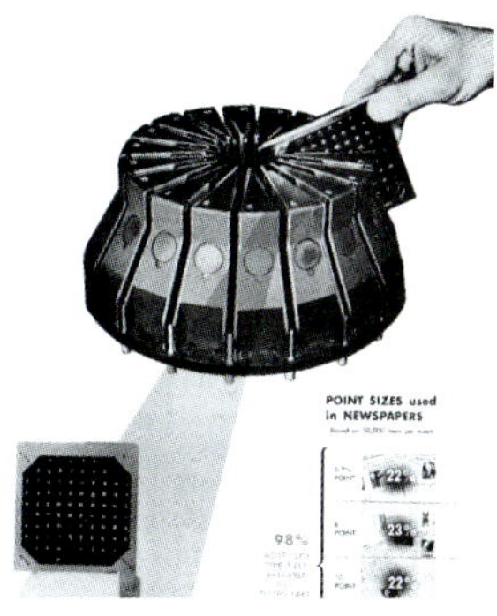

Phototype systems like Linofilm project light through photographic negatives of the letterforms onto a light-sensitive surface which is then used to produce a printing plate. Pictured: the Linofilm's grid turret and a grid font.

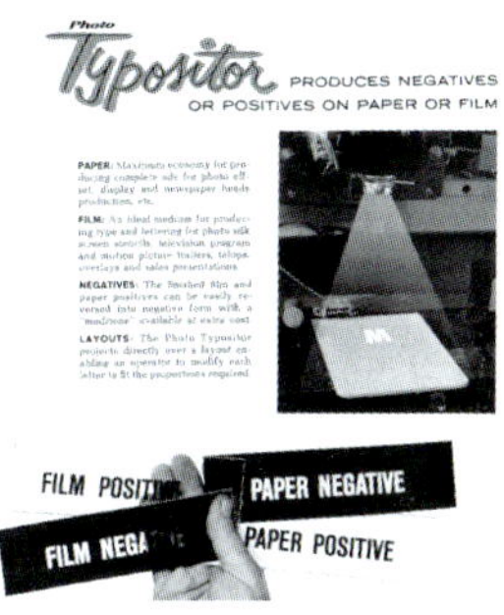

As in film photography, in the photo- type process light projects through **negatives** of individual typographic characters in the desired order, and magnified to the desired size. This exposes photographic paper which is then used to make printing plates.

corona

Corona, the product of Linotype research, was designed and tested to provide top-level printing performance in newspapers and catalogs

· LINOTYPE ·

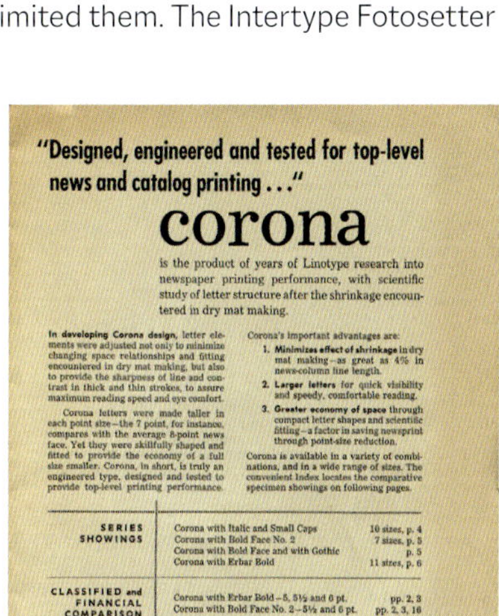

"Designed, engineered and tested for top-level news and catalog printing . . ."

corona

is the product of years of Linotype research into newspaper printing performance, with scientific study of letter structure after the shrinkage encountered in dry mat making.

In developing Corona design, letter elements were adjusted not only to minimize changing space relationships and fitting encountered in dry mat making, but also to provide the sharpness of line and contrast in thick and thin strokes, to assure maximum reading speed and eye comfort.

Corona letters were made taller in each point size—the 7 point, for instance, compares with the average 8-point news face. Yet they were skillfully shaped and fitted to provide the economy of a full size smaller. Corona, in short, is truly an engineered type, designed and tested to provide top-level printing performance.

Corona's important advantages are:

1. **Minimizes effect of shrinkage** in dry mat making—as great as 4% in news-column line length.
2. **Larger letters** for quick visibility and speedy, comfortable reading.
3. **Greater economy of space** through compact letter shapes and scientific fitting—a factor in saving newsprint through point-size reduction.

Corona is available in a variety of combinations, and in a wide range of sizes. The convenient Index locates the comparative specimen showings on following pages.

SERIES SHOWINGS	Corona with Italic and Small Caps	10 sizes, p. 4
	Corona with Bold Face No. 2	7 sizes, p. 5
	Corona with Bold Face and with Gothic	p. 5
	Corona with Erbar Bold	11 sizes, p. 6
CLASSIFIED and FINANCIAL COMPARISON	Corona with Erbar Bold—5, 5½ and 6 pt.	pp. 2, 3
	Corona with Bold Face No. 2—5½ and 6 pt.	pp. 2, 3, 16
NEWS BODY COMPARISON	Corona with Erbar Bold—7 pt.	p. 7
	Corona with Bold Face No. 2	
	7½ and 8 pt., 8 pt. No. 1, and 8 pt. No. 2	pp. 8, 9, 10, 11
EDITORIAL COMPARISON	Corona with Erbar Bold—9, 10, 14 pt.	pp. 12, 14
	Corona w Italic and Small Caps—10, 11, 12 pt.	pp. 13, 15

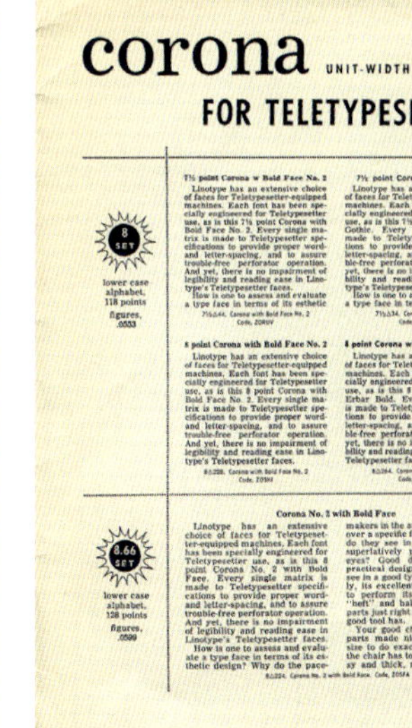

CORONA FOR YOUNG READERS

Large, clear letters
Even color
Compact design
Economy of space

M

"My!" said a Mole to a Miner,
"This hole couldn't be any finer.
If we dig downhill
And never stand still,
We'll surely end up in China."

N

"No, no, no!" said the Nightingale.
"I won't sing in this awful gale!
Indeed I've no choice,
It would spoil my voice,
And I'd be as mute as a snail!"

O

"Oh!" said the Owl to the Ostrich,
"I do wish you and I were rich!
We'd buy a flashlight,
And go out at night
To call on the frogs in their ditch."

K k

The eleventh letter of the alphabet

keep
1. I **keep** my rabbit in a box.
2. George gave me a ball.
I may **keep** it.
keeps kept keeping

kettle
We heat water in a **kettle**.

key
We lock the door with a **key**.

kick
Ronald **kicks** the ball.
kicks kicked kicking

kindergarten
Little children go to **kindergarten**.
The **kindergarten** is in the school.

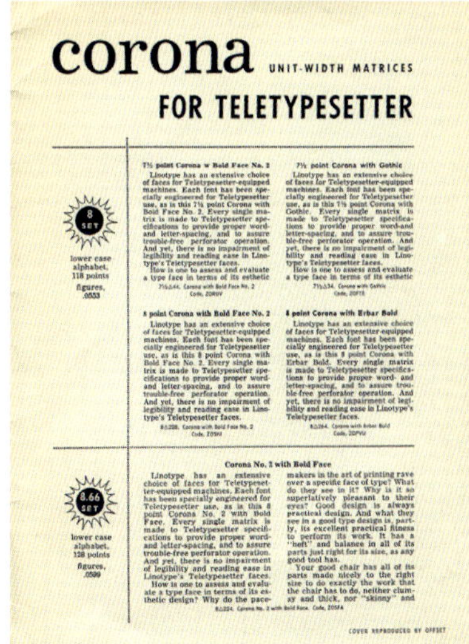

corona UNIT-WIDTH MATRICES

FOR TELETYPESETTER

8 SET

lower case alphabet, 118 points
figures, .0553

7½ point Corona w Bold Face No. 2

Linotype has an extensive choice of faces for Teletypesetter-equipped machines. Each font has been specially engineered for Teletypesetter use, as is this 7½ point Corona with Bold Face No. 2. Every single matrix is made to Teletypesetter specifications to provide proper word- and letter-spacing, and to assure trouble-free perforator operation. And yet, there is no impairment of legibility and reading ease in Linotype's Teletypesetter faces.
How is one to assess and evaluate a type face in terms of its esthetic

7½△44. Corona with Bold Face No. 2 Code, ZORUV

7½ point Corona with Gothic

Linotype has an extensive choice of faces for Teletypesetter-equipped machines. Each font has been specially engineered for Teletypesetter use, as is this 7½ point Corona with Gothic. Every single matrix is made to Teletypesetter specifications to provide proper word-and letter-spacing, and to assure trouble-free perforator operation. And yet, there is no impairment of legibility and reading ease in Linotype's Teletypesetter faces.
How is one to assess and evaluate a type face in terms of its esthetic

7½△34. Corona with Gothic Code, ZOFTE

8 point Corona with Bold Face No. 2

Linotype has an extensive choice of faces for Teletypesetter-equipped machines. Each font has been specially engineered for Teletypesetter use, as is this 8 point Corona with Bold Face No. 2. Every single matrix is made to Teletypesetter specifications to provide proper word- and letter-spacing, and to assure trouble-free perforator operation. And yet, there is no impairment of legibility and reading ease in Linotype's Teletypesetter faces.

8△228. Corona with Bold Face No. 2 Code, ZOSHI

8 point Corona with Erbar Bold

Linotype has an extensive choice of faces for Teletypesetter-equipped machines. Each font has been specially engineered for Teletypesetter use, as is this 8 point Corona with Erbar Bold. Every single matrix is made to Teletypesetter specifications to provide proper word- and letter-spacing, and to assure trouble-free perforator operation. And yet, there is no impairment of legibility and reading ease in Linotype's Teletypesetter faces.

8△264. Corona with Erbar Bold Code, ZOPVU

8.66 SET

lower case alphabet, 128 points
figures, .0599

Corona No. 2 with Bold Face

Linotype has an extensive choice of faces for Teletypesetter-equipped machines. Each font has been specially engineered for Teletypesetter use, as is this 8 point Corona No. 2 with Bold Face. Every single matrix is made to Teletypesetter specifications to provide proper word- and letter-spacing, and to assure trouble-free perforator operation. And yet, there is no impairment of legibility and reading ease in Linotype's Teletypesetter faces.
How is one to assess and evaluate a type face in terms of its esthetic design? Why do the pacemakers in the art of printing rave over a specific face of type? What do they see in it? Why is it so superlatively pleasant to their eyes? Good design is always practical design. And what they see in a good type design is, partly, its excellent practical fitness to perform its work. It has a "heft" and balance in all of its parts just right for its size, as any good tool has.
Your good chair has all of its parts made nicely to the right size to do exactly the work that the chair has to do, neither clumsy and thick, nor "skinny" and

8△224. Corona No. 2 with Bold Face. Code, ZOSFA

COVER REPRODUCED BY OFFSET

Fig 7.1 (left)

***Corona* (Linotype, New York, 1951). Linotype's Teletypesetter inspired new types "engineered and tested" to work well with emergent photographic technologies. Like many of Linotype's phototype publicity materials, Corona's specimen spoke a visual language informed by science and characterized by a beam of light.**

FUTURA BOLD

24 LENS

Photo-composition is the perfect method for modern typography. It presents a cle ar, precise image in a single-step operati

30 LENS

Photo-composition is the perfec t method for modern typograph y. It presents a clear, precise im

36 LENS

Photo-composition is the p erfect method for modern t

48 LENS

Photo-composition i s the perfect metho

60 LENS

Photo - composi tion is the perfe

auto-graphics, inc. Los Angeles • San Francisco • Chicago • New York • Vancouver, B.C.

6 LENS

Photo-composition is the perfect method for mode rn typography. It presents a clear, precise image in a single-step operation on photographic paper or film positive, ready for your paste-up departmen t or camera. By carefully analyzing the purpose of your composition, a proper selection of modern t

8 LENS

Photo-composition is the perfect meth od for modern typography. It prese nts a clear, precise image in a single-step operation on photographic paper or film positive, ready for your paste-up department or camera. By careful ly analyzing the purpose of your co mposition, a proper selection of mode

9 LENS

Photo-composition is the perfect method fo r modern typography. It presents a clear, precise image in a single-step operation on photographic paper or film positive, ready for your paste-up department or camera. By carefully analyzing the purpose of yo ur composition, a proper selection of mode rn type style may be made that will help

10 LENS

Photo-composition is the perfect meth od for modern typography. It present s a clear, precise image in a single-st ep operation on photographic paper or film positive, ready for your paste-up department or camera. By carefully an alyzing the purpose of your composit

12 LENS

Photo-composition is the perfect meth od for modern typography. It presen ts a clear, precise image in a single-ste p operation on photographic paper or film positive, ready for your paste-up department or camera. By carefully an alyzing the purpose of your compositi

14 LENS

Photo-composition is the perfect metho d for modern typography. It presents a clear, precise image in a single-step operation on photographic paper or fil m positive, ready for your paste-up de partment or camera. By carefully anal

18 LENS

Photo-composition is the perfect method fo r modern typography. It presents a clear, p recise image in a single-step operation on photographic paper or film positive, ready for your paste-up department or camera. B

abcdefghijklmnopqrstuvwxyz
ABCDEFGHIJKLMNOPQRSTUVWXYZ
1234567890 .,;:-''' ! ? & ( ) % * — "

FUTURA BOLD ITALIC

CHARACTER COUNT IN PICAS

Lens Size	10	12	14	16	18	20	22	24	26	28	30	34	38	42
6	41	48	55	62	69	76	83	90	97	104	111	125	139	153
8	32	38	44	50	56	62	68	74	80	86	92	114	126	138
9	28	34	40	46	52	58	64	70	76	82	88	110	122	134
10	25	30	35	40	45	50	55	60	65	70	75	85	95	105
12	21	25	29	33	37	41	45	49	53	57	61	69	77	85
14	19	22	25	28	31	34	37	40	43	46	49	55	61	67
18	13	15	17	19	21	23	25	27	29	31	33	37	41	45

PHOTON 200

FUTURA BOLD ITALIC

Disc No. 1

auto-graphics, inc. Los Angeles • San Francisco • Chicago • New York • Vancouver, B.C.

Fig 7.2 (above)

Futura Bold specimen (Auto-graphics, Los Angeles, c1960-65). Words like *perfect*, *modern*, *precise*, and *single-step* described new phototype technology in this Auto-graphics specimen for Futura.

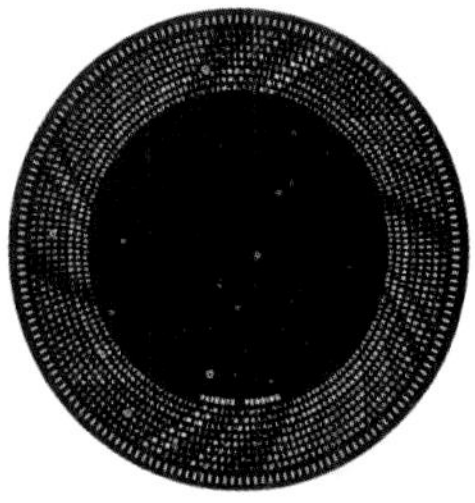

Phototype **discs**, like this one for the Photon Series 540, held tiny negatives of a typeface's characters, which were projected in rapid sequence at the desired size.

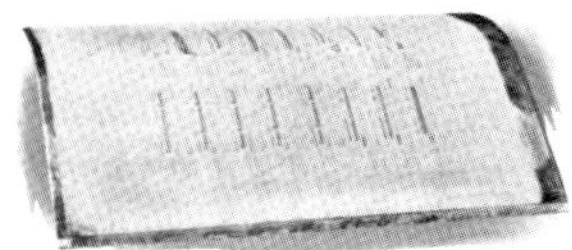

A **printing plate**, produced photographically or electrically (if electroplated), contains all of the typographic and/or image information to be printed on a single, solid plane.

(1950) and Monotype Monophoto (1955), for instance, operated on the same mechanical principles as their makers' hot metal machines, down to details like the shape of individual matrices in the Fotosetter or the size of the Monophoto's mat case.[3] Linotype's Teletypesetter inspired the design of new typefaces, despite its first-generation phototypesetting technology [Fig. 7.1]. Two French electrical engineers with no printing experience reconceptualized typography as a purely photographic process. Their research, funded by the American offset reproduction company Lithomat, led to the Lumitype-Photon, a "second generation" phototypesetter initially introduced to the commercial market in 1949.[4] Unlike its competitors, the Photon (as it was known in the United States) or Lumitype (in France) owed little to the mechanics of hot metal machines. The "matrix" component was a **disc** with rows of negative letter images, usually about 6 points in size; these had been photographed from large (±512pts.) master-images of positive characters, called phototypes. As the disc of tiny letter-images rotated, light shone through it at the precise location needed to expose individual characters, in sequence, onto a photosensitive surface, which was then used to create a **printing plate**.[5] No longer tied to the idea of the physical typographic body, phototype could be scaled, skewed, and spaced at will.

"Photo-composition is the perfect method," an Auto-graphics brochure for Futura exhorted [Fig. 7.2]. "It presents a clear, precise image in a single-step operation." Its physical flexibility and speed—which increased with every new model—ensured that phototype technology spread quickly. By the late 1960s, the year 1963 had been widely acknowledged as "the major beginnings of automatic composition," or the "decline of printing from movable type," pending the reporter's attitude toward new technologies.[6] While hot metal machines set about thirty words per minute, by the mid-1960s phototypesetters achieved 3,600 per minute. By 1973, an international survey estimated "2,000 typesetting computer installations and some 20,000 filmsetters in use."[7] Obvious advantages in speed and economy meant that early adopters were willing to overcome the aesthetic challenges posed by the new technology—or, demonstrably, some were willing to ignore them. In a 1979 photo-composition textbook, digital typesetting pioneer John W. Seybold wrote that "good phototype composition is now inherently superior to 'hot metal' typesetting."[8] His caveat, "good," pointed to a longstanding complaint of professional typographers and printers—that ease of typesetting, facilitated by more widely available technologies, often lead to substandard results both aesthetically and functionally.

"Swift & Exact": how phototypesetting works

The mechanics of phototype machines evolved over time. Smaller, less complex models produced only headline and display copy, while more sophisticated versions sought to replace metal type entirely. As with early printers; manuals and hot metal specimens, those devoted to phototype sometimes explained the new physical processes associated with their products. Intertype pictorialized photo-typographic printing on the cover of *Intertype* (c.1970). A solid white beam of light shone through a clear lens onto a black background [Fig. 7.03]. From its position behind this lens, a film negative produced a printed positive of the uppercase I in Intertype; the white of the letterform linked it visually to the white beam of light. The interior pages prioritized function; they displayed numerals and alphabets for typefaces listed alphabetically, with ordering information below each listing. The page design communicates little about the types' histories, intended uses, or production technology. The selling point is the production method—indicated only on the cover—combined with the availability of all the standard, workaday types printers require.

Varigraph's specimens explained how the Varigraph "sets formal and creative headline lettering" using three components [Fig. 7.4]. The unit itself "fits in a desk drawer" and utilized a matrix or mat for each typeface, with "over 220 mats" available. The operator controlled the pen, guiding it through the engraving

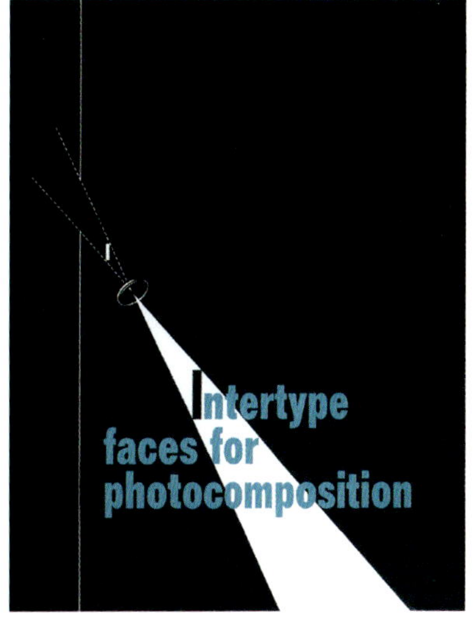

Fig 7.03 (above)
***Intertype Faces for Photocomposition* (Intertype, New York, c.1970). Most hot metal manufacturers attempted some variation on phototype technology, though most were limited by their understanding of type as a metal/physical (rather than optical/film) process—regardless of what images like this one from Intertype might communicate.**

Fig 7.4 (below)
***Type Catalog* (Varigraph, Madison WI, c.1960). Some phototype machines were complex and designed to handle extensive book, magazine, and catalog printing jobs. Others, like the Varigraph, were small and relatively simple, designed mostly for setting headlines and short ads.**

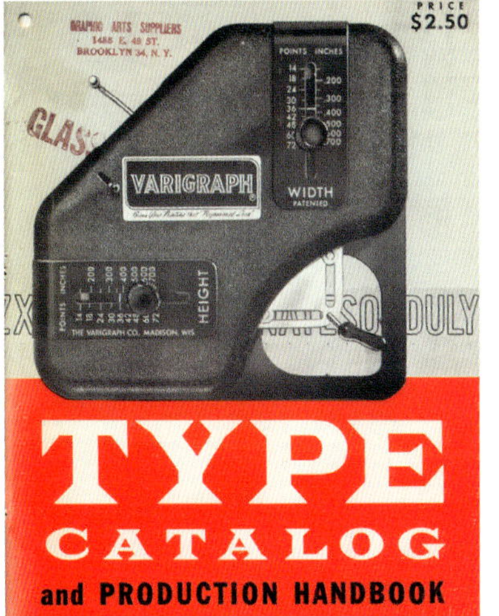

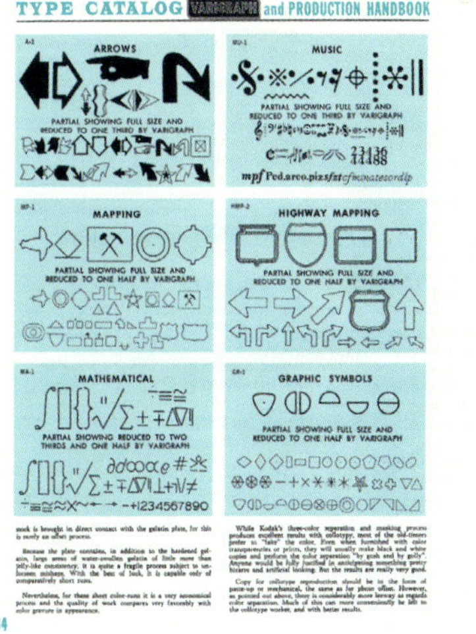

Fig 7.5 (opposite, top)

The idea that phototype technology was "so easy the secretary could use it" permeated ads and specimens alike, as shown in these catalogs for the PROtype (c.1963-9), Varigraph (c.1960), Typro (c.1963), VariTyper 360 (c.1960), and Photo Typositor (1962).

Fig 7.6 (opposite, bottom)

***The Linofilm Converter* and *Linofilm System* (Linotype, New York, ND/1960s). Smiling typists might use a desk-drawer-sized phototype machine to typeset headlines. But at a systems level, phototype technology was always the purview of men in business suits or lab coats, as demonstrated by Mergenthaler Linotype's Linofilm system.**

on the matrix to reproduce the desired letters in ink on film. A single matrix produced a range of styles and sizes—forward and back slanting, compressed or expanded, ranging from 14 to 72 or 96 points. A specimen (c.1960) showed Varigraph type in use, offering "a smattering of possibilities" for composing display type that's stretched, skewed, overlapped, set on curving baselines, and otherwise distorted in ways that had been difficult or impossible to achieve in metal. These gymnastics showcased the unique, technically-derived aesthetic capacities of phototype, but A-Z settings of each typeface weren't included. Instead, readers were instructed to request a *Type Catalog* (1964) for $2.50 plus shipping and handling, cost applied to future orders. The comprehensive printed specimen, instead of a freely distributed advertising tool, had become a professional resource with a (modest) price tag.

Ease of operation led to gender-coded messages about the work of typesetting [Fig. 7.5]. The Photo Typositor depicted the "typesetting miracle of the modern graphic arts" by showing a perfectly-coifed, smiling woman setting headline type, as did the ProType, which boasted "25,000 types styles & sizes ... the world's largest type library!" The VariTyper 360 was so easy to operate that the "office typist" could take over the "tedious, time-consuming" work of producing headline lettering, thus freeing the "skill and time [of] draftsmen to concentrate on more creative assignments." Friden Typro promised that "Anybody can learn to use it in minutes," offering visual proof in the form of a smiling young woman in high heels who operated the desktop model.[9] With the aid of phototypesetting technology, then, the work of typesetting was gendered and devalued—but only in certain contexts.

Linotype advertised its Linofilm System as "swift" and "exact," emphasizing the **systemization** of human workflow aided by scientifically designed mechanical functionality—both visualized as the domain of men. A brochure (n.d.) explaining "the new concept in photocomposition" included a flow chart comparing "the laborious, slow methods of OTHER cold type: non-automatic correction on film, hand cutting and splicing" to "the SWIFT, exact LINOFILM method: correction at keyboard, correction on tape, automatic film correction." Throughout, men—never women—in lab coats or business suits operated the equipment; often their figures were juxtaposed with a diagram, bar graph, or flow chart [Fig. 7.6]. As always, Linotype emphasized systems, speed, and universality. Linofilm was "versatile and flexible" and its "keyboard has been planned by Henry Dreyfuss, noted industrial designer, to conform to the physiology and psychology of the operator." Linotype described operator training as a quick process taking advantage of "skills acquired in hot-metal work." Little attention was paid to the typefaces; the copy described "popular display faces" like "the vast Spartan family," or "prime favorites" for body copy, such as "Corona, the most widely used newspaper body face in the world." All the types were "completely redrawn to take full advantage of the far greater flexibility of photographic composition." Two spreads offered demonstrations of advertising and book composition and job printing, with little focus on annotating the types. This implied that translating Linotype's extensive, up-to-date font library into phototype was the real task at hand—printers could continue the work they'd always done, but with phototype instead of metal type.

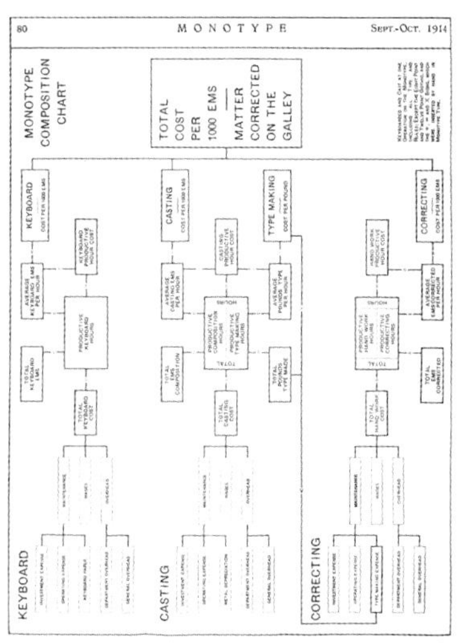

Systemization characterizes all aspects of industrialization and modernity, from the macro to the micro. The design of governments, international corporate entities, cities, buildings, factories, machines, consumer products, corporate identities, typeface families and the systems used to name them—all are organized according to rationalized, intentionally designed systems, like this cost-saving analysis of Monotype composition methods (1914).

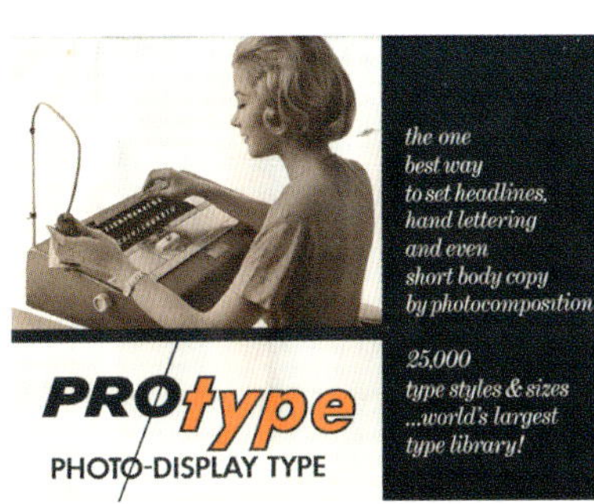
the one
best way
to set headlines,
hand lettering
and even
short body copy
by photocomposition
25,000
type styles & sizes
...world's largest
type library!
PROtype
PHOTO-DISPLAY TYPE

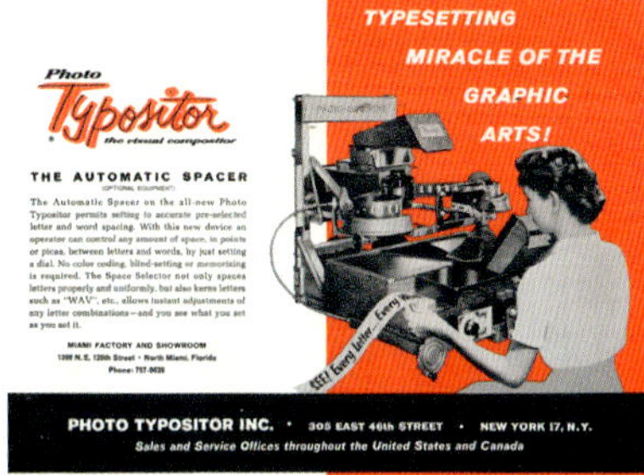
Photo
Typositor
the visual compositor
THE AUTOMATIC SPACER
TYPESETTING
MIRACLE OF THE
GRAPHIC
ARTS!
PHOTO TYPOSITOR INC. • 305 EAST 46th STREET • NEW YORK 17, N.Y.
Sales and Service Offices throughout the United States and Canada

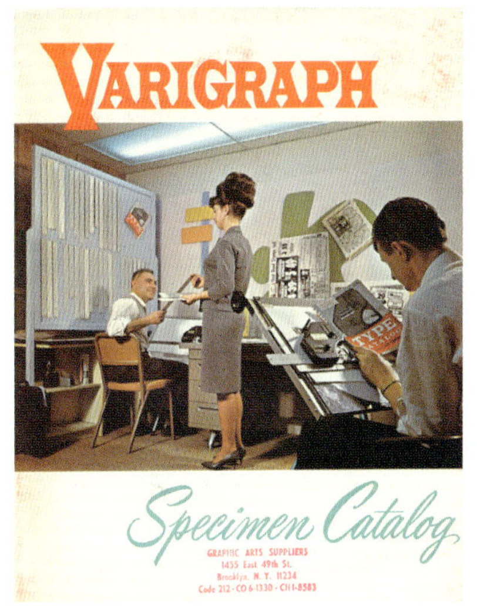
VARIGRAPH
Specimen Catalog

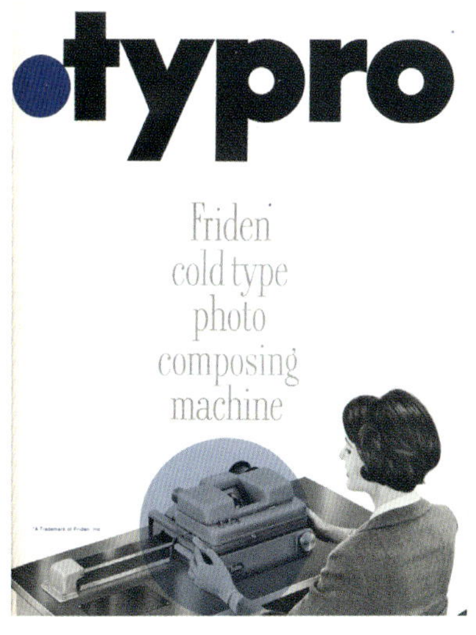
typro
Friden
cold type
photo
composing
machine

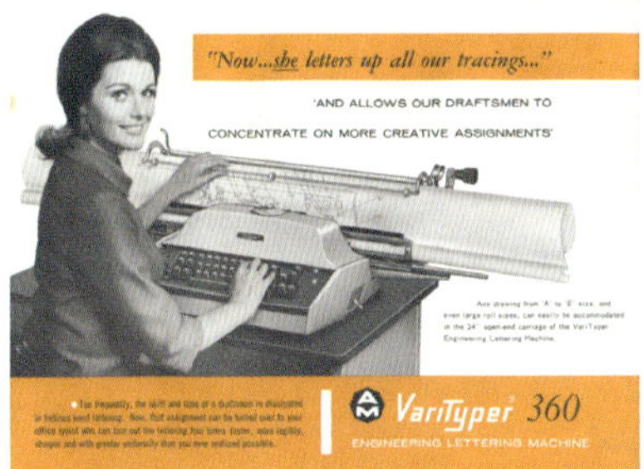
"Now...she letters up all our tracings..."
AND ALLOWS OUR DRAFTSMEN TO
CONCENTRATE ON MORE CREATIVE ASSIGNMENTS
VariTyper 360
ENGINEERING LETTERING MACHINE

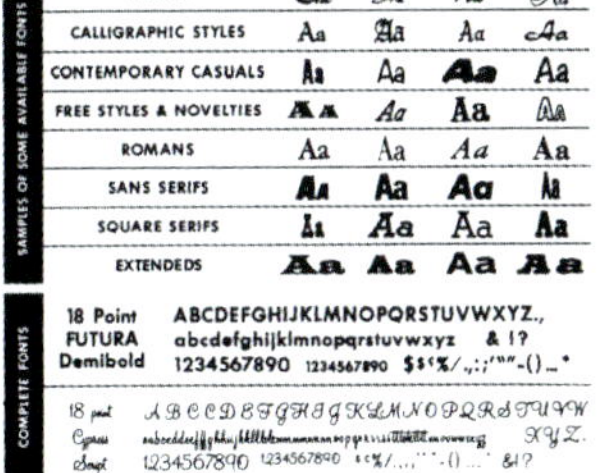
SCRIPTS
CALLIGRAPHIC STYLES
CONTEMPORARY CASUALS
FREE STYLES & NOVELTIES
ROMANS
SANS SERIFS
SQUARE SERIFS
EXTENDEDS
SAMPLES OF SOME AVAILABLE FONTS
18 Point
FUTURA
Demibold
ABCDEFGHIJKLMNOPQRSTUVWXYZ
abcdefghijklmnopqrstuvwxyz
1234567890
COMPLETE FONTS
RETAILER'S FONT

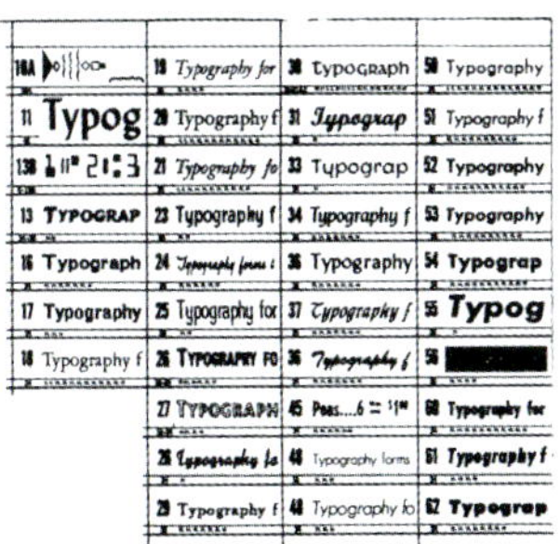

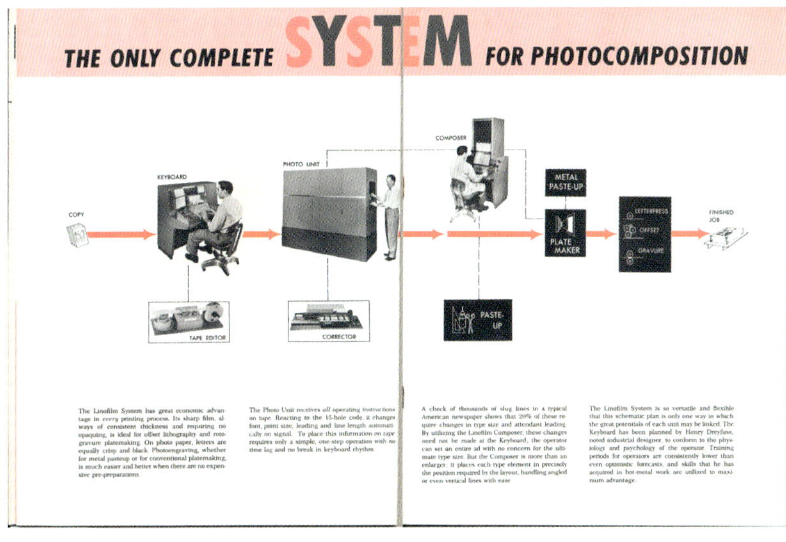
THE ONLY COMPLETE SYSTEM FOR PHOTOCOMPOSITION
COPY
KEYBOARD
PHOTO UNIT
COMPOSER
METAL PASTE-UP
PLATE MAKER
LETTERPRESS
OFFSET
GRAVURE
FINISHED JOB
TAPE EDITOR
CORRECTOR
PASTE-UP

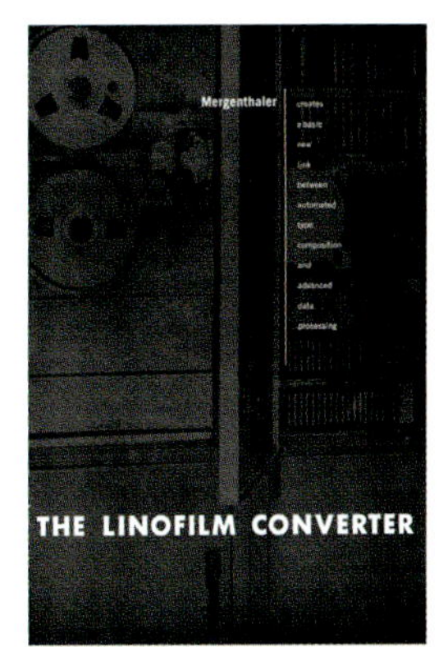
Mergenthaler
THE LINOFILM CONVERTER

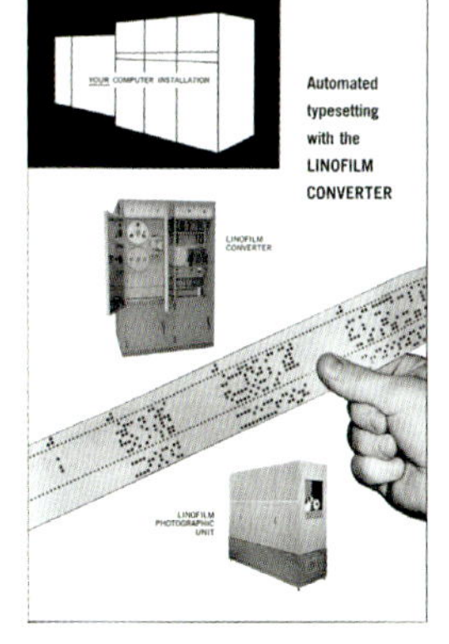
Automated
typesetting
with the
LINOFILM
CONVERTER

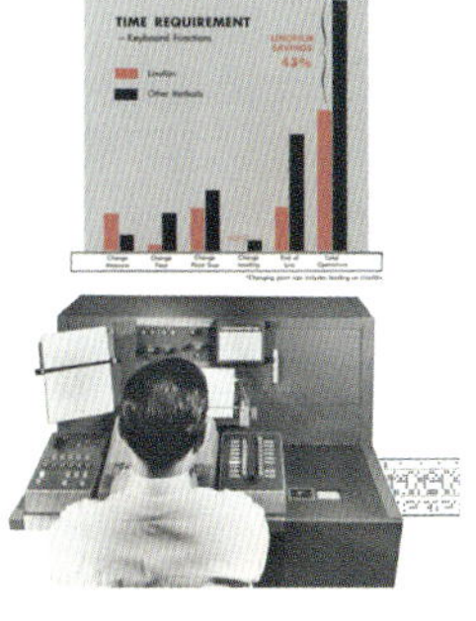
TIME REQUIREMENT

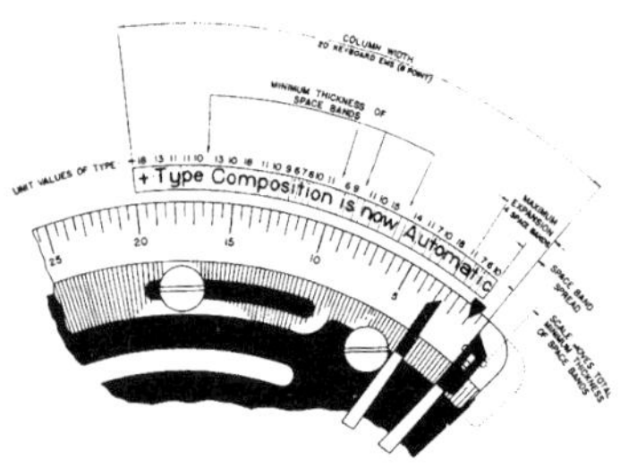

Phototype machines **resized** letters much like photographic enlargers, through a series of lenses. Mechanisms for setting the scale varied by manufacturer; shown, the Fairchild Teletypesetter of the late 1950s.

Typography, dematerialized

Whereas hot metal type did away with the need to store vast quantities of individual sorts, phototype **dematerialized** type as an object entirely, storing font information on film, tape, or disc. Advantages in efficiency and economy aside, this facilitated new aesthetic approaches to type, which could now be **resized**, positioned, and altered at will. Some printers and industry observers embraced these possibilities, while others mourned a decline in typographic standards.

Intertype took care to remind its customers that they "Set the Standard" for quality even as technologies evolved [Fig. 7.7]. Their ad for the late 1960s Fototronic filmsetter achieves two rhetorical goals: reassurance of quality and reconceptualization of type as a photographic medium. First, the language itself—"set the standard of the industry"—makes claims for Intertype's quality and reliability. Historically, foundry and hot metal specimens claimed similar accolades for their products and production methods. Almost since the inception of the specimen as a form, foundries positioned themselves

Fig 7.7 (right)

Intertype Fototronic brochure (Intertype, New York, c.1968-70). A single disc contains upwards of 40 typefaces, pointing to the dematerialization of typography—now stored on film, not cast in metal.

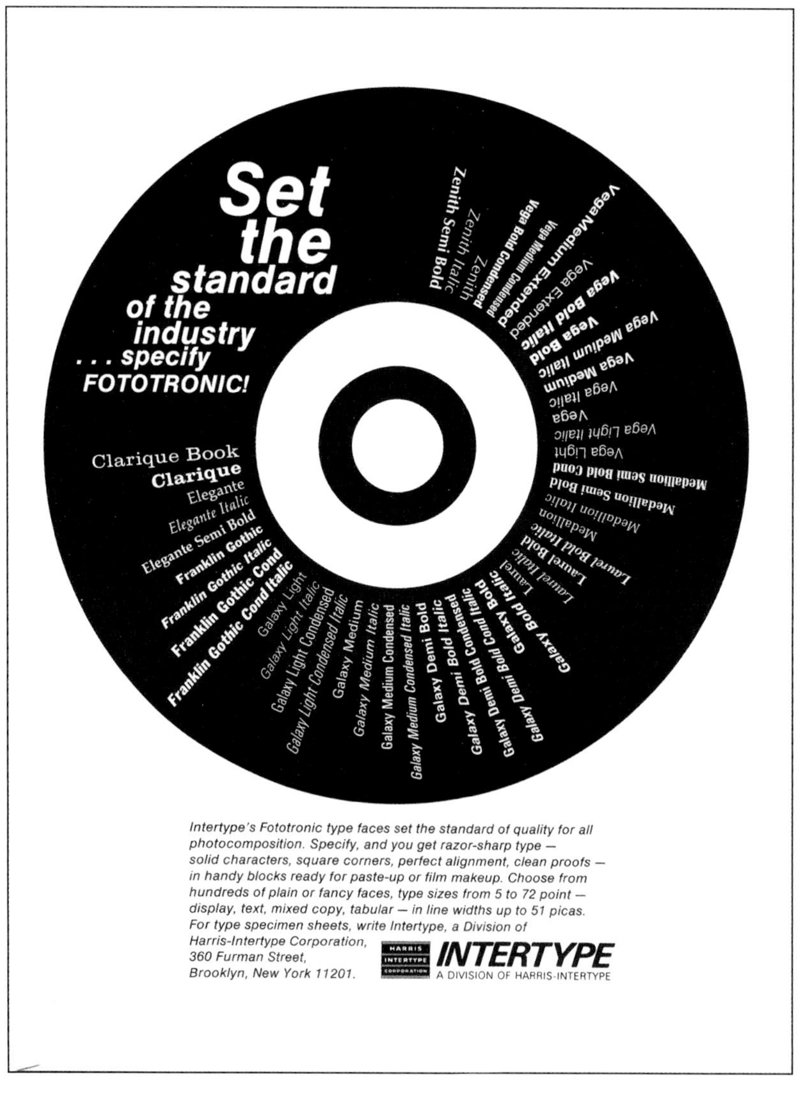

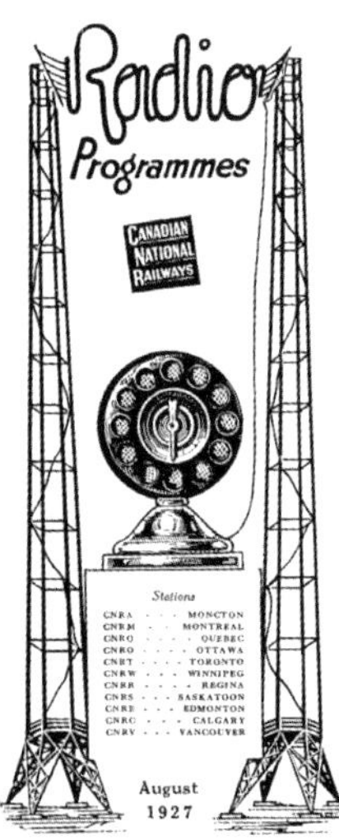

Dematerialization characterized many kinds of new 19 and 20 c. communication and imaging technologies, from telegrams and x-rays to phototype and, later, the internet. Even dematerialized signals require physical infrastructure to create and broadcast them, though, as this 1927 radio program schedule illustrates.

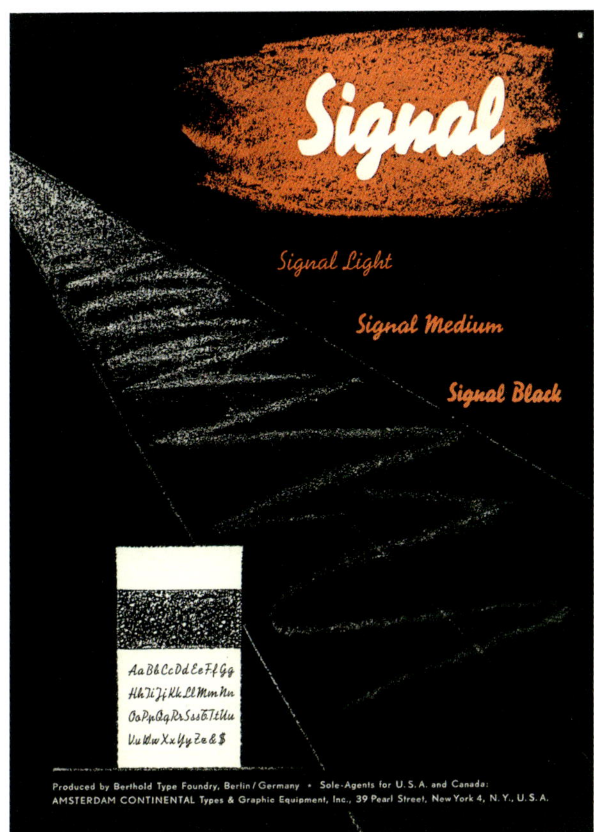

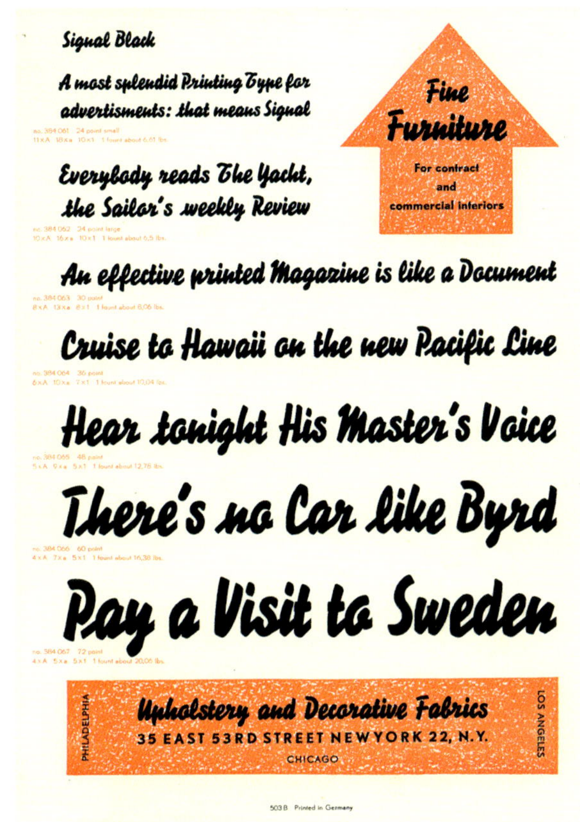

Fig 7.8 (above)

***Signal* (Amsterdam Continental, New York, c.1951). After its use by Germany's Nazi party, Berthold's Signal was re-conceptualized for American audiences as a broadcast signal, carried on airwaves and indicitave of modern, dematerialized communication technologies.**

competitively within the market through such language. Phototype specimens did the same. Second, the visual design suggests ease, efficiency, and variety achieved through photographic production technologies. While the first three were hardly novel claims, the physical form of the production method differs, and this photographic method was what the image emphasizes. Almost four dozen different typefaces radiated from the center of a single disc. The name of each, displayed in its own face, offered the user a compact menu of typographic choices, all held on one small disc.

The dematerialization of typography found its way into the graphic language used to conceptualize individual typefaces, as well. This held true even if the type itself pre-dated phototype, as in the case of Signal [Fig. 7.8]. The typeface, in four styles/weights, had been designed by Walter Wege for Berthold in 1931–4. The Nazi propaganda magazine *Signal* utilized a customized version for its logotype but this didn't prevent its postwar import into the United States, reconceptualized as a contemporary advertising face.[10] Amsterdam Continental's *Signal* specimen (c.1951) leveraged the dematerialized beam or wave motif, traveling through open space, as an abstracted signpost for new technologies. Early ads for Signal had emphasized its handmade qualities; Herbert Bayer's 1932 specimen portfolio for the face featured ink splatters, for instance. But, as always, type foundries and distributors sought to contextualize the faces they sold as contemporary and technologically advanced. Signal's visual transformation into a dematerialized broadcast medium reflects this impulse, divorcing the type from its origins and offering a new translation of its meaning.

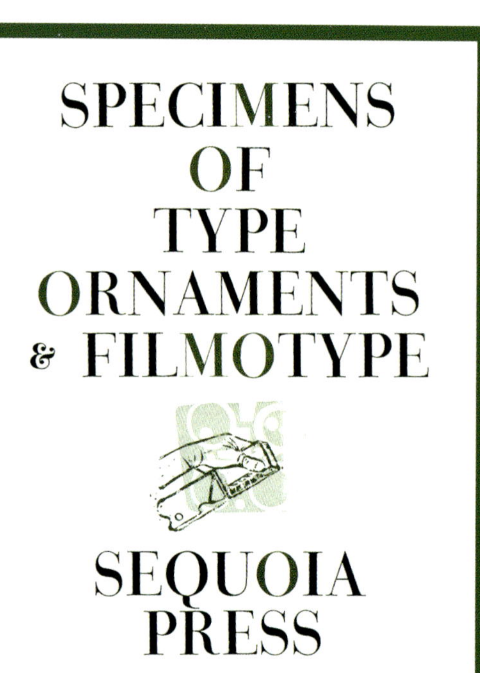

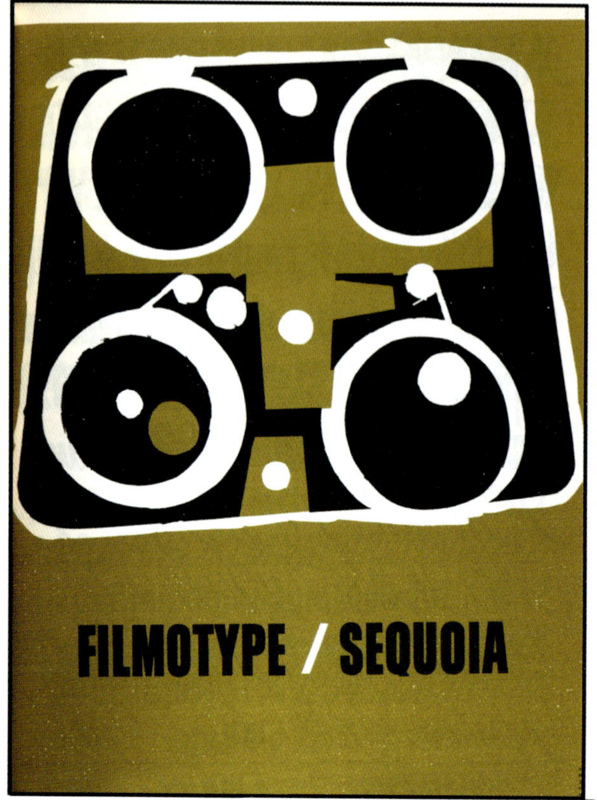

ABCDEGHIJKLMNO!
PQRSTUVXYZ&?abcd
efghjkmoprstuvxyz½%
123456789 $ Standard Light Extended

ABCDEJ
GKORS!
UVXYZ1
259 12345
ALTERNATE GOTHIC

ABCDEFGHIJKL
MNOPQRSTUV
WXYZ abcdefghi
jklmnopqrstuvw
xyz &.,:;!?'""-() $*
1234567890%¢
Venus Italic 36 pt.

ABCDEFGHIJKLMNOP
QRSTUVWXYZ abcdefg
hijklmnopqrstuvwxyz &!?
1234567890 $ % 1234567890
Venus Italic 24 point

Photographic type

FILMOTYPE GOTHIC TYPES / SEQUOIA PRESS

ABCDEFGHIJKLMNOP
QRSTUVWXYZ
abcdef
ghijklmnopqrstuvwxyz
123 Avon 678

ABCDEFGJK
MNOPQRSTUVW
abcdefghij
nopqrstuvwxyz
123 Lancer 456

FILMOTYPE INFORMAL SCRIPT / SEQUOIA PRESS

Attitudes toward technology

Fig 7.9 (opposite)
Filmotype/Sequoia (Sequoia Press, Kalamazoo MI, 196-?). Photographic gradients and popular advertising faces Filmotype specimen

Foundry, hot metal, and photomechanical type coexisted within the printing industry for roughly a quarter-century. Specimens produced during this time embodied attitudes toward evolving production technologies. Some emphasized production processes, while others mentioned them only in passing. Cover images might be the only indication of a specimen's physical production method, but such images offered manufacturers and printers opportunities to contextualize new technologies within a value system. The front cover of Sequoia Press' Filmotype specimen (c.1957–60s) drew attention to phototypesetting as a technology, offering the leaflet's primary indication of its means of production [Fig. 7.9]. The image implied equivalency between metal foundry type and film type, layering a hand-held composing stick over an abstracted image of the Filmotype machine. Inside, a full-page illustration showed the Filmotype, a manually operated phototypesetting machine designed for producing headlines. Simple construction offered relative ease of use; the operator exposed letters one at a time on a film strip, which was then ready to produce printing plates. The interior text repeated either the alphabet running A–Z, or a brief passage from British design educator John R. Biggs, opening with the truism "a love of letters is the beginning of typographical wisdom." Functional faces like Univers, described as "a new integrated series" imported from Europe, sat alongside fat faces, Egyptians, and scripts, staples of mid-century print advertising. In its other advertising literature, Filmotype emphasized high standards. "The Filmotype photo-composition machine produces professional hand lettering and display type," an undated brochure claimed, indicating that quality remained a concern for both makers and users of phototype. Evaluations of the relative merits of each typographic production technology varied; some championed a particular technology as objectively and consistently best, while others argued that different methods suited different purposes.

Inferiority—"the hand is the guide"

Like hot metal type before it, the quality of photomechanical type compared unfavorably to foundry type in purists' eyes. In 1937, Bauer had argued for the supremacy of the human **hand** in the printed page:

> Printing types ... are projections of the human hand. The original and most powerful form of printing types is that which is known as 'foundry,' in which the designs are either cut or drawn by hand, the hand is the guide through all the processes of manufacture, and the hand arranges the completed types in a composing stick for the final act of impressing them on paper.[11]

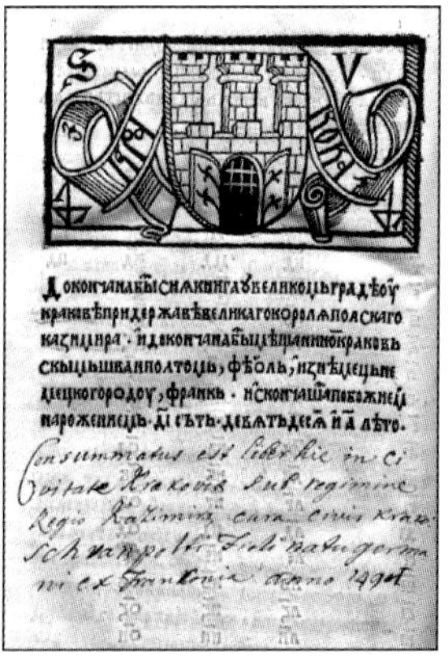

Hand might indicate a manuscript hand (the style in which a manuscript text is inscribed) or, as Bauer uses it here, to mean evidence of the human hand in the printing process. This 1491 Slavonic print by Swietopelk Printing House, Cracow, shows both.

The core of this argument continued to inform postwar attitudes, especially toward fine printing, encouraging a market for foundry type as a specialty product. ATF continued to produce foundry fonts of their historical or "old" types, printers' favorites which hadn't been produced for newer technologies. (ATF didn't introduce a phototype machine until 1958, and it had limited success.) But these old faces remained available under their "regular" and "subscription plan" casting procedures. As a 1953 specimen explained, ATF cast a few high-demand foundry faces regularly in several common sizes, and these could be ordered and delivered at any time [Fig. 7.10]. For lower-demand

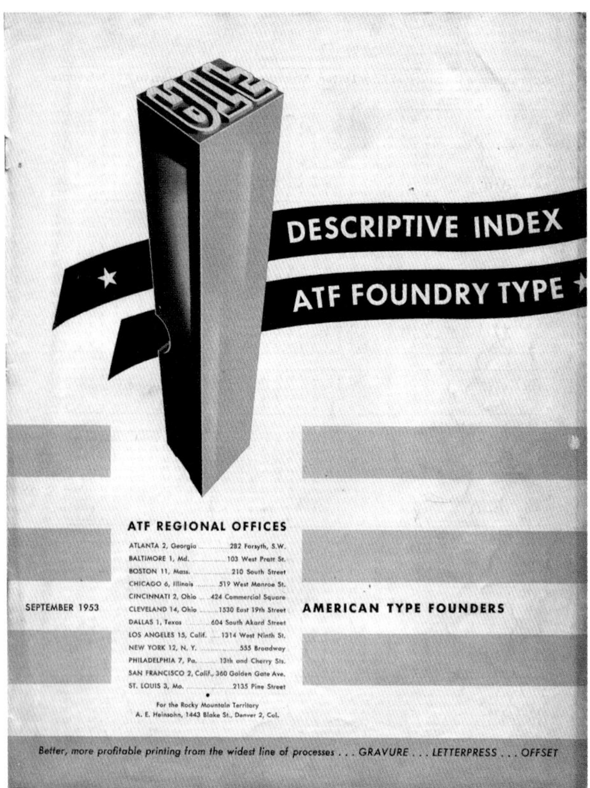

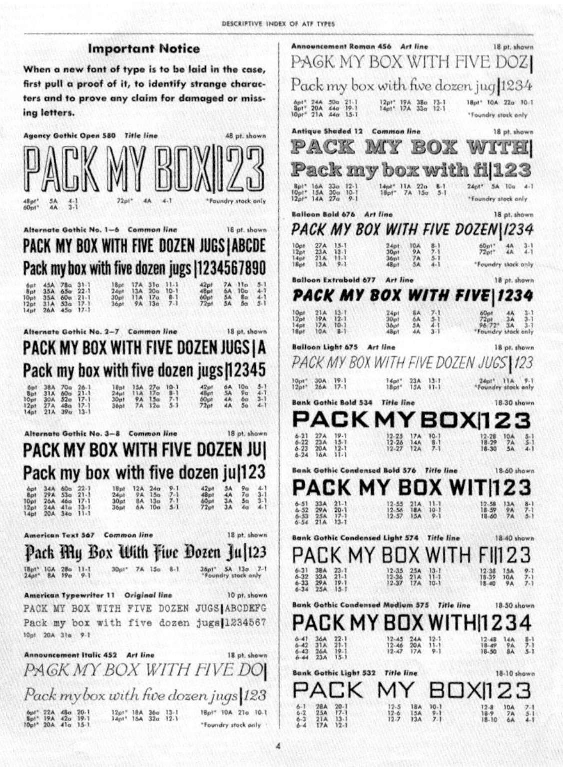
DESCRIPTIVE INDEX OF ATF TYPES

Important Notice

When a new font of type is to be laid in the case, first pull a proof of it, to identify strange characters and to prove any claim for damaged or missing letters.

Agency Gothic Open 580 Title line — 48 pt. shown

PACK MY BOX|123

Alternate Gothic No. 1–6 Common line — 18 pt. shown

PACK MY BOX WITH FIVE DOZEN JUGS|ABCDE

Pack my box with five dozen jugs|1234567890

Alternate Gothic No. 2–7 Common line — 18 pt. shown

PACK MY BOX WITH FIVE DOZEN JUGS|A

Pack my box with five dozen jugs|12345

Alternate Gothic No. 3–8 Common line — 18 pt. shown

PACK MY BOX WITH FIVE DOZEN JU|

Pack my box with five dozen ju|123

American Text 367 Common line — 18 pt. shown

Pack My Box With Five Dozen Ju|123

American Typewriter 11 Original line — 10 pt. shown

PACK MY BOX WITH FIVE DOZEN JUGS|ABCDEFG

Pack my box with five dozen jugs|1234567

Announcement Italic 452 Art line — 18 pt. shown

PACK MY BOX WITH FIVE DO|

Pack my box with five dozen jugs|123

Announcement Roman 456 Art line — 18 pt. shown

PACK MY BOX WITH FIVE DOZ|

Pack my box with five dozen jug|1234

Antique Shaded 12 Common line — 18 pt. shown

PACK MY BOX WITH|

Pack my box with fi|123

Balloon Bold 676 Art line — 18 pt. shown

PACK MY BOX WITH FIVE DOZEN|1234

Balloon Extrabold 677 Art line — 18 pt. shown

PACK MY BOX WITH FIVE|1234

Balloon Light 675 Art line — 18 pt. shown

PACK MY BOX WITH FIVE DOZEN JUGS|123

Bank Gothic Bold 534 Title line — 18-30 shown

PACKMYBOX|123

Bank Gothic Condensed Bold 576 Title line — 18-60 shown

PACK MY BOX WIT|123

Bank Gothic Condensed Light 574 Title line — 18-40 shown

PACK MY BOX WITH FI|123

Bank Gothic Condensed Medium 575 Title line — 18-50 shown

PACK MY BOX WITH|1234

Bank Gothic Light 532 Title line — 18-10 shown

PACK MY BOX|123

4

Fig 7.10 (above)

***Descriptive index* (ATF, Elizabeth NJ, 1953). As a relative latecomer to the phototype scene, ATF continued to market "foundry type," albeit as an increasingly specialized product most suited to the high standards of fine printing.**

faces, ATF held orders for a specific face/size until meeting a quota, at which point they cast the type and filled the accumulated orders.[12] This allowed printers who used foundry type—for whatever reason—to continue restocking.

Other manufacturers and distributors marked foundry type as a specialty product, as well. Chicago's branch of the Acme Foundry offered "American and foreign cast foundry types ... purchased by the line." This allowed printers to "avoid buying high cost fonts, when only a line or two are needed."[13] Acme collaborated with Pittsburgh's **Neon** Type Foundry to release Neon's eponymous typeface in wood (1939).[14] Then, after Typefounders of Chicago acquired Neon in 1959, they too began selling foundry type through their newly named Neon Type Division. [Fig. 7.11], Neon offered types "foundry cast with foundry metal on foundry machines"—both domestic faces from their library and "imported type styles from European foundries." Their 1962 catalog offered "guidance in proper typeface selection for specific printing jobs." Its designers hadn't "adhered to any set format in [its] compilation" or the presentation of its types. "The important factor [wasn't] the style of the book," but its value as a "reference" for measuring "a line of practically any type face." The introduction suggested genuine foundry type offered better outcomes; "changes in graphic arts ... gave birth to the demand for more accurate foundry type—precision cast and micrometer perfect"—just as typographic purists demanded.[15]

NEON (B) CAPS AND FIGURES ONLY

54 Pt.—3A

NEON CAP

42 Pt.—4A

ILLUMINATES 1

30 Pt.—7A

THE TIME TO BUY 3

24 Pt.—10A

THE CONTINENTAL GRILL

18 Pt.—13A

OF THE HOTEL MT. MIRADOR

Neon was an inline sans serif face, not a kitschy script like twenty-first century viewers might associate with vintage neon signs.

To give typographic purists their due, phototype posed specific challenges. The process used a single master font for all sizes in a typeface, overemphasizing thick strokes in larger sizes and causing thin strokes to disappear in smaller sizes.[16] This phenomenon vexes digital revivals, as well; the influence of phototype predecessors on early digital type design was pragmatic as well as aesthetic and philosophical.[17] The ability to size, space, and **skew** at will also led to problems with legibility and **print quality**, as well as debates about what these terms even meant. These questions, too, persisted in early digital type design.[18] Applied expertly, though, phototype's level of precision offered pristine, engineered results. Berthold's promotional literature, for instance, included specimen pages charting the size, spacing, and shading options facilitated by their Diatype machine, introduced in the 1950s [Fig. 7.12]. Such specimens pointed toward the typographic variety and control made possible by new phototype technologies.

The Barco foundry of Illinois persisted into the twenty-first century as a distributor of metal type, remaining committed to the medium even after it passed from common use. The cover of their undated, mid-century specimen

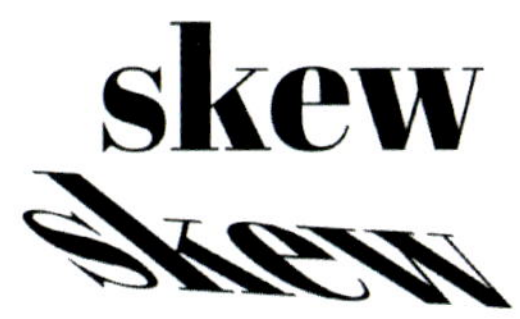

To **skew** a typeface is to bend it, non-proportionally alter its width/height ratio, or otherwise alter its appearance in opposition to its original construction principles.

abg

In 1966, DigiSet released the first truly digital typesetting equipment, a technology initially plagued by low resolution and poor **print quality**, as seen in this sample.

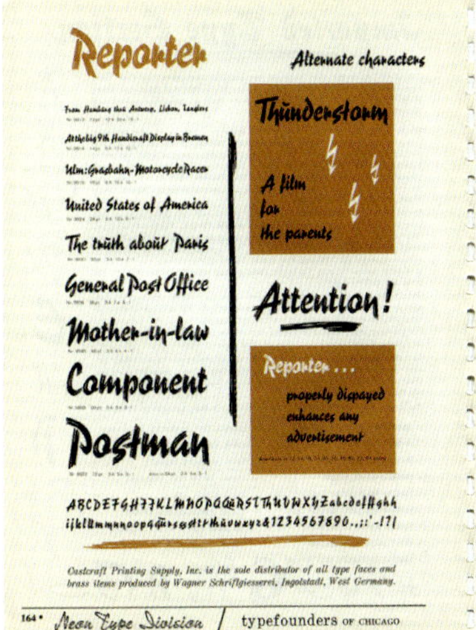

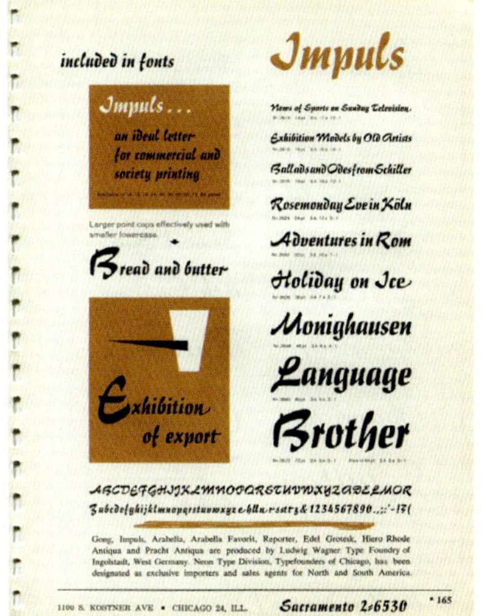

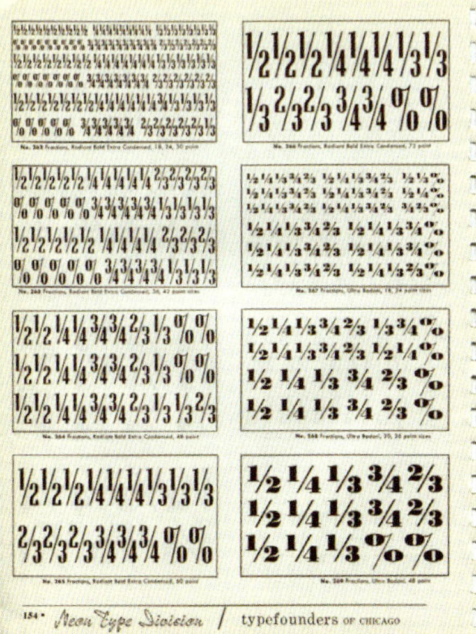

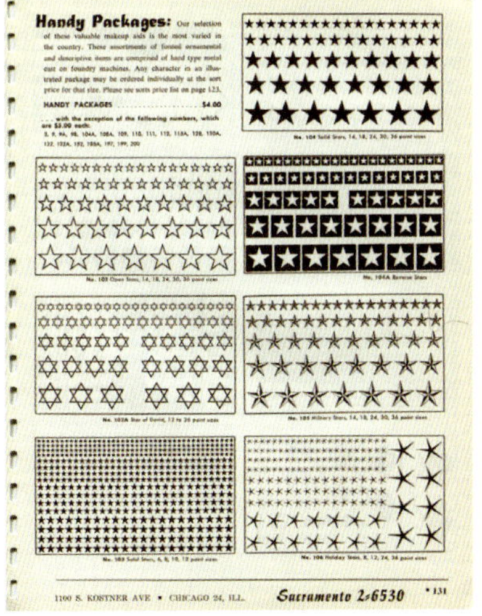

Fig 7.11 (left)

Type Specimens by Neon Type Division **(Typefounders of Chicago, Chicago, 1962). ATF wasn't alone in advertising foundry type to purists who demanded accuracy, high standards, and the material qualities of a letterpress-printed page. When Typefounders of Chicago acquired Pittsburgh's Neon Foundry, they started marketing all of their imported foundry faces using the Neon name.**

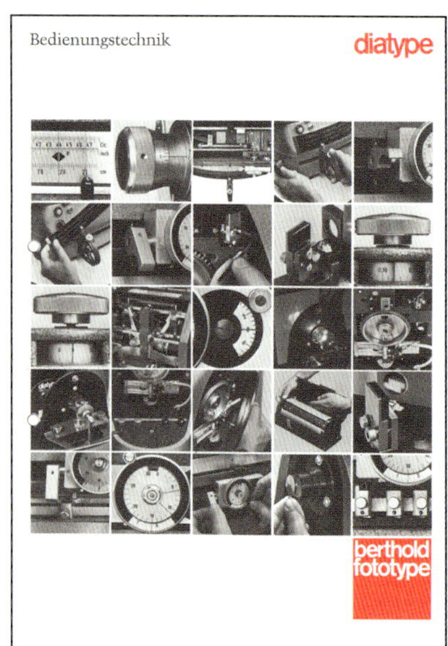

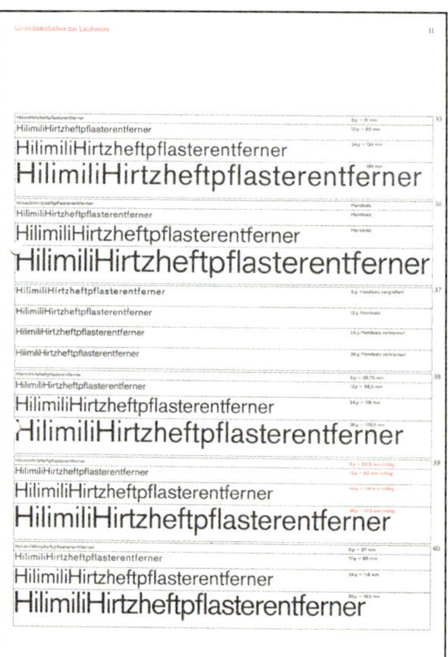

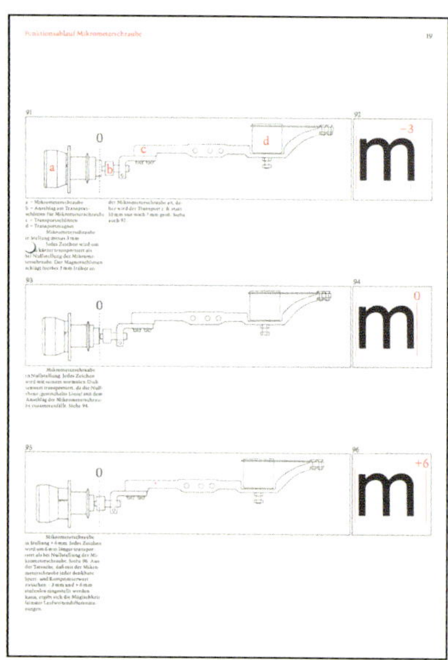

Fig 7.12 (above)

Berthold Fototype Diatype Bedienungstechnik **(Berthold, Berlin, 1950s). While phototype was an easily abused technology, when applied with care it lent crisp, precise, almost engineered results, as demonstrated by this Berthold Diatype specimen from the 1950s.**

booklet leaves no doubt as to the product being sold [Fig. 7.13, top rows]. It emphasizes the physicality of metal type, showcasing a single sort in three-quarter profile view. The large uppercase B feels monumental within the space, a wordless commentary on the permanence and status of metal type. The specimen promises "clean, sharp, clear impressions guaranteed due to highly skilled and trained type craftsmen" but otherwise doesn't comment on industry-wide changes in production technology. The cover image does most of the semiotic work. A 1954 Intertype **Fotosetter** specimen likewise relies on its cover image to communicate its technology, with the interior pages designed for functionality rather than articulation of process [Fig. 7.13, bottom row]. Here, an abstracted beam of light pierces an eye-shaped lens, its dotted lines becoming solid when they meet the vertical rule along the left edge of the picture plane. While the introductory note informs readers that "Fotosetter composition has opened the door to new concepts in typography for the modern printer," the specimen doesn't demonstrate any of these, not even the "connected scripts and beautiful kerning italics" it describes. *Barco Type Founders and Intertype Fotosetter*[19] utilized remarkably similar page design tactics. The name of each type serves as its sample's title, followed by alpha-order lines of uppercase then lowercase letters, with numerals to the right. Each page shows about eight faces, and both catalogs organize types alphabetically, starting with Alternate Gothic and running to Times Italic (Fotosetter) and Wedding Text (Barco). Nothing inherent to the specimens' design differentiates between metal and photomechanical type. Only the cover images, and brief introductory notes, indicate the significant difference in production processes and attitudes toward them.

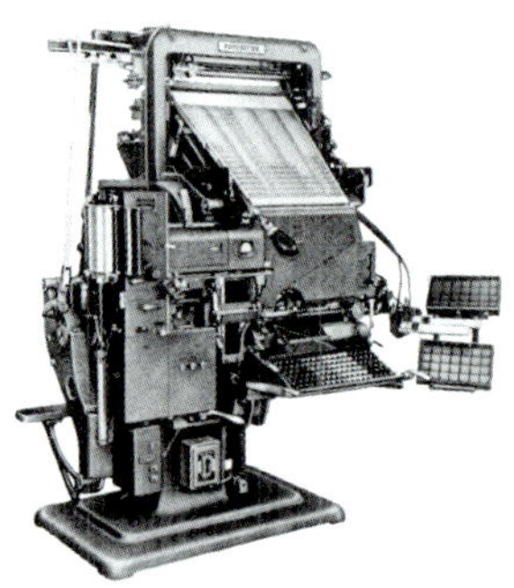

Intertype's **Fotosetter**, a first generation phototypesetting machine, looked much like the manufacturer's hot metal machines.

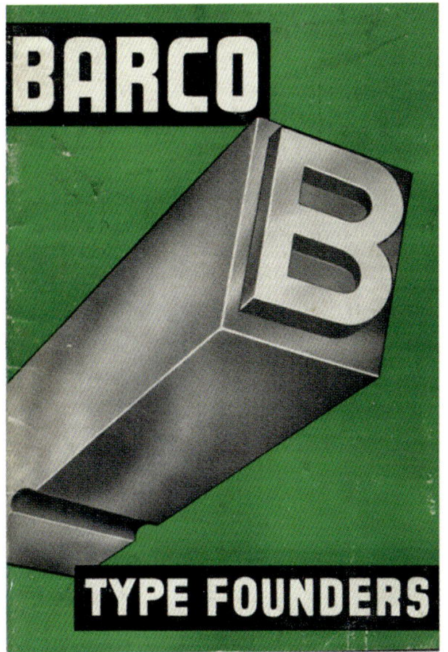

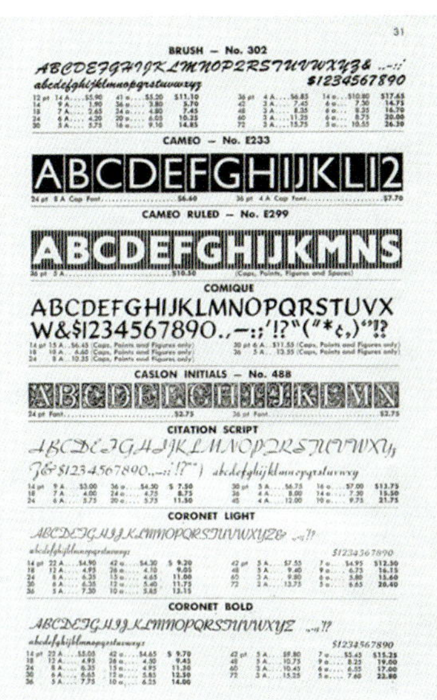

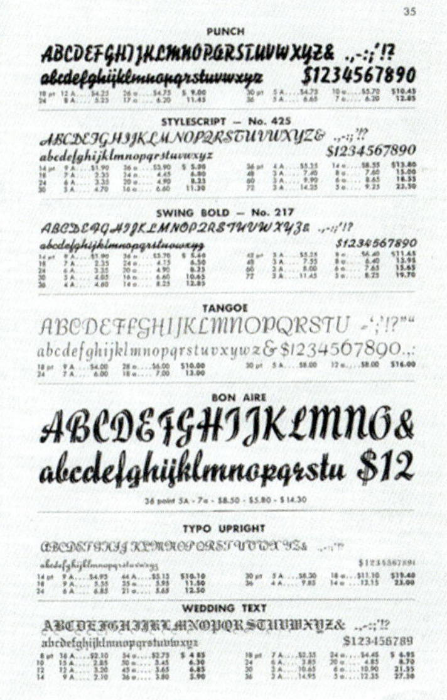

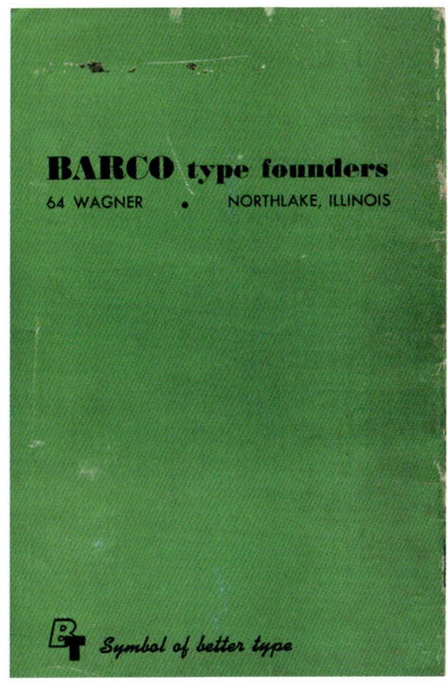

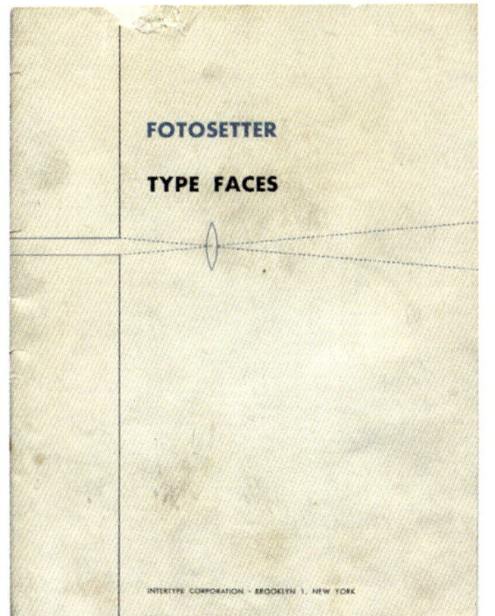

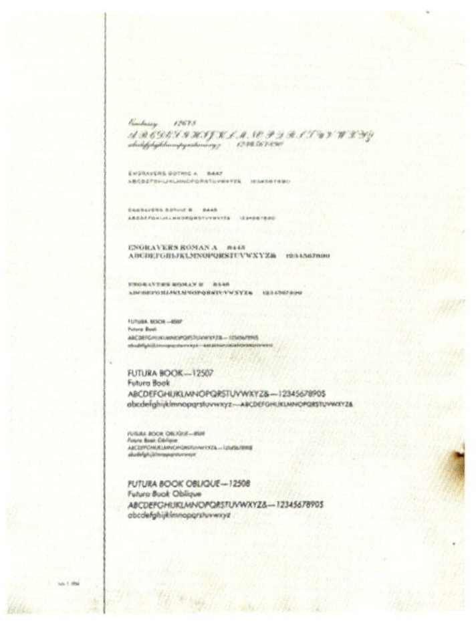

Fig 7.13 (above and left)

***Barco Type Founders* (Barco, Northlake IL, ND/before 1963) and *Fotosetter Type Faces* (Intertype, New York, 1954, bottom row). At times, cover images were the only indication of a specimen's production technology while interior pages were generic and unremarkable in design.**

Innovation—"interesting possibilities"

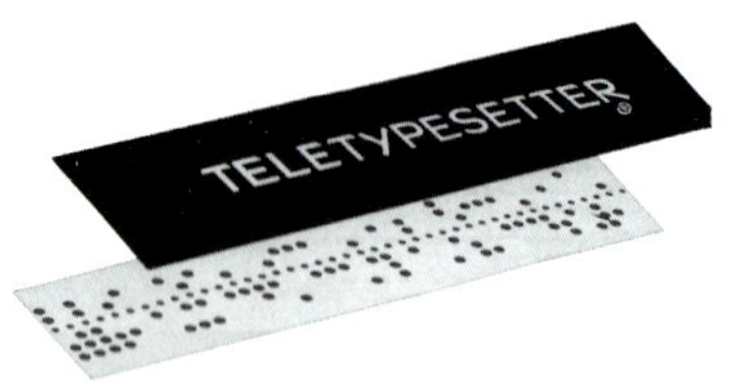

Punched **tape** represents each sort with a unique, machine-readable series of punched holes. Early tape-punching solutions used tape to control metal typecasting, later models to control fully computerized systems.

Phototype, though its critics decried its low quality and disregard for typographic conventions, offered what Linotype's Linofilm advertising called a "new concept" in typesetting. Monotype, meanwhile, "freed [letterforms] from the mechanical limitations of type metal" with Monophoto, offering designers the flexibility to mix sizes and styles at will. As a medium, phototype offered opportunities for experimentation, as Monotype was quick to point out; "[i]nteresting possibilities are suggested by multiple exposures to combine common character elements" into novel forms. Because Monophoto was "built on [the] fundamentally sound and proven principles" of its hot metal predecessors, Monotype predicted it would become the "standard" tool for producing "quality typography."[20] Despite often-lengthy prose descriptions, much of the promotional literature left out *visualizations* of phototype's formal possibilities. Instead, images of the machines and their storage and communication mechanisms dominated, visualizing it through discs, punched **tapes**, binary code, computer systems, and the ever-present signal-wave motif.

Fig 7.14 (right)

Phototype made it possible to skew, distort, and overlap letterforms with ease. Yet signal waves, discs, and punched paper tapes dominated cover images, like these advertising Swiftape (Ludlow, mid-1960s), Linofilm (Mergenthaler Linotype, 1960s), the TSS Teletypesetter, an additive operating unit (Mergenthaler Linotype, 1951), and the Photon (Photo Typositor Inc, c.1965).

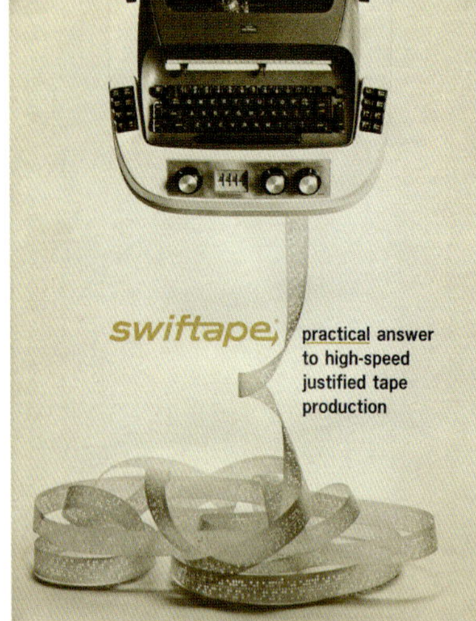

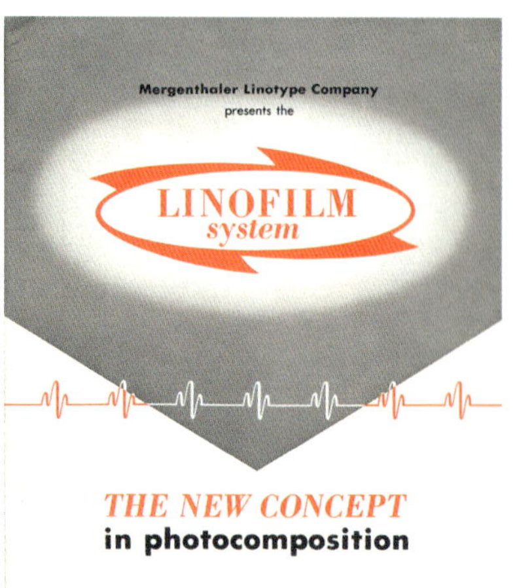

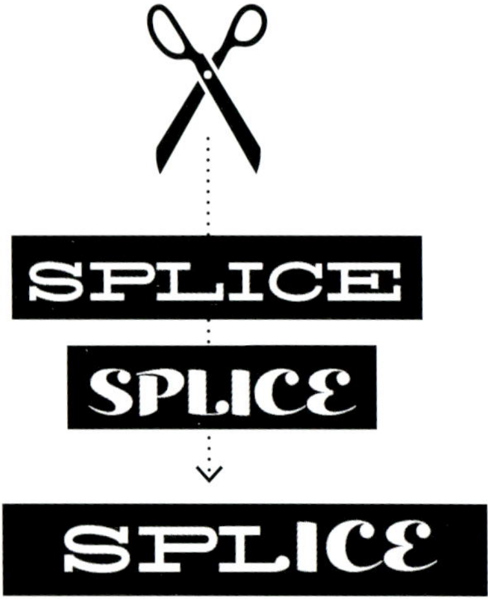

Splicing photo-typographic negatives allows the typesetter or graphic designer to cut apart and recombine letterforms easily and intuitively—not always to ends appreciated by traditionally trained typographers.

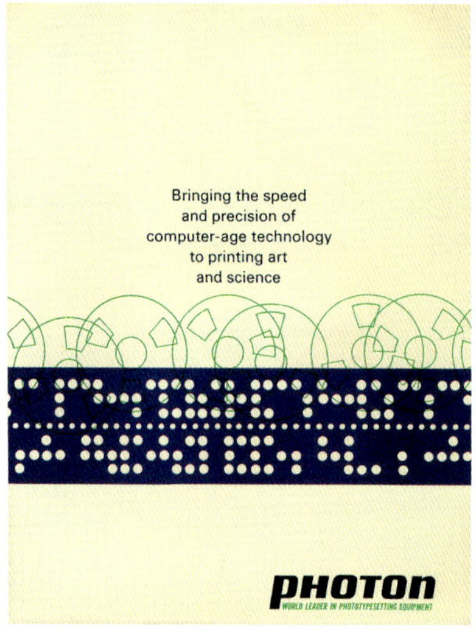

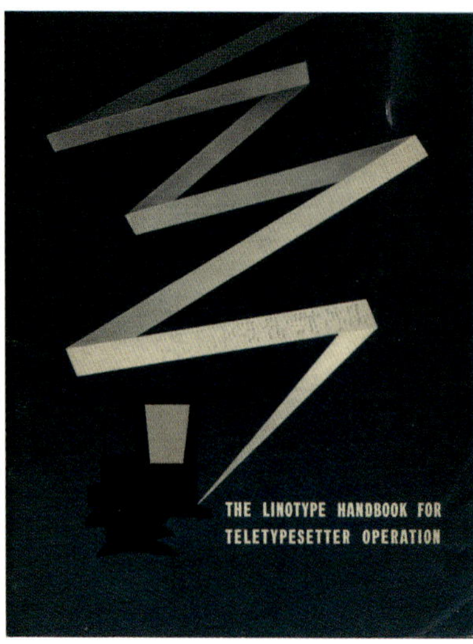

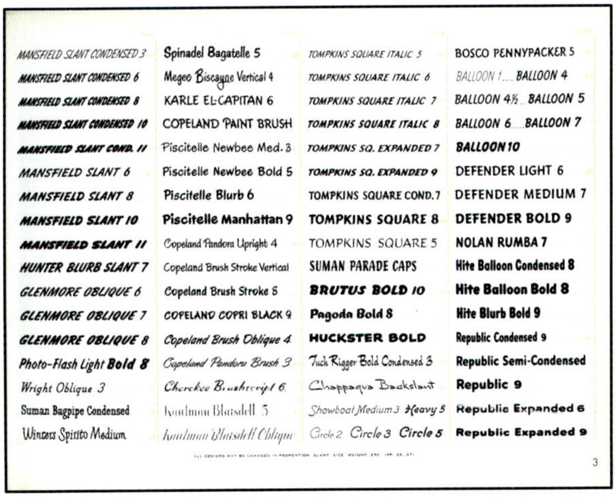

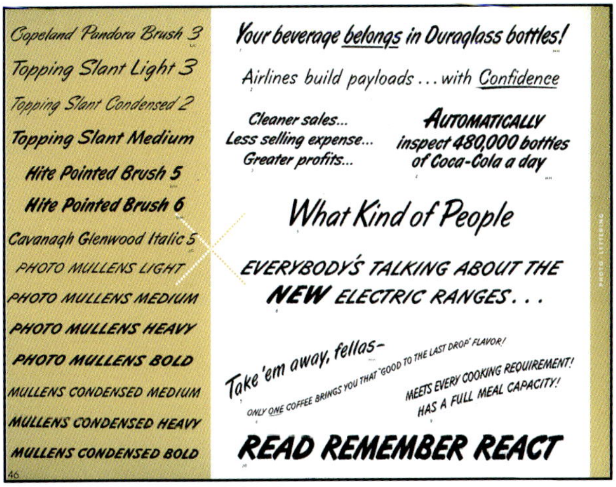

The physical possibilities of printing with phototype, though perhaps not as common a motif as the mechanics of the system, did appear in specimen posters, booklet covers, and advertisements. A 1960 Lumitype poster design by Rémy Peignot bent letterforms, curved baselines, and skewed the viewer's perspective to imply the zooming function of a camera lens. Roger Excoffon's booklet cover for a specimen of his Antique Olive family (1962-5, Fonderie Olive) applied color gradients to large letterforms, suggesting the overlapping capacity and inherent transparency of film. Ladislas Mandel used overlapping, transparency, and **splicing** to conceptualize his typeface Antique Presse (1964, Deberny & Peignot), an evocation of nineteenth century wood type reimagined for film. A poster for Adrian Frutiger's Univers (1954-7, Deberny & Peignot) used hundreds of overlapping, radiating U's on incrementally tilting baselines to advertise a typeface conceptualized initially for film. The rhetorical work accomplished by such images reminded viewers of phototype's radical compositional possibilities.

On their interior pages, specimen books frequently highlighted a few examples of how **photographic manipulation** might work, then left the rest to the viewer's imagination. Photo-Lettering Inc. (est. New York, 1936) depicted "circoflare" and "perspective" techniques in their three-volume Alphabet Thesaurus, demonstrating how type could be warped and skewed through photographic reproduction [Fig. 7.15].[21] They showed the available typefaces in their standard form, however. Similarly, the Photo Typositor, manufactured by the Visual Graphic Corporation (VGC), allowed designers to "enlarge or reduce; condense, expand, heighten or shorten; slant letters; apply Benday shadows; step up or down; bounce, stagger, arc, curve; interlock or letterspace." VGC's promotional literature illustrated each technique with a handful of type samples, offering designers a preview of the equipment's possibilities [Fig. 7.16]. The core operating principle of phototype—that a single master font could produce nearly-unlimited variations—made displaying each typeface in all its variations impossible. So specimens often consisted of a single line for each type, showing only its most basic form and relying on users to recall the permutations available.

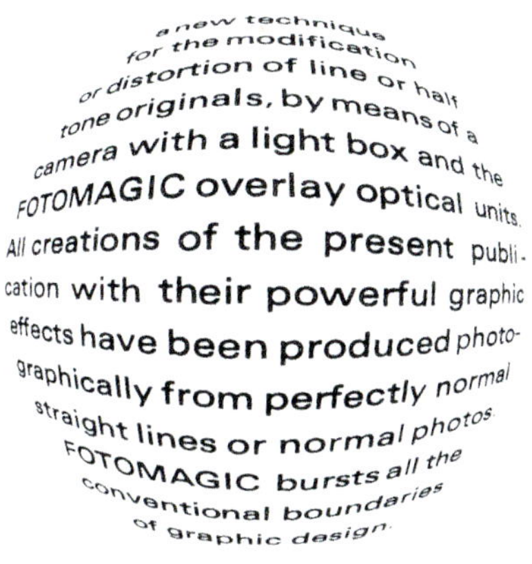

Fig 7.15 (above)

Photo lettering catalog (Photo Lettering Inc., New York, c.1960). Informal types that felt hand-lettered could, with phototype, be bent, skewed, twisted, and otherwise manipulated into unexpected shapes.

Photographic manipulation allows the designer to warp, bend, pixelate, blur, wrap, or otherwise alter standard letterforms. This example from *Understanding Photo Typesetting* (Kleper, 1976) utilized FOTOMAGIC optical overlays.

Multiplicity—"for case, matrix, and film"

The radiating u-forms on Frutiger's **Univers** poster pictorialized its ties to photocomposition, but this wasn't the only form the typeface took. Deberny & Peignot released Univers (1957) in three formats, after a four-year design and production process. Underscoring the notion that typefaces exist independently from delivery technology, a single bifold advertises Univers for "case, maxtrix, [and] film" [Fig. 7.17]. Univers was the first typeface designed intentionally for flexibility not only of width, weight, and size, but across all three available typesetting platforms. Its designer, Adrian Frutiger (1928–2015), worked throughout his long career in the technology of his day and designed typefaces specifically for metal, photographic, and digital methods, as well as typefaces like Univers which spanned multiple **production platforms**. Technology didn't dictate his philosophy, per se, but rather made new things possible. "Casting a font in lead was very expensive," Frutiger reflected in a 1999 interview about his design process for Univers, which he'd pitched to Deberny & Peignot as an alternative to Futura developed specifically for use with the **Lumitype**-Photon. "Now suddenly I only needed to prepare drawings, and I could place sixteen alphabets photographically on one plate." Fruitger explicitly tied Univers' wide range of styles to its position within his own typographic development: "suddenly, there is a new technology, phototypesetting," for which he, a young designer at the time, proposed "a phototypeset font which no longer represents the old trinity—the roman, italic and semi-bold—but instead a system with 21 variations!"[22] These variations played an important role in Univers specimens, which visually referenced the periodic table of elements to indicate a rational, organized system. And despite its origin in the need for a functional, flexible, less-geometric (than Futura) sans serif for phototypesetting, D&P released Univers for foundry type, hot metal type, and phototype simultaneously, as its specimens made clear.

Univers (1957) took advantage of the phototypesetting technology pioneered by Lumitype. Its systematic progression of sizes, widths, and weights offered significant flexibility for designers of its day.

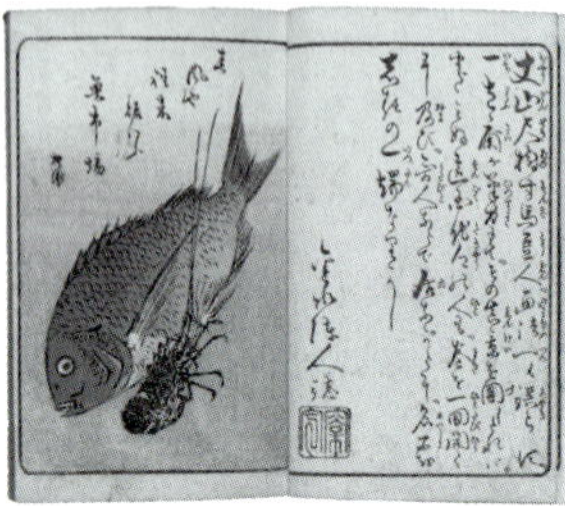

Historically, books have been made via many **production platforms** — including relief, intaglio, and lithographic printing and large-scale manuscript production. Pictured, a woodblock book printed in Japan 1850-68, *Ehon Edo miyage*.

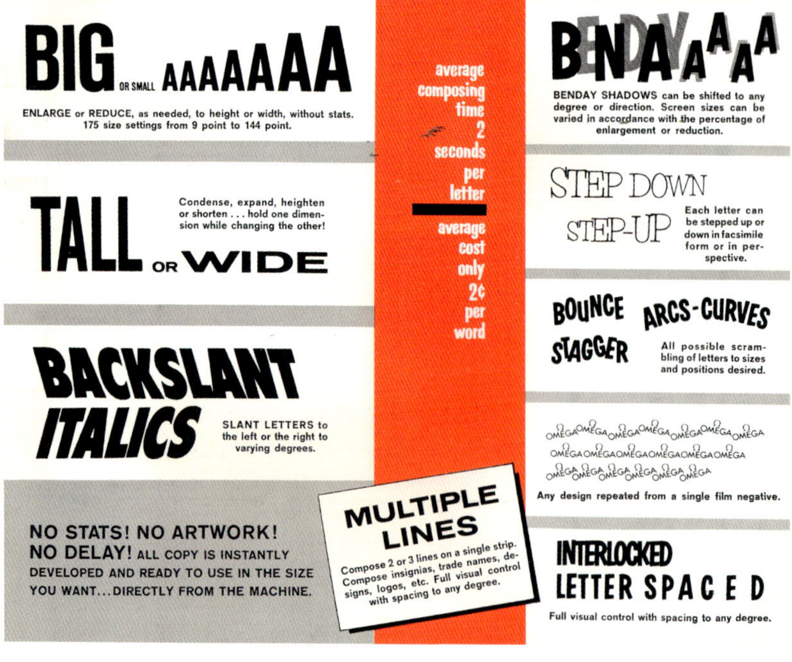

Fig 7.16 (right)

The Photo Typositor, the "typesetting miracle of the graphic arts" (Photo Typositor, New York, c.1962?), accommodated a wide range of photographic techniques, producing letterforms that bounced, staggered, arced, curved, and interlocked.

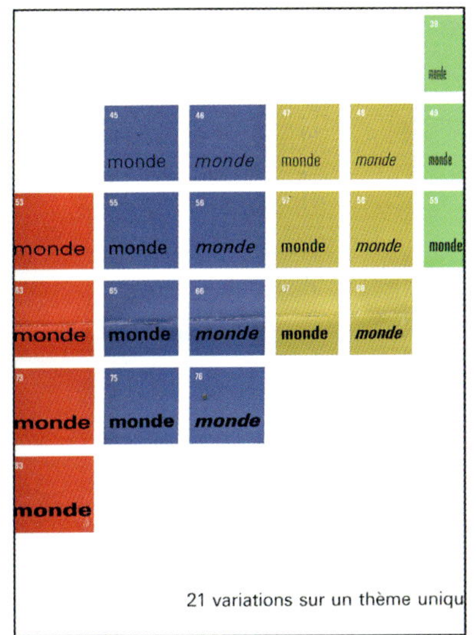

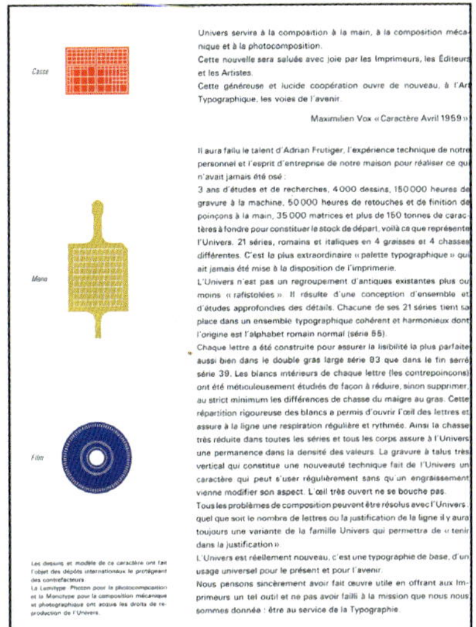

Univers servira à la composition à la main, à la composition mécanique et à la photocomposition.
Cette nouvelle sera saluée avec joie par les Imprimeurs, les Éditeurs et les Artistes.
Cette généreuse et lucide coopération ouvre de nouveau, à l'Art Typographique, les voies de l'avenir.

Maximilien Vox « Caractère Avril 1959 »

Il aura fallu le talent d'Adrian Frutiger, l'expérience technique de notre personnel et l'esprit d'entreprise de notre maison pour réaliser ce qui n'avait jamais été osé :
3 ans d'études et de recherches, 4 000 dessins, 150 000 heures de gravure à la machine, 50 000 heures de retouches et de finition de poinçons à la main, 35 000 matrices et plus de 150 tonnes de caractères à fondre pour constituer le stock de départ, voilà ce que représente l'Univers. 21 séries, romains et italiques en 4 graisses et 4 chasses différentes. C'est la plus extraordinaire « palette typographique » qui ait jamais été mise à la disposition de l'imprimerie.
L'Univers n'est pas un regroupement d'antiques existantes plus ou moins « rafistolées ». Il résulte d'une conception d'ensemble et d'études approfondies des détails. Chacune de ses 21 séries tient sa place dans un ensemble typographique cohérent et harmonieux dont l'origine est l'alphabet romain normal (série 55).
Chaque lettre a été construite pour assurer la lisibilité la plus parfaite aussi bien dans le double gras large série 83 que dans le fin serré série 39. Les blancs intérieurs de chaque lettre (les contrepoinçons) ont été méticuleusement étudiés de façon à réduire, sinon supprimer, au strict minimum les différences de chasse du maigre au gras. Cette répartition rigoureuse des blancs a permis d'ouvrir l'œil des lettres et assure à la ligne une respiration régulière et rythmée. Ainsi la chasse très réduite dans toutes les séries et tous les corps assure à l'Univers une permanence dans la densité des valeurs. La gravure à talus très vertical qui constitue une nouveauté technique fait de l'Univers un caractère qui peut s'user régulièrement sans qu'un engraissement vienne modifier son aspect. L'œil très ouvert ne se bouche pas.
Tous les problèmes de composition peuvent être résolus avec l'Univers : quel que soit le nombre de lettres ou la justification de la ligne il y aura toujours une variante de la famille Univers qui permettra de « tenir dans la justification ».
L'Univers est réellement nouveau, c'est une typographie de base, d'un usage universel pour le présent et pour l'avenir.
Nous pensons sincèrement avoir fait œuvre utile en offrant aux Imprimeurs un tel outil et ne pas avoir failli à la mission que nous nous sommes donnée : être au service de la Typographie.

Les dessins et modèle de ce caractère ont fait l'objet des dépôts internationaux le protégeant des contrefacteurs.
La Lumitype Photon pour la photocomposition et la Monotype pour la composition mécanique et photographique ont acquis les droits de reproduction de l'Univers.

Fig 7.17 (left)

Univers (Deberney & Peignot, Paris, 1957). As one of the first typefaces designed specifically with the considerations of phototype in mind, Univers took a systematic approach to visual variation and a flexible approach to production technology. Deberney & Peignot advertised it as equally suited to "case, matrix, and film," adaptable to all three environments.

Conclusion—toward a digital future

The earliest explorations of digital typographic tools took place while phototype emerged into market dominance, though at first phototype and **digital** type weren't explicitly connected.[23] Soon, however, the two technologies began developing in relationship to one another.[24] ITC, the International Typeface Corporation (est. 1970), created and distributed *only* photomechanical and **computerized** type, becoming the first foundry established entirely without metal type. ITC was a collaboration between Push Pin Studios designer Herb Lubalin, type designer Aaron Burns, and Photo Lettering cofounder Edward Rondthaler. *U&lc* (upper and lowercase), ITC's "house organ," displayed and promoted their types. Like its metal type predecessors, it included articles, trade news, and formal type specimens, all set in ITC types and annotated for easy identification. Famous guest designers and editors often appeared on its tabloid-sized newsprint pages. ITC distributed *U&lc* free of charge as a marketing vehicle for its types. In 1999, a decade after purchase by new owners, publication ceased. But during its quarter-century of publication, *U&lc* functioned as "a defining voice in international graphic design."[25] Its specimens introduced ITC's types within a carefully designed and stylistically recognizable context that spoke directly to practicing professionals.

Editorial content clearly articulated the magazine's purpose, which echoed historical forerunners like the *Inland Printer* or the *Monotype Recorder*. "Each issue of *U&lc* will introduce new ITC typefaces for use in text and display," the magazine's second issue informed readers, advising designers to collect the "[h]andsomely designed and colorful type specimen booklets [that] will be prepared for each new typeface." Available upon order, the "booklets will be the foundation of your future library of ITC typefaces."[26] Adjacent ads painted a vivid picture of the industry's transitional status in the early 1970s. RyderTypes of Chicago ran a full-page ad claiming that in a "tough town [w]e still settle certain problems with hot lead." In smaller print, they boasted "one of the largest selections of Hot Metal faces in the midwest." Meanwhile, TypoGraphics Communications (TGC) of New York argued that "It doesn't matter how it's set. What counts is how it looks." They went on

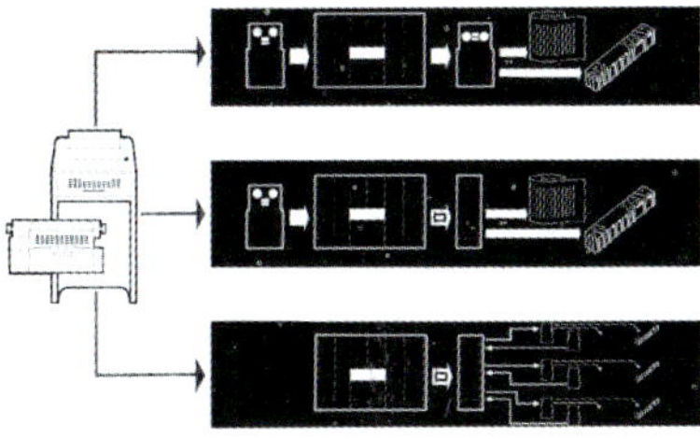

Early **computerized** typesetting systems, like this RCA Newscom system, used low resolution and poor-quality typefaces, which impacted legibility — but improvements were quick to materialize.

Mrs Eaves (1996)
Matrix II (1986/2007)

Digital types might be designed to take advantage of emergent digital technologies (as the original Matrix was in 1986 as personal computers and dot-matrix printers were introduced to everyday design practice) or to update classic faces for digital use (as in the case of Mrs Eaves, a Baskerville homage named for Sarah Eaves, Baskerville's live-in housekeeper and eventually his wife). Both were designed by Zuzana Licko, a pioneer of digital type design and co-founder of the Emigre digital type foundry.

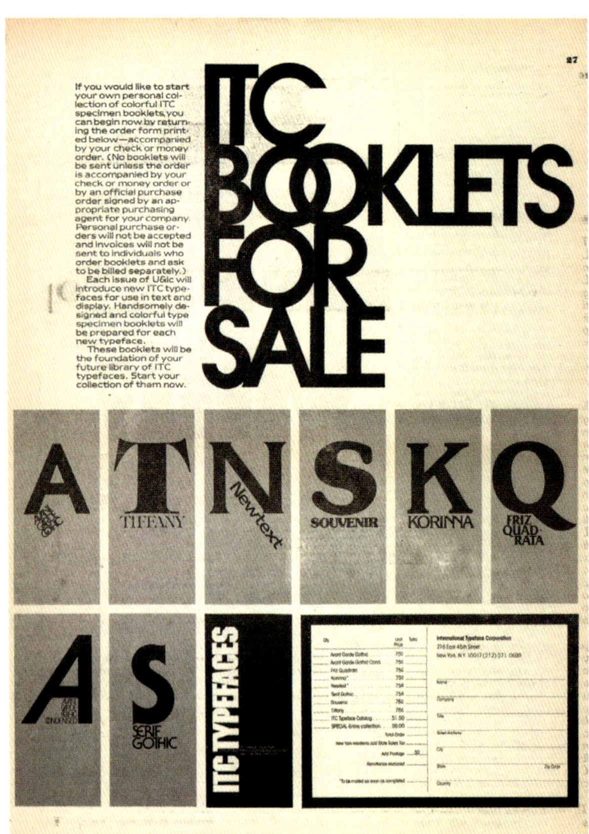

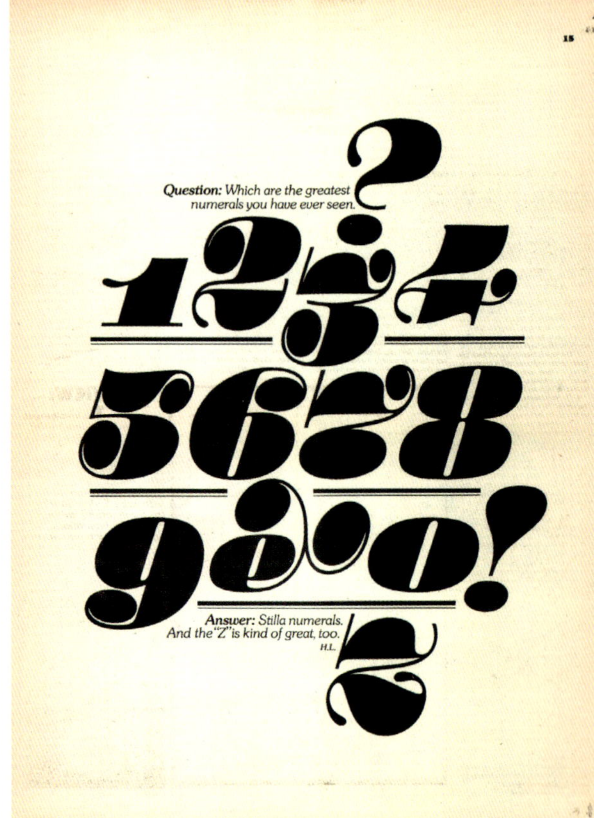

Fig 7.18 (above)

ITC booklets ad and ITC Stilla specimen (*U&lc* 1.2, 1974). As the first type foundry exclusively dedicated to film and then digital types, ITC used its house organ, *U&lc* magazine, to popularize its faces among designers and printers. In a pluralist and playful spirit, ITC produced everything from historical revivals to funky display faces, and released a specimen booklet dedicated to each.

Fig 7.19 (right)

Front cover and page from the appended 1996/7 ITC specimen catalog (*U&lc* 23.2, 1996). By the mid to late 1990s, ITC had shifted its attention entirely to digital type, echoing contemporary trade practices. Yet the printed specimen remained a vital tool for designing printed texts.

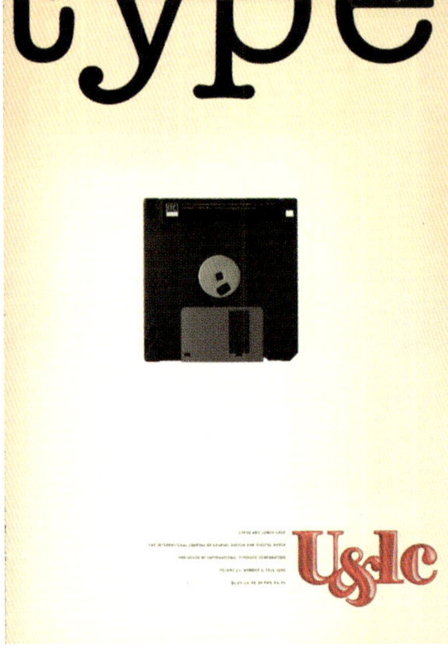

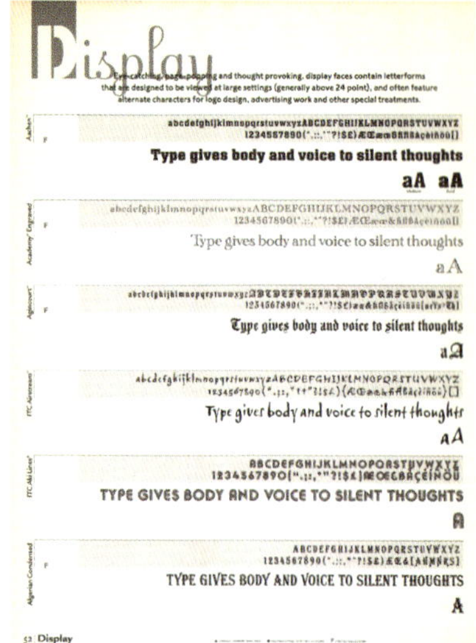

to describe the "revolutionary hardware" they'd introduced, like "a space-age phototypesetting system" that "set[s] type faster, for less money, and with better quality."[27] Clearly, technology mattered—but to printers, not their clients. Specimens ran the gamut from Helvetica—with newly available outlined and drop-shadowed versions; to Korina, a revival of a 1904 Berthold type with four weights and an outline version added; to Stilla, a fat face with decorative numerals [Fig. 7.18].

By 1996, near the end of its run, *U&lc*—like most of its audience—was exclusively digital, and ads emphasized this with images of **CD-ROMS** and **floppy discs**. Yet typesetting and reading still retained strong ties to printing, indicated by the continued presence of specimen books. Though the fonts were digital, seeing them in print remained crucial. Precision Type advised readers, "To pick the right font, get the right book."[28] The same issue's appended 1996/7 ITC catalog offered "a comprehensive 64-page supplement" of printed fonts, displaying each with an upper and lowercase alphabet and the phrase "Typography gives body and voice to silent thoughts," a quote from German Romantic philosopher Friedrich Schiller [Fig 7.19]. As an "easy-to-use visual reference to ITC's broad range of ... typeface styles," the supplement performed a traditional job—gathering all of a foundry's faces into one place for quick access. But it did this work in service to the new and soon to be dominant format of digital fonts. Soon, rapidly improving and increasingly accessible software would facilitate digital type-making not only by professional typographers but also by the *users* of digital type—aficionados, students, designers, programmers, gamers, and readers whose languages, reading practices, and physical capabilities weren't being accommodated by existing types. Many such typographic explorations are now available online through open access platforms and creative commons licensing [Fig. 7.20]. But screen-based type specimens are a subject unto themselves and a horizon for future research.

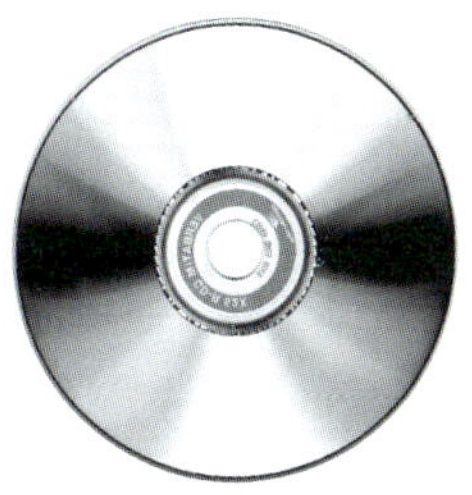

The **CD-ROM** was introduced commercially in 1984. It stores data externally from the computer's hard drive, holding 700MB in comparison to a 3.5 inch floppy disc's 360-720KB.

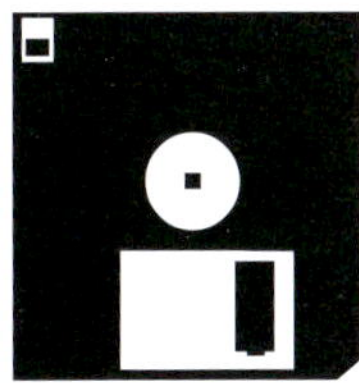

The 3.5 inch **floppy disc** remains iconic as an indicator of external computer memory, though the most common format stored only 1.44MB when introduced to market in 1986.

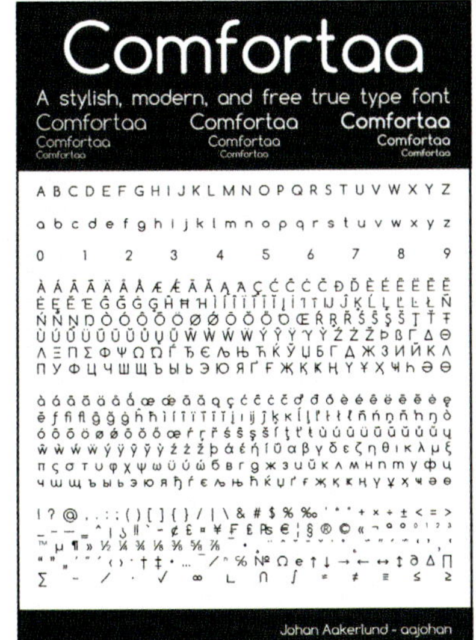

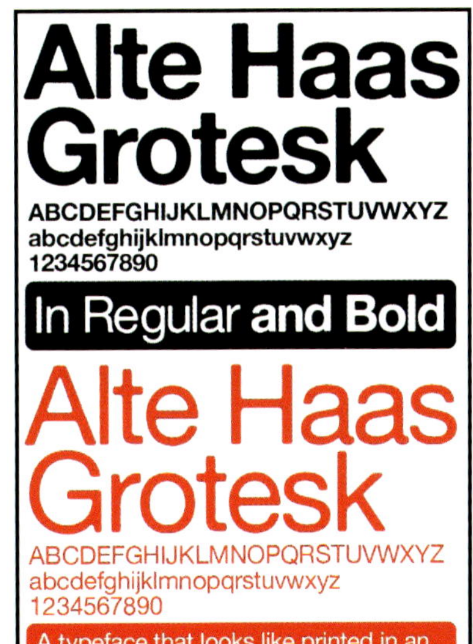

Fig 7.20 (left)

Comfortaa by AA Johan (released to the Creative Commons in 2008 via Deviant Art) and Alte Haas Grotesk by Yann le Coroller (released to the Creative Commons in 2007 via Font Zillion) are both open source digital fonts, freely available for public use.

1 Michael L. Kleper, *Understanding Photo Typesetting* (Philadelphia: North American Publishing Company, 1976), 23-25, http://archive.org/details/UnderstandingPhotoTypesetting.

2 "Photoline," *The International Stereotypers and Electrotypers Union Journal* 16, no. 12 (Dec 1921): 32.

3 Southall, *Printer's Type in the Twentieth Century*, 80-86.

4 John W. Seybold, *Fundamentals of Modern Photo-Composition* (Media, PA: Seybold Publications, 1979), 72-75, http://archive.org/details/FundamentalsOfModernPhotoComposition; Alan Marshall, *Du Plomb à la lumière: La Lumitype-Photon et la naissance des industries graphiques modernes* (Paris: les Éditions de la Maison des sciences de l'homme, 2003).

5 Southall, *Printer's Type in the Twentieth Century*, 79-86.

6 Mary Elizabeth Stevens, *Automatic Typographic-Quality Typesetting Techniques: A State-of-the-Art Review* (Washington, D.C.: U.S. Government Printing Office, 1967), 7, http://hdl.handle.net/2027/uc1.b4195061. Stevens, generally positive about phototype, here quotes a 1964 *Penrose's Annual* editorial that takes a dimmer view.

7 United States Bureau of Education, *Public Libraries in the United States of America: Part I, 1876 Report* (Urbana-Champaign: University of Illinois Graduate School of Library Science, 1965), iii; Albert George Holzman, Allen Kent, and Jack Belzer, eds., *Encyclopedia of Computer Science and Technology: Minicomputers to Pascal*, vol. 5 (New York: M. Dekker, 1976), 343.

8 Seybold, *Fundamentals of Modern Photo-Composition*, 8.

9 Photo Typositor Inc, *Photo Typositor* (New York: Photo Typositor Inc, 1962), http://archive.org/details/TNM_Photo_Typositor_Brochure_20170621_0001; PROtype, *PROtype Photo-Display Type* (New York: Electrographic Corp., 1963), http://archive.org/details/TNM_PROtype_Photo-Display_Type_0520; VariTyper, *Presenting the New VariTyper Type Face Series 470 Gothic Light Cond.* (New York: VariTyper, 1963), http://archive.org/details/TNM_VariTyper_type_faces_20180309_0008; Friden, Inc., *Typro, Friden Cold Type Photo Composing Machine* (San Leandro [CA]: Singer Co., 1963), http://archive.org/details/TNM_Typro_Friden_cold_type_photo_composing_machin_20171229_0137.

10 Steven Heller, "Dubious Typeface For Sale," *Print*, May 16, 2013, https://www.printmag.com/post/signal-magazine-typeface.

11 Bauer Type Foundry (N.Y.), *Human Touch: The Bauer Type Foundry* (1837-1937) (New York: Bauer Type Foundry, 1937), n.p.

12 American Type Founders, *Descriptive Index: ATF Foundry Type* (Elizabeth [NJ]: American Type Founders, 1953), n.p., http://archive.org/details/ATFDescriptiveIndex1953.

13 Acme Type Foundry, *Handy Index of Foundry Type Faces: Line Service or Reproduction Proofs* (Chicago: Acme Type Foundry, 1948), https://archive.org/details/AcmeHandyIndexOfFoundryTypeFacesPostCatalog10.

14 "'Neon' in Wood Type" [advertisement], *The Graphics Arts Monthly* 11, no. 12 (April 1939): 70.

15 Typefounders of Chicago, *Type Specimens by Neon Type Division [of] Typefounders of Chicago* (Chicago: Typefounders of Chicago, 1962), 1-3, http://archive.org/details/NeonTypeDivisionTypefoundersChicago1962pt1.

16 Meggs and Carter, *Typographic Specimens*, 7.

17 For example, Philip Meggs' review of ITC Founder's Caslon, designed by Justin Howes in 1998, discussed this design challenge. Philip B. Meggs, "Caslon Redux," *Print* 53, no. 1 (February 1999): 26.

18 The most famous example is probably 1990s postmodernist designer David Carson. *The End of Print: The Graphic Design of David Carson* (London: Laurence King, 1995).

19 Barco Type Founders, *Barco Type Founders* (Northlake [IL]: Barco Type Founders, ND), http://archive.org/details/BarcoGreenSpecimen.

20 Mergenthaler Linotype Company, *Linofilm System, Photocomposition* (Brooklyn: Linotype, N.D.), n.p., http://archive.org/details/TNM_Linofilm_System_photocomposition_-_Mergenthal_20170912_0073; Monotype Corporation, *The Monotype: How It Works* (New York: The School, 1957), 10, 14-15, http://archive.org/details/MonotypeHowItWorksEtc1957.

21 Photo-lettering Inc. and Edward Rondthaler, *Alphabet Thesaurus*, vol. 3, 3 vols. (New York: Van Nostrand Reinhold, 1971), http://catalog.hathitrust.org/api/volumes/oclc/246758.html. Vols. 1 and 2 were published 1960 and 1965, respectively.

22 Yvonne Schwemer-Scheddin, "Reputations: Adrian Frutiger," *Eye*, spring 1999, http://www.eyemagazine.com/feature/article/reputations-adrian-frutiger.

23 Labovitz, "The Electric Typesetter," 55-58.

24 Loretta Staples, "Typography and the Screen: A Technical Chronology of Digital Typography, 1984-1997," *Design Issues* 16, no. 3 (2000): 19-34, https://www.jstor.org/stable/1511813; P. McJones and D. Spicer, "The Advent of Digital Typography," *IEEE Annals of the History of Computing, Annals of the History of Computing, IEEE, IEEE Annals Hist. Comput.* 42, no. 1 (January 1, 2020): 41-50, https://doi.org/10.1109/MAHC.2019.2929883; Donald Day and Charles Bigelow, "Digital Typography," *Scientific American*, 1983, 106.

25 Steven Brower, "Herb Lubalin's *U&lc*, the First Magazine for Typeface Lovers," *Eye on Design* (blog), March 26, 2015, https://eyeondesign.aiga.org/design-history-101-herb-lubalins-ulc-the-first-magazine-for-typeface-lovers/; John D. Berry, *U&lc: Influencing Design & Typography* (Brooklyn: Mark Batty, 2005).

26 Advertisement, *U&lc* 1, no. 2 (1974): 27.

27 Advertisements, *U&lc* 1, no. 2 (1974): 33, 46.

28 Advertisement, *U&lc* 23, no. 2 (1996): 109.

ATF High-speed Photographic Typesetter B, 1963

Though ATF's phototype systems weren't very successful in commercial terms, their specimen design and visual communication of technology were superb. Here, a 1963 booklet shows the disc that stores tiny, photographic images of typographic characters, replacing metal matrices and metal slugs and/or sorts alike. It also shows the paper control tape that carries binary code information from where it's input (at the keyboard, by an operator) to where it's output (onto photosensitive paper or film, which is developed and then used either for direct paste-up or to expose a printing plate). Compared to metal type, phototype was a short-lived technology. Dominant by about the time this brochure was published, phototype was quickly rendered obsolete when digital typesetting emerged in the late 1980s and early 1990s.

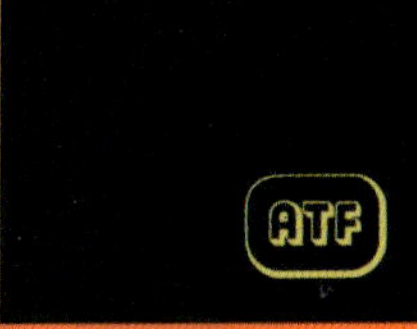

atf high-speed
photographic typesetter model b

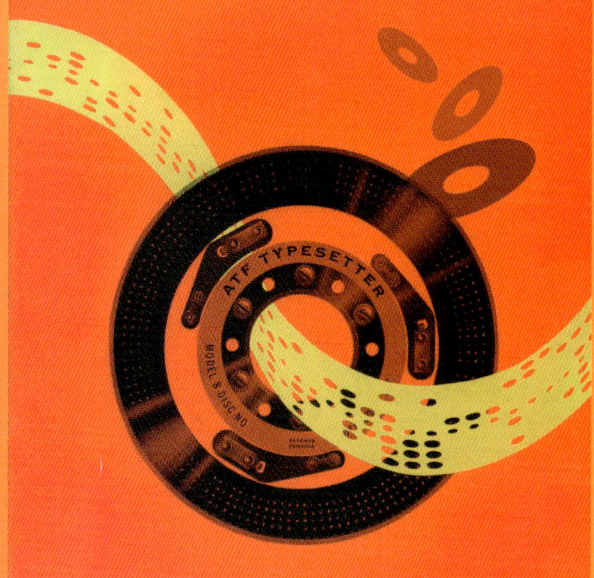

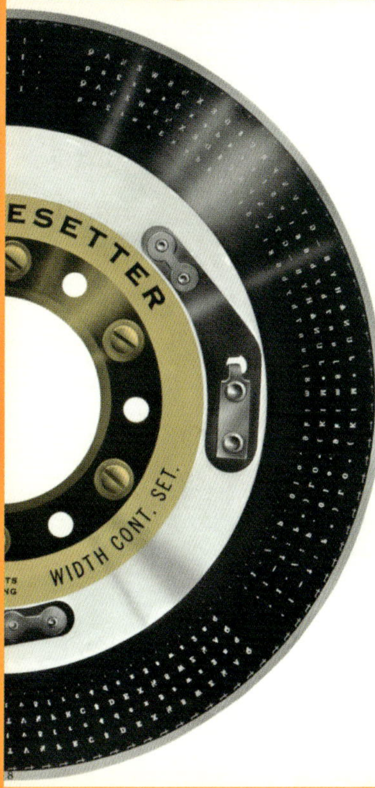

Faster than ever:

NEW
HIGH-SPEED
TYPE DISCS

Establish new standards for
text and tabular production

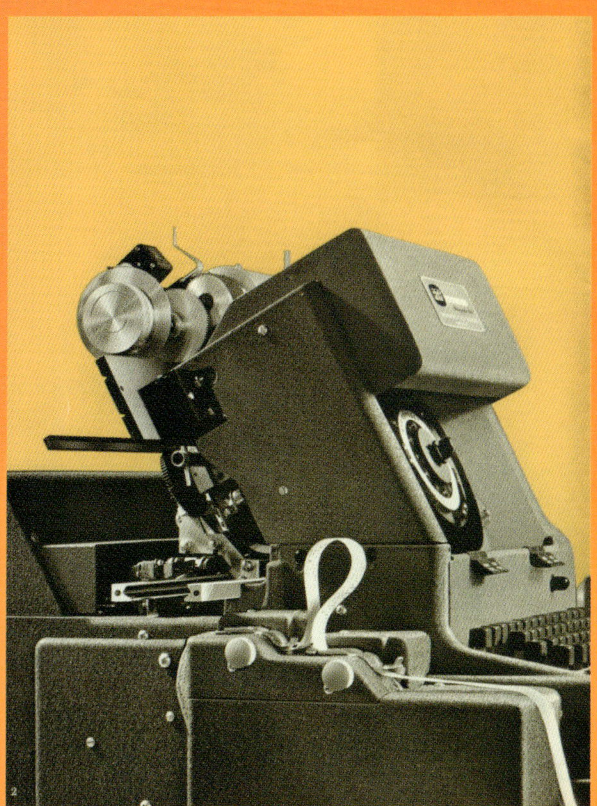

2

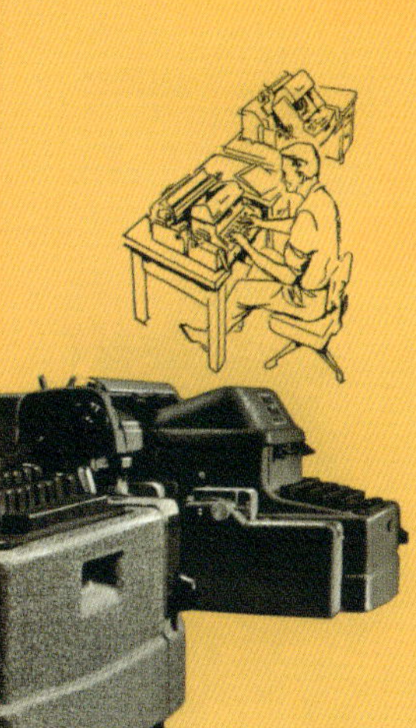

This text was set by the light beam of a 40-watt lamp; a photographic lens; and a transparent disc that weighs less than two ounces, changes in less than ten seconds, carries 168 different type images, packs the composing power of a double-letter font of hot metal mats, and costs less than an *empty* hot metal mat magazine.

It was set on a unit that weighs under 125 pounds; takes up less floor space than the average office desk; runs on an ordinary electric light circuit; and uses less power than a portable TV.

It was set automatically, under coded tape control. The unit that cut the tape simultaneously typed a compositor's proof that enabled the Comp to catch most errors at once, and to correct all visible errors before photosetting.

It was set on low-cost sensitized paper and could just as readily have been set directly on film. It was developed and ready for paste-up in less time than it takes to proof and correct the average hot metal galley.

It was set, automatically justified and leaded, at a production rate that can average ten 11-pica lines of 8½ point Century Schoolbook a minute.

It was set without a pound of pressure and without an ounce of metal.

It was set without leads, slugs, galleys, chases, quoins, furniture, stones, saws, proof presses or furnaces.

It was set on the fast new ATF Model B Typesetter—the logical, field-proven way to set professional-grade text for any process that prints from plates.

3

POSTLUDE: DIGITAL TYPE, DIVERSE FUTURES

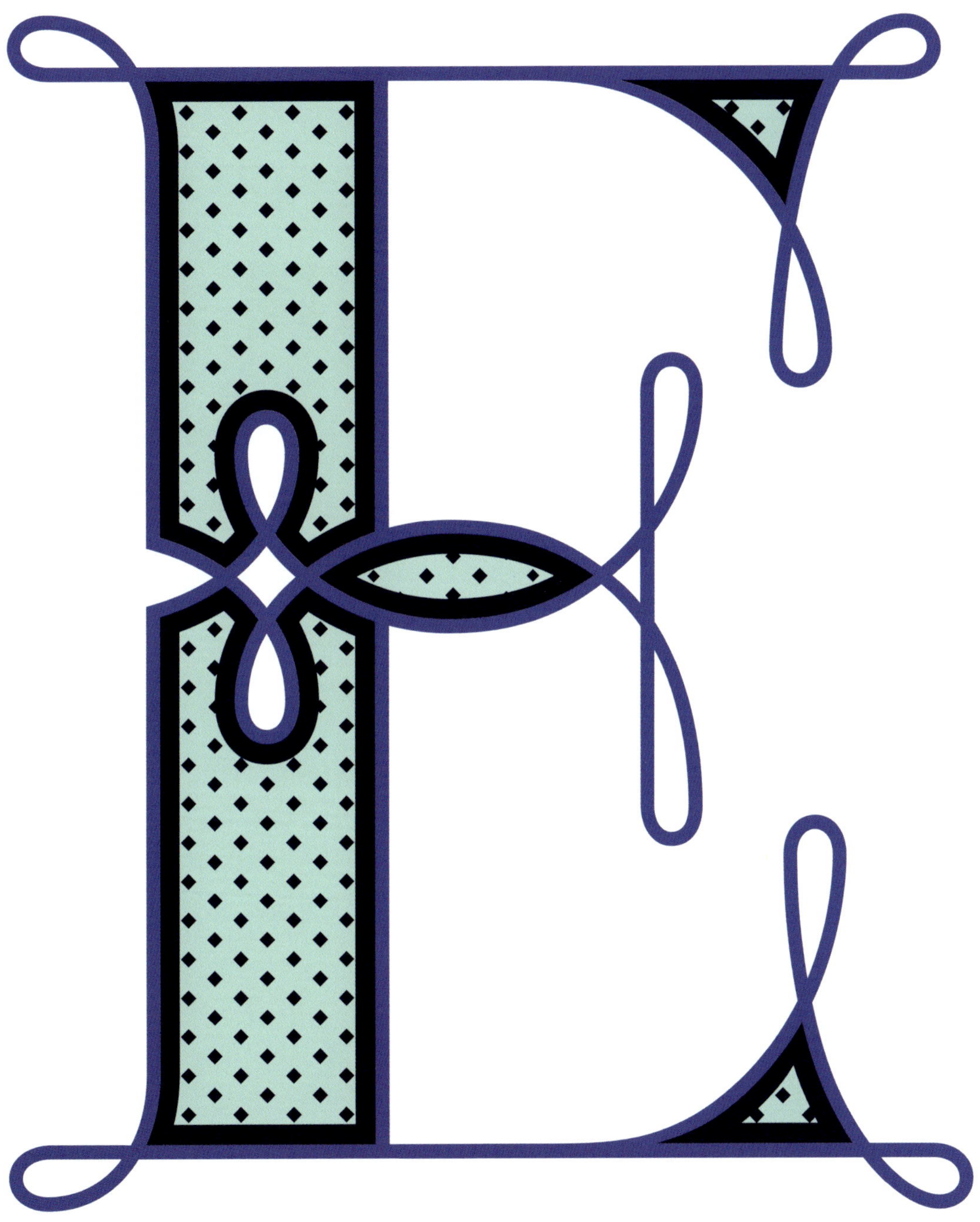

MARCONI® STD BOOK - 3 VARIANTS

Marconi

MARCONI® STD BOOK ITALIC - 4 VARIANTS

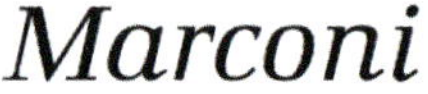

MARCONI® STD SEMI BOLD - 4 VARIANTS

Marconi

MARCONI® STD SEMI BOLD ITALIC - 4 VARIANTS

Marconi

1975 – Germany

Hell releases Marconi, the first original digital typeface, designed for them by Herman Zapf.

1984 – USA

Emigre

Emigre's Triplex Serif Condensed Black

& Triplex Serif Light

1985-9 – USA

Emigre releases Triplex Serif, designed by Zuzana Licko and John Downer.

1989 – USA

Font Bureau
Hoefler & Co

1990 – Netherlands

Dutch Type Library

1991 – Brazil & UK

Dalton Maag

1993 – Germany

Lineto

USA

House Industries

1994 – France

Typefonderie

USA

T.26

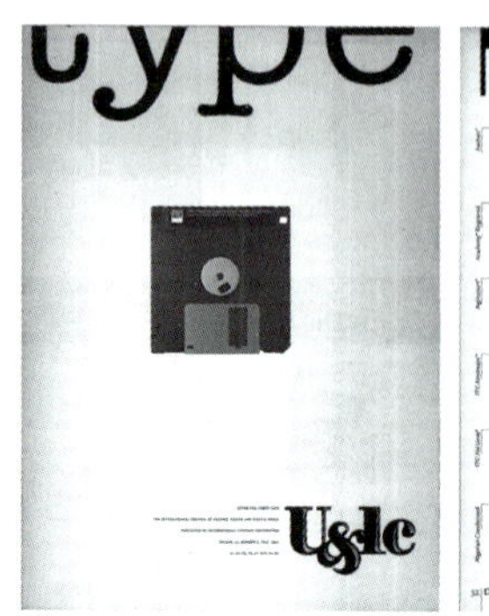

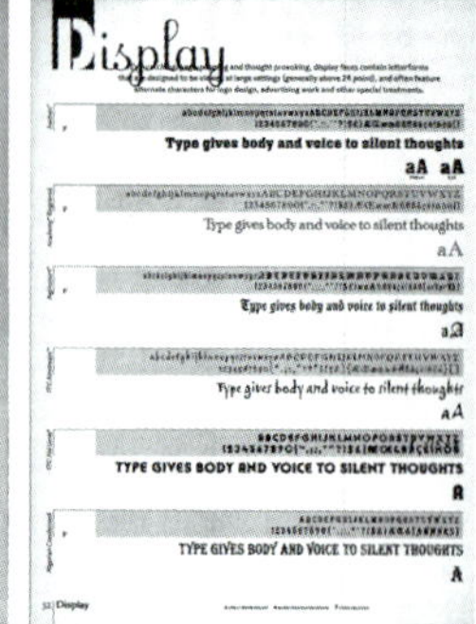

1996 – USA

ITC's print catalog offers a font library that ships to users on floppy disc.

1998 – Switzerland

Optimo

1968 – Japan

OKI Wiredot, first commercially available dot-matrix printer with character generation (CG).

1969 – USA

Laser printing invented at Xerox.

1975 – USA

Xerox launches first graphical user interface (GUI).

1978 – USA

Donald Knuth's TeX digital typesetting program released; vector-based.

1979 – USA

Donald Knuth's Metafont digital typesetting program released; raster-based.

1984 – Japan

CD-ROM announced by Sony.

USA

Apple Macintosh personal computer.

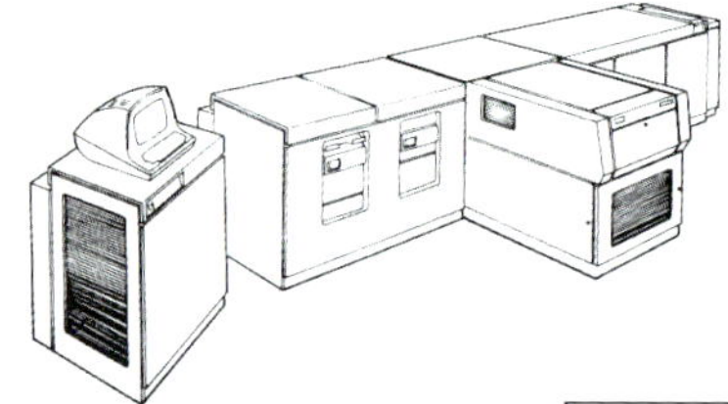

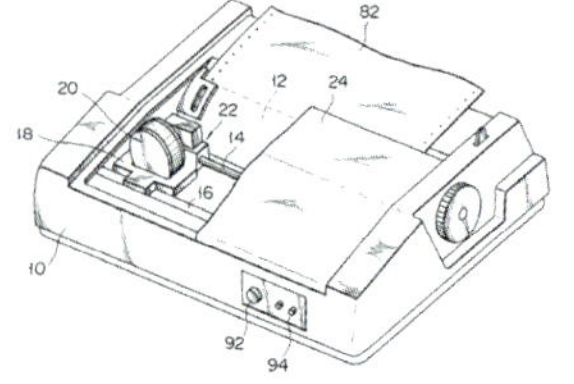

TEX

METAFONT

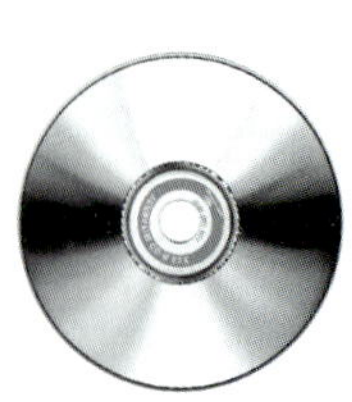

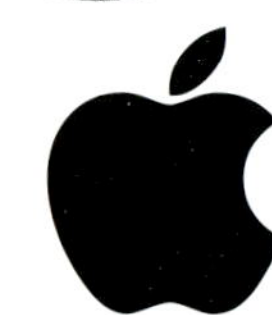

2003 — USA

Neutra

2004 — USA & UK

Commercial Type

2005 — India

Ek Type

New Zealand

Klim

2006 — Czech Republic

Type Together

2009 — Argentina

Tipo

Netherlands

LettError

USA & UK

Colophon

USA

TypeKit
(Adobe Fonts)

2010 — USA

Google Fonts

2011 — Canada

Lost Type CoOp

Switzerland

Grilli

2012 — Ireland

Signal

Korea

AG Typography Institute

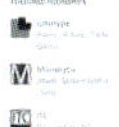

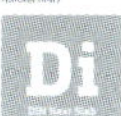

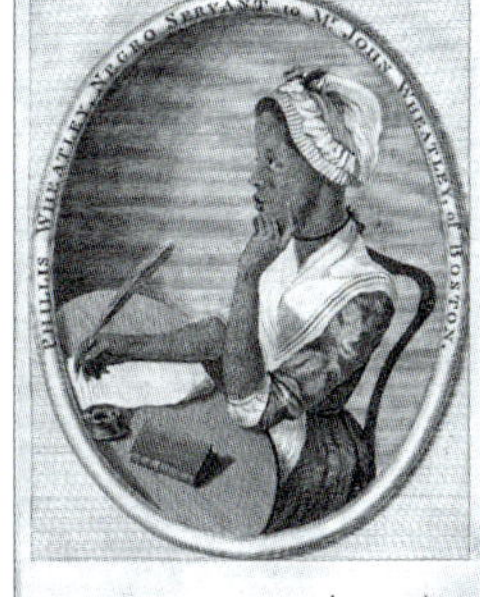

اور بازار سے لے آئے اگر ٹوٹ گیا

ساغرِ جم سے مرا جامِ سفال اچھا ہے

2012 — USA

Launch of Google Noto, fonts for all languages; shown, Nastaliq Urdu (2014).

2012 — USA

Early African American Print Culture by L. Cohen & J. Stein published; shown, Phyllis Wheatley (1772).

2020 — USA

Monotype launches Monotype Fonts, www.fonts.com.

1985 — USA

PostScript typesetting language.

1987 — USA

Quark XPress desktop publishing software program.

Adobe acquires digital license for Linotype's full library.

1988 — USA

Adobe Photoshop raster graphics editing software program.

1995 — USA

IBM's 3.5″ high-density floppy disk marketed.

1996 — [internationally]

OpenType scalable computer fonts.

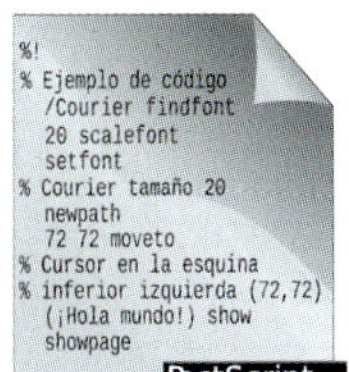

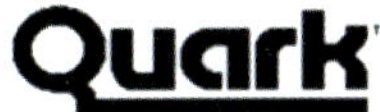

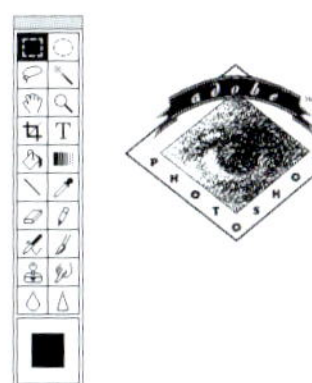

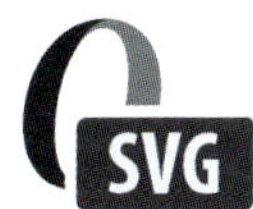

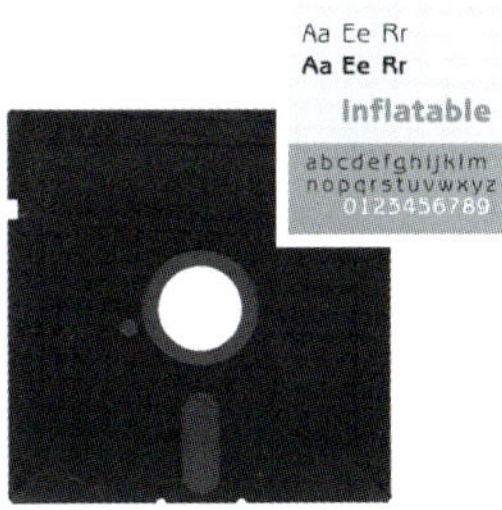

Digital type specimens differ profoundly from printed specimens in their delivery format. Yet their purpose remains familiar: seeing, analyzing, choosing, and acquiring typefaces fit for specific tasks, audiences, and contexts. In a time when readers—viewers—increasingly encounter type on screens, the digital specimen is uniquely suited for this work. Designers typically agree that printed typography is best evaluated from a printed sample; type for screens is best evaluated on (many) screens. In the midst of what might be described as a golden age of digital type design, many pioneers of digital type-founding retain a strong market presence: Dutch Type Library, LettError, and Typotheque in the Netherlands; Adobe, Émigré, and H&Co. in the United States; Typefonderie in France; and FontFont (now FontShop) in Germany are but a few examples. Newer yet still widely revered foundries include Commercial Type, Font Bureau, GrilliType, House Industries, Lineto, Lost Typye CoOp, and T.26. AG Typography Institute in South Korea, Ek Type in India, Hebrew Typography in Israel, Klim in New Zealand, Tipo in Argentina, and Type Together in the Czech Republic demonstrate an ever-growing geographic diversity in type-founding. The digital environment is inherently disembodied and ephemeral—digital specimens vanish easily if not intentionally preserved. For the moment, though, a quick internet search uncovers a goldmine of noted and notable digital type foundries.[1]

Though they cause preservation challenges, digital tools provide opportunities not only for new formats, but also for multiple voices to be heard—often, voices that have been ignored, excluded, or violently suppressed historically. The Latin script dominated typographic production in metal and photographic formats, to the extent that producers and users of typography uncritically embraced the binary term "non-Latin" as a generic descriptor.[2] Thankfully, global languages and their many scripts flourish digitally, though developing a non-binary script classification system remains problematic. Even close, careful, scholarly studies in the twenty-first century continue to deploy the term.[3] Despite remaining inequities, type designers who are women, ethnic minority, and/or working in a global multi-script context now have access to systems of creation and distribution.[4] Contemporary typographers are engaged with the work of making, contextualizing, and distributing typefaces to facilitate vibrant, diverse, respectful global communication.[5] New archival, analytical, and narrative type specimen projects rooted in digital tools fall outside the scope of "printed typographic specimens" and this brief nod to their existence isn't a survey by any means.[6] The typographers who follow offer only a very brief introduction, primarily in their own voices, to the work happening as this book goes to press. Often, their typefaces have ideological goals. They evoke the human hand, promote access, advocate for equity, and facilitate global multi-script communication.

Fig 8.1 (bottom left)
Magasin typeface and specimen by Laura Meseguer

Fig 8.2 (below)
Green Fairy Font Family and specimens designed by Maria Montes, 2018. www.mariamontes.net

Digital types for a handcrafted aesthetic

Magasin by Laura Meseguer (2015) is a high-contrast display typeface inspired by the pointed pen and copperplate calligraphy, yet with a retro-chic twist [Fig. 8.1]. It combines a sense of script with geometric and slightly condensed structures, resulting in idiosyncratic curves softly connecting the vertical elegance of its forms. It's ideally suited to use in large sizes for magazine headlines, posters, or packaging. Magasin boasts a rich set of OpenType features that provide a better flow such as Ligatures, Stylistic Alternates,

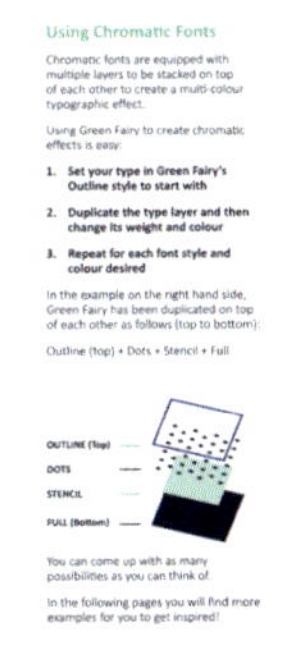
Using Chromatic Fonts

Chromatic fonts are equipped with multiple layers to be stacked on top of each other to create a multi-colour typographic effect.

Using Green Fairy to create chromatic effects is easy:

1. **Set your type in Green Fairy's Outline style to start with**
2. **Duplicate the type layer and then change its weight and colour**
3. **Repeat for each font style and colour desired**

In the example on the right hand side, Green Fairy has been duplicated on top of each other as follows (top to bottom):

Outline (top) + Dots + Stencil + Full

You can come up with as many possibilities as you can think of.

In the following pages you will find more examples for you to get inspired!

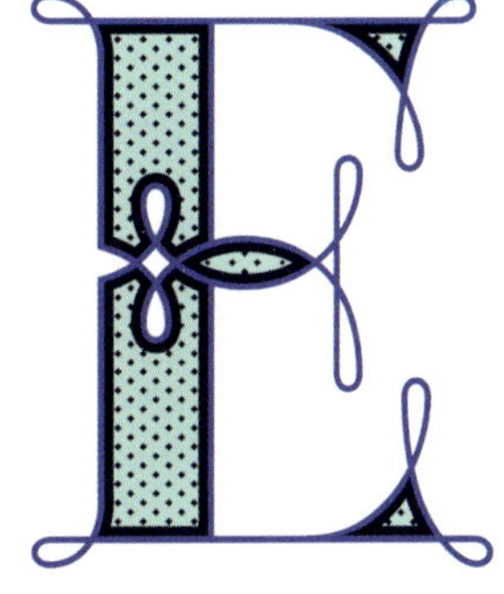

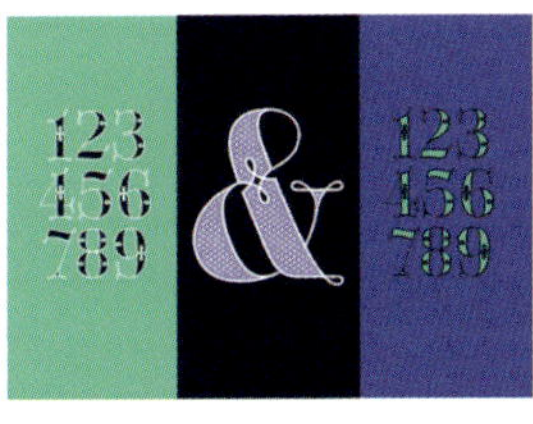

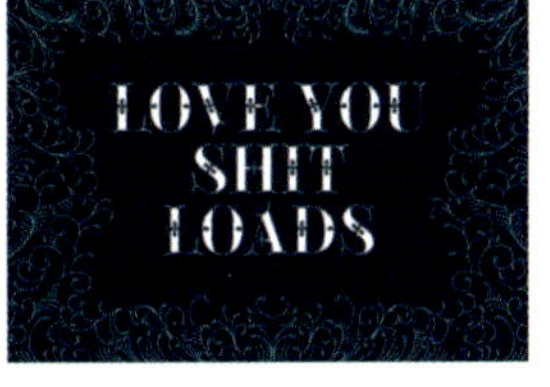

Fig 8.3 (opposite)
Dyslexie typeface (2008-20) and specimen (2020) by Christian Boer.

Contextual Alternates, and Final Forms. It also includes a set of capital Swashes. Magasin wants to achieve the obvious accuracy that can be seen in any calligraphic work, but with a close attention to the creative combination of linked letters when creating words digitally, bringing a lettering flavor.

Maria Montes' Green Fairy (2018) is a chromatic font family that's highly ornamented for display purposes [Fig. 8.2]. It combines the detail and energy of historical chromatic faces with a contemporary letterform architecture and the capacity offered by digital typography tools. Montes describes Green Fairy's characters as specifically designed to accommodate its loops and ornaments within a modern typeface structure. The font has four weights: Green Fairy Outline, Dots, Stencil, and Full. The outline weight has been created as the base for the other weights. Designers can combine these weights and add colors to obtain multiple styles and effects. Green Fairy has also three combined weights (combos) to simplify work flow, for occasions when designers want to use a single color in the font: Green Fairy Dots Combo, Stencil Combo, and Full Combo. The typeface can be purchased online.[7]

Types—and typographic tools—for access

Dyslexie by Christian Boer [Fig. 8.3] is designed to facilitate character recognition. Dyslexie began as a student project in 2008 but evolved as Boer professionalized his design practice. Today the typeface reflects a process of sustained scientific and visual research, as well as Boer's empathy and compassion—as a dyslexic reader, he built the face to accommodate the visual experiences he and other dyslexics face. As the font's online landing page puts it, "reading with dyslexia can be quite a challenge, and Dyslexie offers people with dyslexia a unique typeface to make reading, learning, and working easier—always, everywhere, and on every device." As a dyslexic, Boer "knew from experience why a special typeface was needed for people with dyslexia." During research on strategies for improving readability, "he saw for the millionth time words turning and letters mirroring and swapping, and suddenly he knew how to solve the problem: with a typeface that would prevent these 3D letter movements. He started designing, and the Dyslexie typeface was born."[8] Dyslexie holds multiple typeface design and accessibility awards and appeared onstage at TEDx New York in 2015.

Democratic access to tools opens up possibilities both serious and playful, making the technologies of type design and production available to novices as well as experts. Beginning typography student Elaina Buffkin designed Bubble Divers (2020) as both a functional display face for digital game branding and a form of personal typographic play [Fig. 8.4]. The custom font is designed for the Bubble Divers mobile app, developed with Buffkin's brother.[9] Players battle strange sea creatures while sinking into a watery crevasse, while the pixelated art style of the heroes and villains complements gameplay to create an arcade video game feel. When designing the font, Buffkin considered both its nautical and retro features—hence the clunky, asymmetric quality of the type's characters. She began with complete pixilation to match the overall look of the game, but when this seemed too mechanized, she explored more organic elements: the occasional rounded edge, mismatching stroke weights within the individual characters. The font evokes the quirks that characterize Bubble Divers, completing the aesthetic of the game.

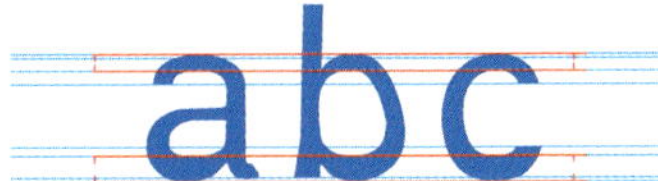

Heavier bottoms

Each letter has a clear baseline, which creates a visual center of gravity and prevents letters from being turned upside down.

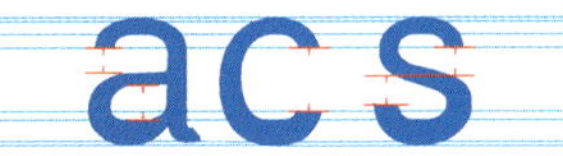

Bigger openings

The openings of the Dyslexie Font letters are enlarged. Here for letters can be easily recognized by their shape.

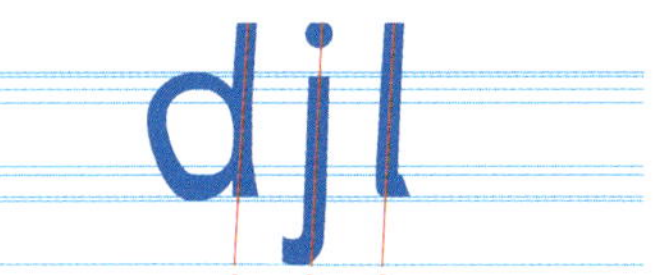

Inclined letters

Letters that look alike are slightly inclined. This way different letters are easier to distinguish.

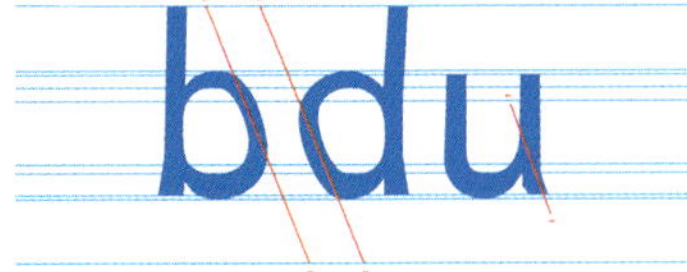

Different shapes

The shapes of the letters are adjusted subtly. This way the chance of turning, mirroring and swapping letters is minimized.

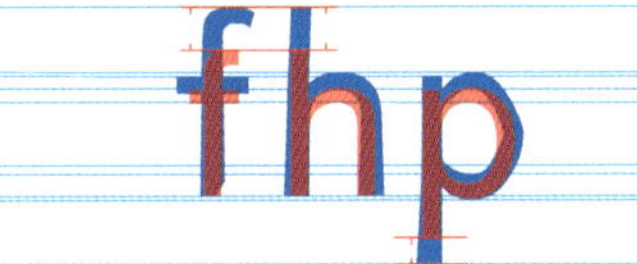

Longer sticks

Some Dyslexie font letters have longer sticks, which helps to decrease switching and swapping letters while reading.

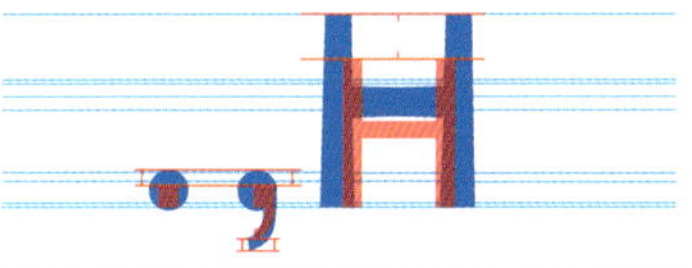

Capital letters and punctuation

Punctuation marks and capital letters are bold, emphasizing the breaks, endings and beginnings of phrases.

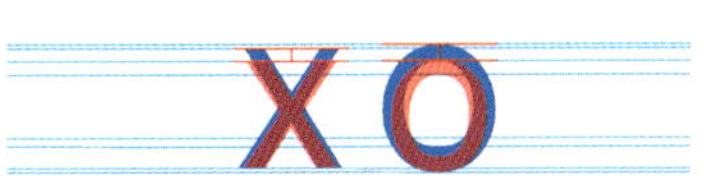

Higher x-height

The height of the letters is increased, whereas the width isn't. This adds 'air' to the Dyslexie font letters, making them easier to distinguish.

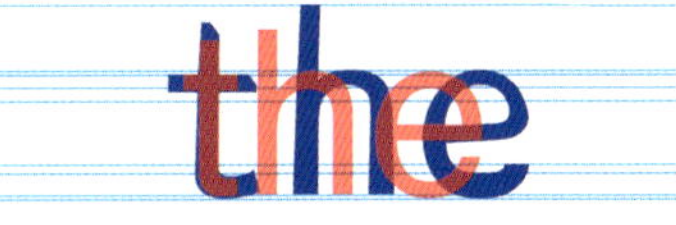

Better spacing

The distance between individual letters and words is enlarged, which makes reading more convenient and avoids the crowding effect.

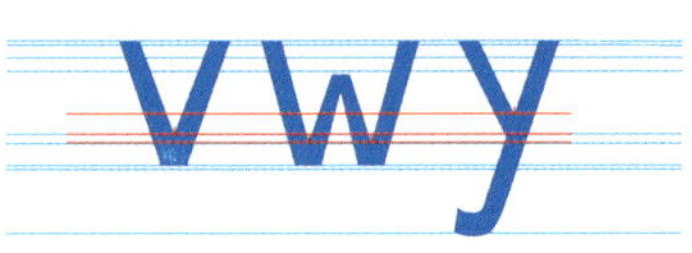

Various heights

Letters that look alike are differentiated by several levels. This way each Dyslexie font letter is a unique character, avoiding letter swapping.

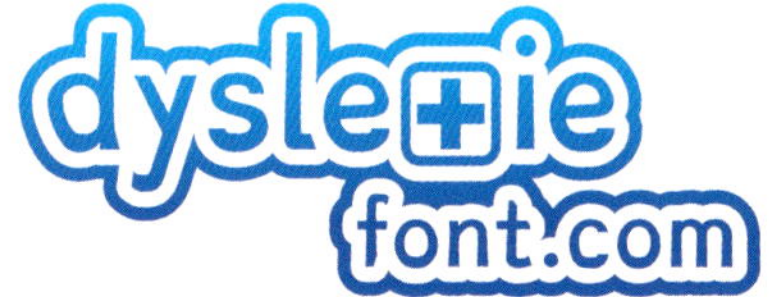

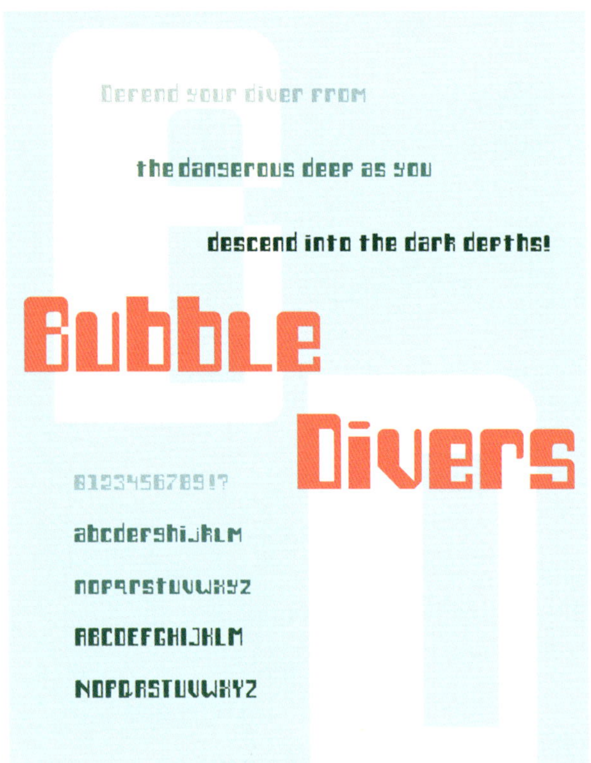

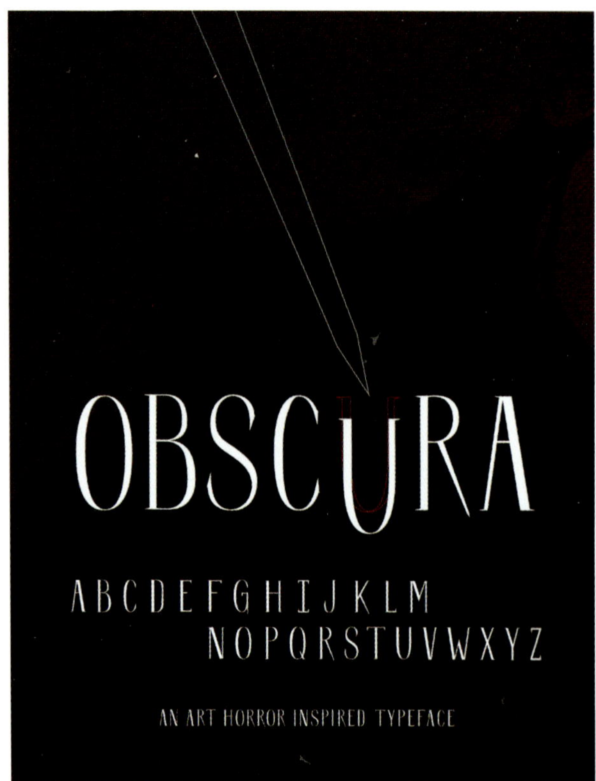

Fig 8.4 (above)
Bubble Divers by Elaina Buffkin, 2020.

Fig 8.5 (top right)
Obscura by Megan McCormick, 2019.

Professional designer and advanced degree student Megan McCormick created Obscura (2019) in response to an empirical study regarding the impression of emotion in typographic design [Fig. 8.5]. The study was designed to measure audience response to typographic information utilized in poster designs for cinematic horror. Viewers weren't given access to additional visual information often provided in poster design, such as photographs of actors or movie-specific scenery, and viewers might or might not be able to read the language in which the type was set. The appearance of serifs, line weight variation, and narrowness of the overall letterforms tended to yield a higher amount of "fear" responses from participants. These results led McCormick to design the typeface's knifelike serifs, line weights shifting uncomfortably within the letterforms, and a looming appearance.

Types for equity

Leandro Assis' "Power to Black People" poster (2020) is part of a graphic series with eleven other Black artists in support of the Black Lives Matter movement [Fig. 8.6]. The project was organized by the Fine Acts platform, which gathered twenty-four posters to be used by anyone and distributed online to everyone, for free.[10] Assis' bold, handcrafted letterforms send a message of power, shared humanity, and protest against institutionalized racism. The letterforms can't be divorced from their genesis in the BLM social protest movement. Unlike a handlettered font, these letters live exclusively in Assis' posters, where their heavy, rounded, graphic forms feel human, urgent, and demanding.

True Woman by Dina Benbrahim (2020) is a typeface for feminist activism [Fig. 8.7]. Women's rights advocate Margaret Fuller rejected sex roles and codes among other women. She wrote, in *Woman in the Nineteenth Century* (1843), that "there is no wholly masculine man, no purely feminine woman"—introducing the concept of fluidity. True Woman is inspired by Margaret Fuller's statement and intends to push the boundaries of sexism as well as mock the concept of true womanhood that dictates the behavioral code of a "good" woman. This typeface is a single-weight display face, geometric and rounded, condensed and bold, as well as bottom heavy and unconventional with slightly asymmetrical strokes. True Woman was initially designed to be laser-cut and to serve as a frame to hold messages directed to harassers during creative experiences that facilitate dialogues, ideation, and agency for self-identified women to reclaim their right to exist safely in the public space. For more information on using the typeface, visit the designer's website.[11]

Fig 8.6 (bottom left)

Power to the Black People poster with custom lettering by Leandro Assis, 2020.

Fig 8.7 (below)

True Woman, designed and released by Dina Benbrahim, 2020.

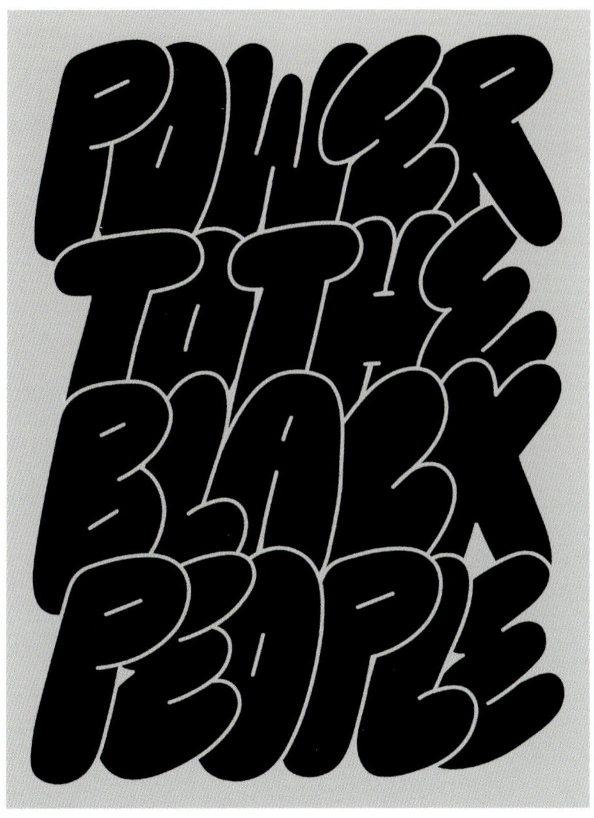

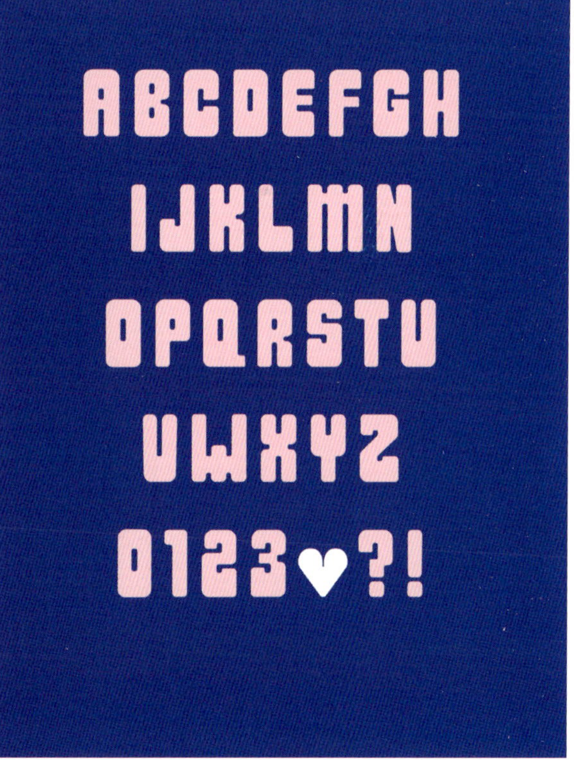

Fig 8.8 (below)

Noto Sans Nüshu, designed by Lisa Huang 黄丽莎 for Google Fonts, 2020.

Fig 8.9 (opposite)

Ploni, designed by Avraham Cornfeld, released by AlephAleph Aleph, 2018.

Types for all languages

Noto Sans Nüshu (2017), designed by Lisa Huang, was the first digitally available Nüshu script [Fig. 8.8]. The Noto family from Google Fonts "aims to support all languages with a harmonious look and feel."[12] Huang was commissioned to design Noto's Nüshu scripts, as its some 396 glyphs were added to the Unicode Standard encoding in 2017. Nüshu is the only writing system in history to be invented, developed, and used by women. The script emerged from a small, remote region in Southern China's Jiangyong county, Hunan. In feudal China, when gender separation was even greater than today, women were considered of a lower social rank than men. They weren't allowed to read or write Chinese characters, *Hanzi*, a privilege that was exclusive to men—thus the need for Nüshu. Apart from the historical uniqueness of this script, no digital version of it existed before Noto Sans Nüshu. Huang's biggest challenge with this project was to set up "standard rules" as guidelines to a consistent and harmonious design—crucial requirements for a typeface—while keeping the script's nature intact. More information is available from the designer online.[13]

AlefAlefAlef's digital foundry is "a group of ambitious, independent designers, whose passion for typography led each of us to seek out this virtual space." They offer "fresh" Hebrew typefaces "crafted ... with a great deal of diligence, punctiliousness and thought." Some faces were inspired by "architecture, mythology and children's books, while others were designed with an emphasis on functionality, for use as convenient and legible body text" in print and digital environments. Avraham Cornfeld describes his typeface Ploni (2018), in both Hebrew and Latin scripts, as "a precise, geometric bilingual typeface.

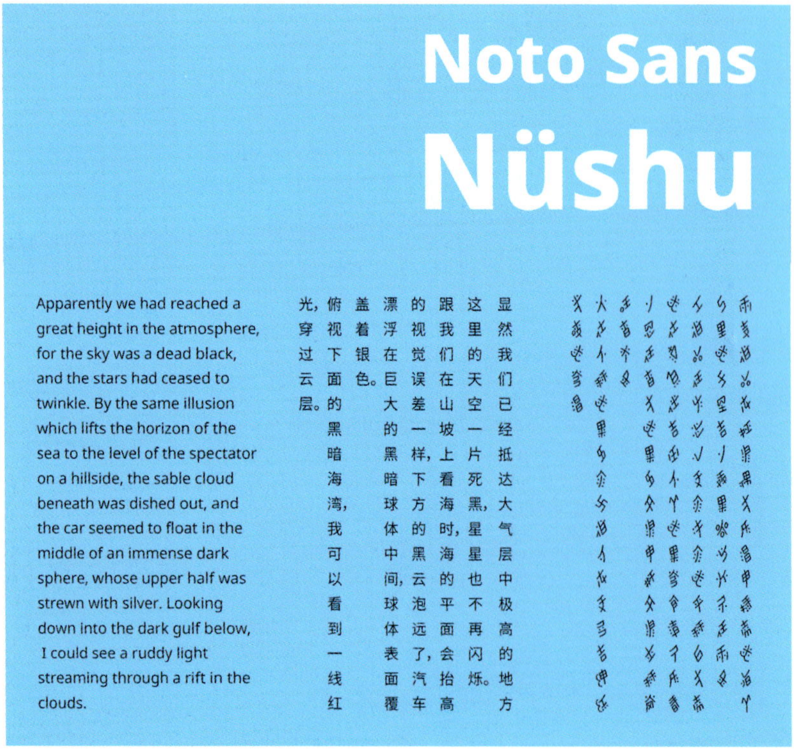

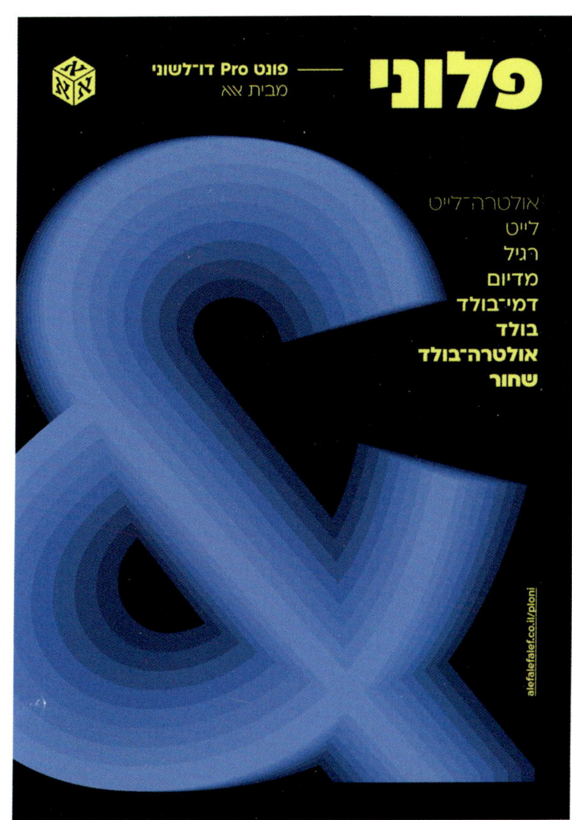

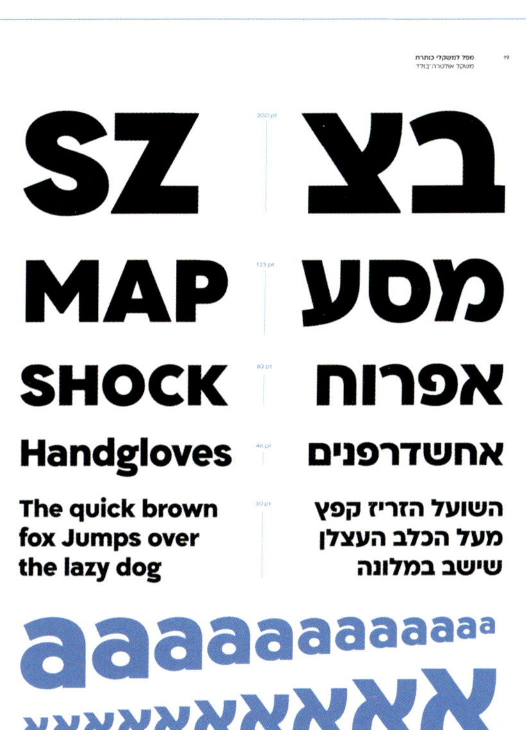

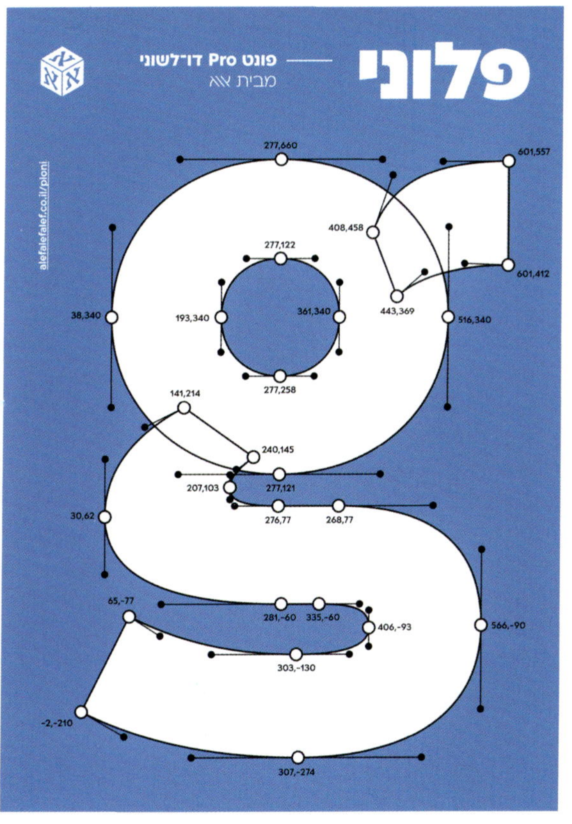

אבגדהוזחטיכךלמ
םנןסעפףצץקרשת
1234≠5678≠1234
AaBbCcDdEeFfGg
ŤßĐãìļðŧþÿşĦé
%^!?:;"'.=↕+@&({[
₰$☯§₹№Ω☆₹←
₿∞*ﬅ%‰*¶?
ÆØQAÅAªǫ¤Œ
☑☮❞☺◈✪≈*♥

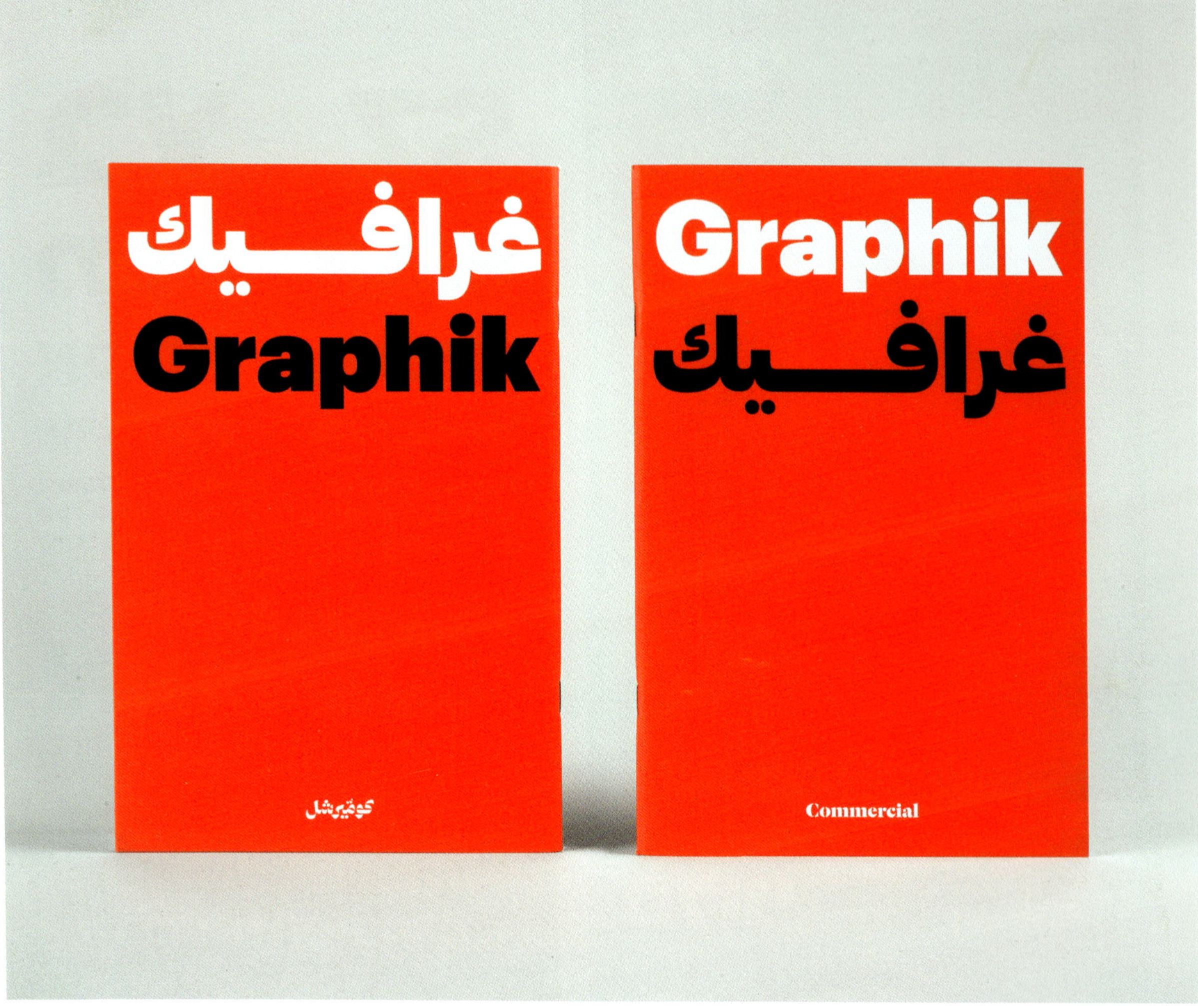

Fig 8.10 (above)

Grafik Arabic Typeface and Specimen design by Khajag Apelian (Debakir) and Wael Morcos (Morcos Key), 2017; Graphik Latin designed by Christian Schwartz. Published by Commercial Type.

It contains many glyphs and fully supports 146 Latin languages—which makes it an ideal font for the side-by-side use of Latin and Hebrew characters." His specimen for the font highlights Ploni's multiscript, multilingual capabilities [Fig. 8.9].[14]

Graphik Arabic (2017) by Wael Morcos and Khajag Apelian was designed in harmony with Christian Schwartz's Graphik Latin [Fig. 8.10]. Inspired by lesser-known mid century Modern typefaces, the Graphik family is distributed by the online foundry Commercial Type. Graphik Arabic "aims to be a meaningful departure from calligraphic detailing and presents a utilitarian workhorse with a plain style."[15] Its simplicity cooperates with many Latin grotesques, not just Graphik Latin. But it doesn't abandon the structure, fluidity, and proportional relationships of the Arabic script. Bold, minimalist specimen posters showcase the visual dialogue between Graphik Arabic and Graphik Latin without prioritizing one script over the other, pointing the way to a post-binary typographic world.

1 As a shortcut, visit http://type-foundries-archive.com/ for a listing of 350+ foundries in 45+ countries.

2 Soulaf Khalifeh, "Latin & Non-Latin," Medium, August 4, 2020, https://medium.com/@soulafkh/latin-non-latin-5a7378ecf725.

3 Fiona Ross and Graham Shaw, *Non-Latin Scripts: From Metal to Digital Type* (London: St Bride Foundation, 2002); Thomas S. Mullaney, "Facing the World: Towards a Global History of Non-Latin Type Design," *Philological Encounters* 3, no. 4 (November 27, 2018): 399–411, https://doi.org/10.1163/24519197-12340050.

4 Alphabettes, "It's Time to Act," blog, *Alphabettes* (blog), June 14, 2020, http://www.alphabettes.org/its-time-to-act/; Tanya George, "Reflections on THAT Article," Alphabettes (blog), July 8, 2020, http://www.alphabettes.org/reflections-on-that-article/. See also Amber Weaver, "Femme Type – Celebrating Women in the Type Industry," 2020, https://femme-type.com/; Stephen Coles and Noemi Stauffer, "Database of Black Type Designers," 2020, https://www.notion.so/Database-of-Black-Type-Designers-4bd9315ec77d4f2f9ea07821efa211f7.

5 One example among many of self-contextualization: Nadine Chahine, "More Than Letters: Nadine Chahine on Her Typographic Practice," *Design and Culture* 11, no. 2 (2019): 237–44, https://doi.org/10.1080/17547075.2019.1632552; Monotype GmbH, "TEDx Talk with Font Designer Nadine Chahine," *Linotype Blog* (blog), 2016, http://blog.linotype.com/2016/07/tedxtalk-with-fontdesigner-nadinechahine/.

6 A diverse handful of very recent examples to whet the digital appetite: The People's Graphic Design Archive is a crowd-sourced expansion of graphic design history. "The People's Graphic Design Archive," PeoplesGDArchive, accessed August 4, 2020, https://www.peoplesgdarchive.org. Mark Boulton's Digital Type Specimens is an online research and image collection project launched in 2020, doing exactly what its title says; "Type Specimens," July 30, 2020, https://typespecimens.xyz/. Alphabettes is a woman-centered digital network of type design and research launched in 2015 and continuing to release timely and vital content as of this writing; "Alphabettes," July 21, 2020, http://www.alphabettes.org/.

7 www.mariamontes.net

8 www.dyslexiefont.com

9 Bubble Divers is available free of charge on the App Store.

10 https://fineacts.co/blm

11 https://meaningfuldialogues.myportfolio.com/

12 www.google.com/get/noto/

13 www.lisahuang.work, Twitter @LisaLisaHuang, InstaGram @hellolisahuang

14 www.alefalefalef.co.il

15 https://commercialtype.com/catalog/graphik_arabic

Bibliography

Acme Type Foundry. *Handy Index of Foundry Type Faces: Line Service or Reproduction Proofs*. Chicago: Acme Type Foundry, 1948. https://archive.org/details/AcmeHandyIndexOfFoundryTypeFacesPostCatalog10.

Adi, Einat. *New Types: Three Pioneers of Hebrew Graphic Design*. Edited by Ada Wardi. Jerusalem: Israel Museum, 2016.

Alphabettes. "Alphabettes." Alphabettes, July 21, 2020. http://www.alphabettes.org/.

——. "It's Time to Act." Blog. *Alphabettes* (blog), June 14, 2020. http://www.alphabettes.org/its-time-to-act/.

American Mission Press. *Barnāmaj Al-Matba'at al-Amīrikānīyah / Illustrated Catalogue and Price List of Publications of the American Mission Press, Beirut*. Beirut: American Mission Press, 1887. http://www.dlir.org/archive/items/show/11122.

——. *Illustrated Catalogue and Price List of Publications of the American Mission Press, Beirut, Syria*. Beirut: American Mission Press, 1896. http://archive.org/details/illustratedcata00missgoog.

American Type Founders Company. *American Line Type Book, Borders, Ornaments: Price List Printing Material and Machinery 1906*. Chicago: American Type Founders, 1906.

——. *Descriptive Index: ATF Foundry Type*. Elizabeth [NJ]: American Type Founders, 1953. http://archive.org/details/ATFDescriptiveIndex1953.

——. *Specimen Book and Catalogue 1923*. Jersey City: American Type Founders, 1923. http://archive.org/details/1923AmericanTypeFoundersSpecimenBookCatalogue-Hi-resolution.

——. *Specimens of Printing Types*. New York: American Type Founders, 1897. http://archive.org/details/specimensofprint00amerrich.

Amsterdam Continental Types. *A Handbook of Types*. New York: Amsterdam Continental Types, 1960.

Annenberg, Maurice. *Type Foundries of America and Their Catalogs*. New Castle [DE]: Oak Knoll Books, 1994.

Auji, Hala. *Printing Arab Modernity: Book Culture and The American Press in Nineteenth-Century Beirut*. Leiden: Brill, 2016.

Axel-Nilsson, Christian. *Type Studies: The Norstedt Collection of Matrices in the Typefoundry of the Royal Printing Office: A History and Catalogue*. Stockholm: Norstedts Tryckeri, 1983.

Aynsley, Jeremy. "Politics and Design: Reaction and Consolidation, 1933-45." In *Designing Modern Germany*, 112–43, 2009.

Barco Type Founders. *Barco Type Founders*. Northlake [IL]: Barco Type Founders, ND. http://archive.org/details/BarcoGreenSpecimen.

Barnhart Brothers & Spindler. *Book of Type Specimens*. Chicago: Barnhart Bros. & Spindler, 1907. http://archive.org/details/BBSSpecimenNo9_1907.

Barnhart Brothers & Spindler. *Type Faces, Border Designs, Typecast Ornaments, Brass Rule, Superior Specialties, Machines and Materials, Cabinet Equipment*. Chicago: Barnhart Bros. & Spindler, 1925.

Bauer Type Foundry (N.Y.). *Human Touch: The Bauer Type Foundry (1837-1937)*. New York: Bauer Type Foundry, 1937.

Baurao, Nayak S. Epigraphy, *Typography Of Devanagari*. Vol. 2. 2 vols. Bombay: Directorate of Languages, 1971. https://archive.org/details/epigraphytypographyofdevanagaribauraonayaks.volume2_927_x.

Beamer, George C., Lawrence D. Edmonson, and George B. Strother. "Improving the Selection of Linotype Trainees." *Journal of Applied Psychology* 32, no. 2 (April 1948): 130–34. https://doi.org/10.1037/h0056649.

Beaujon, Paul, and [Beatrice Warde]. "The Garamond Types: Sixteenth and Seventeenth Century Sources Considered." *The Fleuron*, no. 5 (1926): 131–79.

Benton, Linn Boyd. *Benton's Self Spacing Type [Typographic Specimens]*. Benton, Waldo and Company, 1886. http://archive.org/details/BentonWaldoSpecimenBooklet1886.

Benton, Megan L. *Beauty and the Book: Fine Editions and Cultural Distinction in America*. New Haven: Yale University Press, 2000.

Berry, John D. *U&lc: Influencing Design & Typography*. Brooklyn: Mark Batty, 2005.

Bigmore, E.C., and C.W.H. Wyman. *A Bibliography of Printing: With Notes and Illustrations*. Vol. 1. 3 vols. London: B. Quaritch, 1880. https://archive.org/details/bibliographyofpr01bigmrich.

——. *A Bibliography of Printing: With Notes and Illustrations*. Vol. 3. 3 vols. London: B. Quaritch, 1886. https://archive.org/details/bibliographyofpr03bigmrich.

Binny & Ronaldson, and Carl Purington Rollins. *The Specimen Books of Binny and Ronaldson, 1809-1812, in Facsimile; with an Introduction by Carl Purington Rollins, and Facsimiles of Some Early American Types*. Columbiad Club: New Haven, 1936.

Birrell & Garnett, and Henry Graham Pollard. *Catalogue of I Typefounders' Specimens II Books Printed in Founts of Historic Importance III Works on Typefounding Printing & Bibliography*. Brighton: Tony Appleton, 1928.

Blades, William. *Some Early Type Specimen Books of England, Holland, France, Italy, and Germany*. London: J.M. Powell, 1875. http://archive.org/details/someearlytypespe00bladrich.

Bodoni, Giambattista, Giovanni Mardersteig, and Herman Cohen. *Manuale tipografico, 1788*. Editiones Officinae Bodoni. Verona: Officina Bodoni, 1968.

Boulton, Mark. "Type Specimens." Typespecimens, July 30, 2020. https://typespecimens.xyz/.

Brenner, Naomi. "Milgroym, Rimon and Interwar Jewish Bilingualism." *Journal of Jewish Identities* 7, no. 1 (February 2, 2014): 23–48. https://doi.org/10.1353/jji.2014.0009.

Bryans, Dennis. *A Survey of Australian Typefounders' Specimens*. Blackburn [Australia]: Golden Point Press, 2014.

——. "The Beginnings of Type Founding in Sydney: Alexander Thompson's Type, His Foundry, and His Exports to Inter-Colonial Printers." *Journal of Design History* 9, no. 2 (April 1996): 75–86. https://doi.org/10.1093/jdh/9.2.75.

Burke, Peter, and Asa Briggs. *A Social History of the Media: From Gutenberg to the Internet*. Cambridge: Polity, 2005.

Burke-Gaffney, Brian. "Information and International Exchange in Meiji-Period Nagasaki." *Journal of Socio-Informatics* 4, no. 1 (2011): 5–16. http://www.ssi.or.jp/eng/pdf/Vol4No1.pdf.

Bussotti, Michela, and Han Qi. "Typography for a Modern World?: The Ways of Chinese Movable Types." *East Asian Science, Technology, and Medicine*, no. 40 (2014): 9–44. https://www.jstor.org/stable/eastasiascietech.40.9.

Carson, David. *The End of Print: The Graphic Design of David Carson*. London: Laurence King, 1995.

Carter, Harry. *A View of Early Typography: Up to about 1600*. London: Hyphen, 2002.

Caslon, William. *A Specimen*. London:

W. Caslon, 1734. http://archive.org/details/McGillLibrary-rbsc_caslon-william-speciman-colgate3-C377C377S51734-17593.

Chahine, Nadine. "More Than Letters: Nadine Chahine on Her Typographic Practice." *Design and Culture* 11, no. 2 (2019): 237-44. https://doi.org/10.1080/17547075.2019.1632552.

Chappell, Warren, and Robert Bringhurst. *A Short History of the Printed Word*. 2 Rev Upd edition. Point Roberts, WA: Hartley and Marks Publishers, 2000.

Coakley, J. F. *The Typography of Syriac: A Historical Catalogue of Printing Types, 1537-1958*. New Castle [DE]: Oak Knoll Press, 2006.

Cochrane, Chas. H. "Composing Machines of Today." *American Printer and Bookmaker* 29, vol. 5 (January 1900), 256-7. https://www.google.com/books/edition/American_Printer_and_Lithographer/7WU-AQAAMAAJ?hl=en&gbpv=0

Cohen, Lara Langer, and Jordan Alexander Stein. *Early African American Print Culture*. Philadelphia: University of Pennsylvania Press, 2012.

Coles, Stephen, and Noemi Stauffer. "Database of Black Type Designers," 2020. https://www.notion.so/Database-of-Black-Type-Designers-4bd9315ec77d4f2f9ea07821efa211f7.

Consuegra, David. *American Type: Design & Designers*. New York: Allworth Press, 2004.

Continental Typefounders Association. *Specimen Book of Continental Types*. New York: [Continental Typefounders], 1929. https://catalog.hathitrust.org/Record/100952584.

Cost, Patricia. *The Bentons: How an American Father and Son Changed the Printing Industry*. Rochester, N.Y: RIT Cary Graphic Arts Press, 2010.

Cot, Pierre, and Douglas C. McMurtrie. *The Pierre Cot Type Specimen of 1707: With a Reproduction in Facsimile of the Original Specimen*. Chicago: R.O. Ballou, 1924. https://catalog.hathitrust.org/Record/001161141.

Day, Donald, and Charles Bigelow. "Digital Typography." *Scientific American*, 1983, 106.

De Vinne, Theodore Low. *Historic Printing Types*. New York: De Vinne & Co., 1886. https://archive.org/details/historicprinting00devirich.

Didot, Pierre. *Spécimen Des Nouveaux Caractères de La Fonderie et de l'imprimerie de P. Didot, l'ainé: Chevalier de l'ordre Royal de Saint-Michel, Imprimerie Du Roi et de La Chambre Des Pairs, Dédié à Jules Didot, Fils, Chevalier de La Légion d'honneur*. Paris: Didot, 1819. https://catalog.hathitrust.org/Record/011273746.

Dornemann & Co. *Schriften in Glockenmetall Für Die Vergoldepresse [a Catalog of Bell Metal Types for the Gilding Press]*. Marderburg: Dornemann & Co, 1925. http://objects.library.uu.nl/reader/ index.php?obj=1874-284602&lan=en#page//15/03/71/150371523332903 6119724221933 24083907218.jpg/mode/1up.

Downer, John. "*Emigre* Essays: The Art of Founding Type." Emigre Fonts, 1995 2020. https://www.emigre.com/Essays/Type/TheArtofFoundingType.

Dreyfus, John. *Aspects of French Eighteenth Century Typography: A Study of Type Specimens in the Broxbourne Collection at Cambridge University Library*. Cambridge: [John Erhman?], 1982.

Dreyfus, John, Harry Carter, and Hendrik D.L. Vervliet. *Type Specimen Facsimiles: Reproductions of Fifteen Type Specimen Sheets Issued between the Sixteenth and Eighteenth Centuries*. Vol. 2. 2 vols. London: Bodley Head, 1972.

Duff, E. Gordon. *Early English Printing: A Series of Facsimiles of All the Types Used in England during the XVth Century*. London: Kegan Paul, Trench Trubner and Company, Ltd, 1896.

Eason, Ron, and Sarah Rookledge. *Rookledge's International Directory of Type Designers: A Biographical Handbook*. Surrey: Sarema Press, 1991.

Enschedé en Zonen, and Harry Carter. *The House of Enschedé, 1703-1953*. Haarlem, Netherlands: Joh. Enschedé en Zonen, 1953.

Fedirka, Sarah. "Reorienting Modernism: Transnational Exchange in the Modernist Little Magazine *Orient*." *English Language Notes* 49, no. 1 (2011): 77-90. https://doi.org/10.1215/00138282-49.1.77.

Fonderie du sieur Delacolonge, and Harry Graham Carter. *The Type Specimen of Delacolonge: Les Caracters et Les Vignettes de La Fonderie Du Sieur Delacolonge*. Amsterdam, New York: Van Gendt; Abner Schram, 1969.

Fournier, Pierre-Simon, and Harry Carter. *Fournier on Typefounding: The Text of the Manuel Typographique (1764-1766)*. 468. New York: Burt Franklin, 1973.

Fournier, Pierre-Simon, Harry Graham Carter, James Mosley, and Gerd Hoffrath. *The Manuel Typographique of Pierre-Simon Fournier le Jeune: Together with Fournier on Typefounding*. Vol. 3. 3 vols. Darmstadt: Lehrdruckeri Technische Hochschule, 1995.

Frazier, J.L. "Popular Types—Their Origin and Use, No. VI. Caslon." *Inland Printer, American Lithographer* 72, no. 6 (March 1924): 945-50.

Friden, Inc. *Typro, Friden Cold Type Photo Composing Machine*. San Leandro [CA]: Singer Co., 1963. http://archive.org/details/TNM_Typro_Friden_cold_type_photo_composing_machin_20171229_0137.

Friedlaender, Henri. *The Making of Hadassah Hebrew*. Jerusalem: [Typophiles], 1975.

Fry, Edmund, and David Chambers. *Specimen of Modern Printing Types by Edmund Fry 1821: A Facsimile with an Introduction and Notes by David Chambers*. London: Printing Historical Society, 1986.

F.T. Wimble & Co. *New and Second-Hand Printing Type, Material and Machinery*. Melbourne, Australia: F.T. Wimble & Co., 1900. https://nla.gov.au/nla.obj-52845999.

Fyyfe, Aileen. *Steam-Powered Knowledge*. Chicago: University Of Chicago Press, 2012.

Gando, Nicolas, ed. *Epreuve Des Caracteres de La Fonderie de Nicolas Gando*. Paris: De l'imprimerie de Jacques Guerin, 1745.

Gandy, Lewis C. *Bodoni Type; an Historical Sketch of Its Origin, Together with Suggestions as to Its Proper Use*. Boston: Pinkham Press, 1920. https//catalog.hathitrust.org/Record/100191615.

George, Tanya. "Reflections on THAT Article." *Alphabettes* (blog), July 8, 2020. http://www.alphabettes.org/reflections-on-that-article/.

Goudy, Frederic W. *Typologia: Studies in Type Design & Type Making, with Comments on the Invention of Typography, the First Types, Legibility, and Fine Printing*. Berkeley: University of California Press, 1977. http://archive.org/details/bub_gb_s5Js_NPRflwC.

Grafton, David D. *The Contested Origins of the 1865 Arabic Bible: Contributions to the Nineteenth Century Nahda. The Contested Origins of the 1865 Arabic Bible*. Leiden: Brill, 2015.

Gravier, Marina Garone. "Nineteenth-Century Mexican Graphic Design: The Case of Ignacio Cumplido." *Design Issues* 18, no. 4 (2002): 54–63. https://www.jstor.org/stable/1511979.

Gray, Nicolete, and Ray Nasher. *Nineteenth Century Ornamented Typefaces*. London: Faber and Faber, 1976.

Great Western Type Foundry. *Specimen Book and Price List of the Great Western Type Foundry, Chicago, Barnhart Bros. & Spindler, Proprietors*. Chicago: Great Western Type Foundry, 1873.

Green, Nile. "Persian Print and the Stanhope Revolution: Industrialization, Evangelicalism, and the Birth of Printing in Early Qajar Iran." *Comparative Studies of South Asia, Africa and the Middle East* 30, no. 3 (2010 2010): 473–90. https://www.muse.jhu.edu/article/430311.

——. *Terrains of Exchange: Religious Economies of Global Islam*. Oxford University Press, 2015.

Gress, Edmund Geiger. *Fashions in American Typography, 1780 to 1930: With Brief Illustrated Stories of the Life and Environment of the American People in Seven Periods, and Demonstrations of E.G.G.'s Fresh Note American Period Typography*. New York: Harper & Bros, 1931.

Gujarati Type Foundry. *Book of Type Faces and Printers' Auxiliaries*. Bombay: Gujurati Type Foundry, 1937.

——. *New Faces in Types & Borders; Cast in Copper Alloy on the American Point System* ... Bombay: Gujurati Type Foundry, 1924.

Haley, Allan. *Typographic Milestones*. Wiley & Sons, 1992.

Halhed, Nathaniel Brassey. *Grammar Of The Bengali Language*. Hoogly [Bengal]: Halhed, 1778. https://archive.org/details/in.ernet.dli.2015.43675.

Hamilton Manufacturing Co. *Specimens of Holly Wood Type*. Two Rivers [WI]: Hamilton & Katz, 1880. http://archive.org/details/ldpd_12465515_000.

Hansard, T. C. *Typographia: An Historical Sketch of the Origin and Progress of the Art of Printing; with Practical Directions for Conducting Every Department in an Office: With a Description of Stereotype and Lithography. Illustrated by Engravings, Biographical Notices, and Portraits*. London: Baldwin, Cradock, and Joy, 1825. https://archive.org/details/typographiaanhi00hansgoog.

Hargrave, Jocelyn. *The Evolution of Editorial Style in Early Modern England*. Springer Nature, 2019.

Hebrew Monotype Press. *Specimen Book of Hebrew, Yiddish, English, Arabic & Greek Type Faces*. New York: Hebrew Monotype Press Inc., 1927. https://catalog.hathitrust.org/Record/003005325.

Heller, Steven. "Berthold's 1924 Hebrew Type Catalogue." *Baseline*, 2006.

Higgins, Janet. "'And the Wife Helped Also.'" *Southeastern College Art Conference Review* 11, no. 3 (1988): 201–6.

Hilton, Robert. "Introduction of Printing into Russia." *British Printer* 1, no. 5 (October 1888): 15.

Hoefler & Co. "Didot Fonts: History." Typography.com, 2020. http://www.typography.com/fonts/didot/history/.

Hofer, Philip. *A Newly-Discovered Broadside Specimen of Fell Type Printed at Oxford about 1685*. Cambridge: Cambridge University Press, 1940. http://hdl.handle.net/2027/uiug.30112108344406.

Holzman, Albert George, Allen Kent, and Jack Belzer, eds. *Encyclopedia of Computer Science and Technology: Minicomputers to Pascal*. Vol. 5. New York: M. Dekker, 1976.

Hottinger, Johann Heinrich, Alan David Crown, Geoffrey Roper, John Huehnergard, J.F. Coakley, and Balthasar Koeblinus. *Elementale Quadrilingue: A Philological Type-Specimen (Zürich 1654)*. Oxford: Jericho Press, 2005. https//catalog.hathitrust.org/Record/005086900.

Hudson, Graham. *The Design and Printing of Ephemera in Britain and America 1720-1920*. London: British Library/Oak Knoll, 2008.

Huppatz, D.J. "Globalizing Design History and Global Design History." *Journal of Design History* 28, no. 2 (2015): 182–202. https://doi.org/10.1093/jdh/epv002.

Inland Type Foundry. *Specimen Book and Catalog: A Price List of Printers' Supplies*. St. Louis: Inland Type Foundry, 1907. http://archive.org/details/specimenbookcata00inla.

Insetsu-Kyoku. *Katsuji Mon'yō Mihon [Specimens of Printing Types and Ornaments Cast at the Insetsu-Kioku]*. Tokyo: Insetsu-Kyoku [Imperial Printing Office], 1885. http://hdl.handle.net/2027/nnc1.cu13207504.

Intertype Corporation. *Intertype Matrices: Specimens of Two-Letter, One-Letter, Head-Letter and Display Matrices, Border Slides and Border Matrices, Font Schemes and Keyboard Layouts, Classified by Series*. New York: Intertype Corporation, 1920.

James Figgins. *Type Founding and Printing During the 19th Century*. London: Figgins, 1900. https://archive.org/details/Figgins1900TypeFoundingPrinting.

Jannon, Jean. *Espreuve des caractères nouvellement taillez*. Sedan: Jean Jannon, 1621.

——. *The 1621 specimen of Jean Jannon, Paris & Sedan, designer & engraver of the caractères de l'Université, now owned by the Imprimerie nationale, Paris.: Ed. in facsimile with an introduction by Paul Beaujon [Beatrice Warde]*. Paris, 1927.

Japanese Central Association. *An Itinerary of Hokkaido, Japan*. Tokyo: Hakodate Chamber of Commerce, 1893. https://archive.org/details/itineraryofhokka00batc.

Jaspert, W.P., A.F. Johnson, and W.T. Berry. *Encyclopaedia of Typefaces*. 5th ed. London: Cassell Illustrated, 2008.

J.G. Schelter & Giesecke. *Plakatschriften & Holzschriften [Display Type & Wood Type]*. Leipzig: Schelter & Giesecke, 1928. http://archive.org/details/PlakatschriftenJ.G.SchelterGiesecke.

Johnson, A.F. "The Type-Specimen Books of Claude Lamesle and Nicolas Gando." *Library* s4-XVIII, no. 2 (September 1937): 201–11. https://doi.org/10.1093/library/s4-XVIII.2.201.

Johnson, John. *Typographia, or, the Printers' Instructor: Including an Account of the Origin of Printing, with Biographical Notices of the Printers of England, from Caxton to the Close of the Sixteenth Century: A Series of Ancient and Modern Alphabets, and Domesday Characters: Together with an Elucidation of Every Subject Connected with the Art*. Vol. 2. 2 vols. London: Longman, Hurst, Rees, Orme, Brown & Green, 1824. https://catalog.hathitrust.org/Record/.

Johnson, Phillip. "The Japanese Gutenberg." *The Book Lover: A Magazine of Book Lore* 2, no. 9 (December 1901): 390–92. https://www.google.com/books/edition/_/jaA5AQAAMAAJ?hl=en&gbpv=0.

Johnson, Rossiter, and John Howard Brown. *The Twentieth Century Biographical Dictionary of Notable Americans*. Boston:

Biographical Society, 1904.
Johnson Witehira. "Mana Mattauhi: A Survey of Maori Engagement with the Written and Printed Word during the 19th Century." *Visible Language* 5, no. 1 (April 2019): 76–109. http://www.visiblelanguagejournal.com/issue/292.
Johnston, Alastair. *Alphabets to Order: The Literature of Nineteenth-Century Typefounders' Specimens*. 1st ed. New Castle, DE: Oak Knoll, 2000.
Kamei-Dyche, Andrew T. "The History of Books and Print Culture in Japan: The State of the Discipline." *Book History* 14 (2011): 270–304. https://www.jstor.org/stable/41306539.
Katibah, H.I. *Arabic-Speaking Americans*. New York: Institute of Arab American Affairs, 1946. http://hdl.handle.net/2027/uva.x001897252.
Kelly, Rob Roy. "American Wood Type." *Design Quarterly*, no. 56 (1963): 1–40. https://doi.org/10.2307/4047285.
Keystone Type Foundry. *Abridged Specimen Book, Type: Nickel-Alloy on Universal Line Comprising a Price List of Types, Borders, Leads and Slugs, Brass Rule, Brass Galleys; Miscellaneous Cuts and General Supplies for Printers*. Philadelphia: Keystone Type Foundry, 1906. http://archive.org/details/abridgedspecimen00keysrich.
Khalifeh, Soulaf. "Latin & Non-Latin." Medium, August 4, 2020. https://medium.com/@soulafkh/latin-non-latin-5a7378ecf725.
Kim, Sojin, and Somi Kim. "Typecast: Meaning, Culture, and Identity in the Alphabet Omelet." In *Lift and Separate: Graphic Design and the Quote Vernacular Unqote*, edited by Barbara Glauber, 30–37. New York: Herb Lubalin Study Center of Design and Typography, 1993.
Kinross, Robin. *Modern Typography*, 2nd Edition. 2nd ed. London: Hyphen, 2004.
Kleper, Michael L. *Understanding Photo Typesetting*. Philadelphia: North American Publishing Company, 1976. http://archive.org/details/UnderstandingPhotoTypesetting.
Knight, Stan. *Historical Types: From Gutenberg to Ashendene*. New Castle, Delaware: Oak Knoll Press, 2012.
Kohut, George Alexander. "The Contributions of Cyrus Adler to American Jewish History." *Publications of the American Jewish Historical Society*, no. 33 (1934): 17–42. https://www.jstor.org/stable/43058413.
Kornicki, Peter. *The Book in Japan: A Cultural History from the Beginnings to the Nineteenth Century*. Honolulu: University of Hawaii Press, 2001.
Kuskin, William. *Symbolic Caxton: Literary Culture and Print Capitalism*. Notre Dame: University of Notre Dame Press, 2008.
Labovitz, John. "The Electric Typesetter: The Origins of Computing in Typography." *Printing History*, no. 22 (Winter 2017): 46–66.
Lamesle, Claude. *Epreuves Generales Des Caracters Qui Se Trouvent Chez Claude Lamesle, Fondeur de Caracters d'imprimerie*. Paris: Pres la place Maubert, 1742.
Lane, John A., and Mathieu Lommen. *Dutch Typefounders' Specimens: From the Library of the KVB and Other Collections in the Amsterdam University Library, with Histories of the Firms Represented*. Amsterdam: De Buitenkant, 1998.
Lanston Monotype Machine Company, ed. *Monotype Type Faces*. Philadelphia: Lanston Monotype Machine Co, 1904.
——. *The Monotype Pony Specimen Book of Type Faces, Rules, Ornaments & Borders*. Philadelphia: Lanston Monotype Machine Co., 1921. https://catalog.hathitrust.org/Record/008609414.
——. *The Monotype Specimen Book of Type Faces. A Complete Catalog of Matrices Made for Use with the Monotype Composing Machine and with Type & Rule Caster*. Philadelphia, 1922. http://archive.org/details/monotypespecimen00lansrich.
——. *The Monotype Specimen Book of Type-Faces*. Philadelphia: Lanston Monotype Machine Company, 1916. https://catalog.hathitrust.org/Record/004689420.
Laubach, Frank C. *India Shall Be Literate*. Ann Arbor: Jubbulpore/Mission Press, 1940. http://archive.org/details/in.ernet.dli.2015.202272.
Lavi-Turkenich, Liron. "Lettering: Drawing Letters for a Variety of Purposes." In *New Types*, 218–31. Jerusalem: Israel Museum, 2016.
Lawson, Alexander S. *Anatomy of a Typeface*. Boston: Godine, 1990.
——. *Printer's Manuals: From Moxon to the PIA*. Kirkwood [MO]: The Printery, 2002.
Lawson, Alexander S., John Bidwell, and American Type Founders Co. *Specimens of Type, Brass Rules and Dashes, Ornaments and Borders, Society Emblems, Check Lines, Cuts, Initials and Other Productions of the American Type Founders Co [1896]*. Nineteenth-Century Book Arts and Printing History. New York: Garland Pub, 1981.
Leonardi, Alessio, and Jan Middendorp. *A Line Of Type*. Mergenthaler Edition. Bad Homburg [Germany]: Linotype, 2006.
Loop, Jan. *Johann Heinrich Hottinger: Arabic and Islamic Studies in the Seventeenth Century*. Oxford: Oxford University Press, 2013.
Ludlow Typograph Company. *Ludlow Typefaces [Edition D, Copy 1140]*. Chicago: Ludlow Typograph Company, 1940. http://archive.org/details/LudlowTypefacesEditionD1140.
——. *Newspaper Experience with the Ludlow: A Record of Achievement*. Chicago: Ludlow Typograph Company, 1930. http://hdl.handle.net/2027/mdp.39015034743461.
Lyons, Martyn, and John Arnold. *A History of the Book in Australia, 1891-1945: A National Culture in a Colonised Market*. Macmillan, 2001.
Mack, Edward. *Manufacturing Modern Japanese Literature: Publishing, Prizes, and the Ascription of Literary Value*. Duke University Press, 2010.
Macmillan, Neil. *An A-Z of Type Designers*. New Haven: Yale University Press, 2006.
Magata, S. "Motogi Nagabisa: The First Japanese Printer." *The British Bookmaker* 7, no. 75 (1894): 53–56. https://books.google.com/books?id=aaA3AQAAMAAJ&dq=tsukiji+type+foundry& source=gbs_navlinks_s.
Marder, Luse & Company. *Price List and Printers' Purchasing Guide, Showing Specimens of Printing Type Manufactured by Marder, Luse & Co., Chicago, Illinois, U. S. A.* Chicago: Marder, Luse & Company, 1890. https://hdl.handle.net/2027/mdp.39015033790497?urlappend=%3Bseq=13.
Marshall, Alan. *Du Plomb à la lumière: La Lumitype-Photon et la naissance des industries graphiques modernes*. Paris: les Éditions de la Maison des sciences de l'homme, 2003.
Maruca, Lisa. "Bodies of Type: The Work of Textual Production in English Printers' Manuals." *Eighteenth-Century Studies* 36, no. 3 (2003): 321–43. https://doi.org/10.1353/ecs.2003.0030.
McDowell, Paula. "'The Manufacture and

Lingua-Facture of Ballad-Making': Broadside Ballads in Long Eighteenth-Century Ballad Discourse." *The Eighteenth Century* 47, no. 2/3 (2006): 151–78. https://www.jstor.org/stable/41467998.

McJones, P., and D. Spicer. "The Advent of Digital Typography." *IEEE Annals of the History of Computing, Annals of the History of Computing, IEEE, IEEE Annals Hist. Comput.* 42, no. 1 (January 1, 2020): 41–50. https://doi.org/10.1109/MAHC.2019.2929883.

McKeller, Smith & Jordan. *1796-1896: One Hundred Years*. Philadelphia: McKeller, Smith & Jordan, 1896. http://hdl.handle.net/2027/pst.000015538079.

McMurtrie, Douglas C. *Le Moreau-Le-Jeune;a Typographical Specimen with an Introduction*. New York, 1919. http://hdl.handle.net/2027/uiug.30112046998057.

——. *Type Design: An Essay on American Type Design with Specimens of the Outstanding Types*. Pelham [NY]: Bridgman, 1927.

Meggs, Philip B., and Rob Carter. *Typographic Specimens: The Great Typefaces*. John Wiley & Sons, 1993.

Mergenthaler Linotype Company. *Linofilm System, Photocomposition*. Brooklyn: Linotype, N.D. http://archive.org/details/TNM_Linofilm_System_photocomposition_-_Mergenthal_20170912_0073.

——. *Specimen Book of Linotype Faces*. New York: Linotype, 1939.

——. *The Book of the Matrix Announcing Specimen Book of Type Styles*. Brooklyn: Mergenthaler Linotype Company, 1916. http://archive.org/details/MergenthalerSpecimenAnnouncement1916.

Mergenthaler Linotype Company, and Samuel A. Jacobs. *Reviving a Famous Ancient Language Linotype Syriac Faces: Estrangela, Nestorian, Jacobite*. New York: Syriac Press, 1914. http://www.columbia.edu/cgi-bin/cul/resolve?clio12719865.

Messner, Phillip. "Hebrew Type Design in the Context of the Book Art Movement and New Typograph." In *New Types*, edited by Ada Wardi, 21–34. Jerusalem: Israel Museum, 2016.

Middendorp, Jan. *Dutch Type*. Rotterdam: 010 Publishers, 2004.

Mifflin, Jeffrey. "History of the Linotype Company." *Printing History*, no. 19 (January 2016): 35–37. https://www.thefreelibrary.com/Romano%2c+Frank.+History+of+the+Linotype+Company.-a0491612726.

Millington, Roy. *Stephenson Blake: The Last of the Old English Typefounders*. New Castle [DE]: Oak Knoll Press, 2002.

Monotype Corporation. *The Monotype: How It Works*. New York: The School, 1957. http://archive.org/details/MonotypeHowItWorksEtc1957.

Monotype GmbH. "TEDx Talk with Font Designer Nadine Chahine." *Linotype Blog* (blog), 2016. http://blog.linotype.com/2016/07/tedxtalk-with-fontdesigner-nadinechahine/.

Mores, Edward Rowe, Harry Graham Carter, and Christopher B. Ricks. *A Dissertation upon English Typographical Founders and Founderies (1778): With a Catalogue and Specimen of the Type-Foundry of John James (1782)*. Oxford Bibliographical Society Publications, new ser, v.9. Oxford: Oxford Bibliographical Society, 1961.

Mores, Edward Rowe, Richard Gough, John Nichols, and Daniel Berkeley Updike. *A Dissertation upon English Typographical Founders and Foundries*. New York: Grolier Club, 1924.

Morison, Stanley. *A Brief Survey of Printing: History and Practice,*. New York: A.A. Knopf, 1923. http://hdl.handle.net/2027/mdp.39015008145081.

——. *The English Newspaper, 1622-1932: An Account of the Physical Development of Journals Printed in London between 1622 & the Present Day*. Cambridge: Cambridge University Press, 1932.

——. *The History of the Times*. Vol. 1. 7 vols. London: Office of the Times, 1935.

Morison, Stanley, and Harry Graham Carter. *John Fell: The University Press and the "Fell" Types; the Punches and Matrices Designed for Printing in the Greek, Latin, English, and Oriental Languages Bequeathed in 1686 to the University of Oxford by John Fell, D. D., Delegate of the Press, Dean of Christ Church, Vice-Chancellor of the University, and Bishop of Oxford*. Oxford: Clarendon Press, 1967.

Mosley, James. *British Type Specimens Before 1831: A Hand-List*. Occasional Publication 14. Oxford: Oxford Bibliographical Society, 1984. https://catalog.hathitrust.org/Record/000569676.

Moxon, Joseph. *Regulae Trium Ordinum Literarum Typographicarum, or, The Rules of the Three Orders of Print Letters: Viz. the Roman, Italick, English, Capitals and Small: Shewing How They Are Compounded of Geometrick Figures, and Mostly Made by Rule and Compass. Useful for Writing Masters, Painters, Carvers, Masons, and Others That Are Lovers of Curiosity*. London: Printed for Joseph Moxon on Ludgate Hill at the Sign of the Atlas, 1676.

Moxon, Joseph, and Theodore Low De Vinne. *Moxon's Mechanick Exercises, or, the Doctrine of Handyworks Applied to the Art of Printing: A Literal Reprint in Two Volumes of the First Edition Published in the Year 1683*. Vol. 1. 2 vols. New York: Typothetæ, 1896. https//catalog.hathitrust.org/Record/008411043.

Mullaney, Thomas S. "Facing the World: Towards a Global History of Non-Latin Type Design." *Philological Encounters* 3, no. 4 (November 27, 2018): 399–411. https://doi.org/10.1163/24519197-12340050.

Mullen, Robert A. *Recasting a Craft: St. Louis Typefounders Respond to Industrialization*. SIU Press, 2005.

Nemeth, Titus. *Arabic Type-Making in the Machine Age: The Influence of Technology on the Form of Arabic Type, 1908–1993*. Leiden: Brill, 2017.

Nile Mission Press. *Blessed Be Egypt: A Challenge to Faith for the Mohammedan World*. London & New York: Nile Mission Press, Partridge, and Revell Co., 1906. http://archive.org/details/blessedbeegypta00palegoog.

Orii, Yoshimi. "The Dispersion of Jesuit Books Printed in Japan: Trends in Bibliographical Research and in Intellectual History." *Journal of Jesuit Studies* 2, no. 2 (April 9, 2015): 189–207. https://doi.org/10.1163/22141332-00202002.

Palmer & Rey. *Third Revised Specimen Book and Price List of Printing Material*. San Francisco: Palmer & Rey, 1887. https://archive.org/details/thirdrevisedspec00palmrich.

Pankow, David. *The Printer's Manual: An Illustrated History: Classical and Unusual Texts on Printing from the Seventeenth, Eighteenth, and Nineteenth Centuries*. Rochester, NY: RIT Cary Graphic Arts Press, 2005.

——. "The Rise and Fall of ATF [editor's introduction]." *Printing History* 22, no. 1 & 2 (2002): 13–14.

Pankow, David, John Dreyfus, and International Typeface Corporation, eds. *The Art of the*

Type Specimen in the Twentieth Century: An Exhibition Held at ITC Center, 1 March-21 May 1993. New York: Typophiles, 1993.

Pannabecker, John R. "Representing Mechanical Arts in Diderot's 'Encyclopédie.'" *Technology and Culture* 39, no. 1 (1998): 33–73. https://doi.org/10.2307/3107003.

Petity, Jean-Raymond. *Encyclopédie élémentaire ou introduction à l'étude des lettres, des sciences et des arts*. Vol. 2. 3 vols. Paris: Hérissant, 1767. https://www.google.com/books/edition/Encyclop%C3%A9die_%C3%A9l%C3%A9mentaire_ou_introduction/qhdTAAAAcAAJ?hl=en&gbpv=0&kptab=overview.

Pettegree, Andrew, ed. *Broadsheets: Single-Sheet Publishing in the First Age of Print*. Leiden: Brill, 2017.

Pettingill & Co. *Copper Alloy Type Book, Comprising Newspaper, Book, and Display Types, Borders and Ornaments : Also Brass Rules, Dashes, Etc*. Boston: Pettingill, 1901. http://archive.org/details/copperalloytypeb00pett.

Photo Typositor Inc. *Photo Typositor*. New York: Photo Typositor Inc, 1962. http://archive.org/details/TNM_Photo_Typositor_Brochure_20170621_0001.

Photo-lettering Inc., and Edward Rondthaler. *Alphabet Thesaurus*. Vol. 3. 3 vols. New York: Van Nostrand Reinhold, 1971. http://catalog.hathitrust.org/api/volumes/oclc/246758.html.

Plantin, Christophe, and Douglas C. McMurtrie. *Plantin's Index Characterum of 1567: Facsimile Reprint with an Introduction by Douglas C. McMurtrie*. New York: McMurtrie, 1924. https://books.google.com/books?id=catCAQAAMAAJ&source=gbs_navlinks_s.

Pollard, Graham. *Catalogue of I Typefounders' Specimens; II Books Printed in Founts of Historic Importance; III Works on Typefounding Printing & Bibliography Offered for Sale*. London: Birrell & Garnett, 1928.

Printing: An Essay by William Morris & Emery Walker. Park Ridge [IL]: Village Press, 1903. https://archive.org/details/printing.essayby00morrrich.

PROtype. *PROtype Photo-Display Type*. New York: Electrographic Corp., 1963. http://archive.org/details/TNM_PROtype_Photo-Display_Type_0520.

Raffel, Burton, and Ellen Mazur Thomson. *The Origins of Graphic Design in America, 1870-1920*. Yale University Press, 1997.

Redfield-Kendrick-Odell Co. *A Printed Specimen of Caslon Old Style Type, with Appropriate Ornaments*. New York: Redfield-Kendrick-Odell, 1921. http://archive.org/details/printedspecimeno00redf.

Reed, Talbot Baines. *A History of the Old English Letter Foundries: With Notes, Historical and Bibliographical, on the Rise and Progress of English Typography*. London: E. Stock, 1887.

Ringwalt, John Luther. *American Encyclopaedia of Printing*. Menamin & Ringwalt, 1871.

Romano, Frank. *History of the Linotype Company*. Rochester: RIT Press, 2014.

Ronaldson, James. *Specimen of Printing Type, from the Letter Foundry of James Ronaldson, Successor to Binny & Ronaldson*. Philadelphia: J. Ronaldson, 1816.

Ross, Fiona. "An Approach to Non Latin Type Design." In *Language Culture Type: International Type Design in the Age of Unicode*, 65–75. New York: ATypI, 2002.

———. *The Printed Bengali Character: Its Evolution*. Richmond: Routledge/Curzon, 1999.

Ross, Fiona, and Graham Shaw. *Non-Latin Scripts: From Metal to Digital Type*. London: St Bride Foundation, 2002.

Saxe, Stephen O., and Rob Roy Kelly. *Specimen Book of Wood Type*. Madison [WI]: Silver Buckle Press, 1999.

Schonfield, Hugh J. *The New Hebrew Typography*. London: Denis Archer, 1932. http://archive.org/details/Schonfield1932 The NewHebrewTypography.

Schools, International Correspondence. *Design Motifs: Design Composition; Space Filling; Color in Design; Historic Styles*. International Textbook Company, 1916.

Seybold, John W. *Fundamentals of Modern Photo-Composition*. Media, PA: Seybold Publications, 1979. http://archive.org/details/FundamentalsOfModern PhotoComposition.

Shani Avni. "Ismar David's Quest for Original Hebrew Typographic Signs." *Visible Language* 53, no. 1 (2019): 51–75. http://www.visiblelanguagejournal.com/issue/292.

Shaw, Paul, and Jonathan Hoefler. *Revival Type: Digital Typefaces Inspired by the Past*. New Haven: Yale University Press, 2017.

Shields, David. "Considering Rob Roy Kelly's American Wood Type Collection." *Printing History* 7 (January 1, 2010): 21–35.

Shockey, Nathan. *The Typographic Imagination: Reading and Writing in Japan's Age of Modern Print Media*. Columbia University Press, 2019.

Silver, Rollo. *Typefounding in America, 1787-1825*. Charlottesville: University Press of Virginia, 1965.

Sisneros, Katie. "Early Modern Memes: The Reuse and Recycling of Woodcuts in 17th-Century English Popular Print." The Public Domain Review, June 6, 2018. https://publicdomainreview.org/2018/06/06/early-modern-memes-the-reuse-and-recycling-of-woodcuts-in-17th-century-english-popular-print/.

Smallian, Hermann. "Type Systems of To-Day—Part II—the Didot System." *The British Printer* 12, no. 69 (June 1899): 131–32.

Smith, John. *The Printer's Grammar. Containing a Concise History of the Origin of Printing; Also, an Examination of the Superficies, Gradation, and Properties of the Different Sizes of Types ... Tables of Calculations; Models of Letter Cases; Schemes for Casting off Copy, and Imposing; ... with Directions to Authors, Compliers, &c. How to Prepare Copy, and to Correct Their Own Proofs*. London: Wayland & Evans, 1787. http://archive.org/details/b2876058x.

Smith, Virginia. "Chapter 4: Native and Imported Forms." In *Forms in Modernism: The Unity of Typography, Architecture & the Design Arts 1920s-1970s*, 72–91, 2005. http://lp.hscl.ufl.edu/login?url=http://search.ebscohost.com/login.aspx?direct=true&AuthType=ip,uid&db=asu&AN=28545988&site=eds-live.

Southall, Richard. *Printer's Type in the Twentieth Century: Manufacturing And Design Methods*. New Castle, DE: Oak Knoll, 2005.

Staples, Loretta. "Typography and the Screen: A Technical Chronology of Digital Typography, 1984-1997." *Design Issues* 16, no. 3 (2000): 19–34. https://www.jstor.org/stable/1511813.

Stenner, Rachel. *The Typographic Imaginary in Early Modern English Literature*. Taylor & Francis, 2018.

Stephenson, Blake and Company, and Sir

Charles Reed & Sons. *Specimens of Point Line Type: Borders Ornaments Brass Rules &c. &c.* Toronto: Stephenson, Blake & Co., 1908. http://archive.org/details/specimensofpoint00step.

Stern, Adi. "The Design of Hebrew Type in the First Decade of Israeli Statehood." In *New Types*, 34–67. Jerusalem: Israel Museum, 2016.

Stern, Arden. "Freaks of Fancy, Revisited: Nineteenth-Century Ornamented Typography in the Twenty-First Century." *Design Issues* 32, no. 4 (October 2016): 76–90. https://doi.org/10.1162/DESI_a_00418.

Stern, Bernard. "Upper versus Lower Case Copy as a Factor in Typesetting Speed for Linotype Trainees." *Journal of Applied Psychology* 34, no. 5 (October 1950): 351–54. https://doi.org/10.1037/h0054885.

Stevens, Mary Elizabeth. *Automatic Typographic-Quality Typesetting Techniques: A State-of-the-Art Review.* Washington, D.C.: U.S. Government Printing Office, 1967. http://hdl.handle.net/2027/uc1.b4195061.

Stower, Caleb. *The Printer's Grammar; or, Introduction to the Art of Printing: Containing a Concise History of the Art, with the Improvements in the Practice of Printing, for the Last Fifty Years.* London: B. Crosby & Co., 1808.

"The Gentleman's Magazine," no. 159 (May 1836): 557–58.

PeoplesGDArchive. "The People's Graphic Design Archive." Accessed August 4, 2020. https://www.peoplesgdarchive.org.

The Thorne Type-Setting Machine Company. *The Thorne Type-Setting Machine.* Hartford: Thorne, 1894. http://archive.org/details/ThorneTypeSettingMachine1894.

Thompson, John Smith. *History of Composing Machines.* Chicago: Inland Printer Company, 1904. https://books.google.com/books?id=vlQsAAAAYAAJ&dq=history+of+the+linotype &source=gbs_navlinks_s.

——. *The Mechanism of the Linotype: A Complete and Practical Treatise on the Installation, Operation and Care of the Linotype, for the Novice as Well as the Experienced Operator.* Chicago: Inland Printer Company, 1916.

Tracy, Walter. *Letters of Credit: A View of Type Design.* David R. Godine Publisher, 2003.

Tschichold, Jan, Richard Hendel, Robin Kinross, and Ruari McLean. *The New Typography: A Handbook for Modern Designers.* Berkeley: University of California Press, 2006.

Tubbs & Co. *Tubbs Wood Type.* South Windham: Tubbs & Co., 188AD. http://archive.org/details/case_wing_Z250_t884.

Typefounders of Chicago. *Type Specimens by Neon Type Division [of] Typefounders of Chicago.* Chicago: Typefounders of Chicago, 1962. http://archive.org/details/NeonTypeDivisionTypefoundersChicago1962pt1.

United States Bureau of Education. *Public Libraries in the United States of America: Part I, 1876 Report.* Urbana-Champaign: University of Illinois Graduate School of Library Science, 1965.

Updike, Daniel Berkeley. *Printing Types: Their History, Forms, and Use; a Study in Survivals.* Vol. 1. 2 vols. Cambridge: Harvard University Press, 1922. http://archive.org/details/printingtypesthe01updi.

——. *Printing Types, Their History, Forms, and Use; a Study in Survivals.* Vol. 2. 2 vols. Cambridge: Harvard University Press, 1922. https://archive.org/details/printingtypesthe02updi.

Valentine, Jonty. *Printing Types: New Zealand Type Design since 1870.* Auckland [N.Z.]: Objectspace Gallery, 2009.

Van Winkle, Cornelius S. *The Printers' Guide: Or, an Introduction to the Art of Printing, Including an Essay on Punctuation, and Remarks on Orthography.* New York: C.S. Van Winkle, 1818. https://archive.org/details/printersguideori00vanwuoft.

VariTyper. *Presenting the New VariTyper Type Face Series 470 Gothic Light Cond.* New York: VariTyper, 1963. http://archive.org/details/TNM_VariTyper_type_faces_20180309_0008.

Vervliet, Hendrik D. L. *The Palaeotypography of the French Renaissance: Selected Papers on Sixteenth-Century Typefaces.* Leiden: Brill, 2008.

Vervliet, Hendrik D. L., Harry Carter, and Gary Schwarz, eds. *The Type Specimen of the Vatican Press, 1628: A Facsimile.* Amsterdam: M. Hertzberger, 1967.

Vervliet, Hendrik D.L. *Sixteenth Century Printing Types of the Low Countries.* Amsterdam: Menno Hertzberger, 1968.

Wardi, Ada, ed. *New Types: Three Pioneers of Hebrew Graphic Design.* 1st ed. Katalog (Muze'on Yiśra'el (Jerusalem)); Mis. 640. Jerusalem: The Israel Museum, 2016.

Weaver, Amber. "Femme Type - Celebrating Women in the Type Industry," 2020. https://femme-type.com/.

Weidhaas, Peter. *A History of the Frankfurt Book Fair.* Translated by Carolyn Gossage and Wendy A. Wright. Toronto: Dundurn, 2007.

Weisenfeld, Gennifer. "Japanese Typographic Design and the Art of Letterforms." In *Bridges to Heaven: Essays on East Asian Art in Honor of Professor Wen C. Fong*, edited by Wen Fong and Jerome Silbergeld, 2:827–48. Princeton, N.J.: Princeton University Press, 2011.

Willems, Alphonse. *Les Elzevier: Histoire et Annales Typographiques.* Bruxelles: G.A. van Trigt, 1880. http://archive.org/details/leselzevierhisto00will.

William E. Burns. *Science in the Enlightenment: An Encyclopedia.* History of Science. Santa Barbara: ABC-CLIO, 2003.

Wood & Nathan Co. *Unitype One-Man Type Setting Machine.* New York: Wood & Nathan, 1902. http://archive.org/details/UnitypeOneManTypeSettingMachineWoodNathan.

Image credits

Reproduced by permission of the Cary Collection, Rochester Institute of Technology: 1.11, 2.2-2.10, 3.4-3.10, 3.14-3.15, 3.17-3.18, 3.20, 4.24, 5.2, 5.15, 6.1, 6.3, 6.7-6.8, 6.12, 6.14-6.22, 6.28-6.29, 7.2, 7.7-7.8, 7.17, and Salut, page 37; *Typographia*, 59; *Probenauszug*, 61; *Die Hauptprobe*, 97; *Specimen Book & Catalog*, 99; *Specimen Book of Type Styles*, 137; *One Line Specimens*, 165; Reklame, 167. Special thanks to the Cary Collection and their support of this book and its images.

Digitally archived and publicly available in Duke University Broadsides & Ephemera Collection: 1.12.

Reproduced by permission of the Folger Shakespeare Library, CC BY-SA 4.0: 1.2

Reproduced by permission of House Industries: 7.15.

Reproduced by permission of Linotype: 6.4, 7.18.

Reproduced by permission of Monotype: 1.3.

Digitally archived and publicly available in the National Library of Australia: 3.25, 6.6.

Reproduced by permission of Ohio University Libraries Special Collections: 4.11.

Reproduced by permission of St. Bride Library: 4.13, 6.4.

Reproduced by permission of the Updike Collection, Providence Public Library: 1.8, 3.2

Reproduced by permission of the designers: Leandro Assis, 8.6; Dina Benbrahim, 8.7; Christian Boer, 8.3; Elaina Buffkin, 8.4; Avraham Cornfeld, 8.9; Julia Martínez Diana, 1.13; Lisa Huang 黄丽莎 8.8; Megan McCormick, 8.5; Laura Meseguer, 8.1 and page 231; Maria Montes, 8.2; Wael Morcos, 8.10.

Reproduced under CC BY-SA 4.0, *Specimen Caracteres d'Affiches Deberny et Peignot*, available online at archive.org/details/specimen-caracteres-d-affiches-deberny-et-peignot-1937

All other images are in the public domain, published before 1926 or published without copyright notice 1927-1977.

Index

Note: Page locators in *italic* refer to figure captions.